Yinjun Zhang · Nazir Shah

Editors

Application of Big Data, Blockchain, and Internet of Things for Education Informatization

Third EAI International Conference, BigIoT-EDU 2023
August 29–31, 2023, Liuzhou, China
Proceedings, Part III

 Springer

Editors
Yinjun Zhang
Guangxi Science and Technology Normal
University
Laibin, China

Nazir Shah
University of Swabi
Swabi, Pakistan

ISSN 1867-8211 ISSN 1867-822X (electronic)
Lecture Notes of the Institute for Computer Sciences, Social Informatics
and Telecommunications Engineering
ISBN 978-3-031-63135-1 ISBN 978-3-031-63136-8 (eBook)
https://doi.org/10.1007/978-3-031-63136-8

This Springer imprint is published by the registered company Springer Nature Switzerland AG
The registered company address is: Gewerbestrasse 11, 6330 Cham, Switzerland

If disposing of this product, please recycle the paper.

Lecture Notes of the Institute
for Computer Sciences, Social Informatics
and Telecommunications Engineering 582

The LNICST series publishes ICST's conferences, symposia and workshops.
LNICST reports state-of-the-art results in areas related to the scope of the Institute.
The type of material published includes

- Proceedings (published in time for the respective event)
- Other edited monographs (such as project reports or invited volumes)

LNICST topics span the following areas:

- General Computer Science
- E-Economy
- E-Medicine
- Knowledge Management
- Multimedia
- Operations, Management and Policy
- Social Informatics
- Systems

Preface

We are delighted to introduce the proceedings of the third edition of the European Alliance for Innovation (EAI) International Conference on Application of Big Data, Blockchain, and Internet of Things for Education Informatization (BigIoT-EDU 2023). BigIoT-EDU aims to provide a platform for international cooperation and exchange, enabling big data and information education experts, scholars, and enterprise developers to share research results, discuss existing problems and challenges, and explore cutting-edge science and technology. The conference focuses on research fields such as digitization of education, smart classrooms, and Massive Online Open Courses (MOOCs). The use of big data analytics, artificial intelligence (AI), machine learning, and deep learning lies at the heart of this conference as we focus on these emerging technologies to further the role of IT in education.

BigIoT-EDU 2023 had three tracks: the Main Track, the Late Track, and a Workshop Track. BigIoT-EDU 2023 attracted over 700 submissions, and each submission was reviewed by at least 3 Program Committee members in a double-blind process, resulting in the acceptance of only 272 papers across all three tracks. The workshop was titled "Application of Advanced Integrated Technologies in Education Informatics" and co-chaired by Yar Muhammad and Muhammad Al-Ambusaidi from Beihang University, China and University of Technology & Applied Sciences of Oman, respectively. The workshop aimed to focus on the application of the latest cutting-edge integrated technologies for the development and digitalization of education in the modern era.

Coordination with the steering chair, Imrich Chlamtac, was essential for the success of the conference. We sincerely appreciate his constant support and guidance. It was also a great pleasure to work with such an excellent organizing committee team for their hard work in organizing and supporting the conference. In particular, we are grateful to the Technical Program Committee, who completed the peer-review process for the technical papers and helped to put together a high-quality technical program. We are also grateful to Conference Manager Ivana Bujdakova for her constant support along with the whole of the EAI team involved in the conference. We must say that they have been wonderful and it is always a pleasant experience to work with them. Also, we would like to thank all the authors who submitted their papers to the BigIoT-EDU 2023 conference.

We strongly believe that the BigIoT-EDU conference provides a good forum for all researchers, developers, and practitioners to discuss all science and technology aspects that are relevant to emerging trends for digitalization of education. We also expect that the future BigIoT-EDU conferences will be as successful and stimulating as this year's, as indicated by the contributions presented in this volume.

Yinjun Zhang
Nazir Shah

Conference Organization

Steering Committee

Imrich Chlamtac	University of Trento, Italy
Fazlullah Khan	Business Technology Management Group, USA
Mian Ahmad Jan	Abdul Wali Khan University Mardan, Pakistan

Organizing Committee

General Chair

Yinjun Zhang	Guangxi Science & Technology Normal University, China

General Co-chairs

Shah Nazir	University of Swabi, Pakistan
Walayat Hussain	Australian Catholic University, Australia

TPC Chair

Yinjun Zhang	Guangxi Science & Technology Normal University, China

Sponsorship and Exhibit Chairs

Lan Zimian	Harbin Institute of Technology, China
Izaz Ur Rehman	Abdul Wali Khan University Mardan, Pakistan

Local Chairs

Huang Yufei	Hechi Normal University, China
Wan Haoran	Shanghai University, China

Workshops Chairs

Rahim Khan   Abdul Wali Khan University Mardan, Pakistan
Abid Yahya   Botswana International University of Science and
                                    Technology, Botswana

Publicity and Social Media Chair

Aamir Akbar   *Abdul Wali Khan University Mardan, Pakistan*

Publications Chair

Yinjun Zhang   Guangxi Science & Technology Normal
                                    University, China

Web Chairs

Mian Yasir Jan   CECOS University, Pakistan
Syed Rooh Ullah Jan   Abdul Wali Khan University Mardan, Pakistan

Posters and PhD Track Chairs

Mengji Chen   Guangxi Science &Technology Normal
                                    University, China
Ateeq ur Rehman   University of Haripur, Pakistan

Panels Chairs

Kong Linxiang   Hefei University of Technology, China
Muhammad Usman   Federation University, Australia

Demos Chairs

Ryan Alturki   Umm-ul-Qura University, Saudi Arabia
Rahim Khan   Abdul Wali Khan University Mardan, Pakistan

Tutorials Chairs

Wei Rongchang   Guangxi Science & Technology Normal
                                    University, China
Hashim Ali   Abdul Wali Khan University Mardan Pakistan

Technical Program Committee

Shahnawaz Khan	Abdul Wali Khan University Mardan, Pakistan
Mengji Chen	Hechi University, China
Yar Muhammad	Beihang University, China
Mian Abdullah Jan	Ton Duc Thang University, Vietnam
Roman Khan	City University of Information Science and Technology, Pakistan
Muneeb Ullah	Peshawar University, Pakistan
Siyar Khan	Bacha Khan University, Pakistan
Muhammad Bilal	Virtual University of Pakistan, Pakistan
Haroon Khan	Bacha Khan University, Pakistan
Shaher Slehat	University of Technology Sydney, Australia
Xiangjian He	University of Technology Sydney, Australia
Shaheer Jan	University of Engineering and Technology Peshawar, Pakistan
Akbar Khan	University of Peshawar, Pakistan
Malik Ahmad	University of Peshawar, Pakistan
Muzammil Shah	COMSATS University Lahore, Pakistan
Aaiza Khan	Guangju University of Technology, China
Farman Khan	Bacha Khan University, Pakistan
Zia Ur Rehman	Bacha Khan University, Pakistan
Abid Yahya	Botswana International University of Science and Technology, Botswana
Ravi Keemo	Botswana International University of Science and Technology, Botswana
Aaiza Gul	Sirindhorn International Institute of Technology, Thailand
Shahid Ali	Women University Swabi, Pakistan
Muhammad Sohail	Abdul Wali Khan University Mardan, Pakistan
Saad Khan	University of Peshawar, Pakistan
Momin Ali	University of Peshawar, Pakistan
Bilawal Khan	COMSATS University Islamabad, Pakistan
Jamal Shah	University of Leeds, UK
Basit Kazmi	University of Peshawar, Pakistan
Jalal Turk	Staffordshire University, UK
Umer Hussain	Indian Institute of Technology Kharagpur, India
Omer Naveed	Uppsala University, Sweden
Muhammad Ali	Uppsala University, Sweden
Hamza Khan	Hankuk University of Foreign Studies, South Korea
Tariq Khan	Abdul Wali Khan University Mardan, Pakistan

Ehsan Ullah	Abdul Wali Khan University Mardan, Pakistan
Noman Ali	Abdul Wali Khan University Mardan, Pakistan
Ayaan Adeel	Abdul Wali Khan University Mardan, Pakistan
Behroz Khan	Abdul Wali Khan University Mardan, Pakistan
Tariq Khokar	Abdul Wali Khan University Mardan, Pakistan
Awais Marwat	Abdul Wali Khan University Mardan, Pakistan
Naeem Jan	Abdul Wali Khan University Mardan, Pakistan
Anas Akbar	Abdul Wali Khan University Mardan, Pakistan
Mian Ahmad Jan	Duy Tan University, Vietnam
Faisal Ayub Khan	Indian Institute of Technology Kharagpur, India
Faisal Khan	University of Leeds, UK
Yasir Jan	University of California Davies, USA
Ryan Alturki	Umm al-Qura University, Saudi Arabia
Alayat Hussain	University of Technology Sydney, Australia
Muhammad Usman	Federation University, Australia
Naveed Khan	Abdul Wali Khan University Mardan, Pakistan
Azam Khalil	Abdul Wali Khan University Mardan, Pakistan
Hamid Naseer	Abdul Wali Khan University Mardan, Pakistan
Arsalan Jan	Abdul Wali Khan University Mardan, Pakistan
Abdul Samad	University of Nebraska Omaha, USA
Asif Khan	University of Nebraska Omaha, USA
Imtiaz Ali	Quaid-e-Azam University Islamabad, Pakistan
Khadim Khan	Quaid-e-Azam University Islamabad, Pakistan
Usman Nasir	Quaid-e-Azam University Islamabad, Pakistan
Ishfaq Ahmad	Quaid-e-Azam University Islamabad, Pakistan
Jamal Baig	National University of Sciences and Technology, Pakistan
Naseer Baig	National University of Sciences and Technology, Pakistan
Sohail Agha	National University of Sciences and Technology, Pakistan
Raza Hussain	Indian Institute of Technology Kharagpur, India
Ibrar Atta	University of Haripur, Pakistan
Majid Ali	University of Haripur, Pakistan
Afzal Durrani	University of Haripur, Pakistan
Faysal Azam	Indian Institute of Technology Kharagpur, India
Asif Wazir	University of Engineering and Technology Mardan, Pakistan
Talal Agha	University of Engineering and Technology Mardan, Pakistan
Salman Shah	University of Engineering and Technology Mardan, Pakistan

Ibrahim Khan	Iqra University, Islamabad, Pakistan
Raayan Jan	Iqra University, Islamabad, Pakistan
Shameer Shah	Iqra University, Islamabad, Pakistan
Zeeshan Khan	Iqra University, Islamabad, Pakistan

Contents

Application of Artificial Intelligence Algorithms in the Field of Smart Education

Exploration of the Application of Computer-Aided Technology in Intelligent Translation

The Application of Computer Intelligent Proofreading System in English Phrase Translation

Shufen Yang[1,2,3](✉), Jilin Xu[1,2,3], and Siyu Zhou[1,2,3]

[1] Wuchang Shouyi University, Wuhan 430064, China
daisyyang0323@163.com
[2] Huaiyin Institue of Technology, University Business College, Huaian, Jiangsu, China
[3] Ministry of Sports, Nanguo Business School, Guangdong University of Foreign Studies and Foreign Trade, Guangzhou 510545, Guangdong, China

Abstract. Computer intelligent proofreading system has an outstanding effect on the application the accuracy of the mechanical translation system, we can extract the basic meaning, scientifically proofread the English information, and determine whether the results meet the criteria. By replacing the unreasonable translation results, the reasonable translation statement is finally obtained. In the practice of this system, the generative statement for the intelligent translation system is proposed, and the translation that can be processed is compared. The system operation accuracy is significantly improved, and a new spatial system is also created for the subsequent system data structure end optimization, which can be used as an auxiliary tool for translation. The system design has improved, the translation accuracy, but also let the translation efficiency of the same period can be effectively improved.

Keyword: computer intelligence · proofreading system

1 Introduction

With the advancement of globalization and the increasing need for cross-border communication, translation has become an essential part of people's lives. Especially in the fields of commerce, technology, and culture, there is a need for cross-border and cross-cultural communication, and the demand for translation is even higher. However, due to differences in language and culture, translation errors and inaccuracies are inevitable in the process. Therefore, the application of computer intelligent proofreading systems in English phrase translation has attracted widespread attention and research, and will make important contributions to improving the accuracy and efficiency of translation [1].

Computer intelligent proofreading system refers to a language intelligent processing system based on artificial intelligence technology, which can automatically proofread and correct various texts, improving the grammar and semantic accuracy of texts. In the

Y. Zhang and N. Shah (Eds.): BigIoT-EDU 2023, LNICST 582, pp. 3–14, 2024.
https://doi.org/10.1007/978-3-031-63136-8_1

process of translation, the computer intelligent proofreading system can proofread and correct the translation results in real time after the completion of translation through its own Parsing and semantic recognition functions to avoid errors and inaccuracies in translation [2]. At the same time, it can also provide suggestions and reminders for some common translation problems, help translators avoid common errors, and improve translation efficiency and accuracy.

Fast numbers [3]. The accuracy and convenience of the results are also well guaranteed. Under the current Big data, how to do a good job in Internet trend analysis and grasp the functions and operating principles of the current data structure is also the key. In order to better optimize the application of English phrase translation, it is necessary to handle the application features, structure, and operational features well. Created a new open space for modern institutional innovation. In the translation and control of English phrases, adjustments and optimizations are made based on user decision-making content [4]. At the same time, combined with the new English translation proofreading system, intelligent proofreading can be achieved from multiple aspects.

In short, the application of computer intelligent proofreading systems in English phrase translation will have a positive impact on the quality and efficiency of translation, providing more efficient and convenient support for cross-cultural communication [5]. With the continuous breakthroughs and innovations in computer intelligent proofreading technology, it will gradually be widely applied in various fields and continuously improved and optimized.

2   Related Work

2.1   Computer Intelligent Proofreading System

In recent years, English grammar error correction has made an important breakthrough in the field of Natural language processing, and a variety of methods for evaluating GEC systems have emerged. The evaluation method usually compares the output sequence with the gold standard sequence (manually annotated target sentence), and during the comparison process, it is necessary to align the corrected sentence with the target sentence. Previously, the performance of the GEC model was only measured by accuracy, but later on, the GEC system can be measured by the recall rate of M2 and I indicators. Nowadays, the emergence of GLEU and ERANT error toolkits has made the evaluation results of GEC systems more fair and reasonable [6].

(1) Matching score

Max Match score (M2 score) calculates the maximum coverage of model output modifications and standard modifications at the word, word, or phrase level. It is a commonly used evaluation method for evaluating English grammar correction models. This measurement method first adopts an alignment strategy based on Levenshtein distance to align the corrected sentences output by the GEC system with the manually annotated standard sentences, and then calculates the number of operations on the word basis required to convert one sentence into another. Evaluate the system with accuracy (P), recall rate (R), and F0.5 values. The calculation formula is as shown in formulas (1), (2), and (3). Where e_i Å $g_i = \{e \in e_i \mid \exists g \in g_i, e = g\}$, ei is the candidate editing set output by the model, and gi represents the standard corrected editing set.

$$P = \frac{\sum_{i=1}^{n} | e_i \cap g_i |}{\sum_{i=1}^{n} | e_i |} \tag{1}$$

$$F_{0.5} = \frac{P \times R(1 + 0.5^2)}{(0.5^2 \times P) + R} \tag{2}$$

$$R = \frac{\sum_{i=1}^{n} | e_i \cap g_i |}{\sum_{i=1}^{n} | g_i |} \tag{3}$$

(2) I indicator

I index applies a multi sequence alignment optimization algorithm based on marker level between the source sentence, system output, and reference sentence. Unlike M 2, the I indicator provides corresponding scores for error detection and correction. This method defines a special format: each sentence contains annotations and all possible modifications [7]. Each candidate correction that can be selected must be mutually exclusive. In the evaluation, each marker is classified as true positive (TP), true negative (TN), false positive (FP), and false negative (FN). The FPN class represents the case where both FP and FN are satisfied, and the calculation formulas for P, R, and F are:

$$P = \frac{TP}{TP + FP} \tag{4}$$

$$R = \frac{TP}{TP + FN} \tag{5}$$

$$F_\beta = \left(1 + \beta^2\right) \cdot \frac{P \cdot R}{(\beta^2 \cdot P) + R} \tag{6}$$

The I index is calculated using weighted accuracy, punishing unnecessary error correction more than uncorrected errors, and punishing weight ω The default setting is 2. Weighted accuracy WACC calculation formula:

$$W_{sCC} = \frac{\omega \cdot TP + TN}{\omega \cdot (TP + FP) + TN + FN - (\omega + 1) \cdot \frac{FPN}{2}} \tag{7}$$

WACCsys is the result obtained by using system output sentences and standard reference sentences for calculation. WACCsrc is the result obtained by calculating the source sentence and standard reference sentence [8]. The value range of I is $[-1, 1]$, where 1 represents that all incorrect sentences have been correctly corrected, and -1 represents that all incorrect sentences have not been correctly corrected. $I > 0$ represents relative improvement, $I < 0$ does not improve, $I = 0$ does not improve. The calculation formula is as follows:

$$I = \begin{cases} \left[W_{ACC_{sys}} \right] & \text{if } W_{ACC_{sys}} = W_{ACC_{base}} \\ \frac{W_{ACC_{sys}} - W_{AC_{base}}}{1 - W_{AC_{base}}} & \text{if } W_{AC_{sys}} > W_{ACC_{base}} \\ \frac{W_{ACC_{sys}}}{W_{ACC}} - 1 & \text{otherwise} \end{cases} \tag{8}$$

(3) ERANT Toolkit

The ERRANT toolkit extracts the number of edits from the source statement and the corrected sentence, realizes the classification of error types, and helps to evaluate the types of Syntax error. This tool uses the alignment algorithm between source and correction sentences proposed by Felice et al., and assigns error types using a rule-based error type framework [9]. The framework is independent of the dataset and only relies on information such as part of speech tagging. For evaluation indicators such as M2, I, and GLEU, as the output of the GEC system is not annotated, the performance of English error correction can only be measured through recall rate. The ERRANT toolkit overcomes this drawback. Previous evaluation metrics often evaluated the overall performance of the system, but systems with poor overall performance may have an advantage in correcting specific types of errors [10]. The ERRANT Syntax error annotation toolkit puts forward the idea of error type analysis, which can more comprehensively evaluate the performance of the system.

2.2   Model and Reordering Strategy

Currently, excellent language models are mainly built on transformers, such as GPT, BERT, RoBERta, XLNET, etc. The use of Transformer and its derivative models has become the next key technology to improve model performance. For example, Zhao et al. proposed the Transformer model based on the copy mechanism, which can judge whether the system's prediction of the next word comes from the direct copy of the original word or is generated from the thesaurus space. The main way to apply the Transformer model is to pre train the model and apply the pre trained model to different fields [11]. Due to the correlation between the performance of the pre trained model and downstream tasks, it can promote the improvement of downstream task results.

(1) Rule-based model

The typical rule-based GEC method is to summarize and abstract language knowledge, and store it in a specific form. In the process of error correction, combined with the input to be corrected, corresponding rule-based knowledge is selected for inference or transformation. Rules include the analysis rules of the source language, the conversion rules from the internal representation of the source language to the internal representation of the target language, and the conversion rules from the internal representation of the target language to the target language [12]. Boyd et al. used part of speech markers and rule templates to correct Syntax error, as shown in Fig. 1. Part of speech tagging is the task of specifying the part of speech for each word. Common parts of speech are nouns, verbs, Determiner, adjectives and adverbs. Nouns can be further divided into singular nouns and plural nouns, and verbs can be divided into Past tense verbs and Present tense verbs. The more detailed the part of speech markers are, the more difficult it is to find the correct marker for the appearance of a word. In English, many words can be used as both nouns and verbs, so part of speech tagging is a typical disambiguation task [13]. After part of speech tagging, each sentence is segmented into phrase blocks. Match phrase blocks with predefined error rules. If the rules match, the phrase block should contain errors at the matching position. Finally, use the special rules set at the matching position to correct Syntax error.

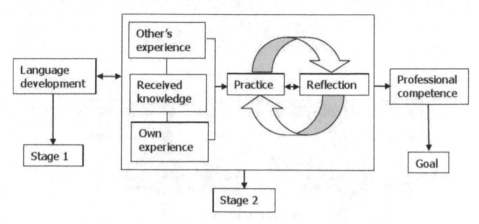

Fig. 1. Rule model

(2) Based on language model

The core idea of GEC task based on language model is that low probability sequences are more likely to contain Syntax error than high probability sequences. A significant advantage of language model based methods is their reliance on minimal annotated data. The goal of GEC based on language models is to convert low probability sequences into high probability sequences as much as possible based on the output probability of the language model, thereby reducing the occurrence of errors. Bryant et al. constructed a GEC system based on a neural language model using less annotated data [14]. By establishing a confusion set for each token in a sentence, each token is replaced, and the generated candidate correction sequence is re rated. By comparing the established threshold, select the best candidate correction sentence as the final output.

The GEC method based on neural language models maps the original unique heat coding vector into a dense continuous vector by embedding a linear projection matrix. Then, by training the neural language model, the weights of the vectors are learned, as shown in Fig. 2. With the increase of training times and the adjustment of parameter weights by backpropagation, the neural network gradually improves its ability to map words in the sequence into word vectors [15]. Finally, the word vector is used to predict the target sequence.

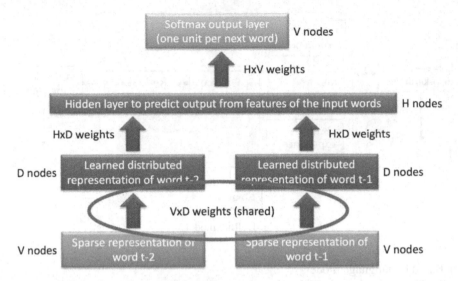

Fig. 2. Neural Language Model

3 Design of English Translation Computer Intelligent Proofreading System

3.1 Overall System Architecture Design

In view of the research process and the application of English phrase translation, the overall structure includes working module, etc., which constitutes the main research content of this system. For the current functional structure and development mechanism mode of the current English translation system, it can quickly control the English translation data in the main system, and it can also be analyzed through the log behavior. The design of the behavior log can be viewed by the background engineers and analyzed by the data structure principle. In this data operation, the whole process of English translation control has been optimized, and the key and difficult parts of English translation are defined. And the translation structure is designed to better ensure the integrity. In the data analysis, the system proofreading effect can also be achieved. English translation, through the replacement of the English structure, in the elimination the incorrect parts, to improve its effectiveness. In addition, the subsequent structure status of the English translation skills is analyzed, to better improve the storage and optimization process of the targeted retranslation module, and to clarify the data functions. It is stored in the working module, which is the English phrases. On this complete the control.

As shown in Table 1, when the proofreading command is proposed, it can be timely analyzed according to the obtained data and view the translation results. Then, it makes the effective adjustment according to the translation process, and realizes the comprehensive design based on the intelligent translation and the process analysis, which also makes the voice control and capture structure of the intelligent terminal more feasible, and truly achieves the overall scale optimization of English translation.

Table 1. Mechanical of Mechanical Structure

phase	Turn over the councillor	proofreading
1	V	
2		V
3	V	

Firstly, a rule-based data augmentation strategy is used to synthesize training data, and the GEG model is trained together with the learner corpus. Afterwards, the GEC model was trained using the training data synthesized by the GEG model and the learner corpus. Inspired by Popel's translation model of alternately training English to Czech language, this paper uses the GEC model to correct the source sentences in the learner's corpus, reconstructs the parallel corpus with the corrected results and the standard reference sentences in the learner's corpus into the GEG model's training data, and trains the GEG model again. The model is trained multiple times until it meets the system requirements, and the operation process is shown in Fig. 3.

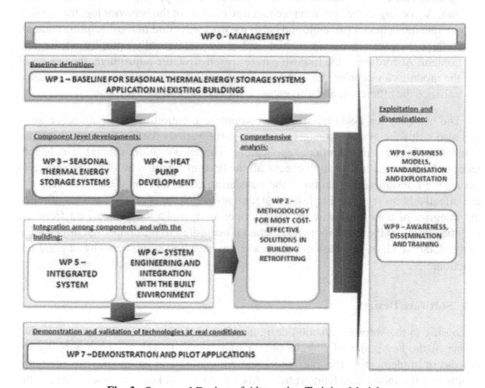

Fig. 3. Structural Design of Alternating Training Models

3.2 Hardware Design

(1) Phrase search module design

The Phrase search module is designed to search and analyze according to the phrase structure and phrase characteristics. In the process of such data function optimization, the basic meaning data characteristics can be adjusted and controlled. In terms of the current design stage, the simulating is updated and optimized for the vocabulary characteristics, so as to provide effective conditions for accurately obtaining the intelligent proofreading results of English translation. The search module is processed after receiving the phrase search task. The search module is designed according to the setting equation to analyze the pending vocabulary, the implementation meaning and the subject content. And to ensure the integrity of the search module data structure, the mapping process in the module design stage is a multi-module processing process. Based on the basis of hardware structure design, it can that all modules can within. Reduce the error rate of user expression, and also innovate the subsequent data structure content.

(2) Behaviour Log

The behavior log is analyzed according to all the behaviors of the user in the system, and is optimized for the structural operation principle of the system data end. According to the operation architecture content of the behavior log, the ray will operate the behavior principle and behavior work structure of the discipline content. Reduce the user expression content, and also systematically optimize all the data content. According to the English phrase search structure adjustment, the design of the module can improve the system for the vocabulary interpretation state, so as to enhance the efficiency, and also enhance the phrase translation.

The behavior log also optimizes the computer operation module data processing, and also helps the system managers to analyze the various data in the English phrase translation. In terms of operational application, manual operation is mainly single sentence, while automatic operation checks all the text information input by the input. To ensure the translation integration of the translation effect and the vocabulary effect, it can effectively exercise the English translation ability of the operators, and also deepen the integrity of their automatic translation operation. Make the comparison from the very beginning of the translation, and extract it according to the contextual information of the database class, in which the automatic proofreading system also has a good use function.

3.3 Software Design

According to the software function design, switching from one formal text to another is one of the key points of English phrase translation. Therefore, the is actually the process of implementing the translation, and comparing and optimizing the efficiency results and the initial translation results. Also through this kind of content, realize the English translation and proofreading structure control. The process of optimizing the translation content of this study through translation structure analysis and proofreading control system also mainly includes as follows.

To facilitate the phrase translation model calculation, the establishment of the system is called the pending vocabulary. If a character exists in it, the characters in the definition to the phrase. Similarly, pending proofreading vocabulary and proofreading vocabulary with the first string, the is to seek appropriate proofreading method, and according to the implementation of the code control, the content improves the effectiveness of the software design, also for the subsequent software control results and difference to create a new space. Under the control structure of this mode platform, it facilitates the synthesis of all data information.

(1) Reduce the detected text to generate new text. The text content is regarded as the object, and it is analyzed according to the accuracy and the data structure of the validity object, so as to better improve the data operation amount of the validity text.
(2) Analyze according to the vocabulary and translation impact size, and operate for the existing data content. Realize the subsequent data function structure optimization, you can build a collective system. At the same time, the comparison of the aggregate city service items and the vocabulary weight size is optimized.
(3) According to different vocabulary relationships, the basic skills of phrase translation are investigated from the system database. At the same time, it controls the word translation structure, function and system advantages.
(4) According to the accuracy design scheme of the system translation, the verification link is added. Combing the translation text with the current context structure can also optimize the various information obtained to ensure the rationality of the translation structure.

4   Experimental Results and Analysis

The 200M training data synthesized by GEG1, GEG2, and GEG3 models and three learner corpora were used to train three Syntax error correction models. The corrective sentences of the corresponding Syntax error correction models were defined as corrective sentence 1, corrective sentence 2, and corrective sentence 3, respectively. The source sentence is a Syntax error sentence, and the reference sentence is a standard corrective sentence.

The Syntax error Generative model GEG3 obtained through alternate training, and the syntax correction model obtained using the training data synthesized by GEG3, can perform up to 0.384 on the F0.5 value, which is about 4 percentage points higher than the F0.5 value obtained using GEG2 model.

If learner corpus is added during the training process of the GEC model for fine-tuning, for pre training the GEC model using 200M data synthesized on the same scale, using GEG3 synthesized data to train the GEC model, the P, R, and F0.5 values reach 0.659, 0.32, and 0.543, respectively. In order to further expand the scale of pre training data, the synthesized 200M training data was mixed with the rule-based data augmentation method to pre train the GEC model, and then three types of learner corpora were used for fine-tuning. According to the experimental results in Table 2, after the data scale was expanded, the values of P, R, and F0.5 reached 0.677, 0.338, and 0.564, respectively, which exceeded the GEC model fine-tuning without using learner corpus by about 20%, 2%, and 13%.

Table 2. Comparison of alternating training results

model	Scale of synthesized data for training GEC		
	P	R	F0.5
GEG1 →> GEC	0.275	0.135	0.228
GEG2 →> GEC	0.359	0.153	0.282
GEG3 →> GEC	0.445	0.123	0.292

In order to better compare with existing work, Lang-8 corpus was added to the three learner corpora, which was only used for fine-tuning the GEC model and further improved model performance. Without the use of multi model integration and reordering, the value of F0.5 reaches 0.62, and the accuracy of GEC model reaches 0.73, which has obvious advantages in the accuracy of correcting English Syntax error.

The performance of *GEGGG* 3 was improved again through alternating training of the GEG model and GEC model. This effect is due to the fact that alternative training constantly strengthens the model to identify errors that are difficult to detect, improves the quality of data synthesized by the error Generative model, and thus improves the performance of GEC model. The improvement of the GEC model also benefits from the multiple use of learner corpus: GEG1 training only uses rule data training, without using learner corpus; The GEG2 model training uses learner corpus fine-tuning on the basis of pre training with rule data; Compared with the GEG2 model, the GEG3 model once again adds data from the GEC model after correcting the learner's corpus.

The 200M training data synthesized using the GEG3 model and the learner corpus were used for pre training and fine-tuning of the GEC model, respectively. Under the same training method, better results were achieved compared to using the GEG1 and GEG2 models, due to the improvement in data quality and the optimization of the model's performance after alternating training. Amplify the pre training data of the GEC model: The use of mixed data with a scale of 400M is significantly higher than that of the GEC model trained with only 200M synthetic data, indicating that the increase in pre training data improves the performance of the model to a certain extent.

This article achieves similar or better results without using model integration or spell checkers, indicating the effectiveness of the proposed method. The main reasons are as follows: firstly, the integration and use of data augmentation strategies. Compared to existing data augmentation work, Awasthi et·al. used rule-based data augmentation methods, Xie et al. used reverse translation data augmentation methods, and Lichtage et al. used round-trip translation data augmentation methods to provide synthetic training data for the GEC model using a single data augmentation method. This paper proposes a fusion strategy of multiple data augmentation methods, which can improve the quality of synthetic data and further improve the performance of GEC model; Secondly, the alternating training strategy plays an important role. With the use of alternative strategies, the model can obtain a more comprehensive semantic representation, which can optimize the generation of Syntax error in data augmentation tasks and the correction of Syntax error in GEC tasks. Xie et al. used the data augmentation method of reverse translation to provide approximately 3.3M training data pairs for the CNN based GEC model. Using only the Lang-8 learner corpus, the F-value can reach 0.49. The model in this article outperforms Xie et al. in terms of accuracy due to the repeated use of learner corpus, and the model's ability to recognize and correct errors is continuously strengthened with alternating training. Secondly, the model can better utilize sentence context information during the correction process. In addition, the model itself has strong feature extraction ability, and performs well in correcting and controlling sentence fluency. The generated sentences are more fluent, and ultimately outperform Xie and others by about 8% in GLEU values. However, there is still a certain gap between the results and those of Kanekol et al. The results indicate that the performance of GEC systems depends to some extent on strategies such as reordering and multi model integration.

5 Conclusion

This system controls the English translation, calculation and proofreading system, uses the search module to analyze the subsequent data side content in terms of hardware part, and will be able to innovate for the advantages of data structure in terms of software. This system has optimized the data structure processing function of the data, and carried out continuous operation according to the data difference module. The accuracy of the subsequent phrase English translation is improved by 27.7%. It can be seen that this English translation can analyze the English continuity skills in different contexts. Adjust the integrity of English translation, and finally make the efficient and systematic advantages of English translation reflected, and proofreading.

References

1. Lan, Y.: Research on computer intelligent proofreading system based on improving phrase translation model. Electron. Des. Eng. **28**(18), 5 (2020)
2. Yue, Z.: Research on Computer Intelligent Proofreading System Based on Improving Phrase Translation Model. Autom. Technol. Appl. **040**(012), 58–61 (2021)
3. Rui, S.: Research on computer intelligent proofreading system based on the application view of english translation. Microcomput. Appl. **2**, 4 (2020)
4. Yundi, D.: The application of computer software translation in English translation (2021)
5. Ideal, Z.: The application of step-by-step principles in translation teaching (2019-16), 1–22021
6. Ning, Z.: Research on non-technical text translation practice based on computer translation technology. Univ. Soc. Sci. (11), 36–38 (2020)
7. History. Computer-aided translation software and practice in the master teaching of English translation and its advantages and disadvantages. Sci. Public: Sci. Technol. Innov. (4), 1 (2020)
8. Min, J.: Research on the application of computer intelligent proofreading system in college english teaching. J. Phys. Conf. Ser. **1915**(3), 032078 (2021). https://doi.org/10.1088/1742-6596/1915/3/032078
9. Zhang, X., Yang, G., Cui, Y., et al.: Application of computer algorithm in fault diagnosis system of RM equipment. J. Phys. Conf. Ser. **2143**(1), 012033 (2021)
10. Mcgovern, E., Mangina, E., Collier, R.: MINI-ME: the application of an intelligent multi-agent system methodology in the design of a mobile managed learning environment (2022)

11. Hadi, S., Rahardjo, T., Pribadi, U.: The application of artificial intelligent in analysing ruling of court for corruption case. IOP Conf. Ser. Earth Environ. Sci. **717**(1), 012034 (2021). https://doi.org/10.1088/1755-1315/717/1/012034
12. Nie G , Xu Y .Research on the Application of Intelligent Technology in Low Voltage Electric Automation Control System[J].Journal of Physics: Conference Series, 2021, 1865(2):022072-.https://doi.org/10.1088/1742-6596/1865/2/022072
13. Su, Z.: The application of intelligent manufacturing technology in CNC tools design and machining. J. Phys. Conf. Ser. **2143**(1), 012045 (2021)
14. Sui, Y.: Computer intelligent proofreading method for english translation based on foreign language translation model (2021)
15. Changda, L.: The application of intelligent technology in traffic automation control system (2021)

Machine Translation Based on Neural Network: A Case Study of Est Translation

Hui Wang$^{(\boxtimes)}$

School of Foreign Languages, Dalian Neusoft University of Information, Dalian 116032, Liaoning, China
wanghui_yy@neusoft.edu.cn

Abstract. Machine translation based on neural network plays an important role in EST translation. EST translation involves the processing of technical terms and complex sentence patterns, which requires accurate translation and fluent language. By building a neural network model and learning a large number of corpora, neural network machine translation can better understand and express the internal logic and semantic information of language, thus improving the accuracy and fluency of EST translation. Global science and technology giants have successively launched neural machine translation systems based on neural network algorithms. Compared with statistical machine translation languages, neural machine translation is more fluent and accurate, optimizing translation services. Machine translation is the process of translating text from one language to another. It has been used for many years and proved to be effective in the field of language translation. Machine translation (MT) is an automatic system that translates text into other languages. It is considered as a form of artificial intelligence (AI). Machine translation software can be used by humans and computers; However, it requires human intervention in order to correctly interpret or modify errors. This paper will discuss machine translation based on neural network. We will compare two methods applicable to different types of data sets: supervised learning method and unsupervised learning method.

Keywords: Neural network · Scientific English translation · MT

1 Introduction

Machine Translation (MT) refers to the automatic translation of a natural language text (source statement) into another natural language text (target statement) with the help of a computer.

Due to the rapid development and iterative progress of neural network models, neural network based machine translation models have made significant progress in recent years. However, the optimization training of neural network based machine translation models still has the problem of inconsistent model training and model testing. In the training phase of the neural network machine translation model, the encoder of the neural network based machine translation model first uses the source input statements as

Y. Zhang and N. Shah (Eds.): BigIoT-EDU 2023, LNICST 582, pp. 15–24, 2024.
https://doi.org/10.1007/978-3-031-63136-8_2

input, while the decoder uses a portion of the target input statements as input. Then, the model optimizes the prediction probability of each positional word at the target by maximizing natural estimation, primarily by minimizing the cross entropy loss function. At the same time, in order to make neural network machine translation models have better generalization ability and robustness, certain regularization methods, such as label smoothing, are generally introduced. However, when a neural network machine translation model specifically translates a certain word, the historical translation it is based on is translated by the model itself. The conditional distribution of these models' own translations is completely different from the data conditional distribution learned during the training phase of the neural network machine translation model, which leads to the neural network machine translation model being overly confident in its own predictions and making incorrect predictions. In addition to the accumulation of errors in natural language generation tasks, incorrect words predicted in the front position can affect the prediction of subsequent position models, resulting in a decline in the translation performance of the final neural network machine translation model. This is a common exposure bias problem in existing work. Exposing bias issues can make neural network machine translation models make overconfident or incorrect choices, and can also affect the normal cluster search process. For example, the distribution probability of error conditions in a cluster is too high, resulting in a relatively low final score for the translation under this path, and ultimately ranking in the optimal model translation position, thereby limiting the translation performance of the neural network machine translation model. Especially when the number of clusters is enlarged, this problem will become even more prominent, namely, the cluster search trap problem. Therefore, mitigating exposure bias in neural network machine translation models has significant and far-reaching implications and research significance [1, 2].

When the traditional machine translation method is used to deal with complex scientific English, semantic ambiguity and inaccurate translation often occur. By learning a large number of corpora, neural network machine translation can better understand technical terms and scientific context, reduce the workload of manual proofreading and post-editing, and improve translation efficiency. In natural language processing tasks, compared with traditional statistical learning, deep learning does not need to do a lot of feature engineering by analyzing texts, because deep learning methods can automatically mine the abstract semantic information contained in texts that are difficult to extract manually by training/learning on a large number of texts, thus improving the prediction ability of the model. At present, in many tasks in the field of natural language processing, methods related to deep learning have been widely concerned and applied, and their performance has improved compared with traditional rules, statistical machine learning models and other methods, such as text classification, language models, information extraction, question answering, machine translation, etc. [3]. Although the deep learning method can automatically learn the feature representation of data, there is a risk of over fitting when the amount of data is not large. However, the data set of machine translation quality estimation task is relatively small, so applying neural network and deep learning to machine translation quality estimation task and effectively alleviating the over fitting problem of deep learning model is one of the research focuses in this field at present.

2 Related Work

2.1 Neural Network Machine Translation Model

The development of neural network machine translation promotes the process of globalization. Through accurate scientific English translation, scientific and technical workers from different countries and regions can communicate and cooperate better, which promotes the progress and innovation of science and technology. A typical original NMT model is mainly composed of two sub models: encoder and decoder. The function of the encoder is to map the sentences of the source language into a fixed length vector, which theoretically contains all the relevant information about translating the sentences of the source language into the sentences of the target language; The main function of the decoder is to decode the vector obtained from the encoder to obtain the sentence of the target language. Figure 1 shows the structure of a typical original NMT model [4]. The encoder inputs the source side statement X = (X1, X2, X3, X4, <eos>) and encodes it into a fixed vector, from which the decoder decodes the target language statement Y = (y1y2, y3, y4, y5, <eos>). Where <eos> represents the end identifier of the statement.

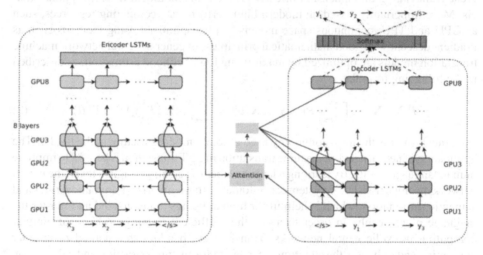

Fig. 1. Neural Network Machine Translation Model

Minimum Risk Training (MRT): Firstly, this method trains a preliminary baseline model based on the ordinary maximum log likelihood method, and then continues to perform training steps on this baseline model. In the subsequent training process, the model will first perform an inference operation, that is, a translation process. After obtaining the translated version of the model to the source side of the training data, the similarity between the model translation and the standard translation of the target side of the training data is measured. Here, a BLEU score is generally used, and then the BLEU score is converted into the risk of the corresponding translation of the model. Then, a new training goal of the model is to minimize empirical risk, and a model gradient retransmission operation is performed. However, due to the need to perform reasoning operations during the training phase of this method, the training speed will have a certain degree of impact. Formally, the reward function for minimum risk training is defined as follows:

$$R(\theta) = \sum_{s=1}^{S} S \sum_{y \in S(x^{(s)})} Q\left(y|x^{(s)}; \theta, \alpha\right) \Delta\left(y, y^{(s)}\right) \tag{1}$$

where $x^{(s)}$ and $y^{(s)}$ are the source and target ends of the translation data, and S (x ('x) is a subset of the sampling space. $\Delta\left(y, y^{(s)}\right)$ reflects the degree of difference between the model translation y and the standard translation ys). In this article, the commonly used BLEU indicator based on the quaternion grammar is used.

Secondly, the continuous representation space of neural network models has more powerful representation capabilities. Statistical machine translation models treat the process of word by word translation as the derivation of phrases or rules, while neural network models can replace traditional distance discrete word representations with distributed representations in real space, so that a sentence can be described as a real vector. In this way, translation can be carried out in a continuous spatial representation, greatly alleviating the dimension disaster problem of traditional discrete spatial models. More importantly, based on modern high-performance computing resources, such as GPU and TPU, continuous space models can be optimized using methods such as gradient descent with good mathematical principles. In general, neural network machine translation models are optimized by maximizing log likelihood estimation, as described in the following formula:

$$P(\mathbf{Y} \mid \mathbf{X}) = \prod_{t=1}^{n} P(y_t|\mathbf{y}_{<t}, \mathbf{X}, \theta) = \sum_{t=1}^{n} \log P\left(y_t|\mathbf{y}_{<t}, \mathbf{X}, \theta\right) \tag{2}$$

Transformer is the most commonly used efficient model structure in the field of The application of neural network machine translation in EST translation is helpful to improve human language ability. By learning a large number of scientific English texts, the neural network machine translation system can automatically summarize grammatical rules and semantic information, which is helpful for human beings to understand and master the language more deeply. In order to avoid the inefficient training problem of circular computing in cyclic neural networks, Transformer abandons the method of circular computing and only uses the attention mechanism for feature extraction and calculation. The calculation process is as follows:

$$\text{Atention}(Q, K, V) = \text{softmax}\left(\frac{QK^T}{\sqrt{d_k}}\right) V \tag{3}$$

among O Represents query, K represents key, and V represents value. First, query and key calculate the similarity, and then calculate based on the similarity score and value to return the final result. Multi header refers to the fact that the computing process of the attention mechanism described above is divided into multiple subspaces for parallel computing, while increasing the representation ability of the Transformer model.

Formally, the calculation method of the multi headed self attention mechanism is as follows:

$$s(u, v) = \frac{r_u \cdot r_v}{\|r_u\|_2 \|r_v\|_2} = \frac{\sum_i r_{u,i} r_{v,i}}{\sqrt{\sum_i r_{u,i}^2} \sqrt{\sum_{i=i} r_{i,i}^2}} \tag{4}$$

The feedforward fully connected neural network is the main model parameter of Transformer, which is mainly composed of a two-layer fully connected neural network and a RELU activation function. Its calculation method is as follows:

$$p_{u,i} = \bar{r}_u + \frac{\sum_{u' \in N} s(u, u')(r_{u',i} - \bar{r}_{u'})}{\sum_{u' \in N} |s(u_n u')|_{\bar{v} = \bar{v}_i \in \mathbb{Z}_i \in \mathbb{Z}}} \tag{5}$$

Unlike cyclic neural networks, which can automatically encode the location information of input statements, Transformer requires additional location coding to sense the location relationship of input statements, typically by adding the following location coding:

$$\hat{r}_{ui} = \mu + b_i + b_u + q_i^T p_u \tag{6}$$

The structure of the decoder Decoder and the encoder Encoder are similar, except for an additional cross attention mechanism sublayer. The cross attention mechanism is designed to focus the target sentence on the words that are most similar to the source and themselves through certain implicit mechanisms. The infrastructure of multi-layer encoder and decoder stacking constitutes the Transformer model framework. There are generally two variants of the Transformer model, namely, Transformerbase and Transformerpig, which have the same model layers, but the latter has wider network parameter settings. At the same time, many researchers have recently focused on how to deepen the depth of the encoder and maintain stable training of the model.

2.2 Neural Network Machine Translation Model with Attention Mechanism

The attention mechanism in neural network machine translation model is very similar to word alignment in statistical machine translation, which can be regarded as a kind of soft alignment. In the neural network machine translation model with attention mechanism added, before each target word is generated in the decoding stage, the correlation between the words of the target end to be output and the words of each source statement is calculated, and the encoding information that focuses on the words in some source statements and changes with the decoding process is calculated for each target word to be output, The encoding information is a weighted average of all or part of the words in the source statement. Attention mechanism is proposed and applied in the field of computer vision, such as image classification. Technical English involves a large number of technical terms, which require accurate translation. Neural network machine translation can accurately understand and express these technical terms by learning a large number of corpora. This is because the attention information reflects the importance of each source word to predict the current target word, which can shorten the distance between the target word and the related source word, and reduce the burden of the encoder. Instead of the original neural network machine translation model, no matter which target word is predicted during decoding, it corresponds to a fixed context vector [6]. The pre training is shown in Fig. 2 below.

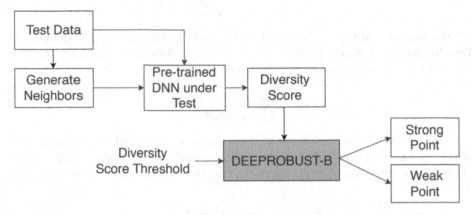

Fig. 2. Pre training

In computer science, cluster search is a heuristic search algorithm that mainly exThere are a large number of complex sentence patterns in EST, such as long sentences and passive sentences. Neural network machine translation can reasonably split and combine sentence structures by learning language models, and ensure the fluency and accuracy of translation [7, 8].

Improve work efficiency: The translation of technical English is completed in an automated way, which reduces the time cost of manual editing and proofreading, and improves work efficiency.

Promote information dissemination: Accurate scientific and technical English translation facilitates the dissemination of information across languages, enabling more scientific and technological workers to share the international cutting-edge scientific and technological achievements and technological progress.

Promote language learning: Through the learning process of machine translation, you can deeply understand the internal logic and semantic information of the language, which can help promote the development of language learning.

3   Machine Translation of Scientific English Based on Neural Network

EST often involves specific context and background knowledge, such as scientific experiments, technical applications and so on. Neural network machine translation can better understand the context and improve the accuracy of translation through the processing of context information.Due to the sequential execution of each decoding position at the target end of the cyclic neural network, that is, the later decoding position depends on the state transition of the earlier position. Therefore, it is relatively straightforward and easy to execute a scheduling sampling algorithm on a recurrent neural network, which is a common structure for scheduling sampling algorithms on recurrent neural networks. The model reads in the input statements one by one in the order of input, and then performs corresponding semantic transformations. Assuming that at the t-th decoding position, in conventional training methods, the model will follow the teacher-forcing training model, using words from the first position to the t-1 position as historical clauses as input at the t-th moment, and then maximizing the probability of correct prediction at the t-th position through model training. A sampling of the Bernoulli distribution is performed for each location of the model to determine whether the model uses the standard translation as input at the current location or the prediction of the model at the previous time as input. However, due to the existence of exposure bias, that is, the standard historical translation used in the training phase of the cyclic neural network cannot be obtained during the actual inference testing phase. Therefore, the model will see a data distribution that has never been seen by the model itself, which can easily lead to prediction errors and overconfidence prediction problems in the model. When a model makes a prediction error at a certain location, due to the natural sequence in natural language, the incorrect prediction at the previous location can also affect the prediction of the model at subsequent stages, leading to the continuous accumulation of errors. In a scheduling sampling algorithm based on recurrent neural networks, it is only necessary to simply change the historical input on which the model is based at the prediction time, so that the model is no longer overly dependent on standard historical translations. Generally, using the prediction of the model itself at the historical time as the input at the current time can simulate the input of the model at the inference testing stage. Due to the fact that the model can see standard translations during the training phase, it is possible to use inputs that may contain errors, and then optimize the model towards the correct translation direction, enabling the model to learn to resist its own translation errors, alleviate exposure bias issues, and thereby improve model translation performance.

The encoder is responsible for outputting the semantic representation vector of the source statement after encoding and feature extraction of the source input statement through two sub layer neural networks. Then, the source semantic representation vector output by the encoder is further used as input to the two round decoder. The first round decoder is a standard Transformer decoder, which consists of three sub layers, namely, the target side self attention mechanism, the cross attention mechanism, and the feedforward fully connected neural network. The target side's self attention mechanism is similar to the source side's self attention mechanism, except that it encodes input statements from the target side and has different input embedding layers. The target side's self attention mechanism accepts the previous standard translation of the current location as input, that is, the labeled teacher-forcing. Due to the fact that future information is not visible in the actual translation reasoning process, it is necessary to use a certain masking mechanism to mask future target words. After the target side's self attention mechanism encodes the target side's input statement and outputs the corresponding semantic representation vector, the target side's semantic representation vector is further used as a query for the query, and the source side's semantic vector is used for cross language attention mechanism calculations. First, query performs a certain semantic transformation, and then divides it into multiple headers for parallel computing. Finally, the source side semantic vector is used as memory for similarity retrieval calculations, and the resulting value is returned. The third self layer is a feedforward fully connected neural network. This part of the model parameters is responsible for fully fusing the semantic information of the source and target ends. After multi-layer encoder semantic transformation and feature extraction, the Transformer model performs the final translation prediction at the top level, first performing a multiplication operation through a two-dimensional softmax matrix. The dimensions of this matrix are the dimensions of the implicit state of the model and the size of the target vocabulary. After semantic transformation of this matrix, the Transformer model outputs the logits of the predicted word, also known as the probability value without logarithmic transformation. The final logits are converted into the final prediction probability of the model through the softmax normalization operation, and the cross entropy loss value is calculated with the standard translation. During the first round of decoding of the model, the structure is basically consistent with the standard Transformer encoder and decoder.

English for science and technology is well structured, well regulated, standardized and objective in description. It is different from other English styles in terms of vocabulary, syntax and textual features. Professional discipline determination is only one of the major points of thermal power, and many technical terms are used in scientific English. These terms reflect the phenomenon of a certain field abstractly, and should be accurate in translation; Secondly, in scientific English, there are often "nobody says" sentences, but few people use "person" sentences. This is because the purpose of scientific and technological texts or reports is to introduce scientific achievements, technological inventions or new concepts. The focus of expression is to state natural phenomena, research findings, scientific and technological creation and other contents, which are generally expressed from an objective perspective rather than a subjective level [9]. Therefore, passive voice is widely used in scientific and technological English. Thirdly, the language of scientific and technological style is concise and clear, and the words are accurate to express a specific or meaning. Most of the sentences are long sentences. For example, Along with the development of polymer technology, PCMs will occur in the form of microcapsule, because of the appropriate shell of microcapsule are acquired, and the produce technology simplify This long sentence has a total of 29 words. In the sentence, professional terms such as polymer technology are used. This word belongs to the field of chemical engineering, refers to polymer synthesis technology, and there is a passive voice.

4 Google Translation Example Analysis

Data preparation: Collect a large number of original technical English texts and corresponding translations to build a corpus.

Model training: Neural networks are used to build language models, learn from corpora, and train model parameters.

Prediction generation: Enter the technical English sentence to be translated, and calculate the corresponding translation through the model.

Post-processing: Post-processing is performed on the generated translation, such as denoising and smoothing, to improve the accuracy and fluency of the translation.American regulators are trying to catch up with Europe to promote "biosimilars", which is a general approximation of patented drugs.

When American regulators promoted the "biological analogues", the general analogues of patented drugs, their momentum quickly caught up with that of Europe.

Momentum has a variety of understandings. Specifically, it means power, momentum, momentum, etc. It is intended to indicate the efforts made by American regulators, so it is more appropriate to translate momentum. Approvals have the meaning of approximation, but in this context, it should be translated freely. It is more appropriate to translate them into general analogues. Literally translating them into general approximation will cause difficulties in understanding. In this sentence, the translation of approximations is not accurate. Although Google translation does not affect the understanding of the original meaning, there is a certain gap between Google translation and the Chinese language expression habits, especially when translating long and difficult sentences, it will be split. Due to technical limitations, the translation may only achieve formal equivalence and basic sentence fluency. The simulation results are shown in Fig. 3 below.

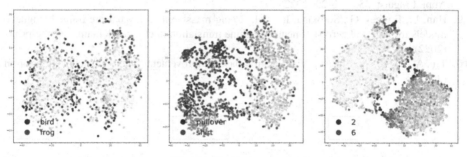

Fig. 3. Simulation result

5 Conclusion

AI has greatly promoted the development of translation services, making it convenient for people to quickly understand the general content of languages other than their mother tongue, and to some extent, no longer rely on human translation. Neuro machine translation is no longer a translation of "words are relative to words". It can better understand long sentences with complex structures from the whole, and convert the source language to the target language in combination with the context. However, due to the differences between the source language and the target language, it is found that there are some semantic deviations from the original sentence through the above examples of scientific English translation, and there is a gap between machine translation and manual translation. Machine translation still cannot achieve perfect translation. Therefore, at present, machine translation has certain application value, but it can not completely replace human translation.

References

1. Dankers, V., Bruni, E., Hupkes, D.: The paradox of the compositionality of natural language: a neural machine translation case study (2021)

2. Li, L.: On Chinese and English metaphors of taste based on conceptual metaphor theory: a case study of taste word translation in fortress besieged. Int. J. Appl. Linguist. Transl. **7**, 69 (2021)
3. Babaali, B., Salem, M.: Survey of the Arabic Machine Translation Corpora (2023)
4. Tong, Q.: Optimization of English machine translation algorithm based on internet information technology (2021)
5. Xiang, L.I., Sun, Y., Jingwei, L.I., et al.: Method and device for compressing a neural network model for machine translation and storage Medium. EP3825924A1 (2021)
6. Hayashi, H., Shibanoki, T., Tsuji, T.: A neural network based on the Johnson SU translation system and related application to electromyogram classification. IEEE Access **9**, 154304–154317 (2021)
7. Song, G.: Accuracy analysis of Japanese machine translation based on machine learning and image feature retrieval. J. Intell. Fuzzy Syst. Appl. Eng. Technol. **2**, 40 (2021)
8. Grabowski, U., Groom, N.: Functionally-defined recurrent multi-word units in English-to-Polish translation: a corpus-based study. Revista Española de Lingüística Aplicada/Span. J. Appl. Linguist. **35**(1), 1–29 (2022)
9. Han, L., Erofeev, G., Sorokina, I., et al.: Using massive multilingual pre-trained language models towards real zero-shot neural machine translation in clinical domain. arXiv e-prints (2022)
10. Tm, A., Dv, B., Pk, B., et al.: Visualization-based improvement of neural machine translation (2021)

Modal Verbs in Learner Corpus Based on Feature Extraction Algorithm

Jianjia Zhang and Jianbo Xu(✉)

Foreign Studies College, Xiangnan University, Chenzhou 423000, Hunan, China
tonyxu5132@126.com

Abstract. The use of modal verbs is a very important grammatical item in English, and it is also a difficult point in Chinese learners' learning. The study of modal meaning has always been the focus of linguists' attention, and modal verbs, as an important means to realize modal meaning, have attracted more and more attention. Chinese learners' use of English modal verbs can show their English proficiency to some extent. Linguists believe that it is of great significance to language communication, and argumentative paper is a genre article that analyzes and discusses a certain problem or matter, and then expresses the speaker's own views, attitudes, positions and opinions. It can best reflect personal feelings, so the expression of modality is obvious in argumentative paper. Based on the corpus, this paper investigates the semantic acquisition of modal verbs by Chinese college English learners. It is found that there is a significant difference between the frequency distribution of English modal verbs used by English learners in written language and that of English native speakers, that is, the semantic acquisition of modal verbs by college English learners is not authentic. Therefore, the purpose of this study is to investigate the choice tendency, semantic choice and usage of typical sentence patterns of modal verbs by Chinese English learners, and to analyze the empirical research methods of the usage characteristics of modal verbs. Corpus-based approach provides reliable linguistic evidence for language research, helps learners pay attention to the usage norms of native speakers and make choices of modal verbs close to those of native speakers.

Keywords: Learner corpus · Modal verbs · Feature extraction algorithm

1 Introduction

With the rapid development of the Internet and the sharp increase of various electronic text data, people are more and more accustomed to searching and publishing information on the Internet, which accelerates the surge of information to some extent [1]. In the face of vast information, how to effectively manage and utilize it has become a hot issue in the field of information technology [2]. Modal verbs and modal verbs have always attracted the attention of many scholars. Modal verbs are a very important part of speech in English. Among them, based on English native language corpus, the semantic frequency distribution of modal verbs is different in different language environments [3].

Y. Zhang and N. Shah (Eds.): BigIoT-EDU 2023, LNICST 582, pp. 25–33, 2024.
https://doi.org/10.1007/978-3-031-63136-8_3

Modality refers to the state between "yes" and "no", which can be divided into "modality" and "modulation" according to the communicative purpose of "information" and "service", which respectively correspond to modal modality and responsible modality distinguished in logic [4]. However, most English modal verbs have polysemy and overlapping meanings. Coupled with the influence of cultural differences, modal verbs are often difficult to learn. Generally speaking, modal modality is the speaker's uncertainty or lack of commitment to the true value, which belongs to cognitive type and is the speaker's response to the existing knowledge state of the stated proposition [5].

In addition, some studies have shown that there are significant differences in the distribution of semantic use frequency of modal verbs between non-English native speakers and native speakers [6]. The responsible modality expresses the obligation, need or allowed behavior felt by the subject. The event is controlled by the external environment of the sentence subject, and the ability comes from the external permission. It involves the actions of the speaker or others, which belongs to the responsibility type [7]. However, as the written expression of human natural language, the inherent characteristics of synonym confusion and polysemy ambiguity of data greatly affect the accuracy of classification algorithm. Its high-dimensional sparse characteristics lead to high time complexity of classification algorithm. In addition, few studies have investigated the semantic frequency distribution of can, an English modal verb with high frequency of use, and there are few studies on the semantic acquisition of English modal verbs in the written language of Chinese College English Learners. Semantic feature extraction is the optimization technology that meets this demand. At present, in the direction of semantic feature extraction, vector space model, VSM) and latent semantic index, LSI) are mainly used for text representation [8]. Include text semantic understanding technology based on natural language understanding, word segmentation matching technology based on keyword list and professional dictionary, and meaningless text decomposition technology based on pure statistical method.

The purpose of semantic feature extraction is to filter data noise features, select the optimal feature subset to optimize the text representation, reduce the dimension of text data and improve the class separability of reduced dimension text representation. There is a difference between the semantic frequency distribution of English modal verbs in the pen language of Chinese College English learners and that in the pen language corpus of English native speakers [9]. It can be seen that there is a strong correspondence between the sentence pattern of modal verbs and modal semantic types. The modal semantic attributes of modal verbs can be predicted according to different sentence patterns, and the characteristics of learners' use of English modal verbs and their modal sequences can be investigated with reference to English native speakers' corpus or other L2 learners' corpus with different backgrounds.

2   An Empirical Study on the Characteristics of Modal Verbs

2.1   A Study on the Characteristics of Modal Verbs in Learners' Corpus

With the development and popularization of applied computer technology and the establishment and improvement of various corpora, using retrieval tools to explore the real use of natural corpora provides a new perspective for language research [10]. The polysemy of modal verbs is a verbal fact. Although the polysemy model objectively and concretely describes the modal meaning, the lack of explanation of the semantic position of modal verbs ignores the ambiguity and compatibility between meanings. The polysemy model of modal verbs is shown in Fig. 1 below.

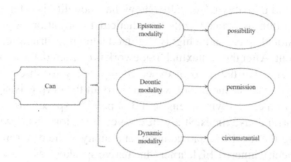

Fig. 1. Polysemy patterns of modal verbs

While using information, we must also fully consider the large number of synonymous and polysemy phenomena in language, as well as the tendency of praise and criticism, which often play a key role in feature extraction. Because the separation of words is not obvious, there are many ambiguities, and the freedom of word order and word order is high in Chinese, there are some difficulties in the application of semantic understanding technology and word segmentation technology in Chinese text environment. People's memory of language is not a simple accumulation of words and grammar, but the probability of these words and grammar items in the language at the same time. Second language learners generally overuse modal verbs when expressing modal meaning. The main reasons are learners' oral use of written language, mother tongue transfer and the influence of teaching. Therefore, the choice of form in language use is to a greater extent determined by the language user's choice of a continuous word collocation sequence to express meaning. However, the use of modal verbs is very complex. Although the overall survey is helpful to understand learners' use of modal verbs from a macro perspective, the research on a specific modal verb is often not deep enough. Therefore, the research on modal verbs has changed from the traditional intuitive experience method to the method based on experiment and statistics, and from the qualitative research on the semantic and pragmatic functions of modal verbs to the quantitative research based on a large number of real corpus.

First of all, in order to study the semantic frequency of modal verbs used by Chinese college English learners, the British National Corpus is selected, and a sub-corpus is established as a reference corpus, which is named as the written language database of English native speakers. Including the basic background information, the time and space information of the presentation center, the author's reference point, purpose, and the tendency of praise and criticism. Accordingly, the word collocation researchers designed a method to extract word cluster. Then randomly select 100 sentences with English modal verb can from WECNES. After the researcher inputs the key words, and then chooses to set the length of the word cluster, the continuous word cluster composed of the word and other words can be extracted. This method provides an accurate and objective basis for in-depth analysis of the causes.

2.2 A Study of Modal Meaning in Semantics

The subjectivity and unreality of modality show that modality is often related to untrue information and often associated with hypothetical information. Context framework is a three-dimensional space and a highly digitized semantic structure, so it is a highly abstract text content. After the contextual framework is extracted, the expected frequency of each word cluster and the ratio of expected frequency to observed frequency are calculated to judge whether the use of word clusters in the corpus is significant. Select the class conjunction cluster with a length of 3–4 parts of speech and set the minimum frequency of occurrence as 5 times. Study the class conjunction cluster with the extraction frequency ranking the top 10%, and compare and analyze the differences in the use of modal verbs between Chinese EFL learners and native speakers, as well as the differences in the use of modal verbs between Chinese EFL middle-level learners and high-level learners. Make necessary adjustments to the original text representation and the trained classifier to ensure the classification performance of the content text classifier, and adjust the text classification system to the best working state. Figure 2 shows the automatic text classification system based on text content.

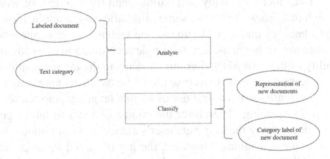

Fig. 2. Automatic text classification system based on text content

Because the contextual framework comprehensively describes the content of the text from three aspects: static category, semantic relationship between features, and favorable and unfavorable tendency among features, it can better reflect the internal relationship of the text by using it as a feature of the text. Word Smith and Ultra Edit-32 corpus retrieval and analysis software are mainly used to retrieve the data needed for research from the corpus, which provides reliable data basis and corpus support for statistics and analysis. In the expression of modal meaning, compared with native English speakers, Chinese English learners use modal verbs with serious overuse and underuse. Methodologically, all modal verbs in the English part of the self-built corpus are retrieved, and their frequency distribution as obligatory modality, cognitive modality and their corresponding modal sequences are investigated.

Obligatory modality is to make a judgment on the possibility of an event according to the credibility of knowledge, but no matter how certain the speaker makes a judgment on the possibility of the event, the event does not necessarily occur in reality. The self built corpus and the target language corpus will be investigated respectively, not only starting from the interlanguage, but also searching and investigating the learners' corresponding mother tongue thinking expression when using the obligatory modality. The advantage of corpus is that it simplifies the unstructured or semi-structured text processing into vector operation in vector space, so it can carry out various mathematical processing and has good operability. Although word clusters are not collocations in the real sense, the extracted use frequency is higher than that of written language [11]. The overall frequency of modal verbs used by Chinese English learners is higher than that of English native speakers, indicating that Chinese high-level English learners show a strong tendency of colloquialism in written language.

3 Unsupervised Discriminant Rules Based on Manifold Mapping

3.1 Feature Extraction Based on Principal Component Analysis

Feature extraction not only obtains the most favorable features for classification from the original information, but also these features greatly reduce the dimension of the sample data and ensure the maximum maintenance of the data description information compared with the original sample data information. The algorithm flow is shown in Fig. 3 below.

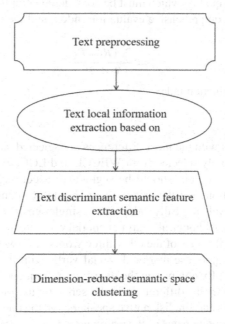

Fig. 3. Analysis of feature extraction algorithm based on principal component analysis

According to the classification of modal verbs, nine core modal verbs are taken as the research objects of this study, and the examples of each modal verb in WECCL and LOCNESS are retrieved by using Ant Conc software. Look for its hidden meaningful low-dimensional data structure in the high-dimensional observation sample data space, and analyze and explore the inherent law of things. Macroscopically, the original frequency of core modal verbs in two corpora and the standard frequency of core modal verbs per 10,000 words are counted, and modal verbs with significant differences are obtained by log-likelihood statistics. Assuming that there are m texts, the accuracy formula is:

$$R_i = \frac{N_{cpi}}{N_{cl}} \tag{1}$$

R_i–Recall rate

N_{ci}–The number of m texts that experts think belong to c_i category.

N_{cpi}–The number of texts considered by experts and procedures to belong to category c_i

The research of linear feature extraction algorithm focuses on the dimensionality reduction of complex data, which is closely related to the high dimensionality of sample data. For nonlinear feature extraction, great progress has been made in both theoretical research and application development in recent years, but its application is limited by the complexity of its theory and calculation, and linear feature extraction still plays a leading role in the application field. Achievement strategies, that is, learners adhere to the original communication task, but take measures to make up for the lack of second language knowledge. At this time, they often turn to their mother tongue and use modal verbs to reflect their emotions. The accuracy rate and recall rate reflect two different aspects of classification quality, which must be considered comprehensively. Therefore, there is a test value of comprehensive evaluation index, and the calculation formula is as follows:

$$F_{1i} = \frac{2 * R_i * P_i}{R_i + P_i} \tag{2}$$

F_{1i}–Comprehensive evaluation index

R_i–Recall rate

P_i–Accuracy rate

Several modal verbs with the most differences are selected as research objects, and 100 examples are randomly selected from WECCL and LOCNESS corpus as analysis samples. Firstly, the text corpus should be segmented according to Chinese, English and paragraph punctuation, and the original text should be segmented into paragraph sequences, that is, relatively logically independent single sentences or paragraphs. Then segment each paragraph. Although all marginal modal verbs are overused, except for used to (ll value + 5.83), the ll values of the other three words are lower than 1, which shows that Chinese English majors use marginal modal verbs with the same frequency and order as native speakers. By comparing the distribution frequency of semantic use, this paper statistically analyzes the differences in the semantic use of modal verbs between Chinese English learners and English native speakers. On the one hand, it simplifies the description of the main components of the original data, and on the other hand, it retains the main features of the original data.

3.2 Feature Extraction Based on Fisher Discriminant Analysis

Discriminant analysis is a statistical method to distinguish the type of data samples. Discriminant analysis is that the known research objects are divided into several types or groups, and the observation data of a batch of known samples and training samples of various types have been obtained. On this basis, the discriminant is established according to some criteria, and then the unknown types of samples and test samples are discriminated and classified. For example, the level semantic relationship in the field of professional activities and the contribution of each role to the sentence group. Finally, the contextual framework is extracted through dynamic memory The processing block diagram is shown in Fig. 4.

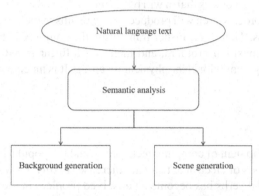

Fig. 4. Context extraction framework

The semantic analysis of modal verbs in 200 sentences randomly selected from WECNES, CELIC and CCELWE is carried out with reference to 10 senses, and the frequency distribution of senses in each corpus is counted with the help of Excel software. Fisher's core idea is to find an optimal feature vector space, so that the intra-class divergence matrix of the projected pattern sample is the largest and the intra-class divergence matrix is the smallest, so that the pattern has the best separability in this space. In English grammar teaching, the accuracy of grammatical form is always emphasized instead of the appropriateness in pragmatic sense, while modal verbs have no inflectional changes in word form, and subsequent verbs have no changes in person and number, which makes it more convenient for learners to use. Therefore, they tend to use modal verbs in writing. Chinese English learners significantly overuse the two modal sentences of "VM + Dynamic Verb" and "Conscious Subject + VM", while the other six modal sentences are significantly less used. MR, MP and MF1 are used to represent the macro recall rate, macro accuracy rate and macro value in the macro average, and then the macro average calculation formula of the classification system is as follows:

$$MF1 = \frac{2 * MR * MP}{MR + MP} \tag{3}$$

MF1–Macro F_1 value

MR–Macro recall rate in macro average
MP–Macro accuracy rate

Analyze 174 sentences with "NENG" randomly selected from CCLC, and count the semantic frequency distribution of "NENG" in sentences with the help of software Excel. Here, it is assumed to be a smooth and compact dimensional Riemannian manifold and embedded in a dimensional Riemannian geometry. Use ant conc software to observe the context of the sentence retrieval line, and refer to the interpretation of the Oxford Advanced English Chinese dictionary and the research results of Biber (1999) on the corresponding relationship between modal verb sentence patterns and modal semantics to determine the semantics, so as to deeply analyze the distribution of Chinese English learners and native speakers in the semantic use of modal verbs. However, feature words with a length greater than or less than n will be segmented, resulting in some deviations in semantics and word order, which will produce wrong results in the subsequent retrieval or classification process. Therefore, Fisher transforms the complex optimization problem into a matrix decomposition problem, and then into a linear transformation to obtain the optimization judgment with clear physical meaning. It is an enduring data judgment algorithm.

4 Conclusions

With the rapid development of computer technology and the popularization of databases and networks, all kinds of electronic text data increase sharply. How to improve the use and research of modal verbs has become an unsolved problem in the field of intelligent information science, so the study of modal verbs in learner corpus based on feature extraction algorithm came into being. There is a significant difference between the frequency distribution of semantic usage of English modal verbs in Chinese college English learners' written language and that in the written language corpus of native English speakers. This paper attempts to deal with ambiguity in the text, focusing on the favorable and unfavorable tendencies in language. The use of modal verbs is very complicated, which is a "problem area" in English learning. It is understandable that there are significant differences between Chinese English learners and native English speakers in the frequency of using modal verbs. With the improvement of language proficiency, the frequency of cognitive modality expressions used by second language learners has not greatly increased. These findings have certain implications for the teaching of modal verbs, and also have certain significance for the further study of modal verbs. Therefore, in English teaching, we should pay full attention to the semantic category of modal verbs and guide students to accurately grasp the multi-layer meanings of modal verbs. We should not only pay attention to the accuracy of their grammatical forms, but also emphasize the appropriateness of their pragmatic meanings, so as to improve students' communicative competence.

References

1. Dai, Z.: Comparison of the use of modal verbs and the use of common words pretty in the English Learner Corpus and the English Native Corpus. Overseas Engl. (2), 2 (2017)

2. Wang, X.: From the dimension of modal verb usage to explore the corpus differences between English learners and native English speakers. Campus Engl. (33), 1 (2016)
3. Sheng, X.: A comparative study on the use of modal verbs between Chinese English learners and English speakers. Writer's World (19), 2 (2019)
4. Long, S., Fu, H., Chen, T., et al.: Characteristics of the use of modal verbs in argumentative essays of professional students. J. Fore. Lang. (1), 8 (2016)
5. Lin, Q., Zheng, J.: Investigating the use of core modal verbs based on corpus interlanguage comparative analysis. J. Fujian Normal Univ. Fuqing Branch (1), 7 (2016)
6. Chang, Z.: Research on modal verbs and modal sequences in Chinese English learners' written language. J. Lanzhou Inst. Technol. **26**(2) (2019)
7. Xiao, Z.: Based on corpus to explore the differences in the use of English modal verbs caused by gender differences. Vision (15), 1 (2020)
8. Ma, Y., Kang, L.: A comparative study on the usage of obligatory modal verbs in English composition of Chinese and Foreign college students. J. Hebei North Univ. Soc. Sci. Ed. **32**(5), 5 (2016)
9. Chang, Z.: Research on modal verbs and modal sequences in Chinese English learners' written language. J. Lanzhou Inst. Technol. **26**(2), 4 (2019)
10. Wang, L., Zhang, L.: Research on the classification method of learner corpus: reflection and enlightenment. J. Ocean Univ. China (Soc. Sci. Ed.) **000**(002), 107–113 (2016)
11. Biber, D., et al.: Longman Grammar of Spoken and Written English. Foreign Language Teaching and Research Press, Beijing (1999)

Design of English Translation Model
for Intelligent Recognition of Fu Tea Culture
Based on Improved GLR Algorithm

Cuiying Wang[1]([✉]), Xiaozhe Yu[2], and Pengying Sui[2]

[1] Xianyang Normal University, Xianyang 712000, Shaanxi, China
wangcuiying0428@163.com
[2] No 1 Middle School of Dalian Economic and Technological Development Zone,
Dalian 116000, Liaoning, China

Abstract. This paper focuses on the design of an English translation model for intelligent recognition of Fu tea culture based on the improved GLR algorithm, the particularity of the connotation of Chinese Fu tea culture, the main translation strategies of Fu tea culture, and focuses on the application of literal translation, free translation and translation compensation in the English translation of Fu tea, It aims to show the material and spiritual cultural connotation of Chinese Fu tea and promote the smooth spread and exchange of national culture. The model can be designed by the following steps: (1) the input text is divided into sentences and phrases, and then each sentence or phrase is further divided into words; (2) Arranging words into a tree structure to form a word frequency index; (3) Create a dictionary file containing all words and their definitions; (4) Using this dictionary, the probability of occurrence of each word in each sentence or phrase is calculated based on its frequency in the entire text file. This probability value will be used as a parameter to determine whether the word should appear in the sentence/phrase.

Keyword: Improved GLR algorithm · English translation · Fu Tea Culture

1 Introduction

In recent years, the tea planting area and output have increased rapidly. Fu tea, as a representative product, has also been recognized by the tea industry and praised by the public consumers. Reasonable development and utilization of Fu tea cultural tourism resources can not only accelerate the development of Shaanxi Fu tea industry, but also greatly improve the utilization rate of tourism resources and cultural connotation, thus optimizing the overall industrial structure and promoting the comprehensive development of economy [1].

Chinese tea culture originates from the process of drinking tea and is a traditional culture with typical Chinese characteristics. As one of the birthplaces of tea, China retains various customs and habits such as making, tasting and drinking tea [2]. Nowadays,

Y. Zhang and N. Shah (Eds.): BigIoT-EDU 2023, LNICST 582, pp. 34–44, 2024.
https://doi.org/10.1007/978-3-031-63136-8_4

Chinese tea culture has become an important part of Chinese traditional culture and has great cultural dissemination value.

The role of culture in society and economy has received increasing attention and gradually become the "soft power" of a nation or even a country. With the increasing marketization and internationalization of China's economy, people are increasingly accepting foreign cultures, such as foreign fast food such as KFC, Starbucks Coffee, which has become the spokesperson of "petty bourgeoisie", rock music popular, and Japanese and Korean TV dramas dominating the screen. Under the conflict between Chinese and foreign cultures, traditional Chinese culture is gradually lacking, and traditional consumer goods are gradually being replaced by a variety of "foreign goods" [3]. In this situation, China has begun to emphasize cultural self-confidence.

The study of the relationship between culture and industry began in the 1960s. The cultural industry has a strong sense of experience, has become a new force in the advanced industrial industry, and has also received widespread attention from the international academic community [4].

Since the centenary of the Canadian Federation in 1967, Canada has embarked on a cultural boom. The government has participated in the formulation of cultural policies, and many cultural institutions have emerged that interface with industrial and social management departments, playing a positive role in using culture to promote social stability and production development. Some scholars in the United States believe that consumers have a natural curiosity mentality towards exotic cultures. He concluded from the development trajectory of the Spanish Flaming Song and Dance Culture Complex that unique regional culture is an indispensable element in the development of local industries, and even an important weight for local industries to enter the world market [5]. Russia's narrow understanding of the concept of culture has led to a reduction in the legal and social status of culture and a smaller investment in the cultural industry. Through a study of the potential of developing creative industries in Russia, the author proposes that culture can become a "landscape" of creative industries, enhance the connotation of industrial brands, and become a consumption engine. Therefore, it is recommended that Russia establish cultural clusters to lay a foundation for the development of creative industries.

Chinese tea culture originates from the process of drinking tea and is a traditional culture with Chinese characteristics. As one of the birthplaces of tea, China still retains various customs and habits such as making, appreciating and drinking tea. Nowadays, Chinese tea culture has become one of the most important components of Chinese traditional culture and has high cultural transmission value.

It highlights the cultural significance of Chinese Fu tea. It focuses on the translation of Fu tea culture loaded words, explores effective and practical translation methods, and aims to make contributions to the international dissemination of Chinese culture [6]. Through the study of Fu tea culture loaded words, this paper highlights the cultural significance of Chinese Fu tea. It focuses on the translation of Fu tea culture loaded words and explores effective and practical translation methods in order to make contributions to the international exchange of Chinese culture.

2 Related Work

2.1 Machine Translation Model

The study of English machine translation models has always been an important research direction in the field of natural language processing [7]. At present, research on English machine translation models mainly focuses on the following aspects:

1. Model based on Statistical Machine Translation (SMT): Statistical Machine Translation is one of the early machine translation methods, which is based on large-scale bilingual parallel corpora and establishes translation and language models for translation. In recent years, neural network-based methods have been widely applied in statistical machine translation, such as introducing neural networks as feature functions to extract richer language features.
2. Neural network-based models: With the development of deep learning, neural networks have made significant progress in machine translation. Neural network-based machine translation models such as Neural Machine Translation (NMT) have achieved significant improvements in translation quality and efficiency. The NMT model typically consists of an encoder and decoder, which learn the representation of input statements and generate translation output [8]. For English Chinese machine translation, researchers have also attempted some specific improvement measures, such as introducing attention mechanisms to handle long sentences and alignment issues.
3. Transfer learning and multimodal translation: In order to overcome the problem of data scarcity, transfer learning has been widely applied in English machine translation. Transfer learning improves the performance of machine translation by utilizing trained models from other tasks. In addition, multimodal translation has also become a research hotspot, which combines images or other non textual information with translation tasks to improve translation quality through joint learning.
4. Reinforcement learning: In recent years, reinforcement learning has been increasingly applied in machine translation. By treating the translation process as a decision-making process, reinforcement learning algorithms can be used to optimize translation decisions and improve translation quality.

The research on English machine translation models is constantly developing towards higher quality, efficiency, and accuracy in translation. The application of neural network-based methods and transfer learning and multimodal translation technologies is expected to further improve the performance of English machine translation [9]. In addition, with the continuous development of deep learning and natural language processing, new technologies and methods will continue to emerge, bringing more innovation to the research and application of English machine translation.

At present, the mainstream framework of machine translation model is seq2seq framework, which has made excellent achievements in machine translation, speech recognition, text summarization and other fields [10]. The seq2seq framework is composed of an encoder decoder structure. Its core idea is to encode the source language input sequence through the encoder to obtain the hidden vector, decode the hidden vector through the decoder, and output the target language result in turn. The encoder and decoder can be composed of RNN, CNN, transformer and other structures. The transformer structure is proposed to form the seq2seq framework, and the model structure is shown in Fig. 1. The core of transformer structure is the multi head self attention structure [11]. Through the self attention mechanism, the importance and global relationship of each word to the target word can be obtained, while a variety of different self attention structures can obtain different syntactic and semantic features of other words corresponding to the target word. Experiments also show that the seq2seq model composed of transformer structure is far better than the seq2seq model composed of RNN structure in the past.

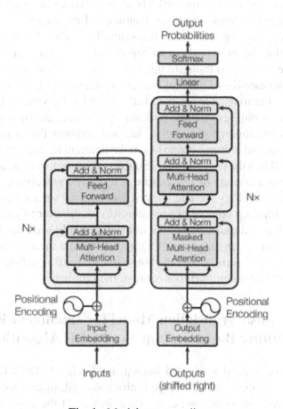

Fig. 1. Model structure diagram

Although the transformer model based on seq2seq has achieved better translation results, there are still shortcomings. As the machine translation task is a resource dependent task, the translation effect of the model is very dependent on parallel corpora. However, there are several problems in parallel corpora [12]: 1) the number of parallel corpora is small and it is difficult to collect; 2) The scope of parallel corpus is narrow, and most of them are concentrated in news, government reports and other fields; 3) The uneven number of corpora in different fields makes the translation results tend to be biased; Due to the above-mentioned problems, the machine translation model trained with such parallel corpora may have rare word translation errors, inaccurate entity noun translation, and the translation results tend to be most words in the corpus, which will affect the final translation results [13].

2.2 Translation of Tea Culture

The text of tea culture needs to be placed in the context of modern culture, adhere to the attitude of inheriting and carrying forward the excellent culture of Chinese ethnic minorities, integrate the original author's writing intention, the context state, the target language readers and the target audience of the text, and select the words and sentences, structural expression and translation methods of the text, so as to finally achieve the purpose of communication between the two languages. Language reflects culture and is restricted by culture. Language translation is essentially a cultural translation. Under the guidance of adaptation theory, it is also a process of continuous selection and adaptation to study tea culture works and translate this kind of text with strong national characteristics from the perspective of cultural context adaptation [14]. In order to adapt to the cultural context, the translator needs to fully consider the various factors involved in the culture, such as politics, history, philosophy, science, customs and habits, religious beliefs, mode of thinking, geography, etc., and combine the dynamic changes of language components and cultural context to make continuous choices in terms of language and strategy. When the two cultures are universal in one aspect and basically equal in function, the surface content of this culture is directly transformed, and the factors such as humanism, psychology and deep-seated unconscious values are less considered. For the language with deep cultural connotation, if it is difficult to understand or seek equivalence in another cultural context, the translator should seek the indirect equivalence between the source language and the target language in the process of seeking cultural context [15]. At this time, we can choose to use free translation, free translation annotation and other translation methods to solve the problem.

3 Design of English Translation Model for Intelligent Recognition of Fu Tea Culture Based on Improved GLR Algorithm

Traditional Fu tea is brick shaped, also known as "Fu Brick Tea". Currently, it has developed into cake shaped, column shaped, block shaped, biscuit shaped, as well as loose Fu tea, bag tea, instant tea, and canned tea drinks. At the same time, there have emerged flavored health tea, Fu tea food, Fu tea wine, and Fu tea daily necessities, such as rose Fu tea, chrysanthemum Fu tea, and cordyceps Fu tea, spicy wood Fu tea, Hexiang Fu tea, Du Zhong Fu tea, and Forsythia Fu tea. The market price of Fu tea varies, and the shape of Fu brick tea is still more common among the product types. Therefore, the price is generally based on "pieces". Generally, each piece of Fu brick tea is 500 g or 1000 g, and the selling price ranges from less than 100 yuan to over 1000 yuan. Due to the storage and transformation value of Fu tea over a certain period of time, the price of old tea (aged tea, aged tea, and vintage tea) of the same grade and quality is generally higher than that of new tea. Different shapes of Fu tea, such as block, column, bag, or loose Fu tea, also vary in price depending on weight, raw material, and year.

The processing technology of Fu tea includes traditional hand building technology and modern mechanism technology. The traditional "Fu brick tea making technique" is a provincial intangible cultural heritage, and its main process is: picking and picking → chopping tea → sifting tea → boiling glaze → weighing tea → stir-frying tea → potting → building tea → bundling → shaping → blooming → drying. The traditional process of Fu tea mainly relies on the experience of tea makers and environmental conditions. The underground well water used for frying Fu tea is relatively special, and its salty taste may be one of the reasons why Fu tea cannot be successfully processed elsewhere (Li Gang 1997). According to scientific testing results, the pH of groundwater is 6–8.5, which meets the optimal acid-base condition for sporulation culture medium of T. coronatus (pH = 7) (Lu Jiazuo et al. 2015), which is conducive to the growth, development and reproduction of T. coronatus. In the modern process of Fu tea, stir-fried tea is replaced by steamed tea, and hand made tea is replaced by machine pressing. At the same time, product acceptance procedures such as inspection and packaging have been added. In recent years, innovative flower development technologies such as loose tea flower production, brick surface flower production, and artificial inoculation flower production have also emerged.

Based on the uniqueness of Fu Tea couplets, the language of Chinese Fu Tea couplets is very simple, with few numbers and rich connotations. In translation, we original meaning and concise expression, but also pay attention to the formal beauty and phonological beauty of the original couplet, and combine the traditional Chinese culture. Only in this way can we express the form, spirit and culture of the original couplet. Language adaptation occurs in the context and is affected and restricted by the specific context. In translation, on the basis of combining the context of the original couplet and accurately conveying the meaning of the original couplet, free translation should be adopted at all linguistic levels, from phonemes, syllables, words to the whole tea couplet, so as to achieve structural adaptation and finally translate a translation that conforms to the expression habits of the target language.

At present, in English Chinese machine translation algorithms, the method of matching segmented phrases with phrase corpora and using the matching results as the final translation result does have some limitations. This method often overlooks the analysis of the context in which the phrase is located, and overly relies on the part of speech analysis of the phrase corpus, which may lead to inaccurate final translation results.

The meaning and translation of phrases may be influenced by the context, especially for polysemous words or ambiguous translations. If only relying on the method of matching phrases with phrase corpora, contextual information cannot be fully considered, and incorrect translation results are prone to occur when dealing with situations with contextual semantic correlations.

Overreliance on phrase corpus for part of speech analysis also carries certain risks. The part of speech tagging of phrase corpora may have errors or inaccuracies, especially for uncommon phrases or new words, which may not be accurately labeled. Such errors may affect the accuracy of phrase matching and translation.

To improve these issues, it is possible to consider introducing more contextual information and language models for translation. For example, for translation models, neural network-based methods can be used to translate phrases by considering contextual sentence information. In addition, more language resources, such as bilingual sentence alignment and parallel corpora, can be integrated to provide richer language contextual information for translation.

In current English Chinese machine translation algorithms, there are certain limitations in only matching phrases with phrase corpora as the final translation result. In order to improve the accuracy of translation results, we can consider introducing more contextual information and language models, and comprehensively using multiple corpora and resources for translation, in order to better handle the contextual and semantic relationships of phrases. Fig. 2 shows the flow of phrase corpus information.

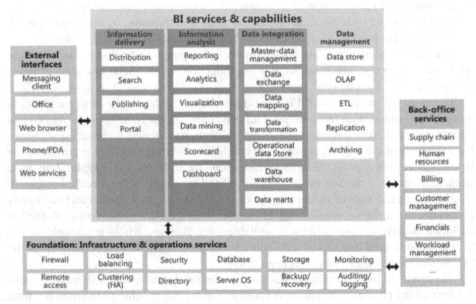

Fig. 2. Phrase corpus information flow

In this article, we constructed a phrase corpus to support intelligent recognition of English translation models. This corpus contains 740000 words and uses three labeling methods, namely data, hierarchy, and processing methods. We use text format to represent data in the corpus. This means that we use text files to store sentences and words in the corpus. The advantage of this format is that it is easy to understand and process, and can facilitate subsequent corpus analysis and research work. We used a hierarchical structure to label words in the corpus. Specifically, we adopted the methods of part of speech tagging and alignment tagging. Part of speech tagging can help us understand the part of speech and grammatical roles of words in sentences, playing a crucial role in subsequent semantic analysis and machine translation. Alignment markers can be used to align words in phrases or sentences, helping us establish semantic and grammatical relationships between words.

We used a specific processing method to process this phrase corpus. The specific processing methods may include steps such as data cleaning, preprocessing, and feature extraction, aiming to make the data more suitable for training and optimizing intelligent recognition of English translation models.

Through such data, hierarchy, and processing methods, we have constructed a rich and useful phrase corpus, providing strong support for the development and improvement of intelligent recognition English translation models. This corpus can not only be used for training models, but also for researching and evaluating the performance of models, providing useful resources and references for researchers and engineers in related fields.

4 Translation Service Framework

In intelligent machine translation, the role of phrase part of speech recognition is not limited to handling grammatical ambiguity, but also helps to solve the translation problem of polysemy. The same word may have different meanings in different contexts, and phrase part of speech recognition can accurately mark the meaning of the word based on the context, providing more accurate translation results.

Syntactic analysis transforms the dependency relationships of phrases into syntactic trees of sentences, further extracting structural information of sentences. This syntactic analysis helps machine translation systems better capture the associations between words in sentences, thereby more accurately interpreting the meaning and expression of sentences. In addition, part of speech recognition and syntactic analysis are particularly important for processing phrase corpora. Phrase level processing can better capture the grammatical and semantic relationships between phrases, effectively improving the efficiency and quality of phrase processing. This is particularly important for large-scale machine translation systems, as it can help the system translate more quickly and reduce errors during the translation process.

The application of phrase part of speech recognition and syntactic analysis plays a crucial role in intelligent machine translation. It not only improves the timeliness and accuracy of machine translation, but also can handle a large number of grammatical ambiguities and deal with complex sentence structure and semantic problems. By introducing this step, machine translation systems can better understand and translate various types of sentences, and improve the processing ability of phrase corpora. In the future, with the continuous development of deep learning and natural language processing technology, the application prospects of phrase part of speech recognition and syntactic analysis in the field of intelligent machine translation will be even broader.

Phrase part of speech recognition and syntactic analysis play a crucial role in intelligent machine translation. They provide more accurate translation results and optimized processing capabilities by analyzing the structure and semantics of sentences. With the further development and innovation of technology, methods and models for phrase part of speech recognition and syntactic analysis will continue to be improved, bringing more breakthroughs and progress to the development of intelligent machine translation.

The improved GLR algorithm implements the likelihood calculation of the preceding and following phrases using a quad cluster, as shown in Eq. (1):

$$GE = (V_N, V_T, S_{,a}) \tag{1}$$

Assume that P is α Any action in and P exists in V, can be derived from Eq. (2):

$$P \rightarrow \{\theta, c, x, \delta\} \tag{2}$$

The English translation usually composed of one or more translation servers running Moses programs and one web server running Apache. Different translation servers generally handle translation services between different languages, and can also establish a distributed server system to support large-scale translation services. The translation server is managed by the web server and provides an access interface for the client. This system has built a Moses translation server and a web server. The online translation system runs on the Moses server. The web server provides a set of HTTP interfaces for the client to query online. See Fig. 3 for the server architecture.

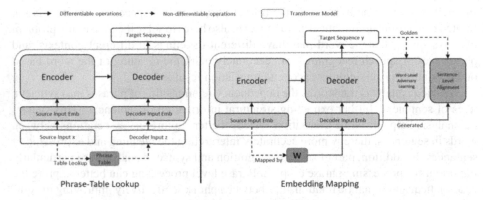

Fig. 3. Translation service framework

Isenweb is a complete set of web server system. The system is developed with PHP and provides Web server and online translation pages. The system server customizes the system interface on the basis of isenweb to make the interface meet the needs of the client. Isenweb needs the support of Apache, PHP and netcat, so it needs to ensure the above software and installation.

The construction of the statistical machine translation system. The is to count the data needed to calculate the maximum probability in the huge parallel corpus, and the decoding step is to find the solution with the maximum probability according to the data obtained from the training. In the training process, the training data is obtained through the statistics of sentence pairs in the parallel corpus. In the decoding step, the input sentence is searched for the translation result with the maximum probability according to the training data through the decoding algorithm.

5 Conclusion

This article designs an intelligent recognition and translation model for Fu tea culture by improving the GLR (Generalized LR) algorithm. Firstly, a detailed introduction was given to the principle of GLR algorithm and its application in grammar analysis. Subsequently, an enhanced GLR algorithm was designed based on the characteristics of intelligent recognition and translation of Fu Cha culture. This algorithm improves the accuracy and efficiency of syntactic analysis by introducing contextual information and semantic analysis. Then, an intelligent recognition and translation model for Fu Cha culture was constructed, combining the improved GLR algorithm with other natural language processing technologies. Through experimental verification, the model has achieved excellent performance in the task of intelligent recognition and translation of Fu tea culture, with high accuracy and ability to understand context.As for the translation of culture loaded words, due to the differences between language and culture, when translating words and sentences with strong cultural background, the corresponding expressions and images are often not found. Even if there are parallel texts for reference, the translation will be inconsistent. However, the adaptation theory holds that in the process of translation, the translator will make some adjustments consciously or subconsciously at the linguistic level and the extra linguistic level in the face of two different language systems and cultures.

Finally, the main contributions of the research work were summarized and the potential application value of improving the GLR algorithm in the field of natural language processing was pointed out. This study provides an effective solution for the intelligent recognition and translation of Fu Cha culture, and provides useful insights for researchers in related fields. In the future, the model can be further optimized to enhance its applicability and practicality.

References

1. Deng, T.: Design of intelligent recognition English translation model based on improved machine translation algorithm. In: Jain, L.C., Kountchev, R., Tai, Y., Kountcheva, R. (eds.) 3D Imaging—Multidimensional Signal Processing and Deep Learning. Smart Innovation, Systems and Technologies, vol. 297, pp. 233–244. Springer, Singapore (2022). https://doi.org/10.1007/978-981-19-2448-4_23
2. Sui, Y.: Computer intelligent proofreading method for English translation based on foreign language translation model (2021)
3. Liu, L.: Intelligent system of English composition scoring model based on improved machine learning algorithm. J. Intell. Fuzzy Syst.: Appl. Eng. Technol. 40(2) (2021)
4. Li, H., Yang, J.: Design of fire alarm system of intelligent camera based on fuzzy recognition algorithm. J. Intell. Fuzzy Syst.: Appl. Eng. Technol. (3), 41 (2021)
5. Wang, Y.L., Wu, Z.P., Guan, G., et al.: Research on intelligent design method of ship multi-deck compartment layout based on improved taboo search genetic algorithm. Ocean Eng. 225(2), 108823 (2021)
6. Pan, L., Hu, L., Li, Z.: Simulation of English part-of-speech recognition based on machine learning prediction algorithm. J. Intell. Fuzzy Syst. 40(2), 2409–2419 (2021)
7. Wang, Z., Li, L., Deng, J., et al.: Magnetic coupler robust optimization design for electric vehicle wireless charger based on improved simulated annealing algorithm. 5(1), 14 (2022)
8. Wang, Q., Pan, F.: Research on the design of computer scoring system for chinese college students' English translation. J. Phys.: Conf. Ser. 2021(3), 032085 (1992)
9. Yang, Y., Ko, Y.C.: Design and application of handicraft recommendation system based on improved hybrid algorithm. Int. J. Pattern Recogn. Artif. Intell. (2), 36 (2022)
10. Ruan, Y.: Design of intelligent recognition english translation model based on deep learning. J. Math. 2022 (2022)

11. Shi, N., Zeng, Q., Lee, R.: The design and implementation of intelligent English learning chabot based on transfer learning technology. ASTES J. (5) (2021)
12. Deng, M., Yang, L.: Intelligent translation recognition model supported by improved GLR algorithm. In: Sugumaran, V., Sreedevi, A.G., Xu , Z. (eds) ICMMIA 2022. Lecture Notes on Data Engineering and Communications Technologies, vol. 138, pp. 472–479. Springer, Cham (2022). https://doi.org/10.1007/978-3-031-05484-6_59
13. Lian, Y.: Design of intelligent response system for business english (training) based on improved GLR algorithm. In: Sugumaran, V., Sreedevi, A.G., Xu, Z. (eds) ICMMIA 2022. Lecture Notes on Data Engineering and Communications Technologies, vol. 136, pp. 11–18. Springer, Cham (2022). https://doi.org/10.1007/978-3-031-05237-8_2
14. Meng, J., Wang, Z.: Design of intelligent recognition model for english translation based on deep machine learning. In: Sugumaran, V., Sreedevi, A.G., Xu , Z. (eds.) ICMMIA 2022. Lecture Notes on Data Engineering and Communications Technologies, vol. 138, pp. 774–779. Springer, Cham (2022). https://doi.org/10.1007/978-3-031-05484-6_100
15. Zhao, Z.: Design of English multimedia intelligent translation system based on neural network algorithm. In: Xu, Z., Alrabaee, S., Loyola-González, O., Zhang, X., Cahyani, N.D.W., Ab Rahman, N.H. (eds.) CSIA 2022. Lecture Notes on Data Engineering and Communications Technologies, vol. 123, pp. 1043–1050. Springer, Cham (2022). https://doi.org/10.1007/978-3-030-96908-0_129

Accuracy Correction of English Translation Based on Fuzzy Clustering Algorithm

Qin Meng[1(✉)], Weiqing Liu[1], Cui Yun[1,2], and Haifeng Xu[2]

[1] School of Humanities, Shandong Agriculture and Engineering University, Jinan 50100, Shandong, China
165220073@qq.com
[2] Modern College of Northwestern University, Xi'an 710130, China

Abstract. As an international mainstream language, English is an important means in the process of international cultural interaction. Therefore, in recent years, countries have increased the training of English translation talents. The cultural differences objectively existing between different language systems have a great impact on the accuracy of translation. Translation does not simply transform one language into another, which involves deeper cultural exchanges. People expect to improve the accuracy of English translation, which correspondingly challenges English translators. Therefore, it is of practical and guiding significance to further study the improvement of English translation accuracy. In order to achieve the clustering and integration of English translation index parameters, this paper designs an English translation intelligent recognition algorithm based on FCM (Fuzzy Clustering Algorithm), corrects the English Chinese structural ambiguity in the part of speech recognition results according to the syntactic function of the parsing linear table, and finally obtains the recognition content. From the comprehensive evaluation results, the recognition accuracy based on FCM is 90.62%. This proves that this method has better information fusion analysis ability and improves the accuracy of translation.

Keywords: Fuzzy clustering algorithm · English translation · Corpus · Accuracy correction

1 Introduction

Translation involves the contradiction between the content and form of two languages in the process of translation, or rather, translation is mainly to solve the contradiction between the content and form of the original and the translation [1]. Under different cultural backgrounds, people have different ways of thinking. Different ways of thinking will also have an impact on English translation. Due to cultural differences, various translation errors are likely to occur in English translation, which will affect people's understanding [2]. When people communicate orally or in writing, they will express complete and accurate sentences as much as possible. In this process, people will subconsciously be affected by grammar and consciously follow the rules of grammatical

Y. Zhang and N. Shah (Eds.): BigIoT-EDU 2023, LNICST 582, pp. 45–54, 2024.
https://doi.org/10.1007/978-3-031-63136-8_5

sentence formation [3]. The traditional machine translation method is to use a continuous process pipeline to perform partial marking and grammatical analysis of letters to obtain English grammatical structure, which will cause repeated transmission errors between translation tasks and limit the accuracy of the structure, thus reducing the accuracy of English literary translation [4]. The thinking in translation, that is, translation thinking, is mainly based on the continuous acquisition and application of language materials. English and Chinese multi-language materials constantly act on people's brains, and then form a basic freeze frame in their minds, and finally form a relatively fixed bilingual conversion trend [5]. In English translation, we should fully consider the influence of cultural factors, especially the cultural differences, and avoid the phenomenon of imperial mistakes in the process of translation [6]. In addition, regarding the definition of word meaning, polysemy is quite common in business English [7]. Generally speaking, if a term has multiple meanings, it is often applied to different disciplines, fields and specialties, and is the jargon and technical term of the field or industry [8]. Therefore, as to guarantee the accuracy of the translation, we must understand the specific professional meaning of a word and the relevant knowledge of the profession. After all, technical terms are words used to correctly express scientific concepts, and they exclude polysemy and ambiguity [9].

There are also many researches on applying clustering algorithm to English translation. For example, Morchid et al. made use of the semantic network based on automatic translation model, used the automatic translation method of carriers based on statistical semantic combination and the carrier translation rules used to determine the similarity between two different carriers, and obtained accurate translation quality assurance results [10]. Miyaji I et al. proposed that if syntactic error is detected in translation, the linear table should be parsed using syntactic analysis geometric structure linear call to identify the content of the phrase. Then, the principle of local optimization is used to improve the quality of the content, which is transmitted through different identification channels to identify symbols and improve the precision of the recognition results [11]. AF Llitjós overcomes the problem that fuzzy clustering algorithm is sensitive to initialization and easily falls into local minima. Combined with modern optimization methods, many hybrid algorithms have been proposed. In order to overcome the slow convergence speed of fuzzy clustering algorithm, a core-based fuzzy clustering algorithm has also been proposed [12].

2 Correction Path of English Translation Accuracy

2.1 Analysis of Influencing Factors of Accuracy

English translation is a very extensive way of application, and its importance in communication is gradually highlighted. The content formed through translation is not only an interpretation of language, but also a kind of cultural exchange and transmission. If the accuracy of English translation is not in place or cannot match with the cultural connotation, there will be errors or obstacles in the transmission of various cultures.

(1) The influence of different ways of thinking on English translation. In British culture, people are influenced by free thought, and when thinking about problems, they often start from the individual point of view, which is obviously different from the eastern

culture's emphasis on the whole point of view. In addition, westerners' expressions are outspoken and undisguised. In the expression, you can directly show your personal views and clarify the communication points, which are mainly reflected in different emotional aspects. The oriental way of thinking tends to think in images, so in the process of language expression, we often adopt a more obscure way of expression. It is this kind of cognitive difference that will affect the accuracy of English translation to a certain extent.

(2) The influence of differences in living habits on English translation. In Western culture, in the process of interpersonal communication, it is generally rare to ask questions about privacy, such as age, weight, etc., but in China, it is different. Chinese people think that the question about privacy is mainly about you. In terms of cultural habits, there are often some conflicts between British culture and Chinese culture. For example, red in British culture is not auspicious or festive.

(3) The influence of definition and association differences on translation accuracy. There are also obvious differences in sentence creation between China and the West due to different living environments. Third, there are cognitive differences. There are also obvious differences between Chinese and Western people in the psychological process of cognition, and they show regional characteristics.

2.2 Corpus-Based Translation

Corpus is an important basic resource for corpus linguistics research, and it can also provide content support in language translation research methods. With this in mind, if the content cannot be accurately proved or the attitude of language users cannot be directly expressed, we can solve this problem with the help of appropriate translation forms in the corpus. This will play a buffer role to a certain extent for both sides of communication. Because of the support of corpus content and theory, the explicit and implicit English translation can perform well in terms of accurate expression. Especially in the process of translation, different cultural contexts cause great differences. But even if it is difficult, it should be as accurate as possible. To achieve this accuracy, it is not

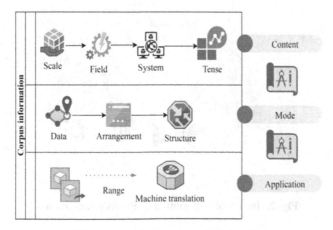

Fig. 1. Translation corpus information

enough to translate the literal meaning only. It is necessary to express its underlying meaning. However, translating through corpus information can effectively improve the translation accuracy (Fig. 1).

In the above image, the mark is composed of three parts: data, grade and processing method. Type is the shape of text. Select a part of a speech and align it in the hierarchy. Perform a series of routine translations in English to make data translation more accurate. In order to ensure the communication between Chinese and English, the language similarity between the translated sentence and the native language vocabulary that need computer network input is calculated, and the accuracy of translation is improved.

3 Introduction to Algorithm

This paper plans the overall model design based on the functions that the English intelligent translation model established by the algorithm needs to achieve (as shown in Fig. 2). In the process of running this model, the pointer type must be identified before the termination character is replaced. The operation of each step uses a variety of shift instructions and simplified operations, and the beginning and end of each operation are displayed using the special envoy's standard. In the process of phrase translation, when the algorithm does not detect syntactic ambiguity, it will restart the duplication and calibration operations. If syntactic ambiguity is detected, it is necessary to use the geometric structure linear table of syntactic analysis to call the analytic linear table and identify the content of the phrase. The optimal content is provided according to the local optimal principle, and transmitted to different recognition channels for symbol recognition. The optimal result is selected according to the recognition result.

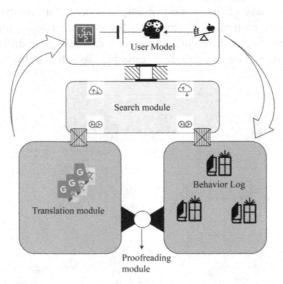

Fig. 2. Intelligent recognition of English translation

Translation can not be separated from the specific text, which is an important basis for training and cultivating translation thinking. For beginners, the moderate degree of difficulty and reasonable length of the text are important conditions to stimulate interest in translation. This paper makes a systematic analysis of the essence of translation in the form of appropriate theoretical analysis, data statistics, and other forms, with reference to translation studies, linguistics, and relevant cultural theoretical knowledge, and probes into the process and phenomenon of translation.

Words are the knowledge carrier and basic operation unit of natural language text, while there is no obvious segmentation mark between words in written English text, so word segmentation is the first step in automatic English classification. Based on the actual requirements of the translation system, the feature function and corresponding privilege weight are automatically set, and the optimal translation with the highest score for the generated translation is obtained according to the formula. The conceptual similarity of words p_1 and p_2 is expressed as:

$$similar(p_1, p_2) = \frac{\alpha}{t + \alpha} \tag{1}$$

In the vectorized representation of English statements, two statements are first represented by equal length vectors. For example, for statements s_1 and s_2, all words in the two statements are combined into a joint word set R, as shown in the following formula.

$$R = R_1 \cup R_2 = \{w_1 \cdot q_1, w_2 \cdot q_2, \cdots, w_n \cdot q_n\} \tag{2}$$

Combine the two sentences, delete the exclamations in the two sentences, keep a real template word, record the same word, and merge the sentence. In this paper, we analyze a tense problem in English translation-automatic translation based on semantics will lead to more original verbs.

For a given sentence f_I, translation e_I is formed. The maximum entropy translation model is:

$$e_I^\alpha = \sum_{i=1}^{n} \lambda_n h_m(e_I \cdot \alpha, f_I) \tag{3}$$

Clustering algorithm is an important part of data mining process. In traditional systems, when faced with a large number of word translation cache packets, clustering algorithm has a large resource cost, resulting in low efficiency of clustering algorithm. This system uses the fuzzy clustering algorithm to choose the sentence with the highest similarity as the final answer. The process is as follows.

When the sample points are sparsely distributed, if the samples in the sample set are used as the cluster center, certain errors will inevitably occur. If the cluster center is assumed to be a "floating point", there must be a neighborhood k around the cluster center, and the neighborhood k of other samples reaching the cluster center should be the smallest. It is necessary to find more reasonable clustering division results from many possible clusters, so it is necessary to establish isolated fuzzy clustering objective criteria and correlation functions:

$$\min(U, P) = \sum_{k=1}^{n} \sum_{i=1}^{c} (U_i P_k)^2 \tag{4}$$

In formula (4), P represents the representative vector of each cluster class, that is, the cluster center.

Suppose that the sample labels of the k neighborhood of the i cluster center are respectively $l_1, l_2, \cdots, l_k$, then:

$$a_{lj} = \frac{\frac{1}{n} \sum_{i=1}^{m} b_{ji} - b_{lj}}{\frac{1}{n} \sum_{i=1}^{m} b_{ji}} \tag{5}$$

The phrase center is used to analyze the phrase structure, reduce the coincidence probability of data points, and improve the accuracy of part of speech recognition. Using quaternion cluster computing to improve the phrase context likelihood of clustering algorithm.

$$G_e = (V_n, V_t, S, \alpha) \tag{6}$$

where, S is the start symbol cluster, V_n is the cyclic symbol cluster, V_t is the termination symbol cluster, and α is the phrase action cluster.

4 Experiments and Results

In order to fully verify the effectiveness of the intelligent recognition model of English translation, the English translation proofreading test of the model in this paper is realized through experiments, the data in the experimental process is recorded, and the performance of the system is analyzed. In the experiment, there are 500 characters proofreading vocabulary, 200 short articles proofreading quantity and 25 kB/s vocabulary recognition speed. However, the word set of the experimental text after word segmentation is very large, so it needs dimension reduction. Dimension reduction methods include feature selection and feature extraction. Dimension reduction can not only speed up the calculation of clustering algorithm, but also improve the classification effect and avoid over-matching. Due to the limited capacity of the system translation cache, the code blocks generated in the translation process will fill the translation cache within a certain time. In this case, a certain number of translation blocks need to be removed to make room for the translation cache. The ideal removal target is the translation blocks that will not be used in the future or will not be used for the longest time in the future.

In this document, the simulation used to test the accuracy of English translation requires the statistical analysis method to evaluate the performance of large-scale data analysis to evaluate the accuracy of data translation and sampling. Table 1 provides the accuracy of the evaluation and other indicators of test results. The analysis shows that the method proposed in this paper is more accurate and effective.

To confirm the effectiveness of this system, an English-based experimental translation of corpus was conducted. Table 2 compares the translation results of this document, the automatic translation system based on semantics and open statistical data sources and the automatic translation system.

Table 1. Performance test comparison

Evaluation cycle	Methods in this paper		Literature [1] Method	
	Accuracy	Utilization	Accuracy	Utilization
1	94.44	92.44	88.44	86.08
2	91.16	95.15	81.99	80.27
3	90.61	96.18	80.09	84.93
4	96.56	95.44	83.57	85.67

Table 2. Test results of different translation systems

Translation system	BLEU value	NIST value
Semantic based translation system	31.26	5.214
Based on statistical translation system	34.22	5.254
Text system	35.36	5.311

Semantics have different degrees of fuzziness, so if it is used as a communication tool, the word meaning is not necessarily equal to the objective reference. As long as it does not affect communication, the words we use naturally do not need to be clearly defined as objective things or concepts. The higher the number of matching segments calculated by BLEU(Bilingual Evaulation Understudy) in Table 2, the better the accuracy of the translation to be evaluated. NIST is used to evaluate the quality of unit translation. The higher the value, the better the translation quality. From this analysis, it can be concluded that the performance of the translation system based on this algorithm is better.

From the system structure level, it can be seen that extracting the information feature values of standard files using software algorithms is the basis for accurate translation under different semantic environments. Through sentence similarity calculation, the degree of sentence differentiation can be found. Translate 500 randomly assigned network statements, and then compare the translation results with algorithms to get the following Fig. 3.

Obviously, the algorithm in this paper has obvious performance advantages over other algorithms. This paper analyzes the accuracy of translation correction under different algorithms from the perspectives of word order expression, grammatical rules and sentence structure. Although the translation results of this algorithm only extract temporal conjunctions for sentences with temporal conjunctions, they do not mark temporal information in the representation. However, the semantics meet the requirements with high accuracy (as shown in Fig. 4). Moreover, the corpus translation system established by the algorithm has higher accuracy and recall rate in the sentence translation process, especially in the English translation process of prepositions, function words and tenses, which has higher translation efficiency and accuracy.

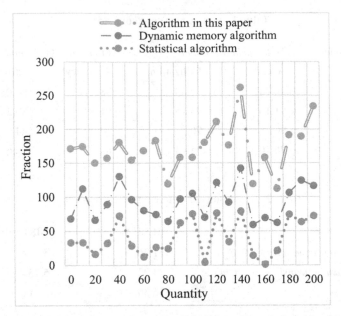

Fig. 3. Evaluation Results of Four English Chinese Translation Algorithms

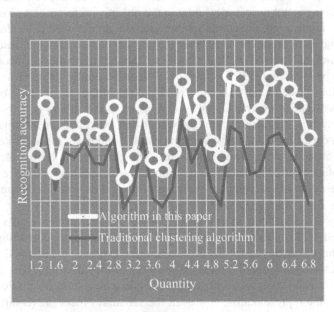

Fig. 4. Comparison of accuracy of two algorithms

To sum up, the traditional clustering algorithm model translation recognition results have data points overlap, and the accuracy cannot be effectively guaranteed. In order to recognize words correctly, we designed the English translation recognition algorithm based on FCM algorithm. The fuzzy structure of English and Chinese is a part of the confirmation letter, which is corrected by analyzing the grammatical functions in the linear form and the final confirmation letter. From the comprehensive evaluation results, the recognition accuracy based on FCM algorithm is above 90.62%. The algorithm overcomes the disadvantages of traditional clustering, and the relative statistical algorithm and dynamic memory algorithm improve the accuracy of English translation.

5 Conclusions

In the context of globalization, language differences and the cultural differences behind them have become one of the factors hindering accurate communication between different countries and regions. To achieve barrier free communication, we must pursue the effective integration of language and culture as much as possible. Proper and accurate translation of the source language can make the language expression tend to be accurate and objective, and achieve the ideal expression effect. In order to effectively correct translation accuracy, in the process of talent training, we should strengthen the penetration of English culture and minimize the impact of cultural differences on translation accuracy. This paper studies how to determine the relevant semantic extraction rules based on the FCM corpus, and uses the vector space model standard through the English sentence similarity algorithm. The similarity of sentences and words is taken as a vector element to find the degree of sentence differentiation and distinguish the various contents of sentences. Finally, it is proved that this method has good information fusion analysis ability and improves the accuracy of translation.

References

1. Lou, X., Li, J., Liu, H.: Improved fuzzy C-means clustering algorithm based on distance correction. J. Comput. Appl. **49**(1), 3 (2021)
2. Wu, F.: Translation accuracy evaluation of english complex long sentences based on multi-label clustering algorithms. J. Inf. Knowl. Manage. (5), 8 (2017)
3. Qu, W.: Algorithm design of translation accuracy correction for english translation softwares. J. Phys. **44**(16), 0044 (2021)
4. Huang, D.: Design of translation accuracy correction algorithm for English translation software. Mod. Electron. Tech. (4), 3 (2019)
5. Xiao, C.X.: Correction of English translation accuracy based on Poisson log-linear model. J. Phys. **36**(8), 4 (2019)
6. Wu, L., Wu, L.: Research on business English translation framework based on speech recognition and wireless communication. Mob. Inf. Syst. (4X), 2 (2018)
7. Miyaji, I., Shimoyama, H.: For correction in system STEJ3 for learning translation from English into Japanese on reading. Ieice Tech. Rep. Educ. Technol. (6), 11 (2018)
8. Ehsan, N., Faili, H., et al.: Grammatical and context-sensitive error correction using a statistical machine translation framework. Softw.: Pract. Exp. (5), 10 (2018)
9. Adriaens, G.: Simplified English grammar and style correction in an Mt framework: the Lre Secc project. In: Aslib Proceedings, no. 3, p.174 (2017)
10. Morchid, M., Huet, S., Dufour, R.: A topic-based approach for post-processing correction of automatic translations. In: 11th International Workshop on Spoken Language Translation, no.18, p. 47 (2017)

11. Miyaji, I., Shimoyama, H., Akiyama, R., et al.: STEJ3: system for learning, evaluation, and correction in translation from English into Japanese on reading. Ieice Tech. Rep. Educ. Technol. (7), 093 (2018)
12. Llitjós, A.F., Carbonell, J.G.: The translation correction tosssol: English-Spanish user studies. Deductive Stud. 24(3), 5 (2017)

Construction and Optimization of English Machine Translation Model Based on Hybrid Intelligent Algorithm

Lirong He[1(✉)], Chun Xie[2], and Yuan Deng[2]

[1] College of International Studies and Education, Tongren University, Tongren 445300, Guizhou, China
Helirong1312366@163.com
[2] GuilinUniversityofTechnology, Guilin 541004, Guangxi, China

Abstract. English grammar is a prerequisite for mastering English, and its complexity and learning difficulty perplex most English learners. Most English learners will encounter all kinds of difficulties in the stage of English learning, so English grammar learning has become a module for English learners to invest energy in learning. The goal correction is to automatically correct grammar errors in the text through computer programs, that is, to identify and correct grammar errors based on the analysis of the context of the input text, so as to ensure the accuracy of the output text and not affect its own semantics.

Keyword: Deep learning · Machine translation · Error correction

1 Introduction

MT and calibration should be carried out according to semantic similarity to improve the semantic allocation accuracy of MT [1, 2]. The goal of English grammar automatically correct grammar errors in the text through computer programs, that is, to identify and correct grammar errors based on the analysis of the context of the input text, so as to ensure the accuracy of the output text and not affect its own semantics [3, 4].

Under the current background of global integration, countries are increasingly connected in many aspects, such as economy, culture and politics [5]. Whether it is cross-regional business cooperation, academic communication or cultural communication, a common language is needed as a medium of communication. As the most widely used, English acts as a carrier of cross-regional communication [6, 7]. Traditional English MT methods based on syntactic analysis can't solve some structural ambiguities in massive English languages in intelligent recognition, and there is a problem of low MT accuracy [8]. Therefore, this English MT model based on hybrid intelligent algorithm. The deep learning algorithm is adopted to automatically optimize the translation errors in the stage of English conversion.

Y. Zhang and N. Shah (Eds.): BigIoT-EDU 2023, LNICST 582, pp. 55–62, 2024.
https://doi.org/10.1007/978-3-031-63136-8_6

2 Design and Improvement of English MT Model

2.1 Generate Countermeasure Network Model

The generator is one of the key components in the GAN model, responsible for generating corrected sentences. In the English grammar correction task, the generator takes incorrect sentences as input and attempts to generate correct sentences that match them. Generators are typically based on recurrent neural networks (RNNs) or Transformer models, using an encoding decoding architecture to generate corrected sentences. The discriminator is another part of the GAN model used to evaluate the quality of sentences generated by the generator. The discriminator accepts sentences generated by the generator and real correct sentences as input, and attempts to distinguish between the two [9]. By evaluating the output of the generator, the discriminator can provide feedback signals on the quality of generated sentences, thereby helping the generator continuously optimize the generation process.

Through adversarial training between generators and discriminators, the generative adversarial network model is gradually improved in English grammar error correction tasks. The generator optimizes the generation process to make the generated sentences closer to real and correct sentences, and the discriminator continuously provides quality feedback to help the generator learn the ability to correct grammar errors. The design of this generative adversarial network model can effectively solve English grammar

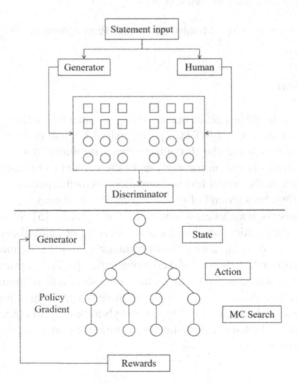

Fig. 1. Adversarial learning architecture

error correction tasks, improve error correction effectiveness, and obtain more accurate translation results. The learning architecture is shown in Fig. 1.

The agent takes the random strategy as the carrier to perform the action, generates the complete corrected sentence, and uses it together with the wrong sentence at the source as the input component of the discriminator to correct the possibility of parallel sentence pairs generated by manual tagging [10]. Output the detailed probability value as a reward and feed it back to the generator in real time, so as to strengthen the learning optimization goal. Adding grammatical errors to English monolingual corpora with high grammatical quality to generate pseudo-parallel sentence pairs has also become a highly respected practice at present. The reason why this method is widely used is that English monolingual corpus is easy to obtain. The MT system includes a variety of components, and each component will provide a variety of different candidate target sentences. Figure 2 shows the relationship judgment process.

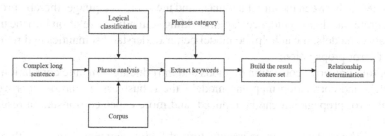

Fig. 2. The relationship determination process

Due to the differences between different languages, the quality of translated texts obtained by MT is not the same, and even many translated texts do not conform to grammatical rules. In addition, in the task of text generation, the output of the previous time step of the model affects the result of the next time step, and the finally generated texts will be selected by conditional probability based on historical results. In order to make the correct sentences produce more real grammatical errors, we will introduce the real errors of English learners to disturb the correct sentences, and add some common part-of-speech errors and other error forms. Specifically, the following disturbance methods are adopted to generate English grammatical errors [11]. Through deep learning, a tree topic vocabulary of English conversion is established, and the sentence structure of English conversion. The elimination of English translation errors and the registration of key words are realized. The deep learning algorithm is used for automatic optimization, which realizes the elimination of English translation errors.

2.2 English Grammar Error Correction

A typical neural model adopts a framework. The overall model includes an encoder and a decoder. The encoder receives sentences with grammar errors as input, and the decoder outputs the corrected sentences. In training, the maximum likelihood estimation is generally used to learn the model parameters. Generating wrong sentences from grammatically correct sentences can not only directly use the noise function, but also be obtained by MT. The generation of grammatical errors can be regarded as the reverse generation model of English grammatical errors, that is, the generation stage of grammatical errors is regarded as the translation of a correct sentence into a wrong sentence [12].

The goal of the semantic correlation detection model is to detect semantic errors in target language sentences during the translation process and correct these errors as soon as possible. This model can model the semantic correlation between the source language and the target language, and determine whether the generated translation is semantically consistent with the original text through semantic similarity calculation. When semantic errors are detected, some strategies can be taken to quickly correct them and avoid error propagation.

The goal of the correlation mapping model is to map the semantic relationship between and the into a representation space and guide the generation process of machine translation models. This model can learn the sentence level or word level semantic correspondence between the target language and the source language, thereby providing more accurate translation guidance. By embedding semantic correlation into the training of translation models, it can help the model better understand semantics and reduce the impact of error propagation.

By optimizing error correction methods and introducing semantic correlation detection models and correlation mapping models, the robustness of can be improved, the impact of error propagation can be reduced, and more expected translation results can be obtained.

Figure 3 shows the translation architecture of fusion segmentation algorithm.

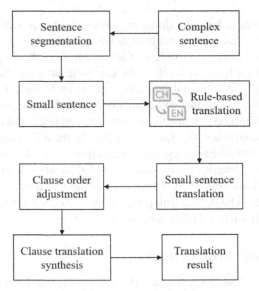

Fig. 3. The translation architecture of the fusion segmentation algorithm

Consider correcting a sentence with grammatical errors. Intuitively, if the corrected sentence output by the neurogrammatical error correction model is difficult to distinguish from the manually marked one, it can be considered that the model has excellent error correction performance. By aligning operations, the positional correspondence between Chinese and English sentences can be established, providing accurate positional information for search statistical machine translation based on noise channel models, ensuring compliance with formula requirements and improving translation accuracy and fluency.

Set any Chinese matrix f and English sentence e, then the probability of e translated into f is $P(e|f)$, then the stage of MT of f into e is:

$$\hat{e} = \arg \max P(e|f) \qquad (1)$$

If the Chinese strings are 1 and n respectively, alignment operations can be performed to describe the positional correspondence between words in Chinese sentences. For example, for each word in a Chinese sentence, positional information can be used to represent its corresponding relationship with words in an English sentence.

If the Chinese string are 1 and m respectively, there are:

$$f = f_1^m = f_1 f_2 \dots f_m \qquad (2)$$

Specifically, an array can be used to represent alignment relationships, with an array length of n. Each element in the array represents the corresponding relationship between. For example, for position i, if the value of the i-th element in the array is j, it means that the i-th word in a corresponds to the jth word in an English sentence.

$$a = a_1^m \equiv a_1 a_2 \dots a_m \qquad (3)$$

Among them, the value interval of each value is [0, 1], then there is:

$$P(f, A|e) = p(m|e) \prod_{j=1}^{m} p\left(\alpha_j \Big| a_1^{j-1}, f_1^{j-1}, m, e\right) \cdot$$
$$p\left(f_j \Big| a_1^j, f_1^{j-1}, m, e\right) \qquad (4)$$

As far as the parallel corpus of error correction is concerned, there are some repetitions in the source error sentences and the target error correction sentences, mainly because generally speaking, grammatical errors are only related to some words of the whole sentence. Through this corpus training, both forward and reverse English grammar error correction models tend to be conservative. we regard the generator as a random strategy with the help of the strategy gradient method in reinforcement learning, and take the feedback of the discriminator as a reward. The optimization goal is to guide the agent to take a series of actions based on the strategy defined by the generator, so as to obtain the maximum expected reward.

3 Result Analysis and Discussion

This article uses the adversarial learning framework generator as the English grammar error generation model, and uses Matlab in the experimental design. Meanwhile, in order to represent the association rule set conversion, OAEI language was used. The

Adversarial Learning Framework Generator is a model based on Generative Adversarial Networks (GAN) that can generate English sentences with grammar errors through adversarial training. This method introduces grammar errors by simultaneously training the generator and discriminator, and continuously optimizes the performance of the generator through adversarial training to generate more compliant grammar errors.

In the experiment, researchers used Matlab for design and implementation, utilizing its rich tools and functions to support the training and evaluation of adversarial learning frameworks. At the same time, in order to represent the conversion, OAEI language is used, which is a formal language used to describe language conversion rules, which can help establish the association rule set and support model evaluation and comparison. The use of adversarial learning framework generators, Matlab, and OAEI languages can effectively generate English grammar errors and conduct relevant experimental research. This research framework helps to improve the occurrence of grammar errors, as shown in Fig. 4.

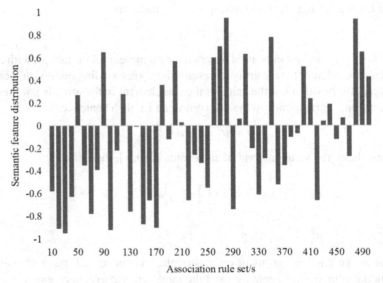

Fig. 4. Simulation results of semantic feature distribution

The sentence structure of English conversion is adjusted to improve the elimination rate. Adjusting the sentence structure of English translation is an effective method to improve the error elimination rate in English translation. By adjusting the sentence structure, it can be made more in line with the grammar rules and idioms, thereby reducing the occurrence errors. For example, it is possible to reorder the components in a sentence, adjust the order of the subject verb object, and make the translation results more accurate. In addition, the improved by adjusting the relationship between clauses and main clauses, applying appropriate conjunctions, and other means.

In addition, it is also possible to consider using parallel corpora, semantic models, and other technical means to assist in sentence structure adjustment. Parallel corpora can provide more comparative data to help machine translation models learn correct sentence structures. Semantic models can further optimize the results of sentence structure transformation by modeling and matching the semantic representation of sentences. By comprehensively utilizing these methods, the error elimination rate in English translation can be improved and more accurate translation results can be obtained.

According to the distribution shown in Fig. 4, the optimization control of English language is carried out, as shown in Fig. 5.

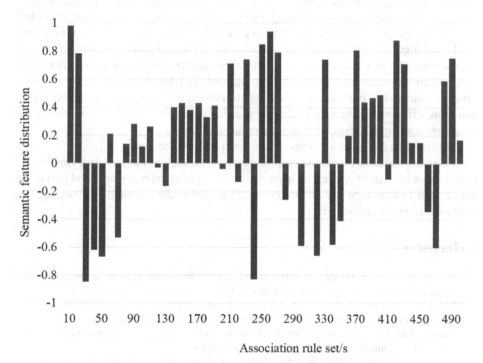

Fig. 5. Characteristic distribution

In this study, the proposed machine translation method adopted special rules to correct grammar errors and set these rules at matching positions to achieve the goal of high error elimination rate. These special rules can help machine translation models better understand grammatical structures and correct them. Continuing to use special rules to correct grammar errors is of great significance for the quality and accuracy of machine translation. These rules can be matched based on grammatical structure and contextual information, and the translation results can be adjusted and corrected. By setting special rules, researchers can correct different grammar errors, including errors in word order, tense, voice, and other aspects. This method can help machine translation models express the original meaning more accurately and improve the overall translation quality. At the same time, this rule-based error correction method can also to some extent avoid generating translation results that do not comply with grammar rules, improving overall translation fluency and readability. By using these rules, researchers can effectively correct grammar errors in translation and improve error elimination rate. The application of this method makes machine translation more accurate and compliant with grammar rules.

4 Conclusions

The goal of English grammar error correction is to automatically correct grammar errors in the text through computer programs, that is, to identify and correct grammar errors based on the context analysis of the input text, so as to ensure the accuracy of the output text and not affect its own semantics. In this paper, an English MT model based on hybrid intelligent algorithm is proposed, which can realize English grammar error correction. Through simulation results, it can be seen that this method has demonstrated good accuracy and error correction ability in eliminating errors in English translation. At the same time, this method also demonstrates strong correlation in translation calibration, which can more effectively adjust and calibrate translation results. This machine translation model makes English translation more accurate and reliable.

This method has good application value in intelligent design of MT.

There are some defects in the proposed algorithm, such as long running time, translation errors in some special cases, such as translation of some rare words and polysemy, which lead to low accuracy of the results. This is the main content that needs to be improved in the next research.

References

1. Al-Sayed, M.M.: Workload time series cumulative prediction mechanism for cloud resources using neural machine translation technique. J. Grid Comput. **20**(2), 1–29 (2022)
2. Shi, C., Guo, S., Chen, J., et al.: Breakout prediction based on twin support vector machine of improved whale optimization algorithm. ISIJ Int. **63**(5), 880–888 (2023)
3. Tao, Y., Tao, D.: Application of intelligent fuzzy decision tree algorithm in english machine translation. Comput. Meas. Control **28**(10), 5 (2020)
4. Zhang, F.: An English machine translation model based on modern intelligent recognition. Mod. Electron. Technol. **41**(16), 4 (2018)
5. Li, N.: Comparative test of English machine translation accuracy under weakened grammar rules. Inf. Technol. **45**(11), 7 (2021)
6. Hu, G.: Research on semantic sequence of English machine translation based on fuzzy theory. Mod. Electron. Technol. **40**(21), 4 (2017)
7. Dong, S.: Architecture of English online translation platform based on C/S mode. Microcomput. Appl. **34**(11), 104–106 (2018)
8. Yu, Y., Nie, F.: Error analysis of online machine translation based on scientific and technological texts. Inf. Record. Mater. **20**(5), 3 (2019)
9. Costa-jussà, M.R., Aldón, D., Fonollosa, J.A.R.: Chinese-Spanish neural machine translation enhanced with character and word bitmap fonts. Mach. Transl. **31**(1–2), 1–13 (2017)
10. Nonaka, K., Yamanouchi, K., Tomohiro, I., et al.: A compression-based multiple subword segmentation for neural machine translation. Electronics **11**(7), 1014 (2022)
11. Chatzikoumi, E.: How to evaluate machine translation: a review of automated and human metrics. Nat. Lang. Eng. **26**(2), 1–25 (2019)
12. Liu, Y., Vong, C.M., Wong, P.K.: Extreme learning machine for huge hypotheses re-ranking in statistical machine translation. Cogn. Comput. **9**(2), 1–10 (2017)

Computer-Assisted Korean Translation is Used in Translation Practice

Hong Sun[1]([✉]), Xiao Guo[2], and Xiaoying Zhang[2]

[1] Shandong Women's University, Jinan 250300, Shandong, China
sunhong808@163.com
[2] Xinjiang University, Urumqi 830046, Xinjiang, China

Abstract. The role of computer-assisted translation in Korean translation practice is very important, but there is a problem of poor translation accuracy. The online Korean translation method cannot solve the problem of the association of sentence translation in practice, and the logic is poor. Therefore, this paper proposes computer-aided construction of Korean translation relationships. First, the difficulty of translation is classified using grammar knowledge, and the Korean content is divided according to the translation standard to simplify the Korean content Processing. Then, grammatical knowledge classifies sentences, forms a Korean translation mapping table, and performs revision analysis of the translated content. MATLAB simulation shows that the accuracy and time of computer-aided translation are better than online Korean translation methods under the condition of certain translation difficulties.

Keyword: grammar knowledge · statements · computer-aided · Translate the results

1 Introduction

As people's pursuit of fashion has been accelerating in recent years, the pursuit of Korean fashion is really threatening [1]. There are many beautiful men and women in Korean dramas, and the clothes on the market are also exquisite, which makes more people have a strong interest in Korean things, but the barrier between languages blocks the communication between the two countries [2], The emergence of the translation industry has also led to economic development and exchanges between the two sides.

With the gradual rise of the translation industry, the translation market is valued by many people, especially in the Korean market. Because Korea is close to China and has a similar culture, it is relatively easy to learn Korean. Korean translation is divided into interpretation and translation. Compared with translation, interpretation is more difficult. Because interpretation requires not only professional knowledge but also the ability to adapt on the spot, it is also necessary to have a good psychological quality on the basis of mastering a lot of Korean knowledge. Now let's introduce the benefits of learning Korean translation.

Y. Zhang and N. Shah (Eds.): BigIoT-EDU 2023, LNICST 582, pp. 63–72, 2024.
https://doi.org/10.1007/978-3-031-63136-8_7

In recent years, Chinese enterprises and more and more Korean enterprises choose to come to China for development. They often encounter language problems when conducting trade with South Korea. But for now, many people choose to learn English, because English is a big language, and Korean is a small number of speakers. However, with the development of China's economy, there is still a shortage of Korean translation talents in the Chinese market, Therefore, due to the lack of professional talents in Korean translation, the market is in short supply, and Korean translation has become a high-tech profession. In the process of learning Korean translation, there are also many people who are interested in Korean. "Interest is the best teacher to learn", because they may be interested in Korean culture, diet, customs and customs, and so on, so they can learn Korean. After learning Korean well, it will be easier to understand Korean culture and so on, without so many obstacles. It is also possible to watch Korean TV more smoothly without watching subtitles.

South Korea's entertainment industry is one of the best in the world. With the popularity of Korean Wave, more and more young men and women want to go to South Korea for further study, learn singing and dancing, and hope to become a Korean Wave star in the future. But because they don't understand Korean, many young people will choose to give up. So if they learn Korean well, it will be more convenient to communicate with others abroad, and will also make their way to study abroad more smooth [3].

From a personal point of view, girls are much more interested in learning Korean translation than boys, because many girls are particularly fond of watching Korean dramas now, because most of the male protagonists in Korean dramas will meet their requirements for boyfriends, so many girls will choose to learn Chinese in order to meet their desire to pursue stars. Secondly, because of the rise of the Korean Wave, many Korean drama shooting sites have become tourist attractions, so many girls will particularly yearn to travel to this place after watching Korean dramas, so South Korea has also experienced a tourism boom in recent years.

In general, Korean is a small language, but with the economic development in recent years and the demand for Korean talents in the market, Korean translation is also very popular, which explains why more and more people want to choose to learn Korean. Therefore, the role of learning Korean well is very important. Work hard to learn, so that your translation level will be excellent, and continuous progress will build you into an excellent Korean translation talent.

Translation effect is one of the important contents of Korean translation practice, and it plays a very important role in Korean translation practice. However, in the actual translation process, the translation results have the problem of poor semantics, which affects the application and evaluation of practice. Some scholars believe that the application of computer-aided to practice can effectively analyze grammar and sentences, and provide corresponding support for the verification of translation practice. On this basis, this paper proposes computer-aided measurement of the practical effect of Korean translation, and verifies the effectiveness of the model [4].

2 Related Concepts

2.1 Computer-Aided Mathematical Description

Computer-aided is to use Korean logic, word relationships and sentence correlation to optimize Korean translation content [5], and based on multi-dimensional indicators in practice. Discover outliers in Korean translations and form a logical table of translations. After integrating the Korean translation results, the logic of the translation results is finally judged. Computer assistance combines grammar knowledge, uses information mining and computer assistance, optimizes the statement results, and can improve the sentence recognition rate.

Hypothesis 1: The Korean translation content is x_i, the Korean translation result mapping table is $\overrightarrow{x_i}$, the professional grammar is y_i, and the judgment function of the translation result is $K(x_i)$ As shown in Eq. (1).

$$K(x_i) = \iint x_i + \xi \tag{1}$$

Computer-aided is to use Korean logic, word relationships and sentence correlation to optimize Korean translation content [5], and based on multi-dimensional indicators in practice. Discover outliers in Korean translations and form a logical table of translations. After integrating the Korean.

The GEC method is to summarize and abstract language knowledge and store it in a specific form. In the process of error correction, combined with the input to be corrected, select the corresponding regular knowledge for reasoning or transformation. The rules include the analysis rules of the source language, the conversion rules of the internal representation of the source language to the internal representation of the target language, and the conversion rules of the internal representation of the target language to the target language.

Combined with Korean part-of-speech mark and rule template to correct grammatical errors. Korean part of speech marking is the task of assigning Korean part of speech for each word. The common parts of speech in Korean are nouns, verbs, determiners, adjectives and adverbs. Nouns can be further divided into singular nouns and plural nouns, and verbs can be divided into past tense verbs and present tense verbs. The more detailed the part of speech markers in Korean are, the more difficult it is to find the correct marker for the occurrence of a word [6]. In Korean, many words can be used as both nouns and verbs. Therefore, Korean part of speech tagging is a typical disambiguation task. After Korean part of speech tagging, each sentence is divided into phrase blocks. Match phrase blocks with predefined error rules. If the rules match, the phrase block should contain errors at the matching position. Finally, use the special rules set at the matching position to correct grammar errors.

Korean grammar error correction method mainly regards the error correction task as a classification problem. In the early stage, it mainly corrected the errors of articles and prepositions. The main idea is to manually implement the feature selection of data, and then mark each type of grammatical error as a different classification label. For example, articles can be divided into four situations: a, an, the, and no article, with labels of 0, 1, 2, and 3 respectively. The classifier uses the selected features to predict the target word, and the most likely prediction result of the target word is used as the final classification output.

2.2 Choice of Translation Method

The function of the encoder is to transform a non-fixed length semantic sequence into a fixed length context vector, and encode the information of the input semantic sequence. The encoder of Transformer is composed of N identical nerve modules, and the output of the previous nerve module is the input of the next nerve module [7]. Each neural module has a multi-head attention layer and a feedforward network layer. The multi-head attention layer is composed of multiple attention layers, and each layer adopts the Attention mechanism. The attention mechanism in Transformer enables the model to focus on valuable information in the context. When encoding a word, not only the current word but also the context of the current word should be considered. Integrate the whole context into the current word vector. The encoder is composed of several layers, and each layer includes two sub-layers, namely, the self-attention layer and the feedforward neural network layer.

The decoder has the same number of layers as the encoder, including the self-attention layer, the code-decode attention layer and the feedforward neural network layer. The code-decode attention layer helps the decoder focus on the relevant part of the input sentence. Each sub-layer in the encoder and decoder adopts residual connection and normalization [8]. The hidden layer in the neural network uses normalization to normalize the output of each layer to the standard normal distribution, and finally accelerates the training speed and convergence speed.

Hypothesis 2: The Korean translation logical selection function is $T(x_i)$ and the statement weight coefficient is $\vec{w}_i$, then the Korean translation logical selection is shown in Eq. (2).

$$T(x_i)=z_i \cdot K(x_i|y_i) \wedge w_i \tag{2}$$

2.3 Processing of Sentences and Phrases

Before performing computer-aided analysis, standard analysis of sentences and phrases in the translation results is performed, and the Korean translation content is mapped In the translation table, determine the content of semantic anomalies [9]. First, the Korean translation content is comprehensively analyzed, and the threshold and weight of the Korean translation content are set for computer-aided is supported by accurate analysis. The Korean translation needs to be simplified, and if the results of the processing conform to the non-standard distribution, the processing is effective Otherwise, the standard processing is redone. In order to improve the accuracy of computer-assisted and improve the level of translation, the translation logic should be selected, and the specific logic selection is shown in Fig. 1.

The Korean translation in Fig. 1 shows that the computer-aided analysis is homogeneous and consistent with the actual semantics. The translation method is not directional, indicating that computer-aided analysis has high accuracy, so it is translated as a Korean

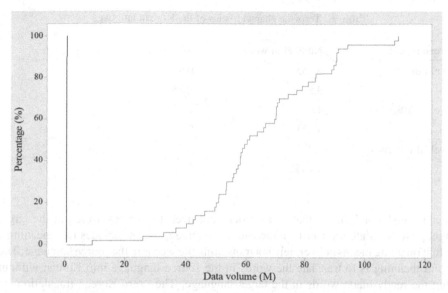

Fig. 1. Processing results of computer-aided analysis

translation practice of translation studies [10]. The translation method meets the mapping requirements, mainly grammatical knowledge to adjust the translation method, remove repetitive grammar, and revise the professionalism to make the whole Korean translation content is more translatable.

2.4   Logic of Sentence Translation

Computer-aided judgment of sentence accuracy and adjustment of corresponding grammatical relationships to optimize Korean translation practices. Computer-aided Korean translation practices are divided into different data volumes and randomly selected by different methods [11]. During the revision process, the translation standards with different data volumes are fitted to the translation method [12]. After the fitting process is completed, different methods are compared for Korean translation practice, and the sentence results with the highest accuracy are recorded.

3   Actual Examples of Korean Translation

3.1   Translation Content

In order to facilitate the analysis of translation results, the number of words and sentences tested in this paper was 2421 based on different types of Korean content, statement 450, as shown in Table 1.

The professional processing process of sentence translation in Table 1 is shown in Fig. 2.

Korean translation of error-free sentences includes zero Korean translation, basic standard Korean translation and identical Korean translation [13]. The so-called "zero

Table 1. Tests the characteristics of the Korean language

Korean type	Number of words	logicality	Practice rate
Level I difficulty	2,2551	0.85	0.6
	3,854	0.65	0.6
Level II difficulty	1,865	0.75	0.6
	4,251	0.69	0.6
Level III difficulty	2,475	0.75	0.6
	1,7852	0.92	0.6

Korean translation" means that Korean does not need to use any words in the target language to translate the words in the source language, which includes two meanings: the first meaning means deliberately not translating the words in the source language; The second meaning is to translate the words in the source language into Korean without using the ready-made words in the target language. The "zero Korean translation" is mainly caused by three factors: language expression differences, cultural differences and source language vocabulary innovation [14]. Basic standard Korean translation means that the meaning of the result of machine Korean translation is basically correct, which is different from that of artificial Korean translation but does not affect the expression.

For the recognition and detection of punctuation errors, the comprehensive performance of model correction. It can be seen from the results that the model has certain ability to identify and correct punctuation type errors. The noise construction method of punctuation errors in this paper adopts a derivative of the replacement rule: if the selected word to be replaced is a punctuation type, then a punctuation is randomly selected from the defined punctuation confusion set for replacement [15]. The advantage of this is that in the real situation of Korean learning, punctuation errors are often punctuation omission and misaddition: the data expansion method proposed in this paper has covered both omission and misaddition to a certain extent. However, it does not achieve the performance of correcting verb, noun and other error types. It is speculated that the reason is that the number of punctuation in the text is less than the number of words, and the probability of randomly selecting punctuation is less than the probability of randomly selecting words, that is, the probability of replacing punctuation is less than the probability of replacing Korean parts of speech.

The recognition and correction ability of the model for spelling errors and adjective-related errors is relatively weak, because the confusion set created for spelling errors is too small, and the Korean part of speech confusion set for adjectives is not created. When synthesizing training data manually, the randomly selected target words do not appear in the constructed confusion set list, and the replacement candidate words can only be selected from the constructed dictionary [16]. Therefore, the independent components of grammar error correction such as spelling checker are applied to the subsequent tasks of GEC, and the overall performance of the error correction system is improved through the collocation of various error correction components.

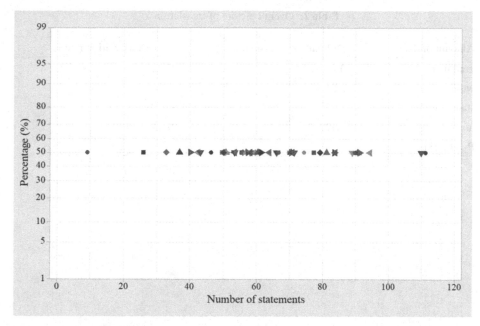

Fig. 2. The process of processing Korean language expertise

Table 1 shows that compared to online Korean translation methods, computer-assisted translation results are closer to actual sentences. Computer-aided online Korean translation methods in terms of Korean translation practice translation professional translation rate and accuracy. As can be seen from the change in professionalism in Fig. 4, computer-aided accuracy is better and judgment speed is faster [17]. Therefore, computer-assisted sentence speed, sentence and translation accuracy are better.

3.2 Outlier Recognition Rate of Statements

Sentences contain notes, specialization, bars. After computer-aided threshold standard screening [21], preliminary statement results were obtained, and statement results were obtained is analyzed logically [18]. In order to verify the effect more accurately, select statements with different data volumes, and evaluate the professionalism of the statements as shown in Table 2.

3.3 Timing and Accuracy of Practice Assessments

In order to verify the accuracy of computer-aided translation, the professionalism of the online Korean translation method is compared as shown in Fig. 3.

As can be seen from Fig. 3, the computer-assisted translation time is shorter than that of the online Korean translation method, but the error rate is lower, indicating that the computer-assisted translation is relatively stable, while the online Korean translation method is relatively stable Translation accuracy varies [19]. The accuracy of the above algorithm is shown in Table 3.

Table 2. Overall picture of translation

Amount of data	Difficulty of translation	Outlier recognition rate
grammar	3.21	93. 23
word	2.01	93.36
statement	3.79	97.29
mean	2.12	92.14
P = 0. 031		

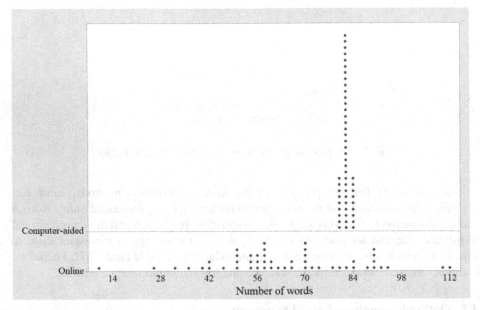

Fig. 3. Translation time for different algorithms

Table 3. Comparison of translation accuracy of different methods

algorithm	Translation time	accuracy	error
Computer aided	92.21	93.79	4.74
Online Korean translation methods	70.25	85.26	6.21
P	0.022	0.032	0.013

Table 3 shows that the online Korean translation method has shortcomings in translation time and accuracy in Korean translation practice, and the accuracy of sentences changes greatly and the error rate is high. Computer-aided synthesis results have higher translation times than online Korean translation methods. At the same time, the computer-assisted translation time is greater than 90%, and the accuracy has not changed significantly[20]. To further verify the superiority of computer-aided. To further verify the continuity of the method, computer-aided synthesis analysis was performed using different methods, as shown in Outcome 4.

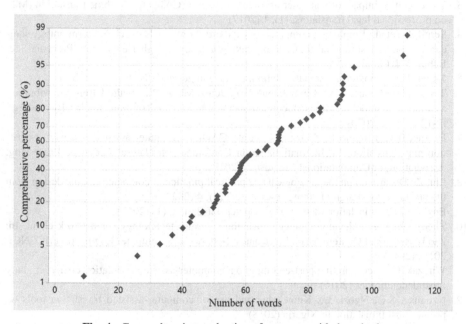

Fig. 4. Comprehensive evaluation of computer-aided methods

As can be seen from Fig. 4, computer-aided professionalism is significantly better than online Korean translation methods, and the reason is that computer-aided increases the sentence adjustment coefficient and sets the corresponding threshold, judging the professionalism that does not meet the requirements.

4 Conclusion

In the context of the development of computer-aided technology, in response to the practical problem of Korean translation, this paper proposes computer-assisted, combined with grammar knowledge, right statement to improve. At the same time, the department and threshold standards of the statement are analyzed in depth, and the mapping table of the statement is constructed. Studies have shown that computer-aided translation can improve the precision and accuracy of translation, and can comprehensively translate sentences. However, in the computer-assisted process, too much attention is paid to the ability to analyze unilateral indicators, and the proportion of sentences is ignored.

References

1. Qu, L.: Measures to improve the operability of computer-assisted translation software in translation practice. China Comput. Commun. (2018)
2. Usmanova, Z.A., Zudilova, E.N., Arkatov, P.A., et al.: Impact of computer-assisted translation tools by novice translators on the quality of written translations (2021)
3. The cognitive impact of computer-assisted translation (CAT) and machine translation (MT) on professional legal translators. (1), 1 (2017)
4. Serpil, H., et al.: Employing computer-assisted translation tools to achieve terminology standardization in institutional translation: making a case for higher education. Procedia Soc. Behav. Sci. (2016)
5. Kugai, K.: Computer-assisted translation. Its advantages and disadvantages (2016)
6. Travieso Rodrguez, J.A., Llum Fuentes, J., Jerez Mesa, R., et al.: Ultrasonic vibration assisted cutting tool for lathe (Machine-translation by Google Translate, not legally binding). ES1253134U (2020)
7. Durme, B.V., Lippincott, T., Duh, K., et al.: CADET: computer assisted discovery extraction and translation. In: International Joint Conference on Natural Language Processing. Association for Computational Linguistics (2017)
8. Liu, Z.: Discussion on the ideological and political practice of computer graphic design from the visual image design of "three cows spirit". (5), 4 (2022)
9. Engliana, E.: Translation theories in computer translation. (1) (2017)
10. Zheng, Z.: Research on computer translation software technology for network client. In: 2nd International Conference on Electronics, Network and Computer Engineering (ICENCE 2016) (2016)
11. Witczak, O.: Incorporating post-editing into a computer-assisted translation course. A study of student attitudes (2016)
12. Nzuanke, S.F., Ngozi, U.: Knowledge and use of computer-assisted translation tools on professional translation in Nigeria (2018)
13. Nzuanke, S.F., Ngozi, C.U.: Technology and translation: areas of convergence and divergence between machine translation and computer-assisted translation (2018)
14. Seljan, S., Erdelja, N.K., Kui, V., et al.: Quality assurance in computer-assisted translation in business environments (2021)
15. Quan, Y.W., Chen, N.N., Han, J.M., et al.: A study on the Chinese translation strategies of Korean medical and cosmetic terms. Educ. Teach. Forum (2019)
16. Liu, L.Z.: The application of news report in Korean translation teaching. J. Shandong Agric. Eng. Univ. (2019)
17. Huang, B., Yang, Y., Gaoda, H.E.: A diachronic investigation of the theory and practice in Chinese-Korean translation. Chin. Sci. Technol. Transl. J. (2017)
18. Han, B.: Translation, from Pen-and-paper to computer-assisted tools (CAT tools) and machine translation (MT) (2020)
19. Chen, S.: Reflections on the development of computer-assisted translation in china under the background of artificial intelligence. Clausius Scientific Press (2021)
20. Samad, S.S., Mohammed, O.S., Mahdi, H.S.: The attitudes of professional translators and translation students towards computer-assisted translation tools in Yemen. Dil ve Dilbilimi Çalışmaları Dergisi **16**(2), 1084–1095 (2020)

Design of Vocabulary Query System in Computer Aided English Translation Teaching

Zheng Mei[✉] and Zhu Lin

Xinjiang Career Technical College, Kuitun 833200, China
28402798@xju.edu.cn

Abstract. Our research focuses on the design of a vocabulary query system in computer-aided English translation teaching. The system aims to provide an intelligent and personalized vocabulary query and recommendation function to help learners better understand and apply English vocabulary. In system design, we applied Bayesian networks to model and analyze semantic associations of vocabulary, and inferred possible meanings and synonyms of vocabulary by observing contextual and historical information. At the same time, we transform the Bayesian network into a factor graph and use the sum product method to efficiently calculate the marginal distribution of each vocabulary, in order to improve the computational efficiency of the system. Through the user's query history and feedback information, we continuously optimize the Bayesian network model and provide users with recommended vocabulary or phrases related to the query vocabulary. Our system aims to provide accurate and targeted vocabulary query and recommendation functions, providing assistance for learners in English translation teaching. Through experimental evaluation, we have verified the effectiveness and positive feedback of the system. This study has made certain progress in the design of vocabulary query systems in computer-aided English translation teaching, and has further research and application potential.

Keyword: Computer assisted · English translation teaching · Vocabulary query

1 Introduction

With the intensification of globalization, English, as an international language, has become increasingly important for learners. In the process of English learning, vocabulary is the foundation for building language abilities [1]. However, learners often face difficulties in understanding and translation when encountering unfamiliar vocabulary. In order to solve this problem, a vocabulary query system has emerged in computer-aided English translation teaching.

The vocabulary query system aims to provide learners with convenient and fast vocabulary query and recommendation functions to help them better understand and use English vocabulary. Previous research has proposed various vocabulary query systems,

© ICST Institute for Computer Sciences, Social Informatics and Telecommunications Engineering 2024
Published by Springer Nature Switzerland AG 2024. All Rights Reserved
Y. Zhang and N. Shah (Eds.): BigIoT-EDU 2023, LNICST 582, pp. 73–83, 2024.
https://doi.org/10.1007/978-3-031-63136-8_8

but most systems only provide simple definitions and example sentences of vocabulary, lacking personalized and intelligent functions [2].

To address these issues, this article designs an intelligent vocabulary query system based on the probability graph model of Bayesian networks. Bayesian networks are widely used in the fields of probability inference and pattern recognition, as they can model and analyze semantic relationships between vocabulary. We transform the Bayesian network into a factor graph and use the sum product method to efficiently calculate the marginal distribution of each vocabulary [3]. By observing the user's query history and contextual information, the system can infer the possible meanings and synonyms of vocabulary, thereby providing more accurate and targeted query results.

At present, the information-based examination system has been developed rapidly. The standardized examination question banks such as GRE and TOEFL have been very mature in foreign countries. These question bank systems can scientifically and reliably test the level of students, which is sufficient to illustrate the feasibility and effectiveness of computer test paper generation. At the same time, the computer test paper generation is incomparable in terms of security with manual test paper generation, And it can manage the examination more effectively and scientifically, and effectively reduce the examination cost. Therefore, the advantages of online examination system with Bayesian network strategy are mainly reflected in the following points: (1) objectivity. When applying the online examination system to group papers, the test questions need to be automatically extracted from the test questions database and generated according to the relevant parameters. The test questions have a wide knowledge coverage, which can effectively evaluate the students' knowledge level, prevent the occurrence of missing questions, and improve the objectivity of the test questions. (2) High accuracy. In the computer-generated test paper, the scores of objective questions can be judged by the computer system, and there will be no problem of manual evaluation, which effectively improves the efficiency of the evaluation of the test paper, and also improves the fairness of the test paper. (3) Comprehensive data analysis. Through the test paper analysis module in the online examination system, the relevant data concerned by schools and teachers can be conveniently and quickly counted, and the evaluation of test papers, the level of students and the teaching effect of teachers can be quickly and effectively analyzed. (4) Safety of test questions. In the process of examination, the method of computer test paper formation on the spot can effectively avoid the leakage of test questions and improve the security of test questions.

With the rapid development of information science and technology and artificial intelligence technology, the traditional examination and manual test paper generation methods will eventually be replaced by the computer examination system represented by Bayesian network system [4]. With the continuous deepening of modern teaching, the demand of Bayesian network system is also increasing. Studying Bayesian network algorithms and systems can use information technology to scientifically manage examinations, And in the examination management and organization, teachers and schools will be freed from the complicated work, and targeted, showing an indispensable value in schools and educational institutions.

The purpose of this article is to introduce the design ideas and key technologies of this vocabulary query system. We will elaborate on the application of Bayesian networks in vocabulary queries, as well as the overall design and functionality of the system. Through experimental evaluation, we have verified the effectiveness of the system in providing accurate, personalized query and recommendation functions. We hope that this study can provide useful references for the design and improvement of vocabulary query systems in computer-aided English translation teaching.

2 Related Work

2.1 Definition of Bayesian Network

Bayesian network is a probability graph model used to model and represent the dependency relationships between variables. It consists of nodes and directed edges, where nodes represent random variables and directed edges represent dependencies between variables. Let $V = \{X1, X2,..., Xn\}$ be a set containing n random variables. Bayesian networks represent the conditional dependencies between these variables through a directed acyclic graph (DAG). Each node in the graph represents a random variable, and edges represent direct dependencies between variables. If the value of variable Xi depends on variable Xj, then there is a directed edge pointing from Xj to Xi in the graph [5]. The Bayesian network also includes a probability distribution table for each node, which is used to represent the probability distribution of each variable given the conditions of its parent node. These conditional probability tables can be estimated based on domain knowledge, statistical inference, or other methods.

The definition of Bayesian networks allows us to infer unknown variables by observing known variables. Using Bayesian theorem and network structure, we can calculate the posterior probability distribution of unobserved variables given observed variables, for inference and prediction. As shown in Fig. 1(a).

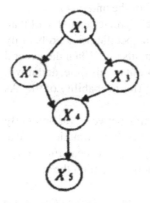

	X_2, X_3	$X_2, \neg X_3$	$\neg X_2, X_3$	$X_2, \neg X_3$
X_4	0.4	0.9	0.5	0.3
$\neg X_4$	0.6	0.1	0.5	0.7

(a) Directed acyclic graph   (b) Conditional probability table of node X4

Fig. 1. Bayesian network

Definition 1. Set $B_1, B_2, ...B_n$ [6], Is the event in the sample space S, then the probability $P(B_i)$ of the occurrence of B in the case of event A can be obtained after re-correction and adjustment according to the prior probability $P(B_i)$ and the observation information. $P(B_i \mid A)$ is usually called the posterior probability. With the continuous change of sample information, the posterior probability is also constantly updated. The previous posterior probability will be used as the prior probability when readjusting, so as to obtain a new posterior probability, which is a process of constant updating and repeated adjustment.

$$P(B|A) = \frac{P(AB)}{P(A)} \tag{1}$$

Let $(\Omega, \mathfrak{R}, \mathbf{p})$ be a probability space, $\mathbf{A}, \mathbf{B} \in \mathfrak{N}$ and $P(A) > 0$, then.
It is called the conditional probability of B when A occurs.

$$P(A_j|B) = \frac{P(B|A_j)P(A_j)}{\sum_{i=1}^{n} P(B|A_i)P(A_i)} \tag{2}$$

To: P (c) refers to a priori probability. Previously, the idea of Bayesian function is different from that of ordinary function. For example, if we toss a coin ten times, it will be positive. Is the next toss positive? This is a conjecture based on statistical probability or parameter distribution. Then, according to Bayesian method, we will think that no matter how many times you toss a coin, Its positive and negative probability will not change, it is 1/2. According to the idea of Bayes, it will think that it has nothing to do with the positive data you throw ten times and the positive data it throws next time. It focuses on what it has verified before [7], That is, "a priori probability". For a given W, whether a guess is good or bad depends on "the priori probability of the guess itself" and "the probability of this guess generating the observed data". So back here, we can see that if the user inputs tha, who will have a greater probability of the and that in the huge thesaurus? Let's assume that, then the prior probability of the is greater than that of that. According to Bayesian method, P(c)*P(W | c), , P (c) Is a specific prior probability [8]. That is to say, according to the above example, the user inputs tha. When the general statistics cannot make a decision, the prior probability stands out at this time, and it will determine the user wants to input the according to the large prior probability of the. As shown in Fig. 2 below, it is a simple Bayesian network:

In factor graphs, local functions represent the relationships between variables. By factoring the global function and representing it as a product of local functions, it can better reflect the conditional dependencies between variables. Each local function is associated with corresponding variable nodes and function nodes, forming the structure of the factor graph [9].

The structure of factor graphs can more intuitively represent the dependency relationships between variables and provide an effective way for probability inference and inference. By using algorithms such as message passing and variable elimination on factor graphs, probability inference can be efficiently performed, and the edge distribution and conditional distribution of variables can be calculated.For example, there is now a

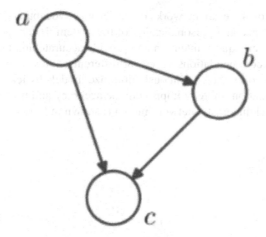

Fig. 2. Bayesian network

global function whose factorization equation is:

$$g(X) = \prod_{E \subseteq Q} f_z(X_z) \tag{3}$$

Factor graph is a graph model used to represent joint probability distributions, where nodes represent variables and edges represent factor functions. By transforming Bayesian networks or Markov random fields into factor graphs, the joint probability distribution can be represented as the product of a series of local factor functions. Then, the sum and integration method (such as variable elimination algorithm) can be used to calculate the marginal distribution of variables.

2.2 Application of Bayesian Network

Bayesian networks can be applied to semantic association and recommendation of vocabulary.

Bayesian networks can be used to model and analyze semantic relationships between vocabulary. By using Bayesian networks, a large number of vocabulary can be represented in the form of nodes, and directional connections between nodes can be constructed using known semantic relationships and contextual information. Then, a probabilistic inference algorithm based on Bayesian networks can infer the possible meaning or synonym of a word from the observed context or other relevant information.

Bayesian networks can be used for vocabulary recommendation in vocabulary query systems. Based on the learned Bayesian network model, conditional probability and prior knowledge can be utilized to provide users with recommended vocabulary or phrases related to query vocabulary [10]. By analyzing users' query history and contextual information, Bayesian networks can more accurately understand users' intentions and provide appropriate recommendation results.

The application of Bayesian networks in the design of vocabulary query systems can improve the intelligence and personalization of the system. It can help the system better understand the user's query intention and provide accurate and targeted vocabulary explanations and recommendations based on different contexts and contexts. Meanwhile, Bayesian networks can continuously optimize models by learning user behavior and feedback information, thereby improving the accuracy and user satisfaction of the system.The Bayesian diagnostic network model is shown in Fig. 3.

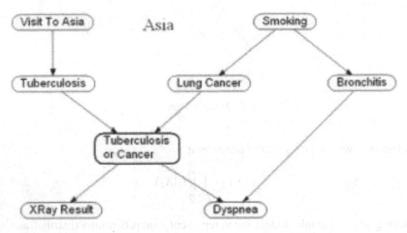

Fig. 3. Bayesian diagnostic network model

Therefore, applying Bayesian networks to the design of vocabulary query systems in computer-aided English translation teaching can make the system more intelligent, personalized, and provide more accurate and helpful vocabulary query and recommendation functions.

3 Application of Bayesian Network in Higher Vocational English Application Ability Test

3.1 Collect and Describe Data

The data collection stage involves determining goals, defining problems, and designing data collection methods. At this stage, we need to clarify the problems we need to solve, as well as the required data types and characteristics. At the same time, it is also necessary to consider ways to collect data, such as survey questionnaires, experimental data, log records, etc. [12]. To ensure the accuracy and comprehensiveness of the data, the collected samples should be representative and collection bias should be avoided as much as possible.

The goal of data preprocessing is to improve the quality and adaptability of data, in order to better apply various data mining algorithms to construct prediction models. Excellent data preprocessing can fully tap into the potential of data and improve the accuracy and effectiveness of models.

In the process of Bayesian network, teachers and other users will put forward various targeted requirements according to the characteristics of higher vocational English teaching and curriculum, mainly including: knowledge points, difficulty, total number of questions, etc. [13]. The basic function of Bayesian network system is to fully meet the needs of users. Applying genetic algorithm to Bayesian network system is the basic idea of this paper. The principle of Bayesian network will be discussed as follows:

Before Bayesian network, the system should establish the state space of the test paper formation process according to its own rules and algorithms. This state space should be composed of various indicators of the test paper. The row in this space represents the index of each test question and can be implemented with binary code. Each column of the space is all values of the index in the question bank. When modeling and inputting the English test question bank, the corresponding attribute value shall be input for each test question, and finally the test question model of the whole test bank shall be generated. Given the Bayesian network or Markov random field shown in Fig. 4 below:

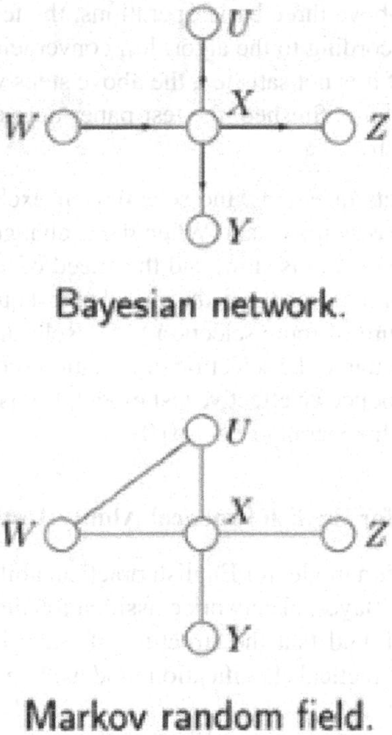

Bayesian network.

Markov random field.

Fig. 4. Bayesian network or Markov random field

After the state space of the English test question database is established, the Bayesian network can be used [14]. The steps of automatic question generation for the Bayesian network test are as follows:

(1) According to the basic needs of teachers and users, the data in the state space of the English test database is planned and filtered, the effective part of the index is retained, and the invalid part of the index is removed. And code the remaining indicators.
(2) Initialize the English test database. And randomly select a group of test questions from the question bank. According to the principle of genetic algorithm, select the appropriate genetic exchange probability and mutation probability, and define the fitness value of the entity as 0.
(3) Continue to extract test questions and match them with control indicators. When the match is successful, the fitness value increases by 1; When the match is unsuccessful, the fitness value remains unchanged.
(4) Take the extracted test questions as the basic data set, execute the elimination operator, and eliminate the fittest to generate a new test model.
(5) Copy the extracted test questions, extract the test questions with a certain exchange probability, and copy the test questions to generate a new test model.
(6) Determine the mutation probability. Based on this value, extract test questions from the question bank and perform gene mutation operation.
(7) After completing the above three basic operations, the test question model can be updated and judged according to the algorithm convergence rules. If it is satisfied, it will be terminated. If it is not satisfied, the above steps will be repeated.
(8) The test paper extraction is finished, the test paper output is finished, and the test paper formation is finished.

When the system selects questions, the selection of exchange probability Pc and variation probability Pm is very important. When the exchange probability is too small, the evolution of genetic algorithm is slow, and the speed of topic selection is reduced. When the exchange probability is too large, the model of test questions will be destroyed, affecting the scientific nature of topic selection [15]. Relevant studies are empirically selected, generally 0.6; Similarly, the selection of mutation probability is also crucial. If it is too small, it will not produce an effective test model. If it is too large, it will generate too many. Relevant research generally selects 0.01.

3.2 A Predictive Model for English Practical Ability Testing

In the design of the prediction model for English practical ability testing, we have made improvements based on the Bayesian network classification model. Based on experience and knowledge, we have found that the structure of Bayesian networks needs to be modified to better adapt to practical classification models. In particular, we have focused on the correlation between.

Based on our practical experience and knowledge, we understand that there is a certain relationship between English grades and gender in vocational colleges [16]. Therefore, based on the network structure learned in Fig. 1, we constructed the Bayesian network prediction model shown in Fig. 5 for predicting English practical ability testing. In this prediction model, we consider the relationship between gender as a conditional attribute and English proficiency B as a category attribute.

By introducing the conditional attribute of gender, Bayesian network models can better capture the impact of gender on the results of English practical ability tests. In the prediction model, we used a large amount of actual data for training and adjustment to ensure the accuracy and predictive ability of the model.

By improving the prediction model of English practical ability testing based on Bayesian network classification model, we can improve the prediction accuracy of students' English practical ability and better understand the impact of gender on it. This improvement can provide useful references for educational institutions to better target the characteristics and needs of students in teaching and training. However, further research and validation are needed to confirm the effectiveness and applicability of this Bayesian network model.

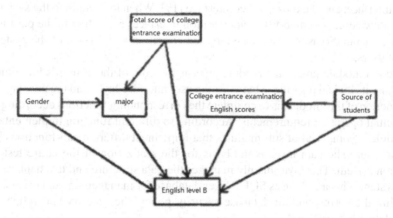

Fig. 5. Test prediction model

The method of evaluating model accuracy can be judged through accuracy evaluation. One of the main methods is to use test set data to test the model, especially for classification models. Subsequently, the predicted results are compared with actual test results to obtain the accuracy of the model.

If the calculation accuracy of the prediction model for students' English application ability testing is greater than or close to 90%, it can be considered that the established model has the ability to classify and predict unknown samples. If the model accuracy is below the threshold, that is, the test results are not accurate enough, you can try to resample and re model until the accuracy standard is reached. Through accuracy evaluation, the predictive ability of the model can be objectively evaluated, and the model can be improved and optimized based on the evaluation results. This evaluation method can provide guidance for model construction and ensure the accuracy and stability of the model. However, it should be noted that the evaluation results should be based on comprehensive test data and undergo statistical analysis to obtain statistically significant results, rather than relying solely on the results of individual test samples.

In the office system of the education system, the introduction of intelligent test paper generation online examination system can greatly improve the fairness, scientificity and accuracy of teacher test paper generation [18]. In order to improve the convenience and flexibility of the system application, increase the expansibility of the system, and facilitate the quick application of the operating user, the system is designed and implemented using the BS structure mode, so that the user's operation interface, the function realization part of the system, and the data storage and management part of the question bank can be effectively processed, mainly based on the hierarchical operation, Thus, the logical structure avoids the functional coupling and correlation between different levels, effectively improves the coding efficiency of the system, and is more conducive to the expansion and maintenance of the system functions.

The authorized operating users can access and use the system at this layer, so as to achieve human-computer interaction and complete the required business functions. According to different system user permissions, three different levels of user interfaces are also set in this layer. They are the system administrator interface, the test paper teacher interface, and the quiz teacher interface [19]. When logging in to the system, the system allows users to enter different operation interfaces according to the permissions of the user name. So as to realize the targeted operation and service of the system for different users.

Function module layer: this module layer is the core of the system's function realization, and its logical position is between the user interface layer and the data layer. The main function of this module is to complete the corresponding functions according to the user's actual operation requirements. According to different function implementations, this module is composed of sub-modules that implement different sub-functions [20].

Data layer: The data layer is the basis for the realization of the entire test paper generation system. This layer mainly manages the data structure and test bank required by the system. This article uses SQL Server database for management and organization. By setting the corresponding database security policy, the security and reliability of system data can be realized.

4   Conclusion

The vocabulary query system in computer-aided English translation teaching is a powerful tool that provides learners with convenient and fast vocabulary query and understanding functions. When designing a vocabulary query system, it is necessary to consider aspects such as user friendliness, database coverage, query speed, and functionality. The following is a summary of these aspects:

The vocabulary query system should also provide rich functionality. In addition to providing basic translation and interpretation functions, other useful functions can also be extended, such as audio pronunciation of vocabulary, display of example sentences, recommendation of synonyms and antonyms, etc. These functions can help learners more comprehensively understand and apply the queried vocabulary, and improve the effectiveness of translation teaching, query speed, and functionality. A well-designed vocabulary query system can help learners acquire vocabulary knowledge more efficiently, improve translation ability, and play an important auxiliary role in English learning and translation practice.

References

1. Zhu, M.: Design of computer-aided English vocabulary query system. Mod. Electron. Tech. (2018)

2. Wang, J., Ondago, O.: Optimization of computer-assisted vocabulary assessment system in international chinese language teaching. Comput.-Aided Des. Appl. **18**(S4), 106–117 (2021)
3. Yasim, I., Lubis, M.A., Noor, Z., et al.: Vocabulary Teaching in English Language Teaching (2016)
4. Huang, Y.T., Meng, C.C., Sun, Y.S.: Development and Evaluation of a Personalized Computer-aided Question Generation for English Learners to Improve Proficiency and Correct Mistakes (2018). https://doi.org/10.48550/arXiv.1808.09732
5. Contrastive Studies of Two Computer-aided Translation Software (26), 1 (2016)
6. Ama, B., Lu, A., Mk, A., et al.: The natural language explanation algorithms for the lung cancer computer-aided diagnosis system. Artif. Intell. Med. **108**, 101952 (2020)
7. Bao, T.: Research on English Vocabulary Translation Technology Based on Dynamic Bilingual Corpus (2020)
8. Sherwani, K.A.: Assessment of Teaching Translation in English Language Learning (2017)
9. The Effects of Grammar-Translation Method and Communicative Approach on Oral English Teaching. 海外英语 (9), 2 (2016)
10. Li, Y.: The Application of parallel corpora based computer-aided translation technology in chemical english translation. C e Ca **42**(6), 2433–2437 (2017)
11. Wang, X.: Building a parallel corpus for english translation teaching based on computer-aided translation software. Comput.-Aided Des. Appl. **18**(S4), 175–185 (2021)
12. Luo, N.: Application of computer aided translation in the ESP discipline and the analysis of its advantages and disadvantages. Autom. Instrum. (2018)
13. Zhongmin, L.I., Liu, H.: The application of computer aided translation teaching system in the translation course of local universities. J. Jilin Agric. Sci. Technol. Univ. (2019)
14. Wu, H.: Multimedia interaction-based computer-aided translation technology in applied english teaching. Mob. Inf. Syst. (2021)
15. Xu, J., Zhao, X.: The design and application of an on-line examination system for computer aided English teaching (2016)
16. Yang, H.: Empirical analysis of vocabulary teaching in college english based on computer-assisted memetics. Boletin Tecnico/Tech. Bull. **55**(8), 723–728 (2017)
17. Xiuming, C.: Design and application of computer-aided english learning system (2016)
18. Yang, C.: Study on english vocabulary based on the computeraided corpus (2016)
19. Wang, M.: Research on the teaching application of computer aided translation course automatic online system based on. Net. Autom. Instrum. (2016)
20. Jihong, Z.: Computer-aided English vocabulary: Based on artificial intelligence and cognitive process model. Agro Food Ind Hi Tech **28**(1), 2403–2407 (2017)

Research on "Online and Offline" Translation Teaching Mode Based on Internet

Yunyun Zhu[1,2(✉)]

[1] School of Economics and Management, Guilin University of Electronic Technology,
Guilin 541000, China
182829464@qq.com

[2] Graduate School, University of Perpetual Help System DALTA, 1740 Las Piñas, Philippines

Abstract. In the past, translation was considered a very tedious and time-consuming task. However, with the progress of technology, translation has become more efficient and time-saving. Translation can now be done through various media, such as written text, audio or video files. The use of computers in translation enables people who are not proficient in two languages to translate documents from one language to another (Kozma & Yildirim, 2018). Translation can also be completed through online platforms such as Google Translate or Bing Translator. The development of information technology has promoted the reform of teaching methods, and the mixed teaching combining the conventional offline teaching and online online teaching has become the development trend of higher education. However, the "representation problem" of the current mixed teaching practice is increasingly prominent, especially the lack of coherence in the design of online and offline tasks, which is easy to lead to poor effect of in-depth learning. This study is about "online and offline" translation teaching mode. This study focuses on different online and offline translation teaching. The purpose is to explore the best way to use the Internet and offline English teaching. Online translation is a method that can be used to teach students how to translate text in real time at work. This kind of teaching is often called "live translation". On the contrary, offline learning is a way for students to read the translation to better understand it. Over the years, this learning method has been widely used in traditional education systems (such as memory).

Keyword: Internet · Translation teaching · Online and offline

1 Introduction

As a new teaching mode integrating online teaching and traditional classroom teaching, hybrid teaching has become the key direction of teaching reform in colleges and universities. In particular, the COVID-19 has further promoted the extensive application of online education, which has greatly improved the application of hybrid teaching mode. The research on the application of blended teaching in foreign language classroom is quite rich. However, in general, although researchers have paid close attention

Y. Zhang and N. Shah (Eds.): BigIoT-EDU 2023, LNICST 582, pp. 84–93, 2024.
https://doi.org/10.1007/978-3-031-63136-8_9

to the implementation of blended teaching in the past 20 years, the research results on teaching strategies are not many. In 2000, the Teaching Syllabus for English Majors in Colleges and Universities clearly proposed that "more task-centered and diversified teaching activities should be carried out" in terms of teaching methods. How to redesign the mixed teaching task based on the task-based teaching theory shows its importance. This chapter includes the research background, research issues, research significance and research methods, and describes the framework of the paper in detail.

With the rapid development of information technology, the application of Internet in the field of education is more and more extensive. Especially in translation teaching, the teaching mode of combining online and offline has attracted wide attention. This model makes full use of the resources and technological advantages of the Internet, aiming at improving the effectiveness and quality of translation teaching. At present, many scholars and educators have studied the online and offline teaching mode, and achieved certain results. However, there are still some problems in practical application of this model. With the rapid development of information technology and the continuous innovation of teaching methods, mixed teaching has quietly penetrated into all kinds of education at all levels. The COVID-19 in 2020 will have a huge impact on traditional offline courses. In response to the call of "suspending classes without stopping classes", colleges and universities have successively carried out online teaching, uploading teaching materials, live teaching, and online discussion using different online teaching platforms. This attempt to combine online and offline teaching has promoted the development of hybrid teaching. Although current teachers have begun to try to carry out mixed teaching practice, they still haven't got rid of the traditional classroom teaching mode in the process of mixed teaching practice. It is common for teachers to copy the traditional course content and teaching form on the online teaching platform. There are also teachers who are confused about the online and offline integrated teaching design. In the process of trying to balance the relationship between reducing the learning burden for students and improving the teaching effect, Be hit to a certain extent. Although scholars at home and abroad have started relevant research on the application of blended teaching in college English courses, relevant research has not put forward the framework and model of blended teaching task design. In the process of mixed teaching design, teachers are too general. They neither make specialized design according to the characteristics of various courses and subjects, nor make full use of teaching theories to guide the design of specific teaching links. Therefore, the effectiveness of their teaching effects needs to be further explored. Under the current situation of mixed teaching, how to design a mixed teaching task framework for a certain class of courses based on the task-based teaching theory and subject characteristics is the development direction of mixed teaching [1, 2].

For students, this study opens a new way for students to explore new knowledge. In addition to judging the usefulness of the curriculum from the perspective of their own learning experience, learners can also judge the value of the curriculum from the perspective of teaching design effect. Students can recognize what design elements affect their willingness to learn, and understand the correlation between gender, major and language level and Internet translation learning, so that they can choose courses and improve their interest in learning [3].

For teachers, this study provides guidance for teachers to implement Internet translation teaching. Teachers can recognize the relevance between the elements of instructional design and what factors affect the instructional design of Internet translation, which provides a basis for teachers to adjust the instructional design. The investigation and Research on learning willingness, students' gender, major and language level can enable teachers to understand the importance of students in teaching design, so as to adopt scientific methods to analyze learners and improve the effect of Internet translation teaching design [4, 5].

2 Related Work

2.1 Connotation of Online and Offline Education Mode

Although the Internet provides abundant translation teaching resources, it is difficult to guarantee the quality and accuracy of these resources, and they are scattered on various platforms and websites, lacking an effective integration and screening mechanism.As the name suggests, "o2o teaching mode" is mainly a teaching mode formed by the combination of "online and offline mode" and "teaching". As shown in Fig. 1, its connotation must be the extension of "online and offline mode" in teaching. Scholars guochuncai and Jin Yifu believe that o2o education mode is a teaching mode integrating offline education and online education, which combines the advantages of offline education and online education. In the whole online and offline teaching process, the roles of teachers and students have changed. Teachers are no longer the leader of the classroom, but the partner of students and the guide of knowledge. Teaching and learning interact with each other, teaching and learning grow together. Teachers and students jointly agree on the learning progress, taking into account the student group and personality. The online and offline learning environment is the combination of traditional classrooms and online learning spaces [6, 7]. When implementing online and offline teaching mode, there is often a disconnection between online teaching and offline practice. After students learn theoretical knowledge online, it is difficult to apply it to practical translation practice.The current technical means can not fully meet the needs of online and offline teaching mode. For example, technical problems such as lack of real-time interaction and untimely feedback still affect the teaching effect.

At present, foreign research on hybrid teaching focuses on the design of resources and strategies at the medium and micro levels, as well as the impact of hybrid teaching on teaching and learning effects. For example, some scholars have divided the computer course into two stages. The first stage adopts the mixed teaching without design, and the second stage adopts the problem-based mixed teaching. The research found that the task-based teaching method can stimulate students' active learning more than the traditional mixed teaching. Some scholars have compared task-based teaching, group peer learning and traditional teaching in the mixed learning environment. The research results show that the application of various teaching methods in the mixed learning environment can improve learners' English practical ability. Other researchers have used the introduction to translation and science and technology translation as research objects to evaluate the effectiveness of the two kinds of translation teaching under the mixed teaching mode, and proposed the way to apply the task-based teaching method to translation

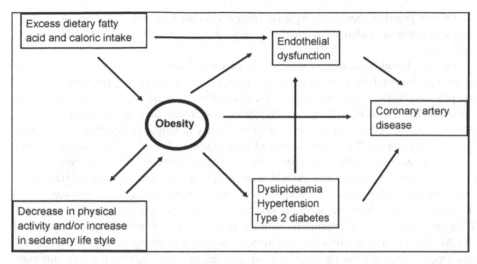

Fig. 1. Online and offline teaching mode

teaching. However, the research has not put forward more opinions on how to design other translation courses. Foreign scholars also put forward the importance of personalized teaching in hybrid teaching in their research. It is a very effective way for teachers to improve students' academic performance through personalized design and providing additional guidance to students. Previous studies have shown that the implementation of blended teaching can improve learners' learning satisfaction and students' participation, but it does not improve students' academic performance. Therefore, the effect of blended teaching remains to be further explored.The "online and offline" translation teaching mode of Internet is a new teaching mode, which has broad application prospects. By strengthening the integration of resources, technical support and cooperation mechanism, the existing problems can be effectively solved, and the effect and quality of translation teaching can be improved. At the same time, it is necessary to constantly explore and practice, and constantly improve this teaching mode, so as to better serve the training of translation talents and the needs of social development.

2.2 Translation Teaching

Resource integration and platform construction: Screening and integrating translation teaching resources on the Internet, and establishing a special online teaching platform or tool to provide students with high-quality learning resources.

Teaching design: According to the teaching objectives and the actual situation of students, formulate reasonable teaching plans and course outlines to ensure the effective connection of online and offline teaching.

Online teaching implementation: use the online platform to teach theoretical knowledge, and strengthen students' mastery of theoretical knowledge through real-time interaction, discussion, homework, etc.

Offline practical teaching: Organize students to carry out practical translation practice, and improve students' practical operation ability through project cooperation and field visits.

Feedback and evaluation: Establish an effective feedback mechanism, collect students' opinions and suggestions in a timely manner, and continuously improve the teaching process. At the same time, reasonable evaluation standards and methods should be formulated to evaluate students' performance objectively and fairly, which will help students experience the applicability and practicality of language learning and enhance learning motivation. The improvement of translation ability cannot be separated from a large number of targeted exercises. Qin Jun stressed that in the after-class stage of the translation course, teachers should arrange appropriate and appropriate translation exercises according to the characteristics of the chapters, so that students can "learn in practice" and achieve the teaching objectives by consolidating the teaching content. With the penetration of Internet technology in the field of learning, the emergence of "Muke" has had a huge impact on traditional translation teaching. Using "Muke" online resources to innovate the training mode of translation ability has become an important way to improve students' translation ability. In Muke learning, students can acquire a large number of cultural background related knowledge according to their own needs, and independently control the learning progress.

Translation teaching is an important part of translation theory and practice. Since Delisle, a University of Canada, first proposed the concepts of "teaching translation" and "translation teaching", there has been a heated discussion in the academic community. As far as delier is concerned, he believes that the purpose of carrying out translation teaching activities is to translate itself, that is, to teach students the knowledge and skills of translation. At the same time, teaching translation is a tool for foreign language teaching. Therefore, translation is only used to test students' understanding of language points. Bao Chuanyun also pointed out that in teaching translation, translation is a vassal of foreign language teaching, a means of teaching rather than a purpose of teaching [8]. Zhong Weihe and Murray, in the form of tables, analyzed in detail the differences between teaching translation and translation teaching from 12 aspects: subject orientation, training objectives, guiding ideology, teaching objectives, communication objectives, translation standards, teacher requirements, language requirements, teaching system, teaching focus, use tools, training meaning, etc. according to the teaching philosophy of translation teaching, they pointed out that the training of translation professionals should be based on language Skills and encyclopedic knowledge, while traditional teaching translation cannot complete the education of translation skills and encyclopedic knowledge. In addition, scholars such as Lin Zhang, Huang Zhonglian and Li Yashu have compared and defined these two concepts. To sum up, the author believes that translation teaching is a traditional means of language teaching, with more emphasis on its translation skills.

3 Internet Based "Online and Offline" Translation Teaching Mode

3.1 Research on the Application of Online and Offline Teaching Mode on the Network Platform

There are many researches on online and offline teaching on the network platform. Based on the investigation and analysis of the current online and offline teaching Provide technical support and training for teachers, so that they can make better use of Internet technology and tools for online and offline teaching.In the online autonomous learning stage, teachers should create classes to learn this lesson on the Internet translation teaching auxiliary platform, group students, build an autonomous learning environment, and publish digital resources of basic knowledge related to the teaching content of this lesson. Digital learning resources can be digital learning resources made in the form of word, ppt, text, pictures and videos, These resources are designed and produced by teachers in advance and uploaded online so that students can study independently. According to these uploaded digital learning resources and the teaching objectives of this class, teachers need to set up tasks for students to study independently. Tasks can be quizzes, the production of simple works, the design of small programs, etc., so that students can learn purposefully with tasks, and can also complete tasks through students, Understand the students' learning situation. When students raise problems in the discussion area, teachers can solve the problems for students in time. At the same time, students' learning progress can also be monitored through the speeches and questions in the discussion area, as shown in Fig. 2.

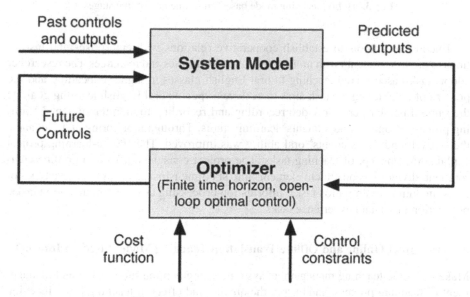

Fig. 2. Internet translation teaching mode

The mixed teaching stage model considers the online and offline links separately, and matches and connects the online and offline links. This is the further development of the mixed teaching ecosystem extending to the meso and micro design. Many scholars have produced some classic teaching models based on specific teaching practices. The two-stage teaching model, represented by Zhang Huanrui, divides teaching into online and offline stages, aiming to help students develop personalized and autonomous learning programs by integrating online activities and offline classroom teaching. The teaching evaluation combines formative and summative evaluation, and sets the evaluation proportion of different links according to the difference of course content (as shown in Fig. 3).

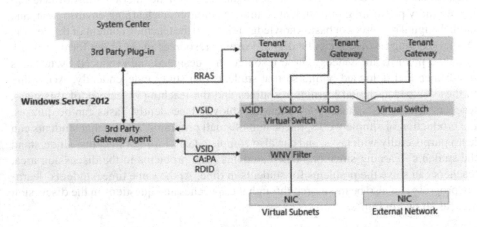

Fig. 3. Hybrid teaching mode based on online and offline stages

Encourage schools to establish cooperative relations with enterprises and institutions to provide students with more practical opportunities and resources.The researcher adopts task-based mixed teaching in oral English classes in higher education, and the process of completing the task aims to achieve a specific oral English learning goal. At the same time, teachers use video recording and recording to monitor students' learning process to understand students' learning status. Through monitoring and guidance, the study found that students' oral ability was improved. The JISC e-learning project explains the concept of teaching tasks. The project considers tasks in an online environment, divides its constituent elements into six dimensions, and explains five types of tasks, including assimilation tasks, information processing tasks, communication tasks, production tasks, and experience tasks.

3.2 Design of Online and Offline Translation Teaching Mode Based on Internet

Make scientific teaching management system, strengthen the supervision and management of teaching process, and ensure the quality and effect of teaching [10]. Teaching work requires educators to plan in advance and divide labor reasonably in an organized and planned way. Teachers' teams first need to complete the distribution of teaching tasks, form teams to complete the tasks of classroom teaching content arrangement, teaching design, resource collection and integration, and discuss specific online and offline teaching measures, so as to ensure that each teacher can supervise and urge the team to improve the overall translation teaching mode while completing their own teaching tasks. Scientific and reasonable teaching design requires the following steps: first, teachers are very familiar with the content of teaching materials, so as to formulate clear teaching objectives, and can appropriately adjust the teaching plan according to the differences of students, and implement personalized teaching targeted. Secondly, teachers should use Internet resources to supplement students with rich extracurricular knowledge while completing the content required by the curriculum standard, so as to ensure the completion of teaching progress and the universality of knowledge accepted by students. Finally, teachers are required to distinguish the differences between online and offline teaching at all times in the teaching process. Online teaching should pay attention to the management of students and the timely cleaning of displayed resources. Online teaching should assist offline teaching and make full use of online teaching to improve the interest of the classroom.

Most students are very resistant to difficult courses, and online teaching allows students to preview classroom knowledge before class. Students can preliminarily feel the classroom content by using the preview of teaching content, setting of teaching objectives, teaching examples and so on set in advance by teachers on the network platform. Students' online teaching and platform can divide the teaching content according to their own learning needs, pay more attention to the explanation of relevant knowledge points that are difficult to understand, search teaching resources on the platform for practice, strengthen knowledge mastery, communicate with classmates about classroom questions, and complete the secondary understanding and innovation of classroom knowledge.

4 Internet-Based Hybrid Teaching Process

Promote communication and learning among educators by sharing and promoting successful online and offline teaching mode cases (Fig. 4).

When implementing the online and offline teaching mode, we should fully consider the individual differences and needs of students and adopt differentiated teaching strategies to meet the development needs of different studentsIn the existing research, the support of task-based teaching based on the mixed environment is mainly reflected in the online autonomous learning and online task reflection stage in the task preparation stage. Based on the mixed environment, Galan and other researchers evaluated the effectiveness of the two kinds of translation teaching methods, taking Introduction to Translation and Science and Technology Translation as the research objects, and proposed the way to apply the task-based approach to translation teaching. Taking Lei Jing's research as an example, task-based teaching is designed based on the CALL environment. The pre-task stage mainly includes warm-up activities and lead-in activities. Teachers play audio or video related to the theme of the text in the warm-up activities, create realistic social reality scenes, and encourage students to participate in various language practice activities. The online task stage is arranged at the end of each unit's classroom study. Students are required to complete letters, survey reports, problem solutions, etc. through the network. Under the resource environment supported by computer network, students' enthusiasm

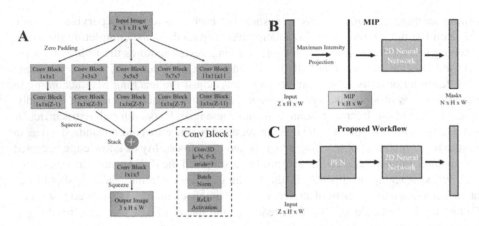

Fig. 4. Matching and integration of task-based and mixed teaching

to explore new knowledge is enhanced, and students' opportunities to contact and use the target language are increased. In Chang Lanhua's research, when the teacher designs and arranges the task, he intersperses the lines from celebrity quotes, speeches, film and television series materials into the teaching work, and requires the students to complete the task according to the division of labor, including collecting data, integrating data, reporting results, etc. In Tian Hui's research, the offline classroom link focuses on the in-depth communication and discussion of students. In order to avoid the situation where a few students speak and other students have nothing to do, teachers should urge students with insufficient initiative to complete the task quickly, and provide help to students with difficulties in completing the task.

5 Conclusion

Education in the new era should be based on the content of teaching materials, fit the psychological characteristics of students, and carry out teaching work in a more information-based and networked way. The rapid development of the Internet and its combination with teaching work are caused by the progressive trend of the times. Teaching workers should actively use this advantage to enrich classroom content and classroom forms and improve teaching efficiency. The combination of online and offline translation teaching mode requires teachers to master the structure of teaching materials, have a clear stage division of teaching objectives, and have higher requirements for students' ability to learn independently and retrieve resources, which is conducive to cultivating applied versatile talents to adapt to social development.

References

1. Yan, C.: Research on the Construction of English Translation Corpus Based on Network Electronic Technology (2021)

2. Li, Q., Song, Y.: Practical Research on Online and Offline Teaching-Taking Baoshan University in Yunnan Province as an Example **5**(8), 6 (2021)
3. Wu, X.: Research on the reform of ideological and political teaching evaluation method of college english course based on "online and offline" teaching. J. High. Educ. Res. **3**(1), 87–90 (2022)
4. Wei, B.: Research on the mixed teaching model in colleges and universities in the context of "internet+". Asian Agric. Res. **12** (2021)
5. Wang, W., Yin, G.: Analysis and research on the application of internet technology in sports track and field teaching. J. Phys. Conf. Ser. **1881**(4), 042026 (7pp) (2021)
6. Pezaro, S., Jenkins, M., Bollard, M.: Defining 'research inspired teaching' and introducing a research inspired online/offline teaching (riot) framework for fostering it using a co-creation approach. Nurse Educ. Today **108**, 105163 (2022)
7. Chi, Q., Song, C., Jiang, X.: Research on online precision teaching based on data analysis. In: IC4E 2021: 2021 12th International Conference on E-Education, E-Business, E-Management, and E-Learning (2021)
8. Qiong, L.I.: Research on the blended teaching mode of "intermediate speaking" based on SPOC. Psychol. Res. **12**(4), 7 (2022)
9. Hellmich, E., Vinall, K.: FL instructor beliefs about machine translation: ecological insights to guide research and practice. Int. J. Comput.-Assisted Lang. Learn. Teach. (IJCALLT) **11** (2021)
10. Zhang, M., Huang, Z.: Crowdsourcing used in higher education: an empirical study on a sustainable translation teaching mode based on crowdsourced translation. Sustainability **14** (2022)

Research on English Chinese Translation System for Tourism Based on Globish

Haihu Zhao[✉]

Guangdong Mechanical and Electrical Polytechnic, Guangzhou 510515, China
935748819@qq.com

Abstract. The 21st century is an information age. With the increasingly frequent international exchanges, the diversity of languages has become a major obstacle to communication. Paul Nerier, a Frenchman, proposed a global language Globish based on English, which brings hope to our realization of language communication among various nationalities. Now, although we can use specialized translators to translate, the high cost and inconvenience are often prohibitive. The design of the English Chinese tourism translation system is developed by the Tourism Translation Institute (TTI) and is based on years of experience in translation services. TTI's goal is to provide effective, efficient and cost-effective services to all customers. All our employees are qualified professional translators who have a good understanding of Chinese language and culture. They are experienced in providing high-quality Chinese English translation and Chinese English translation. We also provide a range of other services, including data entry, document scanning, editing and proofreading.

Keywords: Travel Globish · English Chinese Translation System

1 Introduction

In our daily life, we use language to communicate and communicate every day. Language is the most important tool of human communication. People use language to preserve and transmit the achievements of human civilization. Language is one of the main carriers of information exchange and dissemination. However, the world is so big and there are so many languages. How can people from different languages communicate with each other? This has become a big problem. So some people began to imagine whether they could use a universal language to communicate with this universal language. In this case, a language called Esperanto and a language called Globo came into being one after another [1].

With the continuous in-depth study of machine translation, a variety of translation methods have emerged. At present, the main translation methods are: rule based, corpus based, statistical based, and example based.

Since Warren Weaver published the Memorandum on Translation in 1949, the development and research of machine translation has not been smooth, but has experienced

Y. Zhang and N. Shah (Eds.): BigIoT-EDU 2023, LNICST 582, pp. 94–100, 2024.
https://doi.org/10.1007/978-3-031-63136-8_10

a tortuous development process from optimistic germination period to pessimistic low ebb period to a new understanding of recovery period to a new period of development and prosperity [2].

In summary, the research on Globish based tourism English Chinese translation system is committed to developing a Globish based translation system suitable for the tourism field. By simplifying language and processing domain specific requirements, this system can provide more accurate and understandable English Chinese translation results, promoting the convenience and efficiency of global tourism communication [3]. This study involves key technologies such as corpus construction, machine learning, and natural language processing, as well as important links in user experience and evaluation.

2   Related Work

2.1   Concept of Machine Translation

English machine translation is a technology that utilizes computer and machine learning techniques to automatically translate English text into other languages. It achieves automatic translation by analyzing and processing vocabulary, grammar, and semantic information in the source language (English), and converting it into corresponding vocabulary and sentence structures in the target language.

The development of English machine translation began in the early 1950s, with the goal of achieving the ability to translate minority languages such as English into more common languages such as Russian through computers. With the advancement of computer and natural language processing technology, English machine translation has received widespread attention and research [4].

Traditional English machine translation methods are mainly based on rules and rule libraries, relying on a large number of manually written grammar and semantic rules. The disadvantage of this method is that it requires a lot of manpower and professional knowledge, and it is not effective in dealing with long sentences and complex language phenomena.

In recent years, with the rapid development of machine learning and artificial intelligence technology, data-driven statistical machine translation and neural machine translation have become mainstream methods. Statistical machine translation establishes statistical models between source and target languages by analyzing large-scale bilingual corpora, thereby achieving the translation process [5]. Neural machine translation utilizes deep neural network models to automatically learn the mapping relationship between the source and target languages by training large-scale parallel bilingual data.

The goal of English machine translation is to achieve accurate, fluent, and natural translation results to meet the needs of different fields and applications, such as business translation, technology document translation, tourism translation, etc. Although English machine translation has achieved considerable results in certain scenarios, it still faces challenges such as polysemy processing, language differences, cultural differences, etc. [6]. Therefore, different machine translation methods and technologies are constantly being studied and improved to improve translation quality and effectiveness.

English machine translation is a technology that utilizes computer and machine learning technology to automatically translate English text into other languages. With the development of machine learning and artificial intelligence, data-driven statistical machine translation and neural machine translation have become the main methods, providing new possibilities for achieving more accurate, smooth, and natural translation results.

2.2 Assumption of Globish Based Tourism Translation System

The globalized tourism translation system aims to provide diverse translation results, fully considering the differences in translation platforms and language characteristics. Although the same English input sentence may lead to different translation results, factors such as English and Chinese word order rules and the highest level expression of English adjectives do affect the diversity of translation results in cross language translation. Firstly, there are different word order rules in English and Chinese languages. English usually adopts the word order of subject predicate object, while Chinese tends to prefer the word order of subject object predicate. Therefore, when translating the same English input sentence into Chinese, it may be necessary to adjust the order of words to follow the Chinese word order rules. This adjustment may lead to different translation results [7].

In addition, there are also differences in the superlative expression of English adjectives. The highest degree of an adjective in English usually ends with "- est", such as "the tallest building". In Chinese, the superlative adjective usually uses specific words or expressions, such as' highest. Therefore, for the superlative expression of adjectives, the translation system may produce different translation results based on different language rules and habitual expressions.

In order to achieve diversified translation results, globalized tourism translation systems can rely on machine learning and artificial intelligence technologies. By training models and deep learning algorithms, the system can learn and understand the conversion rules and characteristics between different languages. At the same time, the system can also integrate different translation platforms and resources, comprehensively consider various translation results, and provide richer and more accurate translation choices.

The idea of a globalized tourism translation system can provide users with diverse translation results by considering different translation platforms and language characteristics. Factors such as English and Chinese word order rules and the highest level expression of English adjectives can have an impact on translation results [8]. Through machine learning and deep learning technologies, the system can learn and parse these rules, providing users with more comprehensive and accurate translation choices.as shown in Fig. 1.

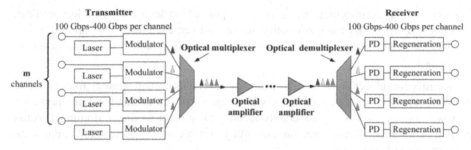

Fig. 1. Communication block diagram of Globish based translation system

3 Main Problems in English Chinese Machine Translation

Through the comparison between English and Chinese, we also understand the difficulties that these differences bring to machine translation.

Ambiguities are mainly manifested in lexical and structural.

On the other hand, it is caused by the lack of direct corresponding expressions in terms of vocabulary and structure between English and Chinese. Lexical ambiguity.

Polysemy and multi category of words are common in both English and Chinese. Moreover, we can also find that words with high frequency of use are often words with serious polysemy. For example, the commonly used word "go" has many different classifications and interpretations in the New English Chinese Dictionary.

Ambiguity of Phrase Structure

A common reason for phrase structure ambiguity is that the attachment methods of nouns and prepositions in noun phrases are not easily determined, leading to different attachment methods that may produce reasonable semantic explanations. When solving the problem of phrase structure ambiguity, we can use the recognition of subject predicate dominant words to help determine the correct attachment method. Subject-predicate dominant words refer to words that occupy a dominant position in a phrase and play a decisive role in the semantics of the entire phrase. Usually, subject predicate dominant words have a high amount of information and semantic importance, playing a crucial role in the meaning and structure of the entire phrase.

By identifying the subject predicate advantage word, we can determine the noun or prepositional phrase it is attached to, thereby determining the attachment method and resolving phrase structure ambiguity. Identifying subject predicate advantage words can be carried out based on the following aspects:

1. Semantic importance: Subject predicate dominant words play a major semantic role in phrases, possessing higher information content and semantic importance. We can determine subject predicate dominant words by analyzing the semantics and context of words.
2. Position and grammatical function: The subject predicate advantage word is usually located at the core position of a phrase, serving as the subject or predicate. By analyzing the position and grammatical function of words in a sentence, it can assist in determining subject predicate dominant words.

3. Context: Context information is also very important for determining subject predicate dominant words. By analyzing other words and sentence structures around words, more accurate results can be obtained for identifying subject predicate dominant words.

Identifying subject predicate dominant words is an important strategy for solving the problem of phrase structure ambiguity, which can help us understand and interpret complex sentence structures. By accurately identifying subject predicate dominant words, we can better solve phrase structure ambiguity and accurately understand and express the semantics of sentences.

4 Design of English Chinese Translation System for Tourism Based on Globish

4.1 Structure of English Chinese Machine Translation System

Each level uses different methods and strategies. Ambiguity is resolved using vocabulary based grammar, semantics, rules and other knowledge. Syntactic analysis does not generate a complete syntax tree, but a sequence of words and phrases in a sentence. Sentences are regarded as the recursion of clauses [9]. As the basic translation unit, clauses are converted through sentence pattern matching. In the analysis, the system uses a framework to describe language units, including grammar, semantics, collocation, rules and other knowledge, and can handle many problems in machine translation in a more intuitive and concise way.

In the knowledge system of the system, the common and procedural knowledge of language is embodied in the algorithm of the program, while the personalized, narrative and control knowledge of language is stored in the machine dictionary for word organization. In addition to grammar, semantics and collocation knowledge, vocabulary disambiguation, structure disambiguation and translation selection represented by rules or conditions are also included under the entries of the dictionary [10]. This organization and representation of knowledge can better solve the representation of different knowledge granularity and avoid the conflict between rules, as shown in Fig. 2.

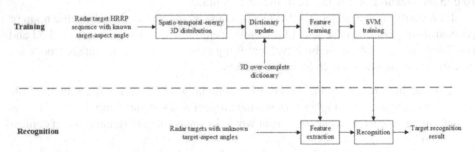

Fig. 2. The structure of english-chinese machine translation system

4.2 Translation Process of English Chinese Translation System for Tourism Based on Globish

The basic idea of this system is to generate translation results based on aligned bilingual tree pair corpus through matching, replacement and combination. The basic process is as follows:

(1) Find the statement ID containing the keyword of the statement to be translated from the keyword index table, and Sort the number of words.
(2) Use the statement editing distance algorithm to calculate the statement editing for all the found statements and the statements to be translated Distance. The found statements are sorted in reverse order according to the calculated editing distance from the statement to be translated. Thus, n statements with the minimum editing distance are selected as the basic statement sequence.
(3) The basic sentence sequence obtained in the previous step is filtered by editing the distance, and then it is combined with the sentence to be translated.

   The improved edit distance algorithm (adding semantic similarity calculation) mentioned in this paper is used to calculate the semantic similarity of sentences. Select the sentence with the greatest semantic similarity as the basic sentence found.
(4) The basic statements obtained from 3 are converted into alignment tree T according to the alignment information of bilingual alignment library.

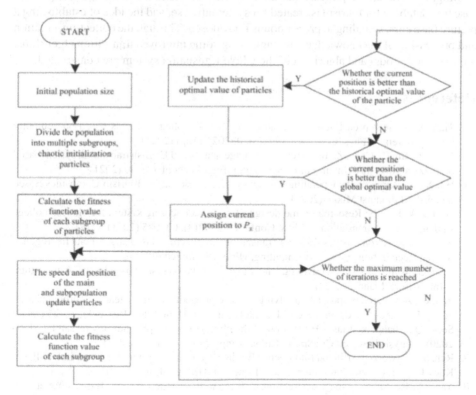

Fig. 3. Basic flow chart of translation

(5) Match the English source statement of T with the statement to be translated through words and part of speech phrases, and replace, insert, and delete in the alignment tree according to the replacement rules of the DOT 2 model.
(6) Reorganize the statement tree obtained by 5 after replacement, insertion and deletion into translated statements.
(7) Translated statements obtained from output 6.

The basic flow chart of the translation process is shown in Fig. 3.

5 Conclusion

Machine translation has always been a difficult subject to tackle. In the early days of machine translation research, people once imagined to create a "universal translation system" that can translate in all fields. However, many years of research shows that this goal is impossible at least in the near future. Due to the infinity of natural language itself and the limitation of human understanding of natural language, empirical methods face serious data sparsity in general fields; The rational approach always faces a large number of exceptions. What this paper systematically implements is only for English Chinese translation in the field of tourism. According to the language characteristics of Globish itself and the field characteristics of tourism terms, a knowledge base including a bilingual dictionary, a professional dictionary for tourism, and a bilingual alignment case tree database for tourism is created for systematic use, and the idea of establishing a picture base corresponding to proper nouns is proposed. Through the collection, creation and processing of the knowledge base, and using some improved translation algorithms, the structural model and algorithm of the whole translation system are constructed.

References

1. Tian, X.: Research on English translation of Chinese college students based on computer scoring system. J. Phys. Conf. Ser. **1992**(3), 032021 (5pp) (2021)
2. Yuan, Z., Jin, C., Chen, Z.: Research on language analysis of English translation system based on fuzzy algorithm. J. Intell. Fuzzy Syst. Appl. Eng. Technol. (4), 40 (2021)
3. Hu, X.: Research on the Operating Efficiency of Chinese Listed Tourism Companies Based on DEA-Malmquist Model (2021)
4. Wang, Q., Pan, F.: Research on the design of computer scoring system for chinese college students' english translation. J. Phys. Conf. Ser. **1992**(3), 032085 (2021)
5. Xu, Y.: Research on Business English Translation Architecture Based on Artificial Intelligence Speech Recognition and Edge Computing. Hindawi Limited (2021)
6. Chai, G., Wen, Q.: An interactive english–chinese translation system based on GLA algorithm. J. Inf. Knowl. Manag. (2022)
7. Yan, C.: A research proposal on applying chinese phonetic system in teaching pronunciation of english words to older chinese EFL adult learners. J. High. Educ. Res. 3(1), 21–25 (2022)
8. Song, Q., Zhang, N., Liang, H.: Review of the chinese internet philanthropy research (2006–2020): analysis based on CiteSpace. China Nonprofit Rev. 13(1&2), 4 (2021)
9. Ren, S.: Networked Artificial Intelligence English Translation System Based on an Intelligent Knowledge Base and Translation Method Thereof. Hindawi Limited (2021)
10. Yan, C.: Research on the Construction of English Translation Corpus Based on Network Electronic Technology (2021)

Design of English Translation Model Based on Recurrent Neural Network

Xinxin Guan$^{(\boxtimes)}$, Yuehua Li, and Ren Yuankun

Yantai Vocational College, Yantai 264670, Shandong, China
`xingege0531@163.com`

Abstract. English is a language that is spoken by almost every person on this planet. It has become the most important language for all the people of this world. English is not only used in business but also in personal life. People from different countries use English as their first language and they want to communicate with other people who are using other languages. This paper aims to discuss about how machine learning can be used to design an effective model for translation between two languages like English and Russian, which will help us to improve the services provided by machines as well as human translators. The create a model that can both predict and generate the meaning of English sentences. This is done using a recursive neural network (RNN). RNN works on sequential input, which encodes information according to the previous example. The proposed RNN model is based on three different layers: input layer (layer 1), which uses context and word embedding as features; The middle layer (layer 2) containing LSTM units is used to predict new words according to the context of new words and previous contexts; And the output layer (layer 3), which considers the meaning of words and their context information. Based on these inputs, RNN will output the next word or sentence, even the paragraph that should be used to predict the meaning. The model was created using the Keras library, which makes it easy to use recurrent neural networks.

Keywords: English translation model · Recursive neural network · English vocabulary

1 Introduction

With the rapid development of information technology, English translation plays a crucial role in cross-cultural communication and international cooperation worldwide. The demand for automated translation systems has made deep learning based translation models increasingly important and widely used. The English translation model based on Recursive Neural Network (RNN) has great potential in translation tasks due to its powerful sequence processing and text modeling capabilities [1].

This article aims to design an English translation model based on recurrent neural networks, which will learn and model the grammar and semantic structure of input English sentences, and generate corresponding target language translations. Specifically,

Y. Zhang and N. Shah (Eds.): BigIoT-EDU 2023, LNICST 582, pp. 101–111, 2024.
https://doi.org/10.1007/978-3-031-63136-8_11

the model will consist of the following main components: 1 Word embedding layer: This layer will encode the semantic information of vocabulary by mapping the input English words into low dimensional vector representations. This vector representation can capture the semantic similarity and correlation between words, thereby providing richer semantic information. 2. Recursive Neural Network Layer: This layer will utilize a recursive neural network model to capture the syntactic structure and semantic features of input sentences by parsing and combining them word by word. The iterative calculation process of recurrent neural networks allows the model to preserve contextual information while modeling long-term dependencies, thereby improving the performance of the translation model. 3. Translation layer: On the basis of the recurrent neural network layer, the translation layer will use techniques such as attention mechanism or encoding decoding architecture to convert encoded English sentences into target language translation. The attention mechanism can allow the model to generate different attention weights based on different parts of the input sentence while generating the target language, and better capture the corresponding relationships between sentences. 4. Decoding layer: The decoding layer will generate target language translation text based on the output and contextual information of the translation layer. The decoding layer can use statistical machine translation models or neural network-based sequence generation models to generate translation results by selecting the target language word with the highest probability [2].

By using a recursive neural network-based English translation model, we can model English sentences from the perspectives of grammar and semantics, achieving more accurate and fluent translation results. The iterative computation and contextual memory capabilities of recurrent neural networks enable the model to infer and make decisions based on contextual information, improving translation accuracy and semantic coherence. In the following chapters, we will provide a detailed introduction to the design and implementation details of each component in the model. Through experimental evaluation and comparative analysis, we will verify the performance and effectiveness of the model in English translation tasks, and further optimize and expand it. Ultimately, we hope to contribute to the research and application of automated translation systems by designing an English translation model based on recurrent neural networks, and improve the efficiency and quality of cross-cultural communication and international cooperation.

2 Related Work

2.1 Recurrent Neural Network

Recursive neural network (RNN) is a special series of neural networks, which aims to deal with serial data, such as a series of texts or stock market fluctuations. In reality, there are many sequential data, such as text, voice and video. These sequential data often have temporal correlation, that is, the output of the network at a certain time or several times. Recursive neural network has a certain memory function [3]. This network is closely related to sequences and lists, and can be used to solve many problems, such as speech recognition, language model, machine translation, etc. Compared with cannot handle this kind of correlation well, because it has no memory ability, so the output of the previous time cannot be transferred to the subsequent time [4]. It deals with the information of sequence structure. The shown in Fig. 1 below:

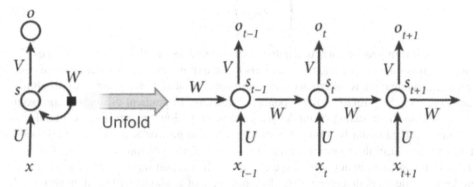

Fig. 1. Model structure

Algorithm process:

1. Use the CNN DeCNN trained on ImageNet to generate rough significant area detection results.
2. Generate the input image sequence of RNN with spatial transformation matrix, and the image in the sequence is the sub region of the original image.
3. The sub region image sequence is sent into the two-layer RNN, the output of the first layer of RNN is decoded with DeCNN, and the decoding result is used to refine the part corresponding to the sub region in the coarse significant detection result [5]. The first layer of RNN can be expressed as:

$$\arg \min_{SC} \sum_{i=1}^{k} \sum_{x \in C_i} |X - \mu_i|^2 \qquad (1)$$

4. The output of the second layer of RNN is used to generate the spatial transformation matrix. The spatial transformation matrix is used to generate the input image sub region sequence of RNN, and the position where the decoding result of the first layer of RNN generated corresponds to the coarse significant detection result. The second layer of RNN can be expressed as:

$$\|y - \theta_i\| = \min(\|y - \theta_i\|) \qquad (2)$$

RNN has inherent advantages in processing sequence data, and it can accept any variable length input. When the repeated avoided due to the internal state mechanism of RNN. The change caused by input reveals this kind of time series information, and the parameter sharing in RNN further reduces the amount of model parameters.

Although RNNLM can use all contexts for prediction, it is difficult for the model to rely on it for a long time during training. Because the gradient may disappear or explode during RNN training, the training speed will become slow or the parameter value will be infinite.

$$\begin{cases} r_k = Uv_k + Mh_k \\ \quad h_k = f(r_k) \\ \quad w_k = g(Nh_k) \end{cases} \tag{3}$$

When training recurrent neural networks, there may be problems with gradient explosion or vanishing. Gradient explosion refers to the exponential increase of gradients during backpropagation, resulting in excessive updates of model parameters and instability. Gradient vanishing refers to the exponential decrease in gradient during backpropagation, making the updating of model parameters very slow or even impossible. These problems are particularly serious for recurrent neural networks, as this network structure requires multiple iterative calculations when dealing with long sequences. Gradient explosion can cause abnormally large gradient values, resulting in excessive parameter updates and network divergence. The disappearance of gradients will result in very small gradient values, making it difficult for parameters to be effectively updated, resulting in the network being unable to learn long-distance dependency relationships.

To address these issues, common strategies can be adopted. For gradient explosion, we can use Gradient Clipping technology to limit the maximum range of gradients to prevent parameter updates from being too large. For gradient vanishing, some improved activation functions (such as ReLU, LSTM, etc.) can be used, which can better maintain the flow of gradient information. In addition, more complex recursive neural network structures can be used, such as Long Short Term Memory Networks (LSTM) and Gated Recurrent Units (GRUs), which have better gradient propagation properties and can better handle long sequence dependencies. In summary, gradient explosion and gradient disappearance are common problems when training recurrent neural networks. By adopting gradient pruning, improved activation functions, and more complex network structures, these problems can be effectively alleviated and the model's modeling ability for long-distance dependencies can be improved.

2.2 English Translation Data Set

When we cut the bilingual parallel corpus to obtain bilingual fragments, we hope that the source language end and target language end of the bilingual fragments are semantically consistent as much as possible; In particular, if a segment contains a word at the source language end, we require that the target language end of the segment must contain the corresponding word. The task of determining the correspondence of lexical levels from the bilingual corpus of sentence alignment is called word alignment. Word alignment determines the basic and indivisible correspondence between source language sentences and target language sentences in bilingual data, which is the basis of subsequent processing of machine translation.

Multi-language aims to establish a single model for the translation, as shown in Fig. 2. The neural network model is very successful in bilingual machine translation. The multilingual translation model performs factor calculation when translating into multiple languages, and shares information among similar languages. In terms of language similarity, there are similarities between many languages, such as sharing cognate

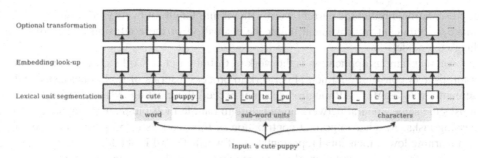

Fig. 2. Multilingual machine translation model

words, similar grammatical structures, and syntactic rules. By utilizing this similarity, we can apply the experience of existing language mining tasks to similar languages, thereby reducing the need for comprehensive mining of each language. This idea of transfer learning can significantly improve efficiency and accuracy. In addition, reverse translation is also an effective technique that can be used to solve the mining problem of zero sample and low resource languages. Reverse translation refers to translating the target language text back into the source language and then comparing it with the original source language. Through this approach, a large amount of existing bilingual data can be utilized to train low resource languages and generate higher quality translation results. By using the reverse translation method, we can utilize existing resource rich languages to generate results as templates, further improving the translation quality of zero sample and low resource languages. This technology can effectively overcome the problem of insufficient resources, enhance the model's ability to mine multiple languages, and reduce dependence on a large amount of manually labeled data. Therefore, which is more than the current bilingual model and has model parallelism. Even it is difficult to track the secondary growth of data caused by the "many to many" setting of parameter expansion. In view of the particularity of the problem, we propose several expansion strategies. In particular, expert hybrid strategy, and uses a new rerouting strategy to train them. The language-specific expert mixing strategy also reduces the need for intensive parameter updates and makes it easier to parallelize in a multi-computer environment [6]. In general, combined with these strategies, we can expand the capacity of the model to 15.4 billion, and still can reasonably.

3   Design of English Translation Model Based on Recurrent Neural Network

Multilayer neural networks were first used to model language models. Bengio et al. proposed a probabilistic language model of multilayer feedforward neural network. Like the traditional n-language model, Begio's model uses a fixed-length history to predict the current word; The difference is that in the neural network language model, words are automatically mapped to the low-dimensional space, and the language is better modeled by exploring the similarity between words. Mikolov et al. further proposed the use of recurrent language. Reproduce the neural network model to build an abstract history representation, predict the current word with infinite length of history information, and make a significant improvement under the evaluation of the confusion degree of the language model.

Another famous application is the work of Collabert et al. Collabert et al. proposed a multi-layer convolutional neural network to process a series of traditional tasks, and semantic role tagging. Although it does not exceed the existing system performance, it uses the same - neural network architecture to handle multiple natural language processing tasks. Another important contribution of this work is to propose a method of fast learning low-dimensional representation of words (Word Embedding), and to learn low-dimensional representation of a large number of words on large-scale text data for the first time. The vocabulary representation learned through neural network contains rich semantic and grammatical information, which is a form of distributed. After that, Huang et al. studied the lexical representation of polysemy; Mikolov et al. proposed a faster training method for vocabulary representation; Dahl et al. proposed a method of learning vocabulary representation with restricted Boltzmann machine.

The language model is the basis of most NLP tasks. For example, in the machine translation (MT) task, the probability of the translation system outputting a specific sequence to improve its fluency in the target language.

Among them, word expression is only a by-product of LM's use to promote other NLP tasks. FFNNLM solves the dimensional disaster by mapping words to low dimensional vectors, and makes FFNN dominate the research of NNLM. Yes, this method still has shortcomings. Before training, the specific size of the context is limited. Words in sequences have temporal characteristics, but FFNNLM cannot be used in modeling. In addition, compared with the nnn meta model, although the fully connected neural network reduces the parameters, there are still a lot of parameters to learn, which is still high cost and low efficiency [7]. The operation model of English vocabulary convolution is shown in Fig. 3 below.

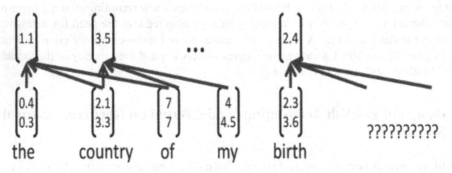

Fig. 3. An operational model of english lexical convolution

This paper introduces how the convolutional neural network is applied in the through an example. In the model as shown in the figure below, first, each word is encoded as a 5-dimensional word vector, and the sentence is represented as a 7 * 5 matrix. Then, three convolution filters (two for each group, i.e., the number of channels out_channels is 2) with the size of 2 * 5, 3 * 5, and 4 * 5 are used for convolution operation. The feature vectors with the size of 6, 4, and 4 are obtained by activating the function [8]. The resulting feature vectors are pooled and combined into each group of feature vectors. Finally, the vector combination obtained by pooling operation is classified as the input of softmax layer.

In the process of training, the setting of parameter configuration depends too much on human experience, and there is neither a recognized standard for reference nor a clear optimal parameter; At present, the neural machine translation system is self-contained and uses end-to-end methods to learn translation knowledge from parallel corpora, which makes it difficult for many external information (such as bilingual dictionaries, part of speech tagging, syntactic analysis, etc.) that are beneficial to translation to be added to the model to improve the translation effect; The differences between different languages have not been fully considered. For example, the differences between Chinese tenses and English tenses should be handled by special components to deal with the adverse effects of such differences between different languages on machine translation [9]. Therefore, although NMT has made great achievements in a short period of time, if the above problems can be solved, further research in all aspects will further improve the quality of translation.

The framework of English machine translation is shown in Fig. 4.

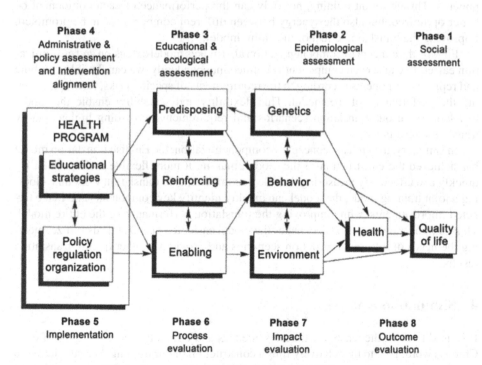

Fig. 4. Framework of English machine translation model

The construction of English translation models usually adopts the concept of componentization, which means that the model can be composed of multiple independent components, each responsible for handling different aspects of translation tasks. This componentized design makes the construction of the model more flexible and scalable, and enables faster evaluation of the role of different components in translation work.

Firstly, by dividing the model into different components, we can clarify the various subtasks in the translation task and design specialized components for each subtask. For example, there can be one component responsible for encoding the grammatical structure of input sentences, and another component responsible for modeling the semantic relationships between sentences. This division enables us to better understand the role and contribution of each component in the model.

Secondly, using componentized model design, we can more quickly measure and evaluate the role of different components in translation work. By enabling and disabling different components on/off, we can evaluate the impact of each component on translation quality individually or in combination. This greatly accelerates the speed of model optimization and the accuracy of effectiveness evaluation, enabling faster identification of key components and targeted improvements.

In addition, the componentized design also promotes joint training of the model, that is, updating multiple components simultaneously during the training process. This training mode reflects the close relationship and interdependence between different components. Through joint training, not only can the performance of each component be better optimized, but also the synergy between different components can be promoted, improving the translation effect of the entire model.

Finally, the concept of componentization also makes model extension and customization easier. Because each component is defined independently, we can flexibly combine and replace components according to the requirements of specific tasks, further improving the performance of the model. This flexibility and scalability enable the model to adapt to various translation scenarios and requirements, providing higher quality translation results.

In summary, through the concept of componentization, the English translation model has achieved the construction of the model, making it more flexible and scalable. By quickly and effectively measuring the role of components in translation work and adopting a joint training mode, the model can quickly identify key components and make targeted improvements, while improving the translation performance of the entire model. This componentized design also makes the model easier to expand and customize, meeting the needs of different translation scenarios and providing higher quality translation results.

4   Simulation Analysis

It is used to mark the tense of Chinese sentences and output the tense category of each Chinese word. Due to the relatively rough construction of our training data set, there is a lot of noise data. We also use the bootstrapping algorithm to strengthen this annotation model, and reduce the impact of noise data by constantly iterating and filtering data, so as to improve the overall effect of the model. After the model has sufficient generalization capability [10]. However, language models are usually trained on different large-scale datasets. Even on the same data set, many preprocessing methods and different training set/verification set segmentation will affect the results of the model. At the same time, the training time is given. The recursive English translation model code is shown in Fig. 5 below.

Algorithm 2: Unsupervised PBSMT

---

1 Learn bilingual dictionary using Conneau et al. (2018);

2 Populate phrase tables using Eq. 3 and learn a language model to build $P_{s \to t}^{(0)}$;

3 Use $P_{s \to t}^{(0)}$ to translate the source monolingual dataset, yielding $\mathcal{D}_t^{(0)}$;

4 **for** i=1 to N **do**

5   Train model $P_{t \to s}^{(i)}$ using $\mathcal{D}_t^{(i-1)}$;

6   Use $P_{t \to s}^{(i)}$ to translate the target monolingual dataset, yielding $\mathcal{D}_s^{(i)}$;

7   Train model $P_{s \to t}^{(i)}$ using $\mathcal{D}_s^{(i)}$;

8   Use $P_{s \to t}^{(i)}$ to translate the source monolingual dataset, yielding $\mathcal{D}_t^{(i)}$;

9 **end**

Fig. 5. Recursive English translation model code

The recursive neural network translation model showed significant improvements in BLEU scores and ALL levels compared to the baseline model in three test sets. This indicates that the model plays a crucial role in aligning information during the modeling process. Especially the influence of bilingual semantic features and sensitive features is more prominent, with semantic features having a more significant impact, while the influence of monolingual semantic features and sensitive features is relatively less significant. Alignment information refers to the correspondence between the source language and the target language, which provides important contextual and reference information for translation models. The recursive neural network translation model can better align the information between the source language and the target language by capturing bilingual semantic and sensitive features, thereby improving translation quality.

Semantic features play an important role in the model because they can capture higher-level semantic information, help the model more accurately understand the meaning of source language sentences, and translate them into corresponding target language sentences. The significant impact of semantic features indicates that the model fully utilizes the semantic relationship between the source and target languages during modeling, improving the accuracy and coherence of translation. The impact of sensitive features in the model is relatively small, which may mean that the model does not have a significant advantage in processing sensitive features, or the impact of sensitive features in the sample is relatively weak. This may also require further research and exploration.

In summary, the recurrent neural network translation model achieved significant improvements in three test sets compared to the baseline model. It fully utilizes the information of bilingual semantic features and sensitive features, especially the more significant impact of semantic features, thereby improving translation quality and alignment process. However, the impact of monolingual semantic features and sensitivity features is relatively small, and further research and optimization may be needed.

5   Conclusion

The design of an English translation model based on recurrent neural networks utilizes recursive structures to handle long-distance dependencies in sentences. The model mainly includes two parts: encoder and decoder. The encoder encodes the source language sentence input word by word into a word vector sequence and learns context representation through recursive units such as LSTM. The decoder generates words for the target language at each time step based on the output of the encoder and the generated part of the target language. In this method, the target sentence is used to manually annotate the initial corpus and a supervised learning algorithm is used to generate its translation. In addition, the model can be improved through attention mechanisms to dynamically focus on the parts of the source language sentence that are most relevant to the current generation position. The recursive neural network translation model performs well in handling long-distance dependencies and alignment issues, providing better translation quality and fluency.

Acknowledgements. Yantai Vocational College Horizontal Project "Community English Education Service Experience Design for the Elderly" (NO:HX202218).

References

1. Shan, Q.: Intelligent learning algorithm for English flipped classroom based on recurrent neural network. Wirel. Commun. Mob. Comput. **2021**(1), 8020461 (2021)
2. Zhou, J., Cao, Y., Wang, X., Li, P., Xu, W.: Deep recurrent models with fast-forward connections for neural machine translation. Trans. Assoc. Comput. Linguist. **4**, 371–383 (2016)
3. Wunier, S., Liu, W.: Mongolian-Chinese machine translation based on CNN etyma morphological selection model. J. Chin. Inf. Process. **32**(05), 42–48 (2018)

4. Devlin, J.: Sharp models on dull hardware: fast and accurate neural machine translation decoding on the CPU (2017). arXiv preprint arXiv:1705.01991

5. Su, J., Tan, Z., Xiong, D., Ji, R., Shi, X., Liu, Y.: Lattice-based recurrent neural network encoders for neural machine translation. In: Proceedings of the AAAI Conference on Artificial Intelligence, vol. 31, no. 1 (2017)

6. Liu, Y.P., Ma, C., Zhang, Y.N.: Hierarchical machine translation model based on deep recursive neural network. Chin. J. Comput. **40**(4), 861–871 (2017)

7. Choshen, L., Abend, O.: Automatically extracting challenge sets for non local phenomena in neural machine translation (2019). arXiv preprint arXiv:1909.06814

8. Tan, Z., Su, J., Wang, B., Chen, Y., Shi, X.: Lattice-to-sequence attentional neural machine translation models. Neurocomputing **284**, 138–147 (2018)

9. Mezzoudj, F., Benyettou, A.: An empirical study of statistical language models: n-gram language models vs. neural network language models. Int. J. Innov. Comput. Appl. **9**(4), 189–202 (2018)

10. Kudinov, M.S., Romanenko, A.A.: A hybrid language model based on a recurrent neural network and probabilistic topic modeling. Pattern Recognit Image Anal. **26**, 587–592 (2016)

Research on the Application of Computer Aided Translation in EST

Jing Li[1,2(✉)] and Lu Jia[1,2]

[1] College of Humanities and Social Sciences, Heilongjiang Bayi Agricultural University,
Daqing 163319, Heilongjiang, China
byndlijing@163.com
[2] Wuhan University of Engineering Science, Wuhan 430060, China

Abstract. This paper aims to introduce the application of computer-aided translation software in EST translation. At present, most scientific and technological academic works, papers and materials are written in English. To master these knowledge, translation is required. At the number of these documents, people put forward higher requirements for scientific and Technological English translation, which requires both accuracy and timeliness of translation. In this case, the can no longer meet people's growing demand for translation. 50. A. kondrakov á et al. (2004) published the first study translation in EST, which is part of the project "computer-aided translation of European legal texts". The purpose of the project is to develop a tool for computer-aided translation of legal texts as an alternative to the traditional Czech translation method. This tool will help translators translate their works more efficiently and accurately, especially when they do not have enough time or foreign language knowledge.

Keywords: computer · English for science and technology · Assisted translation

1 Introduction

Due to the application of new technology and the global flow of capital, the integration of the world has become the general trend. With the deepening of global, exchanges and regions have. After entering the 21st century, China's proportion, and are also receiving [1]. As "science and technology are the primary productive forces". In order to further enhance, mastering core technologies is the key. In order to master core technologies, it is indispensable to vigorously introduce, introduce and learn advanced technologies from abroad. At present, most scientific and technological academic works, papers and materials are written in English. To master these knowledge, translation is required. At the Technology (EST), which requires both accuracy and timeliness of translation. In this case, the can no longer meet people's growing demand for translation [2]. As human beings enter the computer age, using computers to translate a hot research topic. With the research results artificial intelligence technology, as well as the contributions, other disciplines, computers have been widely used in translation. Translators commonly use, computer-aided translation software and so on [3]. The has greatly reduced the workload

Y. Zhang and N. Shah (Eds.): BigIoT-EDU 2023, LNICST 582, pp. 112–122, 2024.
https://doi.org/10.1007/978-3-031-63136-8_12

of translators, improved and quality of translation, and at the same time, the research on them has strong practical significance.

Although there are a large number of translators engaged in EST translation in China, pen and paper have become, and most of the dictionaries have become "what you see is what you get" electronic dictionaries, the degree of computer participation in translation is still insufficient. Translators may have a distrust of computer participation in translation and believe that the read suddenly and cannot be used; Or have computers and hope that they. These misunderstandings stem from the lack of understanding of computer translation/assisted translation technology.

As the author knows, the number of people engaged in EST translation in China has exceeded 1 million (Wang Yanjun, 2000:44). However, the translation efficiency in most manual operations or small work management is very low, because their work will not be repeated in advanced, and can only rely on traditional tools, such as dictionaries, manuscripts, etc. This traditional translation method can not meet the needs of the rapid spread of science and technology, and it is not very helpful for scientific exchanges between China and other countries. To solve this problem, translators, especially those who are committed to scientific translation. We should fundamentally change working translation and make full use of advanced technologies in our work, such as TRADOS, to adapt to and keep up with the pace of the modern world.

Trados. As the leader of similar software in CAT software, it has created the concept and establishment of TM, the core technology in CAT software, and is a prominent breakthrough in the of translation. As the leader of global information management, TRADOS, with its excellent ability and excellent service, undertakes the mission of transmitting the information of companies around the world to different language markets, and promotes the consistency of the company's brand and market (http://baikeb aidu.com/view/650311.htm) It is applied to scientific English translation to speed up translation. However, the output quality of TRADOS has not been evaluated. Therefore, it is necessary to evaluate the output of TRADOS to scientific and technological translation. This is also the reason why the author chose this topic as his postgraduate thesis.

This article aims to introduce the use of computer-aided translation software and, based on the author's experience in using Trados, introduce its advantages and disadvantages. To avoid turning the article into an "operation manual", this article does not provide a detailed description of each step of Trados, as these operations can be easily obtained from the internet or help files provided by Trados. Next, the author will focus on introducing Trados as a well-known computer-aided translation software and sharing their experience using Trados. In this section, the author will explore the advantages of Trados, such as providing a series of functions and tools that facilitate translators to process a large number of translation memory and terminology libraries, thereby improving translation consistency and efficiency. At the same time, the author will also mention some drawbacks of Trados, such as the steep learning curve of the software, which requires some time to familiarize and master, and some operation steps are relatively cumbersome. This information is very valuable for potential users and can help them better evaluate whether to choose Trados as their computer-aided translation tool. In summary, the goal of this article is to provide an overview of computer-aided translation software, introduce the advantages and disadvantages of Trados, and provide readers with useful information to understand and evaluate whether to choose to use Trados as their translation tool.

2   Related Work

2.1   Research Status

The research on sci-tech translation can be said to be very active, but the current research rarely involves computer-aided translation. For example, most of the current researchers start with translation theory; The stylistic features of EST are also discussed from the perspective of linguistics. These studies are beneficial to master the EST and know the translation time of EST [4]. However, it seems that the research on the application of Trados and other software in EST translation is not prosperous, although it is an auxiliary translation software with the highest market share. Through CNKI to search the literature, we can get some short articles that introduce the advantages the software. Among them, the more important is Guo Chuanhui, a postgraduate student, whose master's thesis "Trados translation of English for science and technology translation quality evaluation". In this paper, 822 sentences in 13 different fields of science and technology were translated, and the was counted. It was found that when the matching degree was greater than 59%, the qualified translation based on the content memorized by Trados was 88% of the summary, so the quality of the translation can be guaranteed, This proves that the quality of Trados translation can be guaranteed. However, this paper does not discuss the Trados in EST translation, but only proves the above conclusion [5]. Therefore, this on discussing the Trados in EST translation by integrating its own practice.

2.2   Computer Aided Translation

The idea of computer-aided translation can be traced back to the 1970s. At that time, people proposed the concept of "translation memory", which stores previous translation results in a computer for future repeated use of the same or similar text for translation. Broadly speaking, computer-aided translation still belongs to the category of machine translation, as it utilizes the powerful storage and fast retrieval capabilities of computers, but computers themselves do not actually translate any text.

Computer assisted translation software (such as Trados), as an auxiliary tool, reduces the workload of translators, eliminates unnecessary duplicate translations, and provides efficient translation management functions. It uses a translation memory system as the core technology to achieve the following basic principle: when the software obtains the text that needs to be translated, it first compares it with the content stored in the database. If no matching text is found, the system will take no action and record the input of the translator. If text that reaches the matching threshold is retrieved from the database, the system will provide corresponding prompts. Translators can choose to fully accept the prompt translation, modify the prompt translation, or abandon the prompt translation and re translate according to the actual situation.

The application of translation memory systems makes translation work more efficient and consistent. It provides a reliable basic translation resource library that can quickly retrieve and utilize previously translated text fragments. This not only reduces the burden on translators, but also improves the consistency and efficiency of translation.

In short, computer-aided translation software, as an auxiliary tool, is widely popular among professional translators. It utilizes a translation memory system as the core technology to help translators improve translation efficiency and quality, reducing repetitive labor, or discard the prompt translation and retranslate it, as shown in Fig. 1.

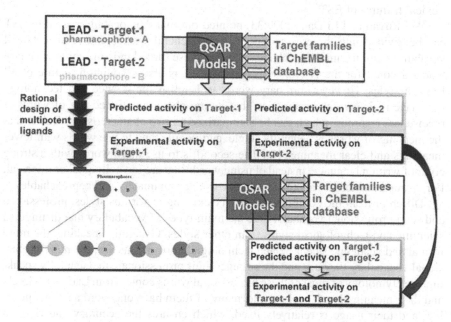

Fig. 1. Structure of computer aided translation system

The terminology database, is. The term base commonly used in translation is generally a bilingual vocabulary. Some term bases can also add subject, industry, part of speech and other labels to the terms the choice of translators. As mentioned earlier, the term base is very important for the translation of EST, because the terms directly affect the quality of the translation. The most important feature of the term library in the computer-aided translation software is that it can be quickly queried and updated in a timely manner. Because of the convenience and rapidity of the query, new words and terms can be added in a timely manner, which can improve the quality of the translation.

The alignment tool module in the computer-aided software. This tool allows translators to align existing translated documents. This kind of processing generally needs to be done manually, which is relatively cumbersome. However, the quality of the aligned corpus is higher, which can better serve the translation practice.

The trend of global integration has for translation work. In high-speed translation, we need not rely on the participation of computer-aided translation technology and software. According to an online survey conducted by Hou Xiaochen and Yan Yuzuo (2008), about 66% of translators use computer-aided translation tools in translation. Obviously, Trados is the most at present. This article also takes Trados 2007 as an example to introduce the in translation practice.

3 Computer-Assisted Translation of Scientific English

3.1 Language Features of EST

(1) Lexical features of EST

Wei Ruyao and Li Dan (2009:33) pointed out that the vocabulary used in EST can be divided into three categories, namely, general vocabulary, semi technical vocabulary and technical vocabulary Among these three kinds of words, ordinary words account for the largest proportion, which is also a common feature of all English styles. However, ordinary words in English for science and technology also have their own characteristics, that is, the above-mentioned use of words is precise and rigorous, which can be summarized as two characteristics. One is that the meaning of words is generally single, and people tend to use words with fewer meanings and clear meanings [8]; The second is to use more words with a strong color of written language, instead of using words that are too colloquial or informal. For example, instead of about, a lot of, we use approximately and approachable.

Different from the common vocabulary existing in various styles, professional and semi professional vocabulary are the main types of vocabulary that distinguish scientific and technological styles from other styles. Generally speaking, the more formal and academic scientific and technological documents are, the more professional vocabulary they use and the stronger their professionalism. Generally speaking, the etymology of most of these professional words comes from Latin and Greek, and their meaning is relatively single, many of them have one word and one meaning, and their usage is relatively fixed, which ensures the accuracy and rigor of the expression of scientific and technological styles. At the same time, because of the relatively fixed meaning of professional words, it is feasible for us to use computer-aided translation (CAT) software to make a glossary.

(2) Syntactic features of EST

English for science and technology is a relatively formal non literary written style, so most of the sentences it uses are relatively complete, and the changes in sentence patterns are not rich. Unlike literary styles, exclamation sentences, antonym questions and other lyrical and pornographic sentence patterns are rarely used in science and technology issues, and rhetoric devices such as euphemism, exaggeration, personification and rhyme are rarely used. Generally speaking, the scientific and technological style has several characteristics at the syntactic level.

First of all, more declarative sentences and imperative sentences are used, more declarative sentences are used in academic papers, monographs and textbooks to strengthen objectivity, and more imperative sentences are used in technical manuals and other documents; Secondly, long sentences are used more often [9]. In order to accurately express objective phenomena, long sentences are often used in scientific and technological literary styles; Third, the tense of scientific and technological style is often used in the general present tense, and the passive voice is often used in the voice.

Because the sentence patterns of scientific and technological problems are not rich, repetitive parts often appear, which is more prominent in documents such as interpreters' manuals and booklets. This feature translation Because CAT software has a translation memory, it can record the sentences that have been translated. When it encounters the same or similar sentences next time, it can prompt the translator to make a choice, which greatly reduces the pain of repetitive work.

3.2 Computer-Aided Translation Process

According to the directly translate Microsoft Word files in a few steps. After the Trados software is installed, the Trados auxiliary translation toolbar will automatically appear in Word. The translator can operate Trados directly. The specific process of using Trados for translation is as follows:

Analyze: This is the pre-processing stage before translation, which can be realized by using. Trados will first use o read the text to be translated into blocks when analyzing, and then compare the translation memory to calculate the number of chunks that are the same or similar to the existing translation, so that translators can intuitively understand the number of chunks that need to be translated in the current text to be translated, so as to know the translation project well, and reasonably arrange the progress. In addition, can also count the chunk repetition rate of the text to be translated. When analyzing the text, the chunks without matching translation are recorded as by Trados; Multiple the same chunk are recorded. During translation, repeated matching only needs to be translated once. When the same text is encountered next time, Translator's will treat the chunk as 100% matching, so as to directly. Generally speaking, the chunk repetition rate is in direct proportion to the improvement rate of Trados for translation efficiency, that is, the higher the text repetition rate, the greater the role of Trados in reducing the repetitive work of translators.

Translate: For the text to be translated with high repetition rate. Pre-translation means that Trados uses the translation stored in the current translation memory and terminology library to automatically replace the perfectly matched chunks in the text to be translated. For the incompletely matched chunks, Trados will save the most similar chunk translation into the text to be translated in the form of annotation. During translation. During translation, the Translator's Workbench will directly give the translation for the completely matched chunks. For the chunks that are different but the matching degree reaches the threshold set by the user in advance, the Translator's Workbench will perform fuzzy matching, and highlight the mismatched parts to remind the translator of the attention. Give the results translation for unmatched chunks to help translators translate to the greatest extent.

Clean up: After to assist translation, the original document is still bilingual. Although the original document is hidden and invisible by default. Therefore, the document needs to be cleaned up after the translation is completed. The purpose of the cleanup chunk marks. Not only that, the cleanup operation actually changes. If the document is completely translated, Translator's Workbench will store the latest the translation memory while cleaning.

The computer-aided translation in Fig. 2.

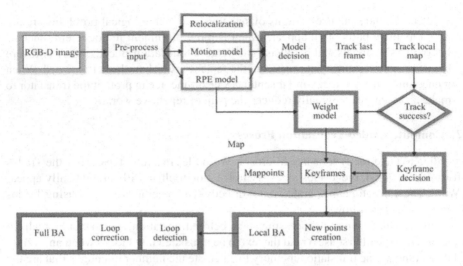

Fig. 2. Computer-aided translation process

4   Application of Computer-Aided Translation in EST

4.1   Preparation Before Translation

Those engaged in translation work first need to read the original text thoroughly and have a correct understanding of the content expressed in the original text. On this basis, they should use another language to accurately and emotionally express the content of the original text. However, sci-tech translation is relatively special and generally highly professional. Many professional terms and some interpretation principles are usually used in the original text, which greatly increases the difficulty of translators' understanding of the original content and requires translators to have more professional knowledge. However, the scope of science and technology is too wide, and the energy and ability of translation staff are limited. It is obviously unrealistic to want to know every discipline. However, before the formal translation, you must also read the literature related to the original text and have a general understanding of the relevant fields [10]. And prepare necessary translation tools. Under the condition that traditional translation tools are increasingly unable to meet the current translation needs, translators need to learn to use modern translation tools to translate scientific and Technological English articles. Trados software is one of the mainstream translation tools at present.

Trados' advantages in processing words are in the processing of terms. Term processing includes term extraction, term import, term prompt and import during translation. As shown in Fig. 3.

Taking the object as an example, technology standard, it involves of electronic industry terminology. If there is no auxiliary translation software, the translator will stop to query the terms from time to time during translation. This will reduce the translation speed on the other hand, it will probably lead to inconsistent terms and reduce the robustness of the translation.

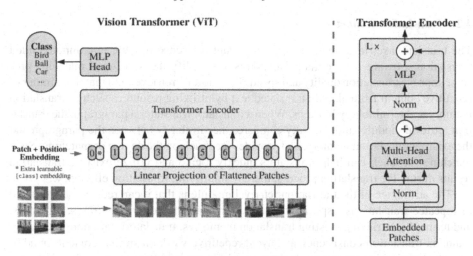

Fig. 3. Trados is processing words

There are two basic methods to use Trados to process terms. One is to import certain industry terms in batches. The effort, because industry terms can be easily downloaded on the network, and once and for all after import; Another method is to use the term extraction component MultiTerm Extract in Trados to extract terms from the documents to be translated before translation, and then import them into the term library after manual recognition and translation. This takes more time than the first method, but is more targeted. The author used MultiTerm Extract to extract the electronic technical documents to be translated, and a total of 1472 suspected terms were extracted. Because Trados extracted the terms according to the frequency of occurrence, so the extracted "terms" are not all technical terms, which need to be checked manually. After checking, 821 terms were obtained, with the extraction efficiency of 55.8%, which is basically acceptable.

Although the batch import, extraction and troubleshooting of terms will take some time, "sharpening the knife will not delay the woodcutter". In the actual translation process, these terms are of great benefit to the translators from the pain of frequent word search and maintain the consistency of terms. Therefore, Trados has obvious advantages in dealing with words.

4.2 Translation Export

The translation retrieval module is an important reference module in computer-aided translation software, whose main function is to simplify the translation matching process, improve translation quality and speed. This module retrieves and matches similar or repetitive content from already translated text by utilizing resources such as translation memory and terminology libraries. When a translator translates a paragraph, the translation retrieval module automatically compares the similarity between the paragraph and the existing translation memory, and provides feedback on the degree of matching. Such matching feedback can help translators quickly locate and utilize existing translation results during the translation process, thereby improving translation efficiency.

The advantage of the translation retrieval module is that it can reduce the workload of repeated translations, especially suitable for handling common phrases, sentences, and terms. By retrieving existing translation memories, translators can more accurately maintain translation consistency and avoid repetitive work on similar content. In addition, the translation retrieval module can also improve translation quality. It reduces the possibility of human errors and omissions, as translators can refer to previously verified translations. Meanwhile, by searching the terminology library stored in the system, translators can more easily maintain the accurate use of professional vocabulary.

Overall, the translation retrieval module plays a crucial role in computer-aided translation. It greatly simplifies the translation matching process, improves translation quality and speed. By utilizing previous translation memories and terminology libraries, translators can more efficiently complete translation tasks and ensure consistency and accuracy in translation. For example, the formula for calculating the similarity between sentences A and B is:

$$\text{Sim}(A, B) = \frac{\text{Max}\big(A_{laugh}, B_{laugh}\big) - d[n, m]}{\text{Max}\big(A_{length}, B_{length}\big)} \times 100\% \tag{1}$$

It can also be called system precompilation or preprocessing module. Its function is to provide preliminary preparation and simplify the process of manual verification. In addition, in the system editing environment, fuzzy matching filtering can be achieved with one click. Find existing words through dichotomy, automatically match similar sentences or phrases, and insert translations for translators. After manual correction, it can be exported as a source document format translation, as shown in Fig. 4.

In actual translation, the ultimate purpose of using Trados tools for translation is to obtain the translation. However, it is impossible to obtain the final translation simply by saving the term base and memory base. In the daily translation process, the translation can not be exported normally, which not only increases the workload of translators, but also brings unnecessary losses to translators.

The fundamental solution to this problem lies in prevention. In the process of using Trados for translation, translators will form some temporary files in the hard disk of the computer, which are the main support for Trados software for translation. Therefore, before using the software for translation, translators must not clean the computer hard disk, and it is better to close the hard disk cleaning program in the antivirus software to ensure that Trados software can export the translation normally.

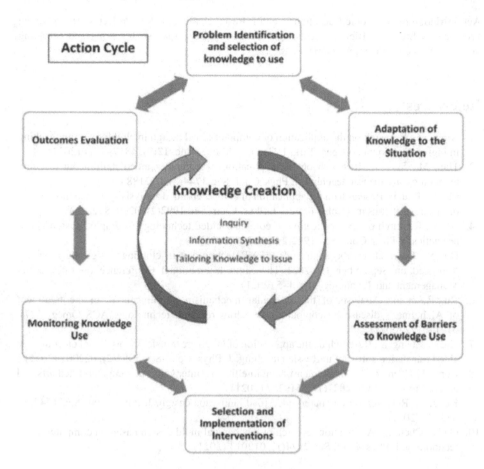

Fig. 4. Export of English translation

5   Conclusion

Computer aided translation technology needs a huge memory bank using "cloud storage technology". This memory bank should be open and shared. People all over the world can freely access and upload their translation memories. Only in this way can it capacity of computer-aided translation technology. Only when human beings understand the nature of language can machine translation technology output a fully satisfactory translation. However, in the foreseeable future, this bottleneck is unlikely to be broken. During this period, computer-aided software is still the mainstream, but to what extent it can play a role depends on the development of Internet storage technology. In the foreseeable future, we are unlikely to break through this bottleneck. At this stage, computer-aided software will still be mainstream, but the extent to which it can play a role will depend on the level of development of internet storage technology.

Acknowledgements. Topic:Education Scientific Research Planning Key Projects of Heilongjiang Province: A Study on Blended Teaching Model in College English Listening and Speaking Teaching Based on Ucampus (GJB1422188).

References

1. Ninga, Z.: Research on the application of computer aided design in clothing design teaching in higher vocational colleges. Turk. J. Comput. Math. Educ. **12**(3), 4817–4821 (2021)
2. Tian, M., Sun, Y.: Research on the application of computer aided multimedia teaching technology in Japanese teaching. J. Phys. Conf. Ser. **1744**(3), 032188 (2021)
3. Ma, Q., Lyu, P.: Research on the application of computer-aided analysis system in the concept of visual aesthetics in graphic design. J. Phys. Conf. Ser. **1992**(2), 022018 (2021)
4. Jia, Y.: Research on the application of computer aided technology in graphic design visual aesthetics. J. Phys. Conf. Ser. **1992**(2), 022096 (2021)
5. Hu, N.: Research on the application of VR technology in clothing design teaching. In: Retracted on September 15, 2021 The Sixth International Conference on Information Management and Technology, pp. 1–5 (2021)
6. Xu, P., et al.: Analysis of the molecular mechanism of punicalagin in the treatment of Alzheimer's disease by computer-aided drug research technology. ACS Omega **7**(7), 6121–6132 (2022)
7. Xu, Y., Zhang, S.: Research on the application of language transfer theory based on computer aided translation software in Russian teaching. J. Phys. Conf. Ser. **1992**(2), 022001 (2021)
8. Deng, J., Chen, X.: Research on artificial intelligence interaction in computer-aided arts and crafts. Mob. Inf. Syst. **2021**(1), 5519257 (2021)
9. Kang, Y.: Research on computer-aided road landscape design. J. Phys. Conf. Ser. **1744**(4), 042071 (2021)
10. Gu, J., Chen, L.: Application research of mechanical mold design based on computer aided technology. J. Phys. Conf. Ser. **2074**(1), 012013 (2021)

Research on the Construction of Computer Technology in English Translation Simulation Training Class

Jia Lu[1,2](✉) and Li Jing[1,2]

[1] Wuhan University of Engineering Science, Wuhan 430060, China
LuJia@wues.edu.com
[2] College of Humanities and Social Science, Heilongjiang Bayi Agricultural University,
Daqing 163319, Heilongjiang, China

Abstract. Translation is generally regarded as a compulsory course for English majors, but it is hardly considered in the process of English teaching in senior high schools. The current national high school English curriculum standards have clear requirements for high school students' translation ability. Through years of English teaching in senior high schools, the author has realized that it is necessary to introduce translation teaching into senior high school English classes, which will help improve English teaching effect and lay a good foundation for students' future development. The use of computers in the 21st century has become a necessity for everyone. Computers have changed our lives in many ways. They are not only limited to the field of work, but also to personal life. In this era, from shopping to paying bills, from writing articles to watching movies, even playing games, almost everything uses computers. It has become a part of our daily life. We can't imagine life without them. However, it is not always easy for non-technical personnel to understand computers, especially when they need to translate into another language. With the continuous application of computer technology in college education, great reforms and changes have taken place in college education. This also better improves the quality of teaching. This article analyzes the current situation of English translation teaching and the application of computer multimedia in English translation teaching. It also explains the application of computer online translation platform in English translation training platform. It mainly studies the design of computer translation platform.

Keywords: Computer technology · English translation · Computer translation platform

1 Introduction

Nowadays, English is one of the languages of international communication, so universities must continue to strengthen the reform of college English teaching. English is a language, so college teachers should increase English training classrooms. They

Y. Zhang and N. Shah (Eds.): BigIoT-EDU 2023, LNICST 582, pp. 123–133, 2024.
https://doi.org/10.1007/978-3-031-63136-8_13

should continuously exercise students' oral English and English communication skills through training classrooms, so that students can learn in an English atmosphere to effectively improve students' learning effects. In addition to strengthening students' oral skills, English teaching also needs to strengthen students' translation skills, which can effectively improve students' English proficiency [1].

Translation courses have been gradually offered for English majors and non-English majors in China's universities, especially since the establishment of translation majors in 2006, and since the establishment of MTI (Master of Translation) in 2007, the research of translation teaching has gradually attracted the attention of scholars. However, the research of domestic scholars in this field focuses on such topics as translation teaching methodology, translation curriculum, translation teaching and translation textbooks. There are still a few scholars who pay attention to the study of translation teachers, and the study of teacher talk in translation classroom is even less.

Compared with other subject classes, English classes have special characteristics in teacher talk. It is because in the classroom, the discourse output by English teachers is not only the main medium for teachers to transmit information, but also an important source of students' second language input. Therefore, teacher talk in English classroom has a profound impact on students' second language acquisition. Domestic scholars have conducted research on the topic of "English teacher talk", but the selected research class types are mainly concentrated in reading, speaking and listening classes, and the research on teacher talk in translation class is few.

Based on the dialogue theory, adaptation theory and relevant research documents, the classroom videos of the nine English teachers who won the prize in the translation course of the translation professional group of the Ninth "Foreign Teacher Service Cup" National College Foreign Language Teaching Contest were transcribed into text materials, and the teacher discourse was classified and frequency analysis was carried out, from teacher code switching, teacher questioning, teacher feedback The main forms and functions of teacher talk in translation classroom are studied from four aspects of teacher talk, with a view to providing reference and inspiration for teacher talk in translation classroom, so as to improve teaching quality and cultivate high-quality translation talents.

In today's era, computer is an indispensable tool in people's life. The continuous development of computer-aided translation technology is an impact on the traditional manual translation method. This is an inevitable choice in the information age, and it will also bring great convenience to people's production and life. With the help of computers, English translation can improve efficiency and save manpower, shorten the project cycle to a certain extent, and its related products will also facilitate people's life and production.

With the continuous development of computer and network technology in recent years, its influence has penetrated into all aspects of people's life. Computer aided translation (CAT) is similar to CAD (Computer Aided Design), which can help translators complete translation work with high quality, efficiency and ease. Unlike previous machine translation software, it does not rely on automatic translation of computers, but completes the whole translation process with the participation of people. Compared with manual translation, the quality is the same or better, and the translation efficiency can be more than doubled. CAT automates the heavy manual translation process and greatly improves the translation efficiency and quality. Computer-assisted translation is a broad and imprecise term, covering a range of tools, from very simple to more complex. In the process of translation, we now know that translation means include two ways: broad sense and narrow sense. Narrow translation is to match the required words through translation memory, and record some words in the translation process, so that translators can carry out computer-assisted work through computers. In a broad sense, translation has completely changed every working link in the translation process, making it basically achieve a fully automated translation level for word count statistics, resource retrieval, terminology identification, format conversion, and fuzzy matching. This paper makes a detailed analysis of the main techniques in computer-aided translation.

2 Related Work

2.1 The Goal of Translation Teaching and the Cultivation of Translation Ability

The core tasks of translation teaching (including translation practice teaching and translation theory teaching) can be summarized as follows: to cultivate students' translation ability and strengthen students' understanding of translation, which is also the basic goal of translation quality education (Liu Miqing, 2003).

The so-called cultivation of translation ability, referring to the discussion of Gagne (1970) on students' "acquisition quality", includes the following five aspects:

First, language analysis and application ability. The object of translation is language, and the purpose of translation is the corresponding transformation of interlingual meaning in line with the expected purpose and communication task, which requires the translator to put all his efforts into language analysis, including semantic (meaning and intention) analysis, grammatical structure analysis and text analysis; Based on the analysis of structure and composition, we can correctly grasp the content and form of language, and can control it freely. It can be said that all plans, measures, curriculum settings, teaching links and process arrangements of translation teaching should aim at cultivating translation ability, and should first cultivate language analysis and manipulation ability.

Second, cultural discrimination and performance ability. Language and culture are closely linked, and semantic analysis cannot be separated from cultural reference. In many cases, word meaning discrimination involves cultural interpretation, which has gone beyond the scope of simple semantic discrimination. Cultural reference has become the fundamental basis for determining semantics. Moreover, the cultural color of language covers words, phrases, sentences and texts, and even includes pronunciation, writing, style, style and other aspects. All this depends on the translator's ability to discriminate.

Third, aesthetic judgment and performance ability. Aesthetic judgment is accompanied by linguistic and cultural analysis. In fact, the aesthetic judgment in translation is not limited to literary and artistic styles. Any style (including official documents, scientific and technological articles, etc.) has a consideration of whether the words and sentences are appropriate and effective, which is aesthetic judgment. Advanced aesthetic tasks (including image, artistic conception and style control) are more complex and need to be systematically cultivated. The ability of aesthetic judgment originates from aesthetic experience and is by no means born famous. The key is to cultivate it.

Fourth, two-way transformation and expression ability. The two-way language expression ability belongs to the high-level language conversion activity. "Two-way" refers to both from language A (source language) to language B (target language) and from language B (source language) to language A (target language). It is not easy to achieve "two-way" in translation, so two-way expression ability is an important indicator of translation ability.

Fifth, logical analysis and correction ability. The logic of thinking is manifested in the scientific nature of concepts, judgments and reasoning (including clarity, orderliness and consistency), which is very important for translation. Sometimes, there is no mistake in grasping the meaning of words and sentences. The problem lies in logic, which makes the whole translation fall short.

2.2 The Current Situation of English Translation Teaching

At present, there is a huge demand for English translators in the market, so colleges and universities should regard English translation as an important content in English teaching. Only by strengthening students' English translation ability can they effectively strengthen their English communication skills. In the process of training English translators, there are still some problems.

(1) Focus on exam-oriented education. The purpose of teaching in the traditional college education model is to comprehensively strengthen students' test scores in various subjects. Therefore, students' study energy tends to be more inclined to the recitation of words, sentences, and articles. They despise the understanding of the cultural connotation of English. This causes students to apply the meaning of words too much in the translation process, and students cannot get closer to the original content without flexible translation [2].

(2) Students lack cross-cultural awareness in English translation teaching. In traditional language teaching, college teachers pay more attention to students' understanding and recitation of theoretical knowledge such as words, sentences, and articles. Therefore, teachers do not explain much about English culture and practical usage of English translation in English classrooms. This makes students unable to understand the background of English culture, as well as a deeper understanding of the characteristics of the English language. Students cannot effectively improve their English level. Under the traditional teaching model, students blindly follow the teacher's education, and the English classroom atmosphere is relatively dull and lacking vitality. Teachers rarely set up corresponding situations, which affects students' interest in learning, and further affects the teaching effect and quality of college English translation teaching [3].

(3) There is not enough application of various new technologies in English teaching. With the advent of the information age, various emerging technologies are constantly being produced and updated, and the development of these technologies has brought a huge impact on all walks of life.Especially for the education industry, the introduction of many computer technology, artificial intelligence technology and multimedia technology have effectively improved the teaching level of colleges and universities. Among them, artificial intelligence technology makes the education system more intelligent, and

multimedia technology makes the teaching classroom more intelligent. It is rich, vivid, and polymorphic, and it effectively enhances students' interest in classroom learning, thereby strengthening students' active learning [4]. However, at present, many college teachers do not pay attention to the application of these technologies, or some teachers are not proficient in the use of these technologies, which makes the English translation teaching lack of vividness and vividness, this greatly affects the quality of English translation teaching.

"Teaching methods", "teaching models", "translation teaching models" and "translation courses" constitute the key words of this topic. First of all, the focus of translation teaching research is the study of "teaching mode" and "teaching method". Based on different teaching theories, scholars have put forward different reform schemes of teaching models and methods. For example, Ye Miao pointed out that the traditional translation teaching method can no longer effectively improve students' translation ability, while the student-centered interactive translation teaching model always has teacher-student interaction, student-student interaction, intra-group interaction and inter-group interaction, which is conducive to improving this situation. In addition, the research of interactive translation teaching mode based on the online "translation review mode", WeChat and QQ network platform has been warmly discussed by scholars, as shown in Fig. 1. Other scholars have also studied translation teaching models from different perspectives. For example, Tan Yesheng proposed a domain-dependent cognitive translation teaching model from the perspective of cognitive psychology and cognitive translatology, and took the teaching experiment design of translation major in an application-oriented undergraduate college as an example to explain in detail the strategies and methods of implementing the domain-dependent cognitive translation teaching model.

Secondly, the relationship between curriculum and translation is also a hot topic in translation teaching research. Some scholars have expressed their views from different angles, and have made in-depth research on the concept and theoretical system of translation courses. For example, Wen Jun first put forward the "problem" of the issue of "translation curriculum research" and advocated the view of "big curriculum theory". On this basis, he thinks about how to improve translation teaching from the perspective of translation curriculum, and puts forward the research framework of translation curriculum. In addition, scholars have also explored such issues as translation curriculum design, translation curriculum design, and translation curriculum group system.

3   The Role of Computer Multimedia Technology in English Translation Classroom Teaching

The content of the new curriculum reform requires college teachers to change the traditional teaching concept, teaching method, teaching content and teaching mode. The use of computer technology combined with new teaching models can effectively improve students' learning interest and learning enthusiasm. In English translation teaching, teachers should do a good job of classroom teaching design in advance. They should fully understand the development characteristics of modern society and the characteristics of contemporary students. Teachers can add some interesting classroom teaching

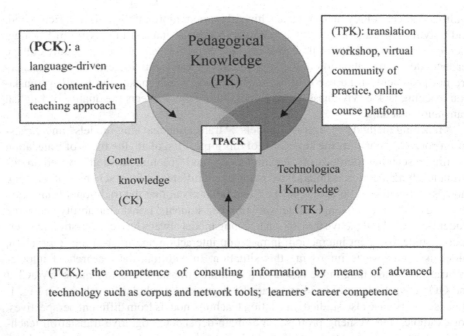

(PCK): a language-driven and content-driven teaching approach

Pedagogical Knowledge (PK)

(TPK): translation workshop, virtual community of practice, online course platform

TPACK

Content knowledge (CK)

Technologica l Knowledge (TK)

(TCK): the competence of consulting information by means of advanced technology such as corpus and network tools; learners' career competence

Fig. 1. Interactive translation teaching mode

situations based on these. This can promote students to actively participate in class-room learning, thereby strengthening students' understanding and application of vari-ous English translation skills. Specifically, the role of multimedia technology in English translation teaching is mainly reflected in the following aspects [5].

3.1   Use Multimedia Equipment to Strengthen Classroom Situational Teaching

Students' English translation ability needs to be improved through strong practical train-ing. In order to strengthen students' understanding of English articles in the translation process, college teachers can use computer multimedia equipment to increase the con-textual teaching methods in the classroom. Teachers can use multimedia equipment to make various abstract knowledge more intuitive through video, classroom games, etc. And contextualized teaching can effectively enhance students' understanding and mem-ory of various knowledge. In the process of English translation teaching, teachers should strengthen students' learning of English translation skills, and use various examples to enable students to master the application of English translation skills more proficiently, thereby strengthening students' English translation ability. In order to create a situation, many teachers use multimedia technology to show some English translation skills in concise electronic courseware. With the help of English videos, students can experience English culture and realize situational teaching [6].

3.2 Make the Content of the Teaching Materials More Vivid

Traditional English translation classroom teaching is mainly done by the teacher in the form of blackboard and chalk based on the teaching materials. In this kind of classroom, teachers can only show the teaching content to students through words and teacher explanations, which makes the teaching classroom too boring, rigid and limited. And students' learning resources are limited to course materials and teacher explanations, which is not conducive to the cultivation of contemporary students. The introduction of multimedia teaching makes the English translation classroom more vivid. Teachers can teach through PPT courseware, online translation-related learning videos, learning audio, and animation effects. This not only enriches students' learning resources, but also makes the entire teaching process simple, easy to understand, and entertaining [7]. Students learn in the process of entertaining and practice the concept of entertaining and entertaining.

Multimedia technology creates two kinds of fast and efficient reading methods for English learners: on the macro level, it can realize an advance organizer through video editing to help students understand the general meaning of the article; At the micro level, students can help students understand and master the words that are relatively difficult to understand through images, texts or videos. The so-called advance organizer strategy (Ausubel) is to present guiding materials to learners before learning tasks. These materials are more general and abstract than learning tasks. With the support of multimedia technology, these advance organizers are presented in the form of visual and dynamic images and videos, changing the traditional presentation in the form of text, making it easier for students to connect and integrate new and old knowledge in the process of learning new knowledge, and understand and master new knowledge. As the main body of learning activities, college students can independently download some reading training software online for practice, such as Ace Reader Pro, MCALL, etc., or read English electronic newspapers to train oral English.

3.3 Make It Easier for Students to Learn

Contemporary students are a group of students who have grown up in the Internet age, so they are more adept at using the Internet to live and study, and the application of multimedia teaching mode in college education makes it more convenient for contemporary students. Students can gain a deeper understanding of various knowledge through multimedia equipment, and teachers generally use PPT courseware for teaching, so teachers can also copy the courseware to students after class, which allows students to understand and review in more detail after class [8].

4 The Design of an English Online Translation Platform Based on Computer Technology

4.1 System Operation Process

The online software platform includes word translation, thesaurus management, word development, system settings, word book, etc. The specific operation process is shown in Fig. 2.

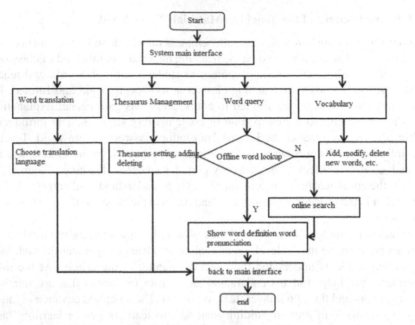

Fig. 2. System operation process

Network Topology Diagram

The network topology is the basis of system operation, as shown in Fig. 3 is the network topology structure diagram [9].

4.2 Architecture Design of Translation Software

English translation platform can be divided into online translation webpage and mobile translation software [10]. The architecture design of mobile translation software is shown in Fig. 4.

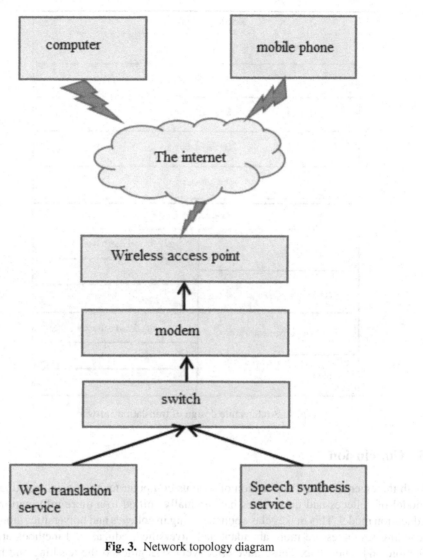

Fig. 3. Network topology diagram

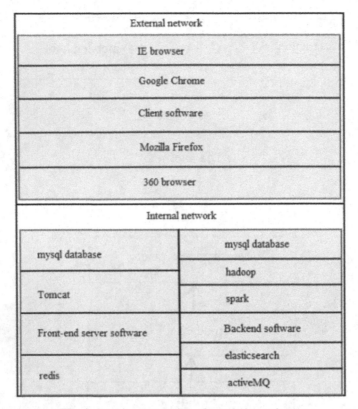

Fig. 4. Architecture design of translation software

5 Conclusion

With the emergence and application of various computer technologies, the educational model of colleges and universities has gradually shifted to a more information-based education model. This makes classroom teaching in colleges and universities more vivid, teaching resources are more abundant and diversified, educational methods are more flexible and innovative. These have effectively strengthened the teaching and training plan of modern students. Of course, the application of computer technology in Chinese universities is not yet proficient, and this requires constant practice by university teachers.

References

1. Xutong, F.: Design and implementation of English online translation platform. Electronic Technology and Software Engineering 63–64 (2019)
2. Di, L.: Exploration of design and implementation based on English online translation platform. Technology Wind 218 (2018)
3. Zhijing, Q.: The application research of flipped classroom in business English translation teaching. House of Drama 180 (2018)

4. Yuhua, D.: A study on the application of multimedia in English translation classroom teaching. China Newspaper 34–35 (2016)
5. Lin, X., Yutao, Q.: The application of "SPOC + physical classroom" teaching model in graduate English translation courses. Theoretical Research and Practice of Innovation and Entrepreneurship 71–72 (2018)
6. Jinghui, S.: Analysis of open-type college English translation classroom teaching. Campus English (Late) 79–80 (2018)
7. Yan, S.: A probe into the effectiveness of college English translation classroom teaching. Curriculum Education Research: Study on Learning Method and Teaching Method 88 (2014)
8. Longlong, L.: Constructing the effectiveness of English translation classroom teaching in higher vocational colleges. Campus English (Late) (2017)
9. Shenling, Z.: Problems and countermeasures in college English translation classroom teaching. Biotechnology World 278 (2016)
10. Zhang, C.: Analysis of college English translation classroom teaching mode in multimedia environment. Biotechnology World 231 (2015)

Construction of Business English Translation Teaching Model in Higher Vocational Colleges Based on Web-Based Learning Platform

Meichun Yang[1(✉)], Ding Miao[1], and Feng Gai[2]

[1] School of Foreign Languages and International Business, Guangdong Mechanical and Electrical Polytechnic, Guangzhou, Guangdong, China
jollyyoung100@163.com
[2] Yunnan Land and Resources Vocational College, Yunnan 652501, China

Abstract. With the formation of economic globalization and the increasingly frequent exchanges between countries in politics, culture, trade and other aspects, the society urgently needs high-level business English translators. Higher vocational colleges bear the important responsibility of cultivating business English translation talents, and cultivate business English translation talents who are suitable for the economic development needs of the "the Belt and Road" and have high professional level, translator quality and communication ability. Which will make them more confident and improve their employability. The project consists of two parts: 1) the development and implementation of training building materials (modules), and 2) the development, design and implementation of web-based training and learning platform.

Keywords: Higher vocational business English · E-learning · Translation teaching

1 Introduction

This year is the 17th year of China's accession to the WTO. China has been fully open to the outside world. China has further integrated into the international economic society [1]. There are more opportunities for cooperation and exchanges with foreign countries, opening up overseas markets, introducing foreign technology and importing foreign products. However, in rural areas where the manufacturing industry in China is developing rapidly, foreign language talents are still scarce, and the management in charge of enterprise decision-making often steps into the business world early and has not received English education.

The construction of a vocational business English translation teaching model based on online learning platforms combines information technology with teaching, providing students with a more flexible, convenient, and personalized learning environment [2]. Through online learning platforms, students can access rich learning resources anytime and anywhere, participate in online courses, conduct practical training, and interact with

Y. Zhang and N. Shah (Eds.): BigIoT-EDU 2023, LNICST 582, pp. 134–141, 2024.
https://doi.org/10.1007/978-3-031-63136-8_14

teachers and classmates [3]. This model can break through the time and space limitations of traditional classrooms and provide a more autonomous, comprehensive, and experiential learning approach. At the same time, the teaching mode based on online learning platforms can fully utilize technological means to provide multimedia teaching, intelligent evaluation, and learning analysis functions, in order to improve learning effectiveness and personalized learning experience.

However, building a vocational business English translation teaching model based on online learning platforms also faces some tests and challenges. Information security, teaching management, and technical support need to be effectively addressed. In addition, the particularity of business English translation requires the teaching mode to be targeted and practical. How to effectively combine theory and practice on online learning platforms is also an important issue in constructing the teaching mode.

Teaching business English on the Internet can overcome the limitations of time and space. Professional business English teachers design teaching plans and record and upload teaching videos. As long as students have a networked computer, they can log in to learn the recorded learning content and complete their homework, and carry out targeted real-time teaching according to the free time of students. Therefore, this article will explore the construction of a vocational business English translation teaching model based on online learning platforms [4]. By fully utilizing the advantages of online learning platforms and combining the characteristics and needs of business English translation, targeted teaching content and activities are designed to cultivate students' business English translation ability and professional literacy. At the same time, we will also explore how to address the challenges and problems in the construction of teaching models to improve teaching quality and student learning outcomes.

2 Related Work

2.1 Introduction and Research Status of E-learning Platform

Electronic learning platform is an online learning platform based on network technology and information communication technology to carry out teaching and learning activities. It provides various functions such as online courses, learning resources, homework submission, discussion and communication, and online testing to support students in learning and accessing educational resources at any time and place.

The research and application of electronic learning platforms have received widespread attention and development in the field of education. The following are some key contents on the current research status of electronic learning platforms:

1. Technical support and platform functions [5]: Research on electronic learning platforms focuses on how to utilize advanced network and information communication technologies to support online learning. Researchers explore how to provide a more efficient, stable, and secure learning platform, increase the diversity and interactivity of learning resources, and provide personalized learning experiences and support.
2. Personalized learning and learning analysis: Research on e-learning platforms also focuses on how to achieve personalized learning, providing personalized learning paths and content based on learners' characteristics, learning progress, and learning

needs. The application of learning analysis technology enables the platform to collect and analyze learning data, and evaluate learners' learning situation and progress through methods such as data mining and machine learning.

3. Social interaction and shared collaboration [6]: Research on e-learning platforms emphasizes the importance of social interaction and shared collaboration. Researchers are committed to developing platform features that can facilitate communication and cooperation among learners, such as online discussions, collaborative projects, and shared resources. At the same time, the application of social media technology has also been deeply explored and applied in the research of electronic learning platforms.

4. Mobile learning and learner experience: With the popularity of mobile devices and the rapid development of mobile networks, research on electronic learning platforms is gradually focusing on mobile learning. The goal of researchers is to provide a learning experience that adapts to different mobile devices, and to utilize mobile technology to increase learning flexibility and convenience.

The research on electronic learning platforms not only focuses on technical support and platform functions, but also on personalized learning, learning analysis, social interaction, shared collaboration, mobile learning, and other aspects [7]. The current research continuously promotes the development and innovation of electronic learning platforms, providing students with more flexible, convenient, and efficient learning methods. In the future, with the further development of technology and changes in educational needs, research on electronic learning platforms will continue to explore and innovate in depth.

2.2   Introduction to Business English Online Learning Platform

The introduction of the business English online learning platform is designed and developed using the Browser/Server model. The teaching content is required to cover all the language skills and professional knowledge contained in the business communication, which is highly professional; Good user interface and visualization; It has good interaction function, convenient communication and strong practicability.

The platform is designed and taught by professional business English teachers, who have good English level, rich international trade operation experience, rich professional knowledge and strong pertinence [8].

The system should have the following five basic functions:

(1) Online teaching: online teaching is realized by uploading and watching teaching videos and courseware.

(2) Homework training: teachers input homework synchronized with class. Some homework requires students to answer online [9]. According to the characteristics of English learning, some homework requires students to complete offline.

(3) Examination test: periodic test to check the learning effect and find out the missing.

(4) Evaluation and Q&A: Evaluation refers to the students' evaluation of classroom learning and teaching teachers and their suggestions. Q&A means that students leave messages to ask questions about the doubts in the classroom, and teachers answer them. Teachers can also actively post the difficulties in teaching on the Q&A interface for college students to learn.

(5) Online voice room. Coaching and oral training. It is necessary to realize the training of multi person online voice dialogue, recording, re reading and following reading.

3 Business English Translation Teaching Mode in Higher Vocational Colleges Based on Network Learning Platform

3.1 System Module Design

The overall design of business English online learning platform has seven basic functional modules, as follows:

(1) Course and platform introduction module.
   It is a plate to introduce the platform and teaching methods. It includes the outline of business English, the characteristics of the platform's courses, teaching and learning syllabus, learning conditions for students, learning methods, etc. This module enables potential users and users to understand business English related knowledge, as well as issues related to the teaching of this platform.
(2) Course content introduction, course introduction of the following six courses, course content and features, teaching plan and teaching methods.
   1. Basic English (Phonetic Alphabet, Pronunciation, Grammar)
   2. Text learning (situational dialogue)
   3. Foreign trade correspondence
   4. Business Negotiation
   5. Business English
   6. Word shorthand (Ebbinghaus memory curve memory method)
(3) Online classes provide students with efficient and intuitive teaching methods. Including video teaching and courseware synchronous playing, classroom communication, and online examination questions.
(4) The homework and examination system provides an online exercise and online examination environment for learning, which is used to remember and flexibly use the content learned in the course, and to test the mastery of knowledge in stages.
(5) The speech training room provides students with an environment for practicing oral English in practice. Regular online training is carried out. The teacher plays the original sound following materials and conducts simulated scene training.
(6) Common downloads and reference materials are available for students to download learning related learning resources, including learning materials, common software tools, test questions and learning videos. At the same time, it provides some e-books and websites related to learning for student users to assist in learning.
(7) Teachers' background management, all teachers' background operations, including recording and uploading learning videos and courseware, publishing homework and exams and marking, editing and modifying the text displayed on the website, publishing news bulletins and articles, uploading common downloads and reference materials, management of student interaction, management of student information, etc.

3.2 System Structure Design

For teaching evaluation systems, the selection of databases is crucial for the stability and performance of the system. Although Access is a lightweight database management system suitable for small-scale data processing and simple application scenarios, it may face some challenges in some more complex systems. Access is suitable for small-scale data processing. For larger datasets and complex data structures, it may lead to performance degradation and extended database response time. Therefore, if the teaching evaluation system involves large-scale data storage and processing, it may be necessary to consider more powerful and scalable relational databases such as MySQL, PostgreSQL, or Microsoft SQL Server. If the teaching evaluation system needs to store and process complex data structures and relationships, such as multiple associations, many to many relationships, and complex query operations, Access's functionality may not be powerful and flexible enough. Other more mature and fully functional database management systems can provide more comprehensive data modeling and query functions to meet the system's requirements.

The concurrency performance of Access is relatively low, and there may be some limitations for situations where multiple users are accessing and operating at the same time, which can lead to deadlocks or performance bottlenecks. If the teaching evaluation system needs to support the demand for a large number of users to access and operate data simultaneously, it may be necessary to consider a more efficient and powerful database system. Although Access is a reasonable choice for small-scale data processing and simple application scenarios, in teaching evaluation systems, especially when dealing with large-scale data, complex data structures, and multi user concurrent access, it is recommended to choose a database management system that is more suitable for large-scale data processing and high concurrent access. Based on actual requirements and system complexity, database systems such as MySQL, PostgreSQL, or Microsoft SQL Server can be considered to provide better performance and reliability. The business English translation teaching system in higher vocational colleges is shown in Fig. 1.

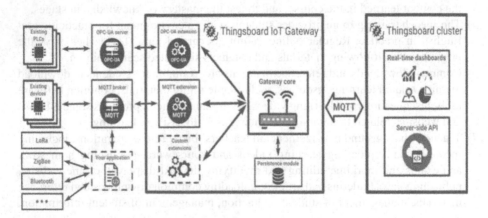

Fig. 1. Business English Translation Teaching System

4 Countermeasures for Improving Business English Translation Teaching in Higher Vocational Colleges

During the selection of business English translation textbooks in vocational colleges, the author believes that the principle of "practicality first" should be adhered to in the selection of textbooks; The teaching materials should be selected according to the actual situation, characteristics and overall level of the students in the local vocational colleges. For competent colleges and departments, teachers can also be invited to compile and revise their own textbooks, which can provide tailored textbooks for business English majors for our school. Because teachers in our school know students' level best, the compilation of textbooks is certainly the most practical [10]. Whether the higher vocational colleges compile their own textbooks or purchase ready-made business English translation textbooks, teachers must understand and master the content of the textbooks.

The following is a further discussion on the importance of adapting to the development of the times, guiding business knowledge, and improving teaching evaluation mechanisms:

1. Adapt to the development and novelty of the times: Business English translation teaching materials must keep up with the times and reflect the latest developments in the business field in a timely manner. With the continuous changes and innovations in global business, students need to understand and respond to new business trends, technologies, and professional terminology. The textbook should include current business cases, authentic business texts, and sample translations, so that students can gain practical application opportunities during the learning process.
2. Business knowledge orientation and pertinence: Business English translation textbooks should be oriented towards business knowledge, helping students master the professional knowledge and skills required in the business field. Textbooks can cover classroom teaching, business culture, business communication, business protocols, and other aspects, and provide corresponding translation practices and training. This targeted teaching content can help students understand business backgrounds, improve translation accuracy and professionalism.
3. Improving the teaching evaluation mechanism: The teaching evaluation mechanism is crucial for improving teaching quality and student learning effectiveness. Teachers can use various evaluation methods, such as homework, exams, oral speeches, project evaluations, etc., to comprehensively evaluate students' translation abilities such as listening, speaking, reading, and writing. In addition, using automatic evaluation systems and mutual evaluation mechanisms, students' evaluation results and feedback can be provided in a timely manner, helping them identify problems, improve and improve.

By adapting to the development and novelty of the times, as well as business knowledge oriented and targeted teaching, students can better cope with the challenges of business English translation and better understand and apply business knowledge.

The blackboard writing design is standardized and reasonable, and multimedia teaching is used. However, the construction of the training room is relatively backward. Teachers can choose teaching methods according to the cognitive rules, optimize the combination of various teaching methods, simplify the number of formative exercises, refine the words, express accurately and facilitate testing. What needs to be improved is that the choice of exercises should be related to the actual situation. The author uses the form to refine the evaluation angle to help teachers improve teaching in all aspects.

5   Conclusion

The construction of a vocational business English translation teaching model based on online learning platforms is an innovative teaching model that meets the needs of modern education. This model provides vocational college students with more flexible, convenient, and effective English translation teaching by utilizing the advantages of online learning platforms and combining the characteristics and needs of business English translation. This "Business English Online Learning Platform" is a self-learning system for business English majors. We should also develop more practical and targeted online teaching platforms, making it easier for more users who crave knowledge and learning skills to enjoy higher quality educational resources. This is a great good thing that benefits society, the country, and the people. It fully utilizes the advantages of online learning platforms to provide students with a convenient learning environment and resources. By combining the characteristics and needs of business English translation with student-centered teaching methods, this teaching model can cultivate students' business English translation ability and professional literacy, while providing comprehensive evaluation and feedback. With the continuous development of network technology and changes in the educational environment, this teaching model based on online learning platforms is expected to be further promoted and applied in vocational business English translation education.

References

1. Zhao, W.: An empirical study of English teaching model in higher vocational colleges based on data analysis. In: Atiquzzaman, M., Yen, N., Xu, Z. (eds.) Big Data Analytics for Cyber-Physical System in Smart City (BDCPS 2020). AISC, vol. 1303, pp. 470–475. Springer, Singapore (2021). https://doi.org/10.1007/978-981-33-4572-0_68
2. Zhang, T.: Study on the mixed English teaching model in higher vocational colleges under the background of big data. J. Phys. Conf. Ser. **1852**(3) (2021)
3. Qian, W.: Research on the innovation of blended English teaching mode based on superstar platform in higher vocational colleges. In: 2021 2nd International Conference on Computers, Information Processing and Advanced Education, pp. 1227–1230 (2021)
4. Yang, Y.: A critical study on the effect of the case-based teaching method in business English reading in higher vocational colleges. Sci. Publ. Group **2021**(2) (2021)
5. Wang, H.: Teaching strategies for improving English effectiveness in higher vocational colleges based on the present situation of English teaching. Learn. Educ. **9**(4) (2021)
6. Huang, S., Cao, H., Yan, L., Chen, H.: Teaching reform of obstetrics and gynecology nursing course in higher vocational colleges based on OBE education concept from the perspective of big data. Biomed. J. Sci. Tech. Res. **37**(2), 29266–29276 (2021)
7. Cui, M.: DRIIS: research on automatic recognition of artistic conception of classical poems based on deep learning. Int. J. Coop. Inf. Syst. **31**(01n02), 2250001 (2022)

8. Bo, Q.: The sustainable development of psychological education in students' learning concept in physical education based on machine learning and the internet of things. Sustainability **14** (2022)

9. Chen, P., et al.: Construction of ZIF-67-On-UiO-66 catalysts as a platform for efficient overall water splitting. Inorg. Chem.. Chem. **61**(46), 18424–18433 (2022)

10. Shike, C.: U.S. Patent No. 11,157,849. U.S. Patent and Trademark Office, Washington, DC (2021)

Analysis Model of Learning Chinese as a Foreign Language Based on Random Forest Algorithm

Qi Zhu[1]([✉]), Maoni Tang[2], and Yuanyuan Chai[2]

[1] International College for Chinese Studies, Nanjing Normal University, Nanjing 210000, Jiangsu, China
absinthzhu@163.com
[2] School of Foreign Language, Jingchu University of Technology, Jingmen 448000, Hubei, China

Abstract. This article aims to propose an analysis model for learning Chinese as a foreign language based on the random forest algorithm. This model aims to analyze students' learning situation and predict their learning performance by collecting learning data, including learning behavior, test scores, learning progress, etc. The random forest algorithm was chosen as the foundation of the model due to its strong learning and prediction abilities. By extracting features from the collected data and training the model, the model can accurately evaluate students' language proficiency and provide personalized learning suggestions and feedback. This method extracts features from four dimensions: basic features, part of speech features, hierarchical features, and grammatical features. The random forest algorithm has potential in improving students' learning effectiveness and personalized teaching, providing useful reference and support for teaching Chinese as a foreign language.

Keywords: Random forest algorithm · Chinese as a foreign language · Learning behavior

1 Introduction

With the development of China's economy, the improvement of comprehensive national strength and economic globalization, China has more and more frequent and close contacts with other countries in the world, and the number of people studying Chinese at home and abroad is increasing year by year [1]. How to improve the teaching quality and learning effect of Chinese as a foreign language has become a key issue of current research [2]. As a place for cultivating students' abilities and qualities, colleges and universities are the main body of learning, and their learning behavior directly affects the effect and quality of learning [3]. Due to the differences in students' educational background, professional differences, personalities, etc., their learning behaviors are also diverse, so it is of great significance to study the learning behaviors of different students [4]. The development of reading ability is an important part of language learning], the

Y. Zhang and N. Shah (Eds.): BigIoT-EDU 2023, LNICST 582, pp. 142–150, 2024.
https://doi.org/10.1007/978-3-031-63136-8_15

importance of reading materials to the development of reading ability is self-evident [5]. In order to ensure that the reading materials meet the proficiency of potential readers, it is very important for educators, authors, publishers, etc. to accurately predict the readability of second language learners' reading materials [6]. However, for second language learners and teachers, predicting the difficulty of reading materials is very time-consuming and often subjective [7]. With the machine learning, the research on text readability has also progressed, and this problem can be solved to a certain extent [8]. Readability is the sum of all elements in a text material that affect readers' comprehension, reading speed, and interest in the material [9]. Transfer, the sum of all actual factors that affect the legibility of the text [10].

Based on the comprehensive observation of the courses offered by universities for foreign students, the Chinese courses for foreign students mainly focus on comprehensive courses and skill training courses. According to different stages of students and learning requirements, elective courses are used as a supplement, which is flexible and changeable [11]. In order to achieve the established teaching objectives and teaching effects, instructional design, as the overall arrangement of a course, is of great significance to the teaching activities and has become the focus of scholars' research [12]. However, according to students' feedback and personal investigation, teachers' teaching design is too idealistic, and there are many deviations in the overall implementation, which neglects students' problems for the overall teaching task of the school [13, 14].

2 Analysis of the Problems Existing in the Classroom of Teaching Chinese as a Foreign Language

2.1 Basic Situation of Chinese as a Foreign Language Classroom

In the teaching stage, teaching tasks can be divided into four levels, and each student needs to complete two tasks.

Listening and Speaking: Listening tasks: Students need to understand and obtain information by listening to recordings or teachers' oral expressions, such as listening to short dialogues, broadcasting news, or listening to story plots. Tasks can revolve around identifying key vocabulary, obtaining the main idea, or answering relevant questions.

Oral tasks: Students need to use Chinese for oral expression, such as conducting daily conversations, discussing topics, and introducing themselves. Tasks can include role-playing, debates, group discussions, etc.

Reading and Writing:
Reading task: Students need to obtain information, understand content, and answer questions by reading Chinese text, such as reading articles, advertisements, briefings, etc. Tasks can involve understanding the topic, searching for details, reasoning and judgment, etc.

Writing task: Students need to express themselves in writing in Chinese, such as writing short essays, diaries, essays, etc. Tasks can include describing things, writing viewpoints, and creating stories.

During the teaching process, teachers can design appropriate teaching tasks based on students' level and needs. Each student needs to complete two tasks in order to fully develop different skills. At the progress in the four skills. By designing teaching tasks tailored to different skills, the comprehensive course of Chinese as a foreign language can promote students' comprehensive development in listening, speaking, reading, and writing. This teaching design can help students improve their skills and provide a richer language learning experience.

The relationship between sex and readability of Chinese as a foreign language is shown in Fig. 1.

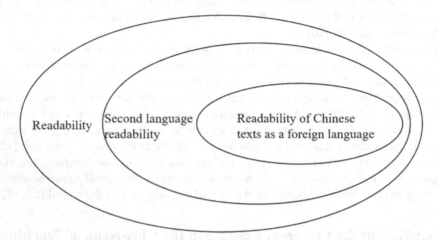

Fig. 1. Relationship diagram of readability, second language readability and readability of Chinese as a foreign language

For students studying a comprehensive course of Chinese as a foreign language, if they believe that the content of the course is not attractive to them and often cannot understand problems in the classroom, teachers can take the following measures to improve teaching effectiveness:

1. Improve the fun of the course: Teachers can increase the attractiveness of the course by adding interactive elements, introducing multimedia resources, and using interesting teaching activities. For example, using stories, games, film and television content to incorporate Chinese into vivid and vivid contexts.
2. Create a friendly learning environment: Teachers can create a relaxed and pleasant classroom atmosphere, encourage students to actively participate, communicate and share learning experiences with each other. Make students feel that their problems and difficulties are understood and supported.
3. Decomposing course content: In response to students' low Chinese proficiency, teachers can appropriately decompose the course content, with a clear structure and clear hierarchy, and improve students' learning understanding through progressive teaching.
4. Introduce concise and clear Chinese expressions: Try to avoid using overly complex language expressions and long sentences. Teachers can use visual means such as pictures and body language to explain and present classroom content concisely and clearly.

5. Personalized tutoring and feedback: Teachers can provide individual tutoring, pay attention to students' learning progress and difficulties, and provide timely and correct feedback and guidance. Pay attention to taking care of students' different needs and provide learning support that is suitable for individual differences.
6. Provide additional learning resources: Teachers can provide students with additional learning resources, such as recordings, text materials, online learning platforms, etc. This way, students can have more opportunities to practice and fill in gaps outside of the classroom.

Teachers need to pay attention to students' feedback and needs in teaching, and make corresponding adjustments and support based on students' level and problems. By using the above methods, students can increase their interest in comprehensive courses of Chinese as a foreign language, reduce learning difficulty, and better master Chinese knowledge and application abilities.

2.2 Teaching Suggestions for Improving the Teaching of Chinese as a Foreign Language

Instructional design is the work content that every teacher needs to carry out. Teachers should formulate instructional design with different characteristics according to the existing teaching objects and teaching contents. Teachers of comprehensive courses in teaching Chinese as a foreign language should determine appropriate teaching methods for different students. For students of different ages, teachers should make necessary adjustments to the classroom content. For some younger students, teachers can choose game teaching; For older college students, teachers can choose more knowledge points to explain. Teachers of comprehensive courses of Chinese as a foreign language should teach according to students' different learning needs. The purpose of students' learning Chinese is different from that of some social people. Teachers should improve the relevant teaching plans after understanding the actual situation. In the comprehensive course of Chinese as a foreign language, teachers should not ask students to answer questions immediately. Because some students have a weak Chinese foundation, they may not be able to understand the meaning of the teacher's questions. If they ask the students to answer the questions immediately, many students will feel pressure. Teachers should give students some time to think, so that students can really understand the meaning of the questions raised by teaching and answer them by applying their own knowledge. Therefore, students need some time to understand when answering teachers' questions. Teachers should give students enough thinking time and ask students to answer after students understand. In the process of questioning, teachers can choose different ways to let students answer different questions. When encountering some simple questions, teachers can randomly select students to answer. The feature selection process is shown in Fig. 2.

At the same time, teachers should increase the interest and interaction of the game according to the teaching content. Only when students are interested can they actively interact with teachers. However, games are only a teaching method, which requires students to master language application ability and improve their comprehensive Chinese ability in the process of games. Teachers should have clear goals and find ways to integrate students into the game process.

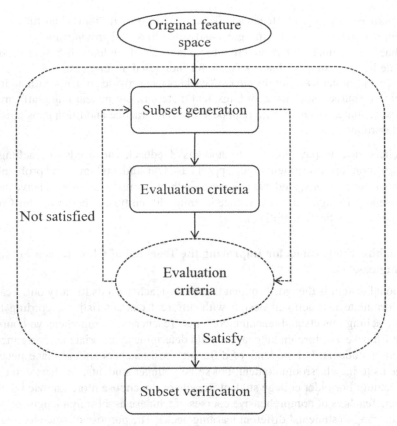

Fig. 2. Flow chart of feature selection

In the aimed at providing a rich learning experience and effective teaching effects. Teachers can use intuitive teaching methods to present vocabulary, sentences, and language application scenarios through images, physical objects, gestures, and other means, helping students understand and remember. This method can improve students' language sense and accuracy. Teachers can adopt communicative teaching methods, emphasizing authentic communication activities and situational simulations. Through dialogues, role-playing, discussions, and other forms, students can actively participate in language communication and improve their oral expression and understanding abilities.

In addition, teachers can also use task-based teaching methods, which are task oriented and allow students to apply their knowledge in practical situations through group collaboration, project research, and other methods to cultivate problem-solving and collaborative abilities. This method can enable students to engage in language output and practice in real-life tasks, thereby improving their language proficiency. In addition, there is an emotional teaching method where teachers can create a positive and relaxed learning atmosphere through resources such as games, music, and movies, enhancing students' interest in learning and emotional engagement.

3 Teaching Curriculum Design Plan

3.1 Introduction to Teaching Courses

Chinese comprehensive course is the main course type that systematically undertakes the teaching task of language ability. It is an important course to further consolidate and improve students' Chinese level. The goal of advanced Chinese comprehensive course should be to cultivate students' language communication skills after completing the basic Chinese course, such as mood, language flow, situational language, identity and distance, which can not be reflected in the teaching materials, but are the cultural factors and teaching factors affecting language communication. The teaching focus of advanced Chinese comprehensive course should release the shackles of syllabus and teaching tasks, and pay more attention to students' language communication quality, rather than simple knowledge learning. Therefore, advanced Chinese comprehensive course can abandon textbooks and teaching materials, reformulate teaching objectives in the form of module teaching, and select and arrange teaching contents. The previous teaching evaluation methods also need to be changed to adapt to this flexible curriculum arrangement.

Integrate the previously divided language skills of students, so that each language skill interacts with each other to form a systematic language system. When building the Chinese system for students as a whole, the study of language knowledge will no longer become the focus of students' learning, but will focus on helping students to establish the awareness of identifying language communication environment and communication identity. This environment is not only the realistic situational environment, but also the interference of culture, communication rules and non-language factors. Advanced students may still have problems in language skills, but language learning at this stage should be an extension of language communicative competence. The whole course should allow students to learn to think for themselves and reflect on the obstacles they encounter in language communication. Teachers are responsible for grasping the direction of the whole classroom, coordinating students' differences, and giving timely training methods for students' weak links. Classroom atmosphere is very important for students' learning. Interesting teaching content can arouse students' interest in learning, relieve students' learning pressure and enliven classroom atmosphere to a great extent. Selectivity, on the other hand, adjusts the curriculum in time according to the specific learning needs of students.

3.2 Analysis of Teaching Objectives

Chinese communicative ability, and Chinese comprehensive course is an important course to systematically cultivate students' language ability. The students in the advanced class often have a prominent level in the training of single language skills, but the overall language level is often unable to achieve balanced development. In the overall comprehensive application, it is difficult to give full play to students' individual language skills. Moreover, language communication itself is the comprehensive use of multilingual skills, and the communication environment is complex and changeable, which can not be successfully completed by a single skill. Therefore, an important teaching goal of comprehensive course is to integrate students' previously split language skills, so that each language skill interacts to form a systematic language system. One of the main orientations of the comprehensive course is the fusion agent, which uses the teaching content and teaching methods to assemble the students' split language skills together to the greatest extent, so that students can use the language skills they have learned to establish their own cognitive system and learning system, and constantly break the obstacles between individual skills through multiple or comprehensive language skill training. It is a supervised learning algorithm. It is famous for its simplicity and efficiency. Random forest only needs to learn classification rules by training on given data, and does not require prior knowledge. The basic idea is: use bootstrap sampling to extract k samples from the training set D; these k samples build k decision trees respectively, and input the test set data T into the k decision trees to get k classification results; Finally, the final classification is predicted through corresponding voting. The random forest algorithm is shown in Fig. 3.

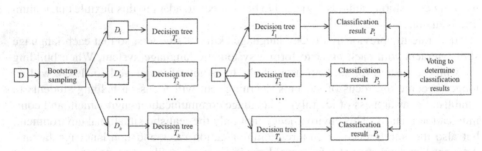

Fig. 3. Schematic diagram of random forest algorithm

Precision rate and recall rate are often used in practical research. However, precision and recall are a pair of conflicting evaluation indicators. When one value increases, usually the other value decreases accordingly. The precision and recall can be calculated by the classification confusion matrix. TP represents the real case, FN represents the false counterexample, FP represents the false positive case, and TN represents the true counterexample The calculation formulas of precision and recall are as follows:

$$precision = \frac{TP}{TP + FP} \tag{1}$$

$$recall = \frac{TP}{TP + FN} \tag{2}$$

Since the precision rate and the recall rate often go up and down, $F_\beta - score$ is introduced again. This is a performance evaluation index that combines the recall rate and the precision rate, and can evaluate the performance as a whole. Calculated as follows:

$$F_\beta = \frac{(\beta^2 + 1) * precision * recall}{\beta^2 * precision + recall} \tag{3}$$

Among them, β represents the weighting coefficient of precision, which is used to adjust the influence of precision in $F_1 - score$. β generally takes the value 1, and the corresponding formula is:

$$F_1 = \frac{2 * \mathrm{Pr}\,ecision * recall}{precision + recall} \tag{4}$$

The learning focus or teaching goal of comprehensive courses in advanced classes is no longer the learning of vocabulary knowledge or grammar knowledge, create real and complex communication situations in combination with real life as much as possible, or select some typical topic rotation or jumping language materials for analysis by teachers and students, So as to investigate and cultivate students' Chinese thinking. Since the comprehensive course no longer focuses on learning vocabulary and grammar, it means that the whole course will no longer restrict students' classroom learning with fixed teaching content and teaching process. This gives students the right to choose learning content. Although many students do not know what specific content they want or need to learn, they have their own clear learning needs. Teachers can roughly understand students' learning needs by designing questionnaires. On this basis, they can help students make choices or list learning contents for students to choose, so as to design their own courses. Of course, teachers have the right to deny the content that deviates from the pre-set teaching objectives or the students deliberately do it. Interest is also an indispensable part of the comprehensive course. It can attract students' attention to a great extent, create a relaxed classroom atmosphere, relieve the pressure of students and teachers, and bring inspiration in other aspects, which is beneficial to students' learning.

4 Conclusions

At present, more and more people in the world are learning Chinese. That students can be motivated to learn Chinese and improve the teaching effect of Chinese. Modern information technology is widely used in the field of education, and the teaching reform based on classroom teaching mode is being carried out drastically. The integration of education and information technology has entered the deep water area. Smart classroom has put forward quite good ideas and practical methods for constructing new classroom teaching mode and improving some problems existing in existing teaching. Classroom informatization is the core of school education informatization, and smart classroom is the key to the concrete implementation of smart education. The fundamental purpose of wisdom education is to improve the existing problems in current teaching, and finally realize the purpose of cultivating students' creative thinking ability and problem-solving ability. Wisdom education is not a simple integration of technology and teaching. To make education truly generate wisdom, researchers and practitioners need to dig and analyze it together. The cultural differences are large, and the learning goals are uneven. Teachers must design reasonable classroom teaching according to the overall situation of the students, especially the teaching of integrated courses. As a comprehensive course, integrated courses have a lot of content to be taught.

References

1. Chen, H.-Z., Tang, G.-Q., Ai, W., et al.: Use of random forest in FTIR analysis of LDL cholesterol and tri-glycerides for hyperlipidemia. Biotechnol. Prog. (31), 6 (2016)
2. Reis, I., Baron, D., Shahaf, S.: Probabilistic random forest: a machine learning algorithm for noisy datasets. Astron. J. (157), 1 (2018)
3. Polan, D., Brady, S., Kaufman, R.: SU-C-207B-05: tissue segmentation of computed tomography images using a random forest algorithm: a feasibility study. Med. Phys. 43(6), 3330–3331 (2016)
4. Sun, H., Liu, M., Li, L., et al.: A new classification method of ancient Chinese ceramics based on machine learning and component analysis. Ceram. Int. (46), 6 (2019)
5. Liu, C., Pang, M., Zhaom R.: Novel superpixel-based algorithm for segmenting lung images via convolutional neural network and random forest. IET Image Process. (14), 3 (2020)
6. Bag, S., Pradhan, A.K., Das, S., et al.: S-transform aided random forest based PD location detection employing signature of optical sensor. IEEE Trans. Power Deliv.Deliv. 34(4), 1261–1268 (2019)
7. Li, X.: Random forest is a specific algorithm, not omnipotent for all datasets. J. Appl. Entomol.Entomol. 50(4), 170–179 (2019)
8. Gao, J., Nuyttens, D., Lootens, P., et al.: Recognising weeds in a maize crop using a random forest machine-learning algorithm and near-infrared snapshot mosaic hyperspectral imagery. Biosys. Eng.. Eng. 170, 39–50 (2018)
9. Qadeer, K., Ahmad, A., Qyyum, M.A., et al.: Developing machine learning models for relative humidity prediction in air-based energy systems and environmental management applications. J. Environ. Manag. (292), 112736 (2021)
10. Özbek, M.F., Yoldash, M.A., Tang, T.-P.: Theory of justice, OCB, and individualism: Kyrgyz Citizens. J. Bus. Ethics 137(2), 365–382 (2015). https://doi.org/10.1007/s10551-015-2553-0
11. Jin, Y., Zhang, L.J., Macintyre, P.: Contracting students for the reduction of foreign language classroom anxiety: an approach nurturing positive mindsets and behaviors. Front. Psychol. 11(1471), 1–14 (2020)
12. Bonilla, C.: Peer interaction in text chat: qualitative analysis of chat transcripts. Lang. Learn. Technol. 21(2), 157–178 (2017)
13. Li, H., Majumdar, R., Chen, M., et al.: Goal-oriented active learning (GOAL) system to promote reading engagement, self-directed learning behavior, and motivation in extensive reading. Comput. Educ. 171(2), 104239 (2021)
14. Zhu, Y., Shu, D.: Implementing foreign language curriculum innovation in a Chinese secondary school: an ethnographic study on teacher cognition and classroom practices. System 2017(66), 100–112 (2017)

The Application of Neural Network
Algorithms in Intelligent Teaching

Development of a Japanese MOOC System Based on Deep Learning

Weizhou Feng[⊠]

School of Foreign Languages, Guangzhou Institute of Science and Technology,
Guangzhou 510540, Guangdong, China
jojoconti@126.com

Abstract. With the advent of the information age and the rapid development of computer technology, internet technology, and multimedia technology, various types of information in the world are growing exponentially, and the growth rate is still accelerating. The amount of data processed by Google servers every day has exceeded 24 PB, which means that the amount of data processed by Google every day is thousands of times that of the paper publications of the National Library of America. Therefore, Lifelong learning has become a widely recognized lifestyle. Since the first year of MOOC in 2012, there has been a global wave of MOOC. The MOOC education model provides equal opportunities for people to obtain high-quality educational resources. MOOC has become one of the hottest research fields, and the era of knowledge sharing has arrived. The application analysis system can realize the retrieval and query of the whole Japanese language structure, but there are also some deficiencies in self-discipline. Neural network needs to be improved by means of neural network, which can make up for the deficiencies in data analysis by weighting. Through the application of BP neural network, we can realize the real-time monitoring and intelligent diagnosis of students' learning behavior, and provide targeted teaching strategies for teachers, thus improving teaching quality.

Keyword: Language system · Use the Internet · Cloud system · You optimize

1 Introduction

Since 2012, led by many famous universities such as Stanford University and Harvard University in the United States, a MOOC storm has been set off around the world. Among them, the most well-known platforms are Coursera, Udacity, and edX. As of December 2016, Coursera has cooperated with universities in 28 countries around the world, including Stanford University and Princeton University, with a total of 2216 courses on the platform; EdX utilizes curriculum resources from Massachusetts Institute of Technology and Harvard University to collaborate with 86 universities in 13 countries around the world, with 950 courses on the platform; Udacity also has over 200 courses [1]. MOOC provides equal opportunities for people to access high-quality educational resources and provides students with more choices. Its characteristics are:

Y. Zhang and N. Shah (Eds.): BigIoT-EDU 2023, LNICST 582, pp. 153–162, 2024.
https://doi.org/10.1007/978-3-031-63136-8_16

(1) It breaks through the limitations of classroom teaching time and space. MOOC adjusts the course accordingly and reconstructs the course content based on knowledge points. The teaching content is based on small videos of about 10 min. Through small videos and occasional short interest detection, it helps learners maintain attention, improve their mastery of knowledge points, and ensure the completion rate of the course as much as possible.

(2) Open for a limited time. All courses on the MOOC platform have a clear starting and ending time. It has a set of teaching plans with a weekly time node. There is a limited time for each class's after class exercises. Finally, students are organized to participate in the course assessment to conduct the final course learning certification, which monitors that students must study on time, and only within the specified time to complete the after class exercises Only those who pass the final exam can obtain credits [2].

(3) Emphasis is placed on interactive practice methods. Students can ask questions online when they encounter problems during course learning, and most of the questions often receive a combination of massive responses and asynchronous discussions; On the other hand, the teacher will screen some meaningful or focused questions for systematic interpretation, and students can find similar questions and answers through keywords; In addition, each learner can also share their learning experience through the network and inspire each other.

(4) Solved the issue of educational equity. According to statistics from the Ministry of Education in 2014, there are as many as in 2824 universities. Most people do not have the opportunity to go to university; Beijing, Jiangsu, Shanghai, Shaanxi, and Hubei have the largest number of key universities, accounting for 48. 5% 9% of high-quality education resources are seriously insufficient and extremely unevenly distributed [3].

(5) Emphasize students' autonomous learning. During the playback process of MOOC videos, students will be artificially "intentionally" interrupted at certain intervals and embedded with exercises to allow them to answer immediately. If students do not complete the exercises, they cannot enter the next stage of learning.

Modern education, with the Internet and multimedia technology as its core, is constantly impacting traditional classroom teaching methods, and has also brought about changes in teaching content and concepts. Our traditional educational ideas and concepts are being greatly challenged.In order to monitor the system thinking and this important retrieval content, the whole data and system can be optimized, and remote data retrieval control should be realized. However, there are its own problems in the retrieval process. It is necessary to set up relevant warrants to meet the real-time dialogue of the whole real system. Neural network can analyze and judge the key indicators in the retrieval system, adjust relevant parameters, complete the overall plan and scale of data, and realize the comprehensive judgment of data.

2 Related Concepts

2.1 Mathematical Description of the BP Neural Algorithm

As a kind of neural network with wide application effect, it can realize the comprehensive facilities and analysis of data by the method of weight parameters, which can provide more support for language retrieval system, and can realize the optimization of data and reduce content to complete the overall analysis of data in the process of carrying out stage. In order to judge the language as a whole, it is necessary to assume the key content, assuming that the data in the language is quantitative data, and the relationship between languages is qualitative data, so the specific calculation process is active.

$$f(x_i) = \lim_{i \to \infty} \sum x_i | y_i \Leftrightarrow \sqrt{\xi^2 - 4xy} \qquad (1)$$

As a comprehensive network method, neural network can optimize various resources and personal relationships in the network, and better analyze and apply data resources. This network is used to measure the teaching effectiveness of the Japanese MOOC The results of your operation are as follows (Fig. 1).

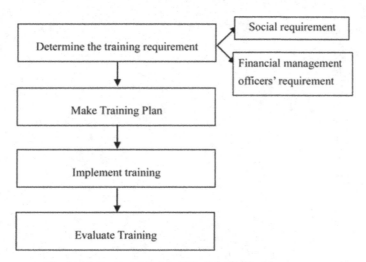

Fig. 1. Evaluation Model of English Interlocking system.

In the process of evaluating the learning effectiveness of a system using BP neural networks, the first step is to normalize various evaluation indicators for the learning effectiveness of the system, and the processing results are used as input vectors for the BP neural network, thereby transforming the learning effectiveness from an abstract form to a quantitative form as output vectors. The second step is to combine the empirical knowledge of relevant experts and use a certain number of training samples to enable the BP neural network to adaptively learn and adjust the weights until the neural network can accurately represent the knowledge [10]. The third step is to apply the properly trained

BP neural network model to the evaluation of the teaching effectiveness of the Japanese MOOC system. According to the various indicators collected by the system for students to learn Japanese, it is possible to conduct a fair, objective, and accurate evaluation of the students' learning.

2.2 Various Monitoring Schemes and Strategies in Personnel Monitoring

In psychological retrieval, the relationship between data and the coupling between data need to be analyzed in order to better carry out language retrieval.

$$F(x_i) = \frac{-x \pm \sqrt{x^2 - 4x\xi}}{2x} + [z_i \cdot \xi] \tag{2}$$

2.3 Distribution of the Results of the Original Retrieval

More in-depth analysis of language retrieval and the content of language retrieval, to the Japanese language monitoring system for data distribution, analysis and verification of the relationship between the data (Fig. 2).

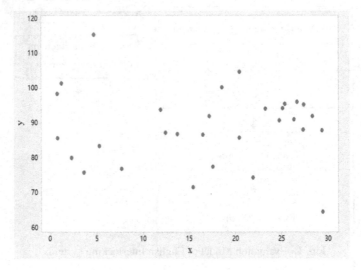

Fig. 2. Analysis results of BP neural algorithm

Through the application of BP neural network, we can realize the real-time monitoring and intelligent diagnosis of students' learning behavior, and provide targeted teaching strategies for teachers, thus improving teaching quality [10–14]. BP neural network can realize personalized recommendation of learning content and self-adaptive learning, so that users can learn according to their own needs and interests, and improve user experience.

3 Overall Architecture Design of Japanese MOOC System

System development refers to the steps of implementing a software project in a certain order. To implement a software project, it is necessary to implement steps such as requirements analysis, analysis and design, system coding, and software testing. Through requirements analysis, it is possible to understand the resources required by the project, the functions to be implemented, and related issues that need to be noted during the process of program codingAs an important retrieval system, it can judge the relationship between data, the idol of data and the comprehensiveness of data, complete the multi-index and content of data, and better optimize the data., question bank, test paper management, system course management, system user management, system settings, and so on. In addition, the system is also required to have characteristics such as non error prone, strong compatibility, stored data with a certain degree of confidentiality, easy expansion of the system in the later stage, convenient migration to other platforms, and easy modification of software.

The detailed procedure of BP neural network algorithm in Japanese MOOC system is as follows,Cleaning, integrating and standardizing the data of students' learning behavior, so as to prepare for the follow-up model training, including the input values ha (j), han (j), ya (j), and ya (j) in the hidden layer, as shown in Eqs. (3) through (5).

$$h_{ih}(j) = \sum_{i=1}^{n} W_{i_i}x_i(j)b_i, h = 1, 2, \cdots, p \tag{3}$$

$$h_{\alpha h}(j) = f(h_\alpha(j)), h = 1, 2, \cdots, p \tag{4}$$

$$y_a(j) = \sum_{k=1}^{p} W_{ba}h_{ab}(j), o = 1, 2, \cdots, p \tag{5}$$

This system uses SSH as the basic framework, and is divided into a user layer, a Web service layer, and a database server, as shown in Fig. 3.

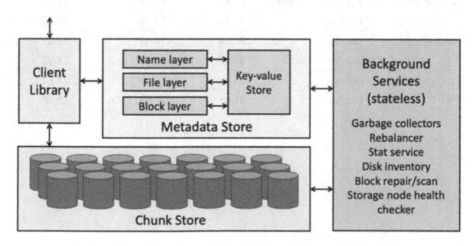

Fig. 3. Schematic diagram of Japanese MOOC system structure

In this article, by using cutting-edge open source development technologies such as LAMP, we have designed and developed a MOOC oriented, B/S structured course assisted learning system. Any user can become a student by registering. After logging into the system, students can maintain personal information, retrieve passwords when they forget them, query and browse courses, conduct course learning and discussion, participate in online exams, and set system attributes.

The user layer mainly includes three aspects of the operating functions of the user application system: students, teachers, and administrators. However, different users have different permissions. The advantage of this design is that it can make the system more secure. The website is also divided into many modules, each of which has different functions, such as finding vocabulary learning modules, testing modules, and student homework modules in the module navigation. In the process of analysis and comprehensive utilization of language retrieval system, it is necessary to analyze the key contents and key indicators in the system, and make use of the database data resources.

4   Key Indicators and Analysis that are Increasingly Extended into the System

4.1   Japanese Language Teaching System

According to the needs of practical problems, choose the appropriate BP neural network structure, such as multilayer perceptron, convolution neural network and so onThis is shown in Table 1.

Table 1. Overall characteristics.

Android data	range	Number of indicators	Horizontal and vertical	Welfare
Make a database	Range of operation	19.47	37.89	18.42
	Cooking	21.58	23.68	16.32
School system	exterior	26.84	19.47	19.47
	interior	31.05	23.00	28.95
According to the search client	exterior	23.68	25.79	18.42
	interior	31.05	22.63	25.26

Statistical analysis of the data in statistics to verify whether it is effective. The specific results are as follows (Table 2).

Table 2. Statistical analysis results of African data.

Data source number	degree of freedom	SD	Mean	F	P-value
1	16.32	18.95	16.34	15.39	24.74
3	25.79	12.62	11.28	17.19	18.15
5	21.58	8.42	21.15	12.23	9.37
error	27.37	12.63	13.38	16.34	16.24

Judging from the analysis results of the whole data, it will be found that the variance, integrity and mean of the whole data meet the requirements, and the distribution standard value of the data also meets the actual situation, so the whole distribution result is normal and meets the final budget requirements.

4.2 The Final Optimization Result of This System

Compile the final optimization results of the system to judge, and realize the comprehensive selection of data results and the classification and analysis of data. By the back propagation algorithm, so that the model gradually fits the data as shown in Table 3.

Table 3. Tracing summary of the whole data analysis.

The rate of change of daily results	TData retrieval level	FThe error rate that eventually exists
25%	5.26	15.79
50%	11.58	9.47
70%	14.74	8.42
mean	7.37	21.05
X2	12.63	11.58
P = 0.042		

4.3 Stability and Accuracy of Japanese Escaping

The training model is evaluated by using test data set, and the prediction performance are analyzed is shown in Fig. 4.

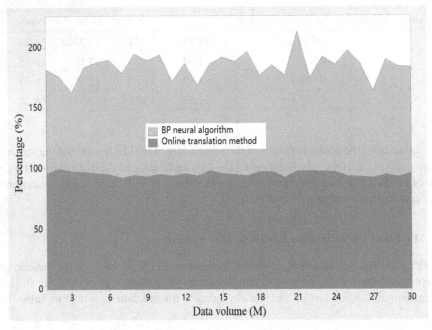

Fig. 4. Volatility of data change in the whole data change process.

Network has the nature of weighted special effects, so it also has certain influence on the whole monitoring system. of MOOC system, such as personalized recommendation, automatic scoring and so on is shown in Table 4.

Table 4. Comparison of indexes in the system.

Analysis of indicators	Optimize stability	According to the target achievement rate	error
If you can put forward it, you can only forget it	91.68	93.63	3.26
Forget the one before the phone call	82.84	82.14	27.89
P	3.25	0.36	0.37

Because the learning data in MOOC system come from a wide range of sources, the types are complex, and the quality of the data is uneven, the training and application of BP neural network are very important, APP neural network analyzes the normality of the final result, analyzes and judges the fluctuation of the result, and the specific result is shown in Fig. 5.

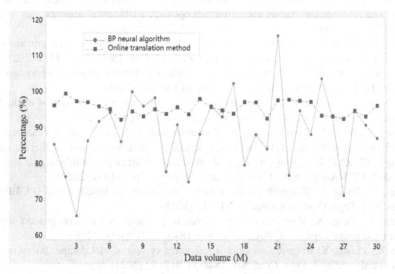

Fig. 5. BP neural algorithm evaluation results

From my whole analysis process, we can find that the data still has strong advantages in fluctuation and leveling force, so the original production method is more in line with the requirements.In the whole process of calculation and data, the integrity is good, which meets the actual requirements and judgments.

5 Conclusion

BP neural network, influence and significance in the development of MOOC system. Through the application of BP neural network, we can realize intelligent analysis and personalized recommendation of learning behavior, and improve teaching quality and user experience. However, in practical application, BP neural network is also faced with challenges in data quality, data security, computing resources and model generalization ability. Therefore, future research should focus on how to solve these difficulties, in order to promote BP neural network in MOOC system development more widely.

References

1. Zhao, X.: Implementation of English ICAI MOOC system based on BP neural network. J. Ambient Intell. Humaniz. Comput. **2021**(1)

2. Xu, Q., Kong, W.: Research on forecast model based on BP neural network algorithm. J. Phys. Conf. Ser. **1982**(1), 012065 (2021)
3. Wang, Y.: Research on E-commerce Big Data Classification and Mining Algorithm Based on BP Neural Network Technology (2021)
4. Xu, X., Peng, L., Ji, Z., et al.: Research on substation project cost prediction based on sparrow search algorithm optimized BP neural network. Sustainability **13** (2021)
5. He, J., Liu, N., Han, M., et al.: Research on danjiang water quality prediction based on improved artificial bee colony algorithm and optimized BP neural network. Sci. Program. **2021**(Pt.14) (2021)
6. Hong, B., Zhang, Y.: Research on the influence of attention and emotion of tea drinkers based on artificial neural network. Math. Biosci. Eng.Biosci. Eng. **18**(4), 3423–3434 (2021)
7. Zhao, S.: Optimization of Human Motion Recognition Information Processing System Based on GA-BP Neural Network Algorithm. Hindawi Limited (2021)
8. Xu, X.H., Ye, L., Pei, Y., et al. : Research on the comprehensive evaluation of the higher education system based on FCE and ARMA models. Complexity (2022)
9. Guerrero Criado, E., Ferriz Valero, A., Baenamorales, S.: Influence of physical activity on cognitive and emotional development in preschool children. A review of the literature (2023)
10. Honglu, C., Zhaoai, Y., Bingyan, Z., et al.: Research on atmospheric lidar signal simulation based on HITRAN database. Chin. J. Space Sci. **40**(6), 1046–1051 (2022)
11. Chen, L., Wang, Y.: Research on the material fire risk index based on the GA-BP neural network. J. Phys. Conf. Ser. **1865**(4), 042125 (2021)
12. Zhang, L., Zeng, X.: Research on transformer fault diagnosis based on genetic algorithm optimized neural network. J. Phys. Conf. Ser. **1848**(1), 012004 (2021)
13. Gan, Y., Zhong, Y.: Research on automatic control system of MR damper based on neural network algorithm. J. Phys. Conf. Ser. **1848**(1), 012152 (2021). (6pp)
14. Dai, N.: Research on evaluation and management mechanism of education management system based on clustering algorithm. In: Hung, J.C., Yen, N.Y., Chang, J.W. (eds.) Frontier Computing. FC 2021. LNEE, vol. 827, pp. 1665–1670. Springer, Singapore (2022). https://doi.org/10.1007/978-981-16-8052-6_245
15. Chen, H.: Research on innovation and entrepreneurship based on artificial intelligence system and neural network algorithm. J. Intell. Fuzzy Syst. **40**(2), 2517–2528 (2021)

Construction and Evaluation of College Students' Psychological Education Evaluation Model Based on Joint Neural Network

Xia Li[✉] and Li Qingfeng

Wuhan University of Communication, Wuhan 430065, China
lixia98733@126.com

Abstract. The construction and evaluation of a college student psychological education evaluation model based on joint neural networks can provide personalized evaluations by analyzing the psychological characteristics and mental health status of different students. This study describes the construction of educational evaluation. This method combines two methods: one is to use the single-layer method to calculate the score of psychological education evaluation; Another approach is to use a multi-level psychological education scoring method. In addition, we also tested whether our method can serve as a substitute for other existing models in psychology. The construction of the model is as follows: Firstly, input data is selected from various psychological tests and other related factors. Then, use a neural network to obtain the output data to obtain the output value. Finally, the evaluation results were calculated based on this method. The evaluation model of college students' psychological education based on the combined neural network combines Natural language processing technology to analyze and study the questionnaire survey of students, and uses neural network technology to train and optimize, so as to achieve accurate evaluation of college students' psychological state. This evaluation model can provide more comprehensive, personalized, and targeted psychological education services for college students, helping them better identify and solve psychological problems, and improving their mental health level.

Keyword: Joint neural network · College Students' psychological education · Evaluation model

1 Introduction

After leaving the care of their parents, newly enrolled college students need to change from dependent life and learning style to relatively independent learning and life style. We need to have necessary interpersonal communication and face the pressure of study and life alone, as well as the pressure of employment. Under these pressures, the way of thinking and behavior of college students has been affected, resulting in some improper behaviors. If the psychological endurance is not strong, it will lead to immaturity, emotional instability, weak self-regulation and self-control, which will lead to different types

Y. Zhang and N. Shah (Eds.): BigIoT-EDU 2023, LNICST 582, pp. 163–174, 2024.
https://doi.org/10.1007/978-3-031-63136-8_17

of mental disorders [1]. The society and family have high expectations for college students. College students have strong self-development ability, but their self-orientation is relatively unstable, and their thoughts are still immature and stable. With the rapid development of modern society, college students will face different types and aspects of pressure, and the challenge of male health is more serious, which has led to a series of psychological abnormalities and other related problems, which the relevant education departments attach great importance to, intelligence and self-esteem. They have higher ideals and pursuits than ordinary people. Therefore, they will face more opportunities and challenges, so they will face greater pressure [2].

As an effective method scientific and effective operating mechanism and evaluation system are the expansion of the management theory of teachers, the improvement of the evaluation system of classroom teaching, and the improvement of the quality and universities. Its functions are as follows:

(1) Diagnostic function. As an important means to measure teachers' teaching quality, classroom teaching quality evaluation can check whether teachers' teaching process is carried out in an orderly manner according to teaching laws and principles by comparing the difference between the actual quality of teachers' teaching and the degree of the need to achieve the goal. In the case of too large a gap, it can also make effective judgments, and summarize lessons and experience.
(2) Feedback function. The teaching process is a "instructing and dispelling doubts".
(3) Incentive function. The evaluation have strong persuasive ability. Through the feedback of teaching information and the horizontal comparison between teachers, the enthusiasm of teachers for teaching work can be stimulated, and the vitality and motivation can be constantly obtained in the competition, which can play an incentive role for teachers [3].
(4) Management functions. The of teaching through and impartial comprehensive evaluation and appraisal of teachers' teaching work. The results can reflect the teaching quality and level of teachers more truly, so that the teaching management department can make a correct judgment on the promotion and evaluation of teachers based on the results [4]. The continuous the development of teaching work to standardization, institutionalization and scientization.
(5) Supervision function. The impartiality evaluation the normal progress provide sufficient basis for judging the correctness and rationality of the teaching work arrangement.

2 Related Work

2.1 Research Status of College Students' Mental Health

As an important turning point in life, college students face many changes and challenges in their physical and mental development, making mental health issues one of the hot topics of concern for college students. In terms of current research on the mental health of college students, domestic and foreign scholars have focused on areas such as anxiety, depression, stress, self-esteem, and self-efficacy.

In China, research on the mental health status of college students mainly focuses on the following aspects: the current situation of college students' mental health problems, factors affecting mental health problems, and analyzing mental health problems from a policy perspective [5]. For example, relevant domestic research has shown that there are obvious problems with the mental health status of college students, with many of them experiencing anxiety and depression, which are more prominent among female students. At the same time, factors such as physical health, learning pressure, interpersonal relationships, and financial burden can also affect students' mental health. Therefore, choosing appropriate solutions can effectively help students maintain their mental health.

In foreign countries, research focuses mainly on the current situation and influencing factors of mental health problems among college students. For example, relevant studies in the United States have shown a significant downward trend in the mental health of college students during their time in school, with stress and anxiety being the main issues [6]. Research has also shown that factors such as social support, personal resources, gender, and cultural background are closely related to mental health issues. In addition, some foreign studies also believe that mental health status is closely related to college students' academic achievements, and efficient learning methods can also help reduce students' psychological burden.

There are also many research results on the factors related to the students. Zhu Rongchun and others found that shame plays an intermediary role in college students' psychological problems, which reduces self-efficacy and self-esteem. In turn, the reduction of high self-esteem and self-efficacy may have an impact on College Students' mental health. A Huiming also confirmed the view that shame plays an intermediary role in college students' psychological problems through research, and also found that there is an interactive relationship between level and their self-confidence level [7]. Fan-fukun et al. Found through investigation and research that college students' self-concept is positively correlated with their mental health, that is, positive self-concept role in improving college students' mental health. Li Hong et al. Also studied the Students' stress and health, and divided college students' stress into internal personal pressure and external academic pressure. The research results show that stress and mental health are negatively correlated [8].

There are also many researches on psychological counseling, especially the counseling model. Most people believe that family education and school training should be combined to form a common psychological counseling mechanism. As the beginning of students' growth, the native family is very important to the formation of students' personal character. Therefore, it is also necessary to contact and communicate with the parents of college students in time, popularize the relevant knowledge of improving mental health to them, and enrich the parents' understanding of the importance of mental health. Schools, on the other hand, comprehensively the combination of curriculum education and after-school counseling, the implementation of group counseling and targeted individual counseling.

2.2 Psychological Problems of College Students

College students have a common living environment and similar learning and job-hunting pressure. They have common characteristics in psychological characteristics, and college students' psychological problems also have their characteristic performance. The investigation of Duan Tao and Zheng Kui shows that the psychological problems of college students are characterized by poor adaptability, excessive attachment, psychological loneliness and anxiety in interpersonal communication, and family poverty causes inferiority, loneliness, emotional anxiety and inferiority. He Rui, Liu Han and others proposed that the psychological characteristics of contemporary college students are the disharmony between the development of cognitive ability and the enhancement of self-concept; The development of sexual consciousness and the lack of communication skills between the opposite sex; The contradiction between the lack of personal practical ability and the urgent social needs. Shanghongjuan's survey shows that college students' emotional disorders mainly include inferiority complex, anxiety, depression, anger and other emotions [9]. Yuan Lingling proposed that the psychological confusion of college students is mainly due to the obstacles caused by their own personality characteristics, cognitive deviation, sexual consciousness confusion, the confusion caused by the impact of multiple cultures, the pressure of employment, and the confusion and pressure from the process of learning and life [10]. At present, the post-90s youth are about to become the main force of college students. As they grow up in the transitional period of society, they receive more extensive information. The survey shows that the status of post-90s is higher than that of our national norm. The post-90s college students' living environment is different from that of any previous generation, so they must have their own characteristics. Zhang Baojun summarized the psychological characteristics of post-90s college students: they showed high autonomy in behavior, longed for independence but were highly dependent, and had poor anti frustration ability; Strong emotion, explicit and publicized, but not deep enough, with the characteristics of emotional mood and poor concealment; They have avant-garde thinking, advanced ideas, "sophisticated and smooth", and have their own unique views on things. When they discuss problems, they have deep views, strict logic, and are good at expressing; Good and evil are distinct, but evil are indiscriminate.

The psychological problems of college students are mainly manifested in the following aspects:

(1) Learning pressure: College students face various academic and life pressures, such as exams, papers, assignments, internships, employment, etc. Failure to achieve satisfactory results in learning will cause Psychological stress and anxiety.

(2) Emotional issues: College students' interpersonal relationships become more complex and their social difficulties increase. Some young people find it difficult to be satisfied with emotional issues, such as a lack of intimate relationships.

(3) Self growth problem: During a critical period of physical and mental development, students need to understand themselves through a large amount of facts and experiences. However, at certain times, students may feel overly sensitive or insecure, unable to master healthy self-assessment methods.

(4) Anxiety and depression: Turbulent emotions are more likely to concentrate on negative emotions. Anxiety or depression may engulf a person's life and make it difficult for them to participate in social activities or enjoy their usual interests.

In response to the above issues, there are many psychological assistance programs provided by mental health service institutions and schools, such as psychological counseling, psychological intervention, psychological counseling, etc., aimed at helping students solve psychological problems, improve their mental health level, and enhance their ability to resist negative emotions. At the same time, college students are also encouraged to actively participate in extracurricular activities such as sports, music, and painting to alleviate the impact of busy academic life on mental health.

3 Psychological Education Evaluation of College Students

3.1 Purpose of Health Assessment

The main work of health assessment is to establish a health assessment model, use health information to evaluate individual health status, analyze health risk factors and future health trends. Through scientific evaluation, it a certain for the scientific implementation of health.

Health assessment can predict high-risk patients and screen out people who need treatment and attention. Every kind of biological information related to health is called biomedical indicators, including height, blood glucose and cholesterol levels, lifestyle, attitude to physical exercise and other information. At present, the medical community has found that what is needed to maintain health is to prevent diseases, not to treat diseases. First of all, health assessment is to assess the health status, and indicate the possibility of disease through the detection of physiological indicators. The second is health risk assessment. Through health risk assessment, the collected data will be transformed into health information, health risk factors will be clarified, unhealthy lifestyles will be corrected, and health management groups will be uniformly classified, so as to implement personalized health education and health guidance.

(1) The openness of the network and the equality of identity and status in cyberspace
   With its rich information resources, the network has shown a new world to college students. Because of its rich content, large amount of information, complete functions, open awareness and other characteristics, it has stimulated people's interest in learning network knowledge and skills. The equality of identity and status in cyberspace has promoted the development of individual personality. Individuals can find fields suitable for their own development according to their interests and hobbies, and display their personality and self in a relatively loose environment. This open space has also promoted the development of their abilities, including the ability to deal with problems, hands-on ability, and exploratory learning ability.

(2) Beyond the limits of space and the infinite expansion of interpersonal relationships
   The network has transcended the boundaries of space and greatly expanded individual interpersonal relationships. The communication between people is no longer restricted by geographical location, and the ideal of "global village" has been truly realized. The Internet has increased the channels for people to communicate with each other. People can open their hearts online, vent their bad feelings and reveal their secrets. However, in the network interpersonal communication, the communication

between people turns into human-machine-human communication. What individuals face is the computer, which is cold and has no emotion. There is no face-to-face communication. In the relatively closed environment of the network, the opportunities of direct contact with classmates, friends and society are reduced, which is easy to cause self-closure and interpersonal communication obstacles; Moreover, there is a widespread trust crisis in online interpersonal communication, which will also affect people's suspicion of sincerity, and then affect the establishment of good interpersonal relationships with others in real life.

(3) Transformation and dreamy state

Sitting quietly in front of the computer and staring at the computer screen, people's consciousness has entered a changeable state. In the virtual multimedia world, people can have their own skills, communicate through ESP (supersensory perception) thousands of miles, and instinctively produce a purpose out of nothing, and sensory experience will become surreal. This virtual state of consciousness is similar to dreams. In cyberspace, it is this changeable and dreamlike state of consciousness that has led to many people's extreme obsession with the Internet, and in serious cases, Internet addiction, manifested as:. When online, people are extremely excited and get a great sense of satisfaction from online behavior, while when offline, they are depressed, have no interest in anything, slow thinking, biological clock disorder, etc.

3.2 Concept of Health Assessment

College students' mental health assessment refers to the evaluation and analysis of their mental health status from multiple perspectives, dimensions, qualitative and quantitative perspectives. By collecting data such as self-report, behavioral observation, and psychological testing, students' mental health status is evaluated and monitored, and corresponding intervention and support measures are taken to help students better adjust their mental state and improve their quality of study and life.

The concept of mental health assessment for college students has the following four main elements:

Firstly, it assesses students' psychological state from multiple perspectives and dimensions. Psychological state is a dynamic concept closely related to factors such as students' life experience, environment, and ideology, and various factors need to be comprehensively considered during evaluation. Conventional evaluation methods include interviews, self filling out scales, behavioral observation, and psychological testing.

Secondly, it is a combination of qualitative and quantitative evaluation. The psychological health assessment of college students can qualitatively describe their psychological state, and can also accurately measure their emotional, cognitive, behavioral and other psychological health indicators through quantitative tools such as scales, in order to better grasp their psychological health status.

Thirdly, evaluation requires comprehensive, meticulous, and objective data collection and analysis. Evaluation includes collecting data from various aspects such as student self-report, behavioral observation, and psychological testing. It requires detailed analysis of the data, mining the information behind the data, identifying valuable and helpful information for intervention, and establishing an objective evaluation system and indicators.

Fourthly, the purpose of attributes presents concern and support for the mental health of college students. The ultimate goal of college students' mental health assessment is to protect and improve their mental health level. Targeted intervention and support measures should be launched as soon as possible based on their different psychological states, to help students adjust their states, enhance their psychological abilities, and improve their mental health level.

The role of psychological health assessment for college students:

Firstly, psychological assessment can help college students detect and respond to psychological problems as soon as possible. The evaluation results can clearly display the psychological status and existing problems of college students, timely identify various psychological problems, including anxiety, depression, stress, etc., help college students respond early, help them overcome negative emotions, better adjust their state, independently solve problems, and act on their own.

Secondly, the mental health assessment of university campuses is conducted for groups, which can help schools understand students' mental health, provide data support for students' mental health, generate valuable information, and provide a basis for school mental health education and intervention.

Thirdly, psychological assessment is targeted and can provide specific interventions for different types of students. Psychological assessment can provide different solutions and coping strategies based on students' different psychological conditions. Therefore, when conducting assessments, different types of students are classified to achieve personalized interventions.

Health assessment is to make appropriate health status assessment, health risk assessment or health follow-up assessment for individuals or groups, and make correct judgments on the health status of individuals or groups. Health assessment includes the evaluation of health through physical or laboratory examination results, as well as the interaction between mental state, social environment, living environment and health. The object of health assessment is groups or individuals. The purpose is to correctly evaluate health by selecting appropriate elements and methods. Health assessment is an important part of health management, and health management is a continuous and dynamic system engineering. Its management object includes not only individuals, but also groups. Therefore, in addition to individuals and families, the object of health assessment should also include larger groups, such as communities, troops, schools, etc. Whether it is for groups or individuals, the purpose of health assessment is to help health management objects understand their own health status, recognize the risk factors affecting health, and provide basis for health promotion means through scientific evaluation [9].

Some people define the concept of health assessment as: "carry out systematic, comprehensive and continuous scientific analysis and qualitative and quantitative evaluation of the health status of individuals or groups and the risk of future illness or death, and predict their current situation and development trend. The focus of health assessment in this paper is the analysis and ordinary soldiers.

4   Evaluation Model of College Students' Psychological Education Based on Joint Neural Network

4.1   Joint Neural Network

(1) Machine learning

Machine learning (ML) is a subject that mainly studies algorithms and statistical models. Computers do not need specific instructions, and can carry out relevant patterns and reasoning through ML methods, etc., so as to have the learning ability similar to human beings. As shown in Fig. 1, the structure diagram of machine learning in structural health monitoring system (SHMS) is shown. The monitoring data obtained by the sensor is used as the machine learning training data sample. The learning model (such as association, clustering, prediction, regression algorithm, etc.) extracts the sample, and finally uses the constructed learning model to identify the monitoring data to be measured, The result of recognition to the learning model to adjust the and improve the structure of the network.

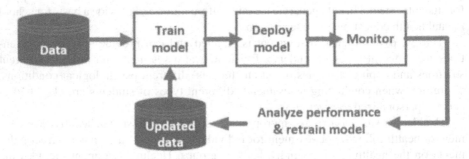

Fig. 1. Machine learning model

Each index of the evaluation is graded, and the theory and method of fuzzy mathematics are adopted. The main operation methods are:

(1) Acquisition of fuzzy evaluation matrix: first make a binary judgment, that is, analyze the grade of each factor of the evaluated object, and then give a conclusion of belonging to or not belonging to a judge, and form the result with a Boolean matrix. Secondly, the obtained Boolean matrices are accumulated to form a degree matrix F. Then the number of judges is used to remove the degree matrix F, and the fuzzy evaluation matrix R expressed by membership degree is obtained:

$$R = \frac{F}{K} \tag{1}$$

(2) Fuzzy comprehensive evaluation: use B to represent the product of the weight of each factor and the fuzzy evaluation matrix R. In this way, the membership of the same grade in the fuzzy comprehensive evaluation forms a value.

$$B = WR = [b_1, b_2, \cdots, b_\pi] \tag{2}$$

where B is the comprehensive judgment matrix, W is the weight of m factors, b'', b. Respectively indicate the subordinate degree of the evaluated attribute to each grade.

(3) Degree analysis: increase the degree belonging to this grade to 1, and reduce the degree not belonging to this grade to 0. It is membership when the evaluated object is rated as a certain level.

In the process of performance evaluation, the fuzzy evaluation method transforms the previously quantifiable qualitative index evaluation into quantitative evaluation through the theory of fuzzy mathematics, builds a bridge between qualitative and quantitative evaluation, solves the problem that qualitative and quantitative evaluation can not be well combined in other methods, overcomes the shortcomings of single and subjective evaluation process, and improves the evaluation method in terms of comprehensiveness, rationality and scientificity, It has solved the difficulty of comparing qualitative indicators in the evaluation process.

(4) Convolutional neural network

In 1962, Hubel put forward the concept of receptive field, of convolutional neural network. In 1989, Lecun first applied convolutional neural network to handwritten font recognition and designed a classic convolutional neural network model. CNN adopts the method of local connection and weight sharing. Due to the low complexity of connectivity and scale, it reduces the number of training parameters and the ability of over fitting the model, so it has better generalization ability for the input data, and avoids the shortcomings and long time consumption. As CNN network is composed of output layer, output layer and so on. First, input the original data to CNN neural network, then extract the features through the alternating action, and use the layer to classify the pooling output feature map. As shown in Fig. 2, the basic structure of network.

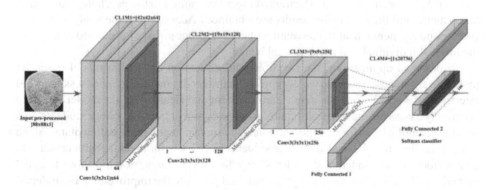

Fig. 2. Convolutional neural network model

4.2 Psychological Education Evaluation Model Based on Joint Neural Network

The psychological education evaluation model based on joint neural network is a new psychological Health assessment evaluation method based on deep learning technology.

This method combines deep learning technology with psychological analysis, and establishes a joint neural network model by training a large amount of psychological data to simulate and predict individual psychological conditions, providing scientific evaluation and analysis methods for mental health education.

The main feature of this model is that it integrates information from multiple data sources, including a large amount of data on learning outcomes, university campus services, social support networks, and subjective feelings. It evaluates and monitors the psychological health status of college students from multiple perspectives, dimensions, qualitative and quantitative perspectives, as shown in Fig. 3.

The implementation process of this model is mainly divided into the following steps:

The first step is to collect data. Establish a unified data warehouse through large-scale data collection, including psychological scales, academic exams, life logs, psychological problem feedback, social networks, and rehabilitation treatment. These data can directly or indirectly reflect the psychological health status of college students, including emotional status, withdrawal habits, psychological torture, psychological recovery status, personal reflection, personal growth, and other aspects of data.

The second step is data preprocessing. The collected data are preprocessed, including Data cleansing, feature extraction, data preprocessing and standardization, to ensure the accuracy and reliability of the data, and the model is established based on interpretability.

The third step is to establish a model. Under the condition of considering multi-dimensional data, establish a joint neural network model, including multi-layer neural networks and self coding neural networks, to integrate various data sources and predict and estimate the mental health status of college students.

Step 4, model training. By training the model, the topology structure, learning speed, and initial weights of the model are determined, and the accuracy and reliability of the model are ensured to improve the credibility and accuracy of the evaluation results.

Step 5: Model application. The trained model is applied to the psychological Health assessment, and the evaluation results are obtained. According to the analysis results, corresponding mental health intervention plans and programs are formulated to improve the level of individual and social mental health.

In practical applications, the psychological education evaluation model based on joint neural networks has been widely applied in university mental health assessment and intervention work. Through in-depth learning of mental Health data, the model can more accurately assess the mental health status and development trend of college students, and provide scientific basis for students' personalized mental health intervention plans. At the same time, this model can also provide valuable data basis for mental health education, help schools better understand students' psychological status, develop more targeted mental health education plans and programs, and promote the improvement of students' comprehensive quality. Major universities and psychological institutions are actively exploring and promoting the application of this model to achieve more effective mental health education and intervention.

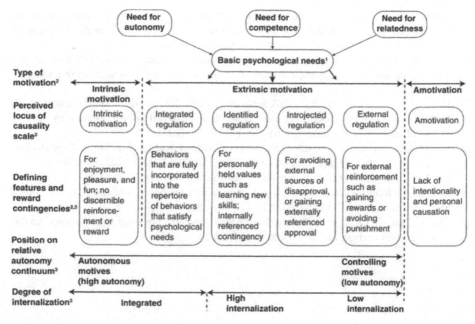

Fig. 3. Psychological Education Evaluation Model

5 Conclusion

In this paper, the joint neural network technology is applied to college students' psychological evaluation modeling, and a college students' mental health evaluation model based on neural network is proposed. Convolution neural network and machine learning are used to establish mathematical models for the mental health of students in our school and evaluate the state of mental health. By analyzing and comparing the evaluation results of joint neural network modeling with those of BP neural network modeling, it is concluded that the mental health state modeling based on joint neural network has better accuracy and adaptability, less error and better fitting of the modeling results, and its modeling results are significantly better than BP neural network.

References

1. Yao, H., Malek, M.: Evaluation of the effect of ideological and political education on psychological crisis intervention for university students based on data mining algorithm. J. Math. **2021** (2021)
2. Yz, A., Hz, B.: Research on the quality evaluation of innovation and entrepreneurship education of college students based on extenics. Procedia Comput. Sci. **199**, 605–612 (2022)
3. Liu, Z., Zhao, Y., Fang, G., et al.: Evaluation and empirical analysis of the influence of disciplinary competition on innovation practice ability. J. Phys. Conf. Ser. **1941**(1), 012040 (2021). (10pp)
4. Liu, L.: Exploration of integrating scientist spirit into college students' ideal and belief construction - based on a questionnaire survey of a normal college in hunan. J. High. Educ. Res. **3**(1), 34–38 (2022)

5. Liu, C., Hu, Y.: Research on the application of the psychological assistance program for college staff: a case study on the psychological health service experience day program for faculty and staff of Jinan University. Open J. Soc. Sci. **10**(4), 12 (2022)

6. Bhatt, R., Jurel, S.K., Chand, P., et al.: Functional and psychological evaluation of premenopausal and postmenopausal women after provision of a complete denture prosthesis. J. Prosthet. Dent. (2021)

7. Doyle, E.K., Sommerville, P.J., Walkden-Brown, S.W.: Development, implementation and evaluation of a hub and spoke multi-institutional national model to tertiary education in sheep and wool science. Anim. Prod. Sci. **61**(16), 1734–1743 (2021)

8. Shi, Q.: Construction of core ideas of ideological and political education for college students based on modern open and distance education. In: CIPAE 2021: 2021 2nd International Conference on Computers, Information Processing and Advanced Education (2021)

9. Han, P.: Multidimensional state data reduction and evaluation of college students' mental health based on SVM. J. Math. **2022** (2021)

10. Qiu, Y., Zhu, X., Li, Z., et al.: Research on the path and effect evaluation of students' quality improvement in private colleges. Complexity (2021)

Human Action Recognition Based on LSTM Neural Network Algorithm

Niqin Jing[⊠]

Department of Computer Technology, Beijing Polytechnic, Beijing 100176, China
jingniqin@bpi.edu.cn

Abstract. As a special recursive neural network, LSTM can avoid the dependency problem of RNN long-term memory to a certain extent. Although the data flow control mechanism is similar, its internal operational logic varies greatly. This makes the LSTM neural network algorithm more conducive to the in-depth study of human motion recognition. In this case, this paper discusses human motion recognition based on LSTM neural network algorithm. Two human motion recognition models based on LSTM neural network and Bi-LSTM neural network with attention mechanism and Dropout are constructed. First, the LSTM neural network is used to identify and classify human actions. Then, the Bi-LSTM neural network is used and attention mechanism and Dropout are introduced to compensate for the shortcomings of the LSTM neural network in human action recognition. The Bi-LSTM neural network can extract more comprehensive information, attention mechanism is used to increase attention to main information, and Dropout is used to prevent overfitting of the neural network. Then compare the two motion recognition models. Orthogonal experiments were used to optimize several main parameters in the neural network, and a high recognition rate was achieved.

Keyword: Long-term and short-term memory model · Neural network algorithm · Human action recognition

1 Introduction

Human behavior is variable and complex, with a flexibility and diversity that no machinery can achieve. Technologies for human behavior analysis and recognition are emerging research directions in the field of artificial intelligence and pattern recognition. In many fields such as medical rehabilitation engineering, somatic games, film and television, virtual reality, professional motion analysis, etc., the technology of human behavior analysis and recognition is widely used and generates great value. Analyzing and recognizing human behavioral actions is a complex project that can create a new way of interaction through gestures [1], hand gestures and other actions to achieve seamless communication and free interaction between human and environment, human and human. The LSTM neural network algorithm has advantages that other human action recognition methods do not have and can provide a reliable solution for the direction of human behavior recognition [2].

© ICST Institute for Computer Sciences, Social Informatics and Telecommunications Engineering 2024
Published by Springer Nature Switzerland AG 2024. All Rights Reserved
Y. Zhang and N. Shah (Eds.): BigIoT-EDU 2023, LNICST 582, pp. 175–185, 2024.
https://doi.org/10.1007/978-3-031-63136-8_18

Human-computer interaction is an important prerequisite for achieving human-computer collaborative manufacturing. Intelligent robots need to recognize human behavior and make judgments to make accurate responses. In traditional manual assembly operations, the efficiency is low, and it is difficult to ensure the assembly accuracy of various parts. Long and repetitive actions can easily lead to fatigue among workers, leading to assembly errors [3]. However, for the use of robots, although assembly efficiency and accuracy are guaranteed, they cannot be assembled for complex parts and complex working conditions, which lacks flexibility compared to manual work. Human-machine collaboration can give full play to the respective advantages of personnel and machines, making the greatest possible use of advantages such as accuracy, efficiency, and adaptability in mechanical manufacturing. In human-machine collaborative assembly, intelligent robots first need to read human behavior data, then need to process the data, and then analyze the data through classification algorithms to judge human behavior. For example, what position the worker is in, what action is being performed, and the possible next action state, and finally respond to complete the collaboration with the worker in the mechanical assembly action. In the entire process, the key is human motion recognition. How to efficiently and accurately recognize human motion is currently a hot topic for scientists around the world [4].

At present, human motion recognition is widely used in various fields of society, in addition to human-computer interaction, it is also widely used in intelligent security, smart home, intelligent medical and other fields. In the field of intelligent security, for the application and processing of video, people often retrieve the video only after the event occurs, lacking real-time performance. Intelligent security systems change traditional passive recognition into active recognition. In the field of smart home, using human motion recognition technology can improve the current smart home, and the overall performance of smart home can be improved through multi information channel fusion [5]. In the field of intelligent medicine, it is possible to analyze human movements through the information already obtained, thereby obtaining the current situation faced by humans, providing technical possibilities for preventing the occurrence of emergencies.

2 Related Work

2.1 Feature Extraction Based on Skeleton Data

Using Kinect depth cameras, in addition to obtaining depth information, it is also possible to combine RGB images to obtain three-dimensional data of human joints. The Kinect depth camera can collect three-dimensional coordinate information of 20 bone joint points of the human body, which can be used to describe the posture of the human body. Using a feature description method based on bone points can not only effectively avoid visual angle changes, light, and scale issues, but also have a small amount of data and good robustness.

As early as 1975, Johnasson began to use bone joint point information for motion recognition. Since then, a large number of scientific researchers around the world have started research on the use of bone information for human motion recognition. Xia et al. used HOT3D (Histograms of 3D Joint Layouts) to represent motion gestures and converted them into spherical coordinates, obtaining excellent results on 3D motion datasets

[6]. Zanfir et al. proposed a velocity and acceleration descriptor based on skeleton joint points, mainly considering the posture and difference components of human joints over a short period of time. On the basis of existing bone representation methods, VemulapalliR et al. proposed a method for describing human limb motion using rotation and translation in three-dimensional space. The proposed bone representation form is a Lie group, which uses the curves in the Lie group to represent human actions, and is ultimately being classified [7]. Wang et al. have improved on the potential lack of information in skeleton information. They proposed an actionlet integration model to represent each type of action and capture intra class variance through occupancy information. In addition, it was found that the relative information between joint points in the skeleton is more representative than the original three-dimensional coordinate information [8].

Liang Yan proposed to use a combination of local joint point spatial information and global information to describe human motion characteristics. Firstly, the obtained joint 3D coordinate information was filtered to eliminate noise, and then recognized and classified after a dimensionality reduction operation. Experiments have shown that for 3D joint point histograms with a single global feature, the fusion of local feature information can effectively improve the recognition rate [9]. Devanne et al. fitted the data collected by the depth camera with the human skeleton model, mapping the motion recognition problem to a computational Riemannian manifold problem. Lv et al. first normalized the skeleton data to eliminate the impact of differences in height and body shape among different individuals. Using multiple important human joint points to form local features and selecting seven sub features to form fusion features for motion classification, ideal results have been achieved. Yao et al. proposed a spatiotemporal motion skeleton descriptor that can describe a complete spatiotemporal view of the human skeleton by integrating the three complementary features of relative geometric velocity, relative joint position, and joint angle between bone joint points [10]. Then interpolate and normalize the descriptors between frames, and finally use principal component analysis to extract the main information in the features to reduce data redundancy. Experiments show that this model can perform better than other bone models.

The quality of human motion recognition models based on skeleton information has a significant impact on recognition, and different models used for classification will yield different results. In general, an excellent action description model should have the following two characteristics: first, it should have strong discrimination and good robustness; Secondly, we should make full use of the temporal characteristics of human motion and use dynamic features to build models based on static models. Skeletal information has the advantages of being less affected by light and having a small amount of data, but it also has some problems and challenges. For example, differences in the height of different objects can lead to significant differences in joint point position data. Currently, two methods are used to solve this problem: feature normalization and adjusting joint point information based on height. Secondly, for some highly similar actions, using common single features is often difficult to recognize or has a low recognition rate [11]. Currently, some scholars have used a combination of depth map and bone information to solve this problem.

2.2 About Human Behavior Recognition

The research of human motion recognition is closely related to human motion analysis. Motion recognition can be performed at different levels of abstraction. So far, many types of classification have been proposed. In this article, we use the levels, primitive actions, actions, and activities proposed by Moeslund. The original motion is an indivisible motion at the limb level. Movement consists of primitive movements that describe periodic or full body movements. Finally, an activity consists of a set of action sequences, which are interpretations of a set of action sequences. For example, moving the left foot forward is the initial action, running is an action, and hurdles are an action consisting of "starting," "running," and "jumping.". In motion recognition, a common method is to extract image features from video and assign corresponding motion categories to these features. Classification algorithms are usually learned from training samples [12]. This paper discusses human motion recognition based on LSTM neural network algorithm.

In general, when the human body is moving, the changes of all joint points of the body with time should be smooth curves in space, and there should be no obvious sudden changes. However, during the acquisition process of raw data, it is inevitable to generate noise due to interference. If the noise is not processed, it is likely to have a negative impact on subsequent action recognition. In this paper, the mean filtering algorithm in image processing is used to smooth the original 3D bone data to eliminate abrupt points in the original data. The basic principle of the mean filtering algorithm is to first calculate the average value of the pixel values in its adjacent region, and then obtain the pixel values of the pixel points [13]. The window of the mean filtering algorithm is the pixel points in the adjacent region. The average filtering algorithm is used for bone data, and the selected window is a window related to time. For data at a certain time, the filtered value is the average value of the sum of the previous period of time and the subsequent period of time at that time. The calculation formula for the x dimension filtering process in the three dimensions of a point space of the original bone data is as follows:

$$P_{m,x} = \frac{1}{N} \sum_{z=m-\frac{N}{2}}^{m+\frac{N}{2}} P_{z,x} \tag{1}$$

For the m-th frame, the filtering process is the average value of the sum of the N/2 frames before the current frame and the N/2 frames after it. In this article, the time window size is selected as 5, and P represents the m-th frame in the x dimension of a certain joint point. After the original bone data is processed by mean filtering, the impact of mutation points can be basically eliminated.

Component limb angle θ The calculation formula for is as follows:

$$\theta_n = \arccos \frac{r_{i1} \times r_{j1} + r_{i2} \times r_{j2} + r_{i3} \times r_{j3}}{\sqrt{r_{i1}^2 + r_{i2}^2 + r_{i3}^2} + \sqrt{r_{j1}^2 + r_{j2}^2 + r_{j3}^2}} \tag{2}$$

Including 11 limb angles θ Represents, n = 1, 2 ..., 11, ri being the first limb vector, and rj being the second limb vector. In this way, based on the angle between the limbs, a complete movement of the human body can be expressed as:

$$A = \left[\theta_{n,1}; \theta_{n,2}; ...; \theta_{n,t} \right] \tag{3}$$

where t represents the frame sequence number in an action sequence.

The construction of joint kinetic energy features selects 13 joint points that contribute significantly to human motion information, namely, the joint points in the human skeleton model. According to the data of two adjacent frames in the motion sequence, the calculation formula for joint kinetic energy is as follows:

$$E_{i,t} = \frac{1}{2}m\left[\frac{(x_{i,j+k} - x_{i,j})^2 + (y_{i,j+k} - y_{i,j})^2 + (z_{i,j+k}, z_{i,j})^2}{k^2}\right] \qquad (4)$$

where E represents the kinetic energy between the two frames of the ith joint point at time t + k and time t, i =, "2... 13,. k is the time length between two frames, m is the coefficient in the kinetic energy calculation formula, which can be regarded as a constant, and (x, y, z) is the coordinate value of the joint point in three-dimensional space.". In this way, based on joint kinetic energy, a complete movement of the human body can be expressed as:

$$C = [E_{i,1}; E_{i,2}; ...; E_{i,t-1}] \qquad (5)$$

The establishment of dynamic features plays a very good role in describing the subtle features of human motion. The above joint kinetic energy and angular acceleration of the limb angle constitute the dynamic features of human motion.

After the above feature extraction, the extracted human motion features are fused, that is, static and dynamic features are spliced to obtain the fusion features of human motion [14]. Combining the data processing and feature construction process in this chapter, the fusion of features is shown in Fig. 1:

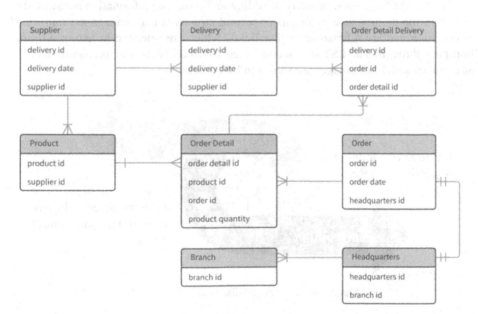

Fig. 1. Feature fusion process diagram

3   Human Action Recognition Based on LSTM Neural Network Algorithm

3.1   LSTM Neural Network Algorithm

LSTM is a temporal recursive neural network that is mainly used to solve long-term dependency problems in RNN (Recursive Neural Network). It is also a special recursive neural network and therefore has a chain structure, but its structure is different from the recursive module of recursive neural networks. It has four neural network layers that interact in a special way, rather than a simple neural network layer. The basic structure of the LSTM neural network is shown in Fig. 2 below.

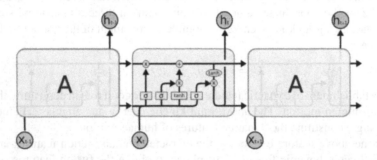

Fig. 2. Basic structure of LSTM neural network

The LSTM has a good property of adding and removing information transferred to and from the unitary state by means of several structures that manage the transfer of information and are referred to as thresholds, which are selective in letting information pass through. The LSTM is mainly used for classification or prediction and the advantages and disadvantages are shown in Fig. 3 below.

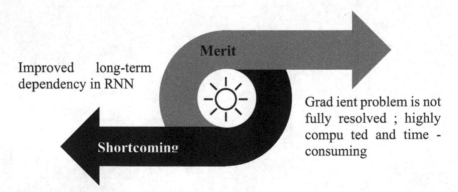

Merit

Improved long-term dependency in RNN

Grad ient problem is not fully resolved ; highly compu ted and time - consuming

Shortcoming

Fig. 3. Advantages and disadvantages of LSTM

The advantages of LSTM are that it improves the long-term dependency problem in RNN; LSTM usually performs better than temporal recurrent neural networks and

Hidden Markov Models (HMM); as a nonlinear model, LSTM can be used as a complex nonlinear unit for constructing larger deep neural networks.

The disadvantages are equally obvious: one disadvantage is that the gradient problem of RNNs is solved to some extent inside LSTMs and their variants, but it is still not enough. Another disadvantage is that each LSTM cell implies four fully connected layers (MLP), which can be computationally intensive and time-consuming if the LSTM has a large time horizon and the network is deep [15].

The human motion recognition based on LSTM neural network classifier is performed based on the constructed human motion fusion features. The constructed fusion feature consists of 11 limb angles, the relative distances of 8 important joint points, the joint kinetic energy of all 13 joint points in the human body model, and the angular acceleration of 11 limb angles. The four features are fused to form a 43 dimensional matrix. Because different action sequences have different frame counts during the acquisition process, the length of each action feature sequence formed after feature construction varies. Finally, the number of matrices formed by feature construction is the sum of the number of training and testing in the next human motion recognition network. LSTM neural networks are particularly suitable for dealing with long sequence problems, and they also correspond to the motion sequences in human motion characteristics. Next, a classifier based on LSTM network is built for human motion recognition, and finally, modifications are made based on LSTM to further optimize the network structure and improve the accuracy of human motion recognition.

This paper uses two dynamic features, joint kinetic energy and angular acceleration of limb angle, to construct a keyframe extraction model. By calculating the Euclidean distance between each joint data in the joint kinetic energy and the joint data in the previous frame, and assigning different weights based on the importance of different joints for motion discrimination, the weighted Euclidean distance of the kinetic energy can be obtained. The calculation formula is as follows:

$$S_{t_i} = \sqrt{\sum_{i=1}^{13} \eta_i (E_{i,t+1} - E_{i,t})^2} \tag{6}$$

Similarly, calculate the weighted Euclidean distance between the angular acceleration of the limb angle and the previous frame, using the following formula:

$$S_{t2} = \sqrt{\sum_{n=1}^{11} \eta_n (a_{n,t+1} - a_{n,t})^2} \tag{7}$$

The final human motion key frame extraction model combines and adds the above two parts to obtain:

$$S_t = \sqrt{\sum_{i=1}^{13} \eta_i (E_{i,t+1} - E_{i,I})^2} + \sqrt{\sum_{n=1}^{11} \eta_n (a_{n,t+1} - a_{n,I})^2} \tag{8}$$

where i represents all 13 joint points, and n represents all 11 included angles, η I and η N is the weight coefficient of the above two items, and different sizes are used depending on their importance. E represents the kinetic energy of the ith joint point at frame t, and an represents the acceleration value of the nth included angle at frame t.

3.2 Improved LSTM Modules

A cooperative LSTM module is designed, and in the new structure, the forgetting gate and the input gate replace the separated update method in the standard structure in a synchronous and complementary way for updating the cell state information, and the changed cell state information update method is shown in Eq. 9:

$$Ct = ft * Ct - 1 + (1 - ft) * C \sim t \tag{9}$$

The internal structure of the S-LSTM module is shown in Fig. 4.

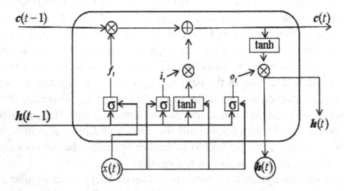

Fig. 4. LSTM cell structure diagram

When the final hidden layer state hT of the LSTM network model is input to the output layer of the model at time T, the final recognition probability of the action is calculated by the softmax function P = softmax (W · hT + b), and the action type is determined.

The network input is a fusion feature composed of four features. After previous feature extraction and processing, each human motion feature becomes a 43-dimensional data x, and the length of the data varies depending on the number of frames of each motion. Before inputting into the network, in order to facilitate processing, each group of data used for training or testing is uniformly processed with equal length, and the remaining sequences are zeroed based on the longest sequence in each group. In each time frame, the data input to the network is a 43 dimensional vector. Next, through the calculation of the LSTM layer, the intermediate value is sent to the output layer. The output layer uses the Softmax function, which judges the action and outputs the probability that belongs to each action tag. The highest corresponding probability value is the final output category of the network.

The main principle of the attention mechanism can be understood as that when humans observe a thing, they do not give the same attention to the entire picture of the thing. They often focus most of their attention on observing a certain part of the thing, which helps humans use limited attention to quickly obtain valuable information from massive resources. Due to the existence of attention, human processing of image information is very efficient and convenient. The attention mechanism is to assign different weights to different parts of things, making them play different roles in the final decision. This weight is generated through the learning process of the network and is constantly updated. In this article, attention mechanism is combined with Bi-LSTM neural network to identify human body movements. Compared with previous LSTM neural networks, attention mechanism added to neural networks can calculate the weight of feature vectors output in different time point networks. Through the size of these weights, important features in the entire human body movement sequence can be found, ultimately improving the accuracy of the entire human body recognition network.

3.3 Human Behavior Recognition Model Based on S-LSTM Network

A human behavior recognition model based on S-LSTM network is constructed, as shown in Fig. 5.

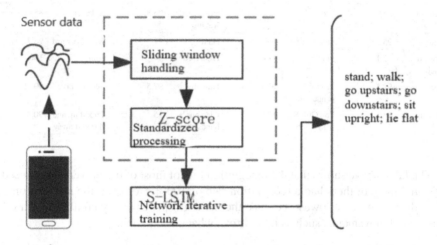

Fig. 5. Human Behavior Recognition Model Based on S-LSTM Network

4 Experimental Process and Result Analysis

First, data acquisition. The data set used is from the publicly available UCI Machine Learning Knowledge Base. The volunteers performed six behavioral activities: three static activities (standing, sitting and lying flat) and three dynamic activities (walking, walking up and down stairs). The sensor signal data were filtered by noise, sampled in a 50% overlapping sliding window of fixed width (2.56 s), and then separated from body acceleration and gravity using a Butter-worth low-pass filter, resulting in 10,929 samples. The dataset used for the experiments is divided into two parts: 70% of the training set and 30% of the test set. The sample labeled data are one-hot processed to correspond to the sample data. Given the limited memory capacity, the mini-batches method is used to perform batch gradient descent. The L2 loss function is better than the L1 loss function because it has been normalized, so L2 is used in the experiments, Adam is used as the optimizer, the learning rate of each model is set to 0.002, and the number of iterations is 1,000.

The set of 10 subjects performed 20 actions sequentially, each action was executed 2–3 times, with a total of 567 samples. The training set and test set were selected by ten-fold cross-validation, i.e., the data set was divided into 10 groups, each group was used as the test set in turn, and the remaining 9 groups were used as the training set. In this method, ten times of ten-fold cross-validation are performed, and the average of the ten times of validation results is taken as the final recognition result (Table 1).

Table 1. Average recognition rate of 20 movements after ten times ten folds

Movement	I% of recognition	Movement	I% of recognition	Movement	I% of recognition	Movement	I% of recognition
High wave	85	Hands	100	Horizontal waving	95.8	Side fist	85
Beat	95.3	Stoop down	100	Hands	71	Kick Forward	96.3
Forward punch	95.1	Side kick	93.4	High throw	94	Run	100
× painting	92.5	Tennis pendulum	90	Drawing	97.5	Tennis serve	90
Drawing circle	98.5	The Golf Swing Club	96.5	Clap one's hands	95	Pick it up and throw it away	90.3

The table above shows that the recognition rate of most of the movements exceeded 90%, and three of them had a recognition rate of 100%. However, the recognition rate of hand grasp was the lowest, because the hand grasp was easily confused with other one-handed movements, such as high throw, whack and punch.

5 Conclusion

In summary, human behavior recognition is the collection and analysis of human body information through computer networks and the results are obtained in the computer to draw relevant conclusions. In this paper, behavioral data based on collaborative LSTM algorithm is studied. The experiments demonstrate the high accuracy when human physiological parameters are predicted using neural networks.

Acknowledgments. Application of neural network in human action recognition.

References

1. Shen, X., Ding, Y.: Human skeleton representation for 3D action recognition based on complex network coding and LSTM. J. Vis. Commun. Image Represent. **82**, 103386 (2022)

2. Ns, A., Mm, B., Sk, C., et al.: Human action recognition based on spatial–temporal relational model and LSTM-CNN framework (2022)
3. Zhuang, T., Zhao, P., Xiao, P., et al.: Multi-stream CNN-LSTM network with partition strategy for human action recognition. In: BIC 2021: 2021 International Conference on Bioinformatics and Intelligent Computing (2021)
4. Yangzhi, L.I., Yuan, J., Liu, H.: Human skeleton-based action recognition algorithm based on spatiotemporal attention graph convolutional network model. J. Comput. Appl. **41**(7), 1915–1921 (2021)
5. Yan, W., Shabaz, M., Rakhra, M.: Research on nonlinear distorted image recognition based on artificial neural network algorithm. J. Interconnect. Netw. **22**(Supp06), 2148002 (2022)
6. Ullah, M., Yamin, M.M., Mohammed, A., et al.: Attention-based lstm network for action recognition in sports. Electron. Imaging **33**, 1–6 (2021)
7. Li, Y.: Research on state-of-charge Estimation of Lithium-ion Batteries Based on Improved Sparrow Search Algorithm-BP Neural Network (2021)
8. Zhimao, Y., Thai, M.T.: Research on the influencing factors of living energy consumption and carbon emissions based on spatiotemporal model (2023)
9. Austine, A., Pramila, R.S.: Hybrid Optimization Algorithm for Resource Allocation in LTE-Based D2DCommunication. Tech Science Press (2023)
10. Wan, B., Shen, Y.: Stock Trend Prediction of Communication Industry Based on LSTM Neural Network Algorithm and Research of Industry Development Strategy: – A Case Study of Zhongxing Telecommunication Equipment Corporation (2021)
11. Wang, H., Zhang, R., Li, Z.: Research on gait recognition of exoskeleton robot based on DTW algorithm. In: CCEAI 2021: 5th International Conference on Control Engineering and Artificial Intelligence (2021)
12. Seo, Y.M., Choi, Y.S.: Graph convolutional networks for skeleton-based action recognition with LSTM using tool-information. In: SAC 2021: The 36th ACM/SIGAPP Symposium on Applied Computing. ACM (2021)
13. Fan, C., Biao, L.U., Ren, J., et al.: An effective action recognition approach used in physical exercise for copd patients. J. Mech. Med. Biol. **22**(09) (2022)
14. Zhang, Y., Tian, Y., Wu, P., et al.: Application of skeleton data and long short-term memory in action recognition of children with autism spectrum disorder. Sensors **21**(2), 411 (2021)
15. Arora, A., Taneja, A., Gupta, M., et al.: Virtual personal trainer: fitness video recognition using convolution neural network and bidirectional LSTM. Int. J. Knowl. Syst. Sci. (4), 12 (2021)

Piano Performance Evaluation System Based on Neural Network and Its Application in Piano Teaching

Xiaolei He[1,2(✉)] and Jijie Liu[1,2]

[1] School of Music and Dance, Sichuan University of Culture and Arts, Mianyang 621000, Sichuan, China
496844336@qq.com
[2] Yunnan College of Business Management, Yunnan 650106, China

Abstract. This study proposes a piano performance evaluation system based on neural networks, aiming to help piano students accurately evaluate their piano performance level and further optimize the quality of piano teaching by utilizing machine learning methods. This system is based on neural network technology for modeling. Through signal processing and feature extraction of piano playing audio signals, the piano playing skills and music performance are evaluated separately, and a comprehensive evaluation result is finally obtained. At the same time, the system supports real-time performance evaluation and standardized evaluation, providing timely and accurate feedback and suggestions for students, and providing effective teaching aids for teachers. Experiments have shown that this system can accurately evaluate the level of piano students' performance skills and music performance, and can provide effective teaching aids for students and teachers. Compared with traditional manual evaluation methods, this system has advantages such as accurate evaluation, fast feedback, and data analysis, which can bring more convenience and benefits to piano teaching. Therefore, the results of this study have practical significance and promotional value, and have broad application prospects in piano teaching.

Keyword: Piano performance · Neural network · Piano teaching · evaluation system

1 Introduction

Piano performance is an art that requires superb skills and good musical expression, and is challenging for various types of piano learners. In the current piano teaching, students need to continuously practice playing according to the guidance and feedback of the teacher, in order to improve their playing skills and musical performance. However, it is difficult for teachers to provide detailed and accurate evaluations of each student's performance when facing multiple students, and at the same time, it is also difficult for students to judge the accuracy and level of their performance during self practice. Therefore, accurate evaluation and feedback on piano performance has become an important issue that needs to be addressed in modern piano teaching.

Y. Zhang and N. Shah (Eds.): BigIoT-EDU 2023, LNICST 582, pp. 186–192, 2024.
https://doi.org/10.1007/978-3-031-63136-8_19

In recent years, with the rapid development of artificial intelligence technology, using computers to evaluate piano performance has become a research hotspot. Especially as a machine learning method with strong learning and recognition abilities, neural networks have demonstrated excellent performance in piano performance evaluation. Based on this, this study proposes a piano performance evaluation system based on neural networks to help students and teachers accurately evaluate their piano performance level, provide targeted feedback and suggestions, and achieve the goal of optimizing teaching quality.

This article is mainly divided into the following parts: Firstly, it introduces the background of piano performance and its importance in piano education; Secondly, it elaborates on the traditional piano performance evaluation methods and their existing problems; Next, the basic concepts and principles of neural networks were introduced; Then, the overall architecture of this system and the main functions and designs of its various components were explained; Finally, the system was evaluated through experiments, and the advantages and disadvantages of this system were discussed, indicating future research directions.

The piano performance evaluation system based on neural networks proposed in this study has the advantages of accurate evaluation, fast feedback, and data analysis. It can provide personalized learning assistants for piano students, optimize the quality of piano teaching, and promote the development and innovation of piano education.

2   Related Work

2.1   Music Visualization Design Strategy for Piano Learning

There are various types of music visualization, and the music information presented in different forms is also different. However, not all forms are suitable for piano learning. The visualization required for piano learning does not require dazzling or novel forms, but rather needs to be able to clearly display the basic information of music sounds, especially the strength related to performance, and can relatively intuitively express the hidden images and emotions in the music, At the same time, feedback can be achieved visually and effectively, thereby improving the learning efficiency of piano learners and enhancing their interest in practicing. Through the analysis of the above music visualization cases, combined with the specific requirements of piano learning, the following design strategies for music visualization suitable for piano learning can be summarized:

(1) Efficiently convey the basic information of musical notes through quantifiable graphics: the basic information of musical notes is the determining factors of explicit musical elements, including pitch, length, intensity, etc. These elements determine which key to press, the duration of pressing the key, and the force of pressing the key when playing the piano.
(2) The emotional appeal of music can be expressed intuitively through color change: music emotion is the essence of music, and playing without emotion can not move people. Only deeply understood music emotion can make your playing appealing. Combining visual case analysis of music emotion, color can intuitively strengthen the emotional expression of music, and has certain scientific basis in color psychology, Therefore, in future research, changes in color will be used to represent changes in musical emotions.

(3) The aesthetic feeling and image of music can be vividly reflected through vector motion graphics: the current music score is relatively rational, and it is difficult to reflect the aesthetic feeling of music in the spectrum of black and white tones, but in the design of intelligent software, a short animation related to the music itself can be made through dynamic vector graphic elements, as the beginning of piano music learning, to show the music image with intuitive graphic elements, Simultaneously increasing the fun of piano learning.

(4) Efficient analysis of music details through the comparison of visual graphics: The many difficulties in learning the piano make it difficult for learners to concentrate and immerse themselves in it [1]. At the same time, it is difficult to only detect errors in playing through hearing during learning. It is difficult to find shortcomings by simply listening to the recording again and again through hearing. Therefore, in the design, it is necessary to provide learners with intuitive analysis of playing details, Compare and juxtapose the visual graphics played by oneself with those played by the teacher.

In summary, using quantifiable abstract graphics to represent the explicit elements of music and using color changes to represent the implicit elements of music are relatively feasible music visualization methods for piano learning. The specific visualization methods and mapping models also need to conduct competitive analysis on current mainstream piano learning software, compare the advantages and disadvantages of different types of products in user learning experience, and form targeted differentiation of their own products in the design, ultimately completing a piano learning software with richer experience and more intuitive feedback.

2.2 Overview of Neural Networks

Based on the above analysis of the basic principles of neural networks, artificial neurons are mathematical models created by simulating the operation mode of biological neurons. It is a nonlinear component with multiple inputs and outputs. Figure 1 shows a neural structure model where one neuron can accept inputs from many other neurons, so it has n neurons as input variables, from 1x to nx being inputs to the neural network. The common role of all neurons determines the current working state of the neurons [2]. The cumulative effect of the final input of this neuron is net, represented by n, where $n = w_1x_1 + w_2x_2 + \cdots + w_nx_n$. N (*) is called the basis function of neurons. The common input of multiple variables and a single output are characteristics of the basis function.

The typical activation function can be linear or nonlinear. Generally, it can be divided into several types: symbolic function, nonlinear ramp function, linear function and S-type function.

(1) Symbolic functions, with an input range of negative infinity to positive infinity and an output range of -1 and 1, are commonly used for classification,

$$f(x) = Sgn(x) = \begin{cases} 1, x \geq 0 \\ -1, x < 0 \end{cases} \tag{1}$$

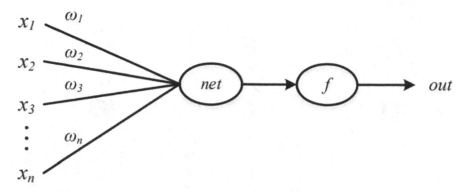

Fig. 1. Neuron structure

(2) Nonlinear ramp function, nonlinear ramp function is a processing method for reducing network performance after linear function is extended back and forth,

$$f(x) = \begin{cases} \alpha, x \geq \theta \\ kx, -\theta < x < \theta \\ -\alpha, x \leq \theta \end{cases} \tag{2}$$

(3) Linear function, linear function is often used to enlarge or reduce the input function,

$$f(x) = kx \tag{3}$$

(4) The S-type function, also known as the sigmoid function, is the most widely used with an output range of (0,1) and is often used for function fitting and optimization,

$$f(x) = \frac{1}{1 + e^{-x}} \tag{4}$$

The overall structure of BP neural network includes three layers, input layer, hidden layer, and output layer. The connection between neurons in each layer is weighted connection. The input layer represents the obtained information, the hidden layer represents the processing information, and the output layer represents the output, as shown in Fig. 2. Among them, the research shows that when the hidden layer in BP neural network is one time, the problem of nonlinear function can be solved.

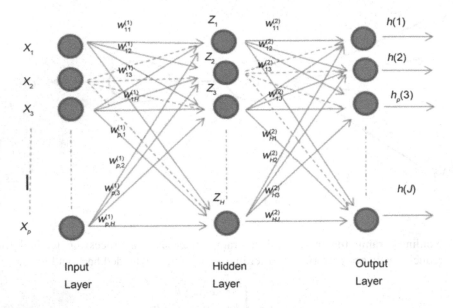

Fig. 2. BP neural network structure

3 Research on Piano Performance Evaluation System Based on Neural Network and Its Application in Piano Teaching

The effect of this sound played by the player the keys are correct, strength and duration. In essence, the features the grasp of strength, duration and whether the keys are correct.

The evaluation of a performance track and highly in the sense of general film. It is impossible to use the box to construct this model. At this time, it is the only way to use the neural network model to construct the component evaluation system. There are many kinds of training algorithms for artificial neural networks, such as BP neural network (feedforward error transfer algorithm) [3], pair transfer neural network and uncertain training algorithm (simulated annealing algorithm). The training of transmission network neural network is very fast, but its performance determines that its application area is very narrow, and the training speed of non deterministic algorithm is very slow, but it can avoid the minimum problem. The comprehensive characteristics of BP neural network for this system are better than other algorithms, and there have been very mature applications. Therefore, this music performance evaluation system plans to use BP neural network model. Design B required P The network solves the problem.

The segments with different duration.

There are no standard rules to apply in this process at this stage, which is mostly determined by experience. Therefore, the choice and quantification of various input and output parameters need to be grouped, and each group needs to be modeled by neural network model. Each model is tested with experimental data, and finally the construction framework of neural network model is selected. As shown in the figure below, 3 bits are staff (Fig. 3).

Fig. 3. Music staff

The primary problem in the application of neural network model in music performance evaluation system is the overall design of the network. The overall network design requirements [4]. Network generalization ability algorithm. Therefore, fully mining generalization ability of the network to a certain extent.

4 Function Realization of Piano Performance Evaluation System

The piano performance evaluation system is an application software based on neural network technology for modeling, which can accurately evaluate the performance skills and music performance of piano students, providing more intelligent and personalized services for piano teaching. This article mainly introduces the functional implementation and algorithm design of the system.

The main functions of this system are as follows:

(1) Audio signal acquisition and preprocessing. The system can collect real-time audio signals for piano performance through a microphone and preprocess the audio signals, such as audio filtering and gain control.
(2) Feature extraction and signal classification. The system uses algorithms such as wavelet transform and wavelet packet decomposition to extract features from audio signals, obtaining multidimensional feature vectors including frequency and time domain features. Then, the techniques of piano performance and musical performance are evaluated through feature vector classification and deep learning techniques.
(3) Real time performance evaluation and standardized evaluation. The system can evaluate students' piano playing skills and music performance in real-time, and provide targeted suggestions and feedback. In addition, the system can conduct standardized evaluation, grading and score statistics of students' performance levels.
(4) Difficulty level and track analysis. The system supports performance evaluation and analysis for different difficulty levels and tracks, in order to better understand the advantages and disadvantages of performance techniques and music performance, and provide better teaching aids for students and teachers.

In terms of algorithm design, this system uses algorithms such as BP neural network and convolutional neural network to evaluate piano performance skills and music performance. In the BP neural network, the time-domain characteristics of speech signals are used to evaluate piano performance skills, including rhythm, speed, force, smoothness, and other aspects. In convolutional neural networks, audio feature vectors are used as convolutional kernel inputs for convolutional operations to achieve fast feature extraction and classification. Using different algorithm models for modeling and training different types of tracks and difficulty levels of performance.

In summary, the functional implementation and algorithm design of this system fully consider various aspects of piano performance evaluation, providing authoritative, accurate, and fast piano performance evaluation services, which can provide better teaching aids for piano students and teachers.

5 Conclusion

This article introduces a piano performance evaluation system based on neural network technology and explores its application in piano teaching. This system has the advantages of accurate evaluation, real-time feedback, data analysis, etc. It can provide better teaching aids for students and teachers, effectively improving the quality and efficiency of piano teaching. To achieve intelligence and personalization in piano performance evaluation, the system adopts algorithms such as wavelet transform and convolutional neural network for feature extraction and classification, and evaluates piano performance skills and music performance separately, achieving fast, accurate, and reliable piano performance evaluation services. This system has performed excellently in practice, providing new ideas and technical support for the development of piano education.

References

1. Yang, S.: Computer Music Production and Digital Audio. Shanghai University Press (2001)
2. Zhang, G.: Design and implementation of CAT system for harmony basic standard keyboard test. Master's thesis of Capital Normal University (2003)
3. Tong, Z.: Basic Music Theory Course. Shanghai Music Publishing House (2001)
4. Liu, L.: Research on piano performance evaluation system. Master's thesis of Tsinghua University (2005)

Prediction Method of College Students' Negative Emotion Based on GA-BP Neural Network

Jun Liao[✉] and Shi Hang

Ganzhou Teachers College, Jiangxi 341000, China
woshify@163.com

Abstract. This study proposes a negative emotion prediction method for college students based on GA-BP neural network. This method uses genetic algorithms to optimize the parameters of the BP neural network to improve the accuracy and precision of prediction. By collecting a large amount of emotion vocabulary and emotion annotation data, establish an emotion dictionary and emotion classifier, and then construct a prediction model. The experimental results indicate that this method can effectively monitor and predict negative emotions among college students, and provide timely psychological intervention measures for schools and individuals. This prediction method based on GA-BP neural network has good adaptability and generalization, and can be applied to other emotional prediction fields.

Keywords: BP neural network · Genetic algorithm · college student · Emotion prediction · mental health

1 Introduction

Mental health is one of the success of college students. From the perspective of these various cases, while we feel sorry for the parties, it is not difficult to find that the improper handling of negative emotions such as anxiety, resentment, sadness, fear, depression and anger leads to or accelerates the occurrence of problems, and emotions have a great impact on a person's psychological growth and development, To explore the current management countermeasures of College Students' negative emotions is helpful to improve their mental health. For college students, managing emotions, regulating emotions, controlling emotions and being the masters of emotions are not only the needs of maintaining physical and mental health, but also the conditions of self-development and personality maturity [1].

College students are at the peak of their youth growth, and their emotions have their particularity. First of all, college students have rich emotions and emotions, showing active, romantic, enthusiastic and creative; Secondly, college students are in what psychologists call "psychological weaning" stage, they are not mature, emotional character is not stable, they have strong impulsivity and explosiveness, and their self-control is obviously weak compared with adults with social experience; Thirdly, the positive and

Y. Zhang and N. Shah (Eds.): BigIoT-EDU 2023, LNICST 582, pp. 193–198, 2024.
https://doi.org/10.1007/978-3-031-63136-8_20

negative, positive and negative, tense and relaxed, loose and calm in college students' emotions are prominent, which are easily affected by the external environment. For college students at this stage, the only child accounts for a large proportion. In the past, parents and school education paid too much attention to the cultivation of IQ, but did not pay attention to the overall development of the individual, including the guidance of negative emotions. Therefore, it is very important to study the prediction method of contemporary college students' negative emotions.

2 Algorithm Information

2.1 BP Neural Network

When the upper layer node is transmitted, the connection weight coefficient WUS is adjusted to enhance or weaken the output, activation and node offset (or threshold). But for the input mode is sent to the input layer node, and the output of this layer node is equal to its input. Note that this kind of network has no feedback, and its actual operation is still unidirectional, so it can not be regarded as a nonlinear dynamic system, but only a nonlinear mapping relationship [2].

The structure of BP network with hidden layer is in Fig. 1. There are q neurons in the of the network.

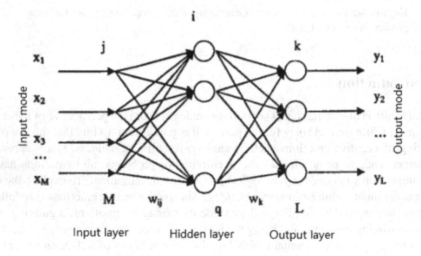

Fig. 1. Structure of BP neural network

One of its characteristics is that the search starts from a population of the solution, so it can effectively avoid falling into the local optimum. Genetic algorithm can automatically acquire and accumulate the search process. The general process of genetic algorithm is to code the individual population and initialize the population; Then according to the selection function is used to select individuals, and finally the conclusion is drawn. Crossover and mutation are carried out simultaneously in selection [3].

2.2 The Relevant Terms Are Explained as Follows

Coding: coding can be understood as setting a unique genome or identification code for all individuals in a population. There are three types of coding: binary coding, floating-point coding and symbolic coding. Here, take binary coding as an example: the chromosome of binary coding has "0" and "1" bases.

Fitness function: also known as the evaluation function, which represents the probability of individuals being selected in the population. The higher the value of the function.

Selection function: the selection function determines the survival of individuals. Commonly used selection functions include random roulette, elite selection mechanism, etc. in general, the probability of being selected by the selection function.

Crossover: crossover operation in genetic algorithm, also known as gene recombination; Crossover is one of the key steps to make the offspring different from the parent. The crossover operation under different coding methods is also different. Here, the binary coding method the crossover operation: the crossover operation under binary coding is similar to the association process of homologous chromosomes of organisms, that is, exchanging codes at the same position to generate new subclass mutation: the mutation operation in genetic algorithm is also known as gene mutation; Mutation and crossover are the same, which will change with different coding methods. The mutation operation of binary coding is that the probability of base change from "0" or "1" to the opposite "1" or "0",

3   GA-BP Neural Network Based on Genetic Algorithm Optimization

Because the traditional has the disadvantages of slow convergence speed, this algorithm the possible negative emotions of college students in pension institutions, The has which in advance, and it depends on experience. In this paper, the parameters of genetic algorithm are selected as: crossover rate: crossover rate affects the efficiency of population renewal, Too small can not effectively renew the population; In this paper, the crossover rate is 90% [4].

Variation rate: variation rate affects the decline rate of population diversity. Too small variation rate will lead to the rapid decline of population diversity, and defective genes will be lost quickly and difficult to repair. Too large variation rate will lead to the increase of damage probability of high-order patterns; The variation rate is 0.8%.

Population size: the probability of morbid genes will increase, which is not conducive to the population. If the population size is too small, it will be difficult to converge and waste resources; The population size of 50.

Evolutionary termination Algebras: termination algebras mainly affect the maturity of the population. Too small termination algebras will cause the algorithm not to converge, and too large termination algebras may cause over fitting; In this paper, we choose the termination algebra as 100.

The specific process as follows

1) Initialize the, code the structure, and randomly generate n individuals, each representing a neural network
2) The individual of current generation is decoded and the neural network is constructed according to the decoding result
3) The neural network is trained with preset parameters and random connection weights
4) According to the training results, the fitness of each individual is calculated, and several optimal individuals are selected to keep the gene to the next generation
5) Using crossover, mutation and other processing methods, the current generation population is processed, and the next generation population is generated
6) Repeat steps 3 through 6 until the termination is met
7) The of BP neural network are initialized individuals.
8) The BP neural network is trained until the termination condition is satisfied

The GA-BP neural network optimized based on genetic algorithm is shown in Fig. 2.

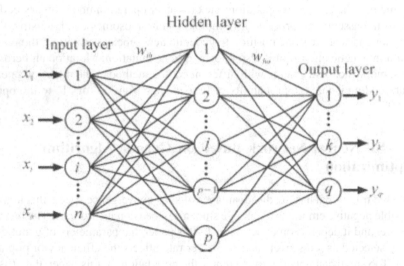

Fig. 2. GA-BP neural network

4   Case Analysis

In the of 2008 in the college students' negative emotion tracking survey data space (Charls) of Peking University open research data platform is selected as the research data. Through removing duplicate values, data normalization and centralization. There are 3047 feature items in the tracking data, including 16954 cases. This paper only uses part of the feature items as the input items. Among them, the selection of the feature items uses the single population t-test to investigate the negative emotion of the output on all the feature items, and selects the feature items with positive prediction effect. The calculation formula of statistics 1 and sample standard deviation s is shown in formula (1).

$$s = \sqrt{\frac{\sum_{i=1}^{n}(x_i - X)}{n-1}} \tag{1}$$

Through single population t-test, 41 characteristic items were selected as input items, including gender, age, years of education, etc.; Five negative emotions identified in the data set were selected as the output items, which were fear, anxiety, loneliness, sadness and depression. Finally, 9889 cases were screened out by removing duplicate values, data normalization and centralization

$$x_j = \frac{x_i - x_{\min}}{x_{\max} - x_{\min}} \tag{2}$$

$x_{\max}$ and $x_{\min}$ in formula (2) are the feature items before and after normalization, respectively. $X_{\max}$ and x_{min} represent x_i in the data space; Corresponding to the maximum and minimum value of the feature term

5   Conclusion

By establishing an emotion dictionary and emotion classifier, a large amount of emotion vocabulary and emotion annotation data is collected, and genetic algorithms are used to optimize the parameters of the BP neural network to improve the accuracy and accuracy of prediction. After experimental verification, this method can effectively monitor and predict the negative emotions of college students, provide timely psychological intervention measures for schools and individuals, and effectively reduce the adverse effects of negative emotions on individuals and society. Specifically, the prediction model of this study utilizes a large amount of sentiment annotation data as the basis, and establishes sentiment dictionaries and sentiment classifiers for sentiment recognition and classification. Using genetic algorithms to optimize neural network parameters can fully consider the local optimization problem of the neural network, improve prediction accuracy and generalization ability. Based on this model, large-scale and efficient emotional prediction and monitoring can be achieved, providing assistance for the mental health of college students. In addition, the model also has good adaptability and can be used for research and application in other fields of emotion prediction and classification. The negative emotion prediction method for college students based on GA-BP neural network has high prediction accuracy and generalization ability, which has positive significance for improving the mental health level of college students. In the future, further in-depth research and application are needed to explore broader research fields and application scenarios.

References

1. Yan, C., Shen, L., Yang, S., et al.: The influence of psychological distance on College Students' moral judgment under different emotional states. Chin. J. Clin. Psychol. **25**(2), 251–254 (2017)

2. Huang, Z.: Application of data mining in college students' Psychological Crisis Prevention. Wuhan University of Science and Technology, Wuhan (2015)
3. Hao, M., Xu, X., Yu, H., et al.: Emotion classification and prediction algorithm based on Chinese microblog. Comput. Appl. **38**(S2), 89, 96 (2018)
4. Qi, Y., Tan, R.: Application of BP neural network based on improved particle swarm optimization algorithm in dam deformation analysis. Water Conserv. Hydropower Technol. **48**(2), 118–124 (2017)

Application of Ant Colony Algorithm in Physical Education Teaching Evaluation

Lei Li[1,2(✉)], Ji Lei[1,2], and Xia Li[1,2]

[1] Nanchang University College of Science and Technology, Nanchang 330001, Jiangxi, China
lileibazx1983@163.com
[2] Wuhan University of Communication, Wuhan 430065, China

Abstract. Ant colony is a bionic algorithm, which is used the of finding the optimal solution in the process of solving. Ant is an example of this algorithm. It can find the in many cases. The main idea behind ant colony is that ants use pheromone tracks to communicate and cooperate with each other. They also use these communication technologies to solve problems such as finding food and avoiding predators. This makes them very effective in solving complex problems without any human intervention. Teachers and students face the problem of how to correctly evaluate physical education teaching through the network interaction of the school's independent campus intelligent education platform, wechat official account, online education platform and so on. Therefore, in the "Internet + education" environment, how to make a evaluation of these emerging classroom teaching and integrate them into the physical education teaching evaluation system is a problem worth discussing. The application.

Keyword: Ant colony Physical education · Teaching evaluation

1 Introduction

As people's pursuit and demand for high-quality education increases year by year, the evaluation of teaching quality in physical education is also increasingly valued. At present, scholars and experts in related fields have conducted a large amount of research, attempting to solve the problem of establishing an evaluation system. In order to improve the accuracy, stability, practicality and fairness of the evaluation, researchers have used a variety of algorithms and models, of which Ant colony optimization algorithms is an important one in recent years [1].

Ant colony optimization algorithms is an optimization algorithm based on Swarm intelligence, which aims to find the optimal solution by simulating the collective behavior of ants in the process of searching for food. Ant colony optimization algorithms is widely concerned and applied because of its strong global search ability, adaptive search mechanism, robustness and computational simplicity [2]. In the evaluation of college physical education teaching, Ant colony optimization algorithms has the following application advantages:

Y. Zhang and N. Shah (Eds.): BigIoT-EDU 2023, LNICST 582, pp. 199–209, 2024.
https://doi.org/10.1007/978-3-031-63136-8_21

(1) Strong ability to deal with complex problems: Ant colony optimization algorithms can deal with multidimensional, multi-objective, nonlinear and complex data types and problems, such as fitting indicators, formulating reasonable classification standards, etc., and can provide good performance in these fields.

(2) Strong global search capability: Ant colony optimization algorithms can transform the search problem into a random walk in the solution space by simulating the collective action of ants when searching for food, which can effectively avoid falling into the problem of local optimal solution.

(3) The model has a wide range of applications: Ant colony optimization algorithms is widely used in machine learning, data mining, optimization problems and other fields, and can be used in the optimization, analysis, evaluation and other aspects of the model.

(4) The algorithm is simple and easy to implement: the implementation and application process of Ant colony optimization algorithms is simple and does not require advanced mathematical knowledge and computer technology support, so it can be widely used in all walks of life.

When using Ant colony optimization algorithms to evaluate college physical education teaching, the following steps need to be taken: first, determine the evaluation indicators, goals and standards, thus forming a natural number Nonlinear programming problem [3]. Then, the corresponding optimization function and constraint conditions are designed according to the planning problem, and the Ant colony optimization algorithms is used to solve the problem, and the optimal evaluation result is obtained. Finally, based on the output results of the model, scientifically evaluate and improve the teaching quality.

In a word, Ant colony optimization algorithms is a widely used and effective algorithm, which can provide scientific and efficient tools and methods for college physical education teaching evaluation [4]. Although there are still some problems and limitations in the practical application of Ant colony optimization algorithms, through continuous improvement and optimization, it is believed that it will have more extensive application and further development in the future.

2 Related Work

2.1 Teaching Evaluation

The explanation of teaching in the Encyclopedia of Chinese middle school teaching · education volume points out that in teaching activities, the effectiveness of both teaching and learning activities. The evaluation is based on the teaching objectives and teaching principles, and then the standard (principle) degree of teaching and learning is evaluated by using various test means and evaluation techniques, so as to provide information, improve teaching or prove the qualification of the evaluated object (teachers or students) [5]. Here, we should not only attach importance to the summative evaluation of teaching work for identification and selection, but also attach importance to the formative evaluation [6]; It the inspection and system by external organizations, but also the self-evaluation of schools.

Teaching the evaluation of the whole in various disciplines. Any educational activity needs to be implemented through the teaching process, and the has become a key link of educational evaluation. Teaching is a purposeful bilateral and students with the course content as the intermediary [7]. Through this activity, students can master systematic knowledge and skills, develop intelligence, physical strength and creative ability in the process, and form a scientific world outlook and moral quality.

Teaching educational evaluation, and it is also an part of the teachers' teaching activities. How to understand teaching evaluation and how to scientifically implement teaching evaluation for teachers to timely regulate teaching activities and improve teaching quality.

The Ant colony optimization algorithms is an optimization algorithm that simulates the self-organization behavior of ants. Its basic idea is to optimize the quality of the solution by simulating the process of ants searching for the shortest path between the food source and the nest while searching for the best solution in the exploration space. In recent years, the Ant colony optimization algorithms has been widely used, and it also has certain application value in physical education teaching [8].

First, in the evaluation of physical education teaching, Ant colony optimization algorithms can be used to optimize the evaluation indicators. The purpose of physical education teaching evaluation is to check the level and progress of students, and the evaluation indicators include basic skills, tactical abilities, physical fitness, psychological fitness, and other aspects. How to choose appropriate evaluation indicators is crucial for the accuracy of the evaluation results [9]. The Ant colony optimization algorithms can be used to optimize the evaluation results by adaptively adjusting the weight of the evaluation indicators to improve the accuracy and objectivity.

Secondly, Ant colony optimization algorithms can also be used to develop personalized education programs. Each student has different levels of physical literacy, interests, and physical characteristics. In order to achieve the best teaching effect, personalized education plans need to be developed for each student [10]. This algorithm can establish a student evaluation model, evaluate based on the level of physical literacy and skills mastered, and then automatically optimize the training plan to develop personalized sports training plans suitable for different students.

Finally, Ant colony optimization algorithms can also be used to optimize and evaluate the teaching effect of teachers. Physical education requires continuous reflection and improvement from teachers, as well as objective and scientific evaluation of the teaching effectiveness of educators [11]. There are also many factors to consider in the evaluation system, such as the rationality of evaluation indicators and the setting of weights. The Ant colony optimization algorithms can be used to optimize, improve the scientificity and effectiveness of the evaluation system, and make it more consistent with the actual teaching requirements.

In conclusion, Ant colony optimization algorithms has a broad application prospect in sports teaching evaluation, which can improve the accuracy and objectivity of evaluation, customize personalized training plans for students, optimize the evaluation of teachers' teaching effects, and promote the development of sports education.

202   L. Li et al.

2.2 Physical Education Teaching Evaluation

Physical is an activity out through rules and the objectives of the course. Physical teaching objectives are the criteria for determining whether physical education teaching can achieve the planned objectives in advance, whether it has achieved the predetermined results in advance, and whether it has completed the tasks; The principle of reference for physical education teaching is to determine whether the teaching work is carried out effectively and whether the basic standards for physical education teaching are met. The above criteria include standardization and objectivity, as well as the educational evaluation; The object of the process and effectiveness of learning and teaching in classes [12]. The key object of evaluation is the specific learning of the educated students, as well as their moral status and learning ability; The will also evaluate the teaching teachers, as well as their professional ethics and teaching abilities; The this subject is the task of measurement and value evaluation. Value evaluation refers to qualitative evaluation, generally assessing whether the teaching direction is correct or not, and whether the teaching method is appropriate; Quantitative evaluation refers to quantitative evaluation, which generally refers to the of quantifiable, such the degree of skill mastery and improvement of physical fitness [13]. The subject evaluation is summarized through the meaning of evaluation, as shown in Fig. 1 below.

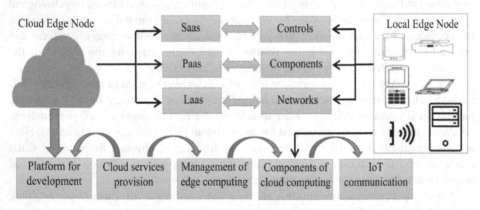

Fig. 1. Research Direction of Physical Education Teaching Evaluation

Physical evaluation is an evaluation itself or the teaching process, which involves teaching objectives,, teaching results and so on. According to the objectives and health, the value and teaching results is judged. On the one hand, we should evaluate. On the should pay more the evaluation of the effectiveness of to achieve, that is, to evaluate the performance of students in learning and the changes before and after learning [14]. It is a specific activities and an of the good and bad effects of physical education teaching.

It includes four clusters: physical education teachers, educational reform, problem solving, and practical teaching. The key words in physical education teachers include practical work ability, emotional experience, teacher teaching quality, etc. The key words in educational reform include physical education institutions, effective teaching, etc. Based on the original teaching concepts, effective teaching is proposed, indicating that focusing on the entire, how many skills and experiences can be learned by students through teaching, and attaching importance to teachers' work ability, emotional experience, and teaching quality the effective application evaluation in teaching. The key words in the questions include suggestions, countermeasures, curriculum reform, and health [15]. The focus is curriculum reform of physical education evaluation. Suggestions are proposed and countermeasures are studied the development teaching. The key words in practical teaching include mode, development, dynamic evaluation, and segmented management. The focus is on the application mode and development evaluation in practical teaching, the research on dynamic evaluation and segmented management, to promote the development evaluation.

3 Ant Colony Algorithm

3.1 Basic Idea of Ant Colony Algorithm

The Ant colony optimization algorithms is an optimization algorithm that simulates the self-organization behavior of ants. Its basic idea is to optimize the quality of the solution by simulating the behavior of ants searching for the shortest path between the food source and the nest while searching for the best solution in the search space. Specifically, the basic idea of this algorithm is:

(1) Ants will release Pheromone in the process of searching for food source, and communicate through the evaporation and deposition of Pheromone;
(2) Ants searching for food sources tend to choose the path with higher Pheromone concentration, which will increase the concentration of Pheromone on the path;
(3) In the exploration space, if the Pheromone concentration of the current location is higher, the probability of ants searching near the current location is greater;
(4) When an ant finds a food source or returns to its nest, it will mark the path by releasing a large number of pheromones, attracting other ants to follow the same path, and strengthening the Pheromone concentration of the path;
(5) As time goes by, Pheromone will gradually decrease due to evaporation and other ants passing by, and the final weight will gradually decrease.

Based on the collective wisdom of ants, Ant colony optimization algorithms guides the search direction through evaporation and deposition of pheromones, and constantly optimizes the final solution. It has a wide range of applications in decision-making, planning, and optimization problems, including path planning, machine learning, data mining, and many other fields.

Specifically, although it is difficult or slow for an ant to reach the food source, it is much easier for the whole ant colony to search the food source. When more, the number increase, and the pheromone strength will increase. The probability of ants choosing the path will increase, which will further increase the pheromone strength of the path. However, the path with less ants will volatilize and less and less with the passage of time. Figure 2 shows a simple example of this:

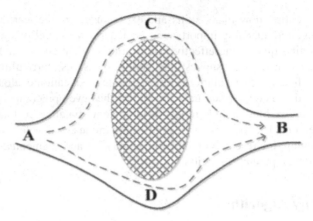

Fig. 2. Schematic diagram of ant colony algorithm routing

3.2 Basic Ant Colony Algorithm Process

From the of specific algorithm design, the as a model-based search algorithms the parameterized probabilistic model. In ant parameterizes the probability, and the parameters of the model are pheromones, so this parameterized. In the generated by searching on a parameterized probability distribution model in the solution space, and the parameters of this model are updated with the previously generated solutions, so that the search. The validity of this method is based on the assumption that high-quality solutions always contain good solution components. Through learning, the influence of solution composition elements on the quality of solutions helps to find a mechanism, and construct high-quality solutions through the best combination of solution composition elements.

Ant colony optimization algorithms is an optimization algorithm that simulates the self-organizing behavior of ants. Its basic process includes initialization, Pheromone update, ant movement and reconciliation update. The basic process of Ant colony optimization algorithms will be introduced in detail below.

(1) Initialize

Before the algorithm starts, it is necessary to initialize the initial Pheromone concentration, the position, state and path of each ant and other parameters. In addition, some parameters need to be set, such as Pheromone volatilization speed, the importance of Pheromone, the number of iterations of ants, etc.

(2) Pheromone update

Pheromone plays an important role in the whole algorithm and is the core of Ant colony optimization algorithms optimization. In the Pheromone update phase, each ant will release Pheromone according to its own search results. These Pheromone will be volatilized and reconstructed over time. When the ant finds the food source or returns to the nest, it will release Pheromone on the path, increasing the Pheromone concentration of this path. When other ants search this path, they will choose the path according to the Pheromone concentration, so as to continuously optimize the final solution.

(3) The Movement of Ants

In the process of ants moving, according to the Pheromone density, they tend to choose the path with high Pheromone concentration, release Pheromone, and strengthen the Pheromone concentration of this path. At the same time, they will also ignore the path with low Pheromone concentration, and continue to optimize the path until the optimal solution is found.

(4) Update of solution

After all ants complete their search, they need to update the solution based on the search results. Throughout the entire search process, the paths of each ant are recorded, which can be used to update the optimal path among the ants. By comparing the paths between different ants, the optimal path is ultimately selected as the solution.

(5) Termination conditions

During the iteration process of the algorithm, it is necessary to set termination conditions. In general, there are various termination conditions, such as reaching a predetermined number of iterations, achieving a predetermined accuracy of the objective function, and the search time exceeding the predetermined time.

$$
p_{ij}^k(t) = \begin{cases} \dfrac{\tau_{ij}^\alpha(t)\eta_{ij}^\beta}{\sum\limits_{j\in N_j^k} \tau_{ij}^\alpha(t)\eta_{ij}^\beta} \\ 0 \end{cases} \tag{1}
$$

Ants leave behind pheromones on the path they pass by, and the remaining pheromones is trail to distinguish it from the path where no ants have passed or where the pheromone has evaporated. The update method for pheromones of each node is as follows:

$$
\tau_{ij}(t+1) = (1-\rho)\tau_{ij}(t) + \sum_{k=1}^{K} \Delta\tau_{ij}^k \tag{2}
$$

Based on AS, the Ant Colony System (ACS) is further improved by adding transformation rules, changing the overall update method, and adding local update methods:

$$
J = \begin{cases} \arg \max_{u\in J_x(i)}\{[\tau_u(t)]^a[\eta_{in}]^q\}\,, & if\ q \le q_0 \\ J & ,\ otherwise \end{cases} \tag{3}
$$

Only the pheromone of the optimal solution path found during each iteration is changed. Here, traversal refers to the time when all artificial ants obtain a feasible solution. The idea of holistic renewal is to reward the best solutions to guide ants in their development and exploration based on these paths.

$$
\tau(i,j) = (1-\alpha)\tau(i,j) + \alpha\Delta\tau(i,j) \tag{4}
$$

As long as there is a path traveled by ants, they change the pheromones on the path. The main idea of local update is to avoid creating an overly strong path that attracts all ants to follow, so that appropriate actions to explore new paths cannot be performed, leading to local optimization.

$$
\tau(i,j) = (1-p)\tau(i,j) + p\tau^0 \tag{5}
$$

4 Physical Education Teaching Evaluation Based on Ant Colony Algorithm

4.1 Characteristics of the Construction of PE Teaching Evaluation System in Colleges and Universities

The construction of the evaluation system for physical education teaching in universities is an important measure to improve the quality and level of higher education. Building a scientific, objective, comprehensive, and diversified evaluation system is the key to promoting the reform of physical education teaching in universities. The following introduces the characteristics of the evaluation system for physical education teaching in universities from several aspects.

(1) Diversification

   The evaluation system of physical education teaching in universities should be diversified, that is, the evaluation should be based on multiple evaluation standards and methods. Evaluation should not only focus on students' physical fitness and motor skill levels, but also consider their comprehensive quality and physical and mental health status. Therefore, in the evaluation system of physical education teaching, various evaluation methods such as classroom interaction evaluation, physical fitness testing, action photography evaluation, emotional attitude evaluation, and mental health evaluation should be fully considered to make the evaluation more comprehensive, authentic, and scientific.

(2) Personalization

   The evaluation system of physical education teaching in universities should reflect the principle of personalization as much as possible, that is, recognizing the individual differences of students in physical education learning, and developing corresponding evaluation strategies based on each student's different physical fitness, preferences, and interests. Some students are born with good physical conditions and can quickly achieve excellent grades, while others may have weaker physical fitness. The evaluation system can develop personalized evaluation plans based on the characteristics of students with different physical fitness to meet the needs of each student's physical health development and interest.

(3) Long-term

   The construction of the evaluation system for physical education teaching in universities is a long-term and gradual process that requires continuous improvement and development. In the process of building an evaluation system, a gradual approach should be adopted, gradually adding new evaluation indicators, methods, and techniques, and regularly assessing and revising the evaluation system. In this way, the evaluation system can be gradually improved to make it more in line with the current requirements of physical education teaching in higher education.

   Core literacy is the ability to cultivate students' personal lifelong development and social development. However, the development process of different individuals is affected by different family, social environment, genetic factors, and other factors. There are certain differences in the psychological and physiological development process of each person. If a physical education teacher adopts a single level teaching evaluation model, it will only allow the top to settle down and stop moving forward, and the poor will become worse, which will affect the development of students. The hierarchical teaching evaluation of learning can ensure that different students can develop forward and cultivate their personal abilities. Layered evaluation teaching for students can greatly stimulate students' initiative in active learning. Evaluating students at different levels under the same teaching content is more targeted and more in line with their own situation. In the process of conducting hierarchical evaluation, students should be encouraged to achieve their goals through their own efforts and given certain rewards. This not only allows students to have in learning, but also helps them cultivate the awareness and ability of autonomous learning, enabling them to in classroom teaching and achieve comprehensive physical and mental development. Hierarchical evaluation meets the psychological in the process of seeking knowledge, allowing each student to learn in an environment with basically the same conditions in all aspects, placing them on the same starting line, and more conducive to helping students integrate into the atmosphere of collective learning.

4.2 Evaluation Process of Physical Education Teaching Based on Ant Colony Algorithm

Ant colony optimization algorithms is an optimization algorithm that simulates the self-organization behavior of ants. Its application in the evaluation process of physical education teaching is mainly to optimize the quality of evaluation results by simulating the behavior of ants seeking the shortest path between food sources and nests. The basic idea of Ant colony optimization algorithms is to use pheromones to assist the evaluation process. According to the concentration distribution of the generated Pheromone, it constantly guides ants to search for the best solution. The following three aspects introduce the application of Ant colony optimization algorithms in the process of sports teaching evaluation. The specific process is shown in Fig. 3:

Based on the collected evaluation results, we need to make result judgments in order to obtain better results of physical education teaching evaluation. In the evaluation process of Ant colony optimization algorithms, the evaluation result is composed of the path selected by more ants in the process of finding the shortest path. Therefore, the evaluation result is too single, and it is necessary to make statistics of various index data and statistical analysis in the process of judging the result, so as to obtain more accurate evaluation results. At the same time, in the process of judging the results, we should also compare and delete the evaluation results based on the standard values of the evaluation indicators, in order to make the evaluation more scientific and accurate.

Physical education micro class teaching is produced with the help of "Internet plus". Its teaching objectives, teaching contents and are traditional offline teaching, so the micro class should also be different. When evaluating the physical education micro class produced, students and teachers can communicate online in real time, Teachers should gradually guide students to discover their own shortcomings and advantages while acquiring skills and knowledge, thereby effectively helping students avoid similar problems in future learning, and helping them better acquire domain knowledge and skills. The evaluation mechanism for micro physical education courses will present a multidimensional, interactive and three-dimensional approach, changing the previous

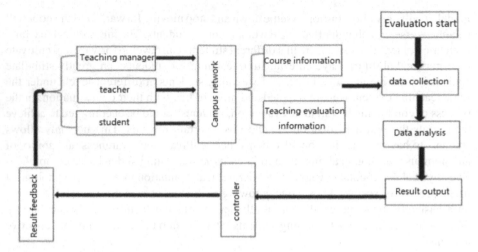

Fig. 3. Evaluation education teaching based on ant colony algorithm

single evaluation method into a comprehensive evaluation of sports emotions, sports skills, sports knowledge, and other aspects, to help students develop their potential. When evaluating micro physical education courses, teachers should also make evaluations and give affirmation based on students' learning and mastery of knowledge. Therefore, the under "Internet plus" may be a hot research direction in the future.

5   Conclusion

Ant colony optimization algorithms is an optimization algorithm that simulates the self-organization behavior of ants. Its application in the evaluation of physical education teaching can achieve more accurate and scientific evaluation results. Ant colony optimization algorithms is mainly used to optimize the evaluation strategy of physical education teaching and realize the optimization of evaluation indicators. Based on the Ant colony optimization algorithms, we can develop a variety of evaluation indicators, and constantly update the evaluation results by observing the Pheromone released by ants in the search path to achieve continuous optimization of the evaluation results. In this process, we can propose more targeted evaluation plans based on the diversity and personalized needs of students, taking into account each student's physical health and interest needs in a more comprehensive and detailed manner. Therefore, the application of Ant colony optimization algorithms in the evaluation of physical education teaching can more accurately evaluate students' performance in physical education learning. Through image data and Line chart, it is intuitive for students' individual performance and advantages and disadvantages. Combined with Ant colony optimization algorithms, it can realize personalized evaluation, reflect students' learning effect more truly and objectively, and improve the scientificity and effectiveness of evaluation.

References

1. Hao, H.: Application of random dynamic grouping simulation algorithm in PE teaching evaluation. Complexity **2021**, 1–10 (2021)
2. Xu, Q., Yin, J.: Application of random forest algorithm in physical education. Sci. Program. **2021**, 1996904 (2021)
3. Chen, Q.: Practical application of improved algorithm of association rules based on computer technology in teaching evaluation (2021)
4. Ding, L., Zeng, X.: Application of decision tree model based on C4.5 algorithm in nursing quality management evaluation. J. Med. Imaging Health Inform. **11**(9), 2359–2366 (2021)
5. Wang, S.: Genetic algorithm and BP neural network for college physical education teaching evaluation. Sci. Program. **2021**(1), 9921960 (2021)
6. Duan, X., Hou, P.: Research on teaching quality evaluation model of physical education based on simulated annealing algorithm (2021)
7. Deng, L., Deng, F., Wang, G.: Application of artificial bee colony algorithm and back propagation neural network in color evaluation of human–machine interaction interfaces. Eng. Rep. **4**(5), e12483 (2022)
8. Iduye, S.: Application of Fawcett's criteria in theory evaluation. Nurs. Sci. Q. **36**(1), 58–63 (2023)
9. Kang, L., Luo, Y., Yang, J.Z., et al.: A primal and dual active set algorithm for truncated L_1 regularized logistic regression. J. Ind. Manag. Optim. **19**(4), 2452–2463 (2023)
10. Zhu, J., Zheng, H., Yang, L., et al.: Evaluation of deep coal and gas outburst based on RS-GA-BP. Nat. Hazards **115**(3), 2531–2551 (2023)
11. Sun, B., Hu, Z., Liu, X., et al.: A physical model-free ant colony optimization network algorithm and full scale experimental investigation on ceiling temperature distribution in the utility tunnel fire. Int. J. Thermal Sci. **174**, 107436 (2022)
12. Zhang, C., Du, B., Li, K., et al.: Selection of the effective characteristic spectra based on the chemical structure and its application in rapid analysis of ethanol content in gasoline. ACS Omega **7**(23), 20291–20297 (2022)
13. He, X., Fu, S.: Data analysis and processing application of deep learning in engineering cost teaching evaluation. J. Math. **2022** (2022)
14. Zhang, C., Hu, C., Xie, S., et al.: Research on the application of decision tree and random forest algorithm in the main transformer fault evaluation. J. Phys. Conf. Ser. **1732**(1), 012086 (2021)
15. Xiaofeng, D.: Application of deep learning and artificial intelligence algorithm in multimedia music teaching (Retraction of Vol 38, Pg 7241, 2020). J. Intell. Fuzzy Syst. Appl. Eng. Technol. **5**, 41 (2021)

Design and Implementation of College Students' Psychological Prediction System Based on BP Algorithm

Hui Yuan$^{(\boxtimes)}$ and Xu Yan

Shandong Institute of Commerce and Technology, Jinan 250103, Shandong, China
yuanhui5681@163.com

Abstract. Because the mental health problems of college students have been paid more and more attention, it is necessary to design the psychological prediction system of college students through BP algorithm, and actually use the system to help carry out psychological intervention of college students. In order to achieve the purpose, this paper will carry out related research, first introduced the basic concept of BP algorithm, then based on the algorithm proposed the design ideas and implementation methods of college students psychological prediction system, and the system has been tested. Through the research, the prediction results of the BP algorithm of college students psychological prediction system are accurate and comprehensive, can help do a good job of college students psychological intervention, so that college students maintain healthy psychological state.

Keywords: BP algorithm · Mental health of college students · Mental prediction system

1 Introduction

In recent years, the mental health problem of college students has become more and more serious, which has a great impact on the current study and future development of college students. Therefore, the majority of the society pays more attention to this problem, and the responsibility of the education field is more significant. But for a long time, the field of education in the face of college students' mental health problems at a cost, that is, educational organizations clearly know how to intervene in college students' unhealthy psychology, or how to help college students to continue to maintain a healthy psychological state, but the application of relevant methods have a necessary premise, that is, to understand the current psychological status of college students, analyze their future may appear unhealthy psychology, only in this way can intervention be carried out according to the symptoms. However, educational organizations are limited here, and it is difficult for faculty members to accurately predict the development trend of college students' psychological conditions. In view of this phenomenon, the research field puts forward a psychological prediction system for college students. Theoretically,

© ICST Institute for Computer Sciences, Social Informatics and Telecommunications Engineering 2024
Published by Springer Nature Switzerland AG 2024. All Rights Reserved
Y. Zhang and N. Shah (Eds.): BigIoT-EDU 2023, LNICST 582, pp. 210–220, 2024.
https://doi.org/10.1007/978-3-031-63136-8_22

the system will break through the current limitations, help faculty members analyze the current psychological conditions of college students, and then give the prediction results. If the results are accurate enough, the mental health problems of college students can be well controlled. At this time, how to ensure the accuracy of the prediction results becomes a topic worth discussing. Under this topic, the research field points out that the accuracy of prediction results largely depends on the algorithm carried by the system. Therefore, through comparison, BP algorithm is considered to be the optimal algorithm. Therefore, it is necessary to study the design and implementation of college students' psychological prediction system centering on this algorithm.

Basic concepts of BP algorithm.

BP algorithm is an algorithm created by imitating the operation mode of people's neural thinking. There are many types of BP algorithm, and the common types are shown in Table 1.

Table 1. Common types of BP algorithm

The name of the	The characteristics of
Feed forward type	Logic forward, do not repeat
Feedback type	Logic repeats, reaching the termination condition after output

Combined with Table 1, because different types of BP algorithm are applicable to different situations, so the practical application should make a reasonable choice according to the situation. This paper mainly selects the psychological prediction problem of college students. Because the problem is a typical linear problem, the logic is not repeated, so the feedforward BP algorithm is selected, and only the concept of this kind of BP algorithm is discussed in detail [1–3].

Like other types of BP algorithms, feedforward BP algorithm belongs to machine learning algorithm, but the difference lies in that the learning process of feedforward BP algorithm only includes two learning mechanisms: forward propagation and error cycle. Among them, forward propagation is a learning mechanism under normalization, which can directly obtain the final result. The error cycle is started when there is a large error between the results obtained under the forward propagation mechanism and the expected standard, which means that the algorithm will carry out the forward propagation process on the basis of the existing results until the final results meet the expected standard [4].

The basic idea of all BP algorithms, including feedforward BP algorithm, is the same, that is, data in the algorithm model will be logically propagated from the input layer, through the input layer will enter the hidden layer to receive layer by layer processing, and the final result will be transmitted to the output layer, which is responsible for display. In this process, if the error cyclic learning mechanism is started, it will fall into the cyclic learning process. The method of error elimination in this process is as follows: The error value between the existing result and the expected standard is evenly divided into other layers of units, thus obtaining the error signal of each layer of units [5–7]. The signal is used as the reference to modify the weight of each layer of units to adjust the weight. The result obtained after each weight adjustment will be regarded as "knowledge" and saved, so as to realize learning, and the error will be reduced with the continuous repetition of the learning process. It is worth noting that the initialized feedforward BP algorithm will cycle without limit after the error cycle mechanism is started, but this may lead to too many cycles, which means the convergence of the algorithm becomes worse, and the calculation process may fall into the dilemma of local optimal solution [8–10]. Therefore, in order to avoid this problem, it is necessary to set a termination condition artificially, and there are many types of termination conditions. See Table 2 for details.

Table 2. Common types of termination conditions after the error cycle mechanism of feedforward BP algorithm is started

The name of the	The characteristics of
Maximum number of studies	Indicates that the number of learning times has a upper limit, and the learning activity is terminated when the upper limit is reached. Adoption of such termination conditions may result in incomplete final results
Maximum allowable error	The error acceptance range of the final result is adjustable. If the value is set to 0, the final result must be completely consistent with the expected standard before output. If the value is set to 3, the error between the final result and the expected standard can be output as long as it is less than 3, and so on
Maximum number of iterations	Indicates that the number of iterations has an upper limit, and the learning activity terminates when the upper limit is reached. Adoption of such termination conditions may result in incomplete final results

According to Table 2, in general, people have personalized requirements for the accuracy of the final results, and generally hope that the higher the accuracy, the better, so it is usually recommended to choose the maximum allowable error. However, in the prediction of college students' mental health, because it is a prediction, the requirement for accuracy is not high, so it is recommended to choose the maximum number of learning or the maximum number of iterations, and the former is chosen in this paper.

Figure 1 shows the basic framework of the feedforward BP algorithm.

Combined with Fig. 1, the forward propagation process of the feedforward BP algorithm occurs between the input layer, hidden layer and output, while the error cycle process occurs between the output and input layer, that is, the output takes the last result as the next input to the input layer and forms a new input node. This is a complete error cycle process. Then the learning process based on the new input node is a new round of forward propagation. In this process, the feedforward BP algorithm mainly needs to deal with the problem of data feature extraction. Its main function is to let the feedforward BP algorithm identify the data for easy learning. The expression of data feature extraction is shown in Formula (1).

$$X1, 2, ...n = \frac{(X + A)/(X + B)/(X + C)}{S} \tag{1}$$

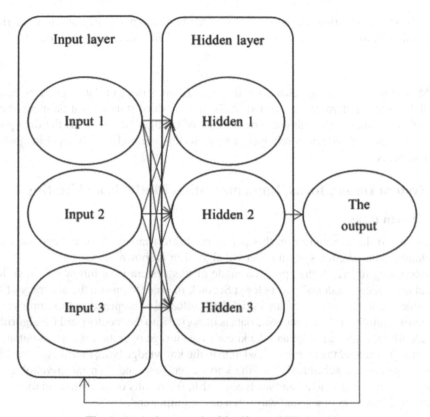

Fig. 1. Basic framework of feedforward BP algorithm

where, X1,2… n is the data feature set, S is the dimension where the data feature resides, A, B and C are X1,2…,n, the feature value items of any X feature are occurrence probability, time ordering and attribute respectively. From this, the A, B and C values of the data in the S-dimension can be obtained.

This rule is to transform all data into [0,1], thereby reducing the impact of magnitude between different data. For a data x, after standardization, the converted result x is:

$$x_i' = \frac{x_i - x_{min}}{x_{max} - x_{min}} \tag{2}$$

When it is difficult to obtain the maximum and minimum attribute values of attribute values, or there are some data that are not within the above numerical range, it is necessary to process them. Usually, the method used is to convert the original overall data using mean and standard deviation. For an outlier data x;, The result x after z-score standardization is:

$$x_i' = \frac{x_i - \mu}{\sigma} \tag{3}$$

In the formula, μ represents the mean value of the original data, and o represents the standard deviation of the original data.

This standardization method achieves standardization by degrading numerical values, that is, moving the decimal point in the data. The calculation formula is:

$$x_i' = \frac{x_i}{10^j} \qquad (4)$$

Maintaining the change characteristics of attribute values of data well is currently a widely used standardization method. Although the third standardization method can simplify the data to fall within a certain range of changes, it only uses the data point movement method, which is relatively rough, so this method is only used in specific environments.

2 System Design Ideas, Implementation Methods and Testing

2.1 Design Ideas

According to the assumption in this paper, the basic framework of college students' psychological prediction system under BP algorithm is shown in Fig. 2.

According to Fig. 2, the operation mode of this system is as follows: first, collect data about college students' psychology; Second, in order to ensure the accuracy of the subsequent calculation results, the initial data collected is preprocessed to improve the data purity; thirdly, the pre-processed data is imported into the feedforward BP algorithm module for machine learning, and the knowledge storage operation is carried out at the same time to transfer the learned knowledge to the knowledge base; Fourth, the machine learning results are scheduled from the knowledge base and then the psychology of college students is predicted and analyzed. Fifth, the results of predictive analysis will be displayed to users in a visual way, such as the output end.

2.2 Implementation Method

According to the basic framework of the system, the realization of each part of the system is as follows.

2.2.1 Data Collection

The system has a special demand for data collection, which cannot be collected by simple methods such as conventional data collection. That is to say, college students' psychology itself does not have the characteristics of output data, and since the mental health problems of college students at the present stage are not significant, it is difficult to obtain effective data from behavior, so we can only understand college students' current ideology, ideology, values and other abstract indicators. Then you have to quantify the results to get the data. According to this requirement, the data acquisition method of this system is as follows: The system is equipped with the learning platform provided by educational organizations, and psychological experts are responsible for the design of psychological questionnaires. The survey questions in the questionnaires are closely related to college students' ideology, ideology and values. Then, questionnaires are issued to college students regularly through the platform, and college students fill in the questionnaires independently, which will generate survey data, and the data will be automatically introduced into the system after submission. Complete data collection.

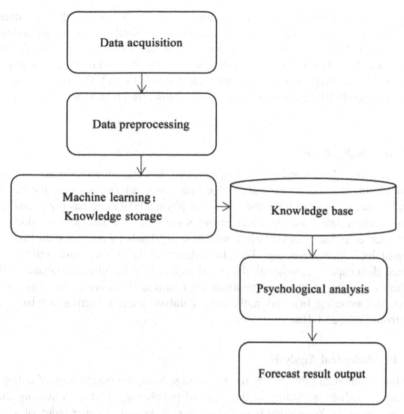

Fig. 2. The basic framework of college students' psychological prediction system based on BP algorithm

2.2.2 Data Preprocessing

Since it is impossible to ensure that all students pay attention to data quality during data collection, the initial data collected may have defects such as duplication and blank. If these data are imported into the algorithm, the accuracy of the final result will inevitably decline, so it needs to be pre-processed in advance. The realization method of data preprocessing is relatively simple, and it is feasible to directly choose the current mature data preprocessing tools. Such tools are various and can solve most of the data quality problems, so it is suggested to choose directly, and there is no need for secondary development. In this paper, two tools of data de-duplication and blank value generation are selected to meet the operation requirements of the following steps of the system.

2.2.3 Machine Learning and Knowledge Storage

In terms of machine learning, the basic framework of feedforward BP algorithm is built according to Fig. 1, and the algorithm is packaged by programming method to form an algorithm module. When the pre-processed data is obtained, the module will start to operate according to the framework logic, which is divided into two processes: forward propagation and error cycle. If the termination condition is reached, the algorithm will stop until a new round of data input. Knowledge is constantly generated from this.

In terms of knowledge storage, output node is mainly set in the feedforward BP algorithm module. The initial value of this stage is [0]. If new knowledge is generated, the initial value of output node will change, and the value is [1]. The value of the output node is returned to [0], and the exported data is transferred to the knowledge base to be saved.

2.2.4   Knowledge Base

The essence of knowledge base is database, but this system chooses the knowledge base for cloud database. The cloud database has many advantages over the traditional physical database. For example, the traditional physical database has high construction cost and limited data capacity, which requires continuous expansion. In addition, the physical server is faulty or damaged, which easily leads to internal data loss, and is not conducive to long-term use. The cloud database has a low construction cost and unlimited data capacity. Although the initial capacity of the cloud database is limited for security reasons, expansion operations are required if necessary, but this operation does not cost anything. In addition, the cloud database itself is a virtual database, which is free from faults and damage.

2.2.5   Psychological Analysis

According to the data provided by the knowledge base, the psychology of college students can be judged according to the logic of psychology, that is, assuming that the BP algorithm in the knowledge base shows that the positive degree index of a college student is -1, and the standard value is 1, which represents that the college student is in a weak degree of negative psychological state, and the analogy can be used to analyze the complex psychological situation. And output an organized result.

2.2.6   Psychological Prediction

According to the results of psychological analysis, it can predict the psychological condition of college students. Taking the weak negative psychological state of college students as an example, according to the logic of psychology, the future psychological development direction of college students may be more serious negative psychology. In this process, the feedforward neural network algorithm will also calculate the development probability of this trend according to continuous data. If the student's psychological positivity for three consecutive days is $-1, -2$, and -2.5 in the calculation of BP algorithm, it means that the probability of the development of this trend is getting higher and higher. In this way, the faculty can make accurate judgment for targeted intervention.

2.3   Testing

Take a college student as the test object, first through the expert manual evaluation to get accurate results, that is, the future development trend of the college student psychology is negative, the probability is 80%–93%, and then adopt this system for evaluation, the results show that the future development trend of the college student psychology is negative, the probability is 91%, out of the expert evaluation range, so the system application is effective.

3 Mental Health Counseling Service Functions

The mental health consulting service function is to provide users with mental health consulting services from a professional perspective, which can further optimize the professional level of the mental health platform. The specific functions of mental health consulting services include psychological testing, expert consultation, psychological information, and psychological community functions. As shown in Fig. 3.

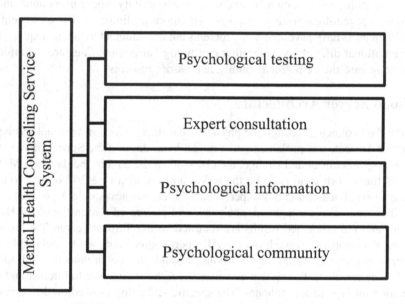

Fig. 3. Mental Health Counseling Service Functions

The psychological testing function provides powerful and comprehensive psychological testing, which covers a wide range of five aspects, including emotion, personality, ability, interest, and specialty. Users can choose the appropriate psychological test according to their preferences, and judge the severity of their psychological problems based on the test results. If they feel that they need it, they can consult a psychological consultant. The professional type of psychological testing is a test question selected by a psychologist from a professional psychological testing question bank, such as the Harvard Professional Aptitude Test Scale. These questions require a certain fee and can receive advice from a psychologist based on the test questions.

The psychological information function is to help users better understand themselves and their opponents, listening to the opinions of a psychological consultant while understanding other people's real cases, thereby solving users' inner confusion. In psychological counseling, case push includes "personality", "happiness", "ability", and other related push items in a case, and providing comments and response functions can improve user interaction.

The expert consultation function, as the name suggests, provides expert consultation services throughout the country, including consultation centers and psychological clinics. These experts can provide professional advice on anxiety, obsessive compulsive disorder, depression, hypochondria, and schizophrenia, ranging from mild to severe. In order to facilitate users' on-site medical treatment, a positioning function is also provided to locate a nearby psychological consultant. Provide a reputation classification based on the user satisfaction of the psychologist. Provide a qualification ranking based on the professional level of psychological counselors, such as national level 2 psychological counselors higher than national level 3 psychological counselors.

The psychological community function is a community where users anonymously publish their psychological status, express their emotions, find confidants, and help each other. When users have psychological problems but are reluctant to talk to acquaintances due to emotional difficulties, unfamiliar psychological communities are a platform to help them release their emotional, family, and work pressures.

4 Cloud Server Architecture

After the data collected through the physiological data collection terminal reaches the web server Tomcat, it is packaged into a model bean through the Spring framework to facilitate logical control and storage, thereby storing the data in the database MySQL. The SSH framework is adopted on the server and the idea of MVC is used to divide the entire server back-end into data persistence layer, business model layer, and control layer. Then, the data is integrated, analyzed, and processed within the cloud Hadoop platform, and the processed results are returned to the Tomcat server. The front-end rendering is performed through the EasyUI open source framework, and displayed to users in browsers (IE, Safari, and Chrome) through the BS architecture. In addition to the B/S architecture, the system also uses the C/S architecture to interact and share information on mobile smartphones. The specific technologies used on the server side are as follows:

The database uses MySQL database, which is an open source relational database management system (RDBMS). It has attracted much attention due to its fast speed, high reliability, and strong adaptability. It also supports multithreading like Java. The database server must ensure both data persistence and integrity and consistency. The massive data of users are stored in the database server. The mental health management system will use the user's basic information, heartbeat characteristic information, real-time chat data, etc. These data are stored in the MySQL database. Through the database server, it is possible to obtain files stored in the file server that store various types of images uploaded by users, various types of video and audio, and records user characteristics. Part of the class diagram design is shown in Fig. 4 below.

Spring uses the concept of a model to encapsulate basic Java classes into beans. Unlike JavaBeans, which must comply with certain specifications, Spring has no requirements for beans. Spring manages these beans as a core container, so that all objects in

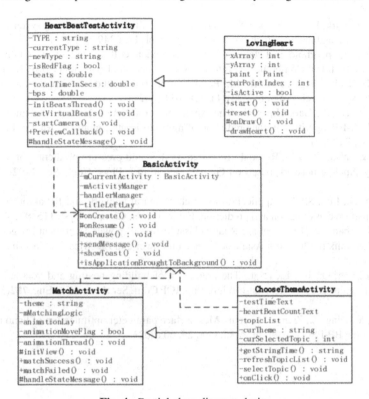

Fig. 4. Partial class diagram design

the Web, including data sources, and basic resources are managed by Spring. Spring provides a lightweight solution for Web development, based on the core mechanism of dependency injection and AOP declarative transaction management, running through the presentation layer, business layer, and persistence layer. At the same time, Spring has many advantages, such as low intrusion design, environmentally friendly code, and independence from other application servers. Spring's IOC container implements loose decoupling between components.

5 Conclusion

To sum up, the results obtained by the psychological prediction system of college students based on BP algorithm are accurate, which can help the faculty understand the psychology of college students, grasp the future development trend of their psychology, and then conduct targeted intervention. In this way, the mental health of Chinese college students can be guaranteed.

References

1. Shi, J., Liu, G., Zhou, J.: Prediction of college students' psychological crisis based on data mining. Mob. Inf. Syst. **23**, 1–7 (2021)

2. Wang, T., Park, J.: Design and implementation of intelligent sports training system for college students' mental health education. Frontiers Psychol. **12**, 634978 (2021)
3. Liu, H.: The psychological status of vocational female college students based on SPSS. In: 2020 International Conference on Information Science and Education(ICISE-IE) (2020)
4. Yao, H., Dahlan Hj, A., Malek, M.: Prediction of college students' employment rate based on gray system. Sci. Program. **2021**(1), 4182011 (2021)
5. Gao, Y., Li, H., Gao, H., et al.: The Application Of Neural Network Technology Based On MEA-BP algorithm in the prediction of microdosimetric qualities. Radiat. Prot. Dosim. **2022**(7), 7 (2022)
6. Xia ,W., Wang, Y., Liu, R., et al.: Research on flow and pressure prediction of urban water supply pipeline network based on GA-BP algorithm.J. Phys. Conf. Ser. **1792**(1), 012045 (2021)
7. Zhang, D., Lou, S.: The application research of neural network and BP algorithm in stock price pattern classification and prediction. Future Gener. Comput. Syst. **115**, 872–879 (2021)
8. He, G., Zhang, Z., Li, H., et al.: Rough classification of power equipment images based on BP algorithm. In: 2021 6th Asia Conference on Power and Electrical Engineering (ACPEE) (2021)
9. Sun, L.,Wei, Q., He, L., et al.: The prediction of building heating and ventilation energy consumption base on Adaboost-bp algorithm. IOP Conf. Ser.:Mater. Sci. Eng. **782**(3), 032008 (2020)
10. Chen, Y., Ding, Z., Zhang, M., et al.: Metasurface parameter optimization of Fano resonance based on a BP-PSO algorithm. Appl. Opt. **29**, 60 (2021)

Research on the Application of BP Neural Network Algorithm in the Practical Teaching of Public Physical Education in Colleges and Universities

Zhenhua Cheng$^{(\boxtimes)}$ and Lihong Shi

Sports Department, Modern College of Northwest University, Xi'an 710130, Shaanxi, China
251721357@qq.com

Abstract. This article studies the application of BP neural network algorithm in practical teaching of public physical education in universities. Through the introduction and exploration of BP neural network algorithm, combined with the characteristics and needs of public sports practice teaching in colleges and universities, this paper puts forward the method of using BP neural network algorithm to monitor and evaluate the state of Student activism' sports, and applies and verifies it in actual teaching. Starting from the research goal of cultivating sports professionals, this paper systematically discusses the important concepts and interrelationships of practical ability, practical ability, and hands-on ability of sports major college students, as well as their understanding and basic viewpoints on this study. The BP neural network algorithm is a multi-layer feedforward network with learning and adaptability. In the monitoring and evaluation of exercise status, BP neural networks can be used to monitor and evaluate students' exercise indicators such as heart rate, electrocardiogram, and posture. Due to the high accuracy and strong robustness of the BP neural network algorithm, it can effectively reduce the error rate of evaluation while ensuring accuracy.

The application results show that the BP neural network algorithm has good effects in the practical teaching of public sports in universities, effectively constructing an efficient and accurate system for monitoring and evaluating sports status. This method provides a more autonomous, fast, and accurate monitoring and evaluation plan for sports status, providing valuable experience and reference for the teaching reform and innovation of public sports practical courses. In summary, this study demonstrates that the application of BP neural network algorithm in practical teaching of public physical education in universities has good results and application prospects. Based on this, it may be necessary to further deepen the research on motion state monitoring and evaluation using BP neural network algorithm in the future, explore more scientific and effective teaching methods, and make contributions to improving the quality and effectiveness of public physical education teaching in universities.

Keywords: College public sports · BP neural network · Practical teaching

Y. Zhang and N. Shah (Eds.): BigIoT-EDU 2023, LNICST 582, pp. 221–231, 2024.
https://doi.org/10.1007/978-3-031-63136-8_23

1 Introduction

With the continuous improvement of people's living standards and the enhancement of public sports awareness, practical teaching of public sports in universities has become an indispensable part of the contemporary university education system. As a discipline that is crucial for students' physical fitness and healthy development, the quality and effectiveness of public sports practice have a direct impact on students' growth and development. However, in practical teaching, the difficulty and complexity of evaluating students' physical condition and exercise effectiveness are relatively high, and there is currently a lack of scientific and effective monitoring and evaluation methods, which brings great challenges to teaching practice. Therefore, this article explores the application of BP neural network algorithm in public sports practical teaching in universities. Through the introduction and application experiments of this algorithm, new ideas and methods are provided for the improvement and innovation of public sports practical teaching. Through the research in this article, we can see that the BP neural network algorithm has obvious advantages in motion state monitoring and evaluation. Using this algorithm to monitor and evaluate the state of Student activism can achieve high precision and strong robustness, improve the accuracy of monitoring and evaluation, and effectively avoid misleading and human interference. The cultivation and development of practical ability is the goal of the whole education, society and family, and the important connotation of lifelong learning and lifelong education. University is an important stage of life-long education and the most important period of systematic learning before college students go to society. promoting students to actively adapt to society are the requirements of the times and the bounden mission and responsibility of higher education [1].

But there are still obvious defects due to the system and mechanism. Mainly reflected in the quality education has not been fully implemented. Many schools talk more about the cultivation of practical ability than they actually do, or it is common to reduce or cancel the practice link on the grounds of insufficient funds and difficult conditions; In the course structure configuration, we should pay more attention to subjects than experiments, and pay more attention to knowledge than skills [2]; In classroom teaching, we should pay attention to the systematization, coherence and logicality of knowledge, and ignore the intersection, integration and practicality of disciplines; In terms of teaching methods, cramming and infusing teaching are still rampant. The facts show that the practical ability of the graduates majoring in Physical Education in China is generally insufficient at present, which is reflected in whether they can recite theoretical knowledge, whether they can do professional skills or not, and what's more, they can neither speak nor do. It shows that they are lack of practical skills, divorced from theory and practice, and are not good at solving practical problems [3, 4].

With social development and human progress, the multiple functions of sports have been continuously developed, and the impact and role of sports on the economy, politics, education, culture and other aspects of human society have become increasingly apparent. Physical quality is an integral part of national quality and an important material basis of national quality. there is an urgent need for all kinds of sports professionals, especially high-quality sports professionals.

In practical teaching, the method proposed in this article has also been fully applied and validated. Teachers can use BP neural network algorithms to monitor and evaluate students' exercise status and effectiveness, dynamically adjust teaching content and methods, improve teaching effectiveness and quality, and achieve the goal of innovating and reforming public physical education practice teaching. In summary, this article provides new ideas and methods for public sports practical teaching by studying the application of BP neural network algorithm in university public sports practical teaching. At the same time, it also makes beneficial explorations and contributions to the theory and practice of sports state monitoring and evaluation.

2 Related Work

2.1 The Meaning of Practical Ability

Generally speaking, The so-called "practical ability" is "the ability to complete practical activities". This paper defines practice as "the process of implementing practical ideas, that is, the objective material activities that actually solve problems or complete tasks". This paper holds that "ability is the psychological and physiological and play a stable role in regulation". Based on the above understanding of practice and ability, we define practical ability as and play a role of stable regulation [5]. This definition includes the following points: first, the bearer of practical ability is the individual; Second, practical ability is embodied in the interaction between subject and object; Thirdly, practical ability is the sum of psychological and physiological characteristics.

Practical ability and ability are both related and different from each other. Ability is the upper concept of practical ability, which includes practical ability and other abilities [6].

In the field of pedagogy, since the mid-nineteenth century, countries with different social natures in the East and the West have focused on cultivating students' practical ability. In the East, the former Soviet Union led the rise of the "combination of education and labor"; In the west, represented by the United States, "learning by doing" germinated. "Combining teaching with labor" and "learning by doing", as two orientations connecting knowledge teaching and students' practical experience, have guided the educational reform in eastern [7–9]. So far, the two educational reform attempts of "combining teaching with labor" and "learning by doing" to cultivate students' practical ability have not achieved the desired results in China.

2.2 Neural Network Evaluation Method

Neural network evaluation method refers to the use of neural networks for data processing and analysis, in order to obtain more accurate and reliable data evaluation methods. Neural network evaluation methods have been widely applied in various fields and application scenarios. This article will analyze the application scope, advantages, and limitations of neural network evaluation methods.

Firstly, neural network evaluation methods have been applied in various fields and application scenarios. In situations where traditional statistical evaluation methods cannot meet the requirements, neural network evaluation methods provide a new approach and approach. For example, in fields such as medicine, finance, and logistics, using neural network evaluation methods can make data processing more accurate and efficient, and improve the accuracy and reliability of data analysis.

Secondly, neural network evaluation methods have many advantages. First of all, neural networks can be Adaptive learning and optimization, can process and analyze large or complex data, and have higher accuracy and robustness. In addition, neural network evaluation methods do not require making assumptions or models in advance, and can effectively handle the nonlinear characteristics of data, improving the overall effectiveness of data analysis.

However, neural network evaluation methods also have some limitations. Firstly, the training and optimization of neural networks require a significant amount of time, computational resources, and data consumption. In addition, the model architecture and optimization algorithms of neural networks also need to be adjusted and optimized in conjunction with practical application scenarios, otherwise errors or overfitting may occur. The topological structure of BP neural network is shown in Fig. 1.

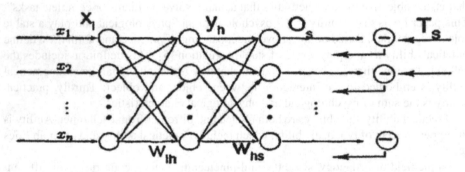

Fig. 1. Topological structure of BP neural network

For different application purposes, the functions they are responsible for are also quite different, so we should be very careful when choosing again.

In Fig. 2, the input information, w; The relationship between them is as follows:

$$Y = WX + b \tag{1}$$

Here:

$$X = \begin{bmatrix} x_1 \\ x_2 \\ \cdots \\ x_n \end{bmatrix} \tag{2}$$

$$W = (w_1, w_2, \cdots, w_n) \tag{3}$$

$$y = \varphi(v) = \varphi(wx + b) \tag{4}$$

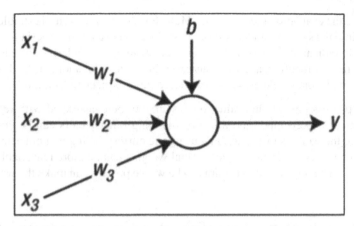

Fig. 2. Schematic diagram of neural network structure of neurons

The φ in the formula is the excitation function mentioned above.

The node between the hidden layer and the output layer is W, and the input variable is X, then the output of the hidden layer and the output layer are respectively:

$$Z_k = f_1(\sum_{i=1}^{n} V_{ki}X_i), k = 1, ..., q \tag{5}$$

$$Y_j = f_2(\sum_{k=1}^{q} w_{ki}Z_i), j = 1, ..., m \tag{6}$$

If p input samples are set, the error function of each input sample is:

$$E_p = \frac{1}{2}\sum_{j=1}^{m} (y_{jp} - y_{jp'})^2 \tag{7}$$

In summary, neural network evaluation methods have wide applications and advantages, as they can improve the accuracy and reliability of data analysis, providing new ideas and approaches for complex data processing and analysis. However, in application, it is also necessary to adjust and optimize the model architecture and optimization algorithms of neural networks based on actual application scenarios to achieve better results.

2.3 Design of Evaluation Index System

Through consultation, The whole process can be summarized as follows: first, collect a large amount of data through consultation, interviews and questionnaires, and then collect, sort out and count the data to in the whole evaluation system, that is, the weight.

(1) Specify the provider of evaluation data. In the above process, this paper has pointed out the evaluation method of combining various opinions. However, in the specific practice process, there are inevitable human factors, so the evaluation method is non-linear. This method is particularly important in this process. It can solve many nonlinear problems in reality, so it has irreplaceable advantages. And the algorithm has been successfully applied to solve practical problems.

(2) Improve the evaluation index system. Multi-level evaluation criteria should be introduced into the system. Students should use different evaluation criteria for PE teaching evaluation and teachers' previous mutual evaluation. And according to different disciplines, different evaluation standards should also be adopted. In this process, so as to make the whole evaluation standard more perfect and sound.

In this process, the whole evaluation system can be constructed with reference to the opinions of experts, and then the corresponding other factors can be constructed. By inputting the weights of experts and using the corresponding computer technology, that is, through network training, the original weights can be more reasonable, and the final results can be objective and accurate. The whole process can make the weight more reasonable.

3 Application of BP Neural Network Algorithm in College Public Physical Education Practice Teaching

3.1 Application of BP Neural Network

There are many applications of neural network evaluation methods in physical education teaching management, which can improve teaching quality and effectiveness. The following will explain from several aspects, including course design, student management, and teacher guidance.

Firstly, the neural network evaluation method can be applied to the design of physical education courses. By collecting students' physical and athletic ability data and analyzing them using neural network evaluation methods, it is possible to objectively understand their physical fitness and athletic level, better grasp their characteristics and needs, arrange physical education courses reasonably, and improve teaching effectiveness and student participation.

Secondly, neural network evaluation methods can be applied to student management. By using neural network evaluation methods to monitor and evaluate students' physical condition and exercise ability, it is possible to timely understand their health status and exercise effectiveness. If abnormal situations occur, effective management measures can be taken in a timely manner to ensure students' physical health and safety.

Finally, neural network evaluation methods can be applied to teacher guidance. By using neural networks to monitor and evaluate students' body data, teachers can better understand their physical fitness and motor ability characteristics, develop personalized training plans and guidance plans for students' shortcomings and problems, and improve teaching quality and effectiveness.

Because BP neural network has excellent nonlinear approximation ability, it has been widely used in many scientific fields since 1994. The following briefly introduces several application fields of BP neural network at present: 1 Information processing field, is shown in Fig. 3.

In short, neural network evaluation methods can play a huge role in physical education teaching management, helping teachers better understand students' physical characteristics and needs, improve teaching effectiveness and student participation, and ensure students' physical health and safety. Relevant departments can conduct specific research and practice, continuously explore the application of this method in physical education teaching management, and explore better methods and means.

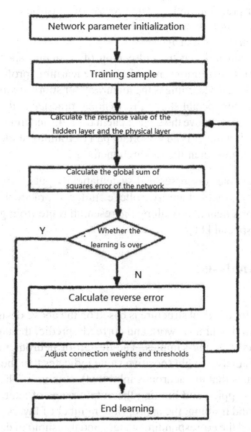

Fig. 3. Neural network physical education practice teaching training flow chart

4 Application of Public Physical Education Practice Teaching in Colleges and Universities

1. The number of colleges and universities offering sports and sports related majors in China is increasing. The types of sports majors in Colleges and universities are developing. Sports colleges and universities are the most concentrated and extensive colleges and universities offering sports and sports related majors.
2. Experience, skill and teacher training are the basic attributes of sports major. Based on this, the training of sports professionals must vigorously strengthen the practical links, and attach great importance to the improvement of sports skills and educational literacy.

3. There are three basic ways to cultivate students' practical ability in physical education institutions, namely, classroom teaching, extracurricular activities and social practice. Extracurricular activities are an important way to guide students' autonomous learning and cultivate their practical ability. The process of must be connected with the real society and social activities, so that students can verify and develop their knowledge and ability in social practice [10].
4. There are three main links in the cultivation of students' special practical ability in physical education institutions, namely, course learning, professional practice and graduation thesis. Course learning is the main way for sports majors to acquire special knowledge and master special skills. Professional practice is the necessary link and important guarantee to achieve the goal of talent training and improve students' practical ability. Graduation thesis is an important part of training students' comprehensive professional ability and scientific research methods.

To sum up, this chapter discusses and systematically puts forward the understanding of practice, ability, practical ability, college students' practical ability and physical education students' practical ability along the research route from general to individual and from general to special [11].

5 Simulation Analysis

Model Building
The design of model topological structure is based on the above design idea. It is the first problem to build a good neural network and correctly predict the target sample through learning 150 students' training samples. The design of neurons must be based on its four core elements, namely, weight (positive value indicates that the neuron is activated, negative value indicates that the neuron is inhibited), sum unit. The excitation function (realizing nonlinear mapping and limiting the output range of neurons) and threshold.

During learning and training, the appropriate number of layers, determined through continuous testing, and the corresponding weight and threshold of each input item can be obtained by this model. In this way, we can use this model to input the learning behavior data of students' courses to predict the final exam results of students, so as to achieve the purpose of predicting their learning effects according to their daily learning behavior.
Model Solving
The experimental environment is built based on python 3.7. This framework can not only well support the widely used Windows, Linux and other major operating systems, Even for mobile phones, it can provide good support. It is also the high-level neural network API of TensorFlow and Theano. Keras library can help developers not to put too much energy into the details of the bottom layer, and enable developers to quickly turn ideas into reality. At present, Keras has been included in TensorFlow, not only becoming the default framework of TensorFlow, but also becoming the official advanced API of TensorFlow [12–15]. The main code of Python program is shown in Fig. 4 below.
Training Boundary Analysis
Neural network structure. After many experiments and modifications. Excitation function. The input layer uses the default ReLu function (Corrected Linear Units) of the Keras library, and the other layers use the sigmoid function.

from keras.models import load_model, Model

from keras.layers import Dense, Activation, Dropout, Input, LSTM, Reshape, Lambda, RepeatVector

from keras.initializers import glorot_uniform

from keras.utils import to_categorical

from keras.optimizers import Adam

from keras import backend as K

from keras.models import Sequential

from keras.layers import Dense, LSTM, GRU

Fig. 4. Main code of Python program

L The expression of ReLu function is: $Relu(x) = f(x) = \{\begin{matrix} 0, x \leq 0 \\ x, x > 0 \end{matrix}$, we can see that the function is a single-measure inhibition function, and its value is 0 for all non-positive independent variables; For arguments greater than 0, the function value remains unchanged [16–20].

The expression of the ll sigmoid function is: sigmoid $Sigmoid(x) = f(x) = \frac{1}{1-e^{-x}}$, function is $[-\infty, \infty]$, , and the value domain is (0,1). The image of the function is an S-shaped curve, sometimes called a growth curve. The function has two very important properties, one is that the function is continuous, smooth, and differentiable everywhere in its definition domain; The second is that the function is centrosymmetric at x−0.5. It is precisely this function that has such good properties [17–20]. This function can not only describe the uncertainty of the decision in a smaller granularity.

6   Conclusion

In practical activities, the general practical ability does not point to the solution of special problems, but runs through all links of solving specific problems and serves as the physiological and psychological basis of the practical process. If the development of the elements of general practical ability is not comprehensive and sufficient, it will directly hinder and restrict the completion of practical activities. General practical ability includes perceptual ability, athletic ability, communicative ability and other elements, which are both independent and interrelated. The practice activities in different fields have different emphasis on the requirements of the general practical ability of the practice subject. The complexity of this problem can be solved by using appropriate algorithms. This paper presents a new method, which can solve this problem conveniently and effectively.

References

1. Tan, X.: Application of random simulation algorithm in practical teaching of public physical education in colleges and universities. In: Jan, M.A., Khan, F. (eds.) Application of Big Data, Blockchain, and Internet of Things for Education Informatization. BigIoT-EDU 2022.Social Informatics and Telecommunications Engineering. LNICS, vol. 465, pp. 298–309. Springer, Cham (2023). https://doi.org/10.1007/978-3-031-23950-2_32

2. Yunan, G., Haiyang, L., Han, G., et al.: The application of neural network technology based on MEA-BP algorithm in the prediction of microdosimetric qualities. Radiat. Prot. Dosim. (7), 7. https://doi.org/10.1093/rpd/ncac062. 07 June 2023
3. Li, Z.: Application of the BP neural network model of gray relational analysis in economic management. J. Math. **2022** (2022)
4. Research on the application of the radiative transfer model based on deep neural network in one-dimensional variational algorithm. 热带气象学报:英文版 **28**(3), 326–342 (2022)
5. Konakoglu, B., Aydemir, S.B., Onay, F.K.: Application of a metaheuristic gradient-based optimizer algorithm integrated into artificial neural network model in a local geoid modeling with global navigation satellite systems/levelling measurements. Concurr. Comput. Practice Exp. **34**(18), e7017 (2022)
6. Al-Abrrow, H., Halbusi, H.A., Chew, X.Y., et al.: Uncovering the antecedents of trust in social commerce: an application of the non-linear artificial neural network approach. Compet. Rev. Int. Bus. J. **32**(3), 492–523 (2022). https://doi.org/10.1108/CR-04-2021-0051
7. Tolgfors, B., Quennerstedt, M., Backman, E., et al.: Enacting assessment for learning in the induction phase of physical education teaching. Eur. Phys. Educ. Rev. **28**(2), 534–551 (2022). https://doi.org/10.1177/1356336X211056208
8. Su, W.: Research on the application of decision tree algorithm in practical teaching of public physical education in colleges and universities. In: Jan, M.A., Khan, F. (eds.) Application of Big Data, Blockchain, and Internet of Things for Education Informatization. BigIoT-EDU 2022. Social Informatics and Telecommunications Engineering. LNICS, vol. 467, pp. 235–245. Springer, Cham (2023). https://doi.org/10.1007/978-3-031-23944-1_26.
9. Ma, Li.: Analysis on the application of BP algorithm in the optimization model of logistics network flow distribution. In: Jansen, B.J., Liang, H., Ye, J. (eds.) International Conference on Cognitive based Information Processing and Applications (CIPA 2021). LNDECT, vol. 84, pp. 67–74. Springer, Singapore (2022). https://doi.org/10.1007/978-981-16-5857-0_9
10. Hagan, J.E., Quansah, F., Anin, S.K., et al.: COVID-19-related knowledge and anxiety response among physical education teachers during practical in-person lessons: effects of potential moderators. Behav. Sci. **12**(3), 83 (2022)
11. Duan, X., Li, X., Liu, Y.: Application of BP neural network in on-board charger fault diagnosis. J. Phys. Conf. Ser. **2290**, 012004 (2022). https://doi.org/10.1088/1742-6596/2290/1/012004
12. Velho, H.C., Vijaykumar, N.L., Stephany, S., et al.: A neural network implementation for data assimilation using MPI. Appl. High Perform. Comput. Eng. (2022)
13. Zhang, X., Shen, Y., Chen, J.: Application of neural network algorithm in robot eye-hand system. In: Macintyre, J., Zhao, J., Ma, X. (eds.) The 2021 International Conference on Machine Learning and Big Data Analytics for IoT Security and Privacy. SPIoT 2021. LNDECT, vol. 97, pp. 112–120. Springer, Cham (2022). https://doi.org/10.1007/978-3-030-89508-2_15.
14. Li, Q., Tu, G., Zhang, X., et al.: Application of a back propagation neural network model based on genetic algorithm to in situ analysis of marine sediment cores by X-ray fluorescence core scanner. Appl. Radiat. Isot. **184**, 110191 (2022). https://doi.org/10.1016/j.apradiso.2022.110191
15. Mei, F.: Application of decision tree algorithm in teaching quality of higher vocational colleges. In: Al-Turjman, F., Rasheed, J. (eds.) Forthcoming Networks and Sustainability in the IoT Era. LNDECT, vol. 130, pp. 89–95. Springer, Cham (2022). https://doi.org/10.1007/978-3-030-99581-2_11
16. Chen, W., Wang, F.: Retraction note: practical application of wireless communication network multimedia courseware in college basketball teaching. EURASIP J. Wirel. Commun. Netw. **2023**(1), 1 (2023). https://doi.org/10.1186/s13638-023-02215-w
17. Chen, B.: Application of cluster analysis algorithm in the construction of education platform. In: Macintyre, J., Zhao, J., Ma, X. (eds.) The 2021 International Conference on Machine

Learning and Big Data Analytics for IoT Security and Privacy. SPIoT 2021. LNDECT, vol. 98, pp. 424–430. Springers, Cham (2022). https://doi.org/10.1007/978-3-030-89511-2_54

18. He, G.: Practical research on computer information technology in physical education teaching in vocational colleges. In: Pei, Y., Chang, J.W., Hung, J.C. (eds.) Innovative Computing. IC 2022. LNEE, vol. 935, pp. 416–425. Springer, Singapore (2022). https://doi.org/10.1007/978-981-19-4132-0_51

19. Xie, X.: Application of BP neural network in the prediction of population aging. In: Macintyre, J., Zhao, J., Ma, X. (eds.) The 2021 International Conference on Machine Learning and Big Data Analytics for IoT Security and Privacy. SPIoT 2021. LNDECT, vol. 98, pp. 660–666. Springer, Cham (2022). https://doi.org/10.1007/978-3-030-89511-2_85

20. Zhang, C.: The application of hierarchical teaching mode based on hybrid criterion fuzzy algorithm in higher vocational English education. In: Jan, M.A., Khan, F. (eds.) Application of Big Data, Blockchain, and Internet of Things for Education Informatization. BigIoT-EDU 2022. Social Informatics and Telecommunications Engineering, LNICS, vol. 466, pp. 424–430. Springer, Cham (2023).https://doi.org/10.1007/978-3-031-23947-2_45

Research on the Prediction Model of off Campus Training Base in Fuzzy Neural Network Algorithm

Jie Zhang$^{(\boxtimes)}$, Xiaohong Zhang, Xiaoyan Quan, Xiaoxiao Fu, and Jinlian Chai

Shandong Institute of Commerce and Technology, Jinan 250103, Shandong, China
191810649@163.com

Abstract. This is a research project aimed at studying the prediction model of off campus training base in the fuzzy neural network algorithm. The main purpose of this study is to find out the relationship between variables and the value of each attribute, so as to predict the future value of this specific attribute. This will help us understand how to use data from past data points to predict future values of attributes. The prediction model of off campus training base is a method to predict the number of students in each class. The main purpose of this research is to find out how many students there are in each class, so that teachers and administrators of universities and colleges can become possible. The study also aims to predict the total number of students who will attend classes so that they can better understand the number of students, which can help them plan their budgets accordingly.

Keywords: Fuzzy neural network algorithm · Forecast model · Off campus training base

1 Introduction

The training base is composed of several experimental training rooms, which is used for students to learn practical skills through the combination of work and learning. The training bases are divided into on campus training bases and off campus training bases. On campus training base refers to the training base located inside the school, while off campus training base refers to the place where students learn practical skills through school enterprise cooperation.

Many enterprises also have their own training bases. In Changqing Oilfield, there are three or four training bases dedicated to training front-line employees, team leaders, etc. [1]. In the training bases, there are actual simulation training grounds, as well as training on enterprise development history, technology evolution, management innovation, ecological civilization construction and other knowledge. It is a centralized platform for enterprises to improve their employees' working skills, business knowledge, ideological education and external display.

In view of the chemical industry, chemical industry plays an important role in the national economy and is the foundation and pillar industry of the country. Chemical

Y. Zhang and N. Shah (Eds.): BigIoT-EDU 2023, LNICST 582, pp. 232–238, 2024.
https://doi.org/10.1007/978-3-031-63136-8_24

industry is also a technology intensive high-risk industry [2]. Raw materials, intermediate products, finished products, etc. are flammable, explosive, corrosive, toxic and harmful, and the process involves high temperature, high pressure, continuous production. The safety risk is high, and production safety accidents are easy to occur, and the consequences of accidents are often very serious. Therefore, it is extremely important to build a chemical training base and carry out staff training.

By reviewing the history of the pre training model, this paper points out the important position of the pre training model in the development of Al [3]. The prediction model of off campus training base is a method to predict the number of students in each class. Considering the continuity of the development of the pre training model, we first introduce the Transformer architecture, the core component of the pre training model, and the typical GPT and BERT pre training models. Further, we summarize the steps of pre training the model, and focus on the improvement of different subsequent pre training models from the perspectives of pre training encoder and pre training task.

2 Related Work

2.1 Fuzzy Neural Network Algorithm

Fuzzy logic reasoning system can apply expert knowledge and experience well, because its foundation is not only fuzzy related theory, but also fuzzy reasoning. During the whole 20th century, PID control was mainly used in the industrial field. Subsequently, finite tuning, adaptive and optimal control methods have also become popular [4]. The reason why the fuzzy control algorithm has become the mainstream control algorithm is that the control in the previous industrial era can not meet the huge needs of social development. Fuzzy control theory plays a very important role in the case of the frequently changing dynamic characteristic system and the lack of clear model. Sampling systems not only use adaptive and optimal control in relatively simple systems, but also are difficult to achieve the desired goals, as well as in complex systems [5]. Therefore, it is particularly important for complex systems to promote the development of new theoretical research. Therefore, the fuzzy control algorithm has developed rapidly. Even when the input variables show dynamic changes, the fuzzy control can also play a stable role. Whether the fuzzy logic system can be stable and high-precision depends on the regulation of the output. As long as we clear up and set up the logical relationship, no matter how the input variables and environment change, the fuzzy control algorithm can adapt to dynamic changes [6]. Figure 1 below shows the traditional fuzzy control structure.

(ArtificalNeural Network, ANN), also known as "neural network". Since its appearance, neural networks have developed many network structures, such as feedforward neural networks, cyclic neural networks, convolutional neural networks, etc. The important thing is that they are all developed on the basis of BP neural network, that is, back-propagation neural network. At present, due to the rapid development of big data and computers, BP neural network has shown great advantages in solving nonlinear complex systems [7]. The principle of BP neural network is that data enters the input layer, through the hidden layer, the hidden layer can have multiple layers, and then the activation function in the hidden layer is used to calculate, and finally the output value is used to calculate the error with the actual value [8]. If the error is less than the original set

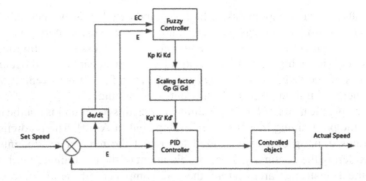

Fig. 1. Traditional fuzzy control structure

value, or the number of iterations is reached, The reverse calculation is not performed. When the error is greater than the original set value, the error is input into the neural network through the output layer, and the activation function of the hidden layer is calculated before entering the input layer, and then the connection weight and threshold value are continuously adjusted until the training process is completed. The structure of BP neural network is shown in Fig. 2:

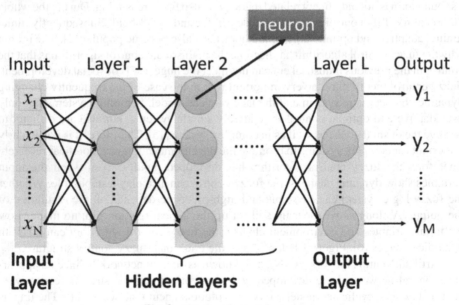

Fig. 2. BP neural network structure

2.2 Off Campus Training Base System

In the process of design and implementation of the training base, different units are funded There are different requirements in terms of land promotion and consistency, and the design and implementation effect of the system will be greatly different. The implementation process of the training system requires the use of the thinter library of the Python off campus training base for system design and development [9]. The tkiner library is a program bank specially provided by the Python off campus training base for the development of graphical interfaces. The system it implements is simple in every aspect and has good human-computer interaction. [10] The software compiled through the tinter library can realize the base training system in real time and quickly, and can meet the requirements of the system for data collection, data analysis and sorting Number training of prediction model.

The upstream task is to increase the number of forecast models by building data and pre training forecast models. Of course, the number of pre training prediction models does not only need to be larger, but sometimes it also needs to be more suitable for downstream tasks, but usually we think that the larger the number of prediction models, the more likely they will bring more benefits [11]. Therefore, some people are trying to build large-scale pre training prediction model number, while others are committed to applying the prediction model number to downstream task debugging.

For task debugging, we found that with the increase of the number of people in the prediction model, the learning effect of small samples of the number of people in the prediction model will be significantly improved [12]. This small sample learning ability is also one of the goals of AI, namely, general AI, which has a very strong learning ability. Therefore, we want to know if we can really realize universal AI if we continue to expand and increase the number of people in the prediction model by an order of magnitude. This is one of the reasons that many researchers in academia and industry are committed to increasing the number of prediction models.

However, it is not easy to increase the number of people in the prediction model. It requires efforts from all sides, including more data, computing power and infrastructure; At the same time, we should also consider whether the ability to predict the number of people in the model is sufficient, and whether the pre training task can support us to get a better pre training forecast model number.

Downstream tasks, that is, the number of people in the existing pre training prediction model will be transferred to the downstream tasks faster and better. In the application of downstream tasks, we also need to study many problems. For example, in terms of efficiency improvement, in the early days, we used the figure method to adjust the number of people in the prediction model, but this method was very inefficient [13]. Therefore, it was proposed in the later stage that whether the efficiency can be improved by simply adding the adapter debugger and adjusting a small part of the parameters or even not, and directly migrating to the downstream task.

3 Research on Prediction Model of off Campus Training Base in Fuzzy Neural Network Algorithm

This paper mainly summarizes the research of the fuzzy neural network algorithm in the prediction of the number of people in the off campus training base of the fuzzy neural network algorithm. The main idea of this study is to use the fuzzy neural network algorithm to predict the number of people outside the school training base, and use it as the decision rule to select the target training base [14]. The proposed method includes two steps: first, we need to use input data and output data to build a fuzzy neural network model to predict the number of people; Secondly, we need to calculate performance indicators as indicators of accuracy. Then we can use these indicators to select the best one according to some criteria such as cost.

On the one hand, the number of prediction models in the future must be growing, and our training data is usually insufficient, so we must use some pre training method to do it [15]. Of course, the connotation of pre training itself is very broad. It is not necessarily the form of predicting the number of people in the model in the off campus training base, but may also be the form of other pre training tasks.

On the other hand, our current prediction model is based on Transformer. Although it is powerful, it has many inherent defects. Therefore, we believe that there may be iterations in terms of the number and structure of the prediction model in the future. But this iteration may become more and more difficult, because when we use a certain prediction model more and more frequently, such as Transformer, and its ecological establishment is more and more perfect, we will have some path dependence [16]. That is to say, when we propose a new prediction model, its actual application efficiency may not be as high as that of Transformer, because our entire architecture has been optimized for Transformer.

However, Transformer has obvious defects, for example, it is not suitable for processing long documents. Therefore, although Transformer may still be the mainstream in the short term, there will be some new forms in the future. Figure 3 below shows the homogenization of the number of people in the large prediction model.

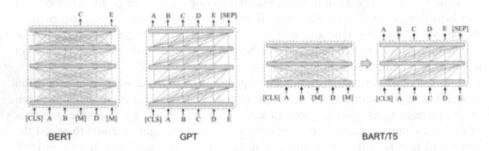

Fig. 3. Homogenization of the number of people in the large prediction model

It can be seen that the homogeneity of the number of people in the large prediction model is becoming more and more serious. Of course, the homogenization of the number of people in the large prediction model is not entirely a disadvantage, it will bring an advantage on the contrary [17].

This advantage is: after the number of people in the prediction model is unified, the number of people in one prediction model can be used to deal with all problems for different tasks in the natural off campus training base; Alternately, Transformer can also be applied to multi-mode or other fields such as visual field and audio field. All problems can be solved with one architecture, including problems at all levels such as perception and cognition [18]. Therefore, it also helps to better blend different disciplines.

In the early natural off campus training base, many people in the prediction model are pursuing the machine learning paradigm, that is, "training error test error = generalization error", which is an end-to-end approach. But after pre training the number of people in the prediction model, we divide the problem to be solved into two steps, namely pre training + fine tuning. However, there is no standard for pre training to predict the number of people in the model, and we do not know how to set the pre training target, so that the test error in the downstream task is small, that is, the training and testing are inconsistent [19]. Therefore, it is not an end-to-end approach. What kind of goals are effective for pre training or for downstream tasks? There is gap between them. But we don't know what this gap is.

Of course, the smaller the number of people in the prediction model of the off campus training base, the better the generalization of its downstream tasks, but this is not completely correct. For example, the training of the number of people in the GPT3 prediction model is not an iterative process, which minimizes the confusion of the number of people in the prediction model in the off campus training base, but ends as long as all the data are seen once. Therefore, this method may make its scheme unclear whether it is pre training or migration. Large factories with rich resources may pay more attention to the error of pre training, while those without many resources may pay more attention to how to reduce the test error of downstream tasks [20]. Therefore, whether there are task indicators that can measure the effectiveness of the pre training prediction model is also one of the problems caused by the large prediction model.

4 Conclusion

The research direction is the prediction model of off campus training base in the fuzzy neural network algorithm. The main objective is to develop a method using fuzzy logic and neural networks to identify and predict the number of students who will participate in after-school training courses based on their previous attendance records at other locations. The research direction is the prediction model of off campus training base in the fuzzy neural network algorithm. The main objective is to develop a method using fuzzy logic and neural networks to identify and predict the number of students who will participate in after-school training courses based on their previous attendance records at other locations.

References

1. Liu, M., Zhang, S.Q., Yu-De, HE.: Prediction of default of credit card clients base on improved fuzzy neural network. Fuzzy Syst. Math. (2017)
2. Zeng, J., Alassafi, M.O., Song, K.E.: Simulation of fuzzy neural network algorithm in dynamic nonlinear system. Fractals **30**(02), 2240106 (2022)
3. Li, T.: Dissolved oxygen prediction model of crab culture industry based on fuzzy neural network. In: International Conference on Mechanical Materials & Manufacturing Engineering (2016)

4. Yafeng, Y., Hua, C., Chuanxin, R., et al.: Analysis and prediction of vertical shaft freezing pressure in deep alluvium based on RBF fuzzy neural network model. J. Min. Saf. Eng. **33**, 70 (2016)
5. Weng, Z., Chen, Q.: Researches on the intelligent database optimization algorithm of the wavelet fuzzy neural network (2016)
6. Muhamediyeva, D.T.: Building and training a fuzzy neural model of data mining tasks. J. Phys. Conf. Ser. **2182**(1), 012024 (2022)
7. Wei, T., Chen, L.: A risk preference model for teaching resource allocation based on functional link fuzzy neural network algorithm classifier. Int. J. Comput. Appl. Technol. **61**(1–2), 88–93 (2019)
8. Zhao, B., Yi, R., Gao, D., et al.: Prediction of service life of large centrifugal compressor remanufactured impeller based on clustering rough set and fuzzy Bandelet neural network. Appl. Soft Comput. **78**, 132–140 (2019)
9. Chen, Y., An, J.M., Yanhan.: A novel prediction model of PM2.5 mass concentration based on back propagation neural network algorithm. J. Intell. Fuzzy Syst. Appl. Eng. Technol. **37**(3), 3175–3183 (2019)
10. Qiao, L., Liu, Y., Zhu, J., et al.: Phase prediction of high carbon pearlitic steel: an improved model combining mind evolutionary algorithm and neural networks. Adv. Eng. Mater. **23**, 2100204 (2021)
11. Xiong, N.Y.: Application of grey neural network model in the prediction of cigarette brand sales (2016)
12. Lin, J., Zhang, S., Lu, Q.: A neural network based method with transfer learning for genetic data analysis (2022)
13. Luo, P.J., He W , Li W , et al. Research on bus arrival time prediction model based on fuzzy neural network with genetic algorithm. Comput. Sci. (2016)
14. Peng, H., Polytechnic, H.C.: Application of intelligent fuzzy neural network algorithm in ultra fast injection machine. Plast. Sci. Technol. (2017)
15. Shen, G., Li, J., Hu, X., et al.: Evaluation and prediction model of agricultural drought based on T-S fuzzy neural network. Nat. Sci. J. Harbin Normal Univ. (2016)
16. Song, S., Wei, Z., Xia, H., et al.: State-of-charge (SOC) estimation using T-S fuzzy neural network for lithium iron phosphate battery. In: 2018 26th International Conference on Systems Engineering (ICSEng) (2018)
17. Fu, T., Wang, T.M., Wu, Y.: Application of wavelet fuzzy neural network in real time traffic flow forecasting. In: 2018 2nd IEEE Advanced Information Management,Communicates,Electronic and Automation Control Conference (IMCEC). IEEE (2018)
18. He, H.: Research on prediction of internet public opinion based on grey system theory and fuzzy neural network. J. Intell. Fuzzy Syst. **35**(1), 1–8 (2018)
19. Yan, W., Zou, C., Li, M., et al.: Design and verification of fuzzy neural network automatic control algorithm in intelligent agriculture. J. Phys. Conf. Ser. **1544**, 012153 (2020)
20. Uyar, K., Ilhan, U., Ilhan, A., et al.: Breast cancer prediction using neuro-fuzzy systems. In: 2020 7th International Conference on Electrical and Electronics Engineering (ICEEE) (2020)

Construction of Basic Education Informatization Evaluation Model Based on Deep Neural Network

Songli Jin$^{(\boxtimes)}$ and Wang Haiyan

Institute of Educational Innovation, Chongqing University of Arts and Sciences,
Chongqing 402160, China
emma628@vip.163.com

Abstract. The transformation of basic education informatization from construction to evaluation, and from level evaluation to benefit evaluation is a new trend in the development of educational informatization in my country. Due to the large differences in the level of educational informatization in different regions, the evaluation of educational informatization benefits presents diversified characteristics. The evaluation of school education informatization is a problem that school principals who implement informatization teaching and management need to actively deal with certain informatization conditions. In this paper, deep neural network is used for statistical analysis of a large amount of data, and through feature extraction in the original data, the accurate output is found from the original data. Using information technology, the big data generated by the user's learning behavior is analyzed by the machine, and the key and effective features are retained, so as to generate a complete and accurate basic education information evaluation. Through the research of this paper, it is concluded that the effect of educational informatization is the achievement of goals in the process of educational informatization construction and application, and it is observable, quantifiable, and explicit educational informatization performance.

Keyword: deep neural network · basic education · informatization evaluation model

1 Introduction

The evaluation of educational informatization benefits has become a consensus as an important means to measure the benefits of educational informatization in a country and a region. However, there are large differences in the level of educational informatization in different countries and regions, and the evaluation of educational informatization benefits is diverse. However, there is still no international universal and authoritative evaluation index system [1]. As an integral part of educational informatization, evaluation is very important in the theory and practice of educational informatization. Moreover, from a long-term perspective, it can provide reference for the planning of educational informatization in the next stage, point out the direction for the next practice, and become an important reference indicator for each country to measure the performance of educational informatization and make investments. Education informatization is an important part of national informatization and an important symbol of educational modernization [2]. With the rapid development and wide application of computer network technology, human beings have entered the information society, and educational informatization is increasingly attracting global attention [3]. If schools initially paid attention to education informatization, they paid more attention to the construction and preliminary application of basic hardware and software infrastructure, then when the investment in informatization has reached a certain scale, the core of schools with these conditions is technology. Effectiveness in practical teaching and management work [4]. Today in the 21st century, the information environment of the whole society has undergone great changes. The Internet is developing rapidly all over the world, and information technology has also been widely valued by all countries in the world. The information industry has become the pillar and condition for the formation and development of a modern economy. The economic development of a country and even the entire international community is of decisive significance [5].

2 Evaluation of Educational Informatization

2.1 Informatization Evaluation

Informatization evaluation started in the early 1960s. With the development and application of modern information technology, people's understanding of informatization evaluation has also undergone significant changes. From the discussion of informatization application to the current value orientation analysis with informatization application as the core and the development of informatization main body as the goal, many evaluation methods with multiple perspectives and cross-fields have evolved [6]. The word "informatization" was first expressed in the Japanese word "Johoka" to emphasize the transformation process of society from "tangible material products" to "intangible information products" driven by information technology. The Delphi method is an expert prediction method produced to overcome the shortcomings of the expert meeting method [7]. In the forecasting process, the experts are back-to-back and not transparent, which overcomes the shortcomings of the expert method, such as insufficient experts' opinions and some experts' opinions being subject to authority [8]. In December 1986, the concept of "informatization" was used by the Chinese government for the first time, and then gradually accepted by various fields in the country, and made different definitions of it. In the Delphi method, experts can really fully express their prediction opinions [9]. In the Delphi method, experts only communicate with investigators, express multiple rounds of opinions, and after repeated consultations, collections, summaries, and summaries, finally obtain the unanimous opinions of experts as the investigation results. There are also many scholars in my country who define this concept from the perspective of "information value".

Informatization is "transformation into a nature with information as the core or a form with information as the basic feature, not only a process, but also a goal". The data envelopment analysis method integrates the knowledge of mathematics, operations research, economics and management. It adopts the mathematical programming method and uses the collected sample data to evaluate the effectiveness of decision-making units and solve multi-objective decision-making problems, especially good at solving multi-objective decision-making problems. The problem of input and multi-output [10]. Informatization refers to the derivation and development of information culture caused by the extensive application of information technology in human society, and finally the process of forming an information civilization and realizing a mature information society. In the data envelopment analysis method, the weight assignment is generated based on the sample data and is not affected by human subjective factors.

"Information" has become the core element of social development and even the transformation of social forms. Specifically, Specific means that performance appraisal should focus on specific work indicators and cannot be general; Measurable means that performance indicators are quantitative or behavioral, and the data or information to verify these performance indicators can be measured; Attainable refers to performance indicators and their The standard can be achieved with hard work and avoid setting high or low goals; Realistic means that performance indicators are real and can be proven and observed; Time-based focuses on completing specific deadlines for performance indicators to avoid overdue completion.

2.2   Evaluation of Educational Informatization

A dimension is a perspective that is used to judge, evaluate, illustrate, evaluate and determine the multi-faceted, multi-level, multi-angle, and multi-level conditions and concepts of a thing. The dimension of educational informatization performance evaluation is to take the development process and status of educational informatization as the evaluation object, and conduct performance evaluation and assessment on it from a multi-level, multi-angle and multi-dimensional perspective. "Education informatization" is a reasonable extension of the concept of "informatization". At present, there is no unified definition for the concept of educational informatization. The structure of performance is mainly manifested as "three effects": one is the effect, which is the degree to which the goal is achieved, whether or not results are achieved, and how much results have been achieved, which is the manifestation of performance; the second is efficiency, which is the relationship between input and output. Relationship is a pursuit of minimizing investment capital or costs; the third is benefit, which is the economic, social and time benefits that the achievement of results brings to organizations and individuals. The hierarchy model of educational informatization needs is shown in Fig. 1.

Basic education informatization is an important part of educational informatization. Therefore, we can define what is basic education informatization according to the concept of educational informatization. Effect, efficiency and benefit represent different levels of performance, which can measure performance comprehensively and accurately, and introduce it into the research of educational informatization performance. The effect of educational informatization is the achievement of goals in the process of educational informatization construction and application, which is observable, quantifiable, and explicit educational informatization performance. Education informatization refers to the process of using computer multimedia and network information technology in education and teaching to promote the modernization of the educational environment,

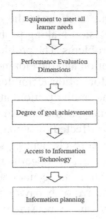

Fig. 1. Education informatization demand hierarchy model

the balance of information resources, and the humanization of management. The cost-benefit diagram of education is shown in Fig. 2. It can be seen from the figure that the employees who have studied are paid more than those who have not studied.

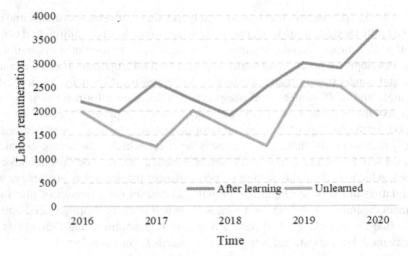

Fig. 2. Education cost-benefit map

The benefit of educational informatization is the gain of the main body of informatization in the process of application of educational informatization, including the obvious benefits of educational informatization brought about by the improvement of students, teachers, informatization managers, principals and other information comprehensive ability and information literacy. At the same time, it also includes the hidden educational informatization benefits brought by the radiation of the main body of informatization to the society. To understand the concept of educational informatization, we cannot one-sidedly believe that the equipment is equipped with various modern instruments and equipment to realize informatization. These facilities are only the hardware foundation of educational informatization construction, and are also the basic guarantee for the technologicalization of educational means.

The efficiency of educational informatization is the time used by educational informatization to achieve goals and gain, and it can also be said to be the degree of development of educational informatization effects and benefits per unit time. The construction of information resources, the application of information technology in education and the management of informatization are the key factors of educational informatization. Only by rationally utilizing information resources and applying information technology to every link of education can we effectively use information technology to promote the quality of education.

3 Evaluation Model of Basic Education Informatization Based on Deep Neural Network

3.1 Teaching Based on Deep Neural Network

With the development of information technology, combined with big data and artificial intelligence technology, online learning has become an increasingly important learning method. This learning method is not limited by time and place, and provides teachers and students with more Many flexible ways to interact. Blended teaching is a kind of blended teaching that combines two teaching methods such as MOOC and traditional teaching. It can not only make full use of the convenience brought by the Internet era to the modern teaching process, but also make teaching more free, intelligent and shared., personalise. The neural network structure is shown in Fig. 3.

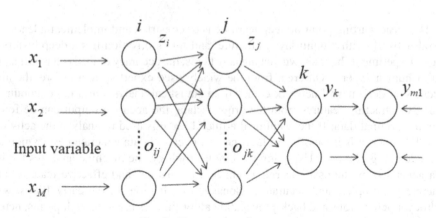

Fig. 3. Neural network structure

Neural network deep learning is one of the latest and hottest advances in intelligence science and technology, and its starting point is to construct a neural network with a structure beyond the typical two-layer structure. With the rapid development of information technology today, deep neural network has become the basis of many artificial intelligence applications. In particular, accurate recognition in graphic image and speech systems has brought rapid development in this field and has also promoted the wide-scale application of deep neural networks. Although personalized learning can simplify the cost and operation mode of learners, there is currently a lack of suitable means to evaluate the teaching effect of personalized learning, especially some unique characteristics exhibited by personalized learning. In this paper, the output value of the hidden layer is averaged, and the feature output is close to the Gaussian distribution, as shown in Fig. 4.

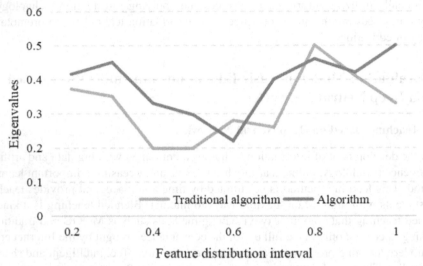

Fig. 4. The average output of multi-dimensional vectors in the hidden layer of deep neural network

The basic starting point of deep learning is to construct and implement a learnable neural network with a multi-layer structure, and this motivation has a deep historical origin. Experiments have shown that in many fields, the accuracy of DNNs has surpassed that of human experts. Different from the widely used expert system before, the high accuracy of deep neural network comes from statistical analysis of a large amount of data. By extracting features from the original data, the accurate output can be found from the original data. If the traditional artificial force is used to analyze the activities of each learner, it is impossible to face the vast ocean of data generated every moment on the learning platform. Using information technology, the machine analyzes the big data generated by the user's learning behavior, retains key and effective features, and generates a complete and accurate personalized evaluation. In the early 1980s, with multilayer perceptrons and back-propagation algorithms as breakthrough points, neural network researchers saw the huge application potential of neural networks.

The feature extraction of clustering data adopts the hidden Markov model based on DNN, which is a forward neural network containing multiple hidden layers. The input layer represents the underlying features of the clustered data, and the output layer represents the slice after dimension reduction. The nonlinear activation function of each node in the hidden layer adopts sigmod, and the nonlinear output value of each node is:

$$y_j^h = Sig(x_j) = \frac{1}{1 + e^{-x_j}}, \quad x = b_j + \sum_i y_i^{h-1} w_{ij} \tag{1}$$

Among them, y_j^h is the nonlinear output value of the j rd node in the h nd layer; x_j is the node input value; b_j is the offset; w_{ij} is the connection weight between nodes j and i.

The DNN training parameters are obtained by iterative training of the BP network propagation algorithm, as shown in Eq. 2:

$$J = (w_1, b_1, w_2, b_2) = \frac{1}{N} \sum_{i=1}^{N} (x_i - x_i)^2 \tag{2}$$

The initial network parameters are initialized by the RBM restricted Boltzmann machine, as shown in Eq. 3:

$$\begin{cases} \frac{\partial \log p(v|\theta)}{\partial w_{i,j}} \approx \frac{1}{N} \sum_{n=1}^{N} \left[v_i^n h_j^{(n)} - v_i^n h_j^{(n)} \right] \\ \frac{\partial \log p(v|\theta)}{\partial b_i} \approx \frac{1}{N} \sum_{n=1}^{N} \left[v_i^n - v_i^n \right] \\ \frac{\partial \log p(v|\theta)}{\partial b_j} \approx \frac{1}{N} \sum_{n=1}^{N} \left[h_j^{(n)} - h_j^{(n)} \right] \end{cases} \tag{3}$$

The core of the evaluation is how to effectively classify the data generated by the learners in the learning process, and to effectively reduce the dimensions of the multi-dimensional data features that describe the learner's behavior in an appropriate way, which can not only ensure the unique representation of the data features, but also can It is guaranteed that the system platform can realize the calculation with the minimum computational cost. There is no doubt that this performance of deep learning will go down in history, and from this moment, those skeptics of the application of deep learning have to face the fact that deep learning is indeed a sword.

3.2 Construction of Basic Education Informatization Evaluation Model

The evaluation of educational informatization is not for evaluation, let alone to get a simple score conclusion. The fundamental purpose of evaluation is determined by the strategic goal of educational informatization, that is, to further strengthen the three functions of education: personnel training, knowledge innovation and social service. Theoretical model is an intermediate layer between the theoretical layer and the practical layer. It is not only a high degree of generalization of the theory, but also a high degree of abstraction of the actual system, and has a theoretical guiding role for practical activities. Because education informatization covers a wide range, it involves informatization infrastructure, informatization applications and informatization safeguard measures. It can measure the degree of realization of the strategic goals of educational informatization, and can provide specific guidance for the further improvement and improvement of educational informatization construction. The beneficiaries of educational informatization are school students, faculty and the general public.

Table 1. Statistics of professional titles of experts

Expert title	Number of people	The proportion
Professor	6	46%
Associate Professor	3	23%
Researcher	4	31%

The higher the professional title of the expert selected, the more authoritative and reliable the research results. It is suggested that the statistics of the professional title of the experts are shown in Table 1.

Taking into account the scientific nature of the research results, when selecting experts, they are mainly selected from experts who have contacted various front-line positions in education informatization. See Table 2 for details.

Table 2. Statistics of expert positions

Expert position	Number of people	The proportion
Educational Technology Teacher	4	44%
Network Center Expert	2	22%
Educational Technology Center Specialist	3	34%

The basic education informatization performance development evaluation model is a theoretical model of performance evaluation and development, which can be used to guide the development of evaluation activities, but cannot be directly applied to evaluation. This needs to be translated into actionable and substantive assessment tools. Informatization infrastructure and its operation indicators refer to the basic implementation and basic operation of informatization construction in colleges and universities, which mainly reflect the level of investment in informatization of the university. The experience and feelings of students and staff on informatization should be reflected in the evaluation index system. Their evaluation of the effect of informatization and the evaluation of the realization of the strategic goals of school informatization are the most direct and objective. The development of evaluation tools is the basis and premise of evaluation work, and is the specific operational object in evaluation implementation. The development of evaluation tools can be based on literature analysis, comparison of results, or based on evaluation models. In the field of basic education informatization evaluation, common evaluation tools include indicator systems and scales. In order to ensure the scientificity and reliability of the research results, in addition to rich experience and influence, the selection of experts should also pay attention to the representativeness of institutions at different levels.

The establishment of educational informatization evaluation indicators can objectively evaluate the level of educational informatization construction, and provide a basis for relevant state departments to understand and grasp the status of educational informatization and make relevant decisions. The indicator system is an organism composed of several interrelated statistical indicators. The development of the index system generally follows the steps of determining the evaluation dimension, determining the evaluation content, forming the evaluation index, optimizing the evaluation index, and assigning the weight of the evaluation index. To build a complete evaluation index system, we must first determine its evaluation index framework, and screen and establish indicators at all levels. The establishment of educational informatization evaluation indicators can enable schools to learn from each other's successful experience, help solve problems in development, avoid mistakes, avoid detours, and identify gaps, so that the decision-making of informatization construction is based on solid foundations. On the basis of reliability, it can ensure the scientificity and safety of informatization construction, improve the efficiency of the use of funds, and play a multiplier effect with half the effort.

4 Conclusions

In today's information age, educational informatization has become an important part of social informatization, and educational informatization has become the direction of educational reform and development. The collection and analysis of annual evaluation reports and periodic evaluation data from countries around the world enlighten us that evaluation data in the era of big data has a good reference for the implementation of evaluation work, and can provide improvement suggestions for the sustainable development of evaluation work. For educational informatization, it is very important to judge whether the information technology introduced in the school has really played its role in improving the teaching effect, promoting the development of students, and enhancing the efficiency of the school. It is of great significance to study the evaluation methods of educational informatization for scientific evaluation of the development level of educational informatization and to correctly guide the development direction of educational informatization. Strengthening the construction of hardware and software, improving the information literacy, technical integration and data analysis capabilities of evaluators and evaluators, and strengthening the power of scientific and technological services are one of the ways to improve the effectiveness of educational informatization evaluation.

Acknowledgements. This work is supported by the 2020 Western and Frontier Regions Educational Youth Fund Project of Humanities and Social Science Foundation of Ministry of Education of China (20XJC880003).

References

1. Kim, S.J., Shin, H., Lee, J., et al.: A smartphone application to educate undergraduate nursing students about providing care for infant airway obstruction. Nurse Educ. Today **48**, 145–152 (2017)
2. Fragneto, R.Y., Gaiser, R.: Labor analgesia: we need to better understand and educate our obstetric patients. J. Clin. Anesth. **41**, 42 (2017)

3. Lilly, C.L.: School climate as an intervention to reduce academic failure and educate the whole child: a longitudinal study. J. School Health 90 (2020)
4. Selleck, C., Jablonski, R., Miltner, R.S., et al.: Partnering to educate nurses in long-term care. J. Contin. Educ. Nurs. **51**(2), 75–81 (2020)
5. Walther, J., Miller, S.E., et al.: A model of empathy in engineering as a core skill, practice orientation, and professional way of being: a model of empathy in engineering. J. Eng. Educ. **106**(1), 123–148 (2017). https://doi.org/10.1002/jee.20159
6. Deal, S.B., Stefanidis, D., Brunt, L.M., et al.: Development of a multimedia tutorial to educate how to assess the critical view of safety in laparoscopic cholecystectomy using expert review and crowd-sourcing. Am. J. Surg. 988 (2017)
7. Merle, B., Chapurlat, R., Vignot, E., et al.: Post-fracture care: do we need to educate patients rather than doctors? The PREVOST randomized controlled trial. Osteoporos Int. **28**(5), 1549–1558 (2017)
8. Lpc, M., Cic, D., Cic, K., et al.: You Use It, You Clean It": a multifaceted approach to educate and engage pediatric healthcare workers in non-critical reprocessing. Am. J. Infect. Control **47**(6), S22–S23 (2019)
9. Ryan, C.J., Bierle, R., Vuckovic, K.M.: The three rs for preventing heart failure readmission: review, reassess, and reeducate. Crit. Care Nurse **39**(2), 85–93 (2019)
10. Young, V.L., Cole, et al.: A mixed-method evaluation of peer-education workshops for school-aged children to teach about antibiotics, microbes and hygiene. Jantimicrob Chemoth **72**(7), 2119–2126 (2017)

Construction of Virtual Simulation Teaching Resources for Tourism Major Based on Neural Network Algorithm

Wenxi Peng[1]([✉]), Zhang Ruyong[2], and Desheng Zhu[2]

[1] Hunan Open University, Changsha 410004, Hunan, China
kjcxdb102@163.com
[2] Shandong Institute of Commerce and Technology, Jinan 250103, Shandong, China

Abstract. The insufficient combination and integration of virtual experiment and physical experiment is not conducive to improving the quality of personnel training and practical innovation ability; Lack of standards and norms and limitations of sharing are not conducive to the overall planning and open sharing of teaching resources. This paper studies the construction of virtual simulation teaching resources for tourism majors based on neural network algorithm, and the resource integration method based on CNN (Convolutional Neural Network). MapReduce in the model adopts an improved MapReduce algorithm framework. In the process of Arduino learning, the design of resource integration method based on CNN mainly consists of two parts: the design of Arduino device identification program based on CNN and the construction of Arduino device learning resource database. The test results show that in Hadoop cluster, the application of the improved MapReduce algorithm model can obviously improve the data access speed and processing performance, and the overall time consumption after the improvement is reduced by 9.326%. This test shows that using this improved algorithm can improve the access speed and data processing performance of the storage model.

Keyword: Neural network · Tourism major · Virtual simulation · Teaching resource

1 Introduction

Tourism vocational education aims at cultivating front-line professionals with certain qualities and skills in service and management. Learning and operating in real post environment is the best way for students to master tourism service skills. This requires universities to set up professional practice in their undergraduate study career. Professional practice is an important part of practical teaching mode of tourism major, and it is also an important stage for tourism major students to get in touch with the actual development of tourism industry in advance and understand the basic skills needed by the industry. Using virtual reality technology to construct virtual simulation resources such as virtual simulation environment and experimental objects can not only reduce the

Y. Zhang and N. Shah (Eds.): BigIoT-EDU 2023, LNICST 582, pp. 249–257, 2024.
https://doi.org/10.1007/978-3-031-63136-8_26

experimental cost, but also be convenient to use, maintain and upgrade. Virtual simulation technology can also be used to realize the experimental contents that are difficult or impossible to fully carry out in physical experimental teaching, such as high-risk experimental scenes, high-cost and irreversible experiments.

In order to solve the problems encountered in the process of university informatization construction in our country, many domestic researchers have also joined in the research of cloud computing massive data storage [1, 2]. This has greatly promoted the development of cloud computing in the field of education, and provided a good theoretical research foundation and a good solution for solving the current problems. Zhou proposed to develop a cloud storage model of teaching resources under the network-based teaching environment, allowing universities to customize teaching management and data storage services based on cloud computing [3]. Zhang believes that virtual reality technology can create various simulated learning environments, provide rich sensory stimulation and natural interaction for learners, and thus bring an immersive learning experience [4]. Bai et al., based on the education system of artificial intelligence, evaluated how helpful such a system is to students [5]. Through the pre-test of the system, the students' difficulties are preliminarily understood, and according to the obtained results, the system is re-compiled by using artificial intelligence algorithm [6, 7]. Limited by objective factors such as capital, technology, time and space, enterprises, etc., it is impossible for schools to provide students with a learning environment that involves all real positions in the major, which leads to many practical teaching dilemmas in the field of vocational education.

Tourism virtual simulation system is a mature training teaching platform based on intelligent tourism. The insufficient combination and integration of virtual experiment and physical experiment is not conducive to improving the quality of personnel training and practical innovation ability; Lack of standards and norms and limitations of sharing are not conducive to the overall planning and open sharing of teaching resources. Based on the construction standards of virtual simulation teaching resources for tourism majors, this paper discusses the relevant principles and specific requirements in detail, in order to promote the orderly and high-quality construction of virtual simulation teaching resources.

2   Research Method

2.1   Overall Construction Idea

Most information-based teaching resources mainly include a large amount of audio data, which generally need a large number of storage devices for data storage. Therefore, some relatively large-scale database management methods are also used to realize the quick query and data retrieval of teaching resources. For example, video, courseware and other teaching resources, instead of just a single transmission from teachers as in the traditional way, which has good interactivity and can make students more active in learning.

Virtual experiment teaching adopts simulation technology, virtual technology, multimedia technology, database technology and network technology to construct virtual scene, experimental environment and experimental operation objects. After the construction task is determined, the relevant center responsible for the task is responsible for organizing the writing of virtual simulation teaching resource scripts, evaluating the project budget and raising construction funds, and managing the project implementation [8]. Each center should pay its own funds for development projects, and at the same time own its intellectual property rights. The developed experimental project should be agreed to open and share on the public platform, and the corresponding remuneration should be obtained according to the sharing degree, production quality and development cost.

Because computer virtual simulation resources need to consume a lot of money and manpower, and at the same time, the complexity of resource construction, therefore, the construction of virtual simulation resources for tourism majors must be carefully selected to make it important, practical and targeted. If you completely rely on the market, it is difficult to buy suitable products, but completely develop it by yourself, you may not have technical strength, and the cost is relatively high. The virtual resources are unified by 3Dmax to build 3D models, and Unity3D to develop virtual interaction. It is required that the shape proportion of the three-dimensional model conforms to the reality, the detail composition meets the requirements, the material is true, and the mapping is correct. The interactive scene is required to realize functions such as multi-view roaming of people, interactive operation of equipment, automatic scene demonstration, free observation of control angles, local zooming, etc. [9, 10].

There are clear requirements for the construction of virtual experimental teaching resources, such as sharing software and instruments, developing technology and application technology, and establishing resource evaluation and evaluation mechanism. It is clear that the main goal is to promote the construction of high-quality experimental teaching resources by establishing a long-term mechanism. The virtual experiment teaching resource pool layer is composed of each module of each project of tourism virtual experiment teaching resource to meet the experimental teaching needs of tourism major. The network layer mainly completes the functions of communication and resource sharing, and consists of wired network and wireless network. It is the login of application layer administrators, teachers, students and other users, and it is the actual combat operation layer. As shown in Fig. 1.

In order to solve the current university's demand for massive teaching resources storage, this paper analyzes the massive data storage model based on cloud computing, and combines the characteristics of teaching resources data to adopt Hadoop, a high-performance, high-reliability massive data storage solution. MapReduce will automatically process these nodes and periodically update the storage and data processing work and status of the whole cluster.

MapReduce in the model adopts an improved MapReduce algorithm framework[11]. The Hadoop mass data storage model under cloud computing is shown in Fig. 2:

This type of storage device can hold a limited number of visiting clients at the same time, and once it exceeds its maximum tolerable limit, it is easy to cause crash or system crash, thus the whole teaching resources cannot be applied.

In the design of the system, we use a general commercial machine as the underlying storage device. Hadoop is used as a platform to build a cloud storage environment, manage the underlying commercial machines, and virtualize a file system, namely HDFS(Hadoop Distributed File System). On the basis of HDFS, an application service

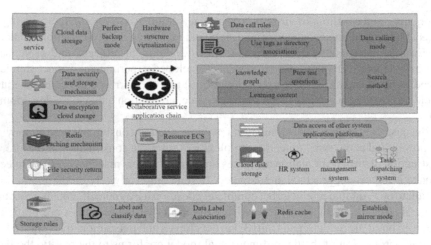

Fig. 1. Construction framework of virtual experiment teaching resources

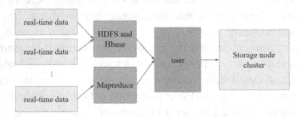

Fig. 2. Massive data storage model

module integrating teaching resources is developed. Internally, a file is actually divided into one or more data blocks, which are stored on a group of Data Node. Name performs namespace operations of the file system, such as opening, closing and renaming files or directories. It is also responsible for determining the mapping of data blocks to specific Data Node nodes. Data Node is responsible for processing the read and write requests of the file system clients. Create, delete and copy data blocks under the unified schedule of NameNode.

Through this cloud platform, not only can a large number of teaching resources be stored in it, but also large resources can be conveniently "cut" into small resources which are more conducive to retrieval and utilization, and they are scattered and stored in electronic computers of multiple nodes, which are organically connected through the network. And the cloud platform not only has the backup function of teaching resources, but also can prevent the teaching resources from being completely destroyed.

2.2 Realization Method of Tourism Virtual Simulation Teaching Resources Construction

Suitable and available computer digital resources not only need the participation and input of front-line teachers, but also need teachers to get rid of traditional teaching methods and make full use of virtual simulation technology for teaching. On the one hand, college students, as a group with high professional quality, can offer advice and suggestions for the reform and development of tourism enterprises during the internship; On the other hand, tourism enterprises can find and cultivate reserve talents by recruiting interns, so as to realize the construction of talent echelon of tourism enterprises. For students, it is not enough to learn the theoretical knowledge only from the classroom. Therefore, it is necessary to enrich the practical experience from the practice process such as enterprise practice and combine the theoretical knowledge with practical ability. Besides, it can also cultivate students' interpersonal skills and improve their social adaptability.

Using virtual simulation technology to carry out practical teaching is the need of deep integration of information technology and higher education. With the development of 3D virtual simulation technology, the current virtual simulation experiment scene is realistic, which is conducive to the demonstration of abstract teaching content. The experimental scenes constructed by virtual simulation technology are rich and diverse, which can improve students' interest in learning. At the same time, integrating all kinds of teaching resources through the experimental teaching platform is conducive to the opening and sharing of experimental teaching resources.

In deep learning, CNN (Convolutional Neural Network) is one of the classic and widely used models. In the process of Arduino learning, the design of resource integration method based on CNN mainly consists of two parts: the design of Arduino device identification program based on CNN and the construction of Arduino device learning resource database. The overall process of resource integration method based on CNN is shown in Fig. 3:

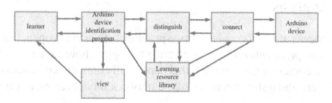

Fig. 3. Overall process of resource integration method based on CNN

In order to reduce the overall bandwidth consumption and read latency, HDFS will try its best to let the reader read the nearest copy. If there is a copy on the same rack as the reader, then read the copy. If an HDFS cluster spans multiple data centers, the client will also read the copy of the local data center first.

Loss is a general index that can describe the gap between the output obtained in the last step of the model and the expected output from the training set.

$$H(p, q) = - \sum_{x} p(x) \log q(x) \qquad (1)$$

p represents the correct answer, while q represents the predicted value.

The input layer x_p is an m-dimensional vector, and the output layer is an n-dimensional y_p-vector. The middle layer is composed of $Z_i, i = 1, 2, \cdots, j$, then the output of the k th hidden layer neuron is obtained by formula (2):

$$y_k = \sum_{i=1}^{j} w_{ik} \cdot \exp\left(-\frac{1}{2\sigma^2} \|x_p, Z_j\|\right) \qquad (2)$$

In order to help the network pruning and make the network weight quickly approach 0, a penalty function should be added to the error function during training, namely:

$$P = (w, v) = \frac{\varepsilon}{2} \left(\sum_{m=1}^{h} \sum_{l=1}^{n} w_{ml}^2 + \sum_{m=1}^{h} \sum_{p=1}^{n} v_{pm}^2 \right) \qquad (3)$$

where: w_{ml} is the connection weight between the l node in the input layer of the neural network and the m node in the hidden layer; v_{pm} is the connection weight between the m th node of the hidden layer and the p th node of the fuzzy output layer; h is the total number of hidden layer nodes; ε is the parameter of the penalty function.

3   Result Analysis

The training process of CNN consists of two processes: forward propagation of information and backward propagation of errors. In order to explore how the setting of parameters will affect the accuracy of CNN model, this paper will conduct experiments. By exploring the parameters, the testing accuracy of the network model can be improved as much as possible.

The number of convolution layers will directly affect the feature extraction ability of the model for the input image. Through experiments, the influence of the number of convolution network layers on the accuracy of the model is explored, and the results are shown in Table 1 and Fig. 4 below.

It can be seen that for the image set in this paper, when the number of layers is less than 5, the model can extract the features of the collected images, and the extracted features can be expressed to some extent, but the abstraction degree has to be improved continuously, the test accuracy of the model is not high, and it is prone to shock, the error loss function does not converge, and the weights cannot reach the optimal solution. However, if the network with too many layers has more parameters than the image data, there will be over-fitting, and the loss function will be negative, which indicates that the network structure design is wrong.

Set the corresponding file weights for the original test data files, and set the number of NameNode master nodes, DataNode data nodes and Job subtasks in the cluster to 1,

Table 1. Accuracy of models with different levels of convolution network

Network layer number	Accuracy/%
2	37.077
4	48.148
6	58.096
8	59.103
10	62.974
12	66.985
14	90.433
16	92.271

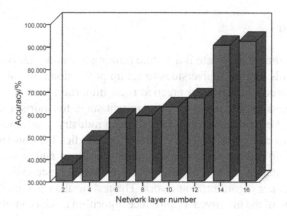

Fig. 4. Model accuracy

3 and 10 respectively. Then, run the test and compare and record the execution speed before and after the application of MapReduce algorithm, and then get the advantages and disadvantages of the test results before and after the improvement through analysis. The specific results are shown in Fig. 5.

The test results show that in Hadoop cluster, the application of the improved MapReduce algorithm model can obviously improve the data access speed and processing performance, and the overall time consumption after the improvement is reduced by 9.326%.

This test shows that the application of the improved MapReduce algorithm in the university mass data storage model based on cloud computing environment is successful, and the improved algorithm can improve the access speed and data processing performance of the storage model.

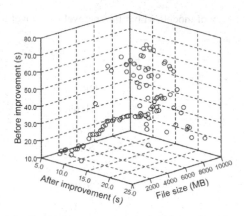

Fig. 5. Performance test results of the algorithm

4 Conclusion

Tourism virtual simulation system is a mature training teaching platform based on intelligent tourism. This requires universities to set up professional practice in their undergraduate study career. Professional practice is an important part of practical teaching mode of tourism major, and it is also an important stage for tourism major students to get in touch with the actual development of tourism industry in advance and understand the basic skills needed by the industry. This paper studies the construction of virtual simulation teaching resources for tourism major based on neural network algorithm, and the resource integration method based on CNN. MapReduce in the model adopts an improved MapReduce algorithm framework. The test results show that in Hadoop cluster, the application of the improved MapReduce algorithm model can obviously improve the data access speed and processing performance, and the overall time consumption after the improvement is reduced by 9.326%.

Acknowledgements. Hunan Vocational Education Teaching Reform Research Project in 2020 "Research and Practice on OBE Teaching Reform of Tourism Management Major in Higher Vocational Colleges from the perspective of Skill Competition" (No.: ZJGB2020406).

References

1. Qian, J.: Research on artificial intelligence technology of virtual reality teaching method in digital media art creation. J. Internet Technol. **2022**(1), 23 (2022)
2. Zhou, L., Tait, G., Chow, S.: Teaching appropriate and high value rheumatology care through simulation: virtual interactive cases. J. Rheumatol. **2016**(6), 43 (2016)
3. Zhou, Y.: Land ecological evaluation based on genetic network algorithm and real-time data monitoring of cloud computing system , no. retraction of vol 14, art no 1572, 2021). Arab. J. Geosci. **2021**(24), 14 (2021)
4. Zhang, Y.: Application of intelligent virtual reality technology in college art creation and design teaching. J. Internet Technol. **2021**(6), 22 (2021)

5. Bai, L., Brown, M.: The improvement of interactive learning efficiency based on virtual simulation technology. Int. J. Contin. Eng. Educ. Life-Long Learn. **2022**(2), 32 (2022)
6. Liang, X., Yin, J.: Recommendation algorithm for equilibrium of teaching resources in physical education network based on trust relationship. J. Internet Technol. **2022**(1), 23 (2022)
7. Li, H., Sun, S.: Research on evaluation model of oral english teaching quality based on cloud computing. Int. J. Contin. Eng. Educ. Life-Long Learn. **2020**(4), 30 (2020)
8. Niveditha, V.R., Usha, D., Rajakumar, P.S., Dwarakanath, B., Magesh, S.: Emerging 5g iot smart system based on edge-to-cloud computing platform. Int. J. E-Collabor. **2021**(4), 17 (2021)
9. Wei, S., Hagras, H., Alghazzawi, D.: A cloud computing based big-bang big-crunch fuzzy logic multi classifier system for soccer video scenes classification. Memetic Comput. **2016**(4), 8 (2016)
10. Weerapanpisit, P., Trilles, S., Joaquín, H., Painho, M.: A decentralized location-based reputation management system in the iot using blockchain. IEEE Internet Things J. **2022**(16), 9 (2022)
11. Mackle, C.: Cloud-based cm system. Insight: Non-Destruct. Test. Cond. Monitor. **2021**(11), 63 (2021)

Development and Utilization of Mathematics Curriculum Resources in Primary School Based on Cyclic Neural Network

Yi Mo$^{(\boxtimes)}$, Jishen Tang, and Qianyue Fu

Hechi University, Yizhou 546300, Guangxi, China
656839540@qq.com

Abstract. Mathematics curriculum resources is a broad concept. It not only refers to math instructional resources, but also includes all kinds of available instructional resources, teaching tools and teaching places. Teachers should make full use of the instructional resources in math instruction to show students a different mathematics classroom. There are many problems in the development and utilization of current primary school math instructional resources, which restrict the smooth implementation of the new curriculum revolution and affect the realization of the goals of the new curriculum revolution. Only by making full use of the potential of existing resources, improving teachers' ability to develop resources, and striving to tap curriculum resources from students' existing life experience, can we create favorable conditions for the realization of the new curriculum revolution. Aiming at the e-learning environment and the data generated by it, the domain knowledge of learners and instructional resources is modeled and represented by using ontology method, and the learning mode of learners is mined by using recurrent neural network (RNN) to obtain the final resource recommendation list. The development and utilization of primary school math instructional resources can effectively improve the quality of primary school math instruction, and should be highly valued. Therefore, according to the experience of primary school math instruction, teachers make a detailed analysis and discussion on the development and utilization of primary school math instructional resources.

Keyword: Circulatory neural network · Mathematics curriculum in primary schools · Exploitation and utilization of resources

1 Introduction

In recent years, the large-scale application of online e-learning environment has promoted the increasing demand of learners for online instructional resources, resulting in the explosive growth of the number of instructional resources on the Internet [1]. IIn math instruction, teachers should make full use of their dominant position, actively develop and use various resources, promote students' understanding of mathematics, and improve students' thinking ability, emotional attitude and values [2, 3]. The development

Y. Zhang and N. Shah (Eds.): BigIoT-EDU 2023, LNICST 582, pp. 258–266, 2024.
https://doi.org/10.1007/978-3-031-63136-8_27

of curriculum resources enriches and interests the teaching content, stimulates students' interest in learning, and finally improves the instructional quality and efficiency. Therefore, it is very necessary and important to develop and utilize the curriculum resources of elementary school math in the classroom teaching of elementary school math. How to improve the instructional quality of elementary school math has always been the focus of the work of most mathematics teachers [4].

The development and utilization of primary school math instructional resources has played a vital role in improving the instructional quality of elementary school math [5]. Therefore, it is necessary to apply the recommendation system in the field of instructional resource recommendation, so as to guide learners to find suitable instructional resources. The preference information of new users on instructional resources is often lacking in the system, and it is difficult to model users; in addition, the number of active users in the recommender system is compared with the number of instructional resources [6]. Therefore, it is prone to cold start and sparse user history learning records, which seriously restricts the effectiveness of collaborative filtering recommendation system [7]. The deepening of educational reform, especially the launch of a new round of curriculum revolution, has brought the renewal of educational concepts. Instructional resources are no longer the only curriculum resources. The importance of developing and utilizing curriculum resources is becoming increasingly prominent. This paper proposes an ontology based neural network recommendation method to recommend online instructional resources to learners. Firstly, the ontology knowledge is used to model learners and instructional resources, and then the TRANSR method is used to embed the entities of learners and instructional resources. Finally, the learning habits of learners are modeled through neural network, and finally the instructional resources are recommended. It effectively improves the recommendation effect, thus improving learners' learning efficiency [8].

2 E-learning Resource Recommendation Model Integrating Ontology and RNN

2.1 Ontology Construction of Learners and Instructional Resources

There is a certain correlation between disciplines. Mathematics discipline can serve the learning of other disciplines as a computing tool, and other disciplines can also provide relevant materials for math instruction [9]. Therefore, teachers should also fully expand subject resources. From the expression form of curriculum resources, math instructional resources can be divided into the following categories: text resources, such as mathematics books and newspapers; Audio visual resources refer to the resources saved by video tapes, multimedia CDs and computer software; Network resources refer to mathematical resources on the Internet; Physical resources, such as mathematical tools, surrounding environment, etc. [10]. In the development of primary school math instructional resources, it is very important to develop existing instructional resources. Teachers should keep in mind the instructional resources and teaching objectives, but in the process of development, they cannot spend all their energy on developing instructional resources. By using new information technology and developing curriculum resources, teachers can greatly broaden students' horizons, cultivate students' logical thinking ability, and enable students to acquire math studies skills. Improve students' ability to analyze and deal with problems.

Each learner's learning style and knowledge level can be obtained by testing the learning style index and basic knowledge level during the account registration process. In this paper, learning style and knowledge level are defined as: learning style = {active/reflective, perception/intuition, visual/verbal, sequential/overall} = {1, 2, 3, 4}; Knowledge level = {beginner, intermediate, advanced} = {1, 2, 3}. And use the survey results to update the learner ontology. In the process of teaching, teachers should always grasp the learning situation of students and formulate different teaching methods according to the actual situation of students, which is also very beneficial to the development of students' physical and mental health and can exercise students' brain power. In this paper, the TransR method is used to embed the above relationship, and on the basis of ontology representation, the interaction between learners and instructional resources is included in the recommendation process. TransR is the current state-of-the-art method for graph relational embedding. The basic flow of TransR is shown in Fig. 1.

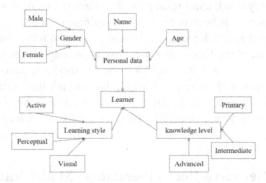

Fig. 1. Ontology of learners and instructional resources

RNN is a kind of neural network with memory function, which can be combined with the input information of all the past moments to calculate when processing continuous time series data. This structure is improved on the basis of feedforward neural network structure, and a recursive connection is constructed, which overcomes the shortcomings of feedforward neural network in solving the problem of sequence data. After entering the twenty-first century, with the large-scale application of the algorithm based on cyclic neural network, the cyclic neural network algorithm has also been optimized and many variant models have been derived. The output of the current output layer and the output of the hidden layer at the previous moment are simultaneously used as the input of the current hidden layer. The self-connection of the hidden layer nodes represents the dependency of the neurons of the RNN in the time dimension, and this feature makes the RNN very suitable for sequence recognition tasks such as speech recognition, machine translation, and handwriting recognition. Figure 2 shows a simple RNN with a single hidden layer structure.

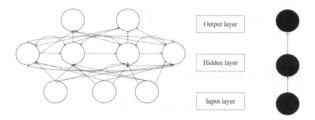

Fig. 2. Structure of cyclic neural network

2.2 Learning Resource Recommendation Strategy

It is an important way to arouse students' enthusiasm for learning mathematics by developing and utilizing their existing life experience, creating vivid and concrete participation situations, and allowing students to learn mathematics in situations. The knowledge of mathematics in primary schools is relatively abstract for primary school students, and the content in class is relatively boring. If teachers don't use proper learning methods, students have no interest in learning mathematics. Now, micro-class is a good instructional resource. In the process of teaching, primary school math teachers can make math knowledge into micro-class, so that the classroom becomes rich and colorful, and various multimedia technologies can be used to display math teaching content. Primary school math instructional resources can be obtained by using information media such as radio, television and Internet. Neural network has been applied to recommendation system in recent years. The use of information media to develop and utilize primary school math instructional resources can not only cultivate students' mathematical thinking ability and mathematical skills, but also cultivate students' ability to acquire and process mathematical information, thereby improving students' mathematical application ability and practical ability. Teachers determine the identification, accumulation, development and utilization of instructional resources. They have the consciousness and high sensitivity of mining instructional resources. In the implementation of the specific teaching process, teachers' personal qualities, educational ideas, teaching experience, knowledge and expertise, emotional attitudes and values can all become important curriculum resources and play an important role in determining the success of teaching. Therefore, from the perspective of curriculum resources, teachers themselves should belong to human resources. For example, in the section "Understanding of kilograms", the river uses its own weight to teach "understanding of meters and centimeters", and can use its own height. The "new curriculum standard" puts forward the idea of using more openness on the original basis, and clearly points out that in the teaching process, we should break the shackles of traditional ideas, adopt advanced teaching ideas, cultivate students' abilities, and promote students' physical and mental development.

In the encoder decoder part, bi-directional *RNN* is used to model the learning sequence, and *GRU* is used as the basic unit. *GRU* unit can effectively learn long-distance dependence and update the hidden layer unit in a more effective way. The activation function of *GRU* unit is linear interpolation, which comprehensively considers the activation function and candidate activation function of the previous unit:

$$h_t = (1 - z_1)h_{t-1} + z_t h_r \tag{1}$$

where the expression of the update gate z_t is given by:

$$z_t = o(W_z x_t + U_z h_{t-1}) \tag{2}$$

The definition of the candidate activation function is as follows:

$$h_t = \tanh(W x_t + U(r_t e h_{t-1})) \tag{3}$$

The update formula for reset gate is as follows:

$$r_t = o(W_r x_t + U_r h_{t-1}) \tag{4}$$

Input1 in the network structure represents the resource sequence that learners used to learn, and is a vector representation obtained by embedding entities. In this system, course teachers can create instructional resources (including lecture videos, syllabus, experimental syllabus, typical cases, analysis of important and difficult points and other multimedia materials) and upload them. Students can access the learning materials in the system after registering for the course. After the final examination of the semester course and before the result announcement, students need to judge whether the instructional resources recommended by the platform website are related to the course according to their actual situation, sort them according to their own learning order, and feed back the instructional resources suitable for their own situation and appropriate learning sequence to the platform. At the same time, at the end of the semester, students' feedback information will be received, including students' annotation of whether instructional resources are relevant or not, and the recommended sequence determined by students according to their own situation. The implementation period of the experiment is 12 months (3 semesters defined by the learning platform). The courses that students can choose are shown in Table 1.

Table 1. Course list and corresponding instructional resource material column

Course name	Learning resources (PCs.)
Fundamentals of computer application	21
Web design and production	29
Introduction to programming	15
Database application	16
Frontier of agricultural science and technology knowledge	14
Cultivation techniques of cash crops	32
Ornamental fish culture technology	20
Artificial culture and breeding technology of bamboo rat	18
Lecture on pest control	22
Cultivation technology of medicinal toad	17
Total	204

Firstly, according to the established ontology knowledge of learners and instructional resources, this paper expresses it as a 50-dimensional vector form. Among them, learners' learning style, education level, gender, etc. occupy one dimension respectively, and the rest dimensions are randomly initialized; The resource form and category of instructional resources occupy one dimension respectively, and the other dimensions are randomly initialized.

3 Development and Utilization of Math Instructional Resources in Primary School

3.1 Develop Curriculum Resources from Students' Life Experiences

Redevelopment and utilization of instructional resources. Textbooks are important curriculum resources, but from the perspective of curriculum resources and the requirements of new curriculum revolution, textbooks are no longer the only curriculum resources, and their role is on the decline. Textbooks are only instructional resources used to achieve curriculum objectives, not the whole curriculum. The so-called "preparation of instructional resources" mainly refers to the redevelopment of instructional resources. The new curriculum highlights an open concept in the use of instructional resources, that is, to break the original instructional resources as the "imperial edict", strictly follow the teaching methods of instructional resources according to the order and content of textbooks, and advocate "teaching with instructional resources", but not limited to "instructional resources". Teachers can directly guide students to use the network platform to find the math instructional resources they need, so as to solve various problems encountered in their math studies.

Under the requirements of the new curriculum revolution, any subject must have good external conditions when teaching, that is, community resources, so that teachers can carry out effective extracurricular activities, so that students can actively participate in extracurricular activities, and finally exercise the mathematics of primary school students. Knowledge application ability and practical ability enable primary school students to transform mathematical knowledge into practical application ability. Therefore, in teaching, teachers must start from the needs and reality of students, change instructional concepts, concentrate on teaching content, save classroom time and let students think and explore. With the acceleration of modernization, an information network era has arrived. Network resources are rich and colorful. Therefore, teachers should actively develop and make use of network information resources to make it a platform for teachers to understand the society and a powerful assistant for students' learning, so as to make math instruction keep pace with the development of the times. Teachers should build a mathematics information resource base by creating a campus mathematics website or personal website, linking other educational websites, especially mathematics education websites, so that teachers and students can learn about mathematics information together, learn from each other, and learn from each other's strengths. Teachers should develop and introduce various multimedia courseware for classroom teaching, and communicate with students through multimedia classrooms to deepen the friendship between teachers and students.

3.2 Development Course Experiment Results

Firstly, the experimental results of the proposed ontology-based neural network instructional resource recommendation system are discussed and compared with the traditional collaborative filtering (CF) algorithm and the ontology-combined collaborative filtering (CF + Onto) algorithm. In this paper, the widely used accuracy, recall and MRR are used to evaluate the performance of the proposed method, and compared with the other two methods. As can be seen from Fig. 3, compared with collaborative filtering (CF) and ontology plus collaborative filtering (CF + onto), the prediction accuracy of

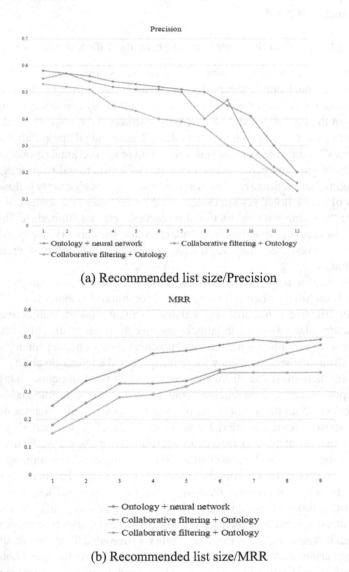

(a) Recommended list size/Precision

(b) Recommended list size/MRR

Fig. 3. Comparison results of recommended results with Precision and MRR methods in various evaluation indexes

ontology based neural network recommendation proposed in this paper is the highest. When n exceeds 20, the growth rate of MRR value slows down. From the above results, it can be seen that compared with recall and MRR, the ontology based neural network recommendation method proposed in this paper is superior to the other two algorithms (CF + onto) and (CF) no matter how the number of recommendation resultschanges.

Therefore, we can find and develop primary school math instructional resources in primary school students' life practice and experience, and make efficient use of them, so as to improve primary school students' mathematical life application ability and practical ability. Teachers should actively change their traditional instructional concepts and methods, especially the traditional instructional concepts of "full house" and "indoctrination", so as to realize students' dominant position in the classroom, thus arousing students' interest in math studies and making them actively participate in the development and utilization of math study resources. Teachers can find the most suitable way for students' math studies according to the age characteristics, cognitive law and life reality of primary school students, so as to mobilize students' enthusiasm and initiative in math studies. In the actual primary school math instruction, teachers should strive to select materials familiar to students and create familiar situations for students, so as to stimulate students' learning interest and motivation.

4   Conclusions

This paper proposes an ontology-based neural network recommendation method, in which the ontology is used to represent knowledge about learners and instructional resources, and then exploits the latent representation of the learner's historical learning data to combine the ontology domain knowledge with the learner's knowledge. Study habits are incorporated into the recommendation process for recommending online instructional resources to learners. The RNN can effectively deal with the sequence problem with time information, and combined with the local *CTC* loss function model, it can realize the stroke level training, without the need to segment the sampling points. Under the background of the new curriculum revolution, elementary school math plays an increasingly important role, which makes many elementary school math teachers constantly improve their teaching methods and change their teaching modes, hoping to improve their primary school math instruction quality and efficiency. The development and utilization of curriculum resources is of great significance. Rational use of curriculum resources can improve the efficiency of classroom teaching. Teachers should take students as the main body to study instructional resources, integrate classroom instructional resources and make flexible use of them, so as to improve students' cognitive level and enrich students' knowledge and experience.

References

1. Huang, R., Li, C.: MBR membrane flux prediction based on differential evolution algorithm and recurrent neural network. Comput. Sci. Appl. **10**(7), 7 (2020)
2. Gou, S.: On the development and utilization of elementary school math curriculum resources. Curriculum Educ. Res. **18**(1), 2020

3. Lu, C., Yang, H., Li, Y.: An online instructional resource recommendation technology based on ontology and recurrent neural network. Intell. Theor. Pract. **42**(2), 7 (2019)
4. Lu, H.: Development and utilization of elementary school math curriculum resources. Primary School Stud. Teach. Pract. (12), 1 (2018)
5. Bi, H.: Thoughts on the development and utilization of elementary school math curriculum resources. Win Future (004), 136 (2018)
6. Gao, M., Xu, B.: Recommendation algorithm based on recurrent neural network. Comput. Eng. **45**(8), 6 (2019)
7. He, X.: Using the source of living water skillfully: on the development and utilization of elementary school math curriculum resources. Math. Teach. Commun. (13), 2 (2017)
8. Ma, Q., Yang, H.: Development and utilization of teaching resources in primary mathematics classroom. Read. Writing **14**(32), 9 (2017)
9. Lan, M.: The development and utilization of mathematics curriculum resources—the application of micro-lecture in elementary school math. Zhonghua Junior (36), 2 (2017)
10. Qin, D.: Strategies for the development and utilization of elementary school math curriculum resources. New Wisdom (19), 1 (2019)

Evaluation Algorithm of New Media Computer-Aided Instruction System Based on BP Neural Network

Xiaoming Wu[✉] and Haihu Zhao

Wuxi Vocational Institute of Commerce, Wuxi 214153, Jiangsu, China
wuxiaoming@wxic.edu.cn

Abstract. With the development of computer network and new media technology, computer-aided instruction (CAI) has begun to develop in a new direction and entered a new stage of new media CAI. Its research and development has been widely valued and rapidly developed. This paper discusses the wide application of multimedia in the auxiliary teaching system, which create new methods for teaching reform. At the same time, the feasibility and system function model of multimedia teaching system are established, and the teaching supporting system based on back propagation (BP) neural network is successfully developed. At the same time, some key points of the algorithm and teaching system are put forward, and the implementation of the algorithm and some functions of the system are introduced in detail, and an example is given. Through the application of this system, the teaching quality of corresponding problems was improved, and the teaching efficiency was increased by 23.14%.

Keywords: New media · BP neural network · Computer aided instruction · System evaluation

1 Introduction

With the appearance of computer, the auxiliary teaching system can use powerful computer as server and application server, which makes the system have faster running speed and more stable running platform [1]. With the rapid progress of database technology, CAI system can be supported by a fully functional database system. With the continuous improvement of network technology and its security performance, the auxiliary teaching system has a solid carrier and a stable application environment [2]. The way to collect feedback information is to provide a lot of test questions corresponding to the teaching content for learners to answer in the teaching process, and then analyze the results of the answers to extract useful information [3]. Computer aided instruction system combines modern education theory and modern information technology, breaks the original teaching restrictions, and brings a new vitality to teaching [4]. It not only makes the content and means of teaching reform, but also breaks through the traditional teaching mode. It promotes a new teaching mode that is student-centered. The CAI evaluation

© ICST Institute for Computer Sciences, Social Informatics and Telecommunications Engineering 2024
Published by Springer Nature Switzerland AG 2024. All Rights Reserved
Y. Zhang and N. Shah (Eds.): BigIoT-EDU 2023, LNICST 582, pp. 267–275, 2024.
https://doi.org/10.1007/978-3-031-63136-8_28

system is mainly composed of three aspects: First, the establishment and maintenance of an open test question bank; Second, the interactive test is automatically generated according to the attribute indexes of the test questions selected by the students; Finally, the comprehensive evaluation of the learners' grasp of the contents is made according to the test results, and the next step of the students' learning is recommended according to the evaluation results [5]. In terms of the current development of CAI, it is mainly divided into two types. One type focuses on students' learning, mainly composed of various courseware and professional auxiliary teaching software. The other type focuses on assessing students' learning, mainly composed of various examination systems [6]. This paper combines these two aspects to evaluate the CAI system and analyze the effectiveness of the algorithm, so as to better achieve the purpose of auxiliary teaching [7].

2   Combination of CAI System and New Media

2.1   CAI System Features and Design Framework

In the design of CAI system, we must fully consider the advantages of computer technology and make use of teachers' subjective initiative and teaching experience [8]. In the whole system development process, database design plays an important role. The whole framework of the system is composed of two modules: courseware management and integrable ware library management [9]. Each module includes the functions of creating and maintaining courseware and teaching material library, as shown in Fig. 1. The specific implementation process of the system is: Firstly, analyze the teaching targets of the course, and formulate the teaching structure based on the learning objectives. Then subdivide the teaching objectives at all levels and add the picture content, and design the questioning questions according to the learning objectives and difficulties, and design the ideal answers and corresponding feedback information [10]. Finally, the contents of the projects at all levels are effectively connected to make teaching courseware [11]. Thus, a set of teaching system that is closer to the current teaching situation is developed from the functional framework and design ideas.

The characteristics of the CAI system are as follows: Based on the information feedback in the students' cognitive model, the CAI system collates and infers in the artificial intelligence system, and finally automatically generates the teaching contents and teaching methods that take the students as the main body and conform to the individual differences of the students. At the same time, it will automatically evaluate the learning ability of students, analyze the wrong behaviors of students in learning, and finally put forward correction opinions and learning methods of learning the old knowledge. In a word, CAI is the product of the combination of modern educational theory and modern information technology. Its appearance has brought a new impetus to traditional teaching methods. It has greatly promoted the progress of teaching methods and means, fully mobilized the enthusiasm of educators and educatees, and played an inestimable role in promoting the development of education.

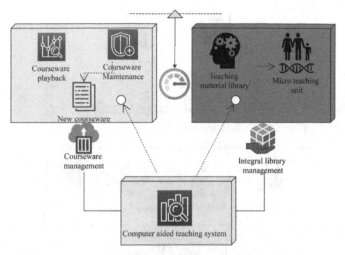

Fig. 1. Design framework of computer aided instruction system

2.2 New Media-Assisted Teaching System Model

For the diversity of new media forms, it is also necessary to condense several new media platforms that should be focused on according to the needs of the curriculum, instead of blindly seeking perfection. The training of new media teaching thinking can enable teachers to accept the diversification of teaching mode in the new era, see the brand-new feeling brought by new media assisted teaching, so as to actively use the new media teaching system to start teaching activities. From the aspects of teacher training, student guidance, mode innovation, platform construction, practice feedback, etc., it promotes the organic combination of new media assisted teaching and traditional teaching, gives full play to the beneficial role of new media assisted teaching, and establishes a complete new media assisted teaching system, as shown in Fig. 2. Another advantage of the new media computer-assisted instruction system is that teachers and students need to interact effectively in the courseware design process, which will greatly improve the subjective initiative of both sides, make every teaching participant feel the courseware planning personally, improve teachers' teaching ability, restrict students' passive psychology, and effectively improve teachers' teaching creativity and students' subjective initiative.

The computer-aided teaching system is mainly for the background management function operation of teachers. After the teachers log in the system, they can manage the corresponding modules in the background of the system. When facing student users, you can view the course schedule and other relevant course information in the system. The main functions for administrators are administrator login and logout, and the management of department information of teacher user information. We should not only vividly show the teaching content from the perspective of "teaching", but also consider the difficulty of acceptance from the perspective of "learning". The new media assisted teaching and traditional teaching are not mutually exclusive, but should be organically combined to give birth to a new teaching mode in the new era.

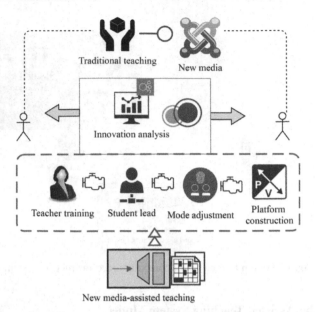

New media-assisted teaching

Fig. 2. New media-assisted instruction mode

3 Algorithm Applications

3.1 Algorithm for Automatic Volume Grouping

The three-dimensional constraint matrix is composed of three attributes, namely, the type of problem, the degree of separation and the degree of difficulty, and then the test is organized. In the test questions database, the method of combining static storage and dynamic index is used to query the test questions according to the types, chapters and knowledge points of the test questions. First, based on the question type and the chapter, all the questions that meet the requirements are extracted. If the number of questions that meet the requirements is greater than 0, the questions that meet the more precise requirements are extracted from the questions that have been extracted under the sub conditions of knowledge points and difficulty. If the number of questions is 0, it will be added to the test paper. If the number of test questions is greater than 1, the test questions will be randomly selected and added to the test paper. If the number of test questions is 1, the test questions will be optimized proportionally to find the most qualified test questions to add to the test paper. If no suitable question is selected based on the question type and the chapter, the information will be returned to ask whether the condition is changed. If the condition is changed, the search will be repeated. Otherwise, the search will end. The specific formula is:

$$\lambda_x = \frac{1}{N}\sqrt{\sum (s\rangle 0, s\rangle 1)} \Rightarrow (s = 0, s = 1) \Leftarrow \qquad (1)$$

3.2   Algorithm of Difficulty Distribution of Test Questions in Random Selection

Before learning, the system is ignorant of the subject's information. In order to solve these problems, the binomial distribution function of discrete random variables is used to establish the mathematical model of topic selection, determine the distribution of topic type and difficulty, and then the random function is used to select topics, and good results are achieved. Therefore, first select a group of test questions with moderate total difficulty from various knowledge points according to the requirements of the test outline, and preliminarily estimate the student's ability according to the examinee's answers. Therefore, it can be considered that the binomial distribution function of the random sampling event in accordance with the discrete random variable is:

$$p(k) = p_k q^{n-k} = p_k(1-p)^{n-k} \tag{2}$$

Among them, $k = 0, 1, 2 \cdots, n$. n is a positive integer. The mean of the binomial distribution is:

$$Q = np \tag{3}$$

On this basis, the random function is used to select topics randomly within this difficulty distribution range, which has good randomness. If the conditions such as question type and chapter range are added, the satisfactory test questions can be automatically selected. If the number of questions in the question bank is moderate and the distribution is reasonable, the composition of the test paper can better meet the requirements of each index. Through the analysis of the test paper and the self-adaptive learning test, the user's learning situation and mastery can be objectively estimated, so as to facilitate the promotion of the next step.

3.3   Evaluation of Teaching System Based on BP Neural Network

Generally speaking, the neural network is a multi-layer neural network composed of three or more layers, and each nerve cell between the left and right layers is completely connected. The neural network is realized by teachers' learning. When a pair of learning patterns are provided to the network, the activation rate will propagate through the intermediate layer between the input layer and the output layer, and each neuron in the output layer will output the corresponding input network response. Suppose we get an accurate evaluation value through the neural network and judge whether it is good or bad according to this value. Therefore, the output of the neural network has only one node. Table 1 shows the training results of the table data in this program:

In the obtained time series data, some valuable information can be obtained. For example, the BP neural network is used to predict the students' grades based on the sequence of the students' homework and the quality of the homework. The process is as follows: First, a set of indicators that affect academic performance is generated. Then, the BP neural network is trained by applying the training set (the time relationship between the grades of former students and the assignments handed in by former students, and the quality of assignments). Finally, the optimized network is used to test the test set, and the output data of the network is inversely normalized to obtain the students' scores

Table 1. Training results

Memory	Comprehension	Analyze	Actual evaluation value
0.93	0.27	0.31	0.36
0.55	0.36	0.78	0.18
0.48	0.74	0.37	0.44
0.33	0.34	0.97	0.43
0.25	0.85	0.6	0.69
0.74	0.12	0.19	0.78

and to stratify the students. Establish the structural model of the corresponding neural network model, determine the learning rate, learning times and error accuracy, and start training the model (see Fig. 3). After training, the corresponding neural network model is established, the test data is read, and the expected value is output by calculating the network.

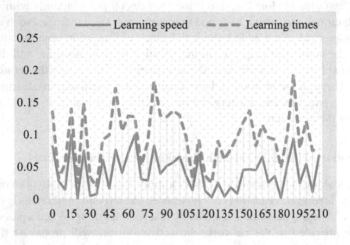

Fig. 3. Comparison of error curves

From the above error curve, it can be seen that the trained network quickly meets the error requirements. Select the basic teaching courseware of the first knowledge point for learning, then draw questions and conduct unit tests. According to the test results, the system will give the evaluation of students' cognitive ability, and write the evaluation value into the updatable dynamic information structure in the student model. Then, according to the evaluation value, the system will give suggestions for the next knowledge point or this knowledge point to learn again, and write it into the student model. Because the error value of the neural network is closely related to the connection weight between the nodes of the network and the adjustment range of the node threshold value, for the sample data set with unreasonable training order, the difference between the two adjacent groups of sample data values may be large, and the connection weight is required to be greatly adjusted during the training process. If the adjustment range is too large, oscillation is likely to occur, and if the adjustment range is too small, the convergence speed will be slow, which will ultimately affect the effectiveness of the algorithm. Next, input the test data to test, and the results are shown in Fig. 4:

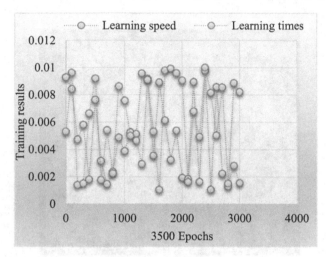

Fig. 4. Training results

Figure 4 shows the current network training function. After multiple training, the network output error is relatively large and the network convergence speed is very slow. This is because the training function is a simple step-by-step training function, the training speed is relatively slow, and it is easy to fall into a local minimum. In the application of neural network, the size of the sample set is also very important. If the number of samples is too small, it is not enough to reflect the feature space, and if the number of samples is too large, the training time will be prolonged. Therefore, we should make a decision after considering factors such as the sample interval, the number of sample elements and the range of variation.

4 Simulation Test

The basic idea of applying BP neural network to the comprehensive evaluation of auxiliary teaching system is to use each evaluation index of classroom teaching quality to form the input vector of neural network, and use the evaluation value, that is, the evaluation result of experts, to form the output vector of neural network, and reasonably design the network structure and training samples. Then, the training samples are input into the network for calculation until the system error meets the specified requirements. The network model obtained is the required evaluation model of the auxiliary teaching system. In order to test the stability of the BP neural network assisted instruction evaluation system, 30 university courses were selected for simulation test, and the performance of the computer-aided instruction evaluation system was tested. The BP neural network assisted instruction quality evaluation system was selected. The traditional university joint teaching is comparable. The RBF neural network is combined with BP neural network, and the BP neural network is combined with the state feedback network to randomly determine the weight of each neural network. The evaluation accuracy of the computer-aided teaching system is shown in Fig. 5.

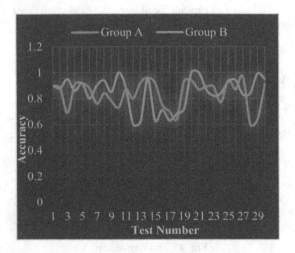

Fig. 5. Correct rate of assessment of the auxiliary teaching system

As shown in Fig. 5, for 30 courses, the accuracy rate of neural network teaching quality evaluation is above 95%, and the overall teaching quality evaluation result is very stable, which can be applied to the actual teaching quality management. In a word, on the basis of tacit knowledge base, cognitive expression, knowledge acquisition and BP neural network, the samples are trained by neural network, the ideal neural network parameters are established, and the self-evaluation system of students is formed. Through the application of this system, the teaching quality of corresponding problems has been improved, and the teaching efficiency has been increased by 23.14%.

5   Conclusions

Like human teachers, CAI system can select the most effective teaching methods for the students according to their understanding of the knowledge in the field of teaching materials, their knowledge level and learning background, etc. to carry out teaching activities, supervise and evaluate the students' learning behavior, select questions for students to answer, and provide help and select supplementary materials in a timely manner according to the students' requirements. This paper studies how to improve the original teaching program with single function into a new media computer-aided teaching system with multiple functions, and integrate the original scattered curriculum teaching resources into the curriculum aided teaching system, so that the system has a whole of information announcement, educational administration and teaching functions. It can be said that the development of CAI system is a revolutionary teaching reform. The new media assisted teaching system realizes the maximum integration and sharing of teaching resources, and enhances the contact and communication among schools, teachers and students.

References

1. Xu, Z., Hu, G.: Research on evaluation algorithm based on new media computer-aided teaching system. Educ. Modernizat. **5**(52), 188–190+221 (2018)
2. Zhang, Y., Zheng, X.: Algorithm analysis of intelligent computer-aided teaching evaluation system. Microcomput. Appl. **23**(2), 4 (2020)
3. Yuan, F., Du, X., Zhang, Y.: Analysis of ICAI system evaluation algorithm. J. Yanshan Univ. **26**(2), 128 (2021)
4. Yang, L., Li, J.: Research and design of TSP teaching aid system based on C-W saving algorithm. Microcomput. Appl. **2**(5), 39 (2018)
5. Wan, M., Guan, Y.: Research on the application of artificial intelligence technology in computer-aided teaching. Microcomput. Inf. (02Z), 4 (2016)
6. Han, Y.: Design and development of mobile new media-assisted teaching platform. Electron. Test. (11), 2 (2018)
7. Zhang, M.: New media-assisted teaching under the concept of CBI to improve students' writing ability. J. Jiamusi Vocat. Coll. (6), 1 (2017)
8. Zhou, J., Li, S., Xiang, W., et al.: Application of new media-assisted teaching in postgraduate teaching of neurosurgery specialty. Chin. J. Med. Educ. Explorat. **20**(1), 4 (2021)
9. Chen, S.: New media assisted teaching: concepts, values and strategies. J. Jiangxi Radio Telev. Univ. **20**(2), 5 (2018)
10. Du, J., Xiao, S.: Challenges and countermeasures of new media-assisted teaching in university education. New Media Res. (13), 4 (2016)
11. Dong, Y.: The auxiliary teaching function of new media and new technologies in mathematics teaching. Exam Weekly (11), 1 (2016)

Optimization Analysis of Higher Mathematics Resources Based on Convolution Neural Network Algorithm

Junyong Gao[1]([✉]), Mingming Wang[2], Hong Leng[3], and Yanyu Chen[3]

[1] Changchun Institute of Architecture, Changchun 130000, Jilin, China
jyg06130613@163.com
[2] Air Force Aviation University, Changchun 130000, Jilin, China
[3] International School, Jinan University, Guangzhou 510632, Guangdong, China

Abstract. Convolution neural network is an artificial intelligence algorithm. It is an algorithm that can be used to solve problems in the field of mathematics. Convolution neural networks have been used to solve optimization problems, such as finding the minimum, maximum or the optimal solution of a given problem. Convolution neural networks have been used to find solutions to optimization problems, such as finding the minimum, maximum or the optimal solution of a given problem. This method was developed by LeCun et al. (1986). There are many ways to recommend advanced mathematics resources, but some algorithms have problems and defects, and the final recommendation results are not reliable and accurate. Therefore, a resource recommendation algorithm for advanced mathematics based on convolution neural network is proposed. Set the weighted fuzzy resource recommendation target, determine the level of collaborative convolution mathematical resource recommendation, construct the convolution neural network mathematical resource recommendation model, and realize the design of advanced mathematical resource recommendation algorithm through the membership matrix. The experimental results show that compared with the traditional fuzzy hierarchical mathematical resource recommendation algorithm test group, the final MSE mean value of the convolutional neural network mathematical resource recommendation algorithm test group designed in this paper is relatively high, indicating that this algorithm has better application accuracy and reliability, and has practical application value.

Keywords: Advanced mathematics · Convolution neural network · resource optimization

1 Introduction

The learning objects of college advanced mathematics courses have generally grown up, and they have their own thoughts and behavior habits that have been developed in middle school. They may not be unfamiliar with information technology, or they may have high

Y. Zhang and N. Shah (Eds.): BigIoT-EDU 2023, LNICST 582, pp. 276–282, 2024.
https://doi.org/10.1007/978-3-031-63136-8_29

information literacy, or they may have prejudice against information technology. In addition, the contents of higher mathematics courses in universities are broader and deeper than those in junior and senior high schools. In addition to professional restrictions and class hour restrictions, students need to master and apply flexibly to practice. It is not enough to rely solely on traditional classroom teaching. Higher mathematics course is the basic course of university and the cradle of cultivating students' innovative ability [1]. The integration of information technology and higher mathematics curriculum is not only to use information technology as an auxiliary teaching or learning tool, but also to emphasize the effective integration of information technology into the teaching process, and to create a new teaching environment, which should be able to support the teaching methods and learning methods required by multiple aspects such as scenario creation, heuristic thinking, information acquisition, resource sharing, multiple interaction, independent exploration, collaborative learning, etc., That is to realize a teaching and learning mode characterized by "independence, exploration and cooperation" that can give full play to the leading role of teachers and fully reflect the main position of students, so as to give full play to students' initiative, enthusiasm and creativity, change the traditional classroom teaching structure, and truly implement the cultivation of students' innovative spirit and practical ability [2].

The author's practice of the integration of information technology and higher mathematics curriculum is to respect the subject of learning, combine the initiative of students with the leading role of teachers, take the improvement of students' scientific quality as the core, and combine the knowledge structure and ability foundation that students have grasped, from scientific knowledge and skills, scientific concepts, scientific methods In terms of scientific attitude and scientific spirit, it is necessary to determine multiple objectives of mathematics classroom teaching, so that students can gradually form a scientific world view and methodology on the basis of mastering basic knowledge and skills. In the process of teaching, we should use traditional media and information technology media to carefully organize teaching activities, make full use of information technology as a media demonstration tool, information processing tool and collaborative organization tool, create conditions for students to actively participate in the whole process of mathematics classroom teaching, and improve teaching efficiency. Strengthen the formation process of mathematical concepts and laws and the practical application process of mathematical experiments, and pay attention to the cultivation of innovative spirit and creative ability while emphasizing the learning of basic knowledge and the training of basic abilities [3]. Pay attention to using the resource environment provided by information technology, break through the limitation that books are the main source of knowledge, and use the information technology platform of higher mathematics teaching to greatly expand the amount of higher mathematics knowledge and cultivate students' personalized learning. And on the basis of practice, the investigation and analysis of the integration effect of information technology and higher mathematics courses are carried out. The investigation results show that the integration of information technology and higher mathematics courses effectively improves the teaching efficiency and the information literacy of students.

2 Related Work

2.1 Modern Information Technology has a Profound Impact on Mathematics and Mathematics Education

The information age is a digital age, in which mathematics plays an important role. In the final analysis, various advanced modern technologies are the embodiment of modern mathematics technology. Modern computer is a magical combination of 0 and 1. The binary system invented by the German mathematician Leibniz in the 17th century promoted the emergence of today's computer. Because mathematics is closely related to the development of human beings with its amazing characteristics, it is involved in the development of technology and integrated into it with its unique identity, and its effectiveness in all aspects is reflected by its accuracy and internal beauty, so mathematics will naturally become the key of key technology and the support point of information technology [4]. On the other hand, due to the intervention of modern information technology with computer and network technology as the core, mathematical science has also been unprecedented expanded in research fields, research methods and application scope. Mathematics is not only a universally applicable technology for people to deal with various practical problems, predict the future and exchange information with each other, but also a basic way of thinking for people to grasp the objective world model and sort out the objective world order.

In front of the computer, because a lot of knowledge becomes dynamic, it can stimulate people's love for mathematics, trigger people to expand the wings of imagination and continue to think and pursue, so that mathematics has a different form from the past - visualization, rapidity, and human culture. Scientific calculation with computer is the most basic function of computer. It can collect and process a large amount of data in a very short time, make judgments, form formulas, and construct theories. The rapid development of computers has put forward many new research topics for mathematical research, such as computer graphics, computer and cryptography, and so on [5]. At present, people have pushed the computing method to the forefront of human scientific activities, and computing, together with experiments and theories, has become the third scientific method. In mathematical research methods, mathematical experiments have been paid more and more attention. At present, many famous mathematicians are increasingly paying attention to the widespread use of computers and the tendency of arithmetization, and have turned to the research of computer algebra, computer geometry and other emerging disciplines.

2.2 Application Status of Online Teaching Platform at Home and Abroad

The teaching mode of sPOC (small-scale restricted online course) proposed by Professor Armando Fox of the University of California, Berkeley is to catch up with students before class, urge students to learn, cultivate interest, strengthen knowledge, expand hands-on ability in class, and interact with each other on the line after class, discuss exercises, and evaluate lectures. SPOC is suitable for elite education in foreign countries. This teaching mode is mainly adopted by many domestic training institutions, and some universities try it out. The BOPPPs model is mainly composed of introduction, objectives, pre-test, participatory learning, post-test and summary [6]. At the same time, it uses the duration of students' concentration to attract students and cultivate their interest in learning. With the rise of online paid teaching, a variety of online teaching modes have also emerged, such as lecture-type online teaching mode, demonstration-type online teaching mode, exploration-type online teaching mode, discussion-type online teaching mode, and information-collection and collation-type online teaching mode. These modes can fully reflect the main position of students and help cultivate students' learning interests Inspire, guide and really mobilize students' enthusiasm, initiative and creativity in teaching. Students can learn independently, control the pace and content of learning by themselves, leave some time and space for their own thinking, and also learn some knowledge points repeatedly to strengthen the learning effect.

Advanced mathematics is a public basic course of science and engineering. The number of students is too large. Teachers can only take into account the overall learning situation of students. Therefore, classroom teaching is no longer teacher-led student learning, but student-led. For students, teacher-assisted learning is also different from each other in terms of speed and understanding of knowledge, and views on the same issue are also different [7]. Compared with elementary mathematics, advanced mathematics is more abstract. However, those abstract definitions and theorems are often important knowledge points that need to be understood rather than memorized. In practical application, solving a practical problem requires drawing inferences from one instance and flexible use of the knowledge learned. However, in the teaching process, for the purpose of assessment, the teacher pays more attention to how to understand these concepts and theorems rather than how to apply them to life and what practical problems they can solve. This has led to the disconnection between the knowledge of higher mathematics and real life, making students more difficult to learn.

3 Advanced Mathematics Resource Recommendation Algorithm Based on Convolution Neural Network

(1) Weighted fuzzy resource recommendation target setting

Before designing the resource recommendation algorithm of advanced mathematics based on convolution neural network, it is necessary to set the weighted fuzzy resource recommendation target according to the actual resource processing. First, build a fuzzy definition, and perform the basic algorithm based on the initial model of C-means clustering. Then, determine the specific weighting coefficient, and set the number of recommended neighbors in the convolutional neural network. In addition, set the strain matrix in combination with the membership of teaching resources in higher mathematics.

However, it should be noted that the set matrix is not fixed, and it changes with the change of resource recommendation type. At this time, the corresponding fuzzy operation rules are formulated, and different advanced mathematics resource recommendation levels are constructed in combination with the recommendation conditions of resources. Each level needs to be guided by a fixed resource recommendation goal, so as to complete the query and acquisition of user resources and lay a solid foundation for subsequent work [8].

(2) Determination of collaborative convolution mathematical resource recommendation level

After setting the target of weighted fuzzy resource recommendation, it is necessary to further determine the corresponding level of collaborative convolution mathematical resource recommendation. Compared with the traditional resource recommendation algorithm, the algorithm designed in this paper has certain complexity, and the execution of the target task is also hierarchical processing, so as to further ensure the stability and reliability of the test calculation [9]. The specific structure level is shown in Fig. 1:

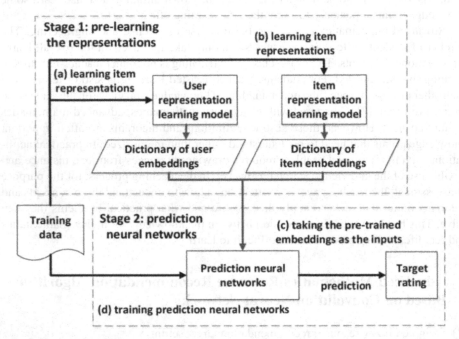

Fig. 1. Hierarchy of collaborative convolution mathematical resource recommendation structure

According to Fig. 1, we can complete the construction of collaborative convolution mathematical resource recommendation structure hierarchy. With the assistance of synergy, the data resources are processed into fixed format, and the weighted fuzzy resource recommendation target is set in the structure level to further optimize and improve the comprehensive application ability of the collaborative convolution mathematical resource recommendation level.

(3) Construction of mathematical resource recommendation model based on convolution neural network

After determining the level of collaborative convolution mathematical resource recommendation, it is necessary to build a convolution neural network mathematical resource recommendation model. You can first set the membership change value range between 1 and 2.5 in combination with the actual resource processing objectives, and at the same time, set the convolution iteration coefficient, as shown in the following formula (1):

$$M = \frac{x+1}{3} - 7\sqrt{r} \qquad (1)$$

In formula (1): M represents convolution iteration coefficient, x represents neural recommendation difference, and r represents cluster termination value. Through the above calculation, the actual convolution iteration coefficient can be finally obtained. Adjust the initial mathematical resource recommendation model. At the same time, combine the convolution neural network, delimit the tested area, locate the convolution recommendation center, and set resource recommendation nodes around to further improve the practical application ability of the model [10].

(4) The design of advanced mathematics resource recommendation algorithm based on membership matrix

After completing the construction of the mathematical resource recommendation model of convolution neural network, it is necessary to combine the membership matrix to realize the design of the advanced mathematical resource recommendation algorithm. First of all, combined with the changing resource recommendation target, feature membership is extracted from each resource processing level, and the actual convex function is calculated, as shown in the following formula (2):

$$T = \frac{2\sqrt{3} - \frac{D}{3}}{A + 0.5} - 5y \qquad (2)$$

In formula (2): T represents the convex function, A represents the preset verification algorithm standard, D represents the convolution neural difference, and y represents the interactive difference. Through the above calculation, the actual convex function can be obtained. Set the edge data recommendation range of the membership matrix to determine the relevant processing accuracy. In addition, adjust the corresponding membership according to the change of resources to improve the overall flexibility of resource recommendation and enhance the comprehensive effect of advanced mathematics resource recommendation.

4 Conclusion

To sum up, it is the design and analysis of the algorithm of advanced mathematics resource recommendation based on convolution neural network. Compared with the traditional resource recommendation algorithm, the algorithm designed in this paper is relatively more stable and flexible, and has accuracy and reliability in the process of practical application. In addition, combined with convolutional neural network, the high-accuracy accounting model can simultaneously process a large amount of information and data, improve the recommendation effect of resources to a certain extent, enhance the comprehensive recommendation quality and efficiency, and then enhance the actual comprehensive application ability.

References

1. Jin, X., Fan, L., Yao, Y.: Convolutional neural network optimization algorithm-based magnetic resonance imaging in analysis of chronic pain caused by the myofascial trigger point. Sci. Program. **2021**(1), 4505147 (2021)
2. Luo, Y., Fan, Y., Chen, X.: Research on optimization of deep learning algorithm based on convolutional neural network. J. Phys. Conf. Ser. **1848**(1), 012038 (2021)
3. Jamshed, A., Mallick, B., Bharti, R.K.: An efficient pattern mining convolution neural network (CNN) algorithm with Grey Wolf Optimization (GWO) (2022)
4. Sato, H., Igarashi, H.: Deep learning-based surrogate model for fast multi-material topology optimization of IPM motor. COMPEL Int. J. Comput. Math. Electr. Electron. Eng. **41**(3), 900–914 (2022)
5. Michel, D.D.E., Beldine, T.N.A., Emmanuel, T.: Propagation model optimization based on ion motion optimization algorithm for efficient deployment of eLTE network. J. Comput. Commun. **10**(11), 171–196 (2022)
6. Cao, J.: An analysis of the optimal allocation of core human resources in family enterprises based on the Markov model. J. Math. **2022**, 7619293 (2022)
7. Shahrokhi, S., El-Shahat, A., Masoudinia, F., et al.: Sizing and energy management of parking lots of electric vehicles based on battery storage with wind resources in distribution network. Energies **14**, 6755 (2021)
8. Pan, Y.: Design of financial management model using the forward neural network based on particle swarm optimization algorithm. Comput. Intell. Neurosci. (2022)
9. Mali, S.D., Govinda, K.: ExpSFROA-based DRN: exponential sunflower rider optimization algorithm-driven deep residual network for the intrusion detection in IOT-based plant disease monitoring. Int. J. Semant. Comput. **17**(01), 5–31 (2022)
10. Li, Z.: Neural network economic forecast method based on genetic algorithm. IET Softw. **4**, 681–693 (2023)

Research on Remote Dance Motion Capture Evaluation System and Dance Injury Prevention Based on Intelligent Terminal

Chen Li[1]([⊠]), Yiyuan Yang[2], Jing Li[2], Weimin Guo[3], and Fang Feng[3]

[1] School of Physical Education and Health, Zhaoqing University, Zhaoqing 526061,
Guangdong, China
gdszqxy123123@126.com
[2] Music College of Zhaoqing University, Zhaoqing 526061, Guangdong, China
[3] Jiangxi University of Applied Science, Nanchang 330100, Jiangxi, China

Abstract. The design of intelligent terminal dance movement supplement and optimization system can systematically analyze the 3 D digital form of dance. And in the subsequent process of folk dance style presentation, we can better understand the characteristics of similar artistic style. This study analyzes the intelligent terminal action supplement technology and dance damage control technology, and shows that the motion capture technology can effectively prevent various dance style problems, produce strong economic benefits in the process of 3 D digitalization promotion, and realize the presentation and optimization of the subsequent dance art style content.

Keywords: intelligent terminal · dance motion capture · dance injury

1 Introduction

Based on the development, in the current process of art style presentation, the dance system and elements can realize the optimization of its intelligent terminal structure operation system, and can better understand the presentation characteristics of intelligent terminal art. Make a systematic analysis of the dance art mode and its construction content, understand the development characteristics of dance art, and in the process of comprehensive digitalization and three-dimensional control of motion capture technology in the movement supplement, so as to make a good analysis for the subsequent inheritance of dance art content. To realize the optimization of intelligent terminal supplement technology, but also in the process of instance control, to strengthen the data structure operation, to create a new open space for the subsequent modern intelligent system terminal adjustment, but also to realize the comprehensive optimization of intelligent dance and artistic style.

Y. Zhang and N. Shah (Eds.): BigIoT-EDU 2023, LNICST 582, pp. 283–291, 2024.
https://doi.org/10.1007/978-3-031-63136-8_30

2 Three-Dimensional Design of Dance Art

2.1 3 D Data Acquisition of Dance

For dance 3 d data acquisition and analysis, it is based on dance capture technology, systematic analysis of dance three data structure, and then according to the concept of dance mapping, for motion capture type, capture mode and so on capture system optimization, understand the development of dance capture technology development view, also create open space for other art synthesis. In the development of motion capture technology, this becomes a comprehensive processing technology. Through the three-dimensional structure of dance art, the camera and standard dance range for acquisition and control. Subsequently, multiple dance action map column forms are used to map the spatial position there. When the computer, the remote operation analysis can be made. Similarly, it can be further reconstructed according to the dancer's point of action and his action diagram, understand the three-dimensional data obtained from the dancer, and finally carry out modeling and structural analysis.

2.2 Intelligent Terminal and Dance Injury Prevention

In the process of building the intelligent terminal system, based on the data capture of each point, from the same perspective of the dance capture system and the construction content of the dance injury prevention system, the content of the data integration can be systematically manually analyzed. Make automatic patching during the manual channel control process. Data repair mode can be composed of two forms, one is to use the own software of the acquisition equipment to process the noise point, and apply the smooth equipment to make the analysis, the other is to use the animation software to supplement and optimize the keyframes. It corrects the data once according to the errors in the animation curve, and realizes the adjustment and control of the structure and content of the data end to ensure the data function and the control structure. Subsequently, the smooth curve is post-processed, and the control structure of all the data function ends is designed to verify and optimize the subsequent data.

3 Associated Imaging Reconstruction Algorithm Based on Web and Intelligent Terminal

The traditional imaging reconstruction algorithm is calculated according to the correlation distance between the target metaphor reference arm, which is calculated by using the weighted average between the target ratio and the reference arm. The matrix and the content of the algorithm are reconstructed. The quality of the algorithm is strong, but the calculation process is very simple, and the subsequent application is also very convenient. A pseudo-heat source is a pseudo-heat light source. Light from the beamsplitter 1:1. After the transmission, it reaches the target and the CCD, respectively. According to the status of the second-order expression work, for the core of the intelligent terminal correlation imaging technology, it is mainly a light input by the light in the object. After the prism transmission, it can constitute the same optical system output data and target. The overall relationship between the two is positively correlated. According to the principle of the reconstruction algorithm, part of it is the data processing system, and the different operations [1]. The results derive the second-order correlation from its GI algorithm, which as follows:

$$T_{GI}(x, y) = \frac{1}{N} \sum_{n=1}^{N} (B_n - \langle B_n \rangle)(I_n(x, y) - \langle I_n(x, y) \rangle) \qquad (1)$$

where N is the total number of acquisitions, x and y are the positions of the pixels, indicating the n th acquisition, and indicating the reference arm in the n th acquisition, $B_n I_n(x, y)$

$$\langle B_n \rangle = \frac{1}{N} \sum_{n=1}^{N} B_n \qquad (2)$$

$$\langle I_n(x, y) \rangle = \frac{1}{N} \sum_{n=1}^{N} I_n(x, y) \qquad (3)$$

The equations the n th mean of the object and reference arms, respectively.

Let's first introduce in detail how to capture dance movements. Then, we will explain how to preprocess the raw data to obtain gesture parameters that are clearly expressed from a body centered perspective. Next, we will point out how DanceTheMusic uses spatiotemporal templates to model and automatically recognize dance characters for a performance, as well as how the system provides visual feedback for that performance. A schematic overview is provided in Fig. 1.

In the calculation process of the imaging formula, the overall principle is still very simple. It is based on the reconstruction algorithm to establish a common function relationship between the two arms. Therefore, when the light intensity in an object ratio is at a fixed value, the data of the other reference arm must also be a fixed value, and the weighted average of the two is the value we need to solve. During, the weight factors in the were essentially the same, and each imaging target was correlated. The target arm constitutes its pixel information, otherwise, the reconstruction results are also very vague [2]. Based formulation, we propose. The proposed algorithm changes the original correlation imaging reconstruction formula, minus, reduces the noise generated during the reconstruction process, and improves effect. The DGI is as follows:

$$T_{DGI}(x, y) = \frac{1}{N} \sum_{n=1}^{N} \left(B_n - \frac{R_n}{\langle R_n \rangle} \langle B_n \rangle \right) (I_n(x, y) - \langle I_n(x, y) \rangle) \qquad (4)$$

The intensity with the reference arm based on the GI formula, $\langle B_n \rangle R_n / \langle R_n \rangle$

$$R_n = \int \int I_n(x, y) dx dy \qquad (5)$$

The n th acquisition of the reference arm. $\langle R_n \rangle = \frac{1}{N} \sum_{n=1}^{N} R_n$ Represents the n th average of the total light, and the reconstruction results have a higher signal-to-noise

Fig. 1. The position of the rigid body on the dancer's body.

ratio than the conventional GI reconstruction results:

$$\frac{(SNR)_{DGI}}{(SNR)_{GI}} = 1 + \frac{1}{\sigma_{rel}^2} \qquad (6)$$

The SNR represents the SNR of the imaging results. The higher the SNR, the better the subsequent quality. σ_{rel}^2 Represents ote the related to the transmission coefficient of the imaging target. It is related to the magnitude of the imaging target. $T(x, y)$ DGI far outperforms GI as high transmission coefficient objects, and DGI reconstruction is similar to GI. By comparing the GI and DGI, Eqs. (1) and (4) show that when light passes through the object, it will small, which gives the DGI little effect to the overall effect, so that the effect is not improved. $\langle B_n \rangle$

The formula for the NGI normalized the weighted coefficients, with the imaging comparable to the DGI. The is as follows:

$$T_{NGI}(x, y) = \frac{1}{N} \sum_{n=1}^{N} \left(\frac{B_n}{R_n} - \frac{\langle B_n \rangle}{\langle R_n \rangle} \right) (I_n(x, y) - \langle I_n(x, y) \rangle) \qquad (7)$$

The reconstruction formulae of GI, DGI, and NGI are all based on the basic theory of association imaging, the second-order correlation formula, computed by weighted average only, with low computational complexity and strong robustness.

Concept reconstruction algorithm can be computed from another perspective. Considering the two-arm structure of the correlation imaging, the object arm is associated with the imaging object, such as formula _ (1), which can be rewritten as the matrix form:

$$B = \Phi T \tag{8}$$

Among $T = \left[T(1,1), T(1,2), \cdots, T(p,q) \right]^T$

$K \times 1$ The dimensional column vector representing the transmission coefficient of the target is calculated according to the coefficient of the imaging data to represent the vector composed of the of the object arm end. $B = [B_1, B_2, \cdots, B_N]^T N \times 1$.

$\Phi N \times K$ It is matrix, which by the arm n times. The data in the parallel data in the collection arm field, and forms the relevant column item vector:

$$\Phi = \begin{bmatrix} I_1(1,1) & I_1(1,2) & \cdots & I_1(2,1) & \cdots & I_1(p,q) \\ I_2(1,1) & & & & & \vdots \\ \vdots & & & & \ddots & \\ I_N(1,1) & I_N(1,2) & \cdots & & \cdots & \cdots & I_N(p,q) \end{bmatrix} \tag{9}$$

Based on the pseudo-inverse correlation imaging algorithm, a PGI (8) [3] $AX = Y$. The phase matrix constitutes a linear equation matrix relation, existing in form. The solution of the objective is transformed into the solution problem of the matrix equation. When the system of equations is the system is the unique solution, the a matrix, and the equation can be solved directly. The observed matrix is neither a full-rank matrix, nor an inverse matrix. At this point, it theory to represent the matrix of the matrix. $A^{-1} X = A^{-1} Y \; \Phi X = A^+ Y A^+$

The architecture of the pseudo-inverse correlation imaging algorithm is shown in Fig. 2. Whose is expressed as:

$$T_{PGI} = \Phi^+ B \tag{10}$$

The GI reconstruction formula can also be expressed in the matrix form:

$$\begin{aligned} T_{GI} &= \frac{1}{N} (\Phi - I\langle \Phi \rangle)^T (B - I\langle B \rangle) \\ &= \frac{1}{N} (\Phi - I\langle \Phi \rangle)^T (\Phi - I\langle \Phi \rangle) T \\ &= \frac{1}{N} \Psi^T \Psi T = A_{GI} T \end{aligned} \tag{11}$$

$\langle \Phi \rangle = \left[\langle I(1,1) \rangle, \langle I(1,2) \rangle, \cdots, \langle I(p,q) \rangle \right] 1 \times K$ Where, it is the row vector, representing the reference arm, and it is a dimensional column vector with all elements of 1. The matrix can finally be called a feature matrix of GI by linking the reconstruction result to the reconstruction T. $I = \left[1, 1, \cdots, 1^T \right] N \times 1 A_{GI} \, T_{GI} \, A_{GI}$.

A_{PGI} In order to unify with the of GI, establish the connection formula between the reconstructed matrices, and obtain the feature matrix of PGI, the of PGI can be changed to writing in a similar form:

$$T_{PGI} = \Phi^+ \Phi T = A_{PGI} T \tag{12}$$

Scalar matrix correlation imaging reconstruction algorithm.

In order to obtain the corresponding relationship between the reconstruction formula, it must be studied according to the correlation characteristics of the reconstruction proof. In view of the reconstruction effect, the matrix is analyzed according to the correlation status. In fact, the feature to the unit matrix, the subsequent effect is. To improve, a scalar matrix-based correlation imaging reconstruction algorithm smgi:

$$T_{SMGI} = A_{SMGI}T = \frac{1}{N}\left(\psi^T - \psi_x\right)\psi T = \frac{1}{N}\left(\psi^T - \psi_x\right)(B - I\langle B\rangle) \quad (13)$$

ψ_x Where, for the correction quantity, it is the feature matrix. It can be reversed according to the constructed feature matrix: A_{SMGI} ψ_x

$$\psi_x = \left(\psi^T\psi - A_{SMGI}\right)\Big/\psi \quad (14)$$

$\psi_x A_{SMGI}$ The Smgi can come over to the matrix, the special features, which will directly affect the reconstruction performance. The robustness of the reconstruction algorithm is enhanced by modifying the scalar matrix. In the process of the original imaging matrix composition, the main diagonal information is basically correlated, and it also has a series of periodic characteristics. And the matrix preserves and improves the compared to PGI.

The reference arm allows for detrimental noise information in the matrix. Effective and relevant noise information is mixed so that the recovered image is not blurred. The Schmidt orthogonal SGI is to eliminate the correlations between each speckle field as much as possible, while ensuring the correlation between the reference and target arms.

Orthogonalization makes independently, eliminating each vector. The target arms and the reference arms were using the orthogonal to obtain the SGI reconstruction, and then multiplied by the correlation algorithm, as shown in Eq. (11) [4].

Φ The following Schmidt orthogonalization of each in the observation matrix:

$$\begin{aligned}
\tilde{R}_1 &= R_1 \\
\tilde{R}_1 &= R_2 - c_{21}\tilde{R}_1 \\
\tilde{R}_1 &= R_3 - c_{31}\tilde{R}_2 - c_{32}\tilde{R}_1 \\
&\cdots
\end{aligned} \quad (15)$$

$$\tilde{R}_N = R_N - \sum_{i=1}^{N-1} c_{Ni}\tilde{R}_i$$

$R_i\tilde{R}_i$ These are the row vectors consisting of the orthogonal ones after orthogonalization. The orthogonal vector minus the redundant information projection of the vector in the direction, which is the proportional coefficient of the p two vectors, whose size can be of the two vectors:

$$c_{ij} = \frac{\tilde{R}_i \cdot R_j}{\tilde{R}_j \cdot R_j} \quad (16)$$

To ensure that the same weight during the process, divide the vector where the vector is located by its own 2-norm.

$$\tilde{R}_i{}' = \frac{\tilde{R}_i}{\|\tilde{R}_i\|_2} \tag{17}$$

To ensure arm, the same transformation is applied at the end of the reference arm. The end object arm has the same parameters as those at the end of the arm. c_{ij}, The proportion the i-th and j-th vectors on the arm was adopted, and was normalized by the 2-norm on the arm (Table 1).

$$\tilde{y}_i = y_i - \sum_{j=1}^{i-1} c_{ij}\tilde{y}_j \tag{18}$$

$$\tilde{y}_i{}' = \frac{\tilde{y}_i}{\|\tilde{R}_i\|_2} \tag{19}$$

The data of arm and the target arms was orthogonally normalized were replaced with the Formula (11) [5]. Unlike the preprocessing method, the vectors of each row of the orthogonal, eliminating redundant information. The formula of the SGI is follows:

$$T_{SGI} = \frac{1}{N}(\tilde{\Phi}' - \langle\tilde{\Phi}'\rangle I)^T (\tilde{B}' - \langle\tilde{B}'\rangle I) = A_{SGI}T \tag{20}$$

Table 1. Scale coefficient between the j vectors

Code name	Coefficient of proportionality
1	2.3
2	2.3
3	2.6

4   Experiments and Results

In the construction process of the dance motion capture system and the dance injury prevention system based on the intelligent terminal, the various data are operational analyzed, and the design points and operation points can be better optimized according to the motion capture system evaluation and the design of the dance injury prevention mechanism. It can also complete the system design in the dance capture motion control and damage adjustment, so that the subsequent dance damage system content can really improve, improve the system synthesis, and realize the remote operation of the capture system and the structural end design breakthrough.

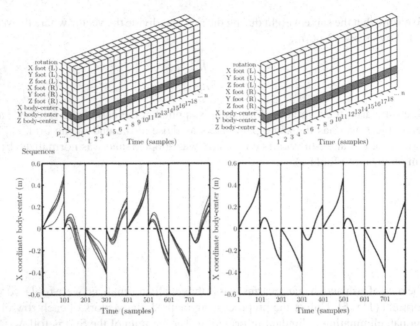

Fig. 2. The representation of discrete values stored in the gray feature array in the upper right corner template.

The rotation of the local body in a fixed coordinate system, with the same direction as the global coordinate system (Fig. 2, middle). The actual situation is that all absolute values (x, y, z) are based on the quaternion numerical rotation of the rigid body connected to the center of the body, which represents the directional difference between the local coordinate system and the global coordinate system.

In the process of intelligent terminal language form control, the motion capture technology is shown in Table 2. In a systematic analysis of the supplementary content of each technology, the following operations need to be completed at the same time [6].

Table 2. Motion capture techniques

Point of capture	Camera 1	Camera 2
An air	X1	X 1
action	X 1	X 2
expression	X 2	X 2

(1) Use the interpolation to calculate the bone and the relative bone position, and transform the matrix.
(2) Analyze the relative bone properties, and understand the transformation situation between different bones.

(3) Calculate the spatial position and orientation features of each vertex in the skin grid.
(4) Analyze the new orientation and grid model for the base position of the bone structure.

Tag

To strengthen the experimental structure design of intelligent terminal, this research makes a systematic analysis of the traditional photo and video recording methods, and obtains the exploration perspective on the development of dance art. In the process of applying computer motion capture technology and dance injury prevention and supplement control technology, the data structure of intelligent terminal and the operation guidance function are analyzed, which is a new view of the mutual integration of culture and technology, and also promotes the reform and breakthrough of digital construction project.

Acknowledgements. 2021 Guangdong Provincial Philosophy and Social Science Planning Project Youth Project: Project No.: GD21YYS14.

References

1. Xun, Z.Y., Wei, X., Rihui, Y., et al.: Research and design of motion capture and image reduction of Dance (2019–9), 37–42 (2021)
2. Yuanzhi, Y.: Research on Tibetan Guozhuang dance based on motion capture. China New Commun. **22**(19), 239–240 (2020)
3. Guoliang, Y.: Research on dance video motion recognition techniques based on motion capture. J. Chifeng Univ. Natural Sci. Ed. **38**(9), 5 (2022)
4. Dong, L., Jianpeng, Z.: Research on portable intelligent power distribution integrated mobile terminal control system based on STM32. Electron. Des. Eng. **30**(20), 7 (2022)
5. Na, G., Wen, Z.: Research on dance virtual visual scene design based on action capture technology (2021)
6. Zongbin, L.: Research on 3 D digital method based on motion capture technology. Fashion Tomorrow **02**, 140–141 (2020)

Comprehensive Evaluation of Students' Self Realization Ability Based on BP Algorithm

Ma Lingya$^{(\boxtimes)}$ and Chen Lu

Hubei Three Gorges Polytechnic, Hubei 443000, China
798543927@qq.com

Abstract. The student ability assessment system is a comprehensive and complex system. Most of the existing comprehensive assessments are based on the results. The better the results, the stronger the ability. However, it is difficult to answer what is strong. Moreover, the phenomenon of students committing suicide has already shown us that we must attach importance to comprehensive development, physical and mental health and psychological education, grasp students' psychological activities more concretely, and correctly guide students. The comprehensive evaluation of students' self realization ability based on BP algorithm is a process of evaluating students' self realization ability by using BP algorithm. The purpose of this approach is to assess whether students understand the subject and identify weaknesses in their knowledge. To achieve these goals, three types of tests were used: 1) basic skills test (TBS), 2) general skills test (TSG), and 3) self actualization ability test (tssra).

Keywords: Students' self realization · BP algorithm · Comprehensive evaluation of ability

1 Introduction

With the development of smart education, the traditional evaluation method based on scores has been unable to keep up with the needs of students' personalized learning, and the capability-oriented education concept has gradually become a consensus in the field of education. Learning measurement refers to the use of information science and data analysis technology to measure and evaluate students' cognitive ability, emotional changes and other aspects. Among them, evaluation is not only an important part of the teaching process, but also a key part of the learning process. In the university classroom, the teacher will arrange a small number of after-class test questions for students to practice, and then check their knowledge and ability level according to the score of the test questions. The model is composed of individual ability parameters and test difficulty parameters. According to the results of the correct or wrong answers of the individual on the test questions, the parameter estimation method is used to solve the model parameters. In this way, the evaluation of students' ability can be transformed into the estimation of model parameters. From the perspective of mathematical statistics, the larger the sample

Y. Zhang and N. Shah (Eds.): BigIoT-EDU 2023, LNICST 582, pp. 292–302, 2024.
https://doi.org/10.1007/978-3-031-63136-8_31

size, the more accurate the model parameter estimation results will be. But in reality, small sample data often occurs. For example, the professional courses in universities are limited to such factors as the compact content of the courses and the wide range of ability points, which lead to the small number of subjects to evaluate students' abilities. How to evaluate students' abilities based on small sample data is a very important demand.

The ultimate purpose of ability evaluation is to take the evaluation results as the feedback of students' ability development and learning process. Students can timely improve weak ability points according to the feedback results, and teachers can also check the students' ability level and adjust teaching strategies in time. Reforming the evaluation model, focusing on data-driven, and improving the scientific and comprehensive evaluation system will play an important role in promoting the comprehensive implementation of capability-oriented education and teaching, and also have guiding significance for the personal development of students.

After the evaluation of students' ability, the following problem is how to improve and train the weak ability points. Personalized test questions can be recommended according to the historical answer records, ability evaluation results and other relevant information of students.Colleges and universities are a special institution. In recent years, colleges and universities have developed and used management information systems for various departments, such as educational administration management information system, library management information system, student management information system and so on. In the school, the students are the main body, and the school is the unit that trains students to become talents. How to manage students' daily learning and life and master their learning and life is the key content of the school. Students ultimately want to go to the society and make contributions to the society. However, the requirements of employment units for the quality of talents are getting higher and higher. Not only do job seekers need to have rich professional knowledge, but also they need to have the ability to be both independent and cooperative [1]. Therefore, how to correctly and completely reflect and evaluate the learning situation of the students in the school, so as to provide some useful and referential opinions and suggestions for the students, teaching and administrative personnel and employers to understand the specific performance of each student's learning and life in school in a timely and detailed manner, so that the students and schools can keep pace with the times, improve their learning and management methods in a timely manner, Talents who can be used by the unit [2]. However, the student information management system developed and used by most colleges and universities only records the student's academic achievements, student file information, comprehensive evaluation, etc. these large amounts of data are fuzzy, diversified, lack of accuracy, and the main body is not prominent. They do not reflect some specific relationships and actual situations, and lack interactivity, and cannot provide enough useful information for the searcher.

The student ability assessment system is a comprehensive and complex system. Most of the existing comprehensive assessments are based on the results. The better the results, the stronger the ability. However, it is difficult to answer what is strong. Moreover, the phenomenon of students committing suicide has already shown us that we must attach importance to comprehensive development, physical and mental health and psychological education, grasp students' psychological activities more concretely, and correctly guide students [3]. The research of this project starts from the actual data of students, integrates the data, and investigates from the perspectives of moral education, intellectual education, physical education, practical ability, hobbies, specialties, cultural and sports activities, and psychological questionnaires. Study whether there are hidden associations between the data and mine potential knowledge, such as the probability of people with medium intelligence and strong practical ability. People with poor grades, how about their cultural and sports activities, etc. Based on this, we can get the decision-making basis: strengthen the knowledge that some students lack. Guide students to develop better [4]. Further, we will continue to collect the work situation of the students in the years after graduation, so as to find the relationship between the school performance and the work after graduation. Provide assistance for future employment of students.

2 Related Work

2.1 Research Status of the Subject

Data mining technology is the result of people's long-term research and development of database technology. It is a popular data analysis technology at present. It has been widely concerned by people and has become a hot spot in the current computer field. Its research focus has gradually shifted from discovery methods to system applications, and it pays attention to the integration of multiple discovery strategies and technologies, as well as the mutual penetration of multiple disciplines. Data mining was first applied in the financial and commercial fields, and its application in the education field is still in the primary stage. Now, the data mining applications based on the education and teaching management information system include decision tree method, cluster analysis method, multi-dimensional association rule method and the campus information management system based on CRM [5]. The developed student evaluation system is either based on a single mining algorithm or a single empirical formula. Can not be very good, comprehensive evaluation of students and predict the development trajectory. At present, in China's educational software market, the information system for predicting students' development trajectory and intelligent evaluation is almost blank, which is specialized in mining various data of students to discover the relationship between intelligence and moral education, intelligence and sports, and even comprehensive quality and work! However, China's education market is huge. If a general law can be found, it will play an auxiliary role in Colleges and universities as well as primary and secondary schools. At least, it can inspire the corresponding managers to pay attention to the aspects of students and assist the managers in making decisions.

In China, every university and class has a set of comprehensive evaluation calculation methods, and the evaluation is conducted once every academic year. But even in a university, different departments have different evaluation methods. However, there is one thing in common, almost all of them are calculating results, and moral education is reflected by adding points [5]. This causes the standards of comprehensive evaluation to be inconsistent, and the evaluation methods are not comprehensive. It is difficult to grasp the psychological activities of college students, and students commit suicide and other extreme behaviors. In foreign countries, college students' psychological education and analysis have been attached great importance, and many research results can be used for reference. They use the principles, methods and tools of measurement and mathematical statistics to analyze student data and guide psychological counselors to provide psychological guidance to students. Nevertheless, there are also incidents of students shooting teachers and classmates. Using data mining technology to analyze student data is the current development direction at home and abroad [6]. The data mining framework is shown in Fig. 1 below.

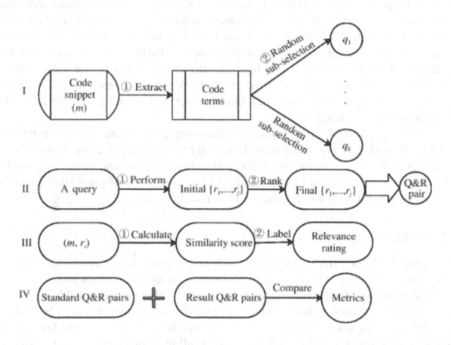

Fig. 1. Data mining framework

Through consulting a large number of domestic and foreign literature on capacity models, it is found that foreign research on capacity models started earlier and has achieved some research results. Franks and others combed the concept of competence dimension in the four dimensions of concept, operation, individual and occupation, and constructed a competence model applicable to human resources. The model emphasizes that knowledge comes from people's cognition, while skills come from practice, and social ability values people's behavior and attitude. Ziffers has constructed a capability framework including cognitive ability, functional ability, personal ability, ethical ability and metacognitive ability [7]. The framework focuses on the field of vocational education and divides abilities into different units according to vocational needs. McCleley believes that competence should be related to job performance and competence, and proposes to use competency assessment instead of score evaluation and competency tendency questionnaire results. He believes that competence should not only have cognitive ability in knowledge content, but also have cognitive and behavioral skills related to work, including communication skills, self-control and setting reasonable goals. Cormackl6l proposed a 360-degree comprehensive ability evaluation model for the ability evaluation of nursing graduate students [8]. Bloom's educational goal classification theory points out that human development is divided into cognitive, action and emotional skills, and uses it as the framework of educational goals to evaluate students' learning effects.

At first, the domestic research on the competency model is from the perspective of college students' employment, using such methods as experience summary, factor analysis and survey statistics to construct the relevant competency model. With the proposal of the concept of capability-oriented education, Zhang Lei? A three-dimensional comprehensive competitiveness model of graduate students based on "logic-skill-attitude" has been constructed, which has played an important role in improving the research climate of graduate students. Du Ruijun I8 attempts to build a college student's ability model based on the individual's ability, the individual's ability to use tools, and the individual's ability to interact with the external environment, and points out that the process of building a college student's ability model should change dynamically with the development of society [9].

To sum up, although many theoretical studies have been done on the construction of capacity models at home and abroad, there are few studies on capacity models for university curriculum content, and higher education has more and more demands for the evaluation of curriculum learning effects. Therefore, it is of great significance to construct a general competency model for curriculum content.

2.2 BP Neural Network

BP Neural Network - BP algorithm, i.e. back propagation. It is a multi-layer network with forward direction. The principle is to transmit the error from back to front.

Characteristics of BP neural network: the hierarchy can be determined by itself, and three layers are commonly used (input layer - hidden layer - output layer); Neurons in the same layer are not connected to each other, and there is no feedback: the connection between layers is complex, and the mode is full interconnection [10]. The specific structure is shown in Fig. 2.

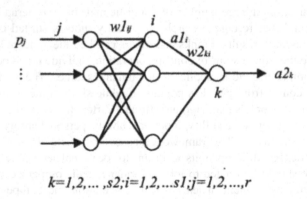

$$k=1,2,\dots,s2; i=1,2,\dots s1; j=1,2,\dots,r$$

Fig. 2. Structure of BP neural network

(1) Forward propagation of input vector

The input vector is transferred from the input layer to the hidden layer, and then to the output layer to generate the output vector. The weight of the neural network does not change during the transmission process. If the expected output is not achieved at the output layer, it will enter the error back propagation stage.

(2) Back propagation of error

The error between the actual output and the expected output of the network is transferred from the output layer to the hidden layer, and then to the input layer. In the error back-propagation stage, the weight of the neural network is continuously adjusted and corrected by the error feedback mechanism, and repeated iterations are made to make the network output equal to the expected output [11].

The main idea of BP learning algorithm is: for q training samples $P^1, P^2, \cdots, P^q$. The corresponding output samples are $T^1, T^2, \cdots, T^q$. The goal of learning is to correct the weight value by making the error between the target vector $T^1, T^2, \cdots, T^q$ and the actual output $A^1, A^2, \cdots, A^q$, so that the actual output $A^l (l = 1, 2, \cdots, q)$ approaches the expected value T, and the square sum of the network error reaches the minimum.

1) The output of the ith neuron in the hidden layer is shown in Formula (1):

$$a1_i = f1(w1_i p_j + b1_i), (i = 1, 2, \cdots, r) \tag{1}$$

2) The output of the k-th neuron in the output layer is shown in Formula (2):

$$a2_k = f2(\sum_{i=1}^{s1} w2_b a1_i + b2_k), (k = 1, 2, \cdots, s1) \tag{2}$$

3) Define the error function, as shown in Formula (3):

$$E(W, B) = \frac{1}{2}\sum_{k=1}^{s2} (t_k - a2_k)^2 \tag{3}$$

Modify the weights and thresholds of each layer in the network, select the next sample in turn, and input the eigenvector of one training sample into the input layer until all the samples in the training set have been learned [12]. You can also learn repeatedly until the error range of the result is within the specified range, that is to say, the continuous number of training is larger than the pre-specified. Save the neural network for next use and end the training.

BP neural network can be widely used in many fields. It can be seen that this neural network not only has the advantages of strong prediction accuracy and simple operation, but also has many advantages:

(1) BP neural network is suitable for solving problems with complex internal mechanism, because its learning and memory ability is continuously improved through continuous learning and training of samples.

(2) Not only has a strong self-learning function, but also the trained network can give a reasonable output for the input of the new data set, which can represent a more logical mapping in any scene, and can learn knowledge from samples, which is convenient for association, synthesis and promotion.

(3) Relevant laws can be abstracted from samples. By solving practical problems and constantly enhancing the ability to discover and remember the rules to be solved, the neural network can quickly complete the nonlinear mapping from the input layer to the output layer [13].

(4) It can process information in parallel and collaboratively. Each neuron in the neural network has the ability to receive, process and output information independently, that is, neurons in the same layer can calculate information in parallel, and the operation results can be output to the next layer of network for further processing, making the network real-time, that is, the characteristics of parallel operation of neural network.

However, BP neural network still has the following shortcomings:

(1) It is easy to fall into local optimum. BP neural network adopts gradient descent algorithm, which converges in the direction of gradient descent of error function. When local minimum is encountered in the process, it is easy to stagnate here. When the network is trapped in the local optimum, the performance of the network cannot be further improved by increasing the number of training, thus the goal of convergence to the global optimum cannot be achieved.

(2) The parameters of the network, such as the number of hidden layers, the number of units in each hidden layer, and the learning rate, are generally determined according to the empirical formula or continuous experiments, and the way to finally select the optimal parameters according to the experimental results. Therefore, in the face of more complex problems, the time of online learning will be longer and the efficiency will be lower [14].

(3) Identify the problem of accuracy. The reasonable selection of network structure will have a great impact on the network recognition ability. The network structure is mainly the determination of the number of nodes in the hidden layer, which will directly affect the mapping ability of the network, thus affecting the recognition accuracy of the network.

In view of the limitations of BP neural network, scholars have made relevant improvements to the BP learning algorithm, such as: additional momentum factor, gradient descent algorithm with adaptive adjustment of learning rate, variable gradient algorithm, elastic gradient algorithm, LM algorithm, quasi-Newton algorithm, etc.

3   Comprehensive Evaluation of Students' Self Realization Ability Based on BP Algorithm

3.1   Principles for Establishing the Evaluation System of Students' Self Realization Ability

Self actualization ability is a multi-level and multi-dimensional complex system. The establishment of the indicator system mainly follows the following principles:

(1) Systematic and hierarchical principles. The self realization ability of students is a system with a specific hierarchy. Therefore, the index system should also have corresponding hierarchical structure and systematicness.

(2) The principle of comprehensiveness and subdivision. Indicators should reflect the attributes of all levels and dimensions of the system; At the same time, in order to reveal its intrinsic essence, the index system should go deep into the structure and meet the principle of independence among the elements of the same layer.

(3) Principle of effectiveness and operability. The model should reasonably and effectively reflect the nature and characteristics of students' self realization ability, and at the same time, the availability of the index system data should be considered.

(4) The principle of combining static and dynamic. The weight of each indicator varies in different stages of the life cycle of students. Static indicators reflect the current level, while dynamic indicators reflect the potential development trend.

The ultimate goal of school teaching is to train a large number of qualified talents with ideals, discipline, morality, knowledge and creativity for the country. Therefore, student quality evaluation is an important part of teaching evaluation. The comprehensive evaluation of students' ability is an important part of teaching design. It guides and regulates teaching to make it in the best state [15]. The objective and correct evaluation of students can also be that students can recognize their learning ability, guide students to constantly adjust their learning methods, and make their learning ability and knowledge acquisition ability reach a new stage. The comprehensive evaluation of students must start with the ability data indicators of students in all aspects, and the relationship between each evaluation index and the overall comprehensive quality is not necessarily a simple linear relationship. Therefore, only by adopting a nonlinear evaluation method can a student's comprehensive quality be correctly and objectively evaluated [16]. However, BP neural network can provide accurate, effective and non-linear evaluation methods to a certain extent. Therefore, the classification analysis subsystem of this system uses the method based on BP neural network to analyze various relevant ability data of students, in order to obtain accurate, objective and high authenticity evaluation results.

3.2 Construction of the Evaluation System of Students' Self Realization Ability

According to the construction principle of the self realization ability index system, the evaluation index system is designed first, then the questionnaires are distributed to the relevant students and experts, and then the collected questionnaires are counted to determine the index weight, eliminate the index dimension, quantify the index value, bring it into the mathematical model, and get the final evaluation results [17].

Use the entropy method to calculate the normalized data and get the initial evaluation results. The entropy method is used to calculate the standardization of the original teaching quality evaluation data, as shown in Formula (4):

$$x'_{iy} = (x_{iy} - \bar{x})/s_j \tag{4}$$

where, is the score of the ith sample in the jth index x'_{iy} is the normalized value, and s_j is the average value and standard deviation of the jth index respectively. In order to meet the requirement of logarithm in the entropy method, the normalized value should be translated, as shown in Eq. (5):

$$Z_{ij} = x'_{iy} + A \tag{5}$$

where Z_{ij} is the value after translation and A is the length of translation.

Quantify the evaluation index of teaching quality with the same degree, and calculate the proportion of the ith sample to the index Py under the jth index, as shown in Formula (6):

$$p_{ij} = Z_{ij}/\sum_{i=1}^{\pi}Z_y (i = 1, 2, \cdots, m; j = 1, 2, \cdots, n) \tag{6}$$

where, Z_{ij} is the translated teaching quality evaluation data.

The entropy method is an objective weighting method. Its basic idea is to determine the index weight by calculating the fluctuation degree of each index value. This method can reduce the deviation caused by human factors and provide a certain basis for the design of neural network. The initial evaluation result determined by this method is used as a prior guidance sample of the BP algorithm model.

How to effectively integrate the ability elements distributed at all levels of students and conduct comprehensive evaluation is the key issue of the evaluation system. Based on the research on the structure of students' self realization ability [18]. We divide students' self realization ability into five first-class indicators and 21 s-class indicators. The specific meaning and composition of level I indicators are as follows:

① Resource force: it is the constituent element of ability. Resource power includes not only human, material, financial, technical and information power, but also intangible assets such as students' goodwill.

② Management ability: refers to the ability of students to effectively combine various resources and abilities by means of organization, planning, control, coordination and other management means. Including system, structure, execution, coordination and leadership.

③ Business ability: refers to the ability of students in the process of transforming their various advantages into market advantages by using business knowledge. Including strategic power, decision-making power, market power and capital operation power.

④ Ethical force: refers to the common value system that unifies people's thoughts and behaviors within the organization. It is the spiritual level of students' ability, including the internal ethics of students, the ethics of business contacts and the external ethics environment.

⑤ Exploratory power: refers to the ability of individuals or organizations to expand their own knowledge. It is the core of students' self realization ability. Including learning, innovation and peak experience. Learning is the input and absorption, innovation is the addition of new knowledge and value, and peak experience is a kind of ability generated in the process of learning and innovation - the ability to achieve self transcendence in the best state and experience the true meaning of life [19].

BP network is a forward network. Although it has nonlinear mapping ability, it is not a nonlinear dynamic system. It has its limitations in function, such as long training time, slow convergence speed and easy to fall into local minima. However, the improved BP network can overcome the above shortcomings by adopting the additional impulse method, that is, adding a potential term [20]. Therefore, this evaluation system adopts the comprehensive evaluation method based on the improved BP network to comprehensively evaluate the students' self realization ability system, as shown in Fig. 3.

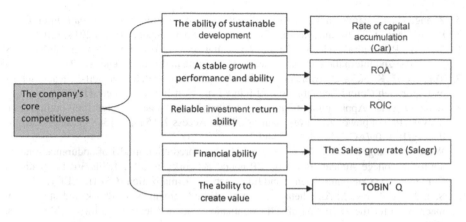

Fig. 3. Evaluation index system of students' self realization ability

4 Conclusion

BP algorithm overcomes the complexity of traditional analysis process and the difficulty of choosing proper function form. It is a natural nonlinear modeling process. Regardless of the given initial weight and initial threshold, in the training, the network weight and threshold can be adjusted repeatedly by comparing the error between the actual output and the expected output, so as to gradually reduce the error, and finally achieve the specified accuracy, and obtain a stable network structure and connection weight. The trained neural network system is to give the evaluation ideas of experts to the network in the form of connecting weights. In this way, the network can not only simulate the quantitative evaluation of students' self realization ability by experts, but also avoid the subjective influence and uncertainty caused by the artificial calculation of weights and correlation coefficients in the evaluation process. Therefore, it has strong objectivity and universality. The maximum relative error between the training result and the expected output obtained by the BP network is 1.0401%, and the maximum relative error between the simulation output value and the expected value of the test sample is 1.448%, which shows that this comprehensive evaluation method is relatively effective and has important practical value for the comprehensive evaluation of students' self realization ability.

References

1. Liu, Y.: Evaluation of students' IELTS writing ability based on machine learning and neural network algorithm. J. Intell. Fuzzy Syst. **5**, 1–11 (2020)
2. Zhang, Q.: The construction and analysis to the evaluation model of the professional ability of the college students. J. Changchun Inst. Technol. (Natural Sciences Edition) (2019)
3. Zhang, Z., Li, Y.: Research and application of the evaluation model of educational technology capability based on BP neural network——Taking PBL teaching situation as an example. J. Comput. Theor. Nanosci. **13**, 6210–6217 (2016)
4. Qingju, T., Jingmin, D., Junyan, L., et al.: Quantitative detection of defects based on markov-PCA-BP algorithm using pulsed infrared thermography technology. Infrared Phys. Technol. **77**, 144–148 (2016)

5. Zhang, H.: Research on vocational college course evaluation based on data mining. In: Proceedings of the 4th International Symposium on Social Science (ISSS 2018) (2018)

6. Wei, W.: Realization and discussion of BP neural network based on C++. In: CONF-CDS 2021: The 2nd International Conference on Computing and Data Science (2021)

7. Turgut C E , Kocaeksi S . Evaluation of the Ability to Cope with Stress, Self-Efficacy Beliefs and Sport Self Confidence Situations of Injured and Non-Injured Athletes[J]. 2019

8. Jiang, Q., et al.: Application of BP neural network based on genetic algorithm optimization in evaluation of power grid investment risk. IEEE Access 7, 154827–154835 (2019). https://doi.org/10.1109/ACCESS.2019.2944609

9. Wang, L., Wang, R., Ying, Y.Q., et al.: Research on prediction model of endurance running ability of college students based on BP neural network. In: 2021 IEEE 3rd International Conference on Computer Science and Educational Informatization (CSEI). IEEE (2021)

10. Sun, J., Yu-Zhong, M.A., Chen, L.H., et al.: Establishment of feedback and application mechanism for the evaluation of self-examination students' learning ability. J. Mach. Des. (2018)

11. Gao, J., Shi, G.: Mental health evaluation of college students based on similar trajectory clustering algorithm. In: 2021 13th International Conference on Measuring Technology and Mechatronics Automation (ICMTMA) (2021)

12. Wei, W., Cao, Y.: Evaluation of government emergency management ability based on BP neural network. Sci. Technol. Manage. Res. (2018)

13. Huang, A.H.: Evaluation of influencing factors on college students' self-control ability in new media era——Based on fuzzy mathematical theory fuzzy evaluation of the influencing factors on college students' self-control in new media era. J. Jimei Univ. (Education Science Edition) (2016)

14. Yang, F., Shi, Y.J., Ding, X.J., et al.: Research on realization method of control model based on bp neural network. Inland Earthq. (2018)

15. Huang, Y., Department, E.E.: Research on temperature compensation technology of optical voltage sensor based on BP neural network and labview software realization. J. Sanming Univ. (2019)

16. Chen, J., Song, D., Gong, Z.Q., et al.: Research on prediction of seed number in the hole based on machine vision and GABP algorithm. Meas. Control Technol. (2017)

17. Shuang, Z., Hu, Q.: Students' comprehensive quality evaluation based on BP neural network optimized by genetic algorithm. DEStech Trans. Soc. Sci. Educ. Hum. Sci. (2017)(eemt)

18. Dan, L.I., Bao, R., Min-Jie, L.I., et al.: Evaluation model of students' ability based on hopfield neural network. Comput. Knowl. Technol. (2018)

19. Zhou, L.: Research on the curriculum evaluation based on students' self-cognition intelligence. Sci. Educ. Article Collects (2018)

20. Yang, B.: Research on the evaluation of college students' employment ability based on decision tree. Mod. Inf. Technol. (2018)

System Design of Student Self-Realization Ability Platform of P Algorithm

Lin Gang[1][(⊠)], Pei Huaiquan[1], Peng Lei[1], HaiE Jia[2], and Xianli Zeng[3]

[1] Changchun Sci-Tech University, Changchun 130600, China
peihuaiquan@126.com
[2] Tibet Agricultural and Animal Husbandry College, Nyingchi 860000, Tibet, China
[3] Student Affairs Office, Guilin University of Electronic Technology, Guilin 541004, Guangxi, China

Abstract. The comprehensive evaluation of students' self realization ability is a process of evaluating and evaluating students' self realization ability. This is based on the concept that a student's self realization ability can be measured by his / her academic performance, attitude, behavior and other factors. The purpose of the assessment is to determine whether the students have reached a sufficient level of self realization ability. The comprehensive evaluation is based on three principles: (1) holistic approach; (2) Pay attention to all aspects of educational experience; (3) Student comprehensive evaluation system. Then, combining the advantages of fuzzy analytic hierarchy process and BP neural network, the fuzzy analytic hierarchy process is used to determine the initial weight of each evaluation index and the comprehensive evaluation value of self realization ability, and then determine the training and test sample output results of the BP neural students' self realization ability evaluation model. The network weight and threshold are constantly adjusted, and a dynamic evaluation model of students' self realization ability based on BP neural network is established, It realizes the prediction of the evaluation value of College Students' self realization ability. The feasibility of the evaluation method is verified by simulation experiments.

Keywords: Students' self realization · BP neural network · Comprehensive evaluation of ability

1 Introduction

The realistic background of College Students' desire to grow up. Most of the contemporary college students are after 00. They were born and grew up in the Internet age. They like to express themselves, emphasize individuality, and have a strong desire to pursue self-development. They want their needs to be seen, recognized and respected, and they also want to be guided if they lack social practice experience. In reality, some college students have lost their ideals and beliefs, and some phenomena such as "Buddhism" have appeared. Individual values of life, money, love and life are distorted [1]. Colleges and universities and the society must attach importance to the guidance of the spiritual

Y. Zhang and N. Shah (Eds.): BigIoT-EDU 2023, LNICST 582, pp. 303–314, 2024.
https://doi.org/10.1007/978-3-031-63136-8_32

needs of college students. As a weapon to guide people's thinking, as an external cause, ideological and political education is bound to work together with the internal cause of students' spiritual needs to guide college students to establish their life ideals, and then become a self-realized person and a free and all-round development person.

Colleges and universities are a special institution. In recent years, colleges and universities have also developed and used management information systems for various departments, such as educational administration management information system, library management information system, student management information system, and so on. In schools, students are the main body, and schools are the units that train students to become talents. How to manage students' daily learning life and master their learning life is the key content of the school. Students ultimately want to go to the society and make contributions to the society. Now the employment units have higher and higher requirements for the quality of talents. It is not only necessary for the candidates to have rich professional knowledge, but also requires the candidates to have the ability to be both independent and united. So how to correctly and completely reflect and evaluate the situation of students in school, so that students, teaching and management personnel and employers can understand the specific performance of each student in school in a timely and detailed manner, and provide some useful suggestions and suggestions for reference, so that students and schools can keep pace with the times, improve learning and management methods in a timely manner, improve learning performance and ability, and employers can hire competent, Talents who can be used by the unit. However, most of the student information management systems developed and used by colleges and universities only record students' academic achievements, student file information, comprehensive evaluation, etc. in detail. These large amounts of data are vague, diverse, lack of accuracy, and the main body is not prominent. They do not reflect some specific relationships and actual situations, and lack interactivity, and can not provide enough useful information for visitors.

The traditional education evaluation method is difficult to adapt to the requirements of the present society for the evaluation of students' comprehensive quality. The expansion of school enrollment and the increase of evaluation indicators have resulted in a large and complex amount of information for students. It is difficult to be competent in manual and simple statistical management methods, and to grasp the ability and development potential of students. Most students lack an objective and correct understanding of themselves and do not know how to revise their development path to face the increasingly fierce competition. During employment, the employer can't judge whether the candidate meets the employment requirements through a rational, objective and effective method.

The student's self assessment system is a comprehensive and complex system. Most of the existing comprehensive assessment is based on the performance. The result is that the better the performance, the stronger the ability. However, it is difficult to answer what ability is strong. Moreover, the phenomenon of students committing suicide has shown us that we must pay attention to comprehensive development, physical and mental health, psychological education, more specifically grasp students' psychological activities, and correctly guide students. The research of this project starts from the actual data of students and integrates the data from the perspectives of moral education, intellectual education, physical education, practical ability, hobbies, specialties, sports activities, psychological questionnaires, etc. Research whether there is hidden association between data and explore potential knowledge, such as the probability of strong practical ability of people with medium intelligence. People with poor grades, how about sports activities, etc. Based on this, the decision-making basis is to strengthen the knowledge that some students lack. Guide students to develop better. Further, we will continue to collect the work situation of students in the years after graduation, so as to find out the relationship between school performance and work after graduation. Provide assistance for students' employment in the future.

The research on comprehensive evaluation of students' self realization ability based on BP algorithm deepens the theory and practice of higher education's educational goal. At present, higher education takes "cultivating morality and cultivating people" as its educational goal and value pursuit [2]. The research on the purpose of Ideological and political education in the perspective of self realization is the embodiment of "people-oriented" and "students' spiritual needs". Only by understanding the students, understanding their spiritual needs, and starting from their actual conditions, can we overcome the disadvantages and shortcomings of traditional university education, be more in line with human nature, be close to the life and reality of college students, reflect humanistic care, promote people's free and comprehensive development, and finally achieve the goal of university education [3]. And thus formed a scientific and human education practice system of higher education in the new era. Stimulate the establishment of College Students' life ideals and their growth motivation. As an important practical activity of human existence and development, ideological and political education has a distinct function of "idealizing human" and forms a spiritual link between individual, society and country with common ideals, emotions, morals and ethics. Establishing a life ideal based on self realization can guide college students to correct their outlook on life, values and world outlook, actively and correctly face emergencies, love life and be happy to learn, so that they can truly grow up [4]. Therefore, the study on the purpose of Ideological and political education in the perspective of College Students' self realization will help them to become the people who distinguish right from wrong and are optimistic and upward, and help college students to establish a correct life ideal.

2 Related Work

2.1 Research Status of Capability Evaluation Methods

In terms of ability evaluation methods, domestic and foreign scholars have done a lot of research, such as factor analysis method and multiple linear regression method using statistical knowledge, such as analytic hierarchy process and fuzzy comprehensive evaluation method in fuzzy mathematics. These methods have achieved good results in ability evaluation. In 2007, Zhang Yang and others designed an online learning evaluation model based on the analytic hierarchy process (AHP) proposed by the American operational research scientist (T.L. Saaty); In 2008, Zheng Xiaowei and Chen Ying improved the fuzzy comprehensive evaluation method to improve the reliability of the evaluation results [5]; In 2011, Jared keengwe and Jung Jinkang adopted the activity theory triangle model in the evaluation method of online learning communication; Xu Lei and Claus

Pahl's evaluation method of online learning is the combination of the analysis model and the website analysis method applied to business websites [6].

Data mining has the advantages of prediction, Interdisciplinary Statistics, pattern recognition, artificial intelligence, database technology and so on. Many scholars have applied data mining technology to the evaluation field and achieved good results. In reference 13, the naive Bayesian network clustering method does not use the label classification method to predict the capability value. BP neural network has good nonlinear mapping ability in dealing with the problems with nonlinear evaluation indexes. More than 80% of the applications use BP neural network or improve BP neural network to achieve the evaluation purpose. The commonly used ability evaluation method is the fusion of optimization algorithm and BP neural network. In order to solve the complex multi factor and non-linear evaluation problem, the evaluation model of university scientific research ability is proposed by combining rough set neural network and collaborative intelligent water drop algorithm; A fuzzy neural network evaluation model based on particle swarm optimization (PSO) clustering algorithm is proposed. Particle algorithm and clustering idea are used to reduce the dimension of indicators, which effectively solves the problems of high dimension of evaluation indicators and difficult extraction rules [7].

2.2 Basic Principle of BP Neural Network

BP (Back Propagation) network is a branch of neural network, also known as error signal feedback network. The BP algorithm of error back-propagation is called BP algorithm for short. Its basic idea is to have a tutor to learn, and can achieve fast convergence by gradient descent method. A typical BP network is a three-layer feedforward hierarchical network (as shown in Fig. 1), that is, the input layer, the hidden layer (middle layer) and the input layer [8]. A three-layer BP network can complete any nonlinear mapping from n-dimension to m-dimension.

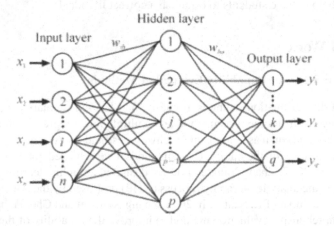

Fig. 1. BP network structure

The learning process of BP algorithm consists of forward propagation and directional propagation. In the forward propagation process, the input information is processed layer by layer from the input layer through the hidden layer and transmitted to the output layer. The state of each layer of neurons (nodes) only affects the state of the next layer of neurons [9]. If the desired output cannot be obtained at the output layer, the error signal (the difference between the ideal and actual output) will be inversely calculated according to the connection path, and the weight of each neuron will be adjusted by the gradient descent method to reduce the error signal. Neural network theory has proved that BP network has strong nonlinear mapping ability, and continuous function or mapping can be realized by three-layer network.

Assuming that the training set contains M samples and the number of units in the middle layer is L, for the P-th training sample ($p = 1 2 \cdots , M$), the actual output of unit j is $O_{p,j}$ and its i-th input is $O_{p,j}$ then:

$$U_{p,j} = \sum_{j=0}^{N} W_{ji} O_{p,j} \tag{1}$$

where w_{ji} is the connection weight between neuron i and neuron j. The output of hidden layer neurons is excited by S function:

$$O_{pj} = f(u_{pj}) = \frac{1}{1 + \exp(-u_{pj})} \tag{2}$$

The error performance index function is:

$$E = \sum_{\rho} E_{\rho} \tag{3}$$

$$E_p = \frac{1}{2} \sum_{j} (d_{pj} - O_{pj})^2 \tag{4}$$

where d_{pj} represents the expected output of unit j for P training samples. The purpose of training network is to find a set of weights and minimize the error function.

2.3 Research Status of Capability Evaluation Model

Generally, it is necessary to establish a competency evaluation model in the process of competency evaluation. The iceberg model proposed by McClelland is a well-known competency model at present. As shown in Fig. 2, although China regards competency as the core task of education, there has been no effective competency model as a guide.

In 1978, Schein suggested effective management of occupations; In 1982, boyatzis put forward the competency model, which is a general competency model; In 1993, Spencer et al. established the employee competency model (i.e., the famous competency iceberg model). In 2002, Shi Kan and Wang Jisheng solved the problem of the ability of senior managers in the communication industry, and the proposed ability evaluation model achieved good evaluation results [10]. In 2006, Cao maoxing, Wang Duan and others established a competency model for enterprise R & D personnel, which solved the problem of R & D personnel ability evaluation. In 2008, Yang Fengrui and Zhao

Ming tried to use it enterprise R & D personnel competency model in enterprise talent recruitment. In 2011, he Jianwen proposed a CSKA model to evaluate the ability of innovative talents of enterprises. With the needs of enterprise development, enterprises pay more and more attention to the development of employees' abilities, especially the higher requirements of developers' abilities. Therefore, more and more scholars are attracted to design the employee ability evaluation model [11]. At present, the more famous and far-reaching models include the ability iceberg model and the ability onion model.

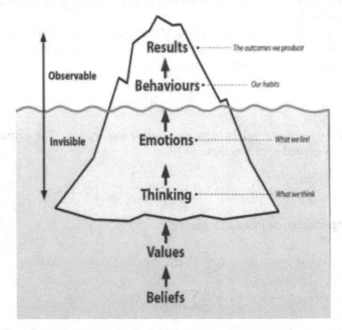

Fig. 2. Capability iceberg model

3   Establishment of Evaluation Index System

The establishment of the evaluation index system is the most basic and important step in the ability evaluation. The following basic principles should be followed in establishing a scientific and reasonable evaluation system.

(1) Scientific principle. Scientificity is one of the most basic conditions for establishing the evaluation index system. The index can objectively reflect the nature and characteristics of the evaluation object, and can be coordinated and unified, which truly conforms to the development laws of cognition, emotion and will of computer major students.

(2) Systematic principle. The evaluation index system can not only reflect the self realization ability of each student, but also reflect the relationship between them. Each indicator is independent of each other and can reflect a certain aspect of self realization ability. However, they are related to each other and form an organic and unified whole.

(3) The principle of comprehensiveness. Select the representative indicators and cover the evaluation contents as much as possible. The establishment of the evaluation index system should comprehensively reflect the students' self realization ability, describe the students' self realization ability from different aspects and angles, and reflect the teaching level of higher education [12].

(4) Guiding principle. The original intention of establishing the evaluation system is to encourage students to develop in a better direction and improve their self realization ability by evaluating the feedback results. Therefore, the evaluation index system can reflect the basic needs of College Students' software development, reflect the development trend of College Students' self realization ability, and guide the training of college software talents.

The most important step in the evaluation of self realization ability is to establish an evaluation model. This paper uses the characteristics of BP neural network to deal with non-linear problems, and proposes an evaluation model of self realization ability of college students based on BP neural network. The first task to determine the model is to determine the structure of BP neural network, and the second is the number of hidden layer neurons. In order to deal with the index data well, this paper introduces the standardization method of the index data and the selection of the evaluation level of self realization ability. Finally, the network is trained by collecting the training samples and test samples of the evaluation model to realize the dynamic adjustment of the network weights and thresholds [13].

Based on the BP algorithm, since the membership function and fuzzy rules have been included in the neural network, such a "fuzzy inference machine" is used for training, and the membership function is constantly modified during learning, and the fuzzy inference model with higher reliability is extracted. The obtained a sample pair {x (a), y (a)} is sent to the fuzzy neural network for learning, and the sample α The corresponding parameter value vector x (a) is used as the input of the fuzzy neural network, the corresponding known output parameter value ya) is used as the ideal output of the network, and Y (a) is the network output calculated at the anti-fuzzification layer. The error energy function of the network is defined as: $E = \frac{1}{2}(y - Y)^2$ minimum, where y is the actual output value, Y is the expected output value, and E is the square error function.

The adjustment of m_v ∂E in the learning process is expressed by the following formula:

$$m_v(n + 1) - m_v(n) = -\eta \frac{\partial E}{\partial m_v} \tag{5}$$

$$\sigma_\varepsilon(n + 1) - \sigma_\varepsilon(n) = -\eta \frac{\partial E}{\partial \sigma_\varepsilon} \tag{6}$$

where n is the learning rate of the network.

For each cycle of sample training, there are two processes - forward transfer process and backward transfer process. In the forward transmission process, the input signal enters from the input end, passes through the intermediate neuron, and is transmitted to the output end. The weight and parameters of the output layer are adjusted by the minimum variance estimation, and then the error of the output value is calculated; In the backward transmission process, the error signal obtained will be transmitted from the output end to the input end, and the parameters of the corresponding layers will be adjusted [14]. Adjust the network parameters through Formulas (5) and (6) to achieve the best effect of the network. When a new object is to be evaluated, it is only necessary to input the index factor vector of the object to be predicted, and then its comprehensive quality evaluation value can be obtained through network calculation [15].

The single hidden layer BP neural network structure of 25-11-1 is determined through experiments, as shown in Fig. 3. Determine the evaluation level, and divide the evaluation results of self realization ability into five evaluation levels: strong, strong, general, weak and very weak.

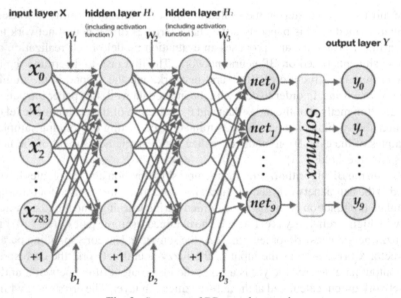

Fig. 3. Structure of BP neural network

The training samples are selected by obtaining the actual programming behavior detection data of the online platform of students and the major course scores of students. The course scores are relatively easy to obtain, but the collection of the students' programming behavior data needs a period of time [16]. Due to the limited ability of the author and time constraints, the number of training samples and test samples is small.

The self actualization ability evaluation system is divided into three main modules: user behavior detection module, user behavior statistical analysis module and self actualization ability evaluation module [17]. Through the analysis and design of the main modules, the self actualization ability of college students is evaluated and presented to the users in an intuitive and visual manner, which meets the user friendliness and real-time, and provides a practical tool for the self actualization ability evaluation of college students.

4 Simulation Analysis

The index values are obtained by testing and investigation, and the comprehensive evaluation values are obtained by expert scoring method. Among them, the performance data of the top 110 students are used as samples to train the sending model. Through continuous learning and training on the network, the past experience and acquired expert knowledge are accumulated into the network structure. The scores of the last 10 students are used as test data.

In this paper, fuzzy rules are divided into five categories by clustering analysis, and m_v ∂E random initial value, set the network learning rate as 0.03, the maximum number of iterations as 1000, and the minimum error as 0.1.

The above recursive process is from the last one to the first one. Of course, it is called the back-propagation algorithm in some books, which is based on the direction of error propagation. It may be better to understand graphically, but it is obviously more appropriate to use formula for algorithm implementation. Of course, the first thing to do in the process of "reverse calculation" is to perform forward calculation according to the signal recurrence formula [18]. Then the error is reversely calculated and written as a function of the program: The project procedure is shown in Fig. 4 below.

```
def back_forward(self,dest):
    self.e[self.layer-1]=dest-self.y[self.layer-1]
    temp_delta=self.e[self.layer-1]*self.d_sigmoid_v[self.layer-1]
    temp_delta=np.reshape(temp_delta,[-1,1])
    self.dW[self.layer-2][:]=np.dot(np.reshape(self.y[self.layer-2],[-1,1]
    self.db[self.layer-2][:]=np.transpose(temp_delta)
    #print(self.dW[self.layer-2])
    for itrn in range(self.layer-2,0,-1):
        sigma_temp_delta=np.dot(self.W[itrn],temp_delta)
        temp_delta=sigma_temp_delta*np.reshape(self.d_sigmoid_v[itrn],[-1,
        self.dW[itrn-1][:]=np.dot(np.reshape(self.y[itrn-1],[-1,1]),np.tra
        self.db[itrn-1][:]=np.transpose(temp_delta)
```

Fig. 4. Project procedures

The simulation results obtained by using the fuzzy neural network for the test sample data are as follows: Fig. 5 shows the comparison between the test sample image and the target image after the last 10 groups of data are modeled. It can be seen from the figure that the two curves basically coincide after the network training. It shows that the fuzzy neural network model has high accuracy and can effectively evaluate the comprehensive quality of students [19]. It is obvious from the figure that the error decline curve basically tends to linear decline, indicating that its convergence speed is fast.

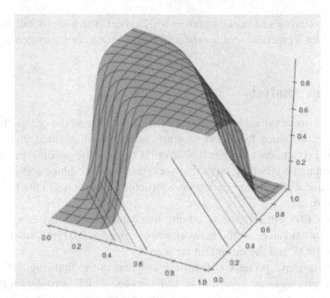

Fig. 5. Simulation curve

Generally, the trained network should also be tested for performance. The test method is to select the test sample vector and provide it to the network to verify the correctness of its processing. The test sample vector should contain the main typical patterns that may be encountered in the future network application process [20]. These samples can be obtained by direct measurement or simulation. When the sample data is small or difficult to obtain, it can also be obtained by adding appropriate noise to the learning sample or interpolating according to certain rules. In short, a good test sample set should not contain exactly the same patterns as the learning sample.

5 Conclusion

BP neural network model for self realization ability evaluation. The relatively simple single hidden layer BP neural network is used, and the training samples are small, which is prone to under fitting. Therefore, in the next work, more college students inside and outside the school are invited to participate in the self realization ability evaluation system, and the learning data of more students are collected as the training samples of the BP neural network, so as to enhance the generalization ability of the network. The evaluation system can reasonably, comprehensively and objectively reflect the students' self realization ability. Through the objective evaluation, the advantages and disadvantages of the students' self realization ability can be found. The evaluation results also help to find the shortcomings in the teaching practice, and then help to adjust the curriculum system structure of the college.

Acknowledgements. Key topic of the Research of Higher Education Teaching Reform in Jilin Province: "Research on the Construction of 2 + 3X + 1 Training Mode under Belt and Road Strategy" (No.: JID9881020190728185953).

References

1. Zhou, P., et al.: Algorithm and system design of video analysis for the violations in food processing in university restaurants. J. Food Saf. Qual. **9**(23), 6320–6326 (2018)
2. Minarro, A., Calvo, M.: A system of student-specific activities of statistics on the internet (2022)
3. Adharini, D., Herman, T.: Didactical design of vectors in mathematics to develop creative thinking ability and self-confidence of year 10 students. J. Phys. Conf. Ser. **1882**(1), 012089 (2021)
4. Chen, S., Yu, S., Lu, J., Chen, G., He, J.: Design and FPGA-based realization of a chaotic secure video communication system. IEEE Trans. Circ. Syst. Video Technol. **9**, 2359–2371 (2017)
5. Yiwen, L.: Innovative research on university teaching quality and evidence-based evaluation system centered on students' 5c core literacy (1), 6 (2022)
6. Uz, M.E., Sharafi, P., Askarian, M., Fu, W., Zhang, C.: Automated layout design of multi-span reinforced concrete beams using charged system search algorithm. Eng. Comput. Int. J. Comput. Aided Eng. Softw. **35**(3), 1402–1413 (2018)
7. Leng, C., Wei, L., Liu, Z., Wang, Z., Yang, T.: Design of epidemic tracing system based on blockchain technology and domestic cipher algorithm. In: Proceedings of the 11th International Conference on Computer Engineering and Networks. Springer (2022). https://doi.org/10.1007/978-981-16-6554-7_51
8. Wu, L.: Realization of feature-fusion-based image retrieval system (2016)
9. Sai Charan, N., Ali Hussain, M., Vineela, P., et al.: Predictive Student Performance Analysis Using Machine Learning and Student Assistance System (2022). https://doi.org/10.1007/978-981-16-7985-8_115
10. Qin, F.K., Meng, F.X.: The control system design of two-wheeled self-balancing car based on linear CCD. Dev. Innov. Mach. Electr. Prod. (2016)
11. Shu-Ping, L., Wang, J., University, H.E.: Experimental system design of two-wheeled self-balancing mobile robot. Lab. Sci. (2018)
12. Greve, D., Davis, J., Humphrey, L.: A mechanized proof of bounded convergence time for the distributed perimeter surveillance system (DPSS) algorithm A. arXiv preprint arXiv:2205.11697 (2022)
13. Darta, Saputra, J., Eliyarti, W., et al.: Improvement of the ability of representation, reasoning, and self-efficacy of prospective mathematics teacher students by using learning with a scientific approach. J. Phys. Conf. Ser. **1776**(1), 012002 (2021)
14. Singh, S., Thirumalai, S., Selvan, M.P.: Realization of self-demand response through non-intrusive load monitoring algorithm. In: 2019 IEEE International Conference on Electronics, Computing and Communication Technologies (CONECCT), pp. 1–6 (2020)
15. Lang, Z.H.: A design of self-study's platform system based on cloud computing. Electron. Des. Eng. **14**, 35–39 (2016)
16. Wang, Y.Q., Xue-Yan, X.U., Jiang, Q.S.: Control design of crane-double pendulum system based on immune PID algorithm. Control Eng. China **23**, 895–900 (2016)
17. Cheng, J.: System design relationship between internal accounting control and administration management of ants colony algorithm. In: Hung, J.C., Chang, J.W., Pei, Y., Wei-Chen, W. (eds.) Innovative Computing. LNEE, vol. 791, pp. 1723–1729. Springer, Singapore (2022). https://doi.org/10.1007/978-981-16-4258-6_222
18. Mao, Y.: Design of calisthenics choreography and recording system based on action recognition algorithm. In: International Conference on Machine Learning, Image Processing, Network Security and Data Sciences. Springer (2022). https://doi.org/10.1007/978-3-031-24367-7_19

19. Rajendran, R.: Enriching the student model in intelligent tutoring system. Doctoral dissertation, Monash University (2022)
20. Surjono, H.: Empirical evaluation of an adaptive e-learning system and the effects of knowledge, learning styles and multimedia mode on student achievement. In: Proceeding of the UiTM International Conference on ELearning 2007 (UICEL), Universiti Teknologi MARA, Shah Alam, Malaysia 12 – 14 December, 2007 (2022)

Application of Artificial Intelligence Algorithms in the Field of Smart Education

Computer Art Pattern Creation and P-filling Algorithm

Weiming Tang[✉] and Xianfeng Meng

Yunnan College of Business Management, Yunnan 650106, China
269286134@qq.com

Abstract. Expert system (expcrt systcm) has been widely used in the application and research field of artificial intelligence in the world. Many of them, molgen system, which studies molecular genetics, have been put into practical use and made remarkable achievements. At present, one of the topics of in-depth research in this field is to combine expert system with CAD, so that its role is not limited to question and answer consultation, but can form an automatic design system, from which we can further directly obtain production materials such as mechanical drawings, architectural schemes, product design and so on. This is obviously of great economic significance. The computer art pattern creation system developed by us is an exploration in this direction. Computer art pattern creation based on p-filling algorithm. This help these products occupy and expand the domestic and foreign markets.

Keywords: Computer · Art pattern creation · P-filling algorithm

1 Introduction

According to the improvement of the standard of living of people, the consumption idea of the people gradually changes, and when the commodity is bought, the people increasingly increase the appearance of the product and the artistry of the molding. For example, the product design of the product, the outline of the outline, the surface pattern, the combination of colors, etc.are heavy, and the product of the system is applied to the technique, and the craftsmen of the performance of the system is the product of the technique of the product, and the people of the product are the products which have the characteristic of the quality of the art, and the product is often the one that is very good.

The 21st century is an era of information technology, and the continuous innovation of computer technology has brought sufficient impetus to the development of society. For example, in the field of animation design, with the continuous innovation of drawing software, great changes have taken place in the means of art design. With the assistance of advanced drawing software technology, animation design has greatly improved its efficiency, developed many new forms of artistic expression, and injected new vitality into traditional animation art design. A plotter is a device that can automatically draw graphics according to people's requirements. It is a widely used peripheral device in

Y. Zhang and N. Shah (Eds.): BigIoT-EDU 2023, LNICST 582, pp. 317–327, 2024.
https://doi.org/10.1007/978-3-031-63136-8_33

computer-aided drafting and computer-aided design, and is also a key device in the manufacturing industry. It can be used to draw various charts, measurement diagrams, design diagrams, circuit diagrams, mechanical diagrams, and so on. The accuracy and speed of its drawing play an important role in product quality and production efficiency. In addition to the industrial field, plotters are also widely used in literary and artistic fields such as artistic creation and poster production, which can enhance the interest of creation. Therefore, the development and design of a plotter has important research value.

With the rapid development of computer technology, computer art design can provide good support to art designers. An excellent computer design system can effectively stimulate designers' inspiration and help designers to quickly and accurately complete the task of art design The creation of the design of computer art is the design of the emerging digital art in accordance with the development of computer technology, and the process of digitization and the mathematics are closely related, and the fractionality is applied in computer graphics [1]. Designers can borrow computers and create designs of fractional art, and because of the similarities of fractionation, they can't be taken, taken and taken over the scales of different scales beyond the symmetry of different scales, and on the scale of design attribution becoming increasingly smaller. It is difficult to produce such an impulsive force, and the traditional art creation method is difficult to generate such an impact force, and the subtype expression based on mathematics has the essence of determinism. The same result can be obtained when walking in the same pattern. A slight change input parameter causes a little change during operation, and if you have a small amount of information, you can get a gorgeous design, apply different colors to each area of the drawing, perform special effects, and appear in front of us is a very beautiful picture.

2 Art Pattern Generation Method

There are many methods to generate patterns, and the fractal patterns generated by different methods have their own characteristics. This paper introduces the generation method of fractal pattern based on p-filling algorithm in detail.

In the process of generating confrontation network training, in order to achieve their respective goals, the generator and discriminator will continuously optimize and improve their abilities, ultimately achieving a Nash balance. Figure 1 shows the basic structure of a generative countermeasures network.

In recent years, generative countermeasures networks have also become the focus of research in the field of computer vision because they have better super-resolution reconstruction capabilities and image generation capabilities than other methods. The objective function of the generated countermeasures network is shown in Formula (1).

$$\underset{}{minmax} \quad GDV(G, D) = E_{x-p_{dance}(x)}\big[logD(x)\big] + E_{z-p_z(z)}\big[log(1 - D(G(z)))\big] \tag{1}$$

At the beginning of training, due to the poor data generated by the generator, D (G (z) is very small, resulting in a small gradient. Therefore, log (1 − D (G (z))) is usually changed to log (D (G (z)).

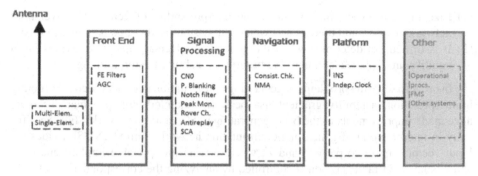

Fig. 1. The Basic Structure of Generative Countermeasures Network

For a fixed G, the optimal discriminator D * (x) is obtained, as shown in Formula (2).

$$D^*(x) = \frac{P_{data}(x)}{P_{data}(x) + P_g(x)} \qquad (2)$$

In the above formula, x represents a real image, which can be thought of as a vector, and Pdata (x) represents the distribution of the real image, that is, the distribution of the set of image vectors. Similarly, Pg (x) represents the distribution of images generated by G. When the number of training times is sufficient, the model will converge, where Pdata (x) = Pg (x), that is, the distribution of the images generated by G is equal to the distribution of the real images, while G and D reach Nash equilibrium. At this point, D cannot distinguish whether an image is real or generated, that is, the probability of determining whether an image is true or false is 0.5.

Compared to other methods, generative countermeasures networks have the following advantages:

(1) Generative countermeasures networks can be combined with deep CNN because any differentiable function can build generators and discriminators.
(2) In terms of super-resolution reconstruction and image generation, it has better results than other pattern recognition and deep learning methods.

On the other hand, although the generative adversarial network has been satisfactory in many aspects, it still has areas for improvement, such as pattern collapse.

"All generated samples are gathered under the first peak, and the generator does not capture the style of the second peak at all. Therefore, the generator only generates very similar samples over and over again, resulting in a pattern loss.".

The problem of gradient disappearance also exists in generative adversarial networks. When the discriminator's discrimination effect is too superior, no matter what kind of sample the generator generates, the discriminator can always correctly determine the true or false of a sample, making it impossible for the generator to learn, resulting in gradient disappearance.

In practice, the following problems still exist in generative countermeasures networks:

(1) Like many deep learning methods, the interpretability of generative adversarial networks is poor, and there is no explicit expression for the final data distribution.

(2) It is difficult to determine when the generative adversary network reaches Nash equilibrium. This leads to unstable training or inability to stop training.

In order to solve the problems of generating confrontation networks such as difficulty in interpretation, instability, gradient disappearance, and mode collapse, many scholars have made improvements to the basic generating confrontation networks. For the difficulty in interpretation of generating confrontation networks, InfoGANl38l divides the input vector z into two parts: c and z′, where c is an interpretable implicit encoding and z is noise. Data generation is controlled by analyzing the correspondence between c and output; To solve the problem of too free training, CGAN inputs constraints into the generator and discriminator, making model training more targeted, but there is still a problem of training instability; WGAN solves the problems of training instability and mode collapse.

Generative adversarial networks are a hot research field, and the research on them is ongoing, and there is still considerable research space, including evaluation criteria for normative models and theoretical exploration. In addition, the application of generative countermeasures networks to new fields is also one of the focuses and hotspots of future research.

2.1 Pattern Generation Method Based on P-filling Algorithm

In computer programming, p-filling refers to a process that directly or indirectly calls its own algorithm.

(1) Direct p-filling call
Void Recur (n)
.....
Recur (m);
.....
//Recur procedure: the recur procedure calls itself internally
(2) Indirect recursive call
Void Recur_ A (n)
{
Recur B (m) / / call procedure recur B
}
Void Recur_ B (n)
{
......
Recur C (m); / / call procedure recur C
}
Void Recur_ C (n)
{
Recur_a (m); / / call procedure recur_a
/*Process recur_ a indirectly calls process recur_ a (i.e. internal call process recur_ B of process recur_ a, internal call process recur_ C of process recur_ B, internal call process recur_ a of process recur_ C)*/

2.2 Drawing Graphics Using P-filling Algorithm

A pattern often contains a huge amount of information, such as 256 × 256 resolution image, each pixel has 16 grayscale (or color), it contains 28 bits of information. Therefore, as described in Sect. 2, the system adopts the key point method to compress the information, which greatly saves the machine processing time and space. The resulting problem is that during pattern display, it is necessary to restore the key points into polygonal color blocks [2]. The filling algorithm completes this function, as shown in Fig. 2.

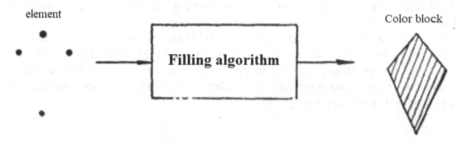

Fig. 2. Filling algorithm pattern generation

If a straight line L is led from a point 0 outside the polygon p to the direction P, it will enter P after the odd times of intersection between L and the edge line of P, and exit P after the even times of intersection (see Fig. 2). According to the parity judgment rule, an algorithm a can be established, which is a very simple color filling algorithm. Unfortunately, for raster scanning display, algorithm a has only theoretical significance. If it is practical, it will be full of errors.

2.3 Overview of Image Superresolution Reconstruction

The nearest neighbor interpolation method is a commonly used image interpolation method for interpolating grayscale values between discrete pixels. The core idea is to find the pixel closest to the interpolation point and assign the grayscale value of that pixel to the interpolation point.

The specific steps are as follows:

1. Calculate the Euclidean distance between the interpolation point and each pixel point.
2. Find the pixel closest to the interpolation point, which is the pixel with the smallest Euclidean distance.
3. Assign the grayscale value of the nearest pixel to the grayscale value of the interpolation point.
4. Repeat the above steps to process all points that require interpolation.

The advantages of nearest neighbor interpolation method are simplicity and high computational efficiency, as it only needs to find the nearest pixel point and assign values. However, its disadvantage is that the interpolation results may exhibit jagged edge effects and do not take into account the grayscale distribution of surrounding pixels.

The process of the nearest neighbor interpolation method can be represented by formula (3).

$$D(x, y) = D(x + a, y + b) \tag{3}$$

In formula (3), (x, y) represents the target interpolation point, $(x + a, y + b)$ represents the point with the smallest Euclidean distance from the target interpolation point, and D represents the grayscale value.

The nearest neighbor interpolation method is the easiest method to achieve image super-resolution reconstruction, but the reconstructed image has serious aliasing effects, and the reconstruction effect is also the worst among interpolation based methods. (2) Bilinear Interpolation.

The core idea of bilinear interpolation is to obtain the gray value of the target interpolation point by weighting and summing the gray values of the four pixel points adjacent to the target interpolation point. The process of bilinear interpolation is explained in detail below. Figure 3 shows the target interpolation point P (x, y) and the four adjacent points $Q_{11}(x_1, y_1) \cdot Q_{12}(x_1, y_2) \cdot Q_{21}(x_2, y_1)$.

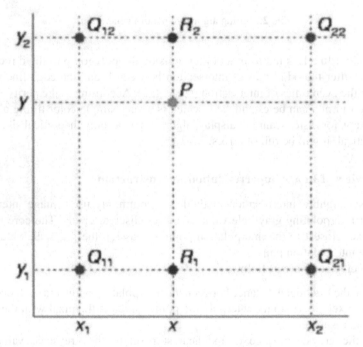

Fig. 3. Bilinear interpolation

First, calculate the interpolation in the x direction, namely $R_1(x, y_1)$ and $R_2(x, y_2)$. The grayscale values $f(R_1)$ and $f(R_2)$ of R_1 and R_2 are shown in (4) and (5), respectively.

$$f(R_1) = \frac{x_2 - x}{x_2 - x_1} f(Q_{11}) + \frac{x - x_1}{x_2 - x_1} f(Q_{21}) \tag{4}$$

$$f(R_2) = \frac{x_2 - x}{x_2 - x_1} f(Q_{12}) + \frac{x - x_1}{x_2 - x_1} f(Q_{22}) \tag{5}$$

Compared to the nearest neighbor interpolation method, the bilinear interpolation method has a slower generation speed, but it utilizes more neighborhood information and produces a smoother image.

3 Application of Computer Art Pattern Creation

3.1 Software Development Tools

Image processing software is one of the commonly used tools in computer art pattern creation. Such software allows artists to edit, transform, and apply filters to images. Some common image processing software include Adobe Photoshop, GIMP, etc.

The development of image processing software requires consideration of the following requirements:

User friendly interface and operation: The software should have a simple and intuitive user interface, allowing artists to easily perform image processing operations.
Powerful image processing algorithms and functions: The software needs to provide rich image processing algorithms and functional options to meet the creative needs of artists.
High performance and efficiency: Artists usually need to process a large amount of image data, so software needs to have high performance and efficiency to achieve fast image processing operations.

The development of vector graphics editing software requires consideration of the following requirements:

Powerful vector graphics processing function: The software should provide rich vector graphics editing tools, such as line drawing, curve editing, shape transformation, etc., to achieve diversified artistic pattern creation.
Vector graphics save and export format support: The software needs to support common vector graphics save and export formats, such as SVG, EPS, etc., to facilitate artists to apply their works to different media and platforms.
Intelligent layout and alignment tools: Software should provide intelligent layout and alignment tools to help artists quickly and accurately create complex pattern designs.
By writing code, artists can achieve custom and interactive pattern generation. Some common code generation tools include Processing, OpenFrameworks, and so on.

In summary, the development of application software for computer art pattern creation needs to consider user-friendly interfaces, powerful functions, high performance, and diversity. It is easy to learn, easy to operate and powerful (Fig. 4).

3.2 Main Function Modules of Software

At present, a pattern is provided in 1 to 5 min. If you use other languages, the speed can be improved. The system has 60 knowledge and elements, and can generate hundreds of millions of different pictures. If the learning function is taken into account, this number

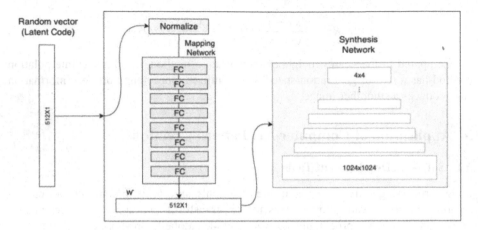

Fig. 4. Generator Network Structure

is even larger [3]. Due to the information compression technology, the whole system can be put into a 5-h floppy disk, and there is still room to store hundreds of generated pattern works. Due to the limitation of the interface and display, the resolution of the display screen is only 64x64, resulting in rough patterns. Now we wait to configure a high-resolution color display for practical use.

The mapping network of the StyleGAN generator includes eight fully connected layers, outputting a vector w' of 512 * 1. The function of the mapping network is to perform feature unwrapping of the input Latent Code. Hidden spaces represent the features of data, but these features are interrelated and highly coupled, making it difficult for models to clarify their relationships [4], making learning inefficient. Therefore, it is necessary to find the underlying relationships hidden under these surface features, and the features obtained by decoupling these relationships are called hidden codes. Multiple hidden codes form a hidden space.

In addition to providing patterns, this computer art pattern creation system can also be developed into an automatic textile pattern preparation center to directly output patterns, plate making and other media to production; It can also be used by artists to study the laws of composition and color. Art knowledge is rich and complex. For example, there are three-dimensional art knowledge to express three-dimensional patterns and animation knowledge to express animal posture, and it is also necessary to establish pattern generators suitable for them. This system only makes a preliminary attempt in the creation of written geometric patterns. A large number of contents need to be further studied.

According to the generation process of fractal art pattern, the main functional modules of the computer system are shown in Fig. 5.

3.3   Operation Steps

Koch curve is a fractal curve composed of infinite subdivision and repeated processes. The key steps to drawing Koch curves using the p-filling algorithm are as follows:

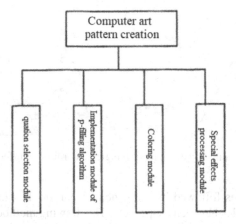

Fig. 5. Functional module diagram of computer art pattern creation system

1. Given the coordinates of the two endpoints of the initial line segment.
2. Divide the initial segment equally into three equally long sub segments.
3. Replace the middle sub segment with an equilateral triangle (with that segment as the base).
4. Repeat the above steps to recursively subdivide and replace each sub segment until the required number of iterations is reached.

The specific steps for the p filling algorithm when drawing Koch curves are as follows:

1. Set the coordinates of the two endpoints of the initial line segment to $(x1, y1)$ and $(x2, y2)$.
2. Calculate the length of the initial line segment: $L = \mathrm{sqrt}\,((x2 - x1)\wedge 2 + (y2 - y1)\wedge 2)$.
3. Calculate the coordinates of an auxiliary point P1: $(x1 + L/3, y1 + (y2 - y1)/3)$.
4. Calculate the coordinates of an auxiliary point P2: $(x1 + 2L/3, y1 + 2\,(y2 - y1)/3)$.
5. Calculate the coordinates of an auxiliary point P3: $(x1 + x2)/2 - (y2 - y1) * \mathrm{sqrt}(3)/6, (y1 + y2)/2 + (x2 - x1) * \mathrm{sqrt}(3)/6)$.
6. Draw three line segments: $(x1, y1)$ to P1, P1 to P3, P3 to P2, and P2 to $(x2, y2)$.
7. Repeat the above steps to recursively subdivide each line segment until the required number of iterations is reached.

These steps can be applied in each recursive call to draw increasingly refined Koch curves. By increasing the number of iterations, more complex and refined Koch curve shapes can be obtained. Figure 6 is a fractal graph generated by the same generator (equilateral triangle) and different operation rules.

The basic generator can take various forms, including simple shapes composed of lines, two-dimensional planes, three-dimensional shapes, and even any object in real life. These generators can be used to create various fractal art shapes. When the basic generator is a 3D graphic, the generated fractal art graphics are also 3D. They can have more depth, perspective, and three-dimensional effects, making artistic graphics more rich and three-dimensional.

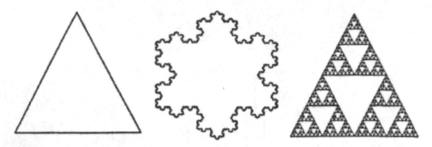

Fig. 6. Patterns generated by equilateral triangles according to different operation rules

The operating rules followed by the generator can be drawing methods, coloring methods, matching rules between shapes, etc. The drawing method refers to generating the shape and structure of the basic generator based on rules and algorithms. The coloring method is to add colors and textures to the generated graphics to enhance artistic effects. The matching rules between graphics can be used to control how the generated graphics are connected and combined, in order to create an overall harmonious artwork.

These operational rules can be defined and adjusted by artists, designers, or programmers based on their own creativity and needs. By combining and changing different operating rules, we can create ever-changing fractal art graphics, creating infinite possibilities. The basic generator can be in the form of lines, two-dimensional planes, or three-dimensional graphics, and the generated fractal art graphics can also present corresponding dimensions. The operating rules followed by the generator include drawing methods, coloring methods, and matching rules between shapes. By defining and adjusting these rules, a rich and diverse variety of fractal art works can be created.

4   Generate Pattern Analysis

The following are the applications of computer art patterns in image generation mode analysis:

Pattern recognition and classification: Computer art patterns can be used to generate various patterns and forms, including geometric shapes, textures, colors, etc. Applying these patterns to the pattern recognition and classification process of images can help us identify and distinguish different patterns and structures.

Feature extraction and description: By generating different artistic patterns, features can be extracted from images and described. These features can include information such as edges, textures, and color distribution, allowing for a more detailed and comprehensive analysis of the image.

Data visualization: Computer art patterns can be used to visualize the features and patterns of image data. By combining image data with artistic patterns, patterns, trends, and relationships in the data can be more intuitively displayed, enabling a better understanding and analysis of the data.

Image enhancement and restoration: Computer art patterns can be applied in the process of image enhancement and restoration to improve the quality and clarity of images. By generating artistic patterns and combining them with the original image, operations such as denoising and enhancing details can be performed on the image, thereby improving its appearance and quality.

It achieves high-resolution image reconstruction by training the Generative Adversarial Network (GAN). Training ESRGAN requires a large amount of data and computing resources, as well as a longer training time. In ESRGAN, using pre trained models can be a fast solution. The trained model has been trained on large-scale datasets and has a certain degree of universality. This means that using such a model for image reconstruction may result in similar results to ESRGAN trained using other datasets.

However, it should be noted that using trained models may not necessarily meet all requirements. It may not fully adapt to the details and features on a specific dataset. If there are specific requirements or you want to optimize the results, it is best to continue training or fine-tuning the model based on the trained model to better adapt to the specific dataset. ESRGAN can provide fast high-resolution reconstruction capabilities using trained models. If there are no specific requirements or time constraints, using other datasets for training may yield better results. However, based on the specific situation, taking into account factors such as time and accuracy, suitable methods are selected for ESRGAN training and application.

5 Conclusion

The creation of computer art patterns is a creative and technical task that combines elements of computer graphics and art. In this process, the p-filling algorithm plays an important role. The p-fill algorithm is used to fill closed areas in computer images to create different patterns and texture effects. Its principle is to scan pixel by pixel and determine the fill color of the pixels. Among them, the most common p-filling algorithms are the scan line algorithm and the seed filling algorithm. The scan line algorithm is an efficient filling algorithm. It identifies boundaries by scanning each row in the image and searching for adjacent pixels of different colors. Once the boundary is found, the algorithm will start filling the color from the boundary until it encounters pixels of the same color. This algorithm is suitable for filling continuous areas. The creation of computer art patterns relies on the use of p filling algorithms and other graphics and art techniques. The continuous development of these algorithms and technologies provides us with more possibilities to create beautiful and complex patterns. Through continuous practice and exploration, we can create stunning works of computer art.

References

1. Su, L.: Justification of algorithm governance in intelligent era. Yunnan Soc. Sci. (03) (2021)
2. Jin, Y., Wang, X.: Risk prevention of algorithm technology being controlled and abused in the era of big data. Internet World (06) (2021)
3. Yin, J., Yin, Q.: The beauty of fractal geometry - one of the philosophical explorations of fractal theory. J. Luoyang Univ. **20**(4), 27–30 (2005)
4. Sun, X.: Application of computer art in teaching. Vocational Education Forum (1999)

Computer Simulation of Sports and Design of Auxiliary Training System

Xianfeng Meng[1]([✉]), Chaofeng Yang[1], Donghui Wang[1], Baisong Lin[1], Weiming Tang[2], and Bingtao Wei[2]

[1] Xinjiang Vocational and Technical College of Communications, Urumqi 831401, Xinjiang, China
mxf455410007@126.com

[2] School of Artificial Intelligence, Wenshan University, Wenshan 663000, China

Abstract. Motion analysis technology is a very broad field, which involves many fields such as computer vision, artificial intelligence and pattern recognition. It is a highly interdisciplinary subject. Because of its high application value, it has always been a research hotspot. Computer simulation of sports is a computer-based method used to study the effect of training and performance. It allows researchers to assess how different training methods affect an individual's performance in a particular sport. Coaches, athletes, coaches, and researchers use computer simulations to determine whether various techniques help improve their performance. Computer simulation of design system is a modeling technology, which helps designers and engineers create models of real objects using computer software. Designers use certain parameters (such as size, weight) to create models so that they can be tested according to the actual design without building the model first.

Keywords: athletic sports · Computer simulation · Auxiliary training

1 Introduction

Sports computer simulation and auxiliary training system is an important technology in the field of sports, and its emergence provides new ways and tools for sports training and competition. By utilizing computer science and virtual reality technology, this system can simulate real sports scenes and training environments, helping athletes improve their skills and tactical awareness [1]. This article will introduce the design principles and key technologies of motion computer simulation and auxiliary training systems, and explore their application prospects in sports training.

With the continuous improvement of sports competitive level and the intensification of competition, traditional training methods can no longer meet the needs of athletes. At the same time, the rapid development of modern technology has provided new opportunities for the field of sports [2]. The motion computer simulation and auxiliary training system, as an advanced technological means, effectively compensates for the shortcomings of traditional training and has important practical value.

Y. Zhang and N. Shah (Eds.): BigIoT-EDU 2023, LNICST 582, pp. 328–338, 2024.
https://doi.org/10.1007/978-3-031-63136-8_34

The design of a motion computer simulation and auxiliary training system is based on computer graphics, virtual reality technology, and kinematic principles. The principle is to establish a virtual sports scene and training environment, immersing athletes in a virtual world, and assisting athletes in technical and tactical training by simulating various sports actions and situations [3]. The design of the system first requires the establishment of a real motion model, which can include information such as the athlete's body structure, muscle strength, and joint activity. Then, the motion model is transformed into a virtual three-dimensional motion entity through computer graphics and virtual reality technology. Athletes interact with virtual environments by wearing devices such as sensors and headsets.

The computer simulation and auxiliary training system for sports relies on various key technologies. Motion capture technology can collect athletes' motion data in real-time, and sensors and camera devices can record information such as speed, acceleration, and angle of motion. Virtual reality technology can create realistic visual effects and tactile feedback, allowing athletes to have an immersive experience.

This system has been widely applied in multiple sports fields. For example, the passing, shooting, and defensive movements in football training can be simulated and trained through motion computer simulation and auxiliary training systems. Technical actions such as shooting and blocking in basketball training can also be simulated and trained through the system [4]. Even in the field of medical rehabilitation, systems can help rehabilitation patients undergo exercise recovery training and improve rehabilitation outcomes.

Sports computer simulation and auxiliary training system is a cutting-edge technology in the field of sports, which helps athletes train and compete by simulating real sports scenes. This system has important application value in sports training and medical rehabilitation. Despite facing some challenges, its application prospects are broad and it is expected to have a profound impact on the field of sports.

2 Related Work

2.1 Research Status

Human research in the field of motion analysis technology has gone through a long process of development, and its history can be traced back to the 15th century. However, the emergence and development of modern computer vision technology have brought tremendous changes and progress to human motion analysis.

In the early stages, human motion analysis relied more on human eye observation and manual measurement. Researchers analyze and evaluate athletes' technical level by observing and recording their movements. This method has been widely used in training and teaching in the field of sports, but it is limited by subjectivity and subjective judgment.

With the development of computer technology, especially the advancement of computer vision and image processing, human motion analysis gradually relies on computers to achieve automation and objectification [5]. Computer vision technology can extract image information from video sequences and use image processing and pattern recognition algorithms to analyze and recognize human movements. This provides new avenues and tools for motion analysis.

At present, modern computer vision technology has been widely applied in human motion analysis and has made significant progress. Motion capture systems and 3D reconstruction technology can capture and reconstruct human motion in real-time, providing accurate motion data. Machine learning and deep learning algorithms can learn and understand the patterns and laws of human motion from a large amount of data. The development of these technologies has provided more accurate, objective, and automated methods and tools for human motion analysis.

The emergence of modern computer vision technology has brought tremendous changes and progress to human motion analysis, making analysis more accurate, objective, and automated [6]. With the continuous development of technology, human motion analysis will play an increasingly important role in fields such as sports training, medical rehabilitation, and virtual reality. VR football sports simulation training is shown in Fig. 1 below.

Fig. 1. VR Rugby Sports Simulation Training

In the research of human motion analysis, model-based human motion analysis methods rely on prior knowledge and the establishment of 2D or 3D models of the human body. When using this method, it is first necessary to establish an accurate human model, in which information such as joint structure and motion constraints are defined. Then, by processing and analyzing the input image or video sequence, feature vectors are obtained from the model to describe human motion.

The feature vectors of model-based human motion analysis methods are mainly obtained from the constructed human model, which can include information such as joint angle, joint velocity, and joint position. By analyzing and processing these feature vectors, quantitative evaluations of human posture, action effects, etc. can be obtained. However, the establishment of a human body model is a relatively complex and time-consuming process that requires a large amount of prior knowledge and professional technical support [7]. Therefore, in practical applications, model based methods are often rarely used.

In contrast, modelless methods do not require the establishment of a human body model in advance. This method directly extracts features from the input image sequence to describe human behavior. Features can include human body contours, key point positions, human motion trajectories, etc. By extracting and analyzing these features, it is possible to describe and analyze human motion. Model free methods are relatively simpler and more flexible, but there are also some challenges, such as the accuracy and robustness of feature extraction.

Model based human motion analysis methods require establishing a human body model and extracting feature vectors from it, which is more complex in practical applications. In contrast, model-free methods are more direct in describing human behavior by extracting features from image sequences. The choice of method depends on actual needs and research objectives.

2.2 Research on the Characteristics and Difficulties of Human Motion Analysis

Human motion analysis is a large subject category, which contains a considerable number of technical knowledge points. According to the current research technology level, the research on human motion analysis technology is mainly based on visual motion analysis. Vision based motion analysis can be divided into monocular vision based and multi vision based. The image sequence based on monocular vision contains two-dimensional motion information, while the image sequence based on monocular vision contains more three-dimensional motion information. Whether it is two-dimensional information or three-dimensional information, human motion analysis is in the final analysis and research for image sequences, not just for image analysis and processing [8]. Human motion analysis is shown in Fig. 2 below.

Therefore, the current research work on human motion analysis mainly has the following difficulties:

(1) Image sequence, the research object of human motion analysis, although image sequence can contain more abundant information resources than a single image, it also has high requirements for information processing ability when it has rich information, which poses a great challenge to the computer's ability to calculate and process big data and the ability to optimize motion analysis algorithms.

(2) When analyzing the image, we can easily describe and extract the features of the image, and then we can naturally carry out the subsequent analysis. However, for image sequences, it will be difficult to extract features, because it is impossible to extract features directly from image sequences [9].

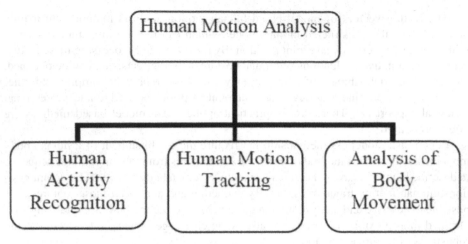

Fig. 2. Human Motion Analysis

(3) As a research object, human body has its unique attribute, that is, non rigid, compared with cars, faces and other objects. Human motion is a typical non rigid body motion. Even under the same conditions, the two human motions before and after cannot be exactly the same. In addition, the external environment in the process of human motion, such as the influence of light, has brought great difficulties to human motion analysis and recognition.

2.3 Sports Evaluation

The quantitative evaluation of students' movement performance is the key to subsequent content feedback, guidance feedback, and skill level updates. According to the order of the processing program and the degree of data extraction, motion evaluation can be divided into three levels: motion capture, feature extraction, and motion evaluation.

Motion capture is the use of sensors or camera equipment to collect student motion data. Sensors can record data such as joint position, body posture, and movement speed, while camera devices can record visual information of movements. By processing and analyzing the captured data, a digital representation of students' actual actions can be obtained [10].

In the feature extraction stage, key feature information is extracted from the captured data. These features can be the angle, speed, acceleration, etc. of the action, or other statistical indicators related to the quality and effectiveness of the action. Feature extraction aims to reduce the amount of data and extract the most representative information.

Based on the feature information obtained from the feature extraction stage, the motion evaluation stage quantitatively evaluates the actions of the trainees. This can be achieved by comparing it with professional proficiency, standard actions, or other reference data. The evaluation results can be used to provide feedback and guidance, help students understand their motor performance, and provide updates on their skill levels.

The relationship of the three levels can be expressed as formula (1)

$$J_m(U, V) = \sum_{j=1}^{C} \sum_{i=1}^{N} u_{ij}^m d_{ij}^2 \tag{1}$$

tor V is calculated by the following formula:

$$v_j^{(t)} = \frac{\sum_{i=1}^{N}(\mu_{ij}^{(t-1)})^m x_i}{\sum_{i=1}^{N}(\mu_{ij}^{(t-1)})^m} j = 1, \ldots C \tag{2}$$

Data fusion for common indicator values:

$$\mu_{ij} = \frac{1}{\sum_{k=1}^{C}(\frac{d_j}{d_k})^{\frac{2}{(m-1)}}} i = 1, \ldots, N j = 1, \ldots C \tag{3}$$

$$F(U, V) = \frac{1}{J_m + \varepsilon} \varepsilon > 0 \tag{4}$$

Selection of exercise content Selection of exercise content includes two levels: group and difficulty. The selected group needs to be able to exercise the skills that the trainees currently lack. The specific formula is listed in (5). The difficulty of the exercise will be positioned as the trainees' progress during the last exercise in that group. When a trainee's immediate performance at a certain difficulty level in a certain group meets the requirements, their difficulty progress in that group is updated, and the corresponding skill level is updated.

$$D = \frac{\sum_{i=1}^{C}\|v_i - v_j\|}{C} \tag{5}$$

The selection of feedback instructions is related to the selection of feedback instructions. In numerical terms, instruction preference can also be equivalent to a posterior probability that instructions will help trainees. Since feedback instructions have a strong correlation with exercise content and real-time performance, the initialization of preferences for each feedback instruction can be obtained by calculating the distance of {ca: (X, pi)). Equation (6) provides a method for initializing instruction preferences, where d (x, p;), ix, pl) represents the distance function between two "content performance" combinations.

$$f = J_m(U, V) + D \tag{6}$$

$$F'(U, V) = \frac{1}{J_m(U, V) + D} \tag{7}$$

However, this is not enough. A scheme that only relies on initialization to determine command preferences at least has problems that real-time performance cannot fully cover, and trainees have different command receiving habits. For this reason, this paper introduces an instruction preference correction method for different effects after instruction feedback: When the immediate performance after instruction feedback is better than before, the instruction preference increases; If the immediate performance before and after feedback does not differ significantly or becomes worse, the preference for the command is reduced accordingly. The correction range of command preference depends on the specific situation.

3 Sports Auxiliary Training System Based on Computer Simulation

3.1 System Design Principles

The design of this system is based on the following design principles, aiming to provide an information-based management platform for coaches and athletes:

1. User friendliness: The system interface should be concise and intuitive, and easy to use, to facilitate coaches and athletes to quickly get started. At the same time, the system should consider the user's usage habits and personalized needs, and provide customizable interface settings and functional options.
2. Real time: The system should be able to monitor and record athlete data and performance in real time, so that coaches can keep track of athlete training progress and performance at any time. This can conduct timely data analysis, provide personalized feedback and guidance, and help athletes adjust their training plans in a timely manner.
3. Data security: The system should have a high level of data security to ensure that the personal information and training data of coaches and athletes are not leaked or abused. The system should adopt appropriate data encryption and access control measures to ensure the confidentiality and integrity of data.
4. Multi platform compatibility: The system should support use on different devices and operating systems, including computers, tablets, and mobile phones. In this way, coaches and athletes can use the system anytime and anywhere, improving the efficiency of data collection and management.
5. Data analysis and visualization: The system should have the ability to analyze and visualize data, and be able to collect and analyze athlete data, and present it to coaches and athletes in the form of charts, images, and other forms. This can help coaches better understand and evaluate athletes' performance, and develop effective training plans.
6. Personalized Customization: The system should have the function of personalized customization, providing flexible and adjustable functional modules and training plans according to the needs of coaches and athletes. Coaches and athletes can set and adjust according to their own needs to meet personalized training goals.

In summary, the design of this system is based on design principles such as user friendliness, real-time performance, data security, multi platform compatibility, data analysis and visualization, and personalized customization. By following these principles, this system will provide an efficient, reliable, and personalized information management platform for coaches and athletes, promoting the improvement of training effectiveness and the professional development of athletes.

3.2 System Function Design

Combined with the problem of athlete training, this paper divides the functions of the system into four subsystems: basic information management, training management, evaluation management and medical management. Its specific functional design is shown in Fig. 3.

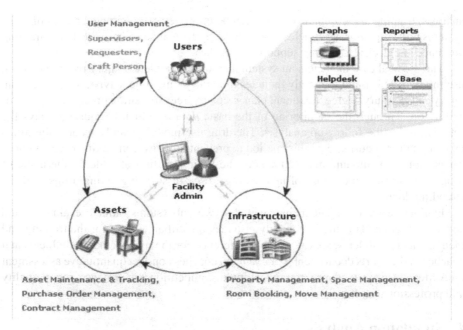

Fig. 3. Computer simulated sports auxiliary training system

Basic information management mainly includes the recording and management of personal basic information of athletes and coaches. This information includes name, gender, age, contact information, physical fitness assessment, etc. In addition, athletes' relevant technical information also needs to be recorded, such as professional skills, team positions, training results, etc. At the same time, it is also necessary to maintain the sports competition arrangements and results that athletes have participated in over the years, in order to conduct performance evaluations and further training arrangements. The system should also have the function of modifying personal basic information and updating files to ensure the accuracy and timeliness of information. In addition, some additional information, such as athlete flexibility, can also be recorded and managed.

The training management system includes four functional modules. Firstly, the training plan management module is used to arrange and manage athletes' training plans, including training objectives, schedules, training content, etc. Secondly, the training effectiveness analysis module can track and evaluate athletes, including the analysis and evaluation of training results, in order to provide guidance for subsequent training. Thirdly, the athlete technical action analysis module can record and analyze the athlete's technical actions, helping coaches identify and improve technical issues. Finally, the pre competition skill state analysis module can evaluate and analyze the skill level of athletes before the competition, in order to develop appropriate training strategies and preparation plans.

The basic information management and training management system is an indispensable part of athlete training. By effectively recording and managing personal information, and utilizing training management systems for scientific training plans and technical analysis, training and competitive skills can be improved. The implementation of these systems will help improve athletes' competitive performance and provide better training guidance and decision-making support for coaches.

The medical care management system includes the athlete's injury record and drug use module. This module mainly includes the injury time, injury type, injury location, injury cause, injury degree, treatment plan, recovery, reexamination time, nursing doctor and so on. Through the monitoring of the basic data of athletes' injuries, it lays the foundation for the follow-up analysis. The drug use module mainly records the drugs taken by athletes during the injury period to prevent athletes from taking drugs without permission. This module mainly includes the basic situation of athletes, the name of drugs used, dose, time, cause of taking drugs, time of stopping taking drugs, and the attending doctor.

Evaluation management mainly includes two subsystems: athlete evaluation and coach evaluation. This module mainly provides quantifiable basis for the training and management of athletes, so as to provide reference for the management of athletes and coaches in the sports department. For example, coaches conduct quantitative assessment on Athletes' daily attendance, training attitude, competition performance, moral quality and professional skills.

4 Simulation Analysis

The implementation difficulties and error factors of applying computer simulation training to sports examples have been explained in Sect. 3. However, the digitization and automation of sports, or any other sports training, is still fraught with challenges, which are embodied in two aspects: first, the complexity of sports itself, with rich dimensions in various parts, from exercise content, real-time performance, to skill indicators, and complex conceptual expression, distance calculation, and mapping relationships between them. There are no directly available conclusions in existing research; The second is the long-term periodicity of sports training. Regardless of the ideal situation of the trainee from the initial level to the expected goal, it is necessary for the trainee to have a long usage time of the system just to be able to observe the visible progress of the trainee. Table 1 below shows the comparison between the two experiments of horizontal kick and flying kick.

Table 1. Experimental Comparison

category	male			female		
	Before the experiment	After the experiment	P	Before the experiment	After the experiment	P
Flying kick	29.25 ± 3.45	32.88 ± 3.48	0.06	27.75 ± 1.67	32.00 ± 1.77**	0.00
Cross kick	27.00 ± 1.31	52.63 ± 1.41**	0.00	18.63 ± 1.06	18.63 ± 1.06	0.00

From Table 1, it can be seen that in the comparison of test data before and after the experiment, the physical fitness of the boys and girls in the control group has improved, but the statistical analysis value $P > 0.05$ indicates that there is no significant difference in physical fitness before and after the experiment, and the increase is not significant; In terms of specific quality, the test results can be seen that the scores of male and female students have significantly improved before and after the double flying kick experiment at 27.00, 52.63, and 18.63, respectively, for male and female students, and there is a significant difference in the scores before and after the experiment ($P < 0.01$). What is noteworthy is that the scores of male and female students before and after the high flying kick experiment at 29.25, 32.88, and female students before and after the high flying kick experiment at 27.75, 32.00, respectively, Although the scores of both male and female students have improved, the analysis value of $P > 0.05$ for boys indicates that there is no significant difference before and after the experiment, while $P < 0.01$ for girls indicates that there is a very significant difference in the scores of high level horizontal kicks before and after the experiment.

In summary, through the pre and post comparisonit was found that both VR assisted training and routine training had a trend of improving students' physical fitness, but the improvement was not significant; In terms of specific qualities, and the control group in the scores of high level horizontal kicking and double flying kicking, indicating that both VR assisted training and conventional training methods have a significant impact on the improvement of the girls' scores in these two items; The boys in the experimental group and the control group have extremely significant differences in the performance of the double flying kick. However, although the performance of the high level horizontal kick has improved through comparison between the groups, the improvement difference is not significant. However, through self comparison of the high level horizontal kick performance before and after, it is shown that the boys in the experimental group have extremely significant differences, while the boys in the control group have no significant differences, This indicates that virtual reality assisted training and conventional training have a significant impact on the improvement of boys' performance in both flying and horizontal kicks, with VR technology assisted training having a more significant training effect.

5 Conclusion

The design of a sports computer simulation and auxiliary training system aims to utilize computer technology to provide an interactive virtual environment for athletes to improve their skills and abilities. This system allows athletes to train and practice in a virtual environment by simulating sports scenes and related parameters. In system design, it is necessary to collect and organize relevant data, and use computer graphics and physical simulation technology to transform it into a visualized virtual scene. At the same time, the system should also provide appropriate interaction methods and feedback mechanisms to simulate real motion environments. This system design helps to provide a more realistic and personalized training experience, helping athletes achieve better training results in a shorter period of time, and improving their competitive ability.Therefore, it has attracted the majority of scientific researchers at home and abroad to invest tirelessly in the research of motion analysis technology. As an important branch of motion analysis technology, human motion analysis is also increasingly sought after by people. At present, great technological breakthroughs have been made in the motion analysis technology of rigid bodies, and a relatively complete technical theoretical system has also been established; However, the research on human motion, a typical non rigid body motion, is not very in-depth and needs further research.

References

1. Fujimoto, H., Oshima, Y., Ando, M., et al.: Dark matter Axion search with riNg Cavity Experiment DANCE: design and development of auxiliary cavity for simultaneous resonance of linear polarizations. arXiv e-prints (2021)
2. Luo, J.: Online design of green urban garden landscape based on machine learning and computer simulation technology. Environ. Technol. Innov. **24**(3), 101819 (2021)
3. Jiang, L.: Research on auxiliary methods of swimming training virtual simulation technology based on embedded computer. Microprocess. Microsyst. **82** (2021)
4. Chowdary, V., Srinath, D.R., Narendra, D.G., et al.: Design and simulation of robot hand for writing and correction assistant applications. Int. J. Intell. Unmanned Syst. (2021). ahead-of-print(ahead-of-print)
5. Su, J., Lou, J., Jiang, X.: Optimized design of aluminium bumper by impact test and computer simulation analysis. In: Journal of Physics: Conference Series, vol. 1952, no. 3, p. 032067 (2021)
6. Lin, Z.: Design of Colleges and Universities Mechanical Simulation System Based on Computer VR (2022)
7. Chen, Z., Lei, B., Qin, L., et al.: Computerized design, simulation of meshing and stress analysis of external helical gear drives based on critical control points. Energies **15** (2022)
8. Jeschke, S., Mueller-Fischer, M., Chentanez, N., et al.: Systems and methods for computer simulation of detailed waves for large-scale water simulation. US20210232733A1 (2021)
9. Chanoui, M.A., Bouganssa, I., Sbihi, M., et al.: Design and simulation of a median filter for a cubesat image processing application using an FPGA architecture (2022)
10. Langreck, J., Wong, H., Hernandez, A., et al.: Modeling and simulation of future capabilities with an automated computer-aided wargame. J. Defense Model. Simul. Appl. Methodol. Technol. **18**(4), 154851291987398 (2021)

Application of Artificial Intelligence Technology in Learning App Evelopment

Ping Xie[1,2(✉)], Thelma D. Palaoag[1], and Kailing Sun[1]

[1] University of the Cordilleras, Baguio, Philippines
314379984@qq.com, tdpalaoag@uc-bcf.edu.ph
[2] Xianyang Normal College, Xianyang 712000, Shaanxi, China

Abstract. Learning Learning APPs are designed and developed specifically for people with learning needs to learn relevant knowledge or skills. Nowadays, the integration of artificial intelligence technology into learning APPs has become a trend and a trend, and this article analyzes the currently popular learning APPs and deeply investigates the application of artificial intelligence in the development process of learning APPs. The article analyzes and discusses learning APPs from several aspects such as personalized learning, automatic tutoring, intelligent assessment and game strategy, etc. By analyzing the experience of different users and by analyzing the way of integrating APPs with artificial intelligence, the article gives a deeper understanding of the combination of learning APPs and artificial intelligence technology, and makes effective guidance for the development direction and function expansion of learning APPs, making Artificial intelligence applied to the design and development of learning APP becomes more intelligent and closer to users, so that parents and schools can see more educational possibilities, so that teachers can get richer resources, and so that students' learning will become more personalized and specific.

Keywords: learning app · application of AI · personalized learning · design and development

1 Introduction

The ultimate goal of education is to ensure inclusive and equitable quality education and to promote lifelong learning opportunities for all. Access to quality education is the foundation for improving people's lives and achieving sustainable development. Learning apps are currently an important part of the education sector, providing more people with better quality education, breaking time, geographical and economic constraints, and further promoting sustainable development of education for the benefit of society and humanity [1]. At present, there are many learning APPs in the market, such as: Homework Help, Ape Tutor, Zebra AI, Fluency, StudyTalk, Little Bear Art, etc. These APPs are more users in the market with better feedback, they all have a common feature: the development of the app needs the support of artificial intelligence technology.

© ICST Institute for Computer Sciences, Social Informatics and Telecommunications Engineering 2024
Published by Springer Nature Switzerland AG 2024. All Rights Reserved
Y. Zhang and N. Shah (Eds.): BigIoT-EDU 2023, LNICST 582, pp. 339–352, 2024.
https://doi.org/10.1007/978-3-031-63136-8_35

This paper focuses on the application of AI in the process of learning app design and development, mainly from different users and different learning apps, summarizes and analyzes the part of user experience that is closely related to AI, as well as the AI technology used in learning apps, so as to help users better choose the right app for themselves, and help designers to be more clear about the positioning of the app, and also hope to continue to do this part of the research in the future, to further promote the integration of AI technology into learning apps, optimize educational resources, and achieve "AI+ Education" [2].

An excellent learning app must use AI technology and combine digital technology, big data technology, etc., including personalized learning, automatic question and answer, voice recognition and other functions, such as: online human-computer dialogue, voice scoring, viewing records, etc., which must be the integration of learning app and artificial intelligence.

The users of learning apps are mainly divided into two types, students and teachers, students mainly look at the issue of course categories and resources, while teachers, more importantly, need the content, complexity and depth of the course [3]. The article will elaborate the application of AI related to the process of learning app development from the user needs, combined with AI technology. The research framework diagram is shown in: Fig. 1.

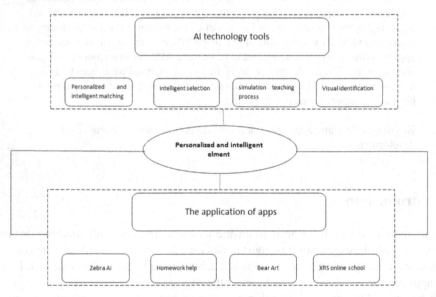

Fig. 1. Research Frame

Faced with the difficulties of information processing, more and more scholars are investing in research. The classification of information is the first solution proposed by scholars. By dividing similar information into the same field, people only need to select the field they need to view all information in that field. However, with the increasing number of information, classification is no longer sufficient to accurately classify all information, so search engines have proposed. Search engines summarize all information, which can more quickly and accurately classify information compared to classification methods [4]. When users clearly know their information needs, they only need to input them into the search engine to obtain a lot of relevant information. Search engines are more suitable when users are clear about their interests, but recommendation systems are more suitable when users are not clear about their interests and needs.

The application fields of recommendation systems involve various aspects, including shopping, social networking, short videos, and so on. This article will focus on the role of recommendation systems within the domain of application programming interface (API) recommendations. In recent years, with the emergence of the open source community, developers are willing to share their code on more platforms. When software features interact, developers begin to realize whether the same data or functionality can also be easily used by another software [5]. As a possible solution, API came into being. After the API has been widely promoted and used, it has received great support from many developers on many platforms. Currently, the website known to have the largest public access to APIs is Programmable Web, which has 22914 APIs up to now, and the number is continuously increasing [6]. However, for users, the huge number of APIs can lead to users being unable to find the best API for themselves.

2 Related Work

2.1 Recommended Algorithm Evaluation Method

In the process of implementing recommendation algorithms, it is often necessary to design some experiments to test the effectiveness of the algorithm and use some algorithm evaluation indicators to determine whether the recommended results meet expectations. This section will introduce commonly used experimental methods and some commonly used evaluation indicators for recommendation [7].

The online experiment is an experiment conducted after the recommendation system goes online. That is, the online experiment is mainly aimed at the recommendation system, and the final result is also made for the recommendation algorithm in a certain recommendation system [8].

(1) Experimental methods

AB testing is a classic online experimental method. The basic principle is to match different recommendation algorithms to different users and count their performance in the system. This performance can be based on user clicks on the system or user views on the system. The performance of the corresponding recommendation algorithm can be displayed through the performance of these different groups of users.

Figure 2 shows the flow of a simple AB test [9]. When a user enters the traffic distribution system and is uniformly assigned to different experimental groups, when the user performs some operations on the system, the system log will automatically record the user's operation behavior and store it in the log database [7, 10]. Due to the different operational behaviors of different users, if the system cannot resolve some non-standard behaviors of the user, it may have an impact on subsequent experimental data. Therefore, after the experiment is completed, it is necessary for the experimental personnel to sort out the user's behavior to remove some illegal behavior operations, leave behavioral data useful for the experimental evaluation, and generate an experimental report, Analyzing the user behavior data in the experimental report can determine the performance of the recommendation system under the current user batch test conditions [11]. The final performance of the system will undergo multiple experiments, and the average value of the performance will be taken as the test result of the online experiment of the system.

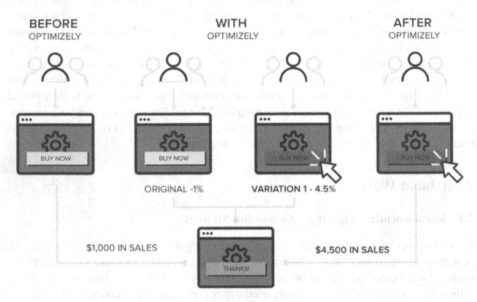

Fig. 2. AB Test Process

(2) Accuracy index

Accuracy indicators are commonly used in ranking prediction tasks in the recommendation field, mainly including accuracy, recall, and coverage. These indicators typically reflect the proportion of predicted data in the test set to determine whether the model can accurately make recommendations. Therefore, they are often used for recommendation algorithm tasks that require ranking prediction [12].

1) Accuracy

For user u, record R (u) as the recommended set data for the target user, and T (u) as the set of items that the user likes in the test set. Accuracy refers to the proportion of items recommended to the user that belong to the test set. The higher the proportion, the higher the recommendation accuracy, as shown in formula (1).

$$\text{Precision} = \frac{\sum_u |R(u) \cap T(u)|}{\sum_u |R(u)|} \tag{1}$$

2) Recall rate

For user u, record R (u) as the recommended set data for the target user, and T (u) as the set of items that the user likes in the test set. The recall rate is defined as the proportion of the test set in the items recommended to the user [13]. The higher the recall rate, the more accurate the items recommended to the user, as shown in formula (2).

$$Recall = \frac{\sum_u |R(u) \cap T(u)|}{\sum_u |T(u)|} \tag{2}$$

(3) Scoring indicators

Scoring indicators are commonly used in scoring prediction tasks in the recommendation field, mainly including mean absolute error (MAE) and root mean square error (RMSE). Due to the fact that scoring prediction is usually a specific numerical value, such indicators judge the accuracy of prediction by comparing predicted values with actual values, so they are widely used in scoring prediction and recommendation tasks.

For user u and item i, R. represents the user u's score for item i, and R represents the user u's score for item i predicted by the recommendation algorithm [14]. A smaller RMSE indicates a more accurate prediction, as shown in Eq. (3).

$$RMSE = \sqrt{\frac{1}{N} \sum_{u,i} \left(R_{u,i} - \hat{R}_{u,i} \right)^2} \tag{3}$$

2.2 Review of Literature

We make a comprehensive reference to several papers related to learning apps, including: user surveys of learning apps, including the development of learning apps, applications of learning apps, and papers related to AI app development, as Table 1 As shown in the table, the table analyzes and compares the information of these articles from the perspectives of the functions of learning apps in the current market, the development technology of apps, and the development of apps related to AI technology, so as to synthetically obtain the viewpoints of the papers [15].

3   Methodolgy

The article uses the survey method to understand several learning apps. The following criteria are used to screen learning apps including: number of users in the market, type of users, future development prospects, and subject categories. The survey includes: user experience, product services, learning reports, etc. Using comparative operations on data, including sorting, comparing, and summarizing, we quantitatively analyze these data from each category and discover the information needed to be elaborated in the article from the data.

We observed and interviewed different users' experiences with learning software at school, at home, at the park and at work, including parents and teachers around me, my friends, my students and children around me, etc. We chose 10 people in each different capacity, and interviewed 50 people in total, all of whom use different learning software,

Table 1. Literature review

TOPIC	CONTENT	SYNTHESIS
Based on the App Inventor2 App design and development of ancient Chinese poems	Mobile learning App application more and more widely, the user demand for the application of App in the individuation, differentiation	App Inventor2 are main tools in the development of App, the application of ancient Chinese poems App is to use the App Inventor2 design and development, to meet user demand for App application of ancient Chinese poems, and provide a reference for design and development of mobile learning App
Curriculum based on mobile terminal App design and development of the research	People's time showing the characteristics of fragmentation, and mobile devices is also closely related to people's life and learning, the effective integration of traditional education and Internet information technology, and has made remarkable achievements, has become the research emphasis in the process of modernization of education development	Current mobile terminal technology applied in the field of education is still relatively weak, as mobile terminal learning has received extensive attention of the society from all walks of life, and its application scope of development in the future will be further expanded
Based on the interest to learn oral English APP AI intelligence design and development of research	New semester and job hunting season is coming, many students and professionals, have a need to learn English, and this product is design for university students to launch a new oral English APP - new sound swim	Based on COVID - 19 during the outbreak of the "Internet + education" online learning mode as well as the students groups for oral English learning interest and employment demand, the module design, customized learning solutions, Al content in such aspects as the introduction of intelligent learning mode to make a certain innovation

Table 1. (*continued*)

TOPIC	CONTENT	SYNTHESIS
One's deceased father grind auxiliary application based on mobile terminal design and development	In this paper, in order to help ready to take an examination of grinding student to cope with the problem of recruitment of students information and test data, processing in one's deceased father grind preparation process of personalized questions, a questionnaire is designed	According to the 363 valid receipt, from many different colleges and different undergraduates, collecting on one's deceased father grind willingness, understanding of one's deceased father grind auxiliary APP and look forward to relevant information, on the basis of analysis of the obtained information, design the "home page" "information" "learning", "my" four pages, initially developed for each page "register/login" "calendar" "examination countdown" "one's deceased father grind common sense" dynamic "colleges" "politics news" "collection", and other functions
Mobile collaborative learning based on the theory of the unicom study APP design and implementation	On demand now for people online photography base course, mobile learning is user interaction of a single, such problems as lack of feedback learning process and learning results, based on unicom learning theory is proposed for this design method of mobile collaboration learning APP	By setting the function such as BBS, group collaboration, photography activities, strengthen students' learning motivation, improve teaching efficiency. Through to the various functional modules test results show that the mobile learn APP can meet the needs of teachers and learners
College students' innovative learning English APP design	This project is an innovative APP in learning English, American English learning through interpretation and analysis of the test examination skills to promote English learning ability and technology	Improve interest in English learning at the same time, combined with China's own culture background and market research results, to develop a different from market existing English learning software design of the APP

such as StudyTalk, Smart to, Zebra AI, Homework Help, etc. We qualitatively analyzed the experience of using intelligent learning APPs with different users' subjective experience, and analyzed different users' different needs for APPs to summarize the application characteristics and development direction of artificial intelligence in learning apps.

Application programming interface (API) refers to predefined interface programs that are required due to the different forms of combinations between different modules during software development. The emergence of APIs facilitates code redundancy in the programming process for developers. For some highly repetitive functions, it is only necessary to call APIs to implement them. In order to facilitate the invocation of different functional APIs by various developers, the features of APIs are often subdivided into more complex and complex features. On the one hand, it is indeed convenient to use, and on the other hand, searching for APIs also makes finding the most suitable API a challenge. Programmable Web is a website that integrates the vast majority of APIs on the market. Currently, the number of APIs included on this website has exceeded 15000, and the information on APIs is relatively complete, including the creation time, label, profile, and company affiliation of the API. However, there is currently no public dataset, so it is necessary to crawl the API data of this website.

In terms of the selection of crawler technology, this article adopts the form of distributed crawler. Compared to other forms of crawler, the distributed crawler method distributes the crawler task on multiple hosts, and under the same crawler task, the efficiency of the distributed crawler will be faster. The overall architecture process of the distributed crawler is shown in Fig. 3.

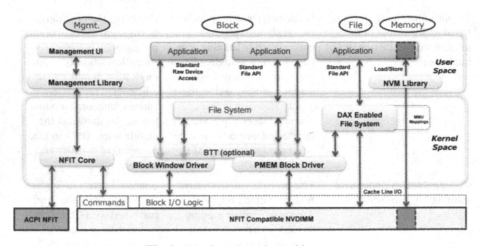

Fig. 3. Distributed crawler architecture

Due to the fact that the crawler task is on different hosts, when a network failure occurs on one of the hosts, it will not affect the crawling of the other hosts, effectively mitigating the need to re crawl due to interruptions to the crawler due to other reasons such as the network during the crawling process.

There are various ways to combine models, such as adding the regularization term of user relationships and the regularization term of API relationships to the LFM loss function at the same time. This method results in a longer loss function, and due to the many parameters involved, different parameter combinations can have a certain impact on the final training results of the model. Another way of combining is in the form of linear combinations. This form was once used in the paper proposed by Zheng et al. The author combined User based CF and Item based CF in the form of linear combination to form a new algorithm and named it Web Service Recommendation (WSRec). Through practical verification, it is shown that this algorithm significantly improves the accuracy of recommendations, and has become a relatively classic recommendation algorithm.

4 Results and Discussion

4.1 Results

Surveys information is summarized as follows: Table 2, the table from p the survey of learning APPs, shows the statistics of different groups of people, different positioning of learning APPs, integration with AI, and the number of learning APP users installed. In the survey, we counted various different types of APPs separately, selected the ones with better user experience and evaluation according to the number of user downloads, and summarized and analyzed them to emphasize the necessity of deep integration of APPs with AI. By describing the integration positioning and usage of different learning APPs with AI technology, it can be seen that the application of AI technology in learning APPs is crucial.

Through observation and interviews, the specific information is summarized as follows: Table 3, the table elaborates different user experiences of each of them for using learning apps from different users, and summarizes where the app needs to be improved and strengthened, all of which are related to AI in large and small ways, and together with Table 1, they answer the article needs to Some of the questions that need to be elaborated.

Through literature review, surveys, observations and interviews, we can know that , Artificial intelligence technology applied to learning apps mainly includes the following aspects: personalized learning, automated tutoring, intelligent assessment, simulation and gamification platforms, and educational decision making, etc. It is not an exaggeration to say that AI has changed the education industry, allowing traditional thinking to be combined with cutting-edge technology, and the feasibility of tailoring education to the needs of the students has been dramatically improved.

a. Personalized learning.

Collecting student's learning data, predicting students' future performance, and intelligently recommending the most suitable content for students, ultimately improving learning results efficiently and significantly.

b. Automated Tutoring and Answer. Questions

It has also become a supplement to face-to-face teaching by teachers. From big data evolution to artificial intelligence, the development of voice recognition, image recognition, handwriting recognition, speech analysis and other technologies make

Table 2. The integration of learning apps and AI

Serial number	Learning App	locate	Integration with artificial intelligence	Number of user installations (times)
1	English Fun Dubbing	Original videos, huge amount of material, professional guidance, fun, convenient and useful language learning platform	Speech recognition, smart scoring, smart word book, smart customization	100 million
2	fluency	A fun and effective English speaking learning software for children, adults and professional English speakers	Personalization, adaptive learning, AI English teachers, speaking assessments	400 million
3	Zebra AI	An all-round ability development platform for loving children aged 3–8	Virtual reality, personalized learning, intelligent assessment, smart interaction	100 million
4	Learning Pass	Course learning built on microservices architecture, providing a one-stop learning and working environment	Data statistics, school monitoring, personalized services	300 million
5	homework helper	Efficient and smart learning tutoring app to solve learning problems that you won't do during the tutoring process	Image recognition technology, intelligent recommendations	3.1 billion
6	ape tutoring	Online online class platform, teacher-student interaction, post-class Q&A	Virtual reality, personalized learning, intelligent assessment, smart interaction	100 million

Table 3. Learning app users' observation interview

1	Yang*	4 years old, middle kindergarten class, user of learning apps for EYFS (Dr. Panda Teacher Literacy, Baby Bus, Companion Fish Children's English)	It was refreshing to use and there was a lot to learn, including numbers, Chinese characters and life lessons	Designers should be more attentive to young children's use of electronics: time management for young children, smart operation, etc.
2	Zhang**	7 year old, 1st grade elementary school student, English, math, reading, art learning app user (VIPKID, Ape Tutor, Little Bear Art, Little Leaf Chaperone)	Although the lessons are interesting, I still need my parents to accompany me in thelessons	The child's self-awareness requirements require features such as permission settings and voice recognition in the app
3	Cao**	19 years old, current college student, professional learning app user (StudyTalk, Know, Fluent, etc.)	Currently many of the courses in the app that I want to self-study are paid for, and although the school teachers will give us some free learning opportunities, it still feels like there is a lack of resources	There are more paid courses on the market, and if you want to meet the requirement of free self-study, you can do so through school-enterprise cooperation and management of different levels of users
4	Zhang*	39 years old, working for a biotech company, tutoring kids with homework related learning app users (Box Wizard, Fun Dub, Homework Help, etc.)	Some apps are not stable enough, and some apps do not have features like smart scoring that can affect the experience	With AI incorporated into the app, both stats, and scoring only, can be well addressed
5	Yan**	48 years old, working at Xianyang Normal College, teaching-related learning app user (StudyTalk, Know, MU)	The level of personalization of learning apps still does not meet the needs of students with different learning situations	Artificial intelligence can automatically search for student learning data, predict learning, and intelligently recommend learning content

it possible for machines to simulate people to answer questions and do services, and there will be more and more applications of this kind.

With the development of information construction and artificial intelligence, big data, text recognition, speech recognition, and semantic recognition make the scale of automatic correction and personalized feedback towards reality. How to use artificial intelligence to reduce the pressure of correction and achieve large-scale yet personalized feedback on homework is an important attack point for future education, and a market that many companies at home and abroad are looking at.

c. Simulation and gamification strategies

Simulation and gamification is also one of the modern education concepts The future of education will have to learn from the entertainment industry how to engage users on a large scale, while improving quality and value. Platform applications of technology will include virtual reality, computer vision, machine learning, etc.

d. Educational Decision Making.

Chinese students have a high rate of poor educational decision making, especially when it comes to choosing a college school as well as a major. According to some data, 70% of students regret their choice of majors. If massive data can be collected to provide a basis for decision making, AI algorithms can help students find the optimal theoretical path to a more suitable school and major.

Finally, education can be divided into four categories: early childhood education, K12, higher education, and vocational education. After entering the AI era, the R&D threshold for early childhood education has undoubtedly increased again. The threshold of children's robots is not in the technical level, but in the content, interaction methods.

As we can see from the above, learning apps will allow students to have access to real-time feedback and automated tutoring; parents will be able to see their children's real-time learning and clearer career prospects in a convenient and affordable way; teachers will be able to harvest richer teaching resources and personalized student learning data to tailor their teaching to their needs; schools will be able to provide high-quality education; and governments will have an easier time providing affordable and more balanced education for all.

4.2 Discussion

The importance of artificial intelligence for learning apps has been self-evident, but if AI is to serve learning apps better, there is a need to strengthen the humanistic approach to AI technology. We need to know and care about the nature of AI, ultimately, the data becomes the direct production of the learner's data, in AI education is the "raw material" of the algorithm, to affirm the existence of the value of data, but at the same time, we should pay attention to the source of data production is the user, only by investing in emotion, can the data play the most value, into the human feelings The AI is what the user wants most, that is, the AI learning APP must be to maintain human autonomy.

We know that the AI into education technology are photo search, layered scheduling, oral assessment, homework review, learning effect test, error analysis and so on. These things, indeed, bring convenience and improve efficiency to parents and teachers, and schools, teachers and parents are willing to pay the financial cost for this. However, the application of AI technology in artificial intelligence education from the technical level of depth, is relatively shallow, only the periphery of some of the more standardized aspects of education, to achieve a deep level of artificial intelligence applications, still need the joint efforts of the government, enterprises, schools and other sectors of society.

Compared to the real artificial intelligence, AI education is mainly 2C, we can also call it pseudo-artificial intelligence education. Because of this, we are more optimistic about it, because it has a good market and future development prospects, there are already many governments, enterprises and individuals invested in the field of AI education, there is a market and investment, I believe that the future AI+ learning APP will be better and better, more and more recognized by more and more people.

5 Conclusion

The importance of artificial intelligence for learning apps has been self-evident, but if AI is to serve learning apps better, there is a need to strengthen the humanistic approach to AI technology. We need to know and care about the nature of AI, ultimately, the data becomes the direct production of the learner's data, in AI education is the "raw material" of the algorithm, to affirm the existence of the value of data, but at the same time, we should pay attention to the source of data production is the user, only by investing in emotion, can the data play the most value, into the human feelings The AI is what the user wants most, that is, the AI learning APP must be to maintain human autonomy.

References

1. Lee, Z.Y., Karim, M.E., Ngui, K.: Deep learning artificial intelligence and the law of causation: application, challenges and solutions. Inf. Commun. Technol. Law **30**(3), 255–282 (2021)
2. Khanagar, S.B., Vishwanathaiah, S., Naik, S., et al.: Application and performance of artificial intelligence technology in forensic odontology - a systematic review. Legal Med. **48**, 101826 (2021)
3. Wang, S.: Application of artificial intelligence in university sports risk recognition and identification. J. Intell. Fuzzy Syst. Appl. Eng. Technol. **40**(2), 3361–3372 (2021)
4. Huang, N., Kong, D.: Research on the application of children's reading analysis based on artificial intelligence-take small "raccoon reading" and "Jiao Jiao reading" as examples. J. Phys. Conf. Ser. **1848**(1), 012121 (5pp) (2021)
5. Nazari, N., Shabbir, M., Setiawan, R.: Application of Artificial Intelligence powered digital writing assistant in higher education: randomized controlled trial. Heliyon **7**(5), e07014 (2021)
6. Nia, B.B., Khorrami, M., Farahbakhsh, I., et al.: Application of artificial intelligence and machine learning in desalination: a bibliometric and review study (2021)
7. Fu, X., Krishna, K.L., Sabitha, R.: Artificial intelligence applications with e-learning system for china's higher education platform. J. Interconnection Netw. **22**, 2143016 (2021)
8. Song, Y., Zhao, Z., Zheng, Y., et al.: Investigation and application of high-efficiency network fracturing technology for deep shale gas in the Southern Sichuan Basin. ACS Omega **7**(16), 14276–14282 (2022)
9. Chdil, O., Bikerouin, M., Balli, M., et al.: New horizons in magnetic refrigeration using artificial intelligence (2023)
10. Sun, H.: Research on the application of artificial intelligence technology and cloud computing in smart elderly care information platform (2021)
11. Hou, A.: The practical application of artificial intelligence technology in electronic communication. In: Atiquzzaman, M., Yen, N., Xu, Z. (eds.) BDCPS 2020, vol. 1303, pp. 99–105. Springer, Singapore (2021). https://doi.org/10.1007/978-981-33-4572-0_15
12. Chen, L.: Application of artificial intelligence technology in personalized online teaching under the background of big data. J. Phys. Conf. Ser. **1744**(4), 042208 (2021)

13. Yang, X., Li, H., Ni, L., et al.: Application of artificial intelligence in precision marketing. J. Organ. End User Comput. **33**(4), 209–219 (2021)
14. Ji, J., He, Y.: Application of artificial intelligence in computer network technology. J. Phys. Conf. Ser. **1881**(3), 032073 (5pp) (2021)
15. Yu, L., Shi, Y., Cai, N.: Application and potential of the artificial intelligence technology - ScienceDirect. In: Hybrid Systems and Multi-Energy Networks for the Future Energy Internet, pp. 217–234 (2021)

The Integration Path of AI Technology and Inclusive Preschool Education Quality

Yufang Huang[(⊠)] and Xingping Lan

Department of Preschool Education, Xi'an Fanyi University, Xi'an 710000, China
`573361441@qq.com`

Abstract. Since the implementation of the first three-year action plan for preschool education in 2011, inclusive private kindergartens have developed rapidly. Since its emergence, inclusive kindergartens have been hotly debated in the field of preschool education. However, there is not much research on the educational quality and quality assurance of inclusive kindergartens in China, and most of the research objects are relatively single, either targeting a specific system, or only studying inclusive kindergartens in the region, or only targeting private or rural inclusive kindergartens. There are still many problems in the integration of AI tech and inclusive preschool education, which is difficult to support the effective amelioration of the quality of preschool education. On account of this, this paper first analyses the development status and problems of inclusive preschool education, then studies the necessity and path of the integration of AI tech and inclusive preschool education quality, and finally gives the form and specific strategies of the integration of AI tech and inclusive preschool education quality.

Keywords: Integration Path · AI Tech · Inclusive Preschool Education

1 Introduction

"Generalized System of Preferences (GSP) was originally a tariff system that originated in international trade, referring to" non discriminatory and non reciprocal preferential tariff policies adopted by developed countries when importing manufactured and semi-finished products from developing countries or regions. ". Over time, inclusivity has gradually been applied to the field of education. It is widely believed in the academic community that "inclusivity" is essentially the extension and refinement of educational equity in the new social environment. "Inclusiveness" means universality, fairness, and preference [1]. In the sense of preschool education, "inclusiveness" is reflected in the following aspects: First, expanding the total amount of educational resources while ensuring quality. Ensure equal opportunities for school-age children throughout society to enjoy high-quality preschool education as much as possible; The second is government regulation [2]. The government, through the regulation and control of preschool education resources, seeks a balance between developed and underdeveloped regions, cities and rural areas, public and private preschool education to narrow the gap. However, it is not a mechanical balance like peak shaving and valley filling, but based on and

Y. Zhang and N. Shah (Eds.): BigIoT-EDU 2023, LNICST 582, pp. 353–363, 2024.
https://doi.org/10.1007/978-3-031-63136-8_36

premised on ensuring quality. It can be seen that "inclusive" also reflects the universality and parity advantages of preschool education. Extensiveness refers to the universality of service objects, that is, inclusive preschool education is aimed at school-age children in the whole society; Parity refers to the moderate or preferential admission fees, but it does not mean that the low fees reduce the quality of the park.

With the iterative progress and maturity of computer tech, it has been widely and deeply studied and popularized in many fields, especially the utilization of computer tech represented by AI in the field of inclusive preschool education, which greatly accelerates the quality of inclusive preschool education [3]. AI tech mainly relies on the simulation of human behavior to bring innovation and change to many industries in theory, method and tech. With the continuous expansion of AI tech and function, it has been widely used in many fields as shown in Fig. 1, which greatly facilitates people's life and production process [4]. At present, the integration of AI tech and preschool education is developing in the direction of intelligence, which makes the education represented by inclusive preschool education progress and develops rapidly in the direction of intelligence and diversification.

There are still many problems in the integration of AI tech and inclusive preschool education, which are mainly manifested in the lack of in-depth integration of AI tech and preschool education, and the relevant guarantee conditions and measures are still not in place, which is difficult to support the effective amelioration of the quality of preschool education [4]. Secondly, the information literacy of preschool education teachers is generally low, and it is difficult to give full play to the function and value of AI tech. In view of the common problems in preschool education, such as the shortage of teaching materials and students' lack of interest in learning, the use of AI tech can create a more specific sense of experience and interactive teaching atmosphere, optimize the learning conditions of inclusive preschool education, and comprehensively ameliorate students' comprehensive quality from the aspects of language, art and knowledge literacy [5].

In addition, the integration of AI and inclusive preschool education is a complex system engineering, which needs to be adjusted from the design, management and operation levels to accelerate the quality and efficiency of the integration [6]. As an emerging tech with revolutionary influence, AI tech is playing an important role in the field of education, which can effectively lead the reform and innovation of preschool education. Inclusive preschool education as an important measure to accelerate the balanced development of education, its teaching quality is not only related to the fairness of education, but also an important representation of the construction level of modern education public service system. Therefore, it is of great practical value to study the path of the integration of AI tech and inclusive preschool education quality.

2 The Current Situation and Problems of Inclusive Preschool Education

2.1 The Development of Inclusive Preschool Education

This article believes that the so-called inclusive preschool education refers to inclusive preschool education, which uses government regulation as a means, and collects nursery and accommodation fees at government guidance prices as a method to expand the

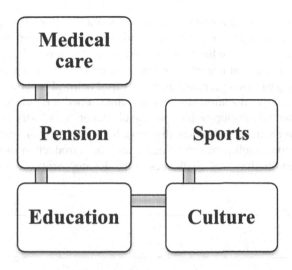

Fig. 1. Utilization fields of AI tech

total amount of preschool education resources and achieve fair distribution of preschool education. Inclusive kindergartens include two types: one is a public kindergarten established by the education department or other departments or collectives, and the other is a inclusive private kindergarten. In addition, based on the needs of the research object of this article, the author distinguishes between inclusive kindergartens and inclusive private kindergartens. Inclusive private kindergartens refer to inclusive kindergartens run by private forces, and inclusive private kindergartens belong to inclusive kindergartens [7]. Through the above conceptual analysis, it can be seen that inclusive preschool education has the following characteristics: (1) a strict and complete approval process. The kindergarten has passed the preliminary review by the municipal education administrative department and the final review by the education department. It has established a kindergarten with complete certificates and passed the annual inspection and annual review, and has behaved appropriately and maintained high-quality education quality. (2) Reasonable fees. Under the guidance of the government, each district/county uniformly sets the price for its own jurisdiction based on the economic situation, the average price level of kindergarten care and education fees, costs, and other realistic conditions. The pricing of inclusive kindergarten care and education fees in more developed urban areas can be appropriately raised based on the specific situation, but the upward float standard should not exceed half of the care and education fees. After pricing, it should be reported to the municipal education, price, finance bureau, and other departments for filing and implementation. (3) Standardization of financial and personnel management. Comply with the national financial and financial policies, and do not collect sponsorship fees or donation fees from student families that are not priced in disguised form [8]. Sign personnel contracts according to law, and purchase social insurance and provident fund for teaching and administrative staff according to law.

With the progress of society and the continuous amelioration of people's living standards, all walks of life pay more and more attention to the investment in education, especially the parents' preschool education for children, which makes the scale of preschool education institutions expanding [9]. The market size and growth of preschool education institutions in the past seven years are shown in Fig. 2 below. From the Figure, the quantity scale of preschool education structure has maintained a rapid expansion speed in recent years. After the development of preschool education industry in recent years, its quantity scale has entered a stable growth period. In the Internet era, with the loading and assistance of various intelligent technologies, and the introduction of various policies, it brings new opportunities and challenges to the development of preschool education industry.

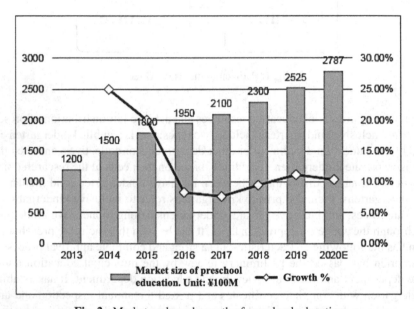

Fig. 2. Market scale and growth of preschool education

2.2 Problems in Inclusive Preschool Education

At present, with the increase of the number of preschool children, the phenomenon of difficult and expensive entrance for children of age is more prominent and common, which greatly aggravates the burden of parents. There is still a great space for optimization of the structure stability and the standardization of preschool education industry [10]. Secondly, the standard and standard of inclusive preschool education is not detailed enough to guide the development of preschool education effectively. Especially under the modern information condition, how to guide the integration of preschool education and information platform and carrier becomes the blank of standardized management and operation. In addition, the level of teachers in inclusive preschool education institutions is low, especially the poor information literacy, so it is difficult to effectively apply modern teaching carriers and platforms to better accelerate the professional, professional and diversified development of preschool education quality [11].

At the educational content level of inclusive preschool education, the current teaching content has not been effectively optimized according to the characteristics of school-age students, resulting in uneven teaching materials and teaching content. Some teaching methods and teaching contents that are not suitable for children's development still exist in the development of inclusive preschool education. Therefore, inclusive preschool education institutions still need to be ameliorated systematically; comprehensively and scientifically to ameliorate the teaching quality and connotation, so as to better guarantee the teaching quality [12].

With the development of basic scientific and technological environments such as big data, the Internet, and cloud computing, the continuous expansion of the total amount of knowledge not only makes existing knowledge and skills face upgrading, but also makes significant changes in the structure of knowledge and skills that people need to master. In any future industry, cultivating a single knowledge and skill structure cannot meet the needs of the intelligent era, and it also violates the development trend of intelligent education. The author learned from face-to-face interviews with relevant leaders and front-line teachers of preschool education in the surveyed schools that there are many shortcomings in the cultivation of preschool education professionals, which is even more inconsistent in the context of smart education. For example, the current goal of cultivating pre-school education professionals is relatively single, and most of them are positioned to enable students to master knowledge and skills such as early childhood care and teaching [13]. The scope of their careers is also concentrated on caregivers and teachers in early childhood education institutions, resulting in a lack of competitiveness for students in the future. Currently, too much emphasis is placed on artistic skills such as playing, jumping, and painting, while ignoring the cultivation of students' digital literacy, technological innovation, application, and scientific literacy, which may lead to the inability of talents trained in preschool education to meet the needs of the diversified preschool education market in the future. The curriculum content of preschool education majors is still dominated by public basic courses and professional skills courses [14]. At the same time, many preschool education majors offer redundant and difficult curriculum content, which is divorced from the actual life of students. The continued use of teaching methods makes it difficult to reflect students' participation in the teaching process. Due to the limitations of external conditions such as technology, the current teaching evaluation of preschool education majors generally occurs after teaching and learning. It pays too much attention to students' current academic performance and ignores the entire learning process of students. The evaluation dimension is single and lagging [15]. With the support of intelligent education concepts and technology, these demands can be responded to to to a certain extent.

3   The Integration of AI Tech and Inclusive Preschool Education Quality

3.1   The Necessity of Integrating AI Tech with Inclusive Preschool Education Quality

The development of science and technology has changed people's lifestyles, concepts, and ways of thinking. People have become accustomed to dealing with electronic products and using digital technology to collect and manage information. With the development of artificial intelligence and information technology, people with only a single knowledge and skill will face elimination. On the contrary, with the rise and development of intelligent education, intelligent talents with good value orientation and high thinking quality and strong thinking ability will be increasingly favored. Many kindergartens and early childhood education institutions have opened courses such as Lego robotics and early childhood programming, emphasizing that young children should be more hands-on while using their brains, emphasizing the "integration of theory and practice", and the curriculum content is more diversified, integrated, and enlightening in science, paying more attention to the cultivation of scientific qualities and innovative abilities.

In addition, too much emphasis is placed on the teaching of theoretical knowledge in the context of interdisciplinary courses, with emphasis on skills such as piano, chess, calligraphy, painting, and playing, as well as jumping and playing. Figure 3 shows the curriculum architecture of the surveyed school.

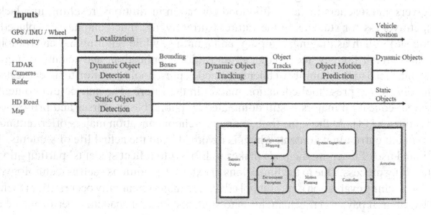

Fig. 3. Curriculum architecture

Through the above research and analysis, it is found that intelligent education brings new opportunities to the field of preschool education. In the future, the products of online and offline early childhood education will be extremely popular. To provide a rich multimedia resource database and online course editing environment, not only technical talents but also content oriented talents are needed. The development of technology has changed the industry pattern, while providing new employment opportunities, creating a new talent demand gap. Vocational colleges and pre-school education majors need to base their talent cultivation goals on the actual situation of the university, Formulate talent cultivation goals and programs that meet the needs of the local preschool education market, rather than being uniform. Smart education puts forward new requirements for the cultivation of preschool education professionals.

The integration of artificial intelligence technology and inclusive preschool education can effectively improve the imbalance of educational resources, optimize the content and form of preschool education, and help inclusive preschool education move towards rationality. Aiming at the problems and shortcomings in the quality of inclusive preschool education in the current information and intelligent environment, the use of artificial intelligence technology can effectively combine market demand and policy guidance to enhance the strength of preschool education and better meet the practical requirements for improving the quality of preschool education. In addition, the integration of artificial intelligence technology and inclusive preschool education can make teaching content more targeted, match and optimize the growth characteristics of school-age children, thereby helping students teach according to their aptitude. Artificial intelligence technology can also become the technical card and symbol of educational quality for inclusive preschool education institutions, helping them establish a brand image and better accelerate the development of inclusive preschool education.

3.2 Utilization Value of AI Tech in Inclusive Preschool Education

First of all, as an important function module of AI tech in preschool education; logical reasoning is a relatively long-lasting field of AI tech utilization research. Through automatic programming, it can realize the description of different purposes and realize the automatic correction and development of the system. Secondly, the expert AI expert system uses a lot of expertise and experience for reasoning and judgment to simulate the decision-making process of education experts in order to solve complex problems. Its structure is shown in Fig. 4 below.

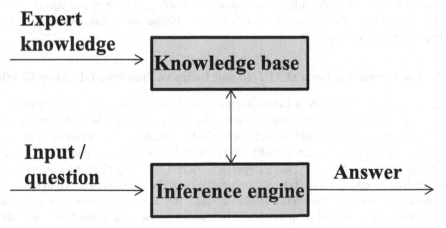

Fig. 4. Functional architecture of AI expert system

In addition, AI expert system can effectively solve the problems of interpretation, prediction, diagnosis, design, planning, monitoring, repair, guidance and control in inclusive preschool education.

In carrying out the integration and application of artificial intelligence technology and kindergarten education activities, the "Learning and Development Guide for Children Aged 3–6" points out that education activities should comply with the laws and learning characteristics of children's physical and mental development, advocate the harmonious development of children's physical and mental health, and respect individual differences in children's development. This clarifies the dominant position of children in early childhood education activities, and the role of teachers as guides and leaders. The integrated application of artificial intelligence technology and kindergarten education activities should involve both teachers and young children, and the role of teachers in activities should be a guide and leader, Is a "guide" for young children "From this perspective, paying attention to the needs of each child is an important issue that must be addressed in preschool education during the application of artificial intelligence technology. From the perspective of educational theory, each child has certain personalized characteristics, so in the process of integrating artificial intelligence technology with preschool education, we must pay attention to the needs of young children. Specifically, artificial intelligence technology can address the different needs of learners." To provide reasonable learning methods for different personalized situations, such as the level of thinking ability, learning ability, understanding ability, and learning interest points. In other words, the greatest value of artificial intelligence technology lies in mobilizing the learning enthusiasm and initiative of young children. Therefore, in the process of integrating artificial intelligence technology and preschool education practice, educators must not blindly pursue high-tech and deviate from the center of education work - young children. Young children should always be considered as the main position for all educational and teaching work, and artificial intelligence technology should be flexibly introduced based on their learning characteristics, information receiving ability, and information receiving level, in combination with the personalized needs of different young children. Through artificial intelligence technology, children can absorb knowledge, expand their abilities, inspire intelligence, cultivate awareness, and assist in their comprehensive development.

3.3 The Integration Form of AI Tech and Inclusive Preschool Education Quality

The integration of AI tech and inclusive preschool education quality mainly includes education robot, autonomous online learning platform and automatic evaluation system. Among them, as the assistant of preschool teachers, educational robot can assist teachers in teaching, and ameliorate the quality of preschool education in content, process and teaching guidance. Secondly, the independent online teaching platform can carry out personalized teaching for the typical characteristics of the students of the right age, so as to guide the students to constantly ameliorate their initiative and enthusiasm, especially for the thinking ability of the pre-school students to develop the pre-school curriculum and foster their emotions. In addition, the automatic evaluation system can evaluate the quality of inclusive preschool education, evaluate and feedback the activities of preschool education in real time, help teachers optimize the effect and ameliorate the quality of inclusive preschool education.

4 Strategies for the Integration of AI Tech and Inclusive Preschool Education Quality

4.1 A.Driving Factors of Deep Integration of AI Tech and Inclusive Preschool Education

The deep integration of AI tech and inclusive preschool education is the result of the highlight of the nature of education, the remodeling of education structure, the balance of educational resources and the increase of educational opportunities. Among them, in the aspect of highlighting the essence of education, the deep integration of AI and preschool education is to return to the essence of education in the aspect of humanistic spirit, and its ultimate goal is to serve students. Secondly, in the reconstruction of the education structure, AI tech has a huge impact on the preschool education structure, enriching the teaching resources from the internal and external aspects, promoting the co construction and sharing of resources, and transforming to the intelligent education mode.

In addition, at the level of balanced educational resources, inclusive preschool education has been facing the dilemma of insufficient resources for a long time. The integration of AI tech and preschool education is conducive to promoting the balance of educational resources, realizing the co construction and sharing of high-quality educational resources, covering all teaching actors and running through the whole process of teaching. In the increasing level of educational opportunities, AI tech information space makes educational resources more sufficient, and teachers' teaching potential is maximized and liberated. In the open level of education ecosystem, AI tech organically connects teachers, school-age students and learning environment, and accelerates inclusive preschool teaching to develop in the direction of personalization, accuracy and intelligence.

4.2 A.Strategies for the Integration of AI Tech and Inclusive Preschool Education Quality

First of all, at the level of government and education administrative agencies, it should further refine the utilization standards and planning of information tech, ameliorate relevant laws and regulations, and ensure the healthy development of inclusive preschool education quality. Secondly, it is necessary to further ameliorate teachers' information literacy, so as to develop more teaching content matching with AI environment and acceptance of school-age students, and return to the physical and mental development of preschool students. In addition, it is necessary to ameliorate the campus AI infrastructure, create AI learning atmosphere, establish and ameliorate the supervision mechanism in the utilization of AI education, clarify the positioning of teachers, and reasonably intervene in the value of AI tech in inclusive preschool education quality integration. Finally, it should update the concept of education and teaching, and pay attention to the dynamic and interaction in the teaching process, and it should pay attention to the dynamic and diversified teaching evaluation, and establish a scientific and efficient management system.

Infrastructure is the foundation and prerequisite for carrying out various types of education and teaching work. In terms of the integration and application of artificial intelligence technology and kindergarten educational activities, the most important thing for kindergartens is to do a good job in supporting the construction of infrastructure, as well as the corresponding equipment, network software, computers, AI equipment, etc. for the application of artificial intelligence technology. All of these require the kindergartens to spend corresponding financial and material resources to achieve. Therefore, kindergartens must attach importance to the allocation of resources related to the integration of artificial intelligence technology and kindergarten education activities, give full play to the advantages of multiple resources such as the kindergarten itself, the government, and society, and do a good job in supporting the construction and purchase of infrastructure related to artificial intelligence technology, providing effective protection for kindergarten to carry out the integration of artificial intelligence technology and kindergarten education activities. Only in this way can we make better use of artificial intelligence technology to maximize the effectiveness of early childhood education.

5   Conclusion

In summary, as an emerging tech with revolutionary influence, AI tech is playing an important role in the field of education, which can effectively lead the reform and innovation of preschool education. This paper analyzes the necessity of the integration of AI tech and inclusive preschool education quality through the research on the development status and problems of inclusive preschool education. Through the analysis of the path of the integration of AI tech and inclusive preschool education quality, this paper studies the form of the integration of AI tech and inclusive preschool education quality. Through the research on the strategy of the integration of AI tech and inclusive preschool education quality, this paper analyzes the driving factors of the deep integration of AI tech and inclusive preschool education.

Acknowledgments. Research on the current situation of Inclusive Preschool Educational Resources and Effective Expansion Countermeasures in Shanxi Province.

References

1. Ran, F.: Research on the integration of new media technology and ideological and political education teaching (2021)
2. Fang, G.: Research on the integration design of algorithm teaching and mathematics curriculum under information technology. In: Jan, M.A., Khan, F. (eds.) BigIoT-EDU 2022, vol. 466, pp. 331–343. Springer, Cham (2023). https://doi.org/10.1007/978-3-031-23947-2_36
3. Sun, L.: Research on the integration model of information technology and agricultural college students' ideological and political theory course teaching. J. Phys. Conf. Ser. **1744**(3), 032153 (2021)

4. Dong, X., Qin, Z.: Research on the Integration of the new generation of information technology into the curriculum system of business education (2022)
5. Megapanou, N.: Preschool teachers' views on the outcomes of preschool inclusive education for students with special educational needs and typically developing students. Open Access Libr. J. **9**(3), 1–17 (2022)
6. Palla, L., Roth, A.C.V.: Inclusive ideals and special educational tools in and out of tact: didactical voices on teaching in language and communication in Swedish early childhood education. Int. J. Early Years Educ. **30**(2), 387–402 (2022)
7. Khlevnoy, O.V., Kharyshyn, D., Nazarovets, O.: Problem issues of evacuation time calculation during fires in preschool and secondary education institutions with inclusive groups. Fire Saf. **37**, 72–76 (2021)
8. Bulut, A.: Metaphoric perceptions of preschool teachers towards inclusive education. Acta Educationis Generalis **11**(2), 112–128 (2021)
9. Ge, H., Li, B., Tang, D., et al.: Research on digital inclusive finance promoting the integration of rural three-industry. IJERPH **19**, 3363 (2022)
10. Tang, Z., Liu, P.H., Peng, S.Y., et al.: Research on the construction of "theory and practice integration" professional classroom based on information technology (2021)
11. Zhou, X., Tsai, C.W.: Handbook of research on digital content, mobile learning, and technology integration models in teacher education. Int. J. Technol. Hum. Interact. (1), 17 (2021)
12. Wang, D.J., Guo, J.: The research on the test technology of ammunition-feed system based on the integration of shooting simulation and driving simulation. J. Phys. Conf. Ser. **1721**(1), 012047 (8pp) (2021)
13. Zhang, H., Meng, F., Wang, G., et al.: Research on the automation integration terminal of the education management platform based on big data analysis. Adv. Data Sci. Adapt. Anal. Theory Appl. (1/2), 14 (2022)
14. Han, T., Cao, Z., Zhao, X., et al.: Research on the implementation path of "specialty and innovation integration" course in higher vocational colleges (2021)
15. Sorsdahl, K., Naledi, T., Lund, C., et al.: Integration of mental health counselling into chronic disease services at the primary health care level: Formative research on dedicated versus designated strategies in the Western Cape, South Africa. J. Health Serv. Res. Policy **26**(3), 135581962095423 (2021)

Artificial Intelligence Lyric Creation Based on Natural Language Processing

Youqian Zhong[1,2](✉)

[1] Jinan University, Guangzhou 510632, China
yauhin@163.com
[2] School of Liberature, Jinan University, No. 601, West Huangpu Avenue, Guangzhou, Guangdong, China

Abstract. As an emerging intelligent algorithm, natural language processing has many advantages and has been widely used. In terms of songwriting, the automatic speech synthesis technology based on the speech model has been greatly developed, and it has been applied on a large-scale in real life. From the perspective of text generation, this paper deeply discusses the concept, application field and technical principles of natural language processing, and deeply analyzes the basic theories of RNN and LSTM.

Keyword: natural language processing · artificial intelligence · lyric creation

1 Introduction

With the continuous development of artificial intelligence technology, intelligence is the trend of development in today's society, and the application of intelligence has also penetrated into all aspects. Such as human-computer interaction, human-computer chess playing, A I word writing and so on. With the rapid development of intelligent technology, the art of artificial intelligence and lyrics is more widely and profound. On the Internet, AI words are being produced more and more, for example, in the talent show "The Voice of China", She also promotes the A I word production of the startup company. The rise of artificial intelligence has had a great influence on the traditional music industry, and the lyrics and writing of artificial intelligence has also become a hot topic of people research. This paper takes the lyric production of artificial intelligence as a hot topic and expounds its application in natural language processing.

Music based on artificial intelligence can accelerate the creation and save a lot of time and energy. In the past, when the composer composed the music, the composer usually wrote the editor's score first, then copied the editor's score into several parts, and then the band rehearsed it. In this way, the composer spends not only a lot of time and effort in writing, but also in tone and drawing. During rehearsals, the composer repeatedly revised the score until a satisfactory result. At the same time, musical works and songcreation

Y. Zhang and N. Shah (Eds.): BigIoT-EDU 2023, LNICST 582, pp. 364–374, 2024.
https://doi.org/10.1007/978-3-031-63136-8_37

are usually done by different authors, so the cost of communication between authors will also increase the burden of musical creation. In addition, the composers' understanding of music is also very different, resulting in the differences in their creative style, and even produce the completely opposite situation. Therefore, composition often takes a lot of time and energy. Using the artificial intelligence method can save creators a lot of time and energy, reduce communication, reduce unnecessary expenses, and enable people to create better works faster and more efficiently. The application of artificial intelligence to music creation can help composers to better understand the ideological connotation and emotion of their works, thus enhancing the appeal of the work.

With the continuous development of deep learning technology, people are increasingly using feedforward neural networks based on natural language processing estimation, cyclic neural networks, and other algorithms to generate lyrics. During training, these models can update parameters through back propagation. However, when using natural language processing estimation methods to generate lyrics sequences, there is a problem of exposure error: the model iteratively generates a sequence and predicts the next word based on its previously predicted words that may never appear in the training data. This difference between training and reasoning will accumulate as the sequence increases, and become significant as the length of the sequence increases. Generating adversarial networks (GAN) can alleviate the above problems. Since its inception, generating adversarial networks has been widely used in various scenarios, including the idea of game theory. Its basic principle is to make the false samples generated by the generator close to the real samples, which are used to deceive the discriminator, which aims to improve the ability to distinguish between data and real samples. Combining the two networks for training, after a certain number of training times, the data obtained by the generator is very close to the real sample. However, the development of generating confrontation networks in image processing is becoming faster and faster, but it is relatively stagnant in the field of natural language processing. Due to the discrete nature of text data, the model cannot feedback parameters to the generator through back propagation, thereby achieving gradient updates.

However, this does not mean that the idea of generating confrontation cannot be used in the field of natural language processing, because artificial intelligence itself is a very decentralized discipline that can apply knowledge from one aspect to another. Now, there are two ways to deal with the above problems: The first is to combine the generation confrontation model with the strategy gradient in reinforcement learning, making the text generation problem a continuous decision-making problem. The sequence generation countermeasure network proposed by Lantao YuF et al. is a good example, which can handle discrete data well. The second solution is to use the original generated adversarial model to solve the problem, which is improved on the basis of the original algorithm. Both TextGANl4 and Gumbel-softmax GANlSI algorithms use a simple argmax operation and Gumbel-softmax algorithm, which can achieve continuous approximate discrete distribution on the text, thereby ensuring end-to-end differentiability of the model. This method can reduce the gradient variance.

(1) In order to control the meaning of key words, the generator of generating confrontation networks from original sequences is improved to explore the infinite possibilities of generating confrontation networks in the field of lyrics creation.
(2) Excellent lyrics and music cannot be separated from good lyrics creation. Lyrics are the embodiment of the wisdom and Chinese culture of the lyricist. While creating

lyrics, people can not only feel the charm of Chinese culture, but also enhance their cultural accomplishment. Starting with lyrics creation and combining modern technology, it can bring new vitality to Chinese culture.

(3) The creation of lyrics requires high literary attainments and a deep creative foundation. Especially for beginners, the creation of lyrics is very difficult. Research on natural language processing technology and its application to the generation of lyrics can assist people in their creation and promote public love for creation.

(4) The study of automatically created lyrics can not only promote the development of natural language processing, but also provide unlimited possibilities for using computers to achieve automatic lyrics creation.

In the highly free age of the Internet, everyone can become a musician and get more resources, so that the music and information of all people are no longer asymmetric. Everyone can upload their music works online anytime and anywhere, and everyone can realize their music dreams. In this context, the traditional music communication mode has also changed greatly, from the traditional radio station, newspapers and other media to the mass communication, to various forms of network media. This progress is amazing, truly pushing music into society [1].

2 Related Work

2.1 Overview of Natural Language Processing

(1) Natural Language Process (N L P) is an emerging discipline of artificial intelligence. It mainly includes two main categories: the reading and expression of natural language. Natural language is an advanced function unique to the human brain. It is processed by computer technology, presented in text and speech, and through the corresponding computing program. Processing and processing by multiple methods. The processing of natural language is divided into two categories: pre-processing and semantic understanding, which can also classify the classification and deconstruction of speech. Its application scope mainly includes mechanical transformation, emotion analysis, andspeech production,Intelligent q & A, information extraction, voice input, public opinion analysis, etc. (1) Machine translation.

Machine translation is a transformation of a natural language into a special language (target language), which is a very special, very practical technology. At present, the more popular youdao translation, Baidu translation, Google translation, etc.

(2) Emotional analysis

In some annotated applications, sentiment analysis is very useful to classify a variety of different evaluations into different sentiment types based on the analysis. For example, the positive or negative assessments, according to certain rules, are shown in the user's comments.

(3) Intelligent question and answer

On some Taobao, Tmall, Jingdong and other online shopping platforms, intelligent Q & A is very useful. Intelligent q & A is a kind of man-machine dialogue based on artificial intelligence and combining the thinking method of natural language. For those questions that do not need to be done manually, the intelligent question answering system can effectively deal with the above questions, thus saving a lot of human resources.

(4) Language generation

Language generation is mainly used in news, sports commentary and other fields. The system adopts the natural language processing method to allow the narrator to translate his lines into text and display them as an App in real time, facilitating the audience to quickly accept the text narrator.

(5) Information Extraction

In the retrieval process, information extraction is mainly used to screen the key information after eving massive data, so as to realize the automatic classification of data. Information extraction technology is a key link of the search engine. For example, using the news as an object for web page retrieval, and then using the information extraction algorithm for topic analysis, different news can be divided into different topics.

(6) Voice input

Voice input is the most convenient input way as well as the simplest input way has been widely used. With the continuous development and popularization of speech recognition technology, speech recognition technology has also been obtained. Asus technology's voice input is one of the best in the world, introducing instant simultaneous translation of Chinese and English, which is widely used in a variety of large conferences and competitions [2].

(7) Public opinion analysis

Public opinion analysis is a valuable public relationship, and Obama used opinion polls many times in the United States, and so was the money. Make adjustments in areas such as advertising to create efficient canvassing strategies. In the Internet era, public opinion analysis is a brand new research field, which will have a profound impact on the traditional public relations work. Using natural language to conduct public opinion investigation will greatly improve the work efficiency of media and public relations.

2.2 Lyrics Creation Generation Model

In the field of computer vision, images can be represented using continuous vectors. However, in the field of natural language processing, text is discrete, so it is necessary to convert text into a computer-recognizable form. This topic uses Skip gram to pre train word vectors, while Word2Vec is developed based on one hot coding.

2.2.1 Single Heat Indication

At the beginning of the rise of natural language processing, words were represented using one dot. It is a relatively intuitive method, which uses binary one-dimensional vector representation. When the vocabulary size is N, the one dot encoding of each word is represented as a one-dimensional vector with a length of N. The specific method is to mark the words in the text with a unique sequence number i. The vector of the words is represented as only having a value of 1 at the position where i is, and having a value of 0 at the rest of the positions.

It is not difficult to find that this encoding method is inherently sparse, resulting in a significant waste of space. At the same time, too long coding can also make training slow. Although the expression of one hop coding is concise and intuitive, when the vocabulary of the corpus reaches a certain level, there may be a problem of dimensional explosion. Moreover, the relationship between any two words is equal, so two vectors cannot represent the relationship between two words. However, the relevance of words between sentences in language is very strong. So in order to address the disadvantages of one hop coding, Word2Vec emerged.

2.2.2   Word2Vec

There are many current word embedding modes, but the most common one is the Word2Vec model proposed by Mikolov et al. 2 in 2013. Word2Vec models can be divided into two categories: Skip gram models and CBOW (Continuous Bag Of Words Model) models, both of which are calculated based on sliding windows (window sizes can be set). Skip gram predicts the context of a word based on a known target word, while CBOW, on the contrary, mainly predicts the target word based on the context words in the window.

The CBOW model consists of three layers, an input layer, a projection layer, and an output layer. It is used to predict the central word from the context. If there are n words in each context of a word in the dictionary, the expression can be expressed as P (w/W rn.....: − t, W + 1,.... W + n). Assuming n = 2, the model training diagram is shown in Fig. 1. The input layer of the model is the surrounding word vector within the target word window, where the window size is 5, then the input layer of the model is a word vector containing 4 words. In the projection layer, the model adds and sums each word vector in the input layer. The output layer is a binary tree, which is constructed by taking the words in the corpus as the leaf nodes of the binary tree, and using the word frequency as the weight value to construct a Huffman tree. The final result needs to be normalized to between 0 and 1 using the Softmax function, where the prediction word has the highest probability.

$$D = (x_1, y_1), (x_2, y_2), \cdots (x_n, y_n) \qquad (1)$$

Including:

$$x_i = (x_i^{(1)}, x_2^{(2)}, \cdots, x_n^{(n)})^T \qquad (2)$$

Skip-gram model is different from CBOW model in that it uses central words to predict surrounding words. In the prediction words in the window, the expression for each word is p (wi/w), t-n < i < t + n. Assuming n = 2, the training process of this model is shown in Fig. 2. The input layer of the Skip gram model is the unique encoding of a given target word, while the output is the unique encoding of the words in the window around the target word. The principle of moving from input layer to projection layer is consistent with the CBOW model, but the difference is the loss function from projection

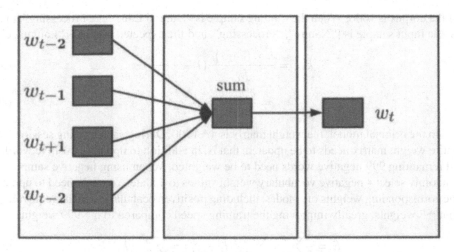

Fig. 1. CBOW mold

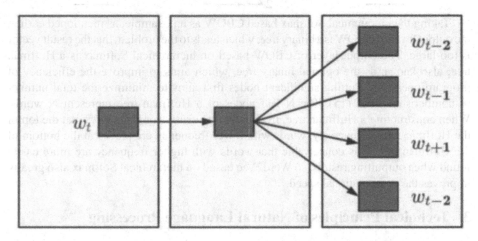

Fig. 2. Skip gram model

layer to output layer, which uses backpropagation and random gradient descent methods to learn weights.

From the above update rules, it can be found that each prediction needs to be calculated based on all data sets in the corpus, which will take up a significant amount of time. Therefore, Word2Vec proposed two methods to reduce training time based on this, negative sampling and hierarchical Softmax.

As the vocabulary increases, the weight matrix also increases accordingly. Therefore, the time and resources required for training have also increased accordingly. Compared with the original model, negative sampling only updates a portion of the weights each time, greatly reducing the workload of training. For example, when the vocabulary size of the corpus is 1000, When the training sample is "Natural Language Processing", that is, the input sample is ["Nature", "Processing", and the expected output is "Language".

$$k'_{dfg} = \frac{n \times (i+1)_k}{f_{er}}(1 - \frac{1}{i+1}) \tag{3}$$

$$w_g = \frac{\partial_{u'} \times e}{u_{rf'}} \otimes \beta \times A \tag{4}$$

In the original model, the weight matrix is n * 1000. During each training session, an entire weight matrix needs to be updated, that is, in addition to updating positive words, all remaining 999 negative words need to be weighted. When using negative sampling, randomly select 4 negative vocabulary weight values to update. You only need to update the corresponding weights of 5 nodes, including positive vocabulary, which is equivalent to n * 5 weights, greatly improving the training speed compared to n * 999 weights.

$$E = \frac{1}{2}\sum_{r=1}^{p}\sum_{j=1}^{n}(l_j^p - y_j^p) = \sum_{r=1}^{p}E_r \tag{5}$$

$$E_p = \frac{1}{2}\sum_{j=1}^{m}(t_j^p - y_j^p)^2 \tag{6}$$

Taking the hierarchical Softmax based CBOW as an example, as mentioned earlier, the output layer of CBOW is a binary tree, which leads to the problem that the result vector is too large. The output layer of CBOW based on hierarchical Softmax is a Huffman tree, also known as the optimal binary tree, which aims to improve the efficiency of program operation. Putting significant nodes first aims to minimize the total number of comparisons by 2 (15). The N leaf nodes of a Huffman tree represent N words. When constructing a Huffman tree, frequently occurring words are placed at the top of the Huffman tree. Conversely, words with lower frequency are placed at the bottom of the Huffman tree. It is conceivable that words with higher frequency are more easily found when outputting results, so Word2Vec based on hierarchical Softmax also greatly improves the computational speed.

3   Technical Principles of Natural Language Processing

Natural language processing is applied in many aspects, and in order to achieve this goal, its technical principles must be deeply analyzed. This paper discusses in depth from vocabulary, grammar, machinery, emotion analysis and text generation.

3.1   Xemmical Analysis

The study of word grammar includes Chinese word segmentation, part of speech annotation and name identification. Most of the word segmentation methods in Chinese rely on manual work. Chinese word segmentation is a word that divides a continuous sentence into a whole. The annotation of word classes allows each word to be given specific words, such as verbs and nouns. A noun is a word or words for something. In the classification of naming language, the segmentation of vocabulary and phrase extraction should be preprocessed first. Using these three steps, a simple classification of natural language can be made to facilitate later processing.

3.2 Syntactic Analysis

Syntactic analysis can use the relationship between words in a sentence to convey the grammar information in a sentence. Grammatical analysis is a major research direction in machine translation and natural language processing. Its main function is to correctly understand the intention of the input, through syntactic analysis, to extract the backbone components of the sentence, so as to make the sentence better understood. The system architecture is shown in Fig. 3 below.

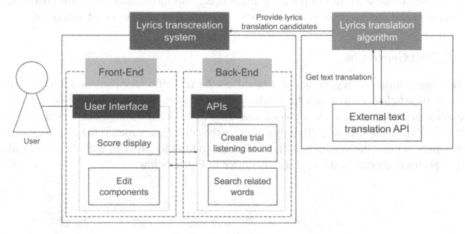

Fig. 3. System architecture

3.3 Main Methods of Machine Translation

3.3.1 Rule-Based Machine Translation

Regular machine translation usually uses word class analysis, word position transformation and other methods to directly translate words or phrases into Chinese, but usually the quality of translation is usually not high.

3.3.2 Machine Translation Based on Statistics

This approach employs statistically relevant principles. First, to have a large corpus, you can calculate the occurrence probability of words and neighboring words when transforming words. Secondly, the most likely translation is selected and output as the largest preset probability, that is, the translation has the highest accuracy. By optimizing the weighting under various conditions, it can somehow achieve the optimal results, so that the accuracy and speed of the translation are improved. This is currently one of the most popular machine translation types.

3.3.3 Instance-Based Machine Translation

When requiring the input sentence for translation, you can find similar sentences, and if abnormal words appear, the final results can be obtained by alternative methods.

3.4 Sentiment Analysis

When it is necessary to enter into a sentence, the final result can be achieved by looking for similar statements instead of an abnormal translation. Emotion analysis is mainly for the user's subjective tendency style, such as the users' evaluation. Emotion analysis is mainly to judge the specific preferences and tendencies of users from the perspective of the form and context of language. Emotion analysis should first classify the main emotional words in the text, and give the corresponding credibility. Emotion analysis can be applied to the website's ranking, promotion, etc. Emotional analysis helps businesses to understand the psychology of users, showing a certain proportion of emotions.

3.5 Text Generation

Text generation can regenerate text based on the text of a keyword or sentence. The focus of articles is on automatic production at the syntactic level. The first step is to enter a keyword, such as a keyword, and then filter out the statement containing the keyword from the database. To judge whether the condition is met, if the condition does not meet, replace the synonym in the thesaurus, and finally proceed with the final result. The preliminary creation screenshot is shown in Fig. 4 below.

Fig. 4. Preliminary creation screenshot

When the text generates synonymous sentences, the input sentence should be divided. If the words of the two sentences are different, they should be divided. If there is no different meaning[3], There is no format conversion premise, to delete the disabled words, and then the rest of the word spacing operation. The similarity matrix of two sentences and the similarity of two sentences. Then select the specified number of sentences based on the number of sentences needed.

4 The Main Method of Creating Artificial Intelligence Lyrics

4.1 Principle of Recurrent Neural Network (RNN) Algorithm

Adding a hidden state h to the recurrent neural network R N N, the characteristics of extracting data from the sequence, that is, the number of inputs can be determined and changed by the number of previous outputs. On this basis, the input and output data are processed and converted into a new input. Secondly, the modeling parameters should be trained. Enter words into x1, x2,...... For xn, this input value is estimated by the operation and the hidden state h[4]And output y 1, y 2 and......y n.Through continuous tests, the forecast results can be gradually optimized. At the same time, various factors should be adjusted to achieve a more scientific and stable purpose. As shown in Fig. 5:

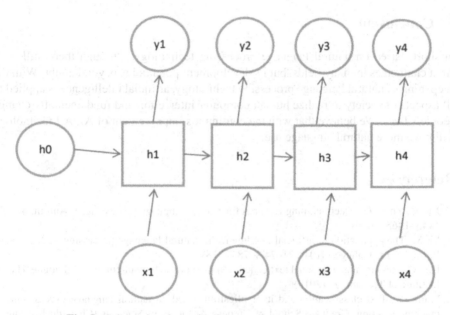

Fig. 5. Schematic schematic diagram of recurrent neural network

4.2 Principle of the Long and Short-Term Memory Network (LSTM) Algorithm

When the data passes through the forgotten gate, the forgotten gate will produce a true value between 0 and 1,1 for integrity and 0 for complete abandonment. This input gate determines the new data to be added, including two phases, the first phase is determining what is updated, and the second phase is the updated vector. The two are combined and upgraded to generate a new candidate that will change with the decision of each upgrade. Ultimately, you must decide which values are output: (1) execute the sigmoid output to determine the status of the unit; (2) use tanh to calculate the last value of the input entry to produce a value and compare it with the sigmoid gate output; and (3) use the required output values needed to generate the text output[5](As shown in Fig. 6).

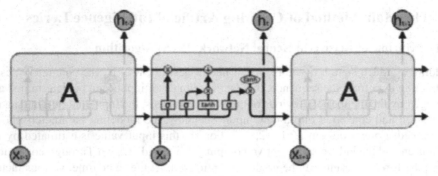

Fig. 6. L S T M technical schematic diagram

5 Conclusion

In short, based on natural language processing technology, although there still exist great challenges in many fields, but its development potential is beyond doubt. With the deepening of natural language processing technology, artificial intelligence is applied to all aspects of society to realize human-computer interaction and fundamentally change people's lives. We believe that with the continuous improvement of AI, A I technology will have more natural language use.

References

1. Xi, X., Zhou, G.: Deep learning research for natural language processing. J. Autom. **42**(10), 1445–1465 (2016)
2. Li, Y.: The application of artificial intelligence in natural language processing. J. Xiangyang Vocat. Techn. College **17**(04), 71–74 + 78 (2018)
3. Fan, C.: Research on emotional text generation methods in human-computer dialogue. Harbin Institute of Technology (2018)
4. Wang, Y.: Text classification and its application based on natural language processing and machine learning. Graduate School of Chinese Academy of Sciences (Chengdu Institute of Computer Application) (2006)
5. Yu, Z.: Research and implementation of natural language generation technology based on LSTM. Beijing University of Posts and Telecommunications (2018)

Undergraduate Talents Training System of Chinese International Education Major Based on Artificial Intelligence

Dongping Chen[✉] and Zhang Jing

Yunnan Technology and Business University, Kunming 65000, China
girlsailor@163.com

Abstract. With the prosperity of the global economy, the languages of all countries are in urgent need of breaking national boundaries to show the world their unique language charm, and at the same time expect that languages can serve the people of the world. The size of the scope of language use determines the influence of a country's national image accordingly. As the representative of China's image, Chinese participates in the competition of world languages. More and more people begin to understand Chinese. Chinese is warming up around the world. Colleges of Chinese International Education have been established in major universities across the country. This paper focuses on the research on the talent training system for Chinese international education undergraduates based on AI, and mainly develops the talent training system based on AI for Chinese international education undergraduates. The research team has developed an intelligent learning management system (ILMS) to support the development process of ILM courseware. ILMS integrates with MOOC platform, student information system and other systems to provide online courses for students majoring in international education or those who want to study.

Keywords: artificial intelligence · Chinese international education · Talent training system

1 Introduction

At present, the language service industry is rising, and the research of language service has attracted the attention of both inside and outside the industry. As an important resource, language has been mentioned many times by the national "Belt and Road" initiative. Professor Li Yuming pointed out that "the Belt and Road Initiative needs language to pave the way", which illustrates the important role of language. Language service can not be separated from language education. International Chinese language education is an important part of language education. Therefore, the development of the business form of international Chinese language education and personnel training will help the development of language education and promote the construction of language service project [1].

© ICST Institute for Computer Sciences, Social Informatics and Telecommunications Engineering 2024
Published by Springer Nature Switzerland AG 2024. All Rights Reserved
Y. Zhang and N. Shah (Eds.): BigIoT-EDU 2023, LNICST 582, pp. 375–381, 2024.
https://doi.org/10.1007/978-3-031-63136-8_38

Modern enterprises need to have certain expertise, good professional ethics, professionalism, certain cultural quality, understanding themselves, good self-regulation ability and strong choice ability. At present, the ability of college students is not enough to adapt to social changes, so in the Outline of the National Medium and Long term Education Reform and Development Plan (2010–2010), it is proposed to vigorously develop vocational education, mobilize the enthusiasm of industry enterprises, and enhance the attractiveness of vocational education; It also requires us to reform the talent training system, update the concept of talent training, innovate the talent training model, and reform the education quality evaluation and talent evaluation system [2]. The outline also clearly points out that "the core of education is to solve the major problems of who and how to train people.".

2 Related Work

2.1 Research Status of Language Services

As an academic concept, "language service" in China originated from the fact that during the preparation for the Beijing Olympic Games, China Translation Association first used "language service" in public. There are many definitions of language services, but there is no clear definition so far. The author has collected and sorted out relevant concepts. For example, Qu Sentinel classified language services into sociolinguistics from the discipline category, believing that they are closely related to pragmatics, and has divided the basic types and attributes of language services [3]. At the same time, he has divided language services into industries, namely, language translation industry, language education services and language support services. He has also divided language services into five systems: language service resource system Language service business system, language service field system, language service level system, language service efficiency system. From the perspective of language resources, Xu Daming pointed out that "language" itself is unconscious, and who it serves depends entirely on the subject who masters and controls it [4]. That is, "language service" should refer to the language service provided by the state for the people, which is a part of all services provided by the state. From the perspective of language service industry, Guo Xiaoyong believes that the emerging industry of language service includes translation and localization services, language technology tool development, language teaching and training, language related consulting services, etc. Zhao Shiju summarized other people's concept of language service and gave his own definition in "The Definition and Type of Language Service from the Service Content", that is, "the behavior and activity that the behavior subject provides help to others or society with the content or means of language", and divided six types of language service: language knowledge service, language technology service, language use service, language rehabilitation service Language education services [5].

At present, there is no clear conclusion on the research of language service in China. The research mostly stays at the theoretical level, without in-depth investigation and research. China has a vast territory, many nationalities, and different regions face different cultural circles of language service. Language service should be promoted in a targeted way when going abroad.

2.2 Nature of International Chinese Education

Language services include language education. International Chinese language education is an important part of language education, so international Chinese language education is an important branch of language services. Language service is a service for the whole human society, which is abstract. Chinese is a universal language in the world and one of the common languages of the United Nations. The international status of Chinese cannot be ignored. The development of Chinese language can not be separated from education. International education of Chinese language is the key for Chinese language to open its doors and integrate into the world civilization [6].

The historical source of Chinese international education in China starts from teaching Chinese as a foreign language. Historically, China has been a great diplomatic country with friendly exchanges with all nations in the world. Since the Western Han Dynasty, there have been ethnic minorities around learning Chinese. During the Eastern Han Dynasty, with the development of the Maritime Silk Road, foreigners from distant seas began to learn Chinese. The prosperous Tang Dynasty ushered in an upsurge of Chinese learning, such as Japanese "envoys to the Tang Dynasty" and Silla foreign students. Chinese has opened up a world In history, Chinese has flourished in the world. In the later dynasties, foreign students came to China to learn Chinese, but for various reasons, Chinese did not prosper. The instinct of Chinese education to serve the language did not play well, although in the Ming Dynasty China's existing Chinese textbooks, such as Lao Qida, Pu Shitong, Xi Ru Er Mu Zi, and the late Qing Dynasty's Language Ziyou Ji, etc., had a great impact. During the Republic of China, there were still many Chinese and foreign exchange students. But Chinese, as a discipline and a language education undertaking, began after the founding of New China [7]. The education of Chinese as a foreign language started in the 1950s and has gone through the initial period (the early 1950s to the early 1960s), the consolidation and development period, the recovery period and the vigorous development period (after the late 1970s). The development of Chinese language education in the above stages has laid a good foundation for Chinese language service. During this period, China established a special leading organization and scientific research team, improved the teaching system and trained special Chinese teachers, promoted the Chinese proficiency test, expanded international exchanges, etc., and made progress in both theoretical teaching and external communication of Chinese.

3 Complex Characteristics of Talent Training System

The elements in the talent training system are people with adaptability and initiative. And the core of complex adaptive system is: adaptability creates complexity. Because of the four characteristics and three mechanisms of the complex adaptive system, the system has the characteristics of adaptability, self-organization, hierarchy, uncertainty and overall emergence in addition to the characteristics of relevance, purposefulness and openness that the system should have.

(1) Adaptive

Characteristics of complex adaptive system: emphasize the initiative and enthusiasm of system members for their own purposes. Students in the secondary vocational talent training system are active individuals. At the same time, there are selection and defense systems in their internal models. They can actively gather among individuals. Through aggregation, individuals and aggregates, aggregates and aggregates interact repeatedly, which has become the motivation for the development and evolution of the system [8]. It can link macro and micro. Through the interaction between students and students, as well as between students and the school system and atmosphere, the change of individual students becomes the basis of the change of the whole system. The system change reacts on individual students, thus changing the internal model of individual students again. This process is an adaptive process. System methodology requires that all parts must be examined uniformly [9].

(2) Self-organization

Self adaptation mainly refers to the change of individual students, while self-organization is a constantly changing process between system subsystems for self adaptation. It refers to the interaction between subsystems within the system, between agents, agents and the external environment through the active role of system agents and the environment, and the result of the interaction. In this process, there is no need for human organization, planning and control. It is the internal driving force of the system movement. Through this movement mode, the subjects and the environment constantly exchange material and energy, so as to achieve the characteristics of self renewal and self generation. For example, the aggregation of students with similar personalities also belongs to self-organization. The needs of students and individual conditions lead to changes in class rules and student cadres' handling methods.

(3) Hierarchy

Hierarchical is another important feature of complex systems. Hierarchical performance makes complex systems relatively simple, and it is divided into different levels for research. Hierarchical is due to the formation of the system's building block logo. When considering the effect of a lesson, it is necessary to consider the level that supports the lesson, such as the knowledge that students have mastered, students' interests and hobbies, teachers' familiarity with the content of the lesson The mental state of students and teachers in this class, and the teaching methods adopted by teachers. These levels should be considered at many small levels. For example, when considering individual students, we should consider their personality, thinking, knowledge mastery, intellectual factors, non intellectual factors, etc. If we can fully understand each level, and do a good job in the corresponding combination work, we can develop to the upper level firmly, and the system evolution can be smooth. Hierarchical performance makes the research of complex systems clearer and the connection between things more obvious.

4 Artificial Intelligence Based Undergraduate Talent Training System for Chinese International Education

4.1 Build a Diversified Talent Training Model

(1) Meet the needs of foreign language talents in domestic universities

The training of college teachers is also one of the contents of language services. College teachers generally require a relatively high level of professional competence. Faced with this demand, colleges and universities in Guangxi should vigorously support the high-level talent training plan, send talents out and bring them back, and help the development of Guangxi's international Chinese education industry. Taking Guangxi Normal University as an example, the proportion of professors and teachers of the Chinese language international education specialty in the school is small, which can not meet the needs of the development of the college. Therefore, the development of international colleges with relatively weak teachers should be supported in the "Belt and Road" development. On the other hand, the demand for high-level Chinese teachers is also shown in the "Belt and Road" language service vision. The language demand is rich and diverse. China's Chinese language resources have huge potential, and quite a number of resources such as pronunciation, vocabulary, Chinese characters, grammar, Chinese culture, etc. are still to be developed. Therefore, colleges and universities need to devote themselves to training a group of teachers who are interested in investing in language and character scientific research, so as to develop and utilize the language service resources and open up the way, Leading development [10].

(2) Meet the needs of independent entrepreneurial talents in international Chinese language education

At present, the country is encouraging the whole people to innovate and start businesses. Many college students are ready to make a move, but they lack experience and ability, so they need to be guided by colleges and universities. The development of Chinese language international education not only requires the efforts of the government and universities, but also the promotion of the social market The development of innovative education industries such as training institutions plays a catalytic role in promoting the spread of Chinese culture. The independent entrepreneurship talents of Chinese language international education are not only the education talents of Chinese language international, but also the language service talents of Chinese language communication. Colleges and universities should properly cultivate them according to the plan.

4.2 Undergraduate Talent Training System for Chinese International Education

There is still a lot of space to explore the talent training model of Chinese language international education. Under the guidance of the "Belt and Road" policy, language service, as a new topic, has a clearer direction for the training of Chinese language international education talents. The language environment and natural environment are also important factors that affect the development of Chinese international education. The structure of the AI based undergraduate talent training system for Chinese international education is shown in Fig. 1.

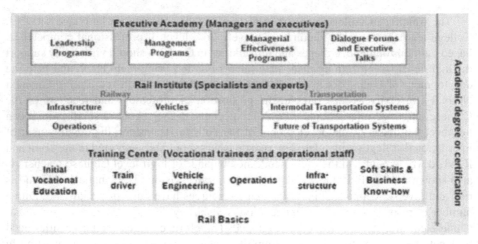

Fig. 1. Structure of talent training system

5   Conclusion

At present, the ranks of Chinese language international education talents in China are uneven. Based on the existing talent training team, appropriately expand the level of Chinese language international education talents. In the undergraduate study stage, appropriately cultivate students' scientific research ability, guide students to move closer to the graduate level, improve the relevant professional master's degree students, expand the types of master's enrollment, and make the disciplines more diversified. The joint training of Chinese students in the training process can not only stimulate Chinese students' interest in learning and understanding different cultures, but also meet the needs of foreign students' Chinese learning context.

References

1. Tao, Y., Feng, J.: Research on the "3+1" talent training mode of application-oriented undergraduate education (2021)
2. Cao, Y.Y., Lv, Q., Cui, L.G.: Research on the training of electromechanical complex talents in higher vocational colleges under the background of artificial intelligence. Destech Publications, Inc (2021)
3. Balfaqih, H.: Artificial intelligence in logistics and supply chain management: a perspective on research trends and challenges. In: Alareeni, B., Hamdan, A. (eds.) Explore Business, Technology Opportunities and Challenges After the Covid-19 Pandemic, pp. 1241–1247. Springer International Publishing, Cham (2023). https://doi.org/10.1007/978-3-031-08954-1_106
4. Della Corte, D., Morris, C.J., Billings, W.M., et al.: Training undergraduate research assistants with an outcome-oriented and skill-based mentoring strategy. Acta Crystallograph. Sect. D Struct. Biol. **2022**(8), 78 (2022)
5. Hanson, P.K., Stultz, L.K.: Linking chemistry and biology through course-based undergraduate research on anticancer ruthenium complexes (2021)

6. Zhao, Y.: Research on the application of university teaching management evaluation system based on Apriori algorithm. J. Phys. Conf. Ser. **1883**(1), 012033 (2021). https://doi.org/10.1088/1742-6596/1883/1/012033
7. Liu, Y.: Research on the influence of artificial intelligence on the training of accounting talents and strategy (2021)
8. Wu, Z.: The training mode of internationalized talents of equestrian management based on artificial intelligence technology (2021)
9. Yang, Y., Xu, Y.: Research on the PDCA quality management model of the undergraduate innovation and entrepreneurship training programs (2021)
10. Li, Z., Wang, L., Liu, Z.: Training of undergraduate physical education professionals in colleges and universities based on competency model (2021)

Research on the High Resolution Remote Sensing Image Target Detection Based on Machine Learning

Yanli Fu$^{(\boxtimes)}$, Yingying Sun, Shuyao Li, Rui Deng, and Hou Linlin

Engineering University of CAPF, Xian, Shaanxi, China
15829379521@163.com

Abstract. With the development of computer technology and the national aerospace industry, remote sensing satellites have been successively projected into the air, and the resolution of remote sensing images is becoming higher and clearer. The surface information contained in remote sensing images can be used not only in civil fields such as forestry, agriculture, water conservancy, but also in the military and national defense fields. Current target detection technologies have achieved good results in natural image detection, but their performance in remote sensing images is poor. This is due to the high resolution of remote sensing images themselves, the small size of key targets in the image, and the dense distribution in multiple directions, while the background information is very complex and covers the entire range of the image, resulting in low detection accuracy and slow speed issues when using traditional methods for target detection. High resolution remote sensing images have a wide range of utilization scenarios. The traditional remote sensing image target detection based on artificial vision recognition and processing has been difficult to effectively cope with and meet the practical needs of large-scale high-resolution remote sensing impact target recognition. Based on this, this paper first analyzes remote sensing image information extraction methods based on machine learning, then studies high-resolution remote sensing image target detection methods based on machine learning, and finally presents the development trend of high-resolution remote sensing image target detection based on machine learning.

Keywords: High Resolution · Remote Sensing · Image Target Detection · Machine Learning

1 Introduction

With the iterative progress and maturity of computer tech, it has been widely and deeply studied and popularized in many fields, especially the utilization of computer tech represented by machine learning in the field of high-resolution remote-sensed image target detection, which greatly accelerates the amelioration of high-resolution remote-sensed image target detection accuracy and efficiency [1]. High resolution remote-sensed

Y. Zhang and N. Shah (Eds.): BigIoT-EDU 2023, LNICST 582, pp. 382–392, 2024.
https://doi.org/10.1007/978-3-031-63136-8_39

image has a wide range of utilization scenarios, which can accurately identify and judge many targets, so it has a high utilization and research necessity. The use of high-resolution remote-sensed images for target detection can effectively meet the needs of target recognition, so as to provide the basis and support for scientific and reasonable decision-making [2].

High resolution remote-sensed image will be affected by a series of factors in the process of target detection, mainly as shown in Fig. 1 below. These factors will cause interference to the detail structure and texture of the image in the process of high-resolution imaging detection, which will affect the imaging quality and greatly reduce the accuracy and efficiency of target detection. On the other hand, with the development of high-resolution remote sensing utilizations, its target detection activities will produce a large number of data to be processed, which brings severe challenges to its data processing ability [3]. It is urgent to ameliorate the image data processing ability, which provides a more suitable practical utilization scenario for intelligent algorithms represented by machine learning.

In addition, for some special utilization scenarios that require high efficiency of target detection, it is not only required to be able to quickly and accurately identify and judge the situation of the target, but also required to be able to quickly process a large number of high-resolution remote-sensed image data. High resolution, high precision and a large number of remote-sensed image processing need intelligent algorithm assistance. The traditional remote-sensed image target detection on account of artificial visual recognition and processing has been difficult to effectively deal with and meet the practical needs of massive high-resolution remote sensing target recognition [4]. Only with the help of intelligent algorithm represented by machine learning, can it adapt to and match the real-time and efficient processing of high-resolution remote-sensed image targets.

In short, in the current situation of high resolution remote-sensed image target detection utilization and utilization needs deepening, intelligent algorithm is needed to solve the interference of background and redundant info in high-resolution image target detection, and help users locate and identify high-resolution remote-sensed image targets quickly [5]. The target detection of high resolution remote-sensed image on account of machine learning algorithm can keep the semantic and target specific areas in the image, and achieve the fast acquisition of the target image details. Therefore, it is of great practical value to study the object detection of high resolution remote-sensed image on account of machine learning.

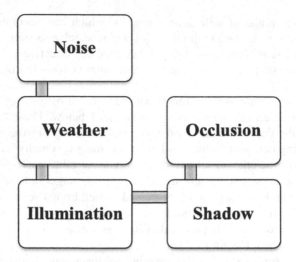

Fig. 1. Influence factors of target detection in high resolution remote-sensed image

2   Remote-Sensed Image Info Extraction on Account of Machine Learning

2.1   The Concept and Connotation of Machine Learning Algorithm

With the remarkable achievements and progress of computer tech and its learning methods in recent years, the utilization of machine learning in high resolution remote-sensed images has also made great breakthroughs. Machine learning can greatly ameliorate the target recognition and detection accuracy of high resolution remote-sensed images [6]. As a kind of unsupervised learning, deep learning combines the lower level features to form a more abstract high-level representation, thus finding the distributed representation of data features. As a distributed expression method, the remote-sensed image data observed by the deep learning algorithm is generated by interaction of various factors, that is, learning a special factor from other factors combination [7].

In addition, the deep learning algorithm involves a wide range of prior beliefs about unknown potential factors. The observation changes of re input are explained by important prior info, and the height of preference for some factors and prediction can be achieved. In fact, deep learning algorithms are the framework of unsupervised learning [8]. Many unmarked images are used to find out the detailed features of remote-sensed images. SVM, as a supervised learning, can map the low-dimensional vector to the high-dimensional space, and then classify the high-resolution remote-sensed image.

2.2   Extraction of High Resolution Remote-Sensed Image Info

The extraction of high-resolution remote-sensed image info is the reverse process of remote sensing imaging process [9]. It is the process of extracting relevant info from the simulated image of remote sensing on the ground and inverting the target image prototype. According to the actual requirements of target detection, we need to use the physical model to interpret the feature marks and practical experience and knowledge, qualitatively and quantitatively extract the physical quantity, space-time distribution, functional structure and other related info. With the continuous amelioration of spatial data acquisition ability, high-resolution remote sensing has gradually become an important source of spatial info for all walks of life and the public [10].

High resolution image data processing, analysis, understanding and decision-making utilization constitute the tech chain of remote sensing utilization, and info extraction and target recognition are the core technologies of remote sensing from data to info and then to develop utilization services [11]. Due to the characteristics of high spatial resolution remote-sensed image, the problem of high-precision and high-efficiency automatic target recognition has always been a great technical difficulty, which has been the bottleneck of large-scale utilization.

2.3 ResNet

In 2014, the Residual Network (ResNet) proposed by He Kaiming and others won the championship in the 2015 competition. The number of network layers reached an astonishing 152, with a record loss value of only 3.57%, which is much better than VGG and AlexNet networks.

Increasing the number of layers can lead to gradient disappearance and degradation in the network. Although the extracted features become more advanced, the image resolution decreases, small target information gradually loses, and the information contained is also reduced layer by layer. If shallow information can be transferred to the deep layer through a bridge, the effect of the deep layer network must not be inferior to that of the shallow layer [12]. ResNet is based on this by adding a direct mapping between the shallow layer and the deep layer, Ensure that the deep layer of the network must contain more image information than the shallow layer. The residual structure in the ResNet network is shown in Fig. 2:

As can be seen from Fig. 2, the residual unit is divided into two parts, one is the residual mapping, which is the part above the straight line in Fig. 2, and the other is the identity mapping itself, which is the straight line part[13]. The 1 * 1 convolution mainly deals with reducing/increasing the dimension of the input feature F1 when the two feature dimensions F1 and F2 are inconsistent, and it can also increase network nonlinearity. The representation of F2 is as follows:

$$F_2 = C(F_1) + f(F_1, W_1) \tag{1}$$

$$F_y = F_x + \sum_{i=x}^{y-1} f(F_i, W_i) \tag{2}$$

Fx and Fy are the inputs of the x th residual cell and the outputs of the (y-1) th residual cell, respectively. Therefore, the gradient of the loss function with respect to F can be derived as shown in Formula (3);

$$\frac{\partial loss}{\partial F_x} = \frac{\partial loss}{\partial F_y} \frac{\partial F_y}{\partial F_x} = \frac{\partial loss}{\partial F_y} (1 + \frac{\partial}{\partial F_y} \sum_{i=x}^{y-1} f(F_x, W_i)) \tag{3}$$

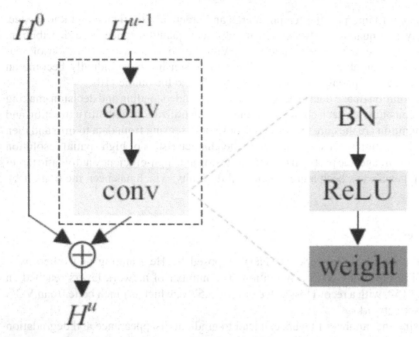

Fig. 2. Residual unit

BN (Batch Normalization) is batch standardization, which can standardize the input data of each layer of convolution uniformly and maintain the same distribution. The purpose is to alleviate the disappearance of gradients, optimize neural networks, and make it easier to learn the laws of data centers[14]. When the network performance reaches saturation as the number of layers increases, you can set the residual part f (F, W) to 0, so that the network performance can always be in a saturated state. Therefore, arbitrarily increasing the number of network layers does not cause network degradation.

3 High Resolution Remote-Sensed Image Target Detection on Account of Machine Learning

3.1 General Tech of Target Detection in High Resolution Remote-Sensed Image

The overall process of high-resolution remote-sensed image target detection on account of machine learning includes remote-sensed image acquisition, remote-sensed image preprocessing, remote-sensed image detection preparation, remote-sensed image target detection algorithm and target detection post-processing. The overall process architecture is shown in Fig. 3.

The object detection of high-resolution remote-sensed image includes two types: large format remote-sensed image and segmented remote-sensed image [15]. In the process of high-resolution remote-sensed image target detection, first of all, it should to preprocess the target image to further ameliorate the accuracy of image detection

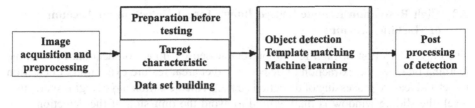

Fig. 3. Overall process of target detection in high resolution remote-sensed image

and obtain stable detection features. Secondly, the preparation of remote sensing target detection mainly includes the following Table 1, so as to ameliorate the detection effect of remote-sensed image target.

Table 1. Preliminary preparation process of remote sensing target detection

Process	Contents	Targets
Prior knowledge acquisition	Preliminary investigation of detection target	Type, specification and shooting conditions
Target characteristic analysis	Image grayscale, structure and texture	Characteristics of target shape and size
Data set building	Training model parameters	Ameliorate the detection effect of the algorithm

High resolution remote-sensed image target detection method on account of machine learning shows significant utilization advantages in the aspect of target image feature and performance representation. The utilization steps of machine learning in remote-sensed image target detection are shown in Fig. 4 below, through the construction of training data set, region extraction, feature design, extraction and processing, training and detection and other process dimensions. The key to the utilization effect of machine learning algorithm in high-resolution remote-sensed image target detection is region extraction, feature fusion, dimension reduction and feature processing.

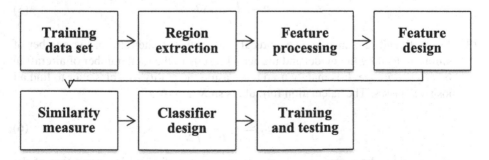

Fig. 4. Utilization steps of machine learning in remote-sensed image target detection

3.2 High Resolution Remote-Sensed Image Target Detection on Account of Machine Learning

The object detection of high resolution remote-sensed image on account of machine learning includes the extraction of detection target area, feature extraction of detection target and feature processing of detection target. In the detection target region extraction level, the sliding window is mainly used to avoid the omission of the detection area, to achieve the selection of complex detection targets and the effective extraction of the region. Secondly, in the feature extraction level of monitoring targets, the high-resolution remote-sensed images are mapped to low-dimensional space, so as to construct effective detection target features. The operation can ameliorate the details of target feature extraction in remote-sensed image, and facilitate the classification and recognition of images.

In addition, in the feature processing level of remote sensing target, the remote-sensed image of the extracted target feature is fused with the latter feature, so as to show all the external info of the remote sensing detection target, and the new feature model is constructed on account of it. In order to reduce the complexity of image processing, the high-dimensional features are compressed effectively by reducing the dimension of the features of remote sensing detection objects.

The effectiveness of target detection depends on the accuracy of the location and category of the prediction box. The evaluation indicators used in this article are the average accuracy rate (AP), recall rate (Recall), and mAP, with the detection of aircraft as the target (only one category is detected). Their respective meanings and calculation formulas are as follows:

(1) MAP: An indicator used to measure whether the category and location of a model's detection frame are accurate, which is the result of the detection of multiple classes, as shown in Formula (4):

$$mAP = \sum_{i=1}^{n} \frac{AP_i}{n} \tag{4}$$

(2) AP: Average accuracy rate, which is the result of each class's detection quality. r represents the recall rate, and p represents the accuracy rate. The calculation formula is shown in (5):

$$AP = \int_{0}^{1} p(r)dr \tag{5}$$

(3) Recall: Recall rate, also known as recall rate, refers to the ratio of the number of aircraft judged by the model and the actual results to the total number of aircraft in the original image. It is mainly used to measure the ability of a classifier to find all positive classes. The calculation formula is shown in (6):

$$Recall = \frac{TP}{(TP + FN)} \tag{6}$$

Precision: Accuracy, also known as precision, refers to the proportion of the number of detection frames identified as aircraft to the number of positive detection frames in all images (positive category numbers) identified by the network. The calculation formula is shown in (7):

$$Precision = \frac{TP}{TP + FP} \qquad (7)$$

Image enhancement actually refers to enhancing or weakening the contrast of some or all pixels of an image to achieve better visual effects and higher performance indicators. The enhancement methods are mainly divided into spatial domain enhancement and frequency domain enhancement. Image enhancement in spatial domain directly acts on image pixel points and performs specified transformations on the pixels to obtain the transformed values of the pixels. The commonly used methods include histogram enhancement and spatial filtering (linear and nonlinear); Image enhancement in the frequency domain is to first transform a spatial image into a frequency domain image through processing such as Fourier transform, wavelet transform, and cosine transform, and then perform enhancement processing on the frequency domain image. After transforming into an enhanced frequency domain transformation, perform inverse operations to convert the frequency domain back into the spatial domain, thereby obtaining an enhanced spatial image. The commonly used methods include low-pass filtering, high-pass filtering, and homomorphic filtering.

When performing feature extraction in a convolutional neural network, multiple convolution operations and pooling operations are performed. During this process (from bottom to top), each time the convolution is pooled, the image resolution becomes lower. Although advanced features are extracted, the information of small targets is gradually lost due to the reduction in resolution, so the accuracy of large scale targets detection is higher, while the accuracy of small size targets is unsatisfactory. Especially in remote sensing images, there are many small targets such as cars, ships, and airplanes, which makes the detection accuracy of small targets using target detection algorithms in remote sensing image detection generally low, and the rate of missed detection is high. For example, R-CNN series networks predict the output characteristics of the last layer, as shown in Fig. 5, so the accuracy of small target detection is not high. If we can combine low-level features of different layers of shallow layers with high-level features of deep layers, and then predict them separately, we can not only predict feature maps on one scale, but also predict multiple combined feature maps of different scales, Then the final feature map not only has more deep features, but also shallow features can be extracted, so that the information of small targets will not be lost in a large amount, which can reduce the missed detection rate and improve the recall rate and precision rate of small targets. The multi scale feature pyramid (FPN) can achieve the output of multi scale feature maps that fuse high and low level features.

High resolution remote-sensed image target detection on account of machine learning will be further expanded to multi-source data and multi feature combination with the development of intelligent algorithm. Secondly, the remote-sensed image target data set will also strengthen the gradual amelioration and target task recognition, especially the one-stage method with high operation efficiency. In addition, from the prior knowledge to the deep learning algorithm, we will gradually introduce the empirical and statistical

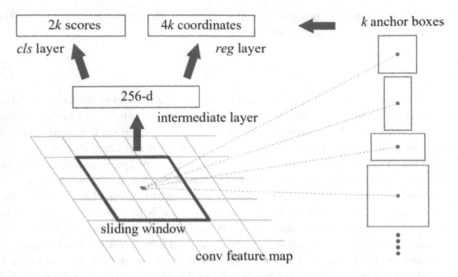

Fig. 5. Single layer feature map

prior info into the deep learning algorithm to ameliorate the remote-sensed image target detection. In addition, the further study of deep learning mathematical theory will also effectively support and guarantee the accuracy and efficiency of high-resolution remote-sensed image target detection.

4   Experimental Results and Analysis

The data sets used in the training and testing process of this article are the DIOR and DOTA data sets, which were integrated and proposed in 2018. The DIOR data set has a size of 800 * 800, and contains 23463 images, which are divided into 20 categories. The number of targets labeled using horizontal annotation methods totals 192472. DIOR is the largest and most diverse data set currently available in the Earth observation community.

Compared with the original Faster R-CNN network, this article first preprocesses the dataset, then selects DenseNet BC for the regional feature extraction network, and introduces CBAM attention mechanism and feature pyramid into the feature extraction network. In this paper, the control variable method is used to conduct experiments on the data set DIOR. The number of training and test sets is 1:1. The original Faster R-CNN network (using VGG-16 for feature extraction network) has a mAP of 56.7% without image preprocessing. The second line is the result of using DenseNet BC to replace VGG-16 network for feature extraction, and its mAP reaches 61.8%, which is 5.1% higher than the original network.

Although other algorithms have their own salient points in some aspects, the overall performance of the network modified in this article is far superior to other networks, with its mAP reaching 78.6%, with the highest value in the table. Target detection in each category is top. Except for the AP in aircraft, tennis courts, ships, and oil tanks, which is slightly lower than YOLOv3, in other categories, whether they are ports, airports, or railway stations with complex backgrounds, "For cars and windmills with small target scales and a large number of them, their AP values are the highest, especially for small target scenarios such as ships and cars. Compared to the original Faster R-CNN network, the AP values for small target detection have increased by nearly two times. These data have proven that attention mechanisms and multi-scale feature pyramids can indeed improve network performance."

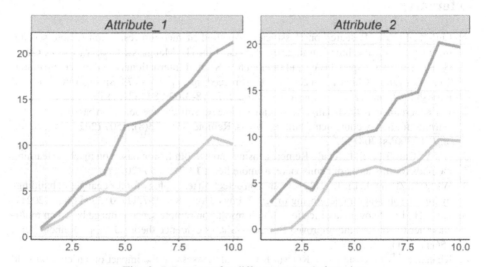

Fig. 6. P-R curves for different network detection

In Fig. 6, the P-R curves of the original Faster R-CNN (upper) and the modified network (lower) in this article are shown, respectively. P represents accuracy, R represents recall rate, and the area enclosed by the P-R curve is the average accuracy AP. The higher the AP value, the better the performance of the classifier. From Fig. 6, it can be seen that the area of the P-R curve corresponding to the network in this article in the six categories of baseball field, tennis court, aircraft, automobile, ship, and port is larger than the area of the original Faster R_ The P-R curve corresponding to CNN is larger, especially in scenes with complex backgrounds such as automobiles, ships, and ports, where targets are small and randomly arranged. Through the introduction of attention mechanism and FPN, the accuracy of target detection has been significantly improved, which proves that the overall performance of the network in this paper has significantly improved.

5 Conclusion

In summary, the establishment of high-resolution remote-sensed image target detection on account of machine learning algorithm can preserve the semantic and target specific areas in the image, and realize the rapid acquisition of target image details. On account of the research of remote-sensed image info extraction on account of machine learning, this paper analyzes the concept of machine learning algorithm and the difficulties of internal and high-resolution remote-sensed image target detection. Through the analysis of high-resolution remote-sensed image target detection on account of machine learning, this paper studies the overall tech of high-resolution remote-sensed image target detection, the machine learning method of high-resolution remote-sensed image target detection, and the development trend of high-resolution remote-sensed image target detection on account of machine learning.

References

1. Liu, X., Li, Ya.: Research on classification method of medium resolution remote sensing image based on machine learning. In: Pan, G., Lin, H., Meng, X., Gao, Y., Li, Y., Guan, Q., Ding, Z. (eds.) Spatial Data and Intelligence: Second International Conference, SpatialDI 2021, Hangzhou, China, April 22–24, 2021, Proceedings, pp. 164–173. Springer International Publishing, Cham (2021). https://doi.org/10.1007/978-3-030-85462-1_15
2. Jia, Y.: A refined method of high-resolution remote sensing change detection based on machine learning for newly constructed building areas. Remote Sens. **13**(8), 1507 (2021). https://doi.org/10.3390/rs13081507
3. Hu, Y., Che, T., Dai, L., et al.: Remote sensing snow depth fusion based on machine learning methods for the northern hemisphere. Remote Sens. **13**(7), 1250 (2021)
4. Wang, T., Zhang, J., Li, T., et al.: Research on detection technology for the changes of buildings by high resolution remote sensing image. J. Phys. Conf. Ser. **1972**(1), 012066 (7pp) (2021)
5. Feng, H.: Land-cover classification of high-resolution remote sensing image based on multi-classifier fusion and the improved Dempster-Shafer evidence theory. J. Appl. Remote Sens. **15**(1) (2021)
6. Khanal, S., Klopfenstein, A., Kushal, K.C., et al.: Assessing the impact of agricultural field traffic on corn grain yield using remote sensing and machine learning. Soil Tillage Res. **208**, 104880 (2021)
7. Yu, X., Zhang, K., Zhang, Y.: Land use classification of open-pit mine based on multi-scale segmentation and random forest model. PLoS ONE **17**(2), e0263870 (2022)
8. Fang, K., Ouyang, J., Hu, B.: Swin-HSTPS: research on target detection algorithms for multi-source high-resolution remote sensing images. Sensors **21** (2021)
9. Huang, F., Shen, G., Hong, H., et al.: Change detection of buildings with the utilization of a deep belief network and high-resolution remote sensing images. Fractals (2022)
10. Kislov, D.E., Korznikov, K.A., Altman, J., et al.: Extending deep learning approaches for forest disturbance segmentation on very high-resolution satellite images. Remote Sens. Ecol. Conserv. (2021)
11. Liu, X., Wu, W., Zheng, L., et al.: Research on target localization method of CRTS-III slab ballastless track plate based on machine vision. Electronics (2021)
12. Chen, J., Li, Y., Cao, L.H.: Research on region selection super resolution restoration algorithm based on infrared micro-scanning optical imaging model. Sci. Rep. **11**(1) (2021)
13. Chen, Z., Wang, Y.: A label- and enzyme-free fluorescence assay based on thioflavin T–induced G-quadruplexes for the detection of telomerase activity. J. Chem. Res. **47**(1), 569–573 (2023)
14. Brook, A.: How the small object detection via machine learning and uas-based remote-sensing imagery can support the achievement of SDG2: a case study of vole burrows. Remote Sens. **13** (2021)
15. Zhang, X.: Research on remote sensing image De–aze based on GAN. J. Sign. Process. Syst. **2021**(5) (2021)

Design of Visual Communication Digital System Based on CAD

Yawei Yu[1](✉), Hanze Guo[1], Jie Xiang[1], and Xue Zhou[2]

[1] Yunnan Normal University, Kunming 650504, Yunnan, China
`yuyawei1224@163.com`
[2] Yinchuan University of Science and Technology, Yinchuan 750021, China

Abstract. Communication is the transmission of information through a certain medium, with the purpose of transmitting information. Communication systems are the generic term for technical systems used to complete the information transmission process, and their role is to send information from a source to one or more destinations. Modulation and demodulation occupy an important position and are indispensable in the process of information transmission, so it is extremely important to study the modulation and demodulation process of a system. The traditional visual communication automation digital system has the problems of poor visual communication effect and low efficiency of visual information transmission, so it can only design a single element and lacks visual order. In order to solve the above problems, a visual communication automation digital system based on CAD is designed, and the hardware and software are designed. The design of visual communication digital system based on CAD is a process involving the creation and development of various graphics and images, icons, logos, symbols and other designs. It also includes the use of computer aided drafting (CAD) software to create these designs from drawings or sketches. The main purpose of creating this type of digital system is to develop an effective way to transmit information in an effective way, with the least errors in spelling and grammar. This is because it can be used as a tool to effectively exchange ideas between different people involved in different projects or activities related to visual communication.

Keywords: Visual communication · CAD auxiliary technology · Digital system

1 Introduction

With the rapid development of digital technology, digital media has become a new media that truly integrates into our life in all aspects. Compared with other traditional media, digital media has its own characteristics in terms of technology and communication form. On this new information communication platform supported by digital technology, visual communication design will inevitably have a new form of design expression corresponding to it [1]. This paper takes digital technology as a clue, seeks for the renewal trend of visual communication in the digital environment by studying the transformation of visual communication design, and makes some basic foresight and theoretical accumulation for the future development of visual communication design in combination with relevant theories.

Y. Zhang and N. Shah (Eds.): BigIoT-EDU 2023, LNICST 582, pp. 393–403, 2024.
https://doi.org/10.1007/978-3-031-63136-8_40

In the field of visual communication design, the rules of objects in the image can reflect the essential characteristics of the image laterally [2]. The essential characteristics of the image can be extracted using statistical extraction technology to achieve the purpose of visual communication. When the system transmits complex multidimensional images, it needs to introduce CAD auxiliary technology, which can simplify and draw multidimensional images to show the structural information of the image [3].

Visual communication under CAD aided technology has three-dimensional and dynamic special effects, which changes the traditional planarization and static characteristics of images, transforms image products into virtual information images, expands the extension of traditional visual communication design, and makes a qualitative leap in visual communication.

The traditional visual communication digital system can not realize the dynamic and multi-dimensional image, and the communication effect is poor. It can only design a single element, and it is difficult to achieve the design of multiple elements. When carrying out automatic visual communication, the system lacks visual order relations, resulting in low efficiency and poor accuracy of visual information transmission [4].

Communication is traditionally understood as the transmission of information. In today's highly informationized society, information and communication have become the "lifeblood" of modern society. As a resource, only through extensive dissemination and exchange can information generate utilization value, promote cooperation among social members, promote the development of social productivity, and create enormous economic benefits [5]. Communication, as a means or means of transmitting information, has become a powerful driving force for the development of the international community and the world economy in the 21st century through the integration of sensor technology and computer technology. Therefore, future communication will have an even greater and far-reaching impact on people's lifestyles and social development.

In the process of information transmission, it is required that the size of the antenna be comparable to the wavelength of the signal in order for the signal to be effectively radiated. For voice signals, the corresponding antenna size should be over tens of kilometers, which is practically impossible to achieve. Therefore, it is necessary to modulate the signal spectrum to a higher frequency range. If the signal is directly radiated without modulation, the frequency of the signals emitted by each radio station will be the same [6]. The essence of modulation is to make signals in the same frequency range rely on different frequency carriers, so that the receiver can separate the required frequency signals without mutual interference.

Sometimes the signal is too complex, and it is difficult to manually calculate its modulation and demodulation process. The analysis of its results lacks visual and intuitive representation, which affects the application of the obtained results in real life. The CAD developed by MathWorks Company in the United States solves this problem. It is used in many fields such as automatic control, mathematical calculation, signal analysis, signal processing, and is also an important tool for domestic universities and research departments to conduct many scientific research. The emergence of MATLAB provides great convenience for the analysis of communication systems [7].

In order to solve the problems of the traditional visual communication digital system, this paper designs an automatic visual communication digital system based on

CAD auxiliary technology. CAD auxiliary technology is used to highlight the structural information of images, so that visual communication has good three-dimensional and dynamic special effects. Hardware and software environments are designed. Through the hardware of the system, image acquisition, processing, transmission, storage and control are completed, and a software development environment is built, Improve the performance of the visual communication automation digital system [8]. Finally, through comparative experiments, verify the effectiveness of the visual communication automation digital system based on CAD technology designed in this paper, and determine the feasibility of the system.

2 Related Work

2.1 Research Status of Digital Visual Communication

In recent years, with the rise of "digital technology" and "Internet", monographs and papers on the development and transformation of visual communication design in the digital era have gradually become the research focus of art design discipline, but it is still a relatively new research direction for the transformation of visual communication design. In its transformation research achievements, there are few monographs, most of which are journal papers, and most of them are under the framework of new media design research, including the research on the relationship between the development of visual communication design and the development of media, and the research on the concept and category renewal of visual communication design [9]. For this, it mainly focuses on the impact of media update on visual communication design.

The earliest discipline of visual communication design in China was named "decoration design", which refers to two-dimensional design, and is relative to three-dimensional design such as architectural design, interior design, interior environment design and industrial modeling design. Later, with the introduction of western ideas, some scholars found that decoration design, as a major of higher education, only subjectively stood in the position of pure aesthetics, and did not add the idea of practical art. Later, it was renamed as graphic design [10]. In his History of World Graphic Design, Mr. Wang Shouzhi summarized the concept of "graphic design", The concept of cognition is "to combine several basic elements on the plane in a way consistent with the purpose of communication, so that they can be mass produced printed materials, which can have the function of accurate visual communication, and at the same time give the audience the visual psychological satisfaction that the design needs to achieve [11]. It also emphasizes that all two-dimensional space in the design category, non film and television design activities are basically the content of graphic design".

Design is the mirror of society [12]. Design should reflect what society looks like. "He is inseparable from the era in which he lives, and represents the spirit of an era, which also indicates the coming of a new era." "The emergence of digital media not only changes our living environment, but also changes the traditional production mode of art design and reconstructs the aesthetic order and paradigm of design art practice". As a part of modern art design, visual communication design also makes great changes in design objects, design means, design thinking and even designers themselves due to the strong intervention of technology [13].

Although the expressive force of the previous visual design is very full, it can not freely convey information at will due to the limitation of traditional media. Due to the involvement of digital technology, the visual communication design in the new era brings the entire communication space into the "bit" environment created by digitalization for information acquisition and editing. In such a virtual world, the audience can be immersive, can make various choices, and can directly access the information needed for editing [14]. At the same time, the addition of multimedia technology enables the design to have a multi-directional sensory experience of hearing, touch, and smell, It has effectively spread and received information.

The visual communication design in the digital environment refers to taking the visual communication design knowledge system as the main body, taking the digital theory as the guidance, using the computer, network and other information technologies in the information age as the media and design tools, in the field of visual design, engaging in various visual information communication activities to achieve the purpose of transmitting information [15]. With the rapid development of science and technology, the distance between people has been shortened, and the concept of national boundaries has gradually become blurred. Faced with the integration of the world economy, digital information, media diversification and many other factors that promote social development, the technology and methods of information exchange have undergone tremendous changes, which also provide a broader and broader development space for visual communication design.

2.2 Overview of Digital Signal Processor (DSP)

With the advent of the information age and the digital world, digital signal processing technology has become an extremely important discipline and technical field today. Digital Signal Processing (DSP) uses computers or specialized processing equipment to process signals using numerical methods such as sampling, transformation, synthesis, estimation, and recognition, in order to extract information and facilitate application. Currently, it is rapidly developing in various engineering and technical fields, and gradually replacing traditional analog signal processing systems in many application fields, such as communication, automatic control, power systems, fault detection, speech, automated instrumentation, aerospace, railways, robotics, radar, sonar, remote sensing, and other fields.

Due to its high accuracy, flexibility, reliability, and ease of large-scale integration, digital signal processing is being rapidly developed and widely used. Digital signal processors (DSP) are emerging to meet this demand and are developing vigorously, which in turn provides impetus for the rapid development of digital signal processing technology. DSP not only has high-speed computing and control capabilities, but also emphasizes real-time processing. In this way, DSP not only has high-speed computing and control capabilities, but also has made significant changes in processor architecture, instruction system, and instruction flow based on the characteristics of real-time digital signal processing:

(1) The Harvard structure, which separates the data bus from the program bus, or an improved Harvard structure, is commonly used.

(2) Most use pipeline technology to reduce the execution time of each instruction.

(3) There are multiple buses on the chip, and convenient addressing methods are provided, greatly improving the execution efficiency of instructions.

(4) Provide high-speed addressing methods, such as cyclic addressing, bit reverse addressing, etc.

(5) According to the characteristics of multiplication and accumulation operations widely used in digital signal processing, independent hardware multipliers and adders are equipped, which can be completed within one instruction cycle

(6) On chip integration of DMA controllers and serial communication ports improves the ability to move data.

(7) With software and hardware waiting functions, it can easily interface with various memories.

(8) Single chip system, low energy consumption, easy to miniaturize and portable design.

Therefore, DSP has extremely high computational speed, and it is important to complete real-time data processing. With the rapid improvement of performance and significant decrease in cost, the application range of DSP continues to expand, and its application almost covers the entire electronic field.

The DSP chip development and programming process is: During the DSP application development process, the development and design section completes the algorithm design and verification. Generally, the simulation is performed using CAD language first, and when the simulation results are satisfactory, the product implementation phase is entered. The algorithm in the development and design stage is implemented in C/C++ or assembly language, and debugged on the DSP target board of the hardware. It is necessary to save the intermediate results of the target DSP program running to the hard disk of the PC through the development tool CCS (Code Composer Studios); Then adjust to the SIMULINK workspace and compare with the intermediate results of the SIMULINK simulation algorithm to find the result deviation caused by design or precision in the DSP program. It is very inconvenient to repeat this process.

In order to gain an advantage in the competition, software developers need to use a high-level integrated environment that is simple and easy to learn to help them overcome the difficulties of underlying design, focus on exploring new algorithms, and achieve technological breakthroughs to adapt to changing technological trends and market conditions. As the most powerful numerical and analytical tool, CAD has long been widely used. The DSP development idea adopted in this paper is: CAD is used for DSP algorithm simulation/simulation, integrating all DSP development tools into CAD. That is, complete conceptual design, simulation/simulation, object code generation, operation, and commissioning in a unified CAD environment. Without losing generality, only the minimization problem is assumed here:

minimize f (x),

subject to:

x represents a feasible implementation ψ,

$$c_i(x) \leq 0, \forall i \in \{1, \ldots, q\}, \tag{1}$$

$$h(t) = A_0\delta(\tau - \tau_0) + \sum_{i=1}^{N-1} A_i(\tau - \tau_i) \tag{2}$$

Using the CAD-DSP system level development environment can greatly save the time and effort spent on programming and correcting errors, freeing developers to follow cutting-edge technology, explore new ideas, and submit first-class product designs.

3   Software Design of Visual Communication Automation Digital System Based on CAD

CAD is the abbreviation of computer aided design. It can use computers and graphic equipment to design images, and assist engineering technicians to design products or engineering drawings through the strong graphic processing ability of computers [9]. In the visual communication automation digital system designed in this paper based on CAD auxiliary technology, CAD auxiliary technology is adopted, which can improve the automation of visual communication, shorten the communication cycle, and improve the communication efficiency. The software flow of the visual communication automation digital system based on CAD technology designed in this paper is shown in Fig. 1.

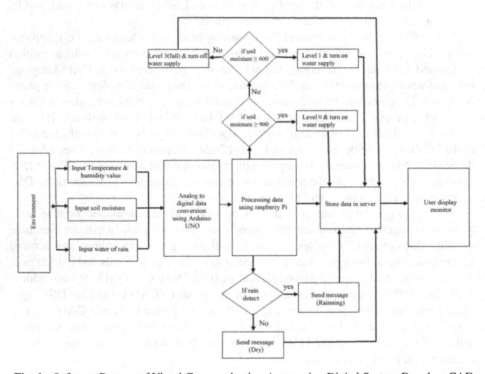

Fig. 1. Software Process of Visual Communication Automation Digital System Based on CAD

Step 1: Manage the image data information base. The image data information library includes image data acquisition, image data information transmission, and image data information reception. Image data acquisition can be realized through the image acquisition processing module in the hardware. When image data acquisition is carried out, image data types need to be classified to improve the acquisition efficiency and shorten the acquisition cycle. The image information is transmitted to the digital system through the image transmission equipment. The image data information receiving is mainly responsible for buffering the collected and transmitted image information, so that the CAD aided technology can be used to design the plane and three-dimensional image information.

Step 2: Display three-dimensional images. After the management of the image data information base is realized, the processed image information is designed in plane and three-dimensional by using CAD auxiliary technology. During the plane design, the images in the panoramic camera are simply spliced, and then the live images are spliced. After the splicing is completed, it is fused with the CAD designed plane image to form a plane panorama and output it. After the formation of the plan, the CAD aided technology is used to carry out the three-dimensional design of the plan to form a three-dimensional and dynamic image. Each point in the image data needs to be mapped into the three-dimensional space, and then the binocular parallax stereoscopic display and true three-dimensional stereoscopic display technology are used to map the original three-dimensional The stereoscopic image is processed. When the binocular parallax stereoscopic display technology is used, when the human eyes see the same image, the images in front of the two eyes are different. Therefore, the images seen by the two eyes are displayed separately. At a certain time, the corresponding left eye view is transmitted to the first camera, and the corresponding right eye view is transmitted to the second camera, Then, the true 3D stereo display technology is used to analyze and process the depth of the two images, combine them with the processed images, and finally display the 3D stereo images.

Step 3: Optimize the three-dimensional image. Because the automatic digital system of visual communication requires high visual communication efficiency, image enhancement technology is used to optimize the three-dimensional image, so that the quality of the displayed three-dimensional image is better, so as to improve the effect of visual communication. According to the different optimization spaces, image enhancement technology includes two image optimization methods, namely, spatial domain based and frequency domain based methods. The frequency domain method is used to optimize each virtual pixel point on the three-dimensional stereo image. The optimization content includes image smoothing and histogram correction. The spatial domain method refers to converting the three-dimensional stereo image to another spatial domain through gray scale transformation, Then, the 3D stereo images stored in another spatial domain are optimized by Fourier transform method. In order to improve the quality of 3D stereo images and the visual communication effect, the depth optimization of 3D stereo images is carried out by combining the space pre-processing method with the frequency domain method.

The relative motion between the receiving and transmitting ends causes a Doppler frequency shift. If the motion speed of the transmitting end is v and the motion speed of the receiving end is v, the transmitting frequency of the transmitting end is f. When the signal reaches the receiving end, the frequency of the received signal, f, can be calculated by the following formula:

$$f_r = f_s \frac{c - v_r}{c - v_s} \tag{3}$$

The simplified analysis method is to treat the signal as a sinusoidal curve shape and continuously advance forward. During the signal's progress, the signal is modulated due to forward scattering, so the frequency shifts when it reaches the receiver. The resulting Doppler frequency shifts can be given by the Carson rule:

$$f_d = 2f_w(1 + \frac{2w\cos\theta_0}{c} h_w) \tag{4}$$

According to modulation methods, it can be divided into baseband transmission and bandpass transmission. The power of digital baseband signals is generally in the low frequency range from zero to a certain frequency (such as 0–6 M), so it cannot be directly transmitted in many practical communications (such as wireless channels). It is necessary to use carrier modulation to shift the frequency spectrum and transform the digital baseband signals into digital frequency band signals suitable for channel transmission for transmission. This transmission method is called frequency band transmission of digital signals or modulation transmission, carrier transmission. The so-called modulation refers to using a baseband signal to control a certain parameter of the carrier waveform, so that the parameter changes with the regularity of the baseband signal to carry messages. Modulating digital signals can facilitate signal transmission; Implement channel multiplexing; Changing the bandwidth occupied by the signal; Improve system performance.

4 Simulation Results and Analysis

By writing M file program, random signals are generated, and each module is programmed in the order shown in Fig. 2. There are statements and explanations that require attention in the program. Run the program to implement the 2ASK modulation and demodulation process. This design adopts analog modulation method (multiplier method) and coherent demodulation method. The graph of post simulation modulation process and demodulation process is shown in Fig. 3.

In binary digital modulation, a binary phase shift keying (2PSK) signal is generated when the phase of the sinusoidal carrier wave varies discretely with the binary digital baseband signal. There are two methods for modulating 2PSK signals, namely, analog modulation and keying. Typically, 0° and 180° of the modulated signal carrier are used to represent 1 and 0 of the binary digital baseband signal, respectively. Analog modulation uses two inverted carrier signals for modulation. Using the phase change of the carrier wave as a reference reference, the phase is 0° relative to the initial phase when the baseband signal is 0, and 180° relative to the initial phase when the baseband signal is 1.

Keying is a modulation method that uses the phase of the carrier wave to carry binary information. Typically, 0° and 180° are used to represent 0 and 1, respectively. The time

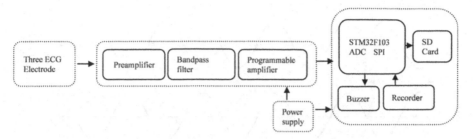

Fig. 2. Modulation and demodulation block diagram

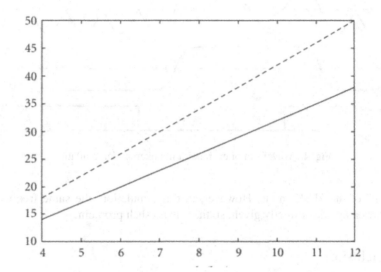

Fig. 3. Modulation process simulation diagram

domain expression is:

$$e_{2PSK} = \left[\sum_n a_n g(t - nT_s)\right]\cos\omega_c t \tag{5}$$

Because the amplitude is constant, coherent demodulation must be performed. The band-pass filtered signal is multiplied by the local carrier in the multiplier, and then the high-frequency components are filtered using a low-pass filter before sampling decisions are made. The discriminator determines by polarity. That is, the positive sampling value is determined to be 1, and the negative sampling value is determined to be 0. The waveform of each point is shown in Fig. 4.

Due to a 180° phase ambiguity in the carrier recovery process of the signal, that is, the recovered local carrier may be the same as the required coherent carrier, or vice versa. This uncertainty in the phase relationship will cause the demodulated digital baseband signal to be exactly opposite to the transmitted baseband signal, that is, will "1" become "0" or "0" become "1", resulting in all errors in the output digital signals of the decision maker. This phenomenon is known as the "inverted π" phenomenon or "inverted phase

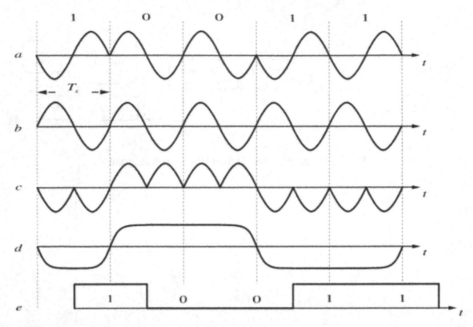

Fig. 4. Waveform of each point in coherent demodulation

operation" of the 2PSK mode. However, in this simulation, the same frequency and phase carrier signal is directly given, so there is no such problem.

5   Conclusion

This paper is a visual communication digital system based on CAD. The architecture of the whole system is realized through the user layer, application layer, service layer and database layer. Among them, the CAD visualization module realizes the visual communication of commodity packaging. The digital liquor packaging designed by this system has good visual communication effect and low packaging energy consumption, which can improve the working efficiency of enterprises and reduce energy consumption in the future. When designing the visual communication digital system, this paper only conducts research from the visual angle of CAD auxiliary technology. In the future research, it can be deeply studied from multiple perspectives to improve the deficiencies in this system. For example, it can analyze from the perspective of software engineering guidance, design relevant research strategies, or design a planned and scientific system for visual communication digital from the perspective of demand.

References

1. Cao, J.: Design and implementation of human-computer interaction system in parallel digital library system based on neural network. Hindawi Limited (2021)

2. Yu, Y., Qiao, Y., Ren, G., et al.: Design of digital recognition system based on FPGA. J. Phys. Conf. Ser. **1885**(5), 052030 (5pp) (2021)
3. Bian, J., Ji, Y.: Research on the teaching of visual communication design based on digital technology. Wireless Commun. Mobile Comput. **2021**, 1–11 (2021). https://doi.org/10.1155/2021/8304861
4. Bai, Y., You, J.-B., Lee, I.-K.: Design and optimization of smart factory control system based on digital twin system model. Math. Probl. Eng. **2021**, 1–16 (2021). https://doi.org/10.1155/2021/2596946
5. Martinez-Manez, R., Climent, E., Rurack, K., et al.: Immunochemical design of antibody-gated indicator delivery (gAID) systems based on mesoporous silica nanoparticles. ACS Appl. Nano Mater. **5**(1), 626–641 (2022)
6. Temmar, M.N.E., Hocini, A., Khedrouche, D., Denidni, T.A.: Analysis and design of MIMO indoor communication system using terahertz patch antenna based on photonic crystal with graphene. Photon. Nanostruct. Fundament. Appl. **43**, 100867 (2021). https://doi.org/10.1016/j.photonics.2020.100867
7. Liu, Y., Liang, C., Xu, H., et al.: Digital art pattern design based on visual material colouring intelligent programming system. Math. Probl. Eng. **2022** (2022)
8. Tehrani, O.S., Zaeri, A., Ghafarioun, E.: Design and implementation of simple speech recognition system based-on digital filters in AVR microcontroller (2022)
9. Karumuri, S.R., Mohammed, H., Guha, K., et al.: Design, simulation and analysis of micro electro, echanical system microneedle for micropump in drug delivery systems (2021)
10. Jing, H.: The Design and implementation of medical image processing system based on DICOM format. China Dig. Med. **2022**(7) (2022)
11. Tian, K., Yingcheng, S., Hyun, K.J., et al.: EvidenceMap: a three-level knowledge representation for medical evidence computation and comprehension. J. Amer. Med. Inform. Assoc.
12. Gao, S., Bhagi, L.K.: Design and research on CADDCAM system of plane based on NC machining technology. Comput.-Aided Des. Appl. **19**(S2), 64–73 (2021)
13. Yu, Y., Sun, Y.: Research on visual communication graphic design information system based on computer simulation. J. Phys. Conf. Ser. **1952**(2), 022032 (2021). https://doi.org/10.1088/1742-6596/1952/2/022032
14. Liu, J., Feng, J.: RETRACTED: Design of embedded digital image processing system based on ZYNQ. Microprocess. Microsyst. **83**, 104005 (2021). https://doi.org/10.1016/j.micpro.2021.104005
15. Ojeda, R.A., Munoz, L.: Optimal design of a heat recovery system based on an organic rankine cycle. SAE WCX Digital Summit (2021)

The Construction of Educational Journalism and Mass Media Platform Based on Genetic Algorithm

Shuyuan Piao[1,2](✉) and Fang Feng[1,2]

[1] Yunnan Engineering Vocational College, Yunnan 650304, China
piaoshuyuan840812@126.com
[2] School of Design and Art, Lanzhou University of Technolo-Gy, LanzhouGansu 730050, China

Abstract. In the modern network era, news media not only undertakes the function of disseminating news information, but also undertakes a certain social education function. We should recognize the differences between news media specialty and traditional education, and make the correct use of the educational function of news media specialty on the basis of understanding. Based on genetic algorithm, the media platform for journalism and the public should have its own unique positioning, that is, the military training field for journalism students' new media employment, the magnetic field for teacher-student interaction, and the public opinion field to show their professional image to all sectors of society.

Keywords: Genetic algorithm · Education journalism · Mass media · Platform construction

1 Introduction

The impact of new media on traditional media is a challenge that traditional media must face, and the integrated development of traditional media and new media is an important task and opportunity at present. In this process, we must pay close attention to the role of technological innovation, because the outbreak of new media is largely caused by the technological revolution.

In the face of the upsurge of running a school of Journalism and communication, the guarantee of journalism practice education mechanism is the most important aspect of journalism talent training. Although there are many successful cases of practical education of journalism in the world, the training of journalists first serves their own country, and the "bringing doctrine" should also be in line with China's national conditions. Therefore, the practical education of journalism specialty should be improved on the basis of absorbing the advantages of the training of Western journalists, combined with Chinese characteristics, and be diligent in practice, hands-on and operation on the basis of news theory, policy line and basic news knowledge, so as to cultivate Chinese journalism talents with strong practical ability and international vision [1].

Y. Zhang and N. Shah (Eds.): BigIoT-EDU 2023, LNICST 582, pp. 404–409, 2024.
https://doi.org/10.1007/978-3-031-63136-8_41

2 Research on Genetic Algorithm

2.1 Overview of Genetic Algorithm Research

The rise of genetic algorithm research was in the late 1980s and early 1990s, but its historical origin can be traced back to the 1960s. In 1967, Bagley first proposed the term genetic algorithm in his paper, and discussed the application of genetic algorithm in automatic game. His operations including selection, crossover and mutation are very close to the corresponding operations in genetic algorithm, especially his meaningful research on selection operation. He realized that the selection probability should change appropriately in the early and late stages of genetic evolution. Therefore, he introduced the concept of fitness scaling, which is a commonly used technology in genetic algorithm. At the same time, he also proposed the concept of self-tuning of genetic algorithm for the first time, that is, integrating the probability of crossover and mutation into the coding of chromosome itself to realize the self-tuning and optimization of the algorithm. The flow of genetic algorithm is shown in Fig. 1.

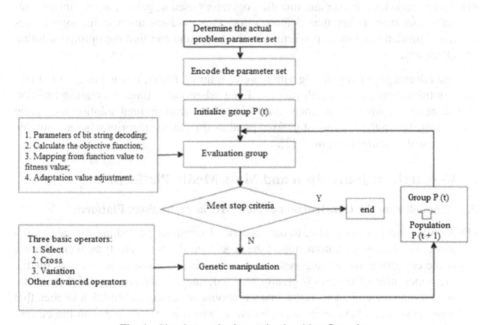

Fig. 1. Simple standard genetic algorithm flow chart

2.2 Characteristics of Genetic Algorithm

Compared with the traditional optimization algorithm, genetic algorithm has the following main characteristics:

(1) The search of genetic algorithm starts from the coding group of the problem solution, that is, many points in the solution space are searched at the same time. We know

that single point search is adopted by the traditional optimization algorithm. It is easy to make the search fall into local extremum and can not jump out, which affects the quality and speed of search. At the same time, evaluating multiple points in the solution space can overcome the defects faced by the traditional optimization algorithm and is not easy to fall into local extremum.

(2) Genetic algorithm uses the information of fitness function to search without other auxiliary information. We know that the fitness function is independent of the search space. It is not limited by the search space, and it is set according to the wishes of users.

(3) Genetic algorithm is to calculate the coding group of problem parameters, not directly on the parameters themselves. With the use of this technology, genetic algorithm can deal with a variety of problems, not just limited to a few, because although the types of problems are different, different problem parameters are encoded in the same way to get rid of the variable set of the original problem. Genetic algorithm only needs to deal with the same form of coding, so that genetic algorithm has a wide range of applications.

(4) The selection, crossover and mutation operators used in genetic algorithm are random operations rather than definite rules. This randomization technology makes the algorithm have more powerful search ability and can find the optimal solution efficiently.

The advantages of genetic algorithm are as follows: firstly, it is not easy to fall into local optimization in the search process. Even when the defined adaptation function is discontinuous, irregular or noisy, it can find the overall optimal solution with great probability. Secondly, because of its fixed parallelism, genetic algorithm is very suitable for large-scale parallel computers [2].

3   Research on Journalism and Mass Media Platform

3.1   Thoughts on the Construction of New Media Technology Platform

(1) A shift from process centric to data centric. Traditional publishing focuses on the process and takes the automation of the process as the core. The typical application is the collection and editing system. However, in the construction of new media, the importance of process is greatly reduced, and the construction of data center has become the core. This is the data warehouse or central information kitchen that many news units have built or are building, which is also in line with the current development trend of big data.

(2) The transformation from closed system to open platform. The information platform of traditional media is basically closed. This closeness has left a deep mark since the era of laser phototypesetting. Platform strategy is an important aspect of Internet thinking. For example, microblog, wechat, JD and Ali, one of the core of their explosive growth is platform strategy. The purpose of platform strategy is to form an ecosystem, Establish a common development alliance on its own platform and let social organizations outside the platform innovate. Now there is no platform company in China's media field. In the future, China's leading media group must be platform type.

(3) Changes from single media to mass media, social media and we media. Media integration is a general trend. In the future, the division of newspapers, radio stations, television stations and websites will certainly be outdated. Media integration is an inevitable trend. At the same time, the explosive development of social media and we media has produced the phenomenon of so-called "citizen journalists". The decentralized media form of social media and we media has strong vitality.

3.2 Principles that News Media Should Pay Attention to in the Process of Information Dissemination

(1) The news media should maintain a certain timeliness of information in news reports. In contemporary society, the occurrence of social events often has a certain sudden occurrence. When reporting social events, the news media must pay attention to the timeliness of information. Only by giving correct reports to the public at the first time can we effectively curb rumors and maintain the initiative in publicity effect. In the current era of unprecedented prosperity of we media, the guiding and educational functions of news media are further reflected. Only by grasping the propaganda position of news media can we effectively increase the public opinion guidance of government departments to social emergencies. In this sense, the news media has played a certain educational significance to the audience,

(2) The news media should keep the authenticity of information when reporting news. In social emergencies, people often guess and even panic to a certain extent because they don't know the truth. The disorganization of Du Hui psychology often has an adverse impact. The rapid dissemination of network information may distort the truth of the event to a certain extent and make some false news popular. Therefore, China's news media should not only have a certain timeliness, but also make the news report have a certain authenticity in the dissemination of relevant social news. Only by ensuring the credibility of the news media can we maintain the educational function of the news media on people's ideas.

(3) The news media should insist on in-depth reporting of events when reporting news. In the era of we media, the information dissemination function of news media has been seriously challenged again and again. People can realize the rapid dissemination of information through mobile phone software, microblog and other forms. In this regard, in the process of news reporting, the news media should not only adhere to a certain principle of timeliness, but also adhere to in-depth follow-up reporting on the basis of events. Because the information dissemination in the era of we media often has certain superficial characteristics and does not have certain authority [3]. News media can make use of their own advantages to report news and spread information on the basis of objectivity and authenticity, so as to make up for the lack of timeliness of news media.

(4) Changes from traditional publishing technology to big data intelligent analysis technology. Traditional publishing technology is mainly to realize digitization and automation, and its ultimate goal is to improve work efficiency and strengthen organizational management and control. The development of information technology has developed from it to DT, that is, the so-called data technology. The key of DT era is to serve the public and stimulate productivity. The intelligent analysis technology of

big data is the core. To effectively realize the association between information and data, information visualization and data news, data mining and analysis, and even prediction.

4 Construction of Educational Journalism and Mass Media Platform Under Genetic Algorithm

4.1 System Platform Architecture Assumption

The media platform of news specialty and mass media is a platform to provide unified broadcasting and resource sharing for each new media business of the group. In terms of specific structure, it should be divided into three blocks: the source subsystem service module that provides signal distribution, format conversion and other signal basic service functions for each service, as shown in Fig. 2; Business operation module composed of various new media business subsystems (the main new media services in phase I include IPTV and streaming media); Be responsible for monitoring and managing the network management system support module of the whole system. Therefore, the overall structure of the whole system is as follows:

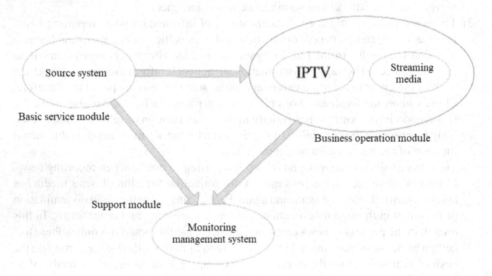

Fig. 2. System platform architecture

4.2 System Workflow Assumption

Since the signals required by the system come from different places and have various forms of digital/analog and SDI/TS, these signal sources should be gathered first, then processed into the signals required by the new media system, and finally distributed to each subsystem. According to the needs of users, the source system of the whole system can be divided into three working modules: signal collection, signal processing and signal distribution. The signal collection module is the collection place of all signal sources of the source subsystem. The signal resources required by each system of new media come from radio and television, which are first summarized into the signal collection module, such as local channel and CCTV channel [4]. The function of the signal processing module is to convert the signals from different formats into the signal types required by each subsystem of the new media after a series of processing. The task of the signal distribution module is to distribute the processed signal to each subsystem of the new media according to the demand. At the same time, all signals are distributed to the monitoring system for monitoring.

5 Conclusion

In modern society, the acquisition of information is of great significance in our life. We are also invisible guided in the acquisition of information. As an authoritative and professional information disseminator, the news media has a certain responsibility and obligation of social education. Based on genetic algorithm, we can better realize the educational function of news media specialty by fully understanding the educational function.

References

1. Wang, A.: Analysis on the role of new media practice platform in Journalism Teaching – Taking wechat public platform as an example. News Res. Guide **2**, 30–31 (2016)
2. Chen, G.: Genetic algorithm and its application. People's Posts and Telecommunications Press, Beijing (1996)
3. Xu, J.: Analysis on the construction of wechat mobile ubiquitous learning platform based on wechat public platform. J. Nann. Vocat. Techn. College **2**, 50–53 (2016)
4. Yuan, Y.: Application of wechat platform in the practice of Higher Vocational journalism students in Ningbo. China Educ. Inform. (6), 39–42 (2016)

An Information Security-Based Youth's Coupling of Scientific Literacy and Creative Arts

Jing Zhang[1,2]([📧])

[1] Modern College of Northwest University, Xi'an, Shaanxi, China
zhangjingbsjs@163.com
[2] Graduate University of Mongolia, Ulaanbaatar, Mongolia

Abstract. There is a natural inherent coupling between the promotion of scientific quality and the expansion of creative art of teenagers based on information security, and the two orientation is the same in the space-time dimension of unity of knowledge and practice, scientific thinking, breaking conventions, speculative life, patriotic orientation, etc. On the basis of current science and technology, an active approach to the coupling path between teenagers' scientific quality and creative art, and to enhance the synergy effect of "aesthetic education" and "intellectual education" is the focus of this paper. Information security is conducive to improving the quality of education and teaching of teenagers, expanding the channels for the integration of production and education, cultivating the patriotic feelings of teenagers, and creating a healthy lifestyle and atmosphere. However, in the process of development, there is still insufficient space for the coupling development between the improvement of scientific quality and creative art of teenagers, and the phenomenon of information leakage and information confusion, so it is necessary to continue to explore the coupling coordination path of high level and high quality.

Keywords: Scientific quality · creative arts · coupled to information · security

1 Information Security Design and Interactive Creative Art

With the in-depth analysis of intelligent technology and interactive creative art, as well as technology-oriented and information security-based, the vigorous development of new forms of art, as the main force of the national scientific and technological team in the future, young people should timely grasp the relevant knowledge, technology and information security awareness, enhance the artistic aesthetic height, and creatively and effectively complete the tasks in the information age. In terms of the educational goal of teenagers, the promotion of scientific quality and the expansion of creative arts promote and complement each other, and serve the fundamental goal of fostering morality and educating people and the construction of innovative art and technology army.

© ICST Institute for Computer Sciences, Social Informatics and Telecommunications Engineering 2024
Published by Springer Nature Switzerland AG 2024. All Rights Reserved
Y. Zhang and N. Shah (Eds.): BigIoT-EDU 2023, LNICST 582, pp. 410–416, 2024.
https://doi.org/10.1007/978-3-031-63136-8_42

1.1 The Unity of Knowledge and Action

According to the age of college students and primary school students, the degree of cognition of information security, and the different cognitive levels of science and art, carry out immersive interactive guidance, "from the small to the big" and "from the big to the small". Enhance each other's scientific quality and information security consciousness. Primary school should not stop at theoretical explanation and classroom teaching, but must enhance the practical height of science and technology and art, and integrate with social development [1]. The university needs to penetrate the creative scientific design process, strengthen the design of information security, transform science and art theory into real knowledge practice, and create effective science projects. Artistic means to promote scientific practice should also uphold the unity of "promoting action by knowledge" and "promoting knowledge by action". Intelligently create real-time interactive "big" and "small" twinning.

1.2 Scientific Thinking

Throughout the development of science, technology and art, critical scientific thinking is the core content of science and art, and also the essential factor to promote the breakthrough of major scientific achievements [2]. When young people are engaged in creative scientific and technological creation, only by adhering to scientific and rational thinking, following the law of scientific development, daring and good at taking "scientific criticism" as the "weapon" to understand and transform the industry in the two stages of primary school and university creation, can they put forward distinctive and original solutions in the context of different voices. To solve the real problem of creativity. Make "big friends" and "little friends" develop each other's scientific thinking habits of "bold hypothesis, careful verification" under different perspectives and forms of scientific thinking, strengthen practical consciousness, and become a new scientific artist of The Times who "dares to criticize and is good at criticizing". The "little master" and the "big engineer" are the common employees of "science and humanity" and "aesthetic education spirit" [3].

1.3 Break the Rules

Creative scientific design in college and scientific cognitive practice in primary school, only by daring to break conventions, dialogue with each other, crossing gaps, giving full play to their strengths, daring to break through the constraints of existing knowledge and scientific thinking patterns, and being good at summarizing or dominating the laws of the development of science and art, can we draw out true knowledge, practice, practical and effective scientific methods on the basis of aesthetics [4]. "From the small to the big", "from the big to the small" immersive interactive guidance, in-depth analysis of the possibilities of art and technology, and breakthrough of the existing science and technology constraints and bottlenecks, in order to achieve the "bridge or boat" safe and fast "cross the river" scientific goals in the practice of "big friends" and "children".

1.4 Think About Life

College students or primary school students have endless cognition of the objective world and endless pursuit of unknown science based on information security and scientific and cultural background. From the perspective of creative science of "little artists" and "big projects", its essence lies in creativity, which requires "big friends" and "little friends" to completely avoid the inertia of empirical scientific thinking, and to use the time, event and potential of science and art to carry out targeted hierarchical thinking. Dialectical cognition and handling of the relationship between "evaluation of the process of science and art practice" and "evaluation of the results of science and art practice" should not only examine the practical problems from the perspective of the results of science and art practice, From the perspective of science and art practice, it is also necessary to investigate whether "big friends" and "children" have the courage to create, innovate, have creative thinking, and realize interactive "big" and "small" twinning, so as to build and protect young people's thirst for knowledge, and assist and stimulate their enthusiasm for creation.

1.5 Patriotic Orientation

We will carry out the creative science quality improvement action of "Little Art Teacher" and "Big Project", guide young people to pay attention to the practical problems of information security, social science and art, further cultivate young people's feelings of home and country, improve the level of science and art, and at the same time, cherish "the great of the country". The immersive interaction of "from small to big" and "from big to small" guides them to integrate their personal ideals into national dreams, give full play to the advantages of all sides, and establish the overall view and professional view in line with the needs of new science and art. Creative art enables "big friends" and "little friends" to enjoy the freedom brought by creativity and to fully experience the sense of achievement brought by scientific innovation and artistic creation. In this way, it can stimulate young people to engage in information design and science and technology to the maximum extent, and give the dreams of "big friends" and "little friends" the wings of scientific information and art innovation. Let the future science and technology of the motherland gather together, let the vast sky of future science shine ".

2 Construct a Service APP for Teenagers' Science Quality and Creative Art Coupling Based on Information Security

The scientific quality and the creative art of the young are not only the imitation and inheritance of painting, design, culture, architecture, or form representation, nor the simple reproduction of some advanced technology, but the redefinition of creativity through the times of the new technology to convey a certain culture, ideas, feelings, spirit, behavior or desire [5]. Creative art can run through the scientific quality education of teenagers through the coupling of rich shapes, winding lines, flying fluidity, profound artistic conception, harmonious interest, yearning spirit and so on. Through intelligent technology to build an interactive and digital feedback information loop, with this intelligent interactive experience to enhance the sense of space, sense of reality and hierarchy, to provide technical support for young people's science and creative arts coupling service APP, breaking the original APP that only relies on computer equipment, breaking the limitations of click interaction, Realize multifunctional real creative experience, here also emphasizes the security of information maintenance design [6].

2.1 Construct the Coupling Model of Teenagers' Scientific Quality and Creative Art

The youth science quality and the creativity art coupling service APP pays more attention to the science quality and the creativity art mutual influence and the close cooperation. From four aspects of cultivation scale coupling, cultivation cost coupling, cultivation information coupling and cultivation culture coupling, it creates new development power and vitality for the scientific quality of the youth and the industrial cluster of creative art education. Using frequency statistical method and theoretical analysis method to construct the index and evaluation system of teenagers' scientific quality and creative art cultivation. Q indicates the coupling degree between scientific quality and creative art, and the Q value is between 0–1. The coupling degree between scientific quality and creative art is divided as shown in Table 1.

Table 1. The coupling degree of teenagers' scientific quality and creative art

Coupling target	Coupling degree interval	Coupling state
Q	0	Teenagers' scientific quality has nothing to do with creative art and develops in disorder
Q	0–0.3	Young People's scientific quality and creative art low-frequency coupling
Q	0.3–0.5	The coupling state between scientific quality and creative art of teenagers
Q	0.5–0.8	Teenagers' scientific quality and creative art run-in stage
Q	0.8–1.0	Teenagers' scientific quality and creative art are highly coupled and develop smoothly
Q	1.0	Teenagers' scientific quality and creative art are benign, orderly, resonant, coordinated and sustainable development

2.2 Construct the Function Model of the Coupling Coordination Between Scientific Quality and Creative Art of Teenagers

The coupling degree between scientific quality and creative art of teenagers can only make a basic judgment on the close relationship and strength between scientific quality and creative art of teenagers, but in the stage of matching and constructing, the orientation of educational goal can not make a corresponding evaluation on the coordinated development, sustainable development and green development level between teenagers' scientific quality and creative art. Moreover, there are inconsistency and differences in the development of the teenagers' scientific quality and creative art, and the coupling degree of the two will be high in the running-in stage, but the other side of the Comprehensive Evaluation Index is relatively low in the complex case [7]. In order to compensate for the one-sidedness of the coupling model assessment and to further explore the level of educational complementarity and coordinated development between adolescents' scientific literacy and creative artists, it is necessary to study the structural coupling coordination model based on the coupling degree of the two. In order to investigate and describe the coupling and coordination degree between the scientific quality and the creative art education system of teenagers more intuitively, and divide it into four levels to divide the coupling and coordination level, j denotes the coupling and coordination degree between scientific quality and creative art, and J value is between 0–1, as shown in Table 2.

Table 2. The evaluation grade of the coupling and coordination between the scientific quality and the creative art of the adolescents

Coupling target	Coupling degree interval	Evaluation grade of coupling coordination degree
J	0–0.4	Young People's scientific quality and creative art coupling low degree of coordination
J	0.4–0.5	The coupling of teenagers' scientific quality and creative art is moderately coordinated
J	0.5–0.8	The coupling of teenagers' scientific quality and creative art is highly coordinated
J	0.8–1.0	The coupling of scientific quality and creative art of teenagers is extremely harmonious

2.3 The Expected Benefits of the Coupling of Scientific Quality and Creative Art of Teenagers

Teenagers are immersed in interactive art exhibitions and information opening, as well as science and art offline "fine lectures" into the campus and society, which can infect more social groups through benign information transmission, so as to pay attention to the improvement of teenagers' scientific quality and the expansion of creative art. The combination of scientific and creative arts among young people will not only drive the rapid development of information and economy in the future [8], but also promote the local arts, intangible cultural heritage arts, technology and culture in urban areas. Let more audience through the organic connection of "small artists" and "big projects", "from small to big" and "from big to small" immersive interaction guide the practice of creative science and technology, innovative interpretation of science and art culture [9]. The information resources of scientific quality education for teenagers should be deeply explored, and the information supply chain of creative arts industry should be extended, as shown in Table 3.

Table 3. The structure of scientific quality and creative art of teenagers

Basic Education	Dig the angle	Education project cooperation
Curriculum system of scientific quality for teenagers	Historical and cultural heritage, ethnic cultural expansion, scientific and technological innovation	We will increase the construction of industrial chains in schools and enterprises, build digital communication platforms, improve the quality of education and teaching for young people, and expand the integration channels of industry and education
The construction of creative art platform	Creative culture, cultural products, immersive interactive exhibition	"From small to big" "From big to small" immersive interactive guidance
An information security path	Fine lectures, exchange activities	The information of "small art division" and "big project" is connected organically

The expected benefits are expected to influence technical professionals to design and modify specific information, scientific and artistic creative products, interactive scientific visual images, so that they can be truly put into processing and production, give full play to the multimodal information coupling of science and art, and fully apply in the ecological chain of science and art industry [10]. Especially in the popular games, products and communication platforms of science and technology and art and culture industries, it pays attention to the setting of information security. Whether it is scene setting, artistic image design, role cultural interaction, event planning, marketing strategy, communication technology and other links, it is necessary to establish the regional cultural characteristic image of Shaanxi Province. The multi-modes of information security, science and art are extended to various fields, and the original simple form of science and technology and the way of information transmission are broken through. It is believed that with the penetration of economic integration, the structure of information security and the continuous development of the western development, the coupling of young people's scientific quality and creative art will continue to develop in the continuous exploration of scientific engineers, art designers, economists. In the wide spread of its application field, information security will attract more attention and love of social groups.

References

1. Zhang, G., Yang, W., Zhao, M.: Prospective analysis of emerging technologies in educational apps from the perspective of "technology enabling learning." China Audio-Visual Educ. **10**, 107–117 (2018)
2. Qian, S., Liu, R., Chu, J.: Res. Indust. Des. **11**, 157–170 (2021)

3. Dai, H., Wei, J.: Empirical study on the coupling coordination degree between rural tourism and rural revitalization strategy in Hubei Province. Hubei Agric. Sci. **61**(17), 155–159, 213 (2022)
4. White paper in 2020. the Chinese quality education industry [EB/OL] (2020). https://zhu anlan.zhihu.com/p/127132618. Accessed 31 Oct 2021
5. Ke, L., Zhang, S.: Sci. Res.**12**, 51–59, 110–111 (2022)
6. Wang, X.: Study on the precise coupling mechanism of party history learning education and ideological and political courses from the perspective of "big ideological and political science." J. Hulunbuir Univ. (in Chinese) **30**(06), 143–148 (2022)
7. He, S.: Evaluation and influencing factors of the coupling coordination degree between digitization and higher education in Chin. J. East Peking Univ. (Soc. Sci. Edn.) **25**(02), 128–135 (2023)
8. Shi, S.: Coupling community: an innovative carrier for the integration of community education resources in open university. J. Yunnan Open Univ. (in Chinese) **24**(03), 22–28 (2022)
9. Yan, H.: A practical approach to the coupling of innovation education and entrepreneurship education in colleges and universities: a review of the theory and practice of innovation and entrepreneurship education in colleges and universities in the new era. China Educ. J. (11), 147 (2021)
10. Hao, Y.: Fusion, inheritance and reconstruction – a study on the coupling of traditional culture and art education. J. Chengdu Univ. Tradition. Chin. Med. (Educ. Sci. Edn.) **23**(02), 47–49, 89 (2021)

Application Research of English Distance Teaching Cloud Platform Based on Artificial Intelligence Algorithm

Xiaoxiao Fu[1], Zhang Jie[2], and Zhang Jun[2(✉)]

[1] College of Information Engineering, Fuyang Normal University, Fuyang 236041, Anhui, China

[2] Department of Economics and Management, Weifang Engineering Vocational College, Qing Zhou 262500, Shandong, China
zhangjun.1220@163.com

Abstract. The arrival of cloud computing has also subverted users' usage concept: instead of buying hardware and software, users buy cloud services. Users are no longer directly faced with complex software and hardware resources, but directly accessible services. Intelligent cloud teaching has brought subversive changes to English teaching, and at the same time, it has provided the possibility to implement online and offline mixed teaching mode in English teaching. This paper studies the application of English distance learning cloud platform based on AI(artificial intelligence) algorithm, and constructs the overall architecture of distance learning cloud platform. A cloud network information DM(data mining) algorithm based on AI adjudication framework mechanism is proposed. By extracting the storage gradient and mining gradient from the cloud network DM process, the volatility of network data transmission and data stream cache are integrated by multidimensional modeling. The results show that among the 104 valid questionnaires, 88 people think that the application of cloud platform for distance education has an impact on their learning effect, accounting for 84.61% of all the respondents. It can be seen that most students think that cloud platform teaching can affect their learning effect.

Keywords: Artificial intelligence · Distance teaching · Cloud platform

1 Introduction

Timely, appropriate and moderate use of modern distance resources to carry out English teaching can cultivate students' listening, speaking, reading and writing ability and open thinking ability, and enable students to learn in real language environment. The integration of information technology into subject teaching is the need of the development of the times, and it has changed the teaching mode [1, 2]. As an important part of language teaching, listening and speaking training is also developing towards automation and intelligence. Teaching in intelligent cloud has brought subversive changes to English

© ICST Institute for Computer Sciences, Social Informatics and Telecommunications Engineering 2024
Published by Springer Nature Switzerland AG 2024. All Rights Reserved
Y. Zhang and N. Shah (Eds.): BigIoT-EDU 2023, LNICST 582, pp. 417–425, 2024.
https://doi.org/10.1007/978-3-031-63136-8_43

teaching, and at the same time, it has also provided the possibility to implement online and offline mixed teaching mode in English teaching [3]. In English teaching, making full use of distance resources without losing any time can enhance the intuition of English classroom teaching, and at the same time cultivate and stimulate students' interest in learning English.

The arrival of cloud computing has also subverted users' usage concept: instead of buying hardware and software, users buy cloud services. Users are no longer directly faced with complex software and hardware resources, but directly accessible services [4]. Lin Xiaonong proposed the construction scheme of education resource base based on Hadoop, and proposed the structure model of cloud storage system [5]. With the deepening of research and the requirements of basic education reform, teaching platform has been introduced into basic education. Zhao Likun et al. found the factors that influence students' choice of learning methods by analyzing the different preferences of more than 2,000 students in nearly 30 schools in online learning platform [6]. Hou Feng uses correlation analysis technology to analyze the web browsing logs of students in the online learning process [7], including content structure, mining usage records, finding effective, novel and potentially useful information, and predicting which web pages students will browse later. At present, the research on cloud platform architecture in the domestic education field mainly focuses on the cloud sharing of digital library resources, while the research on multimedia teaching resources sharing is less.

Intelligent cloud teaching is a kind of teaching activity based on cloud computing technology, which integrates AI(artificial intelligence). Teaching activities in intelligent cloud include comprehensive cloud technology and big data technology of teaching tools, teaching contents, teaching management, teaching supervision and teaching evaluation [8, 9]. Therefore, on the basis of DM(data mining) and analysis of students' behavior, English distance learning cloud platform should comprehensively and objectively analyze each student's learning specialty, learning state, advantages and disadvantages. On this basis, students should be given learning resources suitable for their development accurately.

2   Research Method

2.1   The Design of Cloud Platform for English Distance Learning

In recent years, big data, virtual reality and AI have advanced by leaps and bounds, and the application of new technologies has blossomed everywhere. AI has entered the government work report twice and has become an important part of the national top-level design. At present, the application directions of AI in modern distance education mainly include intelligent teaching platform, intelligent retrieval of teaching resources, intelligent speech recognition aided teaching and evaluation, virtual reality, intelligent simulation, educational robot and so on. On the distance education cloud platform, it is no longer a single process of imparting knowledge from teachers to students, but a process of sharing and learning from each other. It is a new learning mode centered on individual learning, and learners can obtain various learning resources according to their needs and use their own learning methods.

When designing the frame structure of the website, it is necessary to design pictures and video columns, and it has a search function, so that when teachers need any resources, they can display the relevant contents through search. Part of the resources can be downloaded and reproduced from the Internet, which is conducive to reflecting the sharing attributes of resources; Part of the resources should be developed and innovated by ourselves to make the website unique and more suitable for the needs of teaching. With its vividness, interest and dynamic effect, multimedia classroom effectively attracts students' attention, and it is truly entertaining, realizing the efficiency and rapidness of English teaching, and enhancing the efficiency of English teaching.

In cloud computing, users pay according to the amount of services, instead of buying the hardware and software facilities that provide services. Users can access cloud services anytime, anywhere, but they don't know where the servers of services, applications or information provided to them at this time come from. Moreover, users upload information stored in the cloud, and users don't know which server to store the resources on. In order to ensure the security and reliability of services, cloud computing adopts various data redundancy backup mechanisms, and adopts sufficient security management mechanism and flexible and efficient response mechanism to ensure the security, reliability and effectiveness of data services. The hardware facilities of cloud computing can dynamically expand and contract to provide services for users, improve the utilization rate of physical resources and reduce energy consumption. It can be said that cloud computing has greatly accelerated the pace of green data computing.

The remote teaching cloud platform takes private cloud, server, all-in-one machine, wireless network environment and other basic equipment as hardware support, and establishes data support such as basic database, teaching material library and question bank. On this basis, it develops application systems of cloud platform such as teaching management system, student learning system, evaluation and analysis system and teaching assistant system, and then develops various specific applications according to the main functions of each application system. Through B/S architecture, users can realize multi-terminal barrier-free access to cloud platform applications [10]. The overall architecture of distance education cloud platform is shown in Fig. 1.

The multimedia resource cloud sharing platform provides the automatic push function of information resources, which can identify users' preferences individually, automatically identify them according to their usual habit of searching resources, and dynamically push a certain kind of information that users are concerned about to users at the first time. Through the user demand library of cloud platform, users' preferences for a certain category of multimedia teaching resources are known. According to this user demand library, the platform searches the relevant resource stores for information resources that match the user demand library, and then pushes the searched resources to users to realize the automatic push of information.

Private cloud refers to the integration of IT resources in colleges and universities and the establishment of a private cloud computing platform to realize the effective management of IT resources. For colleges and universities with good conditions, they own a large number of software and hardware resources [11]. The shortcomings of cloud computing in university education can be overcome by private cloud. The transmission of the internal core data of the university can be processed and stored on the private

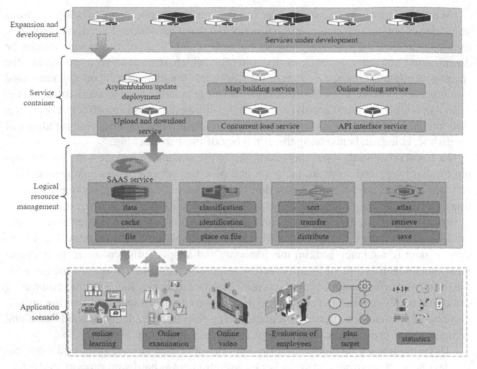

Fig. 1. Overall architecture of distance education cloud platform

cloud through the internal network, thus solving the problem of data security. In this way, the university can completely guarantee the security of data.

Using the test summary and detailed data provided by the distance education cloud platform for teachers, this paper makes statistics on the distribution of test scores, analyzes the reliability and validity of test papers, analyzes the difficulty and discrimination of test questions, and constantly modifies and perfects the test question bank according to these data. You can also explore whether there is a causal relationship between learning behavior and academic performance, explain how learning behavior affects academic performance, or find out whether there is a correlation or interdependence between learning behavior and academic performance.

2.2 AI Algorithm Design

Because the information data in the cloud network has the typical characteristics of big data and streaming, with the new characteristics that the physical transmission media of the cloud network is gradually turning to quantization and the transmission mode is becoming ubiquitous, the data transmission volume in the network is rapidly expanding exponentially. Once the data is in a fluctuating state, the accuracy of DM will be seriously affected, and it will easily lead to network transmission congestion.

In this paper, a cloud network information DM algorithm based on AI adjudication framework mechanism is proposed. By extracting the storage gradient and mining gradient from the cloud network DM process, the volatility of network data transmission and data stream cache are integrated by multi-dimensional modeling.

For any DM node, the interaction with the data stream needs to be realized through bandwidth mining, and the mining process satisfies the following model:

$$E_{sent}(B) = \sum_{t=0}^{B-L} \int f_{sent}(t)dt \tag{1}$$

Where $E_{sent}(B)$ is the total interactive data stream transmission bandwidth, B is the mining cost, and f_{sent} is the DM efficiency corresponding to the computing node, which has a linear correlation with the mining time.

Generally speaking, two learners with identical learning preferences rarely exist. At this time, it is more common to quantitatively calculate the similarity between learner E and other users' preferences, and take those learners who are close to the learning preferences of the target learners as neighbor customers.

For samples with p variables, n samples can be regarded as n points in p-dimensional space. Naturally, it is conceivable to measure the proximity between samples by the distance between points. d_{ij} is commonly used to indicate the distance between the i th sample and the j th sample.

In this example, the Euclidean distance is selected to calculate the similarity:

$$d_{ij} = \frac{1}{2}\left(\sum_{k=1}^{p}(x_{ik} - x_{jk})2\right) \tag{2}$$

At present, for the cloud education platform, the online part mainly focuses on teaching resources, and the online operating system has been online and started to be used on some platforms. Through the network, students can complete the "online homework" within the required time, and then immediately know which questions they have scored wrong. Through the information left in the system during the online assignment of students, such as the time for students to do each question, the improved BPNN (BP neural network) method is used to predict whether students can answer correctly [12] in the given reference time when the difficulty coefficient is different.

Assuming that the input vector of the network is $x \in R^n, x = (x_1, x_2, \cdots, x_n)^T$, the output of the i th neuron in the hidden layer is expressed as:

$$a1_i = f1\left(\sum_{j=1}^{j=n} \omega 1_{ij}x_j + b1_i\right), \quad i = 1, 2, \cdots, s1 \tag{3}$$

The output of the k-th neuron in the output layer is expressed as:

$$a2_k = f2\left(\sum_{i=1}^{s1} \omega 2_{ki}a1_i + b2_k\right), \quad k = 1, 2, \cdots, s2 \tag{4}$$

The error function is defined as:

$$E(W, B) = \frac{1}{2} \sum_{k=1}^{s2} (t_k - a2_k)^2 \tag{5}$$

The algorithm flow chart is shown in Fig. 2:

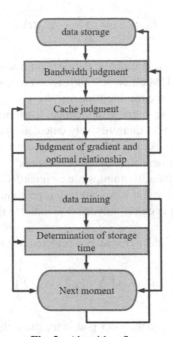

Fig. 2. Algorithm flow

3 Applied Analysis

The classroom teaching of applying teaching cloud platform under AI algorithm is mainly carried out by using intelligent classroom electronic whiteboard, multi-screen interaction between teachers' mobile terminals and students' tablet computers, resource sharing and timely feedback. The whole teaching process is highly interactive. In addition, interaction also involves the mutual communication between teachers in the same discipline, the communication between teachers in different disciplines, the processing and reuse of resources by teachers, and the use of resources by students. Through the students completing the assignments on the cloud platform, teachers can analyze the students' learning situation and summarize the teaching effect through the statistical data provided by the cloud platform system. In addition, real-time and non-real-time interaction can be conducted between teachers and students through the cloud platform, providing personalized learning guidance for students.

In terms of resource integration, universities can upload their excellent resources to the cloud storage according to the unified standards through the unified platform interface. In this way, schools don't need to configure corresponding servers to store resources, which can save a lot of expenses. Moreover, the resources uploaded to the cloud can be accessed by universities, which further improves the efficiency of resource sharing.

Platform administrators only need to manage account management, service directory arrangement, etc. In system management, resources and users are monitored and audited, which improves the security and standardization of the platform. The management of resource storage can mobilize the elastic modules in resource storage to provide storage space for resources, and ensure the efficient and persistent storage of resources in the cloud resource pool. The network plays an important role in the whole cloud service platform. Only through the network, users can enjoy all kinds of services provided by the cloud platform. Therefore, the management of the network by operators is the basis to ensure that the platform can provide services normally.

Through the construction of cloud resource platform, schools can have a platform for sharing resources; Every university can upload its own high-quality resources to the cloud resource platform through the cloud resource platform, or go to the cloud resource platform to find the resources it wants; As long as you can access the cloud platform, you can access the same interface no matter what terminal device you are using or where you are, just like using the same computer. Therefore, users can continue to do unfinished work anywhere, and can also share data with multiple external devices. You can also use the sharing mechanism provided by the cloud platform to share the files obtained from the cloud platform with others. So it is the wisest choice for schools to store data in the cloud. Also, schools don't have to worry about adding storage devices to meet the increasing data volume, and cloud service providers will handle all this.

After the cloud platform for distance education has been used in the classroom for nearly one semester, the author conducted a survey on the use of cloud platform among teachers and students in a school. The object of this survey is 120 students, who use the AI algorithm and the teaching cloud platform in their daily study and life. The theme of this student questionnaire survey is "the influence of teaching cloud platform on learning effect", which is conducted through single choice and subjective narration. The statistical results of the questionnaire are shown in Fig. 3:

The survey results show that among the 104 valid questionnaires, 88 people think that the application of distance education cloud platform has an impact on their learning effect, accounting for 84.62% of all the surveyed people. It can be seen that most students think that cloud platform teaching can affect their learning effect. Therefore, in the application process of distance education cloud platform, it can generally have a good positive impact on the learning effect.

The improved neural network is executed five times continuously, and the prediction result of the optimal network on the test sample set is kept in each execution. Summarize the prediction results of five times and compare them with the expected output to get the possibility of correct prediction of each topic. The results are shown in Fig. 4.

It can be seen that among the five predictions, among the 50 questions, between the actual output and the expected output, 75% of the questions were consistent with the

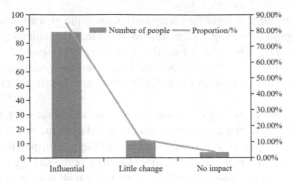

Fig. 3. Statistical results of questionnaire survey

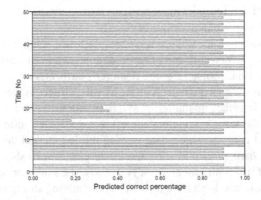

Fig. 4. Predict the correct percentage

expected output in the five predictions, and two questions were the same as the expected value three times during the prediction. Most of the questions that were inconsistent with the expected output appeared in the remaining six questions. This shows that the prediction results of the model are relatively stable.

4 Conclusion

Teaching in intelligent cloud is a kind of teaching activity that integrates AI and is based on cloud computing technology. Teaching activities in intelligent cloud include comprehensive cloud technology and big data technology of teaching tools, teaching contents, teaching management, teaching supervision and teaching evaluation. This paper studies the application of English distance learning cloud platform based on AI algorithm, and constructs the overall architecture of distance learning cloud platform. After the cloud platform for distance education has been used in the classroom for nearly one semester, the author has conducted a survey on the use of cloud platform among teachers and students in the online class of school. The results show that among the 104 valid questionnaires, 88 people think that the application of cloud platform for distance education has an impact on their learning effect, accounting for 84.61% of all the respondents. It can be seen that most students think that cloud platform teaching can affect their learning effect. Therefore, in the application process of distance education cloud platform, it can generally have a good positive impact on the learning effect.

References

1. Zeng, X.: Application research of artificial intelligence detection platform based on cloud platform. China Test. **47**(10), 10 (2021)
2. Chen, Y., Zhang, E., Zhang, J., Lang, N., Yuan, H.: Application progress of various AI algorithms based on imaging in tumor research. Magn. Reson. Imaging **9**(10), 5 (2018)
3. Huang, J., Wang, J.: Optimization of mathematical modeling based on different artificial intelligence algorithms. Autom. Instrument. **2018**(6), 3 (2018)
4. Huang, J., Zheng, J., Gao, S., Liu, W., Lin, J., Dong, Z.: Research on the open source development platform framework of artificial intelligence based on cloud platform. Autom. Instrument. **2020**(7), 5 (2020)
5. Lin, X.: Research on cloud computing resource allocation based on artificial intelligence technology. Mod. Electron. Technol. **43**(21), 5 (2020)
6. Zhao, L., Wang, Y.: A cycle recommendation algorithm of social network user behavior data based on artificial intelligence. Sci. Technol. Eng. **2020**(028), 020 (2020)
7. Hou, F.: Research on the application of artificial intelligence in computer network technology-a review of Cloud Computing System and Artificial Intelligence Application. Forest Produ. Indust. **57**(02), 122 (2020)
8. Zhao, X.: Cloud network information data mining algorithm based on artificial intelligence adjudication. Inform. Technol. **42**(9), 5 (2018)
9. Wang, L., Wen, W.S.: Research on distributed intrusion detection based on artificial intelligence. Comput. Sci. **49**(10), 5 (2022)
10. Wu, G., Wang, Z., Han, J., He, B.: Overview of artificial intelligence verification platform. China Sci. Found. **33**(6), 5 (2019)
11. Ge, Y.: Design of training platform based on artificial intelligence and industrial cloud. Electron. Prod. World **29**(8), 3 (2022)
12. Yao, Y.: Technology, theory, problems of artificial intelligence algorithm patent and China's response. Sci. Technol. Progress Countermeas. **39**(16), 8 (2022)

Development and Application of College English Translation Teaching Software Based on Artificial Intelligence

Xiaozhu Zhang[✉] and Qiutao Qin

School of General Education, Guangxi Vocational and Technical College, Nanning 530226, Guangxi, China
79524013@qq.com

Abstract. This article introduces the development and application of a college English translation teaching software based on artificial intelligence technology. We mainly explored the role and advantages of artificial intelligence technology in college English translation teaching software. At the same time, this article also provides a detailed introduction to the design and development process of a college English translation teaching software. In college English translation teaching software, artificial intelligence technology is mainly used for text translation and voice translation. By utilizing artificial intelligence technology, a large number of English texts and spoken materials can be quickly translated. Meanwhile, compared to traditional artificial intelligence systems, the new type of artificial intelligence system is more intelligent and accurate, and the translation quality has also been greatly improved. In terms of software design and development, this article introduces the development process and technical implementation of college English translation teaching software. We have adopted the B/S architecture and programming languages such as Python to achieve modular design for multiple functions such as speech input, speech recognition, text translation, and speech translation. In addition, we have added functions such as Adaptive learning recommendation system and student learning monitoring system to the software, which makes students' learning more efficient and personalized.

Based on the above content, it can be concluded that the application of artificial intelligence technology in college English translation teaching software can greatly improve students' learning efficiency and translation quality, injecting new vitality and impetus into the intelligence and modernization of English education and teaching. At the same time, the development process and technical implementation introduced in this article can provide useful inspiration and guidance for relevant developers, and provide strong support for the practical application of college English translation teaching software.

Keywords: Artificial intelligence · College English translation · Software development

Y. Zhang and N. Shah (Eds.): BigIoT-EDU 2023, LNICST 582, pp. 426–433, 2024.
https://doi.org/10.1007/978-3-031-63136-8_44

1 Introduction

With the advancement of globalization, English has become one of the most widely used languages in the world, playing an extremely important role in both academic and professional fields. Therefore, the importance of college English education is increasingly being valued [1]. The development and application of artificial intelligence have provided a new teaching mode for college English education. This article will focus on the development and application of artificial intelligence based college English translation teaching software [2]. This software uses artificial intelligence technologies such as machine learning and deep learning, as well as Natural language processing technology to realize the intellectualization and modernization of English translation teaching, and provides a series of technical means, including speech recognition, speech translation, text recognition and text translation. This software is mainly divided into the following modules and functions:

1. Speech input and speech recognition module: Support students to input English sentences or words using speech, automatically recognize speech, and convert speech into text.
2. Text translation and voice translation module: Translate English sentences or words inputted by students into text and voice, and provide synchronous audio reading function, providing convenience and basis for students to recognize English language.
3. Learning Records and Personalized Suggestions Module: The system will record students' learning records and performance, and provide corresponding personalized suggestions and learning resource recommendations based on their learning situation.
4. Group learning module: The software can support multiple people to learn online at the same time, and can establish course groups, homework groups, etc. to encourage and promote mutual communication and cooperation among students.

The above are the main functions of this software, which have important significance for college English translation teaching [3]. The development and application of this software can effectively improve students' English translation ability, enhance their English listening and speaking ability and enthusiasm, increase the fun and efficiency of learning, make education more intelligent and personalized, and contribute to cultivating innovative talents with a global perspective and cross-cultural communication ability. In addition, college English translation teaching software based on artificial intelligence can also improve students' learning efficiency and flexibility, allowing them to independently manage their learning progress and methods, and avoid learning pressure caused by fixed systems and course nature.

However, with the advent of the Big data era, personal information protection and privacy issues are becoming increasingly important. When developing college English translation teaching software based on artificial intelligence, it is necessary to pay attention to personal information confidentiality and security [4]. Effective security measures should be incorporated into the system design to protect the personal information security of students.

The college English translation teaching software based on artificial intelligence injects new vitality and momentum into college English education. This educational application software will become an important component of future college English education [5]. This article aims to provide an understanding and guidance for education departments and related enterprises on the guidance and reference of artificial intelligence based college English translation teaching software.

In short, AI based college English translation teaching software will become an important component of future college English education. This software not only has advanced technological means, but also supports students to manage their learning independently, optimize personalized learning strategies, and has high popularity and practicality. It will be an important direction for the development of future college English education.

2 Artificial Intelligence

2.1 Definition of Artificial Intelligence

Artificial intelligence (AI) is a complex collection of technologies and algorithms aimed at imitating human intelligence and thinking processes, enabling computers to possess learning, reasoning, language comprehension, and other abilities similar to those of humans. In English translation, artificial intelligence has many applications that can greatly improve the efficiency and accuracy of English translation. Firstly, artificial intelligence can help English translators quickly translate a large amount of English text and spoken materials [6]. Machine translation technology can quickly translate one language into another, and the quality of translation is getting higher and higher, which can be comparable to human translation. This technology can reduce the workload of English translators and improve their work efficiency. Secondly, artificial intelligence can also help English translators achieve precise vocabulary selection and grammar proofreading. Machine learning technology can learn from a large number of bilingual corpora, obtaining more accurate vocabulary selection and grammatical structure, helping English translators better understand and translate articles.

In addition, some AI technologies, such as Natural language processing and deep learning, enable computers to accurately understand natural language and context, and generate natural language output [7]. This technology is widely used in English translation, which can help English translators better understand English articles and spoken language, and generate natural language translation results as needed. In short, the application of artificial intelligence technology in English translation can greatly improve the efficiency and accuracy of translation, and help English translators better complete translation tasks. With the continuous development of artificial intelligence technology, it is believed that its application in the field of English translation will become increasingly widespread, is shown in Fig. 1.

2.2 Features of Artificial Intelligence

Artificial intelligence (AI) refers to an intelligent system based on computer programs that can simulate human thinking and decision-making processes. The characteristics of artificial intelligence include the following aspects:

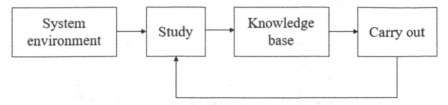

Fig. 1. Basic structure of the learning system

1. Learning ability: Artificial intelligence systems can improve their algorithm models and performance by learning data and experience. It can obtain experience from a large amount of data, continuously learn and adjust models, thereby improving its accuracy and reliability [8].
2. Reasoning ability: Artificial intelligence systems can achieve reasoning and solving complex problems through reasoning algorithms. It can apply known information and rules to new situations, generating new conclusions and solutions.
3. Automation capability: Artificial intelligence systems can automate the execution of a large number of repetitive tasks, greatly improving work efficiency and production efficiency. For example, in image recognition and speech recognition, artificial intelligence systems can automatically process a large amount of data, thereby quickly and accurately completing recognition tasks.
4. Adaptability: Artificial intelligence systems can adaptively adjust algorithm models and behavior based on different environments and tasks, thereby better adapting to different scenarios and needs.
5. Stability and reliability: Artificial intelligence systems can improve the stability and reliability of the system by automatically learning and adjusting data and parameters. It can automatically discover and solve problems, thereby avoiding potential human error operations and program vulnerabilities in traditional systems.

In short, artificial intelligence systems have characteristics such as learning ability, reasoning ability, automation ability, adaptability, and stability [9]. These characteristics make artificial intelligence systems play an increasingly important role in different fields and scenarios.

Regard adaptability as a kind of ability, which is formed in the dynamic process of individual initiative and mutual balance with the environment, including both psychological and behavioral adaptation. College students are the subject of adaptation. Artificial intelligence, is shown in Fig. 2.

2.3 The Application of Machine Translation in English

Machine translation is a translation method realized by computer programs. It uses machine learning, Natural language processing and other technologies to automatically convert one language into another. In English translation, Machine translation technology has made remarkable progress and become an irreplaceable auxiliary tool for a large number of English translation work. Next, we will learn more about the technical process of Machine translation in English translation.

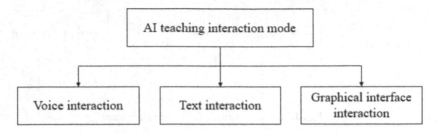

Fig. 2. AI teaching interaction mode diagram

1. Construction of Corpus

When building a machine learning based Machine translation system, a large amount of text data/corpus is needed as the basis for training. Corpus can not only be used to train machine learning models, but also to evaluate the accuracy and fluency of translation results. Corpus can come from various fields, such as news, technology, finance, entertainment, etc., and needs to contain a large number of original texts and corresponding translated texts.

2. Design and training of machine learning models

Machine learning is one of the most important technologies in Machine translation. In the process of machine learning, it is necessary to design appropriate feature extraction algorithms and models. At present, the deep neural network model is one of the widely used models in Machine translation.

Before training the machine learning model, it is necessary to preprocess the corpus, such as word segmentation, Punctuation removal and part of speech tagging, so as to better process the text data [10]. Next, the entire corpus needs to be divided into three parts: a training set, a validation set, and a testing set. The training set is used for model training, the validation set is used for parameter tuning during the training process, and the testing set is used to verify the performance and accuracy of the model.

3. Translation process

The input of the Machine translation system is the English text to be translated, and the output is the corresponding target language text. The translation process can be divided into the following steps:

– Preprocessing: Perform preprocessing operations on the English original text, such as word segmentation, expansion, etc.
– Decoding: Transforming English original text into intermediate expressions in a specific language, using preprocessing to generate "source language text".
– Calculation of translation probability: the process of Machine translation system converting source language text into "target language text" is based on the calculation of translation probability of vocabulary and grammar.
– Generating target language text: the Machine translation system applies the calculated translation probability to the source language text and generates the target language text output.

4. Post processing

After the translation is completed, it is necessary to perform post-processing on the translation results to help them become smoother and smoother. Common post-processing operations include spell checking, grammar correction, and error correction.

In short, Machine translation technology is one of the hot technologies in the field of translation, with a wide range of application scenarios. However, there are still some difficult problems in Machine translation, such as the fluency of translation results, semantic understanding and cultural differences. Therefore, in the research of Machine translation technology, continuous optimization and improvement of its translation accuracy is still a direction that needs constant exploration and efforts.

The automatically recognizes and processes it on this basis. Second, the speech recognition system. The essence of speech recognition is to receive human language by signal, and to operate the content by computer, character sequence and binary coding, and then convert it into readable input information. Database, that is, knowledge base system, by artificial intelligence is preliminarily constructed, as shown in Fig. 3.

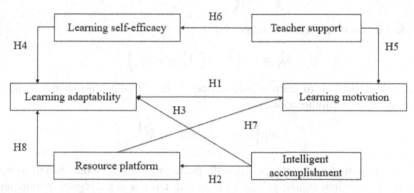

Fig. 3. Hypothetical model of factors influencing college students' English learning adaptability with the support of artificial intelligence

3   College English Translation Teaching Under the Background of Artificial Intelligence

The rapid development of artificial intelligence technology is profoundly changing various fields, including education. In college English translation teaching, artificial intelligence can provide more tools and resources to help students better learn English translation knowledge and skills. Artificial intelligence can support personalized English translation teaching. Through machine learning and Big data analysis, AI can quickly identify students' language preferences and language difficulties, and design personalized teaching content and programs for students. This approach can make teaching more targeted, improve efficiency and accuracy. Artificial intelligence can provide more effective language practice opportunities. In English translation teaching, it is necessary to improve translation skills through practical operations. Artificial intelligence can use virtual reality technology to immerse students in various scenarios and environments, thereby obtaining deeper, broader, and more authentic language practice opportunities. Artificial intelligence can provide better translation services. Through Machine translation and Natural language processing technology, AI can quickly and accurately translate course lists, materials, reports, etc. These translation services can help students better understand subject knowledge and facilitate academic research cooperation. Teachers can also benefit from the support of artificial intelligence technology. Artificial intelligence can analyze and identify students' language strengths and weaknesses, and provide appropriate guidance to support teaching. Meanwhile, auxiliary teaching aids based on artificial intelligence can help teachers better prepare and plan teaching content and methods.

Calculate the output of each neuron in the hidden layer and the output layer of the network:

$$o^l_{Pj} = f_j\left(\sum_j w^l_{ji}o^{l-1}_i - \theta^l_j\right) \tag{1}$$

Calculate the output error of output layer:

$$\delta^2_{Pj} = o^2_{Pj}\left(1 - o^2_{Pj}\right)\left(t_{Pj} - o^2_{Pj}\right) \tag{2}$$

Let the credibility of each sub-condition A_i be $CF(A_i)$, and then calculate the credibility of the combined evidence:

$$\min_f\left\{\|f - f_0\|^2_2 + \alpha\|Cf\|^2_2\right\} \tag{3}$$

$\|f - f_0\|^2_2$ is the fidelity term, which reflects the approximation between the observed signal and the original signal; $\|Cf\|^2_2$ is the regular term, α is the regular parameter and C is the regular operator.

To some extent, students' autonomous learning ability ensures that students can better adapt to learning in the artificial intelligence environment. Therefore, changing "learning method adaptation" to "autonomous learning ability adaptation" is more in line with the adaptive characteristics of students' artificial intelligence supported learning. Moreover, according to the further understanding of constructivist learning theory, learning is a process of actively acquiring knowledge. It emphasizes that knowledge is not taught by teachers, but obtained by completing the meaning construction of knowledge through the process of assimilation and adaptation.

4 Conclusions

College English translation teaching software based on artificial intelligence is an efficient and intelligent teaching tool that can greatly improve students' English translation ability and efficiency. Its research and development can inject new vitality and impetus into the intelligence and modernization of English education and teaching, providing more efficient teaching experiences for teachers and students.

The software can accurately translate a large number of English materials through the application of advanced technologies such as machine learning, Natural language processing, speech recognition, and provides a series of auxiliary functions, such as vocabulary selection, grammar proofreading, cross language communication, to support students' learning and application.

In terms of software development and application, it is necessary to conduct comprehensive and in-depth research and fine-tuning on relevant technologies and platforms, while strengthening consideration and support for diverse student needs, in order to better achieve personalized learning experiences and effects. At the same time, it is also necessary to establish a good evaluation and feedback mechanism to track and analyze the effectiveness of software usage, in order to continuously further optimize and improve.

In short, the research and application of artificial intelligence based college English translation teaching software is expected to provide English learners with a more intelligent and efficient learning method and platform, making positive contributions to the comprehensive improvement and development of English education.

References

1. Tian, J.: Reflections on college English teaching in the background of artificial intelligence translation. Sci. Educ. J. **32**, 3 (2019)
2. Li, X., Feng, Y.: A practical exploration of English translation activity courses in colleges and universities under the background of artificial intelligence. J. Beijing Inst. Graph. Print. **29**(9), 4 (2021)
3. Liang, X.: Practical research on college English translation under the background of artificial intelligence. Standard. Mass. **8**, 3 (2021)
4. Huang, X.: A practical exploration of English translation activity courses in colleges and universities under the background of artificial intelligence. J. Jiamusi Vocat. College **36**(11), 3 (2020)
5. Wei, W.: Reflection and reform of foreign language translation courses in colleges and universities under the background of artificial intelligence. Educ. Inform. Forum **2**(3), 2 (2018)
6. Chen, H., Ji, Z.: Practical exploration of English translation activity courses in colleges and universities under the background of artificial intelligence. J. Beijing Inst. Graph. Print. **28**(1), 3 (2020)
7. He, J.: Research on English learning mode under the influence of artificial intelligence translation. Intelligence **25**, 1 (2019)
8. Ma, W.: Research on the application of artificial intelligence in hybrid college English teaching. New Silk Road: Early Years **9**, 1 (2019)
9. Hou, J.: Strategies for the development of professional competence of college English teachers in the context of artificial intelligence. Campus English **39**, 2 (2020)
10. Wang, Y., Chen, Y.: Undergraduate translation teaching in the age of artificial intelligence. Educ. Res. (2630–4686) **2**(5), 2 (2019)

Analysis on the Application of Artificial Intelligence Technology in College Teaching

Yuankun Ren[1,2](✉), Jiang Wenxin[1,2], and Hailan Lu[1,2]

[1] Shenyang 110036, Liaoning, China
2090800485@qq.com

[2] Nanning University, Nanning 530200, Guangxi, China

Abstract. The application of artificial intelligence technology in university teaching presents broad potential and prospects. Through personalized teaching, artificial intelligence can provide customized teaching materials and guidance based on students' learning styles and levels; Through big data analysis, artificial intelligence provides teachers with detailed information on students' learning situations, which helps to better guide and coach students; At the same time, artificial intelligence can also utilize virtual laboratories and simulated environments to develop safer and more practical learning experiences. In addition, artificial intelligence technology can also provide automated evaluation and feedback, reducing the workload of teachers. In summary, the application of artificial intelligence technology in university teaching can improve students' learning outcomes and teachers' teaching quality, bringing new opportunities for innovation and progress in the field of education. With the further development of technology and the continuous promotion of applications, artificial intelligence will continue to play a more important role, laying a solid foundation for cultivating more outstanding talents in higher education.

Keywords: artificial intelligence · College teaching · Technology application

1 Introduction

First, the purpose of education is the quality specification and standard determined by educators for training talents, which stipulates the direction of talent training and is of great significance in any era. At the same time, the purpose of education guides the work of educators. Teachers should guide students with the purpose of education as the reference direction [1]. Therefore, AI poses a certain challenge to educational content and teachers, which is to challenge educational objectives indirectly. AI era and the major challenges it will bring to education and people who are trained in education, it is particularly important to study the educational purpose of the AI era [2]. Thirdly, AI will bring about changes in the whole society and lifestyle, and correspondingly, the quality and ability of people trained in education will also change.

Y. Zhang and N. Shah (Eds.): BigIoT-EDU 2023, LNICST 582, pp. 434–444, 2024.
https://doi.org/10.1007/978-3-031-63136-8_45

The traditional method of observation and analysis of college classroom teaching process has gone through three stages: (1) manual in-depth classroom observation, combined with the observation form designed in advance, observation and recording, and finally summarizing the observation form for data analysis. (2) After the emergence of audio and video recording technology, some course videos can be used to replace classroom observation, and manual follow-up analysis can be conducted by repeatedly watching. (3) After the emergence of computer technology, many scholars invented special classroom analysis software to replace part of the manual analysis workload.

2 Related Work

2.1 College Classroom Teaching Behavior

Efficient classroom has always been an ideal classroom state pursued by school education. Many education researchers and teaching practices are committed to reducing teaching loss, improving teaching effect and improving the quality of college classroom teaching.

Learning analysis uses various data collection tools and analysis techniques to collect and analyze data such as student input and learning performance in teaching practice, so as to provide basis for guiding teaching and making accurate teaching decisions. Most of the current learning analysis focuses on online learning evaluation data analysis, learning early warning data analysis, ethical privacy data analysis and resource recommendation. The LearnSmart system of McGraw HillEducation Company changes the content of the course materials according to the students' answers to the random tests [3]. Aulck et al. used machine learning methods to collect the scores and demographic data of more than 30000 students, and tested the best factors for predicting students' dropout. Doleck et al. used machine learning algorithms to mine learner behaviors related to diagnostic reasoning, design and guide the maintenance of the system, and improve the adaptability of the learning environment [4].

Indeed, in the development wave of the new generation of information technology represented by artificial intelligence, people's interest in its application and research in the field of classroom teaching in universities is constantly increasing. The current practical research mainly focuses on the development of teaching aids and speech behavior analysis, in order to utilize artificial intelligence technology to provide better teaching tools and evaluation methods.

In terms of teaching aids, researchers are committed to utilizing artificial intelligence technology to develop innovative teaching tools, such as virtual laboratories, teaching games, etc., to provide a richer and more interactive learning experience. These teaching aids utilize the powerful computing and simulation capabilities of artificial intelligence to enhance students' understanding and practical experience of course content, and improve learning outcomes.

In terms of speech behavior analysis, researchers use artificial intelligence technologies such as speech recognition and natural language processing to analyze and evaluate the speech behavior of teachers and students in the classroom. By analyzing teachers' explanation methods, students' questioning and answering language behaviors, teaching effectiveness and learning engagement can be evaluated, helping teachers provide personalized guidance and improvement. In terms of theoretical research, the main focus is on exploring teaching models and assisting in teaching evaluation. Researchers explore how to use artificial intelligence technology to change traditional teaching modes, such as personalized teaching and collaborative learning, in order to enhance students' learning effectiveness and interest. At the same time, researchers are also committed to developing auxiliary teaching evaluation methods based on artificial intelligence technology to comprehensively and objectively evaluate students' learning outcomes and teaching quality.

Although current research mainly focuses on the development and evaluation methods of teaching aids, with the continuous progress of technology and in-depth research, it is believed that the application research of artificial intelligence in the field of classroom teaching in universities will become increasingly rich and mature, providing more powerful support and innovation for teaching.

2.2 Weight Distribution of Teaching Analysis

In order to use artificial intelligence technology to conduct holographic analysis of classroom activities and conduct comprehensive observation of college classroom teaching from multiple dimensions and perspectives, five classic methods for analyzing college classroom teaching behavior and the requirements for college classroom teaching evaluation under the guidance of efficient classroom teaching are combined, The analysis framework of college classroom teaching behavior for AI technology will be constructed through the following two indicator dimensions: observation dimension and evaluation dimension of college classroom teaching behavior for AI.

Consistency test of index weight and hierarchical ranking of primary indicators. For the problem of weight distribution. Finally, 11 points are collected from the effective survey table [5].

$$X = \begin{bmatrix} x_1 \\ x_2 \\ ... \\ x_n \end{bmatrix} \tag{1}$$

$$MI(x, y) = \log_2 \frac{p(x, y)}{p(x)p(y)} \tag{2}$$

It is a common analysis method to judge the weight of indicators through the analytic hierarchy process. Considering the large number of three-level indicators and the urgency of time and tasks, the use of analytic hierarchy process may affect the quality of the questionnaire [6]. In this study, AHP is used to determine the weights of the first and second level indicators, and expert ranking method is used to determine the weights of the third level indicators.

On the basis of the first two rounds of Delphi questionnaires, the selection of experts for this weight allocation consultation is still consistent with the experts in the first two rounds. The experts have a clear understanding of the indicators in the framework, so the weight judgment of each indicator will be more scientific.

On October 17, 2016, NetEase led the release of the Wuzhen Index: Global AI Development Report (2016), which showed that "AI+Education" is mainly to achieve the classification of knowledge, calculate the learning curve for students through big data collection and corresponding algorithms, and quickly match the efficient education model; Based on the teacher community, the application of AI in the field of education can help teachers better achieve intelligent evaluation and personalized guidance [7]. "Domestic research on AI in education mainly focuses on the concept of AI in education and the exploration of the integration of AI and education. Chen Ying (2013) pointed out that AI can provide personalized teaching and optimize teaching effects." "For example, teachers can use AI in English teaching".

It can provide a more authentic context, correct students' grammar and pronunciation, and then reduce the error rate. Wu Wenjun (2017), through research on AI technology, found that AI analysis technology can help teachers understand the overall learning situation of the class, grasp students' mastery of teaching content, and find out the weak links of students' learning. Teachers can adjust the reasonable matching of teaching resources in time according to the basic data provided by AI analysis technology. Wu Tianyu (2018) pointed out in his research that AI can provide convenience for teachers to correct homework and intelligent grading through voice, text, picture recognition and other technologies, and AI conducts big data analysis on students' homework and examination, pointing out the direction for teachers to focus on lectures [8]. "Xu Lixing (2019) In its research, it is pointed out that the premise of teaching design is the analysis of teaching needs". The introduction of AI can help teachers analyze the learning characteristics and learning needs of students. By analyzing a large number of data samples, it can help teachers clarify teaching objectives, improve teaching efficiency and improve teaching quality [9]. Yu Shengquan (2018) pointed out that the development of AI education will not only affect students, but also promote the transformation and differentiation of teachers' functions.

3 Analysis on the Application of AI Technology in College Teaching

3.1 Analysis of AI Technology in Classroom Teaching

Artificial intelligence technology in classroom teaching can provide valuable insights and support by analyzing multiple aspects. Artificial intelligence can analyze the behavioral patterns and interactions between teachers and students. By monitoring the actions, postures, and language communication between teachers and students, artificial intelligence can provide objective and quantitative evaluations of teaching activities. For example, it can analyze the effectiveness of teachers' explanations, students' participation, and the frequency of classroom interaction. This analysis can help teachers understand the effectiveness of teaching and the learning situation of students, so as to make timely adjustments and improvements. Artificial intelligence can analyze students' learning data and performance. By collecting and analyzing students' answers, homework performance, and online learning activities, artificial intelligence can provide insights into students' learning progress, mastery level, and personalized needs. This analysis helps teachers provide personalized guidance and feedback, helping students learn and improve more effectively.

In addition, artificial intelligence can also analyze classroom materials and teaching resources, providing better teaching support for teachers. Through semantic analysis of textbooks and correlation analysis of teaching resources, artificial intelligence can recommend suitable teaching materials and resources, helping teachers better design and prepare for classroom teaching. The analysis of artificial intelligence technology provides comprehensive and objective data and insights in classroom teaching. By utilizing this data, teachers can better understand and meet students' needs, improve teaching effectiveness and learning experience.

Combined with the specific teaching behavior indicators of the observation dimension in the classroom, we can obtain the data of each indicator through the evaluation dimension, and then analyze the teacher activity rate, student activity rate, teacher teaching rate, teacher-student interaction rate and other indirect classroom effects, efficiency and benefits. The specific evaluation dimension corresponds to the following three points: time, frequency, and participants. Figure 1 below shows the analysis of classroom behavior path.

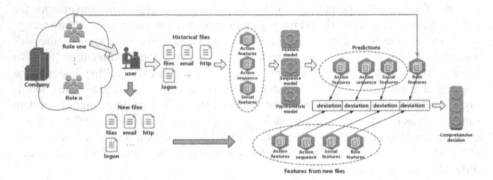

Fig. 1. Analysis of Classroom Behavior Paths

Because college classroom teaching is a system that includes teachers, students, teaching tools, teaching environment and other elements, when analyzing college classroom teaching, it is necessary to identify the objects to be analyzed in the study in combination with the analysis purpose, so as to form a targeted presentation of relevant analysis results.

In the analysis framework of college classroom teaching behavior for AI technology in this study, the indicators of observation dimension comprehensively include the college classroom teaching behavior that widely exists in the classroom environment. However, in the actual analysis of college classroom teaching behavior, due to different observation purposes, it is necessary to collect different data and form different analysis results [8]. Therefore, researchers need to clearly analyze the research object in the research, select the corresponding observation dimension and evaluation dimension in combination with the object, and conduct targeted research.

3.2   Dynamic Teaching Management

The traditional form of teaching organization and management is generally to make "uniform" requirements for students. Facing the era of artificial intelligence, teachers need to start from different students' personality characteristics, knowledge differences, skills differences, and match with different teaching organization and management methods, so that students at different levels can have their own space for survival and improvement in terms of all-round self-development. The development of artificial intelligence has brought dynamic teaching organization and management methods to education, which are mainly reflected in two aspects: one is the dynamic control of teaching process, and the other is the enhancement of the reality of teaching situation.

The first is the dynamic control of teaching process. The traditional teaching organization and management mainly rely on the subjective supervision of teachers, and the teaching process is often disordered or even out of control, thus affecting the teaching efficiency and progress. Facing the era of artificial intelligence, artificial intelligence can conduct face detection, gesture recognition and eye movement tracking for students. By collecting data such as students' facial expressions, learning behaviors, and the rate of head up in class, it can infer students' concentration in class and students' digestion of the knowledge. AI can continuously track the teaching process and dynamically evaluate students' learning behavior. The traditional teaching evaluation is generally carried out after the end of a certain teaching stage, and the evaluation results are also one-sided. The application of artificial intelligence technology in higher education can model every student, combine knowledge atlas, and make timely evaluation for every student. The monitoring of teaching process runs through all links of teaching activities, which helps teachers understand the dynamic change process of students' learning. The teaching organization has gradually changed from traditional summative evaluation to dynamic evaluation and process evaluation, Replace the traditional teaching method of "one test for a lifetime" with process-based teaching data. In terms of teaching tools, the emergence of various intelligent education APPs provides convenience for teachers to realize dynamic teaching management. Teachers analyze students' learning conditions through AI tools, thus establishing a good teaching process detection mechanism. Teachers can realize the sign-in function through intelligent teaching software, upload courseware, homework and test paper after class through intelligent teaching APP, and interact with students online. Through the collection, statistics and analysis of big data, the whole process of learning detection can help teachers identify the key and difficult points of teaching, greatly optimize and improve teaching efficiency, as shown in Fig. 2.

Secondly, the reality of teaching situation is enhanced. From the perspective of pedagogy, education has three basic elements: first, educators (teachers), second, education objects (students), and third, educational media (teaching resources). The current teaching resources are the main media of education, and their characteristics are mainly reflected in three aspects: first, knowledge usually exists in the form of narration, second, the expression of diagrams and words is mainly static, and third, the knowledge involved has certain limitations, which are not conducive to students' independent learning and the cultivation of students' innovative spirit. Only by combining rigid teaching resources with real living environment can a dynamic knowledge system be formed. Under the background of intelligent teaching, students will have a new learning experience in the

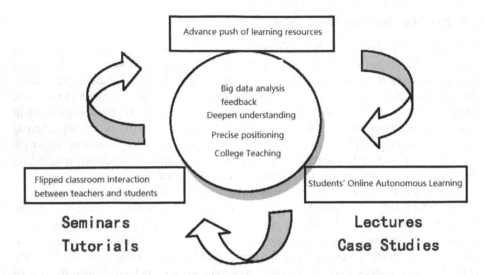

Fig. 2. Dynamic teaching management

classroom. The traditional teaching organization mainly transmits the contents, professional knowledge and professional skills of teaching materials to students through teachers' language, expressions, body movements, etc.; In the teaching of multimedia information technology, teachers can use audio, video, animation and other methods to organize teaching, so as to turn the classroom into static and dynamic, and enhance students' intuitive feelings; For education and teaching in the perspective of artificial intelligence, teachers can use "artificial intelligence+virtual simulation" technology to reproduce various scenes that are difficult to achieve in actual teaching, such as dialogue scenes, free fall scenes, clinical surgery scenes, mechanical operation scenes, etc., so that students can better experience the complexity and diversity of real life and enhance their personal experience. For example, with the help of AI virtual reality intelligent modeling technology, students can clearly observe particles invisible to the naked eye in the real world, facilitate students to intuitively understand the characteristics and composition of small particles, facilitate students to better understand the world, and obtain feelings and experiences that cannot be experienced in books. Another example is that teachers will encounter many abstract and incomprehensible knowledge points in the process of teaching: molecular structure in chemistry teaching, magnetic field problems in physics teaching, anatomy problems in medical teaching, geometry problems in mathematics teaching, etc. The artificial intelligence virtual simulation technology can assist teachers to give students good answers.

4   Simulation Analysis

This framework utilizes convolutional neural networks to analyze and process image information, while recurrent neural networks are used to process speech information to identify and analyze specific activity and speech behaviors. By coordinating and processing the data, evaluation dimension data can be obtained.

Specifically, the evaluation dimension can include indicators such as activity rate and language usage rate. The activity rate can be evaluated by analyzing the behavioral activities of teachers and students in the classroom, such as the frequency of students' questions and answers, and the teacher's demonstration and guidance activities. The language usage rate can be evaluated by analyzing the language used by teachers and students in the classroom, such as students' oral communication and teachers' teaching language.

By comprehensively analyzing the evaluation dimension data, the behavioral characteristics and interaction between teachers and students in classroom teaching can be revealed. Such analysis results can provide guidance and basis for improving teaching methods for teachers, while also providing personalized teaching services for students. Overall, the analysis framework for university classroom teaching behavior based on artificial intelligence technology can improve teaching quality and student learning effectiveness, and promote innovation and progress in education and teaching [10].

This paper uses the EFA method to explore the influencing factors of college teachers' teaching and learning ability. Now 33 variables are described in detail. Through analyzing the contents of the questionnaire, the current situation of college teachers' teaching and learning ability and the content of the impact survey in the perspective of AI are divided into three levels as a whole, and the first level is divided into dependent variables and independent variables, On the second level, it is divided into 4 dependent variable dimensions and 3 independent variable dimensions, and on the third level, it is further decomposed into 33 dimensional variables for evaluation: R1–4 understands teachers' instructional design and development ability through teaching plan design, teaching objectives, teaching content and teaching resources; R5-R9 reflects teachers' teaching organization and management ability through classroom management, teaching environment, teaching regulation, teaching process and combining with practice; R10–R13 shows teachers' teaching evaluation and reflection ability through teaching reflection, teaching philosophy, teaching experience and data analysis; R14–R18 explores teachers' educational technology research and application capabilities through teaching students according to their aptitude, intelligent question answering, homework assignment, courseware production and intelligent marking; R19–R22 understands teachers' own factors through professional attitude, work pressure, teaching reflection and lifelong learning; R23–R27 inspects the comprehensive teaching environment of colleges and universities through teaching environment, training activities, training costs, teaching management and concept updating; R28–R33 analyzes teachers and universities' understanding of AI education application through technology application, data capability, technical capability, training platform, application policy and data ecology. All 33 variables correspond to multiple questions in the questionnaire.

This paper uses KMO and spherical Bartlett test to test the applicability of the collected data, as shown in Table 3.5. KMO statistics are 0.950 respectively, which is more suitable for factor analysis. Dependent variable P The values are all 0.000, indicating that there is a strong correlation between variables. The gravel map is shown in Fig. 3, the total variance interpretation rate table and the rotation component matrix table.

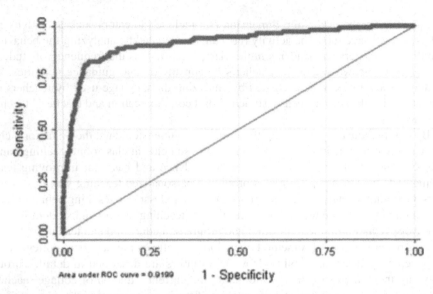

Area under ROC curve = 0.9199   1 - Specificity

Fig. 3. Dependent variable factor gravel map

Artificial intelligence can simulate human thinking through computers, so that computers can replace humans to complete the work that can only be completed through human intelligence in the past, which not only brings great convenience to human life, but also brings better development to the field of education. In order to realize the deep integration of AI and education, college teachers should not only improve their own information literacy, strengthen professional independent development, but also pay attention to the improvement of intelligent teaching ability. According to the relevant survey data in this paper, at present, most education practitioners in China know little about AI technology, even at the level of hearing about it. In order to better promote the high integration of AI technology and education, it is necessary to improve the modern information literacy of university teachers and attach importance to the training and development of their intelligence technology capabilities. University teachers should not only understand the AI technology itself, but also understand and explore the practical application of intelligence technology in higher education. At present, China's research on the use of deep learning technology to support the development of education is relatively poor. Educators do not know what these data can do for education in the face of a series of data generated in teaching. The main reason is that the current education researchers do not understand the relevant technology, so it is difficult to find the appropriate combination point. As an emerging technology, artificial intelligence is not suitable for and experienced by many college teachers in the current new education software and services. This phenomenon is still attributed to the fact that teachers' information literacy and intelligent teaching ability cannot keep up with the development of various new software. The use of all kinds of new software has increased the workload of teachers and raised the requirements for college teachers' intelligent teaching ability. How to effectively integrate new software tools with existing teaching has posed a great challenge to college teachers' intelligent teaching ability. Therefore, facing the education in the era of artificial intelligence, colleges and universities should consolidate the professional development system of teachers, promote the independent professional development of teachers, and improve teachers' intelligent teaching ability. On the one hand, teachers need to constantly improve their information literacy to adapt to the application of various new software; On the other hand, technical researchers also need to consider the needs of teachers in the process of software development to help teachers more easily accept new technologies and quickly integrate into education and teaching.

5 Conclusion

The application of artificial intelligence technology in university teaching has broad potential, which can help students learn better and teachers teach knowledge better. Firstly, artificial intelligence can meet the needs of different students through personalized teaching, providing tailored teaching materials and guidance based on their learning style and level. Secondly, artificial intelligence can also use big data to analyze students' learning data, providing teachers with detailed information about their learning situation, thereby better guiding and tutoring students. In addition, artificial intelligence can also be applied to develop virtual laboratories and simulation environments, providing a safer and more practical learning experience. In evaluating students' learning outcomes, artificial intelligence technology can also provide automated evaluation and feedback, reducing the workload of teachers. Meanwhile, complete behavioral analysis requires the assistance of wearable devices to obtain data samples, and the current infrastructure is not sufficient. Therefore, based on the data obtained during this stage, the technical operations were carried out with the assistance of professional technical personnel. In short, the application of artificial intelligence technology has brought many advantages to university teaching, improving students' learning outcomes and teachers' teaching quality.

References

1. Dong, Y.: Application of artificial intelligence software based on semantic web technology in english learning and teaching. J. Internet Technol. **1**, 23 (2022)
2. Dai, Y.: Research on the application of artificial intelligence technology in the development of sports teaching video compression algorithm (2021)
3. Xiaofeng, D.: Application of deep learning and artificial intelligence algorithm in multimedia music teaching (Retraction of Vol 38, Pg 7241, 2020). J. Intell. Fuzzy Syst. Appl. Eng. Technol. **5**, 41 (2021)
4. Lucic, A., Bleeker, M., Jullien, S., et al.: Teaching fairness, accountability, confidentiality, and transparency in artificial intelligence through the lens of reproducibility (2021)
5. Hao, Wu, Z., Yang: Research on the Construction of Artificial Intelligence Specialty under the Background of 1+X Certificate (2020)
6. Wen, J.: Innovative application of artificial intelligence technology in college physical education. J. Phys. Conf. Ser. **1881**(4), 042028 (2021). https://doi.org/10.1088/1742-6596/1881/4/042028

7. O'Connor, S.: Teaching artificial intelligence to nursing and midwifery students. Nurse Educ. Pract. (2022)

8. The Application of Modern Educational Technology in English Teaching (2020)

9. Liang, B., Yang, Z.: Exploration and application of college students€ management model during the epidemic based on big data technology. Math. Probl. Eng. **2022** (2022)

10. Meng, Q.: The application of pragmatic theory in college english teaching **5**(3), 4 (2021)

The Crisis and Change of Artificial Intelligence Algorithms in Higher Vocational Education

Ning Shi[1]($\boxtimes$), Zhou Jing[1,2], and Xiaoming Wu[1,2]

[1] Jilin Communications Polytechnic, Changchun 130012, Jinlin, China
223064711@qq.com
[2] Wuxi Vocational Institute of Commerce, Wuxi 214153, Jiangsu, China

Abstract. The widespread application of artificial intelligence algorithms has triggered crises and changes. This study evaluates the performance of artificial intelligence algorithms in crisis monitoring and change prediction using MAT-LAB. The results show that artificial intelligence algorithms can accurately analyze crisis situations in vocational education and output accurate change results. Compared with traditional manual judgment methods, artificial intelligence algorithms perform well in terms of error rate. At the same time, the accuracy of the judgment also exceeded 90%, proving its high accuracy in crisis monitoring and change prediction.

In summary, the application of artificial intelligence algorithms in vocational education has brought important crisis perception and change prediction capabilities. The research results of MATLAB indicate that artificial intelligence algorithms can accurately analyze crisis situations and have high judgment accuracy. However, in response to relevant challenges and issues, we need to formulate corresponding policies and measures to ensure the sustainable development of artificial intelligence algorithms in vocational education.

Keywords: distribution network · scheduling · Change · Dynamic · Planning

1 Introduction

The application of artificial intelligence algorithms in vocational education is rapidly developing. The is facing a reality of rapid changes and complex challenges, such as educational policy adjustments, technological innovation, and changes in talent demand [1, 2]. In this context, how to timely identify, evaluate, and respond to crises and bring about positive changes has become an important task faced by universities and educational institutions.

Artificial intelligence, as an advanced technological means, integrates innovative achievements in fields, presenting enormous potential in vocational education management [3]. By constructing intelligent algorithm models and utilizing deep learning techniques, artificial intelligence can efficiently process and analyze massive amounts of data, mining valuable information from them.

Y. Zhang and N. Shah (Eds.): BigIoT-EDU 2023, LNICST 582, pp. 445–452, 2024.
https://doi.org/10.1007/978-3-031-63136-8_46

In terms of transformation, artificial intelligence algorithms and the reform of teaching models. By analyzing students' learning behavior and needs, artificial intelligence can personalized recommend learning resources and teaching content, providing precise learning support and guidance [4]. In addition, artificial intelligence can also provide teachers with intelligent teaching tools and auxiliary decision-making systems, improving teaching effectiveness and quality.

Artificial intelligence algorithms crisis and transformation of vocational education. It can help vocational education institutions respond to crises and achieve change in a timely manner, provide intelligent teaching and management support, and bring new opportunities for sustainable development in the education field. However, we need to comprehensively consider the rationality and potential risks of its application to ensure the effective application and development of artificial intelligence algorithms in vocational education.

2 Mathematical Descriptions of Higher Vocational Education

The main basis of crisis state analysis is teachers, students, teaching content [5], etc.

Definition 1: The crisis state is s_i, the teaching state is l_i, the change indicator is x_i, the result set is set_i, and the number of analyses is c_i. The process of higher vocational education is shown in Eq. (1) [6].

$$\sum_{da_i} set_i = l_i \cdot \sum x_i \cdot c_i \tag{1}$$

Among them, the degree of change is level 4, and the change time is t.

Definition 2: The change function is $f(x)$, a is the constraint of change, and ς is the perturbation rate. The is shown in Eq. (2).

$$f(x) = \sum_{x_i} a \cdot (r_i \cdot x_i \cdot \sin \theta_i) + \varsigma \tag{2}$$

3 The Transformation of Artificial Intelligence Algorithms to Higher Vocational Education

According to intelligent algorithms, data from monitoring points and crisis states are identified, and the results are dynamically calculated [7].

Definition 3: The crisis judgment function $F(s_i|k)$ is calculated in Eq. (3) when a distortion value occurs.

$$F(da_i|k) = \alpha \cdot \Delta k \cdot \sum_s^n s_i \cdot \tan \theta \tag{3}$$

If $F(da_i|k)$ the education is stable in a crisis ^{state}, otherwise, there is a crisis.

4 Practical Cases of Higher Vocational Education

4.1 Case Introduction

In the judgment results algorithms on crisis states, the research objects of higher vocational education institutions were used to judge the crisis and change effects. Among them, crisis states and change measures, and the shown in Table 1.

Table 1. Crisis and state of change in higher vocational education

parameter	State of crisis	The state of change
Degree of comprehensiveness	1~3	1~3
Research directions	Theory → practice	Theory → practice
Scope of analysis	Comprehensive analysis	Comprehensive analysis
Crisis level	Level 3	Level 3
Perturbation rate	18.11	19.65

Figure 1 shows the results of the crisis state in Table 1. Through this chart, we can further observe and analyze the overall situation of vocational education in a crisis state. These data results can be used as a preliminary understanding of the status and trends of the vocational education system, providing a basis for subsequent analysis and decision-making.

However, please note that the data provided in Table 1 and Fig. 1 may only be an overview, and specific analysis and interpretation require comprehensive consideration of other factors and information. Further research and in-depth analysis are necessary for a more comprehensive understanding of the operation of the system in crisis situations. However, vocational education system in crisis situations, further analysis and research are necessary.

In Fig. 1, This indicates that the vocational education system has shown a relatively stable state during this period, and the changes in various indicators are relatively gentle. This situation can usually be seen as a positive signal that the vocational education system has maintained good operation and management during this period. A stable overall state may mean that education policies, teaching plans, faculty, student performance, and other aspects are operating in a good state without significant fluctuations or anomalies.

4.2 Judgment Rate and Accuracy of Crisis State in Higher Vocational Education

The are shown in Table 2.

According to the results in Table 2, in the power allocation and stage is greater than 80%, the rate than 92%, and the interference rate is less than 1%. In contrast, manual judgment methods have a higher stability rate in crisis situations, but lower accuracy, and the interference with the results. This indicates that under the same interference, artificial intelligence algorithms have good performance in terms of accuracy and stability.

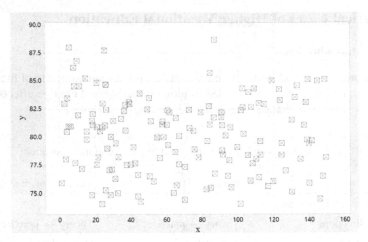

Fig. 1. Distribution of crisis state

In addition, Fig. 2 shows the results of continuous analysis of the crisis in higher vocational education. Through monitoring, artificial intelligence algorithms can quickly identify and respond to crises, providing accurate results and predictions. This further proves the potential and effectiveness of artificial intelligence algorithms in crisis management of higher vocational education.

According to the observation results in Fig. 1, artificial intelligence algorithms have obvious advantages in continuous monitoring, which can effectively improve the accuracy of changes and require fewer. In contrast, stability of manual judgment methods may be limited to some extent. This further proves the potential and advantages of artificial intelligence algorithms in responding to crises in vocational education. Due to its reliance on data and models, artificial intelligence algorithms can quickly identify and capture changes and crises in the field of education. Through real-time monitoring and analysis, artificial intelligence algorithms can quickly adjust and respond, thereby improving overall crisis response capabilities.

4.3   Analysis of the Time of Change in Higher Vocational Education

The time of change is higher vocational education, including content change, teaching plan change, system change and teacher change, shown in Table 3.

In artificial intelligence algorithms, the time required for practical, theoretical, and comprehensive judgment is shorter than manual judgment methods, indicating that artificial intelligence algorithms have significant advantages and efficiency improvements in these areas. In addition, even though the time changes of artificial intelligence algorithms are relatively stable in terms of content changes, teaching plan changes, system changes, and teacher changes, overall they are still significantly shorter than manual judgment methods.

These results further demonstrate the faster and more efficient application of artificial intelligence algorithms in vocational education. Through automated processing and analysis, artificial intelligence algorithms can effectively reduce the time required for

Table 2. Comparison of stability rate and crisis state judgment by different methods (unit: %)

algorithm	The type you are in	parameter	accuracy	Stability rate	Perturbation rate
Artificial intelligence algorithms	Hands-on	Theoretical education	94.33 ± 3. 17	81. 33 ± 2.37	1.73
		Practical education	94.23 ± 3.74	82.34 ± 2.43	1.83
		Compatible with education	95.36 ± 3. 17	83.73 ± 2.36	1.35
	Theoretical line	Theoretical education	93.39 ± 2.73	84.73 ± 2. 53	1.06
		Practical education	93. 16 ± 2.33	83.33 ± 2.32	1.33
		Compatible with education	92. 87 ± 2.73	83.34 ± 2. 53	1.36
Manual judgment methods	Hands-on	Theoretical education	87.23 ± 3.77	68.33 ± 3. 27	3.32
		Practical education	83.36 ± 3.35	66.74 ± 3. 23	3.63
		Compatible with education	85.31 ± 3. 17	65.34 ± 3. 23	3.95
	Theoretical line	Theoretical education	83.23 ± 3.33	69.33 ± 3.03	4.13
		Practical education	83.35 ± 3. 13	69.73 ± 3.07	4.27
		Compatible with education	85.26 ± 3.73	68.33 ± 3.33	4.36

manual judgment and improve work efficiency. This advantage is particularly significant in practice, theory, and comprehensive judgment, effectively shortening the time of the decision-making process.

According to the results in Table 3, artificial intelligence algorithms are significantly superior to manual judgment methods in terms of time, especially in terms of practice, theory, and comprehensive judgment. Although time changes are relatively stable in terms of content changes, teaching plan changes, system changes, and teacher changes, artificial intelligence algorithms still exhibit higher efficiency and speed. These findings once again demonstrate the potential and advantages of artificial intelligence algorithms in vocational education.

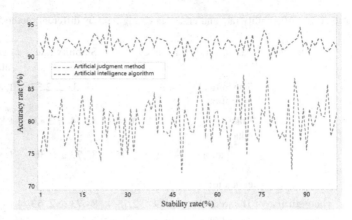

Fig. 2. Comparison of stability rate and accuracy of different algorithm crisis states

Table 3. Higher vocational education time (unit: seconds)

method	parameter	student			Course content		
		Freshman	Sophomore	Junior	practice	theory	synthesis
Artificial intelligence algorithms	content	23.53 ± 1.33	29.35 ± 1.35	45.55 ± 1.35	33.33 ± 1.33	32.35 ± 1.35	35.55 ± 1.35
	teaching plan	27.37 ± 1.55	37.55 ± 1.57	47. 13 ± 1.53	37.27 ± 1.55	33.33 ± 1.57	32. 43 ± 1.53
	system	37.33 ± 3.55	27.50 ± 1.35	47.53 ± 1.37	32.35 ± 1.55	32.53 ± 1.35	32. 17 ± 1.37
	teacher	27. 23 ± 3.55	37.13 ± 1.35	49. 23 ± 1.53	34.33 ± 1.55	32. 13 ± 1.35	34.33 ± 1.53
Manual judgment method	content	47.37 ± 2.33	27.33 ± 2.33	77.55 ± 5.35	77.37 ± 7.33	77.33 ± 3.33	77.55 ± 2.35
	teaching plan	47.37 ± 1.35	27.35 ± 2.55	72.33 ± 2.33	77.37 ± 2.35	72.35 ± 2.55	77.13 ± 2.33
	system	49.35 ± 7.35	79.35 ± 2. 13	74.87 ± 1.37	79.35 ± 2.35	71.35 ± 2.33	73.27 ± 2.37
	teacher	79.35 ± 7.535	70.33 ± 2.35	73.37 ± 2.57	79.15 ± 1.535	73.33 ± 2.35	78.17 ± 2.57

The manual judgment method also performs overall crisis analysis, but the analysis steps are more complicated, and the artificial intelligence algorithm can adopt different judgment schemes for monitoring the situation by simplifying the teaching process, as shown in Fig. 3.

From Fig. 3, it can be seen that based on the understanding of the efficiency and accuracy of artificial intelligence algorithms in processing and analyzing data in general, it is reasonable to speculate that artificial intelligence algorithms may be shorter in time and better than manual judgment methods. Furthermore, based on the provided information, the results in Table 3 further validate the superiority of artificial intelligence algorithms.

However, in order to draw accurate conclusions, it is best to further verify and confirm through analysis of specific data and results. If possible, please refer to Fig. 3 and Table 3 to describe them in a more specific way and further explore the time efficiency and advantages of artificial intelligence algorithms.

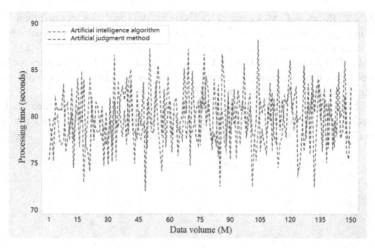

Fig. 3. Processing time for different methods

5 Conclusion

In summary, the application of artificial intelligence algorithms in vocational education is bringing crisis and change. Through MATLAB evaluation of algorithm performance, it was found that artificial intelligence algorithms can accurately analyze crisis states and output accurate change results, which is superior to traditional manual judgment methods. This provides important decision-making basis for higher vocational education decision-makers, making educational decisions more objective and accurate. However, the application of artificial intelligence algorithms also faces some issues, such as privacy protection and data security. Overall, the application of artificial intelligence algorithms has brought important crisis perception and change prediction capabilities to vocational education, but it is necessary to comprehensively consider relevant challenges and formulate corresponding policies and measures to promote the sustainable development of artificial intelligence algorithms in the field of vocational education.

References

1. Coledam, D.H.C., Frotta, B.M., Re, A.H.N.: General versus vocational education in high school: cross-sectional associations with student's health. J. Sch. Health **92**, 570–580 (2022)
2. Miret-Gamundi, P., Bayona-i-Carrasco, J.: Students of immigrant origin in higher secondary education. access to vocational training or baccalaureate in catalonia. Obets-Revista De Ciencias Sociales **17**, 267–284 (2022)
3. Morales-Munoz, K.A., Gonzalez-Burdiles, P., Cisternas-Irarrazabal, C.: Design of a quality management system for a state vocational higher education institution from Chile. Description of a Pilot Experience. Revista Electronica Calidad En La Educacion Superior, vol. 13 (2022)
4. Saadati, F., Celis, S.: Student motivation in learning mathematics in technical and vocational higher education: development of an instrument. Int. J. Educ. Math. Sci. Technol. **11**, 156–178 (2023)

5. Selowa, K.T., Ilorah, A.I., Mokwena, S.N.: Using big data analytics tool to influence decision-making in higher education: a case of south African technical and vocational education and training colleges. South Afric. J. Inform. Manage. **24** (2022)
6. Vieira, M.C.C., Gouveia, R.C., Dias, A.L.: Interdisciplinary teaching activities for high school integrated to vocational education promoting reflections on Industry 4.0 technologies and their implication in society. J. Techn. Educ. Train. **14**, 76–90 (2022)
7. Ye, R., Chudnovskaya, M., Nylander, E.: Right competence at the right time-but for whom? social recruitment of participants in an expanding higher vocational education segment in Sweden (2005–2019). Adult Educ. Q. **72**, 380–400 (2022)

Research on Teaching Reform Model of Computer Public Course Based on Intelligent Algorithm

Shaobing Lu[1,2(✉)], Yunyun Zhu[1,2], and Lei Yang[1,2]

[1] Yunnan Technology and Business University, Kunming 651701, Yunnan, China
lshbyn@163.com
[2] Tianjin Academy of Fine Arts, Tianjin 300020, China

Abstract. With the accelerated development of national information education, the teaching mode of computer public basic courses in colleges and universities is developing rapidly with the characteristics of low age, diversification and specialization. This shows that the basic computer education in China's colleges and universities is moving towards a new and revolutionary stage of development to meet the needs of the times. The research on the teaching reform mode of computer common course based on intelligent algorithm is the research on how to build a computer-based learning system that can help students learn better and faster. The purpose of this project is to develop a new method for teachers to use computers for teaching. This will be achieved by developing an intelligent algorithm that can analyze students' learning processes and then provide them with appropriate courses that suit their needs. This will enable students to learn more effectively in a shorter time than before.

Keywords: Computer Public Course · Intelligent algorithm · reform in education

1 Introduction

The foundation of colleges and universities is to establish morality and cultivate people. To implement the fundamental task of establishing morality and cultivating people in colleges and universities, we need to firmly grasp the three aspects of curriculum, teachers' teaching and students' learning. Curriculum: We need to take the classroom teaching of different disciplines as the channel. The ideological and political theory course should strengthen the affinity and pertinence of its education to meet the needs of students' growth and development. All other courses should combine their own discipline characteristics, keep the responsibility field of the discipline, and make all kinds of courses and ideological and political theory courses go together to form synergy. "In terms of teachers and students: teachers of all disciplines are not only the imparters of single knowledge, but also shoulder the important responsibility of comprehensive education". Each teacher should carry out the ideological and political education of the

Y. Zhang and N. Shah (Eds.): BigIoT-EDU 2023, LNICST 582, pp. 453–463, 2024.
https://doi.org/10.1007/978-3-031-63136-8_47

curriculum with the educational concept of "three complete education". While imparting professional knowledge or technology, fully tap the moral elements in the discipline
teaching, and consciously integrate the ideological and political education content into
the whole process of teaching according to the characteristics of the discipline, Improve
the comprehensive quality of students to achieve the goal of comprehensive education.

As a compulsory course for college students, the public computer course in colleges
and universities has obvious advantages in carrying out ideological and political teaching in the course of teaching and implementing the fundamental task of establishing
morality and cultivating people. The public computer course not only has the function
of cultivating the body, but also its contents of educating people, such as the cultivation of
will quality, cooperation and competition consciousness, are very effective elements of
ideological and political education. Therefore, strengthening the ideological and moral
education in the public computer teaching and deepening the teaching reform of the public computer course under its background is an important strategic measure for colleges
and universities to implement the fundamental task of building morality and cultivating
people.

Currently, Computer network courses are mostly embodied in the separation of
knowledge content and practice from the real situation under the guidance of reduction-
ism. From the perspective of teaching design, the compilation of textbook content is
largely affected by the reductive method, which has weakened the learning efficiency.
Moreover, it is difficult to find an appropriate textbook It can be seen from the 7 textbooks
of computer network courses in the planning textbooks. The structure of chapters is often
"top heavy", which weakens the role of exercises in teaching to some extent. However,
the computer network course is aimed at skill acquisition, and the after-school exercises
after the textbooks have not been effectively designed to promote learners' learning [1].
The teaching mode of domestic colleges and universities is mostly classroom teaching,
so that the limited classroom teaching time makes the role of exercises limited or even
missing. The reason is that traditional education is deeply rooted. On the one hand, it
has led to the neglect of textbook compilation, on the other hand, it has led to different
degrees of weakening in the process of teaching activities. Therefore, it has caused a
certain degree of inefficient learning [2].

The author found from the relevant literature that the research on the concept of
variant exercise was relatively late, and it was not until the 1980s that it became more
and more obvious. In CNKI, there are about 70 studies with the keyword "title = variant
exercise", and nearly 1600 studies with the keyword "title = multiple solutions to one
problem or multiple solutions to one problem"; Less than 30 relevant articles were
searched in Google Academic and Elsevier foreign language journals. These researches
are roughly divided into three directions. One is the experimental research to verify the
facilitation of variant practice on learning, which is particularly prominent in foreign
research; The second is to use the idea of variation or concept to design examples
to guide learners' learning, which accounts for more in the research of mathematics
teaching in China; Third, there is a theoretical study on the concept of variant exercise,
which is related to the memory of declarative knowledge and procedural knowledge.
But in general, its core purpose is to promote learning transfer [3].

This study is expected to summarize and summarize the possible problems and causes of ideological and political education in the teaching through the investigation and analysis of the current situation of ideological and political education in the teaching of public computer courses in colleges and universities, and explore the methods and paths of ideological and political education in the public computer courses in colleges and universities according to the research situation, so as to promote the development of ideological and political education in colleges and universities, The ideological and political education will be injected into the public computer teaching in colleges and universities, so as to realize the all-round development of students.

2 Related Work

2.1 University Public Computer Network Course

The object of this paper is "computer network", a public course in universities, not a "network course" based on computing environment. There is no unified syllabus for computer network courses, but it can be determined that computer network has its contents in two categories, namely computer technology and communication technology. The liberal arts and computer education committee of colleges and universities regards "Computer Network Application Basis" as one of the four modules of the teaching content of the computer curriculum. For the setting of the content of computer network, at the level of basic understanding and application, colleges and universities generally adopt a mixture of such planning textbooks as "Computer Foundation Course" [4]. A small number of colleges and universities, based on the general environment of curriculum reform, Take computer network as a separate public elective course. Some articles put forward the necessity of setting Computer Network as a school level public course due to the rapid development of computer network, the personal needs of learners and the needs of employers, and gave some brief teaching objectives.

Learning strategy is a complex scheme formulated purposefully and consciously by learners in order to improve the learning effect and efficiency. Therefore, the auxiliary strategy given to this learning process is the support strategy. The support strategy is divided into two levels. One is that it does not pay attention to the process of solving problems, and it is an abstract description of problem solving, which is widely applicable; One is to provide a task solving process, that is, a supporting program, such as problem-solving steps and ideas, which is highly targeted [5].

In terms of concept development, by analyzing the relationship between ideological and political computer courses and ideological and political computer courses, experts and scholars' research on the development concept of "ideological and political computer courses" mainly focuses on the following two views. First, although ideological and political computer courses and computer courses differ from each other in terms of teaching content, subject status and characteristics, and teaching advantages, they are also linked in terms of interoperability in specific tasks and objectives, consistency in direction and function, and comprehensiveness in content and requirements, so the two should give play to their respective educational functions and educational advantages, Create a computer course system for ideological and political education in colleges and universities. Second, we should change our thinking in the process of carrying out the ideological and political work of the computer course, form the transformation of "ideological and political computer course" and "computer course ideological and political" in many aspects, jump out of the comfort of the traditional ideological and political education concept in the past, expand the ideological and political education channels, and work together to build a big ideological and political pattern.

To sum up, the development concept of ideological and political education in computer courses is that we should go with each other and give full play to our own advantages; Or should we change our thinking and speed up the unilateral transformation from "ideological and political computer course" to "ideological and political computer course", which is still a problem that needs to be discussed in the academic community. However, different approaches lead to the same goal. The final plan for the development of the concept of "ideological and political computer course" is to train students to become a comprehensive development person.

In the research on the development and construction of "computer curriculum ideological and political work", there are many researches from the aspects of computer curriculum, teachers, teaching resources and system construction. In terms of computer courses, we should promote the ideological and political work of computer courses according to the functional orientation of different types of computer courses. In addition to taking the ideological and political theory course as the teaching carrier, we should also combine the general computer course and the specialized computer course, excavate the ideological and political elements in different types of computer courses, and organically combine the principles, requirements and contents of ideological and political education with computer course design, textbook development, computer course implementation, computer course evaluation, etc. "In terms of teachers and teaching resources, by cultivating the moral education awareness and ability of teachers of various computer courses in the teaching process, accurately mining and integrating the ideological and political education resources in computer courses, creating a case library of ideological and political education resources in different disciplines, and improving the evaluation of teachers' teaching, forming a relatively complete ideological and political education system of computer courses. In terms of system guarantee, the Party Committee and the discipline teaching department of the university were connected to issue programmatic documents for each college under the guidance of "computer curriculum ideological and political" to ensure the implementation of "computer curriculum ideological and political" work.

To sum up, the implementation of ideological and political education in computer courses requires explicit education (ideological and political theory computer course teaching) and implicit education (other disciplines computer course teaching) to go in the same direction, grasp the consistency of discipline teaching direction, discipline education direction and discipline culture direction, combine theory with reality, and plan the construction and implementation of ideological and political education in computer courses in colleges and universities based on practice. From a theoretical point of view, the implementation of ideological and political education in computer courses needs to take computer courses as the carrier, make detailed adjustments to teaching guidance documents and syllabus, and take corresponding policies and systems as the guarantee; From the perspective of concrete practice, it is necessary for teachers of all disciplines to fully explore the elements of ideological and political education in professional courses, and at the same time improve teachers' educational ability and awareness, and all departments of the school work together to achieve a win-win situation.

2.2 Current Situation of Public Computer Courses in Colleges and Universities

Since human beings entered the 21st century, computer has changed from a special tool in the field of cutting-edge technology to one of the indispensable auxiliary tools for modern scientific research, and has also been widely popularized in people's daily study and life. However, the public basic computer courses offered by most colleges and universities are often not targeted and can not meet the students' desire for computer knowledge. After the students enter the society, their computer application ability does not meet the requirements of the society. No matter individuals or units can only spend energy on new training.

The increasing enrollment of colleges and universities has enabled more people to obtain further education opportunities, but many problems have also been highlighted. First of all, some colleges and universities cannot meet the requirements of hardware facilities and software conditions after the expansion of enrollment due to lack of funds and other reasons; Secondly, in the face of a large number of students, the updating speed of university curriculum is slow, and there is a lack of effective quality control. These factors directly lead to the continuous reduction of the gold content of college students' degrees in China, which is accompanied by the chain effect of the declining employment rate and salary [6].

(1) The setting of teaching objectives is seriously divorced from the social needs of students. Students are very interested in computer itself. After all, as a representative of high-tech, computer is indispensable to most human behaviors. However, most colleges and universities can hardly meet the students' needs for computer knowledge. The monotonous and backward teaching contents and methods have greatly hit the enthusiasm of students to learn computer knowledge. With the rapid development of computer application technology, the requirements of employment posts on the computer operation ability of recruitment talents are also greatly improved [7].

(2) The public basic computer education in colleges and universities faces different professional fields for college students to learn, and their mastery of basic computer knowledge is uneven. Therefore, the idea of setting public computer courses should not only take into account the different knowledge bases of students, but also meet the needs of computer knowledge in the professional fields they learn, which has certain complexity and difficulty.

(3) The students' mastery of the basic knowledge of computer application technology is uneven. Most of them studied the public basic computer courses in their first year of college, some of them studied computer application courses in their second year of college, and the vast majority of students studied computer application courses in their third and fourth year of college. It can be seen that during their college study, students cannot use computer technology to successfully and effectively solve problems related to different professional research in the later stage due to the serious lack of computer knowledge [8].

(4) Computer teachers are somewhat divorced from the professional background of non computer major students. They are not familiar with how computer technology plays a role in different majors, and may even be unfamiliar. Therefore, teachers of computer public basic courses are required to have high comprehensive abilities. In reality, as far as the computer teachers in colleges and universities are concerned, there are many teachers who can give full play to the teaching advantages of the computer specialty, but few of them are well integrated with the relevant background disciplines.

3 Ability Training Level of Public Computer Network Courses in Universities

The course of computer network is only taught as a separate course in college education, and the main object is computer and related majors. However, as a public course, the content involved is different. In the teaching of information technology courses in primary and secondary schools, it is mainly about the understanding and shallow application of information technology, focusing on the cultivation of ethics, interest and awareness. The purpose is to understand and master basic knowledge and skills, so as to understand the profound impact of the development and application of information technology on human daily life and science and technology. Therefore, students are required to skillfully browse the news, send and receive emails and find information in their study, life and work, and have the basic knowledge of computer network, which is the most basic level of computer network education. However, some articles define it as the learning level of non computer major students in colleges and universities, and the author cannot agree with it. How to determine the teaching content and the nature of the public computing network course in universities [9]. More than ten years of education informatization construction has made the informatization level of colleges and universities in China have been greatly developed. In order to adapt to the changes of the times, all college students will learn college computer basics and other related courses in their first year of enrollment [10]. For example, the basic course of computer culture has become a compulsory course for non computer majors in colleges and universities. The course also learns computer network related content to a considerable extent, as shown in Fig. 1. However, under the general environment of computer basic teaching in the narrow sense of tool theory, computer network is simplified and even ignored in computer basic teaching [11]. At present, the teaching content of information technology course in primary and secondary schools has a lot of overlap with the teaching content of computer basics in universities, and the computer network knowledge contained in it is an expansion of learners' vision. The author believes that the college public computer network courses should pay attention to the cultivation of practical skills. Table 1 below is a list of common teaching methods for college computer public teachers.

According to the analysis of the survey results, the most common teaching methods used by college computer teachers in the teaching process are the explanation method, the action demonstration method, the practice method and the complete and decomposition method, accounting for 97.4%, 88.5%, 88.5% and 79.4% respectively [12]. As the most traditional teaching method, most teachers will choose explanation method, action demonstration method, practice method and integrity and decomposition method

Table 1. List of common teaching methods for college computer public teachers

teaching method	Sum value	Person (person) adopting this method	Percentage
Interpretive method	746	76	97.4%
Action demonstration method	555	69	88.5%
drill	534	69	88.5%
Completeness and decomposition method	462	62	79.4%
Gameplay	412	60	76.9%
Competition law	230	39	50.0%
Correction and help method	148	26	33.33%
Case teaching method	103	20	25.6%
Multimedia teaching method	87	15	19.2%
Problem-based approach	76	13	16.7%

in the teaching process. There are few teachers using case teaching method, multimedia teaching method and question inquiry method to teach, accounting for 25.6%, 19.2% and 16.7% respectively. However, reasonable use of these teaching methods in the actual teaching process can not only improve the interest of the classroom, activate the classroom atmosphere, but also is a good way to integrate the elements of ideological and political education. In addition, 76.9% and 50% of the respondents chose game method and competition method, which is also a better teaching method to carry out ideological and political courses in teaching [13].

Teaching mode of computer public course

In the whole teaching content, the focus of the overview of computer network system is mainly on the verbal information related to computer network and architecture, as well as a study of the overall attitude towards computer network. The focus of data communication is mainly on the learning of intelligent skills based on the same sex system model, channel, etc. The focus of network equipment is mainly on the study of the transmission structure of computer network system in the real world, the verbal information related to network cards and routers, and how to identify, regulate and other intelligent skills. The focus of network access is to learn the language information and wisdom skills of LAN, WAN and access network [14]. Host configuration, Internet application, networking, network management and other knowledge are learning contents mainly based on skill acquisition.

The improved teaching reform model of computer public course needs to build a teaching information function to describe the proximity between the expected node and the actual computer course information factor node. The teaching information function is called fitness value teaching information function. The fitness value teaching information function reflects the error between the node state and the actual formal state detected by FTU. When the value of the teaching information function is O When, it means that the expected node and the actual computer course information factor status are the same. The performance of the fitness value teaching information function constructed will directly affect the final result of the positioning of the information factors of the computer course [15]. In this paper, the positioning of the information factors of the computer course is transformed into solving the problem of the maximum value of the fitness value teaching information function, that is, solving the minimum error between the two. Therefore, the essence of the positioning of information factors in computer courses is a discrete mathematical problem, whose mathematical model is shown in Formula 1:

$$R^{\dagger} = \arg\min f(X) = \{X^{\dagger} \in N : f(X^{\dagger}) \le f(X), X \in N\}(1) \tag{1}$$

In formula 1, N represents the number of nodes of the computer curriculum factor, $f(X)$ is the real value detected by the teaching information, and $f(X)$ is the switching function. Based on this mathematical model, a fitness value function for course information is proposed, as shown in Eq. 2:

$$f(X) = \sum_{j=1}^{N} |I_f - t_i(s_i)| \tag{2}$$

In the above formula, I_f is the teaching information obtained through real-time monitoring of SCADA, I, (S;) is the value of the teaching function of the ith switch, and S represents the status of each switch in the course information factor. The intelligent algorithm takes the minimum difference of the objective function as the optimal solution, and the output solution space corresponding to the position coded as 1 is the actual location of the teaching accident in the teaching process.

4 Reflections on Offering Public Computer Courses to College Students

4.1 Determine Scientific Training Objectives

Computer education in China's colleges and universities, especially the public basic computer education, which accounts for a large proportion of students, determines to some extent whether talents can apply advanced science and technology to solve their own professional research problems in the future. Therefore, when setting up the public basic computer courses for non computer major postgraduates, we should focus on the cultivation of students' computer ability on the premise of cultivating application-oriented talents. Colleges and universities cultivate a large number of talents with high comprehensive quality through the teaching of computer public courses [16]. Cultivate students' computational thinking ability, conform to the nature, task and function of computer aided research in the new era, and realize its strategic position in the national economy and social development; Grasp the intersection of computer technology and students' related fields, integrate and cultivate the awareness of computing thinking, cultivate comprehensive talents to participate in international competition, and ensure the national competitive strength.

In a word, when promoting the ideological and political construction of computer courses in colleges and universities, it is necessary to excavate the ideological and political education elements contained in computer courses and infiltrate these ideological and political elements into the ideological and political construction of computer courses. But at present, although most teachers have accepted the ideological and political concepts of computer courses, they did not excavate the ideological and political elements existing in computer courses and consciously integrate them into the teaching process while imparting knowledge and skills, which makes it difficult to form the situation of "ideological and political elements in computer courses and education in teachers" [17]. The more important reason for this situation is the lack of the ability to promote the ideological and political construction of computer courses. The ideological and political teaching of computer courses is still at the primary stage, which makes the value guidance and knowledge teaching of students unable to promote in coordination.

4.2 Put the "Practicality" Training Policy Through the Whole Teaching Process

Take "practicality" as one of the teaching objectives to construct the curriculum content. Based on the combination of students' professional background and computer technology application, the teaching system focuses on cultivating students' application ability, integrates theory with practice, and realizes a large number of training of application-oriented talents. Take "ability" as the key of teaching to cultivate students' ability to find, solve and innovate problems. As far as the type of talents is concerned, colleges and universities mainly cultivate technical talents or laborers with high comprehensive quality [18]. The improvement of the comprehensive quality of technical talents is the main sign of productivity development and social progress, and the competition of technological innovation will become the main focus of the future world competition. "Student-centered", instead of using a fixed mode and a fixed way of thinking to teach, we should always encourage students to innovate in their personality: we should emphasize students' independent learning ability and attach importance to the cultivation of students' thinking mode, stimulate their initiative, enthusiasm and creativity, so as to facilitate the cultivation of innovative talents.

4.3 Pay Attention to the Cultivation of Students' Computational Thinking and the Development of Their Innovative Ability

At present, college students' comprehensive quality includes many aspects such as ideological quality, learning ability, physical and mental conditions, and correct thinking ability. Among these qualities, ideological quality is the foundation, physical and mental health is the guarantee, personal ability is the core, and innovative thinking is the driving force [19]. Nowadays, with the rapid development of science and technology, it has also brought about the continuous adjustment of the industrial structure and the wide mobility of occupations, which requires students to maintain their due professional qualities in the changing society.

The spirit of innovation is the soul of a nation's progress and the inexhaustible driving force for the country's prosperity. A nation without innovation ability is difficult to stand among the world's advanced nations. Innovation includes thinking innovation, theoretical innovation, institutional innovation, method innovation, management innovation and other elements, and innovative thinking is the core part of the innovation system [20]. As a centralized system of national knowledge innovation and technological innovation system, the cultivation of innovation ability of higher education institutions is inseparable from the development of their own innovative thinking.

5 Conclusion

This article belongs to theoretical exploration and teaching practice is not deep enough. In the later research process, the author will continue to practice and explore the design mode of variant exercises for college public computer network courses, and propose modification mode according to the problems found in the exploration process, so as to make it more consistent with the purpose of skills acquisition of college students in public computer network courses in China. At present, part of the content of this model is not detailed and clear enough, so there is a lot of room for transformation. I hope that it will be further optimized in future research to make the structure and content more reasonable. As time goes on, new theoretical and practical achievements emerge one after another. At that time, there will be a series of more complete researches to achieve better integration of skill acquisition and variant practice in computer network courses.

References

1. Wang, Z., Wang, G., Mei, G.U.: A research on the teaching reform of electronic technology course based on the intelligent car contest for college students. J. Tongren Univ. (2017)
2. Cao, J.: Computer public course teaching based on improved machine learning and neural network algorithm. J. Intell. Fuzzy Syst. Appl. Eng. Technol. **4**, 40 (2021)
3. Zhang, K., Wang, H.F., Chen, X.Y.: Research on teaching reform of computer course based on computational thinking. DEStech Trans. Social Sci. Educ. Hum. Sci. **2017**(eiem) (2017)
4. Yan, D.: Construction of new model of primary school mathematics education based on computer biological intelligent algorithm (2016)
5. Zhu, L., Mao, H.: A comprehensive teaching evaluation method of computer network course based on TOPSIS algorithm. Revista de la Facultad de Ingenieria **32**(10), 523–530 (2017)
6. Tian, X.: Reseach on college english micro class teaching model based on personalized intelligent adjustment algorithm, pp. 438–442 (2018)
7. Chu, X., Wu, J.: A Discussion on the practical teaching reform of intelligent mobile terminal technology course. **6**(8), 7 (2022)
8. Tan, F.X., Wang, D.M.: Teaching reform about principle of automatic control based on intelligent manufacturing. J. Fuyang Teach. College (Natl. Sci.) (2016)
9. Zhang, P., Liu, N., Chang, J., et al.: A teaching reform about intelligent instrument course based on information technology. Educ. Teach. Forum (2019)
10. Feng, C.M., Liang, M.Y., Zheng, X.J., et al.: Teaching reform and research on comprehensive training of coating production for polytechnic based on intelligent campus. Guangzhou Chem. Indust. (2017)
11. Zhang, J., Junjie, L.I.: Research on the reform of public security college informatization based on intelligent mobile terminal platform. Guide Sci. Educ. (2016)
12. Lin, C.: Reform on the teaching model of "the computer algorithm design and analysis" based on deep learning. Sci. Educ. Article Collects (2016)
13. Wu, Z., Chen, Z., Du, H.: The teaching reform and study of "computer foundation" based on a model of "one basic teaching method,two programming languages and three learning methods. Sci. Educ. Article Collects (2017)

14. Wang, J., Wei, W.: Research on teaching reform and innovation of computer introduction course based on new engineering (2018)
15. Sun, H.: Thinking on the teaching reform of computer basis course for medical specialty under the background of ideological and political education in courses in the intelligent age 5(4), 6 (2021)
16. Li, W.: Multimedia teaching of college musical education based on deep learning. Mobile Inform. Syst. (2021)
17. Lu, S., Wei, X.: Reform of human-computer interaction course based on mobile application interaction design 2021(12), 4 (2021)
18. Sun, J.N., Yong-Feng, L.V., Chen, C.: Pedagogical reform of higher vocational education for machinery design course of mechano-electronic majors base on the model of engineering training. Educ. Teach. Forum (2018)
19. Huang, Y., Song, X., Yang, Y.: Reform and practice of radar control evaluation methods based on computer intelligent assessment. J. Civil Aviat. Flight Univ. China (2018)
20. Zhao, X.L., Xi-Bin, X.U., Liang-Yu, L.I., et al.: Exploration of intelligent teaching reform based on WeChat platform. Mod. Comput. (2016)

A Comparative Study on Piano Robot Playing Classical Piano and Jazz Style Piano

Hong Yang[1,2(✉)], Ping Wu[1,2], and Wenxin Jiang[1,2]

[1] Quanzhou Preschool Education College, Quanzhou, Fujian, China
hy3395@163.com
[2] Beijing Institute of Technology, Zhuhai 519088, Guangdong, China

Abstract. Comparative study of piano robot playing classical and jazz piano. The main goal of this project is to compare the results of a new music learning method based on an artificial intelligence system that can learn from examples. The AI system was developed in cooperation with the University of Pisa (Italy), and successfully tested in the laboratory environment, playing jazz in the laboratory. This paper introduces the experimental results obtained in these tests and compares them with the results obtained by other research groups using more traditional methods to study similar problems., On the basis of in-depth research on the working principle, research status and development trend of humanoid robot equipment at home and abroad, a pneumatic piano manipulator is designed. This manipulator uses the ingenious mechanical structure and the effective cooperation of the pneumatic system, with the control of the software system, to achieve the purpose of playing the piano. Through the study of the piano humanoid manipulator, a multi-degree of freedom, humanoid piano humanoid manipulator is designed. The innovative design of embedded spring is adopted for the joint of the finger, and a humanoid manipulator for playing piano is designed, which is composed of air cylinder, reversing valve, pressure reducing valve, etc. Using ANSYS finite element analysis, the static analysis of the key components of the humanoid manipulator was completed through data sharing between CATIA and ANSYS, and the optimization design was carried out. ADAMS dynamic simulation is applied to simulate the real motion by adding a motion pair, and its motion and velocity curves are obtained, which verifies that the designed structure meets the design requirements. Our results show that our method can be used as an alternative to other methods currently available, because it produces very good performance.

Keywords: Piano robot · Jazz style · Classical piano

1 Introduction

The modern piano is known as the "king of musical instruments" by many musicians, not only because of its largest volume and the most complex internal structure, but also because its excellent and comprehensive performance and extensive use are incomparable with other musical instruments. By pressing the keys on the keyboard, the player

© ICST Institute for Computer Sciences, Social Informatics and Telecommunications Engineering 2024
Published by Springer Nature Switzerland AG 2024. All Rights Reserved
Y. Zhang and N. Shah (Eds.): BigIoT-EDU 2023, LNICST 582, pp. 464–474, 2024.
https://doi.org/10.1007/978-3-031-63136-8_48

moves the small mallet wrapped in felt in the piano, and then strikes the steel wire strings to make a sound. On the basis of full talent, piano players should have more than ten years or decades of training. In addition to a deep foundation of music theory, they also need fingering, creativity and appeal. Therefore, behind the wonderful music is hard work and perseverance [1]. It can be said that the piano is also one of the most difficult instruments to play. As early as 1984, Japanese scientists developed a piano playing robot named WABOT-2. The piano playing robot of Waseda University even includes pedal control. This paper also designs and develops a piano playing robot, which can imitate human beings and play beautiful music on the piano [2]. The core part is a high-speed servo mobile and pneumatic playing structure, which can cover most of the keys on the ordinary vertical or triangular piano, support users to write music by themselves, and also support online real-time performance. It is a high-tech robot product integrating entertainment, technology and art.

Jazz (JAZZ) originated from an encounter - an encounter between European traditions and African traditions - and the creative combination that followed. Its family tree was deeply rooted in the soil of the white continent and the black continent, and a branch that combined into one broke out in 1619. It was in this landmark year that the first batch of black slaves trafficked from Africa landed in Virginia, North America, which brought African black music culture [3]. At that time, black music had foreshadowed some characteristics of jazz music in the future: circuitous notes, repeated syncopation effects, and a series of beats that were regularly separated and always reminded people of dance music.

Most of the original jazz performers did not receive formal music training, and some even did not know music scores [4]. They just developed their performance skills through continuous music performance practice, and played the familiar ragtime, blues and other tunes with the so-called "irregular" sound, timbre and performance methods in textbooks. They freely cut, decorated Imitating the native rough and hoarse voice of black singers has formed a unique style, that is, new voice, new discord, new counterpoint, new dynamic and impact. Therefore, the original jazz music is not so much a new music creation as a new playing style.

Classical music refers to the music from the Baroque period to the Romantic period in the history of western music, which is divided into the pre classical period and the Vienna classical period by the Beethoven period; Classical piano playing and jazz piano playing are two kinds of performing arts based on classical music and jazz music respectively [5].

The pace of life in modern society is accelerating, and people's demand for convenient and intelligent systems is increasing "Robotic technology with the characteristics of information and automation is getting more and more attention". As a cutting-edge science and technology integrating multiple disciplines, since its birth, researchers have been focusing on exploring appropriate application platforms, transforming cutting-edge technologies into productive forces, and promoting social development. For a long time, robot technology has been mainly used in traditional industrial fields such as automobile, aircraft, and shipbuilding. In recent years, robot technology has been developing continuously, and its application fields have also been expanding The fields of unified industry and manufacturing are gradually moving towards society, life People's livelihood and other broader areas [6]. Musical robot is an important direction of robot development, and also a typical representative of the application of robot technology in the civil market. It shows music, the common language of human beings, through robot playing. It is very interesting and can effectively shorten the distance between people and robots. It is a successful example of the expansion of robot application field, and its application prospect is generally optimistic Development is a comprehensive development involving a series of disciplines in different fields, such as automatic control, signal processing, model construction, and material application, which provides a new idea for further expanding the robot application field.

2 Related Work

2.1 Research Status of Music Robot at Home and Abroad

As a new and important development direction in the field of robot application, music robot is attracting more and more attention. Up to now, there are not many researches in this field, and the relevant researches abroad are mainly concentrated in Japan. In order to solve the social problems such as the reduction of the working population, insufficient labor force, and excessive social security expenditure caused by low birth rate and serious aging of the population, Japan has been stepping up the research and development and manufacturing of robots, and has made remarkable achievements [7].

As early as 1977, Waseda University began to research and develop a clarinet playing robot. By 1979, they had successively developed automatic performance robots for violins and cellos, and successfully performed at concerts in 1982. Three years later (1985), Inada University successfully developed an electronic organ autoplay robot and exhibited it at Tsukuba Science Expo. After that, people's enthusiasm for studying music robots gradually became active. Many universities have begun to develop flute, saxophone, trumpet, bagpipe, xylophone, lyre, piano and other instrument playing robots. Among them, WF series flute autoplay robot developed by Waseda University in Japan is widely known around the world. Since 1990, it has been developed [8]. Through the continuous efforts of scientific researchers, the functions of WF series flute playing robots have been gradually improved, and the playing effect has also been continuously improved. The latest WF-5 series robot playing effect has been very realistic. When playing flute, the core part is the coordination of lungs and lips to control the air flow. The original WF-1 robot used an air cylinder with the same vital capacity as a human to act as an artificial lung, simulating a human to exhale and inhale, and then matched with an appropriate lip opening to produce air bundles with a specific flow rate range. The performance function can be realized by adjusting the air velocity within the range. Later, considering that the playing effect cannot be further improved by independently adjusting the pitch by changing the air beam flow rate, a playing posture control mechanism is added to the WF-2 robot to fine tune the length of the air column by changing the playing posture, that is, changing the distance between the lips and the flute mouth. After introducing the performance posture parameters of each interval, the range of robot performance is improved [9].

Relatively speaking, China's research work in the field of performing robots is relatively late. The robot research center in the early stage mainly focused on industrial robots. With the popularization of intelligent technology and the development of social civilization, domestic research is not only limited to service robots, which focus on "practical" research, but also slowly expand its vision to the research of "entertainment" robots. In 2004, the Chinese Academy of Science and Technology launched an entertainment robot that can make a series of expressions through voice control [10]. In 2010, the Department of Electronic Engineering of Taiwan University launched robots that can imitate human expressions and display basic emotions with more interactive experience. In addition to the universities mentioned above, other efficient and domestic enterprises have also carried out a lot of research work on humanoid robots, and have achieved certain results in all aspects, laying a foundation for the research of robots in China.

With the development of intelligent technology, the research on robots has expanded the commercial field. More and more companies have launched robots with different characteristics, such as the Titan robot launched by Cyberstein in the UK, the Alpha egg robot launched by Taoyun Technology and the famous Dajiang unmanned aerial vehicle in China. In this era of industry-university-research flowering, the popularity of UAVs and 3D printers has made more and more high-tech products the choice of millions of households. The number of degrees of freedom of the NAO robot launched by the French company Aldebaran in 2010 is up to 32, which can achieve more complex action tasks [11]. More importantly, because the robot is open and rich in user interfaces, users can not only use it directly, but also conduct secondary development on it, making it more widely used.

2.2 Jazz Piano Music and Classical Piano Music

Jazz piano music is not only an important branch of pop music, but also has a profound impact on the creation of many white classical musicians. Among them, the most famous examples are American musician George Gershwin's Rhapsody in Blue (1924) and Piano Concerto in F major (1925) for piano and band, as well as his piano solo Three Preludes (1926); Copland's "Four Piano Blues" (1926–1946); "Regtam Bess" in the ten Etudes of Virgil Thomson; Even Debussy, a famous French impressionist musician whose position in piano music in the early 20th century was equal to that of Chopin in the 19th century, also widely absorbed the style of jazz music in his works, and created the piano piece "Little Negro", which is still widely circulated today

Jazz piano, as a very important member of jazz music, has experienced more than 100 years of trials and tribulations with the development of jazz music. On the basis of classical piano performance, it has formed its own unique music style and performance skills. Although there are various genres and styles, they all have their common characteristics

(1) Rhythm characteristics

It can be divided into two basic rhythmic forms: straight rhythm and swing or shuffle. The difference is mainly reflected in the way of playing octaves, which also determines the style of jazz piano [12]. The flat rhythm mainly originated from Regtime and later developed into the jazz music of Lat style, such as Bossa Nova, Jazz - Samba and Latin Jazz. In these types of music, the rhythm is based on the octave. In terms of notation, the playing time of the octave is consistent with that recorded on the score. This song

"849 Regtam" is based on the familiar lesson 1 of Cherney's "849 Etude", as shown in Fig. 1:

Fig. 1. 849 Regtime score

The right hand melody part uses a continuous, relatively standard syncopation rhythm based on octaves, especially the first half of the second beat and the third beat, or the second half of the fourth beat and the first beat of the next bar. The syncopation rhythm is formed by connecting lines, which disrupts the stress and sub-stress positions of the original 2/4 and 4/4 beats, and emphasizes it; The left hand accompaniment part uses very regular 4/4 or 2/4 (2/2) beats and medium-speed chords or fabrics with bass. Generally, it uses the harmony rhythm of two beats and one chord, and pays attention to maintaining the flowing bass. The harmony language is very strict, fully in line with the classical harmony norms. This standard Regtam performance directly affects the development mode of pop music.

The swing rhythm is mainly derived from the blues, which is based on the fact that each beat is divided equally into three tones (i.e., triplets). The most common rhythm type is to omit the middle tone of triplets. It creates a sense of swing. Jazz played with this swing rhythm is the most famous "swing music". There are three kinds of notation for swing music:

(2) Jazz scale and chord

The melody of jazz music is mainly composed of major scale and minor scale, which is the result of the influence of European classical music. But at the same time, other characteristic scales are often used, such as a number of medieval scales and a variety of scales based on them. These scales are indispensable "condiments" to make music obtain jazz "taste".

The relationship between chord and scale is very close. In jazz music, the harmony structure often uses the blues scale as melody material, and makes good use of the chord function scale. The so-called functional scale refers to the scale based on the function and structure of chords. Chords are the backbone of the scale, which is an invariable component; And the extrachord is the minor level of the scale, which is a relatively variable component. For any kind of chord, as long as a jazz scale contains the backbone of the chord, the scale can be used as the chord scale of the chord. According to this principle, the scale applicable to each chord is not one, but many.

(3) Form and theme

Jazz piano music is the art of "improvisation". In fact, it is also the art of arranging music. It tends to focus on performers or performers and composers rather than composers. In today's practice, a complete jazz work is often the product of half creation and half improvisation: part of the content of the work is written in advance, and can be read and played; The other part needs the performer to improvise.

3   Structure and Function Analysis of Piano Playing Robot System

According to the functional requirements, the exhibit consists of a piano, a performing robot and a controller, as shown in Fig. 2.

The piano can be the commonly used standing or grand piano. The performance robot is designed in human form. The controller is hidden in the piano stool. The robot sits on the controller to simulate the human playing the piano. The head, arms and hands of the robot can move. The movement of the head can vividly show the intoxicated look of the robot when playing; When the fingers of the rotating arms can not touch the target keys during the performance, the robot arm can rotate at an appropriate angle to adjust the position; In addition, flexible fingers can also cover more piano keys.

Hands are the core of the piano playing robot. Each hand has five fingers. Each finger mimics human fingers and can play piano keys accurately. In order to ensure the flexibility and quick response of each finger, a micro cylinder is used as the actuating element to drive the fingers to press or lift. Each finger is connected with the miniature cylinder through a rotating shaft. When the cylinder is pushed out, the finger is pressed, and when the cylinder is retracted, the finger is picked up. The micro cylinder is controlled by a high-speed solenoid valve to ensure that the fingers can be pressed or lifted in a very short time [13]. Compared with the traditional linear electromagnet finger, this structure

Fig. 2. Schematic diagram of piano playing robot

is simple, reliable, easy to control, and has the advantages of fast action, low noise, long service life and maintenance-free.

The control system includes power supply control, servo motor control and pneumatic actuator control, and there are many kinds of sensors that feed back the status of the actuator and the system operation status to the system respectively for the software system to make decisions, such as Hall sensor for sensing the finger status, air pressure sensor for real-time monitoring of air pressure, when detecting abnormal operation, the system will shut down all functions and actuators to avoid potential safety hazards. The control system also provides external interfaces, including man-machine interface control buttons and operation status monitoring functions. The touch screen provides a window for audience interaction. You can directly click and select tracks or run the functions provided by the software.

The shoulder drive adopts Mitsubishi MR-J4-A series AC servo motor, and uses absolute value encoder mode. It does not need to reset the origin, but directly connects with the control system through RS422 communication mode to obtain absolute value position information in real time.

This paper designs a piano playing robot system, which consists of three parts: mechanical structure design, hardware design and software design. Among them, the mechanical structure design is mainly the actuator design of the mouth control module and the finger control module; The hardware and software parts are used to realize the control function, so that the main control module can send the corresponding code instructions according to the music information to control the action of the actuator, complete the effective control of each module, and achieve the piano autoplay effect [14].

The system structure of the piano playing robot system is shown in Fig. 3, which is mainly composed of five modules: the main control module, the breath control module, the finger control module, the sound acquisition module and the power module.

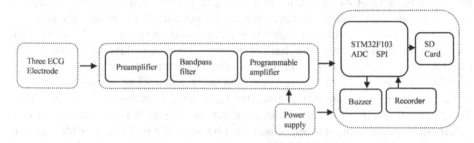

Fig. 3. System Structure Diagram of Playing Robot

In Fig. 3, the main control module is the control center of the entire performance robot system. It sends control commands according to the pre downloaded program, and controls the mouth module and finger module to execute corresponding actions to complete the performance. The sound acquisition module is mainly used to detect whether the piano works normally. The power module is responsible for supplying power to the whole system. The system is powered by batteries with a working voltage of about 24 V.

4   Comparison Between Classical Piano and Jazz Style Piano Played by Piano Robot

4.1   Analysis from the Perspective of Harmony

In the post classicism period of the 19th century, that is, the Vienna classical music period, with the arrival of the prosperous period of classical music, German and Austrian harmony began to form a system and scale, which is still used in the teaching of classical music. After entering the impressionist period in the 20th century, harmony began to become complicated. It is in this environment that the harmony theory of jazz has been developed. Based on the theory of overtone series, continue to list the three and seven chords vertically until the nine chords, eleven chords and thirteen chords. In this way, all seven notes in the major natural scale can be used as the intrachord. Selectivity becomes diversified all at once, and only appropriate omissions can be made when necessary [15]. Jazz is rooted in African Negro singing and development, and there is no strict theory to follow, so jazz harmony is not restricted by the traditional strict theory. After practice and experience, the theory is summarized. Therefore, its harmony has reached a high degree of complexity and liberalization. It not only inherited the progress of T-S-D-T in the traditional German Austrian harmony system, but also derived new theories such as downward five degree loop and replacement chord. The downward five degree cycle is the I-IV-VII-II-VI~II-V-I. In this way, every two adjacent chords have a common sound, not like the S-D in T-S-D-T, because there is no common sound, resulting in a sudden sense of hearing, and each sentence is not so short. In addition, alternative chords are an original theory in jazz harmony. Tritonic substitution is one of its representative theoretical models. "Tritonic" was called "Devil Interval" by early musicians because of its special interval structure. It lacks aesthetic sense in hearing and is extremely discordant. However, among the generic chords in the jazz field, the substitution of those chords belonging to the functional group has not been satisfied, and the substitution of three tones has become the mainstream. Take the C major as an example, the chords are G, B, D, F, B-F from three to seven notes, while the bII chords are bD, F, bA, bC, and F-B between three and seven notes. The three and seven notes of the two seven chords are just inverted, but the interval relationship is the same [16]. Therefore, bII chords can be used instead of generic chords. It is also called "tri tone substitution" because the interval relationship between the root tones of bII and V is tri tone. In practical application, II-V-I progression is a typical harmony short sentence connection in jazz. After understanding the principle of tri tone substitution, level V can be replaced by level bII, which becomes the connection of II-bIT-I. This very tendentious bass progression is the concrete embodiment of the tri tone substitution theory.

Jazz harmony is no more complicated than classical harmony. It comes down in one continuous line with the classical harmony system. Therefore, no matter what style of piano playing you learn, you must also learn the theory of harmony. Only after learning the theory can we understand the content and analyze it [17]. Only in this way can we further improvise and create music.

4.2 Analysis from the Perspective of Improvisation

The essence of improvisation is also the essence of music, that is, horizontal and vertical. The horizontal melody walks and the vertical harmony arranges. The development and progress of melody is not random. In fact, the performance of melodies like flowing clouds and flowing water is also restricted by strict and rigorous logic and theory. So, scale appears as another key point [18]. The scales of classical music are dominated by major and minor modes, harmony major and minor modes, melody major and minor modes, and pentatonic scales. On the basis of the major and minor modes, the jazz scale has developed the church mode scale, the whole tone scale, the minus chord scale, the Alt scale, the Blue scale, etc. The scale of jazz is as complex as the harmony of jazz, and it is ever-changing. It is closely related to the jazz chord [19]. What and what the chord correspond to are scales, and one chord can often correspond to several different scales. Therefore, in the process of the same harmony, everything played by each performer is different, which not only reflects the rich changes in the jazz scale, but also reflects the emotional changes in the performer's heart and the differences in auditory aesthetics. Jazz bands usually write the accompaniment texture, paragraph and harmony in advance when performing. During the performance, the players fill in the improvisation by using the counterpoint of scale and harmony within this "big framework". And then each time can play different content from the last time, making the music sound continuous and flexible, greatly expanding the thinking of the audience and musicians. This theory has also formed a unique "counterpoint" rule in jazz performance.

Chinese music is most influenced by jazz in the creation of urban pop songs. With the popularity of songs, the unique harmony and rhythm of jazz are deeply rooted in Chinese folk music, and jazz piano performance is closely combined with these popular songs and develops together.

Jazz piano performance is mostly based on popular songs at that time, and the melody is mostly a combination of five-tone mode of Chinese folk music and seven-tone mode of western music. The accompaniment part of the harmony is mostly in the form of seven and nine chords, and the rhythm is based on the characteristics of jazz music: either using regtime, or using blues, and the melody is also good at using syncopation to create changes and carry out variations. Its dynamic singing and dancing flavor brings full freshness to urban audiences who are accustomed to Chinese folk music and western classical music. Because most of these musicians are active in entertainment places as accompaniment, it is difficult to find their names now, but some records and films have recorded their classical performances of the year, and some music scores have also been saved [20]. To this day, the "Old Oak Skin Band" in the ballroom of the Shanghai Peace Hotel still retains the playing style of Shanghai-style jazz and plays the pop music of that period.

5 Conclusion

In recent years, with the continuous progress of computer technology and sensor technology, the research and application of robots continue to expand to the civilian market. Musical robots have gradually become a research hotspot in the field of robot research. Up to now, the research on music robot is mainly concentrated in foreign countries, while the research on music robot, especially the automatic playing robot, is relatively less in China. Classical piano performance and jazz piano performance are closely linked and complementary, which can directly reflect the history of music development. Players can choose according to different preferences.

References

1. Horton, J.: Beethoven's Error? the modulating ritornello and the type 5 sonata in the post-classical piano concerto. Music. Anal. **40**(3), 353–412 (2021)
2. Faggiano, A., Ricciardi, M., Pironti, C., et al.: investigation on the deterioration of lead artifacts a case study on piano keys and their degradation products (2022)
3. Sofronievski, B., Gerazov, B.: Scorpiano – a system for automatic music transcription for monophonic piano music (2021)
4. Wang, L., Yue, X., Peng, J.: Modeling and simulation of a tower-of-hanoi-playing robot station based on robotstudio (2022)
5. Zheng, Y., Leung, B.W.: Cultivating music students creativity in piano performance: a multiple-case study in China. Music. Educ. Res. **23**(5), 594–608 (2021)
6. Rustamova, P.: Classical traditions of the piano concerto by ruslan agababayev. Bull. Kyiv Natl. Univ. Culture Arts Ser. Music.Art **4**(1), 130–139 (2021)

7. Rheman, J., Fraune, M.R.: Not in my house!: children playing an online game with robots show low trust and closeness with ingroup robots. In: HRI 2021: ACM/IEEE International Conference on Human-Robot Interaction. ACM (2021)
8. Mishra, N., Tulsulkar, G., Li, H., et al.: Does elderly enjoy playing Bingo with a robot? A case study with the humanoid robot Nadine (2021)
9. Gupta, A., Bridges, N., Kamino, W.: Musically assistive robot for the elderly in isolation. In: HRI 2021: ACM/IEEE International Conference on Human-Robot Interaction. ACM (2021)
10. Dong, L., He, Z., Song, C., et al.: A review of mobile robot motion planning methods: from classical motion planning workflows to reinforcement learning-based architectures (2021)
11. Nyanney, S. Examining piano playing proficiency among selected music students in a ghanaian public university **2021**(17) (2021)
12. Shu, Y.: Influence of piano playing on logical thinking formation of future musicians (2021)
13. Liu, M., Huang, J.: Piano playing teaching system based on artificial intelligence - design and research. J. Intell. Fuzzy Syst. Appl. Eng. Technol. **2**, 40 (2021)
14. Gan, K.Y., Clement, J.B., Sundar, V., et al.: Understanding upper body playing-related musculoskeletal disorders among piano and non-piano players using a photogrammetry. Clin. Ter. **172**(2), 163–167 (2021)
15. Wilhelmi, T.: Hymns: Light Jazz Style-Piano [Paperback]
16. John, V.: Bebop Jazz Piano - Hal Leonard Keyboard Style Series
17. Stefanuk, M.V.: Jazz Album For Piano - 12 Solos in the Style of Jazz Greats
18. Hellmuth, M., Chen, B., Bariki, C., et al.: A Comparative Study on the Combustion Chemistry of Two Bio-hybrid Fuels: 1,3-Dioxane and 1,3-Dioxolane (2022)
19. Kim, K.: A Comparative study on the machine translation accuracy of loanword by language. In: Proceedings of the Korea Information Processing Society Conference. Korea Information Processing Society (2021)
20. Hashimoto, T., Imajo, Y., Funaba, M., et al.: Continuous scanning and inching in ultrasonographic localisation of ulnar neuropathy: a comparative study of sensitivity. J. Hand Surg. (Asian-Pacific Volume) (2022)

English Online Teaching Assistant System Based on Genetic Algorithms

Ling Jiang[(✉)] [iD] and Yuanze Wang [iD]

School of Foreign Languages, Fuyang Normal University, Fuyang 236037, Anhui, China
200407020@fynu.edu.cn

Abstract. Online English teaching can significantly increase the relevance of English instruction, the sharing of English teaching materials, and the quality of English instruction. As a result, this research proposes and investigates an online English teaching assistance system based on a genetic algorithm. First, the English online teaching assistant system's general structure is built, including modules such as network connection, data gathering, bus transfer, and application loading. Second, it creates the system hierarchy, implements the control and structural architecture of the English online teaching system terminal in the user UI interface, and adds different data tables to the system database. The English online teaching assistant system is then optimized using the genetic algorithm. To complete the research of the English online teaching assistant system based on genetic algorithm, chromosome coding and decoding, generation of the initial population, fitness function and genetic operation, and data fairness and genetic material selection are combined. According to experimental verification, the English online teaching assistant system created in this study has strong stability, good data transmission performance, and effectively enhances English teaching efficiency and teaching quality.

Keywords: Genetic algorithm · English online teaching · Teaching assistant system · Genetic manipulation

1 Introduction

Computer technology has been extensively employed in the area of education due to the fast growth of computer technology. Computer technology is solving an increasing number of instructional challenges. The optimization of teaching tactics is a critical link in the educational chain. A new research topic in computer technology applied to education is how to employ computer technology to maximize teaching tactics to overcome the subjectivity and arbitrariness of conventional teaching methods. Online learning has progressively replaced traditional methods of teaching English at major institutions and universities. With the growing number of online English teaching resources, it is critical to analyze and mine the data of English teaching resources effectively, as well as perform intelligent identification in the online teaching assistant system, to achieve the analysis of learners learning behaviour in conjunction with the learners' terminal needs. Provide learners with more relevant resource information based on their choices [1, 2].

Y. Zhang and N. Shah (Eds.): BigIoT-EDU 2023, LNICST 582, pp. 475–488, 2024.
https://doi.org/10.1007/978-3-031-63136-8_49

Currently, most English teaching strategy optimization is based on teachers' self-knowledge and policy promotion, which cannot fulfil the current demands of English teaching and cannot be altered objectively based on the real situation of English teaching. Some quantitative variables make it harder to optimize the English approach. Under these circumstances, a computer simulation-optimization approach to English teaching methodologies may overcome the abovementioned weaknesses. As a result, this research conducts an in-depth examination of the English online-aided teaching system using a genetic algorithm. An ideal answer is produced because genetic algorithms imitate the process of natural evolution [3].

The innovations of this paper are as follows: (1) Designing the overall framework of the English online teaching assistant system, which is composed of modules such as network communication, data collection, bus transmission and application loading. The hierarchy of the system is designed, the control and structure layout of the terminal of the English online teaching system are implemented in the user UI interface, and various data tables in the system database are introduced. Then the genetic algorithm is used to optimize the online English teaching assistant system. The genetic algorithm is optimized by chromosome coding and decoding, as well as the generation of initial population, fitness function and genetic operation. The fairness of the data is combined with the selection of genetic genes. (2) Compared with other online English teaching assistant systems, the online English teaching assistant system designed in this paper is stable as a whole and can effectively improve the sharing of English teaching resources, thus improving the effectiveness of English teaching.

2 Related Work

The use of computer technology in the online English teaching assistance system has become a hot issue among relevant researchers, with some study findings. Liu Dong et al. presented an internet-based online English teaching assistant system to address the issue that conventional online English teaching assistant system user data is disconnected when they join, resulting in unsatisfactory teaching outcomes. First, the particle swarm algorithm is used to optimize the process of data invocation in the database, to assure the ability of teaching resource data interchange, and to effectively optimize the query algorithm of teaching resources in the database. JSP technology is used to augment the functions of each subsystem in the Internet English online teaching assistance system, which increases subsystem performance, maintains the stability of the user's teaching resource data connection, and avoids resource data connection failure. The simulation results show that the designed online English teaching assistant system based on the Internet can ensure the good operation of the teaching resource data without interruption of the teaching resource connection when there are more users. Still, the improvement of the English teaching effect of this method is not obvious [4]. Xie R suggested developing a computer-aided teaching system for online English courses based on data mining to improve the system's flexibility of dynamic information and minimize system response. To begin, data mining technology is used to delve deeply into students' learning abilities, cluster their learning characteristics, and offer suitable English teaching materials to students to accomplish instruction based on their aptitude. This paper establishes the overall framework of the online assisted teaching system through many modules such as the teaching interface, teaching subsystem, and teaching resource pool, divides the role functions rationally according to the user's rights, designs the English teaching process of the assisted teaching system, and completes the design of the online assisted teaching system of English according to the database's construction process database. The experimental findings demonstrate that the developed online teaching assistant system's dynamic information acquisition and clustering effect are more accurate, and the total reaction time is quicker. However, the process is more complicated [5]. Zuo X W built an online English teaching system to increase the degree of teaching resource sharing and scheduling in the English teaching assistant system based on particle swarm optimization. This paper establishes a fusion model of English teaching resources, achieves adaptive scheduling of teaching resources in the English online-assisted teaching system using the fusion particle swarm optimization algorithm, extracts the autocorrelation features of English online-assisted teaching resources, optimizes the fusion of English online-assisted teaching resources using fuzzy-related feature matching and statistical methods, and conducts comprehensive analgesic testing. To accomplish instructional resource scheduling and data fusion, as well as to enhance the management capability of English online supported teaching.

The simulation results show that the designed English online-assisted instruction system has a higher degree of integration of teaching resources, a better ability to schedule resource information, and a significantly improved level of English-assisted instruction management. Still, it needs to improve the English teaching level [6]. Yang X S and co. Analytical Network Online Assistant Teaching System may compensate for the inadequacies of conventional English classroom instruction and is vital in education. Knowledge management theory may bring fresh insights and ideas for designing an online English teaching assistance system. A knowledge management-based online English teaching assistant system focuses on knowledge acquisition, sharing, and communication and the successful conversion of explicit and implicit information to accomplish knowledge innovation. This paper applies knowledge management theory and management methods to the design and development of the English online teaching assistant system, promotes the learner's transition from explicit to implicit knowledge, and presents the basic design principles of the Knowledge Management-based English online teaching assistant system, as well as the design process and system framework model. Applying the findings to the design of an online English teaching assistant system does not increase learners' learning efficiency [7].

3   English Online Teaching Assistant System

3.1   System Architecture Design

The English online teaching assistant system provides services through the Web, with the front end using the Bootstrp framework and the back end using the Springboot framework. The overall architecture of the English online teaching assistant system is illustrated in Fig. 1.

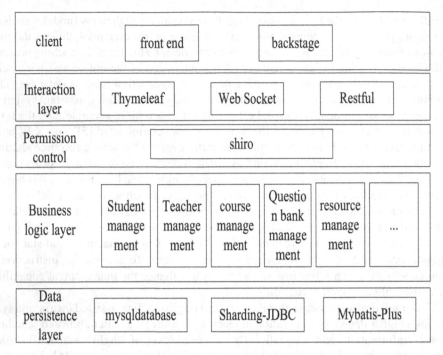

Fig. 1. Overall architecture of online English teaching assistance system

3.2 System Function Module Design

Many modules comprise the English online teaching assistance system, including network connectivity, data collecting, bus transfer, and application loading. Among them, the data gathering role is to build the information perception of the original applicable teaching resources and to upload the English online teaching resources utilizing mass data collection technology. The scope of instruction may be separated into various components. Nodes are classified as backbone nodes, interface nodes, or general nodes during the upload and download of English teaching materials based on the distribution of units as well as the relevance and location of nodes. Wireless radio frequency technology improves the real-time and resource sharing of English online instruction [8, 9].

The network communication function is to realize the transmission and online communication of English teaching resource information. Web technology is used to design the network of English online teaching assistant system, to store, data mining, teaching resource data service and teaching quality feedback of English online teaching resource data.

The English online teaching assistant system is composed of information collection unit, teaching resource data storage database and network application server unit. It uses hierarchical architecture and interface access control to realize the evaluation of data management and network transmission. The function modules of the English online teaching assistant system are shown in Fig. 2.

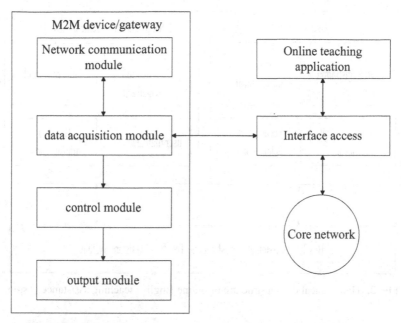

Fig. 2. Functional modules of online English teaching assistant system

3.3 Hierarchical Design of English Online Teaching Assistant System

The hierarchical design of the English online teaching assistant system is divided into user subsystem and background management subsystem. In the subsystem of users, teachers and students can register and login in the system with their own user rights, set user names and passwords in the user interface, students can retrieve and feedback the data of English teaching resources, teachers can upload English teaching resources and control the multimedia teaching system, teachers can use the teaching evaluation software to evaluate the quality of English teaching [10, 11]. The subsystem of background management can also be divided into modules such as classified management of teaching resources, network control, user management and bus data transmission. The user behavior of external data source services can be used to carry out the progress of English online teaching and the evaluation of teaching content and teaching objects. The background subsystem of the English online teaching assistant system and other smart terminal devices are connected to carry out resource data communication and communication according to the service requirements and functional framework proposed by users. The hierarchical design structure of the English online teaching assistant system is shown in Fig. 3.

The terminal control and structure layout of the English online teaching assistant system are carried out in the user interface, the information fusion of English teaching resources is carried out through the campus network and wireless communication technology in the network layer, and the embedded controller is designed to control the transmission of the English online teaching bus between parallel port, serial port and

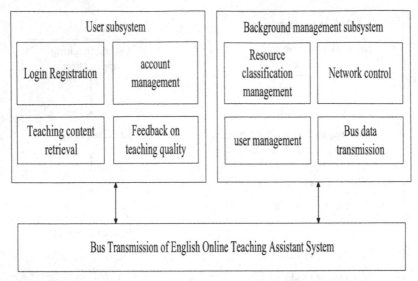

Fig. 3. Hierarchical design structure of online English teaching assistance system

USB port [12, 13]. The corresponding status of the control task identification of the English Online Teaching Assistant System is shown in Table 1.

Table 1. Corresponding Status of Task ID Controlled by English Online Teaching Assistant System

Task Flag	Command status
000	Command initialization
001	Write online teaching information resources
010	Install system applications
011	Send Readiness
100	Explorer Rediscovery
101	Write high-frequency control information
110	Access to network teaching resource database
111	Bus data output

In the management subsystem, under the mode of the Internet of Things, it implements the service of perceived information, the management of perceived information and the control of information service and control information management of English online assisted instruction, establishes the interactive organization of system users, realizes the evaluation and resource sharing of English online instruction information under the Internet and the Internet of Things, completes the hierarchical design of English online instruction assisted system, and the structure of the design is represented by Fig. 4.

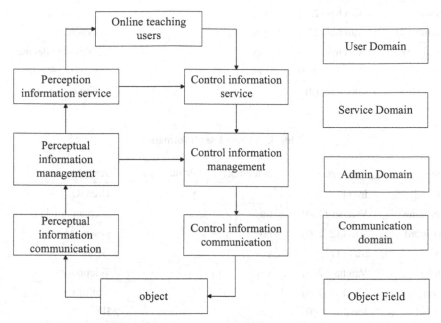

Fig. 4. Hierarchical design structure of online English teaching assistant system

3.4 Database Design

The data tables in the system database are introduced. Because there are many data tables, this paper only introduces the course table and user table.

(1) The course schedule contains information such as the name of the course and the teachers and videos taught, which is indicated in Table 2.

Table 2. System Course Information

title	data type	Is it empty	Primary key	describe
id	Int (10)	no	yes	Course id
name	Varchar (255)	yes		name
video	Varchar (255)	yes		video

(continued)

Table 2. (*continued*)

title	data type	Is it empty	Primary key	describe
kejian	Varchar (255)	yes		Courseware
teacher	Varchar (255)	yes		Teachers
popularity	Varchar (255)	yes		Welcome degree
image	Varchar (255)	yes		Course pictures
Create-time	Tatetime (0)	yes		Creation time

Table 3. System User Information

title	data type	Is it empty	Primary key	describe
User-id	Int (11)	no	yes	User ID
username	Varchar (100)	no		account number
password	Varchar (200)	no		password
sex	Int (11)	yes		Gender
phone	Varchar (200)	yes		Telephone
email	Varchar (200)	yes		mailbox
id-card	Varchar (200)	yes		ID
state	Int (1)	no		state
knowledge	Int (11)	yes		Scope of knowledge
degree	Int (11)	yes		Degree of Difficulty
target	Timestamp (0)	yes		Expected objectives
Create-time	Timestamp (0)	no		Registration time

(2) User table stores information about users in the system, including the names of users in the teaching system, the teaching objectives expected by users and the knowledge they have learned, etc. (Table 3)

4 Research on English Online Assistant Teaching Based on Genetic Algorithms

In conjunction with the above-mentioned English online teaching assistant system, a constraint mechanism that combines the environment of major gene selection in the genetic process with the principle of equal access to resources and the priority of local resources [14, 15].

(1) Chromosome Encoding and Decoding

This paper makes a detailed analysis of the specific features of direct and indirect chromosome coding of English teaching resources, combines them with the characteristics of the English online teaching assistant system, selects the indirect coding method using English teaching resource tasks, considers the number of subtasks of teaching resources as the length of chromosomes, and the number of genes in chromosomes is the number of resources assigned to subtasks. Assume that the number of jobs to be processed by the online English teaching assistant system is J, the number of points to be processed is N, and the English job assignment at t is $TaskNum(t)$. The total number of subtasks for a teaching resource is expressed as:

$$SumTaskNum = \sum_{t=1}^{J} TaskNum \tag{1}$$

It is easier to renumber the English teaching tasks and select the algorithm for the representation of formula (2) [16, 17].

$$m = \sum_{k=1}^{j} taskNum(k) + j \tag{2}$$

Using decoded data and ETC and DTC matrices, the time to complete each English job and the total time to complete all English jobs are calculated.

The time to complete each English job t is calculated as:

$$JobTime(t) = \max_{i=1}^{TaskNum(t)} \sum_{j=1}^{q} TaskTime(j, i) \tag{3}$$

Formula (3) q represents the location of the computing node where task i is assigned in English homework t. $TaskTime(j, i)$ is the time when task i completes the English teaching sub-task j on calculation node q.

The total task completion time for English teaching is calculated as:

$$TotleTime = \sum_{i=1}^{N} NodeTime(j, i) \tag{4}$$

In formula (4), $NodeTime(j, i)$ represents the time at which node j completes its English teaching task i, and p represents the number of tasks at node j.

(2) Initial population generation

Assuming the size of the English teaching resource population is S, with N processing points and J English jobs, there are M English teaching subtasks in total. Firstly, Max-Min algorithm is used to restrict the allocation of resources in the English online teaching assistant system and generate the desired chromosomes randomly. At this time, the number of chromosomes is S, the length is M, and the interval of gene values is limited to $[1, N]$.

(3) Functions of fitness

The genetic algorithm uses the fitness function calculation to carry out the next generation selection and evolution, and then searches for the optimal solution of the problem [18, 19].

The function of the learner's satisfaction with the completion time of all English tasks in Individual i is as follows:

$$f_i(i) = k(i)/J, 1 \leq i \leq S \tag{5}$$

The time fitness function of the total task completion in English teaching is expressed as:

$$f_2(i) = 1/CT(i), 1 \leq i \leq S \tag{6}$$

In formula (6), $CT(i)$ represents the time when individual i completes the overall task of English teaching.

Based on the correlation between formula (5) and formula (6), individuals with larger fitness values can be selected for the next generation.

(4) Genetic Operation

Genetic manipulation is divided into three main operations, selection and crossover, and mutation. It is an important way to select and produce the next generation of individuals [20].

Selection is the basic way to spread good genes in a population. The selection algorithm uses the roulette selection method and calculates the individual probability from formulas (7) and (8) through formulas (5) and (6):

$$P_1(i) = f_1(i)/\sum_{j=1}^{S} f_1(j) \tag{7}$$

$$P_2(i) = f_2(i)/\sum_{j=1}^{S} f_2(j) \tag{8}$$

Variations can create new search spaces. The functions of crossover probability and mutation probability are represented by formulas (9) and (10), respectively:

$$P_C = \begin{cases} k_1(f_{max} - f')/(f_{max} - f_{avg}), f' \geq f_{avg} \\ k_2, \qquad\qquad\qquad f \geq f_{avg} \end{cases} \tag{9}$$

$$P_m = \begin{cases} k_3(f_{max} - f)/(f_{max} - f_{avg}), f \geq f_{avg} \\ k_4, \qquad\qquad\qquad f \geq f_{avg} \end{cases} \tag{10}$$

In the above formulas, f_{max} represents the maximum fitness of the population, f_{avg} represents the average fitness of each generation, and f represents the individual with variation. This process completes the research of the online English teaching assistant system based on genetic algorithm.

5 Experimental Result

In order to verify the validity of the online English teaching assistant system based on genetic algorithm proposed in this paper, a simulation experiment is carried out under the Atlab environment, which is represented by Table 4.

Table 4. Experimental Environment Settings

parameter	data
operating system	64 bit windows10
processor	2.3 GHz, Intel Core i5
browser	IE8.0
Memory	16 RAM, 512G SSD memory
development language	Java

Figure 5 shows the interruption rate of system operation when the system designed in this paper is compared with that in literature [4] and literature [5] when it is used by more than one person.

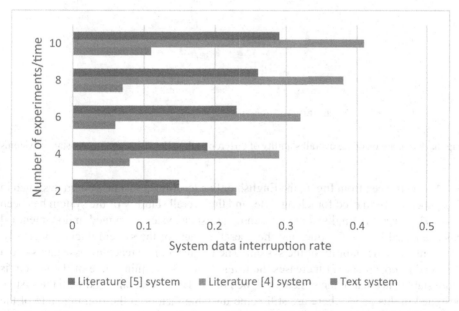

Fig. 5. Comparison of data interruption rate of English teaching resources in different systems

By analyzing Fig. 5, we can see that the interruption rate of the system designed by document [4] increases a lot when there are more users of the system, which indicates that the interruption rate of the system is higher. When there are more users of the English online teaching assistant system designed by document [5], the interruption rate of the system is also on the rise, but on the whole is lower than that of the system designed by document [4]. However, the interruption rate of the English online teaching assistant system designed in this paper fluctuates slightly when the number of users is large, but it shows a decreasing trend as a whole because the system designed in this paper is designed hierarchically to divide the system into user's subsystem and background management subsystem, which reduces the interruption rate of the system. This shows that the system designed in this paper has a lower interruption rate. Ensure the performance of system resource data transfer. Figure 6 shows the overall stability comparison of the design system in this paper with those in literature [6] and [7].

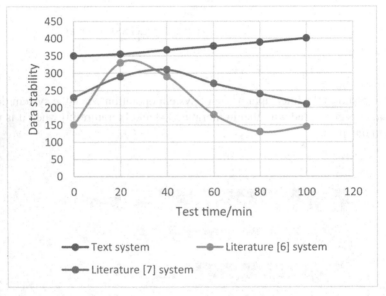

Fig. 6. Comparison of the overall stability of different online English teaching assistance systems

As can be seen from Fig. 6, the English online teaching assistant system designed in this paper has been used for a long time, and the overall stability of the system has been good. However, the English online teaching assistant system designed in document [6] has been used for a long time, and the operating state of the system fluctuates greatly, which reduces the stability of the system. The English online teaching assistant system designed in document [7] increases the usage time. The running state of the system is more stable than that of the system designed in [6]. However, compared with the system designed in this paper, there are still some unstable factors in the running state of the system. This shows that the English online teaching assistant system designed in this paper has strong stability and can effectively improve the learning effect of the learners. Figure 7 shows the teaching efficiency of the system designed in this paper compared with that in the literature [4] and [5].

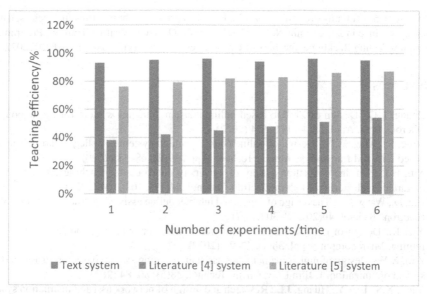

Fig. 7. Comparison of teaching efficiency of different online English teaching assistant systems

According to the analysis of Fig. 7, through six experiments, the teaching efficiency of the document [4] system has been relatively poor, reducing the effect of learners' learning. Although the teaching efficiency of the online teaching assistance system in document [5] has been improved in each experiment, it is not higher than the teaching efficiency of the system designed in this paper. However, the teaching efficiency of the online English teaching assistance system designed in this paper based on genetic algorithm has been relatively high, All of them are above 90%, because genetic algorithms simulate the process of natural evolution, synthesize data fairness and select genetic genes, so as to obtain the optimal solution, and improve the teaching efficiency and quality of English online teaching assistance system.

6 Conclusions

The fast growth of online education is mostly owing to advancements in network and information technologies. Both domestic and international universities have performed extensive studies on this subject to improve institutions' conventional teaching methods. As a result, this research investigates the evolutionary algorithm-based online English teaching aid system. This paper's system design contains network connectivity, data collecting, bus transfer, and application loading modules. Furthermore, experimental verification shows that the overall data transmission performance of the online English teaching assistant system created in this study is excellent, capable of meeting the tailored demands of learners, improving the efficiency of English teaching, and being very practicable.

Funding Statement. This paper is funded by 1. The Undergraduate Teaching Project of Fuyang Normal University (grant No. 2021JYXM0061);2022 Anhui University Student Innovation and

Entrepreneurship Training Program (grant No. 144); Key projects of humanities and social sciences in Anhui Province in 2022 (grant No. 2022AH051290); Overseas Visiting Training Program for Outstanding Young Backbone Teachers of Universities in Anhui (grant No. gxgwfx2022022).

References

1. Zhang, L.Q.: Design of ZigBee based online assistant teaching system for music courses. Microcomput. Appl. **38**(4), 171–174 (2022)
2. Ning, R., Xing, W.N.: Design of online course teaching system in colleges and universities based on VEM framework. Autom. Technol. Appl. **39**(2), 48–51 (2020)
3. Yin, H.L.: On line evaluation system of university micro course teaching effect based on hierarchical clustering. Modern Electron. Technol. **44**(12), 101–104 (2021)
4. Liu, D., Wang, J.S.: The design of web based internet online assisted instruction system. Mod. Electron. Technol. **40**(20), 28–30 (2017)
5. Xie, R.: Design of computer aided instruction system for oncology course based on data mining. Microcomput. Appl. **38**(4), 22–25 (2022)
6. Zuo, X.W.: Design of higher mathematics assistant teaching system based on fusion particle swarm optimization. J. Jilin Univ. Chem. Technol. **38**(5), 80–84 (2021)
7. Yang, X.S., Liu, Y., Huang, J.L.: Research and design of network assisted instruction system based on knowledge management theory. Gansu Sci. Technol. **33**(13), 13–16 (2017)
8. Li, J., Liu, M.C.: Design and implementation of online teaching system based on INM. Comput. Appl. Softw. **34**(4), 23–27 (2017)
9. Guan, H.M.: Design of english writing assistant teaching system based on intelligent cloud service platform. J. Yunnan Univ. Natonal. (Natl. Sci. Edn.) **31**(3), 355–359 (2022)
10. Jin, Y.: Design of japanese CAI system based on natural language processing. Autom. Technol. Appl. **40**(10), 52–55 (2021)
11. Rahman, M.M., Pandian, A.: A critical investigation of English language teaching in Bangladesh unfulfilled expectations after two decades of communicative language teaching. English Today **34**(3), 43–49 (2018)
12. Amin, M.: English language teaching methods and reforms in English curriculum in Iraq; an overview. J. Univ. Hum. Develop. **3**(3), 578–583 (2017)
13. Islam, A.: Deconstruction of method-postmethod dialectics in English language teaching. J. Lang. Teach. Res. **8**(3), 539–547 (2017)
14. Phuong, V.Q.: Rethinking intercultural communication competence in English language teaching: a gap between lecturers' perspectives and practices in a southeast Asian tertiary context. i-manager's J. English Lang. Teach. **7**(1), 20 (2017)
15. Tavoosy, Y.: Evaluation of the intensive English language teaching programme for the fifth grade according to teachers' views. Int. J. Learn. Teach. **13**(3), 106–124 (2021)
16. Hyder, H.: The pedagogy of English language teaching using CBSE methodologies for schools. Adv. Soc. Sci. Res. J. **8**(3), 188–193 (2021)
17. Ramadhana, M.A., Allo, D.K.: Experimental research in English language teaching: a peek from undergraduate students' theses. Jurnal Studi Guru dan Pembelajaran **4**(1), 32–38 (2021)
18. Hashemi, A., Si, N.K.: The barriers to the Use of ICT in English language teaching: a systematic literature review. Int. J. Inform. Commun. Technol. Educ. **3**(1), 77–88 (2021)
19. Hazaea, A.N., Bin-Hady, W.R., Toujani, M.M.: Emergency remote english language teaching in the Arab league countries: challenges and remedies. CALL-EJ **22**(1), 201–222 (2021)
20. Dalilan, E.S., Lestari, D.I.: The practices and obstacles of English language teaching in intellectual disability classroom: a case study at special School (SLB) in Palembang. PANYONARA: J. English Educ. **3**(1), 1–18 (2021). https://doi.org/10.19105/panyonara.v3i1.4319

Algorithm Design of Examination Scheduling in the Teaching of Clinical Medicine in Deep Learning

Changyan Liu[✉]

Sichuan University of Arts and Science, Dazhou 635000, Sichuan, China
603499931@qq.com

Abstract. However, due to the current Chinese medical education, there are some problems in the theoretical teaching and practical teaching. Therefore, the teaching management system of medical specialty in colleges and universities urgently needs a more sound system to improve. Strengthen the echelon construction of clinical medical talents in our hospital, and cultivate qualified professionals in Lin-Song disciplines. With the development of science and the continuous improvement of medical technology, information processing has become an indispensable part of modern medicine. Whether it is clinical diagnosis or teaching and scientific research, clinical medicine has extremely precious value. The credit system first originated in the United States. The credit system in China is gradually popularized and implemented in colleges and universities across the country. The credit system is also known as the "course elective system" in China. Image understanding is mainly to calculate the data abstracted from image analysis, and the result is generally to get more organized and useful information. Therefore, strengthening people's concept of preventing failure to detect the disease in time, increasing clinical medical testing equipment and improving testing efficiency have become the problems to be solved at present. Diversity of course content. In addition to the basic compulsory courses, a large number of elective courses should be set up. While ensuring the backbone of basic theory, some branches and leaves should extend to the forefront of science and technology, and there should be a large number of dense branches and leaves in line with the market. A network model of multi-scale and multi-level input is proposed for nucleocytoplasmic segmentation in clinical medicine. The full convolution network of convolution and deconvolution is used to extract features and complete semantic segmentation. This paper mainly aims at the improvement measures of convolutional neural network in the application of credit system management in clinical medicine in the future, in order to improve the training quality of medical students.

Keywords: Convolutional neural network · Clinical medicine · Credit system · Teaching test arrangement

Y. Zhang and N. Shah (Eds.): BigIoT-EDU 2023, LNICST 582, pp. 489–497, 2024.
https://doi.org/10.1007/978-3-031-63136-8_50

1   Introduction

With the rapid development of China's higher medical education and the gradual deepening of the reform of health undertakings, how to cultivate high-quality medical talents in line with the development of the times is a common concern of medical colleges and universities. However, at present, there are some problems in the theoretical and practical teaching of medical education in China [1]. Therefore, the teaching management system of medical majors in colleges and universities urgently needs a more sound system to improve. Strengthen the echelon construction of clinical medical talents in our hospital, and cultivate qualified professionals in the discipline of Lin Song [2]. Openness of teaching organization. Break the traditional teaching organization of organized classes, organize teaching with curriculum as the center, and allow students to attend classes freely across majors, grades and departments. Therefore, better results will be obtained by analyzing clinical medicine with the related technologies in the field of computer vision, and then by the judgment and analysis of pathologists [3]. With the development of science, medical technology is constantly improving, and information processing has become an indispensable part of modern medicine. Whether it is clinical diagnosis or teaching and scientific research, clinical medicine has extremely precious value. High pressure and fast pace are the challenges that must be faced in the current work. On the one hand, the accumulated high pressure and long working hours make people neglect their physical concerns because of their busy work. The credit system first originated in the United States. The credit system in China is gradually popularized and implemented in colleges and universities across the country. The credit system is also known as the "course elective system" in China [4]. The credit system is a flexible teaching management model based on the elective system, which is a flexible teaching management model based on the elective system, which is a flexible teaching management model based on the unit of credits to measure the learning volume of the course, the minimum necessary credits as the graduation standard, and the management by objectives as the main feature. We try to explore the application of the credit system in clinical medicine to strengthen the teaching management of students, improve this new management method, and cultivate students with more comprehensive knowledge.

In today's society, the detection of most diseases depends on the analysis of medical images. However, the final diagnosis of diseases still depends on the subjective experience of pathologists, which is easy to be misdiagnosed and time-consuming. Image understanding is mainly to operate the data abstracted by image analysis, and the result is generally to get more organized and useful information [5]. For example, similarity detection and matching are performed on the known classified images in clinical medicine and image database to be detected, and the nature and classification of the images to be detected are determined according to the similarity. The large population, insufficient medical equipment and people's weak concept of regular physical examination lead to the inability to find out the illness in time and as soon as possible [6]. Therefore, strengthening people's awareness of preventing diseases from being discovered in time, increasing clinical medical testing equipment and improving testing efficiency have become the problems to be solved at present. Clinical education should constantly adapt to the actual needs of current medical and health undertakings and the development of medical and health talents, in order to comprehensively improve students' comprehensive quality and cultivate their innovative spirit and practical working ability [7]. The credit system is a comprehensive teaching management system that completes the learning tasks of the major through students' self-selected courses to achieve a certain credit score required by the school. Diversity of course content. In addition to the basic compulsory courses, a large number of elective courses are offered. While ensuring the backbone of the basic theory, some branches and leaves should extend to the frontier of science and technology, and there are also a large number of lush branches and leaves that are in line with the market. Clinical medicine can detect these irrelevant information, simplify the data, and enhance the detectability of relevant information [8]. Thereby, the accuracy of operations such as feature extraction is improved, and the accuracy of segmentation and recognition is improved. Kernel-plasma segmentation in clinical medicine proposes a multi-scale and multi-level input network model for feature extraction and semantic segmentation through a fully convolutional and deconvolutional network.

2 The Importance of Implementing Credit System Management

2.1 The Management of Credit System is the Inevitable Trend of the Development of Higher Education in China

The credit system refers to a flexible teaching management system that measures students' academic completion with credits as the measurement unit, that is, the teaching management system that takes students' minimum necessary credits as graduation standard and degree qualification. The remarkable advantage of the credit system is that it can enable students to make their own course study arrangements in the limited study time [9]. The development of higher education is synchronized with the development of human society, and the advanced nature of the credit system is mainly manifested in fully satisfying the concept of "people-oriented" in the development of human society. However, this small number of people will play a key role in the future development of medicine in our hospital's talent team [10]. Therefore, it is of strategic significance to carry out post-graduation education for residents and carry out planned and purposeful training. Due to their different working environments and social experiences, the existing knowledge is quite different; some are the backbone of the grass-roots medical and health units, busy with work, and the contradiction between engineering and learning is prominent. Equivalent to using approximately twice the number of pooling layers, each pooling layer can obtain images of different scales [11]. The information of the image can be better preserved, making the prediction for each pixel more accurate. A convolutional network basically consists of an input layer, a convolutional layer, a pooling layer, a fully connected layer and an output layer, where the convolutional layer, the pooling layer and the fully connected layer can contain multiple [12]. The histogram method first converts the grayscale image into a histogram, and then obtains the threshold by finding the minimum value of the curve. The fixed threshold method is to manually select a fixed threshold as the segmentation limit. The algorithm of a specific theory can calculate a large amount of data, but has a certain dependence on the original image. As shown in Fig. 1.

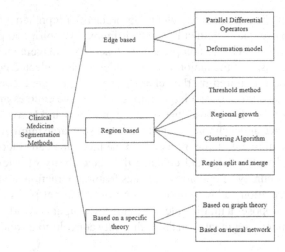

Fig. 1. Classical clinical medicine segmentation method

Credit system is an advanced system, which meets the requirements of talent training, education quality concept and quality education. Implement the people-oriented education management concept and carry out personalized education for students. Therefore, it is the inevitable trend of the reform of teaching management mode in Colleges and universities. The distance is used to calculate the distance between the real boundary value and the boundary of the predicted area. The evaluation formula is as follows:

$$Dice = \frac{2TP}{FP + 2TP + FN} \tag{1}$$

$$PPV = \frac{TP}{FP + TP} \tag{2}$$

$$Sentivity = \frac{TP}{TP + FN} \tag{3}$$

2.2 Credit System Management Meets the Requirements of Personalized Talent Training

Under the condition of market economy, the demand for talents is regulated by the market, especially the "two-way choice" system for college students' employment. Therefore, in order to adapt to the demand of modern society for talents, medical education must meet the market demand and improve its coping ability. It can cultivate students' interest and ability in autonomous learning, and enable students to complete university courses as personal academic tasks, instead of traditional passive learning. Its fundamental task is to cultivate clinical science professionals with both ability and political integrity, and to lay a solid foundation for the overall development and improvement of clinical medical science in the future. With the development of molecular biology technology and the revelation of the mystery of human genome, the medical education curriculum covers a wider range of contents, including not only the multidisciplinary contents of natural disciplines, but also the theories and methods of humanities and social sciences. Through the multi-scale input of the original image, more information of the original image can be preserved, making the segmentation effect better. The features of the image can be better extracted, the amount of computation is reduced, and the training speed of the network model is improved. We can interpret this as we filter small parts of the image through a convolution kernel to get the eigenvalues of these small areas, thus maintaining the relationship between pixels. The purpose of performing convolution is to extract useful features from the input. Such methods rely on edge detection algorithms, and commonly used algorithms include surface fitting, differential operators, etc. The surface fitting method uses the surface obtained by fitting the gray value of the image pixel to find the edge of the image. The credit system is a flexible and flexible study system. Regardless of the length of study, as long as you earn the credits specified in the major, you can graduate normally. Students can choose their majors and years of study independently according to the needs of the market, combined with their own conditions and their own hobbies, so as to achieve personalized training.

3 Deficiencies in Implementing Credit System Management

3.1 The Characteristics of Medical Courses Determine the Limitations of Course Selection

The credit system is implemented in medical colleges. Due to the large number of clinical medicine courses, many compulsory courses and large class hours in medical colleges, it is impossible to compress too many compulsory courses in medical colleges. Due to the large number of courses and large class hours of professional courses set up by medical specialty, students have less scope to choose courses and less time for students to study independently in the credit system. According to the resident's seniority, Isotope Department does in-depth and meticulous work in writing, dealing with difficult problems and imparting experience. The manuscripts prepared by young doctors are carefully and patiently revised so as not to delay the publication time. Conform to the concept of the current transformation of medical education mode, adapt to the situation of rapid development of medical science, the development of health undertakings and the need of medical and health system reform. Give full play to students' enthusiasm and subjective initiative according to the characteristics of adult education objects. The loss of validation set decreases with the loss of training set, and the accuracy of validation set increases steadily in the learning process, which shows that the network is fully trained and the segmentation accuracy is constantly improved. As shown in Figs. 2, 3 and 4.

The original image and label image are operated simultaneously by randomly rotating the image at a certain angle, translating left and right, translating up and down and randomly enlarging or reducing. In order to keep the output the same size as the original input, the network needs to add an upper sampling layer through interpolation or deconvolution. Taking the back propagation process of the original convolution layer as the forward propagation of the deconvolution layer, the convolution network becomes a full convolution network. The appearance of the convolution well solves this problem. The

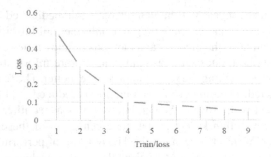

Fig. 2. Training set loss

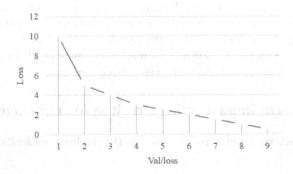

Fig. 3. Validation set loss

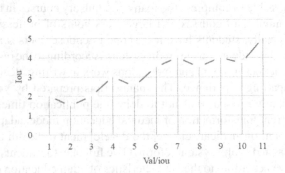

Fig. 4. Validation set accuracy

ordinary convolution kernel uses the cavity, and the convolution kernel is only partially involved in the operation like a sieve. In this way, the coverage of convolution kernel is increased, so that the receptive field is enlarged instead of increasing the amount of computation in each convolution. Therefore, the setting up of elective courses has been greatly restricted, and it is still difficult to set up elective courses with a certain quantity and quality, so the range of students' choices is relatively limited.

3.2 The Basic Teaching Facilities are not Perfect

Under the medical credit system, higher requirements are put forward for the school's teaching facilities. However, the concept of the academic year system is deeply rooted, which makes teaching administrators have a certain influence in adapting to the new credit system. The credit system requires a large number of courses and a sufficient number of teachers. At present, most of the teachers in night colleges in ordinary colleges and universities are part-time teachers. Under the circumstance of full-time full-time or even overloaded work, the establishment of elective courses is bound to be difficult. Under the guidance of senior pathologists, the image is labeled with labeling software. The labeled image includes the original image and label image. The image semantics are divided into three categories: cytoplasm, nucleus and background. The significance of loss function in neural network is the gap between prediction and target value. The smaller the loss function is, the closer the predicted value is to the target value, and the more convergent the neural network is. In order to reflect the advantages of this method, the experiment is compared with UNET network model, and the results are obtained after 50 iterations. As shown in Fig. 5.

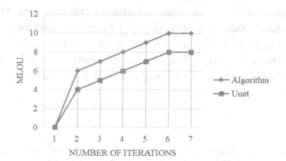

Fig. 5. Comparison of experimental results

The loss is calculated in the forward propagation, and it is also the starting point of the backward propagation. Generally, when processing images, it is desirable to gradually reduce the spatial resolution of features to extract more abstract and advanced feature information. In this way, in a multilayer convolutional neural network. With the pooling operation of each layer, each layer can extract features of different semantic levels and improve them step by step, which plays a very important role in both classification model and segmentation model. The grade point score can reflect the level of students' learning in a learning stage, which not only provides an important reference for students' evaluation and other work. Students choose courses independently, choose teaching process independently, and arrange teaching time by themselves, which effectively alleviates the contradiction between engineering and learning. However, Chinese colleges and universities generally have problems such as shortage of funds and insufficient investment in education funds. The shortage of teaching hardware facilities resources brings difficulties to the school's teaching investment.

4 Conclusions

The credit system fully embodies the new concepts of "people-oriented" and "serving students", solves the contradictions in the teaching management of clinical specialty to a certain extent, and meets the requirements of modern medical education. The particularity of medical specialty makes medical education the top priority of higher education, and medical specialty is the dominant discipline of our university. The implementation of credit system can enhance the talent training ability and discipline construction ability of medical specialty. By using the original multi-scale fusion and multi-scale fusion methods, and using the full convolution neural network of pooling operation, the accurate segmentation of clinical medicine is realized. Convolutional neural network is a kind of artificial neural network. Its weight sharing network structure significantly reduces the complexity of the model and the number of weights. Especially at present, people are reluctant to spend a lot of money on the regular diagnosis of expert doctors, and ordinary physical examination can't effectively diagnose the condition that can't be found in time in the early stage. These factors lead to the late discovery stage of the disease in China, which is also one of the reasons why China can't find the disease in time and the mortality rate is high. The core of these problems lies in the imperfection of the teaching management system matched with the credit system. Therefore, in order to carry out the credit system education in an all-round way and improve the quality of medical personnel training in this school, we should strengthen the research on credit system management in the future, fully mobilize various favorable factors, constantly improve the system and improve the quality of medical personnel training.

References

1. Ma, Q., Xie, L., Li, P.: Application of improved convolutional neural networks in medical image segmentation. Adv. Lasers Optoelectron. **57**(14), 7 (2020)
2. Yang, J., Wang, H.: An efficient fully convolutional neural network for biomedical image segmentation. Small Microcomput. Syst. **42**(6), 7 (2021)
3. Mu, G., Yang, Y., Gao, Y., et al.: Segmentation of head and neck organs at risk based on multi-scale 3D convolutional neural network. J. Southern Med. Univ. **40**(4), 8 (2020)
4. Yuan, Y., Jia, K., Liu, P.: Multi-level context autoencoder for multivariate medical signals based on deep convolutional neural network. J. Electron. Inform. **42**(2), 2020
5. Huang, J., Gao, W., Su, J., et al.: Research on medical imaging data management method based on convolutional neural network and long short-term memory network. Med. Soc. **33**(6), 7 (2020)
6. Li, X., Jia, W., Wu, J.: Deep learning: a new assistant for biomedical research and clinical diagnosis. Int. J. Biomed. Eng. **44**(02), 144–150 (2021)
7. Cao, Y., He, J., Zhu, W., Fu, Y., Fang, M.: Teaching reform of "neurobiology" course under the full credit system. Educ. Teach. Forum **49**, 2 (2020)
8. Wang, M., Duan, X., Han, X., et al.: A preliminary study on the teaching of interventional medicine as a compulsory course for clinical medicine undergraduates. J. Intervent. Radiol. **30**(2), 5 (2021)
9. Guo, Z.: Evaluation of the application effect of the flipped classroom teaching mode in the physiology experimental teaching of clinical medical students. Friends Health **000**(006), 134–135 (2020)

10. Zhou, G., Zhang, Q., Zhang, T.: Teaching methods to improve skills training of clinical medical students. Enlight. Wisdom Educ. **000**(002), 80–81 (2020)
11. Wu, S., Lei, J., Zhang, X.: Reform and effect evaluation of experimental teaching method of "Medical Statistics" for undergraduates in clinical medicine. Chin. J. Med. Educ. Explor. **21**(02), 151–156 (2022)
12. Cao, X., Chen, Y.: A preliminary study on classroom evaluation system under the blended teaching mode of clinical medicine. Mod. Med. Health **36**(9), 3 (2020)

Intelligent Integration of Online Education Resources for Deep Learning

Xiaolan Wei[✉]

Nanchang Institute of Science and Technology, Nanchang 330108, Jiangxi, China
565607996@qq.com

Abstract. The educational informatization of Chinese literature major is an important part of modern educational informatization, and our country It can realize the comprehensive audit of network teaching resources for language and literature majors educational informatization. The construction of educational resources is the core of educational informatization. Using advanced computer technology, communication technology and network technology, we will try our best to build an efficient resource acquisition and learning platform for learners. In recent years, the state has This information resource., and when it comes to Chinese language and literature, it has made many achievements in the In the construction of resources. However, we are soberly aware that the complexity and disorder of information-based educational resources is a difficult problem when we are looking for resources. It has become a bottleneck restricting the development and construction. With the increasing popularity of online education, more and more attention is paid to the integration and utilization of educational resources. Based on this background, the intelligent integration of educational resources of Chinese language and culture majors using cluster analysis algorithm is efficient and easy to use the integration concept and research of cluster analysis algorithm are launched.

Keywords: Clustering analysis algorithm · My whole literature. Network education resources · Intelligent integration

1 Introduction

Professional knowledge is the major specialty of university teaching content, and it can be the focus of research by domestic scholars and relevant personnel, which is General discipline can be a comprehensive judgment of Chinese language, Chinese literature and Chinese literature, so Chinese language and literature can provide support for the in-depth development of Chinese cultural environment and Chinese cultural content [1]. Language major mainly studies language courses and language collation, which has a strong promotion for language mining and realization effect. Moreover, carbon originality also has its own advantages in the process of analysis and mining. Therefore, in the process of regular in-depth mining and analysis, it is necessary to show stronger literariness, and there is another in-depth analysis combined with China's actual situation and

Y. Zhang and N. Shah (Eds.): BigIoT-EDU 2023, LNICST 582, pp. 498–505, 2024.
https://doi.org/10.1007/978-3-031-63136-8_51

natural development, and through temporary inheritance of previous satellite knowledge to better use and realize [3]. The whole study is characterized by diversity and complexity, mainly to promote the actual content of their language and Chinese traditional culture, the status of Chinese language in international exchanges has become more and more prominent. In today's Internet era, the use of network language and network popularity is becoming more and more serious. Under the impact of new media environment, how to optimize the teaching environment, use efficient algorithm tools to intelligently integrate the educational resources of Chinese language and literature specialty, and improve the overall level of Chinese language and Literature Specialty teaching is a problem that Chinese language and literature specialty teachers must seriously think about.

Training methods are mainly based on various system contents and constraints and internal inspection for overall constraints, analysis of relative data and the key points and integrity of the judgment, while requiring the Commission for Discipline Inspection to judge the stage of criminal investigation and discipline direction, so distance equation has strong distance, and can classify distance data, quality relationship and distance attribute, according to the overall process of simplifying data, and solving the relationship between data. The whole is Chinese language teaching, Chinese language professional concentration, and Chinese language learning concept produces research ideas [5]. As one of the important social education that enables the continuation and development of human society, the professional education of Chinese language and literature is also undergoing drastic changes under the promotion of modern information technology. Chinese language and literature plays an important role in the development of Chinese and cultural technology, and can play some of its roles, better analysis of data, and find the relationship between cultural indicators and literary content.. The huge information package capacity of the network provides learning resources for each course, which is far greater than the amount of information that any teacher, any textbook and even any library can provide. As more and more resources are needed, it is easy for users to get lost in the number of resources they need. Because of the complex nature of its information, if it is not clustered and integrated, it is difficult to be effectively used. Looking for information is like looking for a needle in a haystack. In this context, the research on the integration of educational resources of Chinese language and Literature Specialty Based on cluster analysis algorithm is particularly important. Figure 1 shows the cluster analysis process [6].

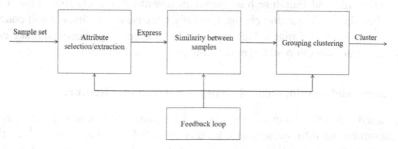

Fig. 1. Cluster analysis process

2   Chinese Language and Literature Major and Network Education Resources

2.1   Concept and Development of Chinese Language and Literature Specialty

Some women have extensive and profound characteristics, which can integrate various languages, including local languages, traditional languages, ancient poetry and other Chinese language and literature. They have a higher level in content and level, and can play a guiding role in other Chinese and Chinese majors. Therefore, Chinese language and literature are in an important position in research and have a guiding and guiding role in other related disciplines. Chinese language and literature have strong advantages in language structure, language structure and language comprehensiveness, so Chinese language and literature have an important educational relationship in the whole society and development, so you can have other majors and cultural courses. work in culture and publicity in news, literature and art publishing departments, universities, scientific research institutions, institutions, enterprises and institutions. Since 1903, eight subjects including literature, law, economics, agriculture, engineering, business, medicine and gezhi have been set up in the capital university hall, and the "literature" subject contains Chinese language and literature. On March 31, 1910, the Capital University Hall established the "Chinese Literature Gate". In 1912, the capital university hall was renamed Peking University [7]. In 1917, after Cai Yuanpei became the president of Peking University, he set up three subjects and fourteen departments of literature, science and law. Fable is a key point in literature, which mainly involves the relevant information in literature, and makes better language judgment and language analysis. It has obvious main characteristics for the head of Chinese language education. Chinese language and literature majors in universities flourished. During the "Cultural Revolution", the development of Chinese language and literature specialty also stopped. In 1977, the college entrance examination system was restored, and the major of Chinese language and literature entered the golden age of development. In 1986, the major of Chinese language and literature was established, which belongs to the major of literature and history. In 1989, Chinese language and literature major was a major in Chinese language and literature, and its professional code was Social Science 0101, which was an undergraduate major in social science. In 1993,Pneumonia has a turning point in its development, and the number of studies has declined. However, after 1998, the overall development of Chinese language and literature has shown an upward trend. On the whole, Chinese language has shown fluctuating changes, mainly because of the diverse and conceptual needs of the market for Chinese language, so Chinese language needs to make clear its own development direction and conduct in-depth research better [8].

2.2   Concept and Development of Network Educational Resources

The so-called network education of Chinese, Literature and Culture specialty refers to These literatures need to master more literary knowledge and data, as well as the key points in literature to enrich their own content. In particular, students of Chinese language and literature should constantly analyze the data, combine the content and data in Chinese language, understand their own Chinese language, and judge the knowledge vocabulary and analysis characteristics in Chinese language. The main technical characteristics of network education are the characteristics of non real-time and Internet-based decentralized teaching. Network education resources are interactive teaching realized through the synchronous transmission of image, text and sound by using advanced video technology and digital audio. The object of online education is for on-the-job personnel (part-time students) and full-time students in the school. Its goal is to realize the opening, sharing and continuing education of teaching resources [9]. With the continuous advancement of the new round of basic education curriculum reform in China, the development and utilization of network education resources, as an important part of teacher education information construction, has become an important breakthrough to improve the level of education modernization at this stage. In recent years, the relevant policy documents issued by governments at all levels have given full attention to the informatization construction, including online education resources. Domestic online education resources have a series of characteristics, such as large demand, wide sources, large quantity and many kinds. On the one hand, online education resources have wide sources and great demand. On the other hand, there are many kinds and forms of online education resources. From the carrier form of network education resources, there are text, image, animation, audio, video, etc.; From the operation platform of network education resources, there are cross platform and special platform resources; From the perspective of the types of online education resources, there are materials, test questions, courses, information, lesson plans, index directories, etc.; From the perspective of the structure of online education resources, there are unstructured original resources, semi-structured resources and structured resources. At present, a large number of online education resources mostly stay in the low-level autonomous sharing. Many online education resources have become discrete and isolated "information islands", which can not be exchanged and shared in a wide range and with high efficiency. This is a The overall waste of resources every year, so we should optimize the overall structure of Chinese language and find the overall changes and trends of Chinese language (Fig. 2).

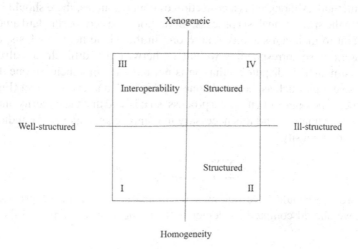

Fig. 2. Classification of the structure and form of online teaching resources

3   Concept of Cluster Analysis Algorithm and Application of Resource Integration

3.1 Overview of Cluster Analysis Algorithm

This analysis process is firstly to collect data, then all the data are standardized to form the initial original data, and then all kinds of data are processed to finally form a buzz head and planning data, and the data of the other party's amount is relatively similar in correlation, the smaller the degree, the better the opportunity, and then the data amount is sorted according to the similarity to form different data nodes, and then the relationship between the data nodes, the prominence of the data and the iteration of the data as a whole are analyzed to find out the final decision. Every accumulation will produce a sentence per bit, so it is necessary to build a unique memory set and compare the optimal solution to judge whether it is the final result of the overall layoutLook at the results If there is no final result, then output the speed results, otherwise, do the calculation results and conduct in-depth and simple analysis (Fig. 3).

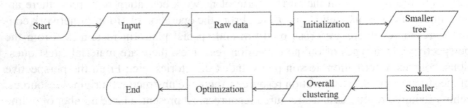

Fig. 3. Flow chart of BIRCH clustering algorithm

In the whole plan, you can classify it fiercely, and then you compare it with the key points in the play in March. Then, the correlation between the negative relationship and coupling analysis established between each node should be analyzed and clustered by clustering method. Although it is a collection of data resources, there should be inseparable data. In the specific analysis process, there should be certain standard analysis, and it is important to maintain stability. Therefore, in the whole fierce analysis, economic analysis should have corresponding weights, otherwise it is difficult to realize its own overall adjustment.This dispute mediation is not only a comprehensive one, but also a comprehensive logic such as the whole one, so this is also a reverse effect (Fig. 4).

This process belongs to an iterative process, so it is said that the integrity and analysis have strong coordination, and it is necessary to compare and analyze the indicators and functions in the intensity.

$$E = \sum_{i=1}^{k} \sum_{p \in G_i} |p - m_i|^2 \tag{1}$$

Therefore, we should have our own focus and center, so in the process of self-discipline, we should compare its center with the field of teaching and the scope of community.

$$M_i = \frac{1}{m} \sum_{j=1}^{m} t_{ij} \tag{2}$$

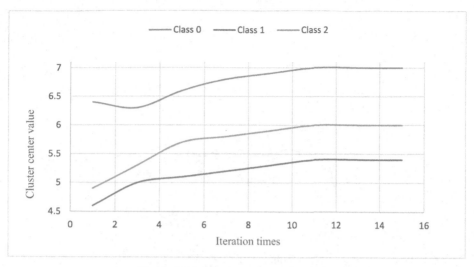

Fig. 4. Initial cluster centers of K-means

the iterative process, so you should form an index in the process of accumulation, decide something, and realize drastic comprehensive judgment and index verification analysis.

$$K_i = (t_{i1}, t_{i2}, ..., t_{in}) \tag{3}$$

Then its mean value, i.e. clustering center of gravity, is defined as:

$$Z_i = \left(\frac{1}{n}\right) \sum_{x,y \in K_i} (x, y)^2 \tag{4}$$

Therefore, we should take the initial point as the center, then expand in a wide range, continuously realize data optimization, and finally form a feasible concrete scheme.

The training analysis method will compare different classes, and then distinguish them to realize the correlation between them. Moreover, in the distance analysis, the correlation should be compared based on the degree of availability, emphasis and regional center, so today's final results are as follows, as shown in the figure (Fig. 5).

3.2 Intelligent Integration of Resources Based on Cluster Analysis Algorithm

The online education resources of Chinese, Literature and Culture specialty have increased rapidly since the beginning of the century. It is estimated that its total amount has exceeded the sum of previous history and has become an important resource in education. Put us in the ocean of information at once, we no longer worry about the "lack" of educational resources for the major of Chinese, Literature and Culture, but we have no choice because of "more". People in the information age are like small boats on the vast sea, like asteroids in space. They have no direction and are full of confusion. As a branch of statistics, clustering is often called cluster analysis and integration, which

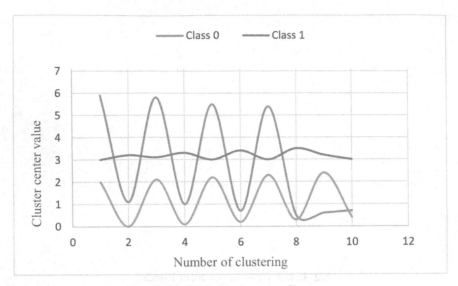

Fig. 5. The final cluster center of k-means

belongs to the process of exploratory network education resource analysis and integration. Cluster analysis integration is just a process of dividing educational resources into different clusters or groups based on some criteria. The most basic criterion is to make the similarity in each resource cluster The idea of partition method is the simplest. First, determine the ideal number of partitions, then create an initial cluster according to the number, and then use iterative relocation technology to continuously optimize and improve the partition integration results through the continuous movement of objects between groups according to the criteria. The retrieval based on resource integration or aggregation obtains all the results with different degrees of correlation, and the real target set may be only a small set. For the intelligent integration of Chinese, Literature and Culture education network resources, text preprocessing is carried out first. When clustering text resources, only when text information is transformed into data information can clustering analysis be carried out. In order to make text information statistics, we must establish a text representation model. The commonly used text representation models include Boolean model, vector space model, probability model and so on. Next, you need to select feature items ① The preprocessed total text file is segmented by word segmentation software to obtain each subject word and its frequency in the document set; ② Stop word processing; ③ Remove low-frequency words, that is, words whose frequency is lower than a certain threshold and has little contribution to the theme of the article; ④ Remove words that are meaningless to distinguish document categories. Secondly, calculate the feature weight, and finally realize the intelligent integration of resources.

4 Conclusions

The deepening of modern education and teaching reform, information technology has gone deep into education and life and become an important way and means for people to obtain information. There are more and more educational resources for, Literature and Culture, which also puts forward high requirements for the integration ability of educational resources. Big data information technology and the country's strong investment in education, the construction of educational informatization is gradually advancing to a high level and deep level. The integration of educational resources of Chinese, Literature and Culture specialty is a beneficial exploration of educational informatization in the field of education. The existing resources can be classified and integrated by using cluster analysis algorithm. Clustering analysis algorithm is to explore other data resources with relevance and use value with the data resource object from the given data education resources. Applying clustering analysis to the data resource set can accurately identify the sparsity and density of the data resource set, so as to better grasp the combination and distribution of the overall resources and the value and strong correlation between the attributes of data resources. The clustering analysis algorithm can also be used to mine the potential Chinese, Literature and Culture education resource information in the web page information. Resource integration and application, the clustering analysis algorithm can not only become an independent use tool, but also realize reasonable classification and planning for the complex and disordered data resource objects, so it is the primary processing means of the data education technology resource mining algorithm of most Chinese, Literature and Culture majors, Make the whole resource integration process more effective.

References

1. Wei, H.: Application of cluster analysis algorithm in wireless local area network optimization analysis. Sci. Technol. Innov. Appl. **6**, 1 (2017)
2. Cao, S., Yang, Z.: Prediction of wireless network traffic based on cluster analysis algorithm and optimized support vector machine. Comput. Sci. **47**(8), 4 (2020)
3. Chen, L., Xu, A., Jiang, Y., et al.: Power information network attack pattern recognition algorithm based on dynamic incremental clustering analysis. China Southern Power Grid Technol. **14**(8), 8 (2020)
4. Shen, X., Yi, J.: Research on adaptive elastic network algorithm for cluster analysis. Comput. Eng. Appl. **53**(009), 175–183 (2017)
5. Fan, S., Zhang, X., Yu, H.: Course evaluation technology based on association rules and cluster analysis. J. East China Univ. Sci. Technol. (Natl. Sci. Edn.) **48**(2), **260** (2022)
6. Xie, H., Wang, X.: Analysis and comparison of several clustering algorithms in data mining. Inform. Comput. Theor. Edn. **418**(24), 71–73 (2018)
7. Duan, J., Guo, F., Zhang, X., et al.: BA network model based on adaptive algorithm and its cluster analysis. Control. Eng. **27**(1), 7 (2020)
8. Shen, X., Yi, J., Shen, et al.: Research on adaptive elastic network algorithm for cluster analysis. Comput. Eng. Appl. **53**(9), 9 (2017)
9. Chen, G., Meng, X., Kang, Q., et al.: Virtual software-defined network mapping algorithm based on topology segmentation and clustering analysis. Comput. Appl. **41**(11), 10 (2021)
10. Sun, W., Du, W., Niu, Y., et al.: Research on interpretation technology of comprehensive geophysical cluster analysis. J. Eng. Geophys. **19**(1), 7 (2022)

Research on Graphic Interactive Visual Online Teaching of Intelligent Algorithm Course

Guixiang Lou[1,2(✉)], Wang Sufang[1,2], and Hongchun Shen[1,2]

[1] Shenzhen Longhua District of Peace Primary School, Shenzhen 518110, China
ld19821129@163.com
[2] School of Art, Sichuan University Jinjiang College, Meishan, China

Abstract. In view of the lack of communication and interaction between teachers and students, students and students due to the separation of teachers and students in time and space, and the fact that teachers cannot supervise classroom order, This paper proposes that based on the "Rain Classroom+Tencent Conference" "The graphic interactive visualization teaching method, innovative teaching concepts, and appropriate changes in teaching strategies and methods. The research on graphic interactive visualization online teaching of intelligent algorithm course is a research aimed at designing and developing an effective learning environment for students in the field of computer science. The main purpose of this research is to provide a platform for students to learn concepts related to algorithms, data structures, programming languages, and software engineering. The platform will Developed through different types of graphical interactive visual tools, these tools will help them understand how to work and how to use them effectively. The main purpose of this study is to ensure that all aspects related to computer science are covered using these different tools.

Keywords: Online teaching · Intelligent algorithm · Courses · Graphic interaction · visualization

1 Introduction

In recent years, computer algorithm programming has been paid more and more attention in the field of education. The target population of education is not only limited to computer majors, but also more and more non computer majors are receiving the curriculum education of programming. At the same time, with the development of NOIP (National Olympic in Informatics in Provinces) and the school's emphasis on quality education year by year, more and more senior high school students and even junior high school students also participate in the learning of algorithm programming [1].

In the information technology curriculum standard for senior high schools revised in 2017, "algorithm and program implementation" is a part of the compulsory module "data and computing", and "data and data structure" is an optional compulsory module. And the students are required to "master the basic knowledge of a programming language,

Y. Zhang and N. Shah (Eds.): BigIoT-EDU 2023, LNICST 582, pp. 506–516, 2024.
https://doi.org/10.1007/978-3-031-63136-8_52

use the programming language to realize simple algorithms. Through solving practical problems, experience the basic process of programming, feel the efficiency of algorithms, and master the methods of program debugging and operation."

The graphic teaching method of algorithm course, also known as "graphic teaching method of algorithm course" and "graphic teaching method", has not been uniformly defined by the academic community, but has basically reached a consensus.

An important scholar who studied the graphic teaching method of algorithm course in the early stage believed that the graphic teaching method of algorithm course was "a medium for transmitting historical knowledge information". Yu Youxi believes that the graphic method of algorithm curriculum refers to "the teaching method of transmitting historical information by means of words, concepts, figures, charts and some symbols". The graphic method of algorithm course is "a method of expressing the system and structure of knowledge itself with concise patterns, symbols, words and colors".

Yan Jiazhen believes that "the algorithm course diagram is actually a kind of outline signal, a concise, vivid and intuitive diagram composed of highly summarized words, numbers, symbols and other 'signals'".

To sum up, we will find that the academic community has the following common points in defining it: first, from the perspective of the constituent elements, including words, numbers, symbols, charts, lines and other forms. Secondly, from the perspective of use intention, it is to reflect the connection between historical knowledge. Finally, from the use effect, it systematizes and visualizes knowledge.

To sum up, the author believes that the graphic method of algorithmic curriculum refers to a teaching method in which teachers use concise words, numbers, symbols, charts, lines and other forms to transmit historical information and systematize and visualize knowledge in the teaching process. Therefore, in terms of its classification criteria, in a broad sense, algorithm picture, algorithm map, diagram and schematic signal algorithm course diagram belong to the category of algorithm course diagram teaching method, but the research on historical picture and historical map is quite sufficient.

Algorithm is a well-defined computing process. There are many ways to express algorithms, such as natural language, pseudo code, flow chart, PAD (problem analysis diagram), programming language, etc., among which pseudo code and flow chart are commonly used. In general, when facing a relatively complex algorithm problem, you should have a clear description of the algorithm before writing the program [2]. This description can be in the form of pseudo code or flow chart. But students may start to write programs directly because they are lazy. For students with poor algorithm thinking foundation and programming ability, it is often difficult to write a correct algorithm program at a time. However, the teacher does not have a good method to check the algorithm description process of students. Therefore, it is often difficult for students to deal with algorithm problems. As time passes, they will have a sense of resistance to algorithm problems, let alone develop good algorithm thinking and programming habits [3]. This is obviously not conducive to the teaching of algorithm programming.

2 Related Work

2.1 Visualization Research Status

Visual programming language is a kind of programming language different from text programming language. Different from text programming language, visual programming language is usually a two-dimensional or more dimensional existence, which uses graphical symbol elements to connect program elements, and contains fewer keywords.

Fischer, Giaccardi and others pointed out in their papers the advantages of graphical languages compared with text languages. They believed that text based languages, because of the existence of grammar and morphology, require people to struggle to master when learning, just like any natural language. The advantage of graphical language is that graphical elements are used to replace some text morphology or grammar that is difficult for people to understand at first [4]. This graphical element acts as a bridge between the reality and the programming world, which clearly indicates the operation rules of the programming world, and reduces the cognitive burden when people enter the programming world. The programming diagram is shown in Fig. 1 below.

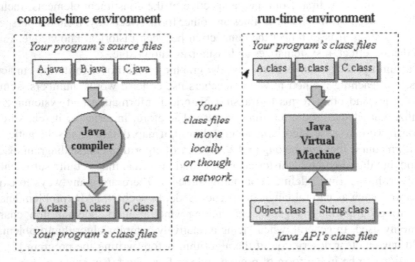

Fig. 1. Programming diagram

Visual programming language is very popular in the programming education of children such as primary school students and middle school students. They do not need to master the knowledge of programming syntax, because visual programming language provides a running environment that is basically free of compilation errors. Another report said that compared with traditional programming languages, visual programming languages can create a more pleasant impression in children's minds, that is, children are more willing to learn visual programming languages [5].

"The diagram of intelligent algorithm course has the function of transmitting information and exchanging ideas. It can simplify the language expression and more intuitively express the essential characteristics of knowledge concepts." Intuitiveness is the most distinctive feature of the diagram of intelligent algorithm course. It transforms the abstract programming concept into an intuitive and vivid diagram structure of intelligent algorithm course through symbols, words and other elements, and transforms the boring textbook knowledge into a more acceptable one for students Direct visual stimulation can activate the enthusiasm and enthusiasm of students to actively learn programming, explore programming and master knowledge. Interest is the best teacher for students. The intuitive and vivid diagram of intelligent algorithm course enables students to deeply understand programming, deepen impression, enhance understanding and promote learning. The data can be customized and initialized as shown in Fig. 2.

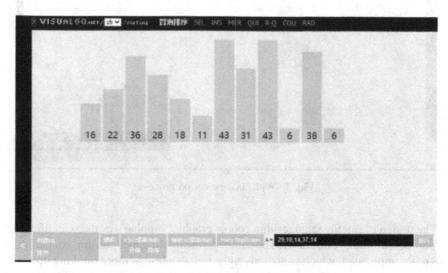

Fig. 2. Data can be customized and initialized

Logic is the internal characteristic of the graphical method of intelligent algorithm course. If teachers want to transform the internal relationship between programming knowledge into the graphical method of intelligent algorithm course, they must rely on its logical relationship. In the classroom summary, the teacher arranges and integrates according to its logic and practical clues, closely combines multiple programming concepts and scattered programming knowledge, so that the teaching system exists in the form of a whole, and the internal logic is connected. Therefore, the graphical method of intelligent algorithm course combines the system and logic to play a collaborative role.

Scientific and accurate is the first essence of the graphic design of intelligent algorithm course. Scientificity means that the logical relationship between programming objects revealed by the diagram of intelligent algorithm course must be correct. "The primary premise of the design of the intelligent algorithm curriculum diagram is scientific and accurate. The illogical and unscientific intelligent algorithm curriculum diagram has no meaning. Teachers should select the content of the textbook according to the requirements of the curriculum standard, and design it as the intelligent algorithm curriculum diagram. As a teaching method, teachers' teaching is for students to learn better. Unscientific intelligent algorithm curriculum diagram can not promote students' learning, even for students It constitutes a wrong guidance, so the design of the intelligent algorithm course diagram must first be scientific and reasonable, and can withstand repeated deliberation. The logical relationship between programming knowledge and knowledge must be organized accurately. According to the selected algorithm and initialization data, it is displayed with animation effect, and in the lower right corner, the code execution process is shown in Fig. 3 below.

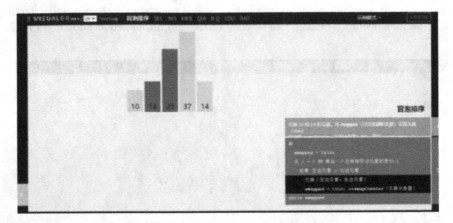

Fig. 3. With code execution process

The design of intelligent algorithm course graphics emphasizes the scientific nature and pursues simplicity and clarity. The cumbersome intelligent algorithm course graphic design is complicated, which is not only ugly, but also brings more thinking operations and reduces teaching efficiency. The simple design is not only to bring students the experience of beauty, but also to make the logical relationship clearer and understand the internal relationship between knowledge.

Hidekuni Tsukamoto et al. also believed in their research that visual programming languages have certain limitations. Visual programming languages for beginners often sacrifice flexibility for simpler syntax. This prevents some advanced students from using visual programming languages to complete advanced exercises. At the same time, students cannot use bottom-up programming. In addition, although visual programming language is widely used in children's programming education, it is not widely used in professional software development. Therefore, at some stage in the future, students will still have to learn text programming language, which will cause a certain secondary learning cost.

2.2   Application in the Field of Education

Many people abroad have made experimental investigations on whether visual programming languages are really effective. In 2006, Jeannette Wing put forward the concept of Computational Thinking, which is defined as the use of computer science concepts to solve problems in any field. In order to clarify the concept of computational thinking,

Wing also listed six principles of computational thinking: 1) through abstract conceptu-alization. 2) It is a basic skill required by modern society. 3) It does not necessarily mean that the problem must be solved like a computer, but includes all the key skills of human beings. 4) It combines mathematical and engineering problems. 5) Mainly concerned with the problems related to labor. 6) It should be a part of everyone's education [6].

At home, Cheng Qianqian of Xi'an Jiaotong University introduced RAPTOR as an important tool for teaching experiments in the college computer basic courses offered in 2012, helping students understand important theoretical concepts of programs and algorithms, and achieved good response.

Zhang Gang, et al. of Tianjin University, opened the course RAPTOR Visual Pro-gramming in 2014, using RAPTOR as a programming tool, and put forward the idea of "RAPTOR flow chart+algorithm design" as a teaching reform to gradually deepen from basic problems to comprehensive problems [7]. By using the "task driven problem solving" training method of "finding problems - analyzing problems - seeking multiple solutions - comparing and optimizing multiple solutions", So as to realize the teaching mode of solving practical problems. And in practice, it has achieved a good response.

To sum up, foreign countries have developed early in the field of visual algorithm design, and many researchers have participated in the research. Whether preschool chil-dren, primary and secondary school students, or beginners learning algorithms, they can find their own visual algorithm design software or environment that can cultivate algo-rithm thinking. However, there is a big shortage of time and space in China. Whether it is a visual programming environment for children or a visual algorithm design tool based on flow chart for algorithm learning, it is either using foreign software or a blank [8]. At the same time, foreign algorithm design tools based on flow chart also have low reuse rate and are not closely integrated with classroom teaching. The purpose of this paper is to study a visual algorithm design method for online teaching, and integrate the evaluation function, so that teachers can design and correct course experiments easily [9, 10].

3 Characteristics and Difficulties of Online Teaching

We can't think of online teaching as simply using the network platform to transfer traditional classes to the network. It is fundamentally different from some online classes in extracurricular tutoring classes, because it is necessary to ensure students' grasp of the professional curriculum system and the learning and mastery of teaching content. In addition, online teaching is fundamentally different from traditional classroom teaching, so it is a great challenge for college teachers [11].

First of all, online teaching is based on Internet media. We mainly adopt the follow-ing three interaction methods to guarantee. (1) Between students and teachers, Rain-class+Tencent Conference+EV screen recording tools are used. In the rain class, the teacher ID is bound with the teaching class and the course, which can realize the man-agement of students during the class, the upload and download of course PPT, in class detection, the arrangement of homework after class, and online examination and other functions. Tencent Conference can accommodate 300 people for online video conference at the same time, and can share the screen, so that students can see the PPT interface that the teacher is currently explaining. EV video recording screen can record high-performance video for unlimited time to meet the needs of micro classes and online classes [12]. The biggest difference between EV video recording and live broadcast software on the market is that its output video file is very small. (2) Between students and learning materials, students can download course PPT through Rain Class, or use WeChat group, QQ group and other tools. (3) Students can use WeChat, QQ and other social tools to discuss cooperation and mutual learning. However, in the course of teaching, teachers may encounter the situation that students cannot smoothly enter Tencent meetings and rainy classes due to weak network signals in remote areas.

Secondly, in the online teaching process, teachers can not be the main lecturer of teaching content in the teaching process as in the traditional face-to-face classroom, and become the protagonist and center of the classroom. The role of teachers in leading the classroom rhythm has been weakened. In addition, students lack the necessary classroom supervision of teachers and classroom discussion atmosphere in home learning. They have a sense of maladjustment and alienation from online teaching. Especially for students with relatively poor self-control ability, it is difficult to ensure normal learning progress and effect due to their own inertia and other factors, as well as certain interference factors from electronic products in the online teaching process. In addition, due to the separation between teachers and students in time and space, teachers cannot know the students' mastery of the knowledge points they teach in real time [15]. All the difficulties above pose challenges to the implementation of online teaching.

But it is undeniable that the characteristics and difficulties of online teaching make it more suitable for the learner centered educational ecology. Students have the opportunity to become autonomous learners, discussion participants, and knowledge builders, which will become a new opportunity and a new starting point for college education. Therefore, college teachers should take this opportunity to adapt to the changes in the teaching environment, get familiar with a variety of online education platforms and tools, and improve their information literacy. In the process of online teaching design, we should not only focus on the teaching of knowledge as the only teaching goal, but also pay attention to the discipline itself, innovate the teaching philosophy, appropriately change the teaching strategies and methods, comprehensively focus on the cultivation of students' key abilities in the discipline, and focus on the establishment of the scientific curriculum system.

4   Research on Graphic Interactive Visualization Online Teaching of Intelligent Algorithm Course

4.1   Pre Class Preview

The pre class independent preview link is mainly divided into two parts: pre class students' independent learning and group discussion, cooperation and interaction. Before class, students complete partial integration of knowledge and find problems, and design theme concept maps for the course content. Teachers push the learning resource package with the help of the rain class and release the preview task [16]. Before class, students take the task designed by the theme concept map, according to the learning resource package released by the teacher, make good use of online resources to complete independent preview, prepare for the classroom content, clarify the basic concepts and knowledge logic, so as to have a deep understanding of knowledge and better adapt to the online teaching mode. Teachers guide and mobilize students' thinking. After group discussion, students give a group level thematic concept cognitive map. For example, for the chapter of Genetic Algorithms (GA) in the intelligent algorithm course, students first learn about the basic biological concepts of GA (including genetics and evolution) through preview, then understand its basic ideas and general processes, draw a personal theme concept map according to the preview data, and summarize the basic concepts and operations related to GA [17]. After the students have completed the drawing of personal theme concept map, through the online discussion of the learning group, they can expand the learning of genetic algorithm based on mutual understanding of personal concept map, discuss the characteristics and application fields of genetic algorithm, further understand the process steps of genetic algorithm, discuss genetic algorithm in combination with their own research direction, and finally summarize and refine the group level concept cognitive map, as shown in Fig. 4.

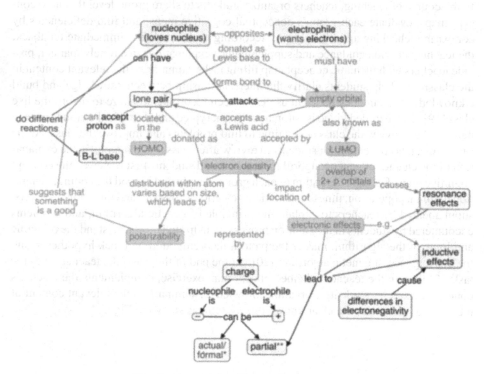

Fig. 4. Genetic algorithm topic concept map

The power to promote these tools lies in the fact that the creators of these tools have a common vision: to liberate the productivity of programmers, decouple interface development and business development, make technology more affinity, and let designers' ideas directly become executable code. But in fact, this is not an easy thing. Because this requires not only mature technology and easy-to-use products, but also the establishment of a series of ecosystems, the training of trainers and the learning of trainees. This is equivalent to creating a new career. As a person obsessed with programming itself, I am very clear about the problems faced by programmers and the reasons for not wanting to make changes. In the interface development, programmers are faced with a large number of duplicate code; In business development, programmers are faced with numerous CRUDs; Even in the so-called field of artificial intelligence, it is nothing more than a white if else... And countless tables [18]. In fact, after careful investigation, this is the essence of the world. We add an acc and whatevername attribute to an existing primitive object, and then use the primativeOp node to add these two attributes, return to the acc attribute, and name the resulting primitive object bPrimitive (Can be used elsewhere) (Primitive is a kind of soap of arbitrary length. Primitive Op nodes operate on each channel in parallel).

4.2 Interaction in Class

In the course of teaching, teachers organize students to share group level thematic concept maps, evaluate each group's conceptual cognitive maps, and find deficiencies by comparing, checking and filling gaps. According to the students' immediate feedback, the teachers provide guidance and supplementary explanations in a timely manner, provide teachers with thematic concept map filling tasks, summarize the relevant content in the classroom, help students clarify the interrelationship between knowledge and build a knowledge system. Teachers can use EV screen recording software to record the live class [19]. The recorded video is automatically encrypted and stored in the cloud space to help teachers review the class at any time to find problems and improve the class. At the same time, it is convenient for students to review after class. For example, in the explanation of the chapter of genetic algorithm, teachers and students first reviewed the concept cognitive map of genetic algorithm of each group, deeply understood the coding, generation of initial population, fitness calculation, selection, crossover and mutation operators, supplemented by teachers to explain the principle of genetic algorithm, and problems encountered by students in the solution process, to help students understand the principle and logic of the algorithm, master the pattern theorem, building block hypothesis, and the convergence of genetic algorithm [20]. At the end of the class, the teacher gives the task of filling in the teacher's theme concept map exercise, complements the teacher's concept map, helps students reorganize knowledge, summarizes the relevant content of the class, and constructs a clear knowledge system, as shown in Fig. 5.

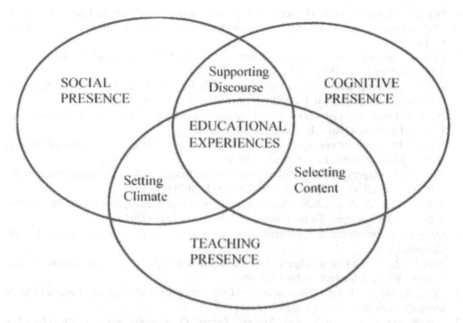

Fig. 5. Online teaching interaction mode

5 Conclusion

The characteristics and difficulties of online teaching make it more suitable for the learner centered educational ecology. The establishment of a scientific online curriculum system plays a crucial role in the realization of the strategic objectives of college education. This paper proposes to apply the schema interactive visualization online teaching mode supported by "Rain Classroom + Tencent Conference" to the postgraduate intelligent algorithm course, divide the teaching content into three modules: pre class discussion preview, interactive live broadcast in class, and after class expansion exercise, gradually build a multi-level theme concept map, reorganize knowledge by means of communication and interaction, improve the construction of knowledge system, and thus form a complete and smooth teaching paradigm, This has promoted the improvement of teaching quality and obtained good effect feedback.

References

1. Yu, H.: Online teaching quality evaluation based on emotion recognition and improved AprioriTid algorithm. J. Intell. Fuzzy Syst. Appl. Eng. Technol. **4**, 40 (2021)
2. Wu, J.: English vocabulary online teaching based on machine learning recognition and target visual detection. J. Intell. Fuzzy Syst. Appl. Eng. Technol. **39**(2Pta1) (2020)
3. Liu, L., Li, M., Wu, Y., et al.: Construction of intelligent interactive education platform for medical image. China Mod. Educ. Equip. (2019)

4. Wang, C.: Design and development of intelligent search algorithm teaching software. In: 2018 2nd International Conference on Systems,Computing,and Applications (SYSTCA 2018) (2018)
5. Fang, C.: Intelligent online teaching system based on SVM algorithm and complex network. J. Intell. Fuzzy Syst. **40**(5), 1–11 (2020)
6. Cao, J.: Computer public course teaching based on improved machine learning and neural network algorithm. J. Intell. Fuzzy Syst. Appl. Eng. Technol. **4**, 40 (2021)
7. Wang, J.: Intelligent system for interactive online education based on cloud big data analytics. J. Intell. Fuzzy Syst. Appl. Eng. Technol. **40**(2) (2021)
8. Wang, Y.H.: Design of intelligent traffic lights teaching experimental platform based on fuzzy control. Mech. Electric. Eng. Technol. (2019)
9. Fang, C.: Intelligent online English teaching system based on SVM algorithm and complex network. J. Intell. Fuzzy Syst. Appl. Eng. Technol. **40**(2) (2021)
10. Yan, H., Han, C., Zhang, X,M.: Research progress of intelligent application of ferrographic technique. J. Chongqing Technol. Bus. Univ. (Natl. Sci. Edn.) (2016)
11. Design and application of intelligent robot online speech control system. Indust. Control Comput. (2019)
12. Wei, D.: Application of intelligent algorithm big data analysis in the construction of smart campus. Wireless Internet Technol. (2019)
13. Pei, Z.S., Shi, B.: Information. research and simulation of intelligent robot visual obstacle recognition method. Comput. Simul. (2016)
14. Luo, R., Wang, H., Chen, Y., et al.: Method of apparel's geometric & floral pattern based on interactive genetic algorithm (2016)
15. Sun, H., Tang, WW.: Construction of intelligent classroom of college literature course based on the mobile intelligent media. J. Guangxi Vocat. Techn. College (2019)
16. Di, W.U., Sheng, L., Gao, Y.F.: Exploration of case teaching in the course of intelligent information processing technology. Educ. Teach. Forum (2017)
17. Hai-Yan, L.V., Zhou, L.J., Jing, H., et al.: Design of intelligent test paper generating genetic algorithm for common online examination system. Comput. Technol. Autom. (2016)
18. Kang, F., Kong, L.: Application of micro-class in teaching of computational geometry algorithm and realization course. Exper. Technol. Manage. (2019)
19. Fan, S.H., Chen, D.M., Fan, K., et al.: Research on case and seminar teaching of intelligent instrument postgraduate course. Sci. Technol. Vis. (2019)
20. Wei, S., Cai, Z.: Proving experimental teaching for course of intelligent control. Guide Sci. Educ. (2017)

Design and Application of Music Assisted Teaching System Based on ARM and SA Algorithm

Rong Zhang[✉] and Xiang Min

Xingtai University, Xingtai 054000, Hebei, China
hangrong123987@163.com

Abstract. In music teaching, there are some tasks that cannot be completed or done well by humans, so it is necessary to develop an auxiliary teaching system to provide help to teachers. This paper will carry out relevant research based on ARM and SA algorithms. This paper introduces the basic concepts of ARM and SA algorithms, and then puts forward the design scheme of music assisted teaching system based on the two algorithms. Finally, the actual application test of the system is carried out to verify whether the application effect of the system meets the expectations. The research shows that, based on ARM and SA algorithm, the music assisted teaching system plays a distinct role, which can provide teachers with good help, complete various difficult tasks and improve the teaching quality.

Keywords: ARM structure · SA algorithm · Music assisted teaching system

1 Introduction

With the continuous development of society, modern people have higher and higher requirements for the quality of music teaching, and their cognition is getting deeper and deeper. As a result, many problems have been exposed in traditional music teaching, so music teaching has been reformed. After the reform, the overall system of music teaching takes on a new look and can achieve expected results in theory, but the practice shows that there are still some gaps between the actual results and the expected results. The reason for this phenomenon is that there are some tasks that teachers cannot complete and do well in music teaching, such as teachers cannot collect the learning data of every student at all times. At the same time, teachers may not be able to analyze the learning situation data with large magnitude, high output, frequent changes, complicated types and complex relationships. Even if they can, it is difficult to avoid the influence of their own subjective factors, which leads to certain deviations in the pertinence, objectivity and rationality of music teaching, and the final result is naturally lower than expected. In the face of these problems, relevant fields believe that a music-assisted teaching system can be designed to complete such work, and also point out that the system design can rely on ARM and SA algorithms to give the system the ability to complete complex work. Therefore, it is necessary to study the system design method.

Y. Zhang and N. Shah (Eds.): BigIoT-EDU 2023, LNICST 582, pp. 517–524, 2024.
https://doi.org/10.1007/978-3-031-63136-8_53

2 Basic Concepts of ARM and SA Algorithms

2.1 ARM Structure

ARM is a microprocessor architecture, which can also be defined as a microprocessor unit. It can be used for the development of machine system control chips and terminals. Its main function is to optimize the software control algorithm in machine control chips or terminals from the perspective of hardware, so that the logic and behavior of machine systems can be accurately controlled. Compared with other micro-processing architectures, ARM has the advantages of low cost, low power consumption and high precision. At the same time, it also has a wide range of applications, which can be used in different fields and can be applied to the design of music assisted teaching system. In this system, ARM is mainly used to develop control terminals [1–3].

According to the application performance of ARM in other systems, it is known that it can simultaneously process the 16-bit and 32-bit instruction set. In the application, it is generally necessary to adopt the embedded method to combine it with the hardware part of the machine system, that is, the controller of the ARM control terminal can be embedded in the control link of the system. ARM controller has high integration, power consumption is not affected. In order to control the machine system through the ARM controller, it is necessary to program before embedding, and then write the program into the ARM controller to ensure the stable operation of the system [4].

In terms of structure, ARM is divided into two hardware layers and software layers. The standard form of the internal structure of the two layers is shown in Figs. 1 and 2.

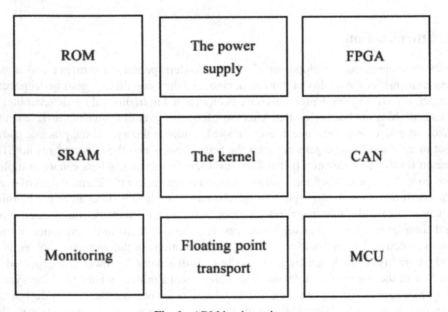

Fig. 1. ARM hardware layer

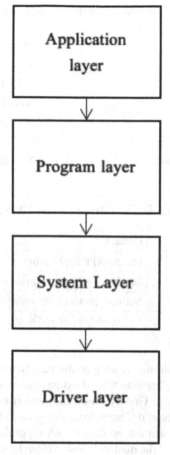

Fig. 2. ARM software layer

Combined with Figs. 1 and 2, the ARM terminal controller relies on hardware startup to promote the software operation, so the performance of the hardware part is very important. To ensure the performance, the hardware selection of the ARM terminal controller should be done well. The selection results in this paper are shown in Table 1. The software part is divided into four layers, and the actual content of each layer depends on the usage requirements, so there is no timing. The content of each layer in this paper is shown in Table 2.

2.2 SA Algorithm

SA algorithm is a random algorithm with the ability to find the global optimal solution, but its optimization ability is not stable, so the final solution is not necessarily the global optimal solution, can only be said to be the global optimal solution. Compared with other random algorithms, the biggest advantage of SA algorithm lies in its speed of finding the approximate optimal solution to the problem. In this regard, almost no algorithm can

Table 1. Hardware selection results of ARM terminal controller

Selection objective	results
Integrated circuit board	STM32F108
Module connection interface	FS, GUI, SP
microprocessor	ARM1176JZ
Power supply module	5 V lithium battery
Communication module	Wifi
Communication monitoring module	TXD pin

Table 2. Contents of each software layer

Layer	Content
Application layer	PC and APP applications
Program layer	Database, API, program development tools
System Layer	Network protocol, operating system, FS
Driver layer	Subroutine driver and related modules

be compared with SA algorithm. As long as the parameters are reasonable, the output speed of SA algorithm is higher than that of exhaustive method [5–7].

SA algorithm is similar to Greedy algorithm, and it is even considered as a kind of Greedy algorithm. However, different from the general Greedy algorithm, there are random factors in the optimization process of SA algorithm, so it can accept a result with a certain probability that the quality is lower than the existing answer, which is the randomness of SA algorithm. May result in a locally optimal solution, or approximately optimal solution. Take Fig. 3 as an example, when SA algorithm optimizes and finds B, B is identified as the global optimal solution, but in fact B is the local optimal solution [8]. At this time, under the action of random factors, B will be accepted with a certain probability and continue to move to the right. If this process is repeated several times, B may reach the peak value between itself and C. I can prove that B is not the global optimal solution, but the local optimal solution, because the peak value means that the solution jumps out of the local minimum, and B is the local minimum.

An important criterion of SA algorithm is the Metropolis criterion, which emphasizes that when the particle temperature is in equilibrium at T, the probability of the particle approaching equilibrium is exp($-\Delta E/(kT)$), where the internal energy is E at T, ΔE is the number of changes in E, and k is Boltzmann constant. According to the description, See Formula (1) for the Metropolis criterion expression.

$$P = \left\{ \exp\left(-\frac{\frac{1}{E(x_{new})} - E(x_{OLD})}{T} \right) \quad if \quad E(x_{new}) < E(x_{old}) \right. \tag{1}$$

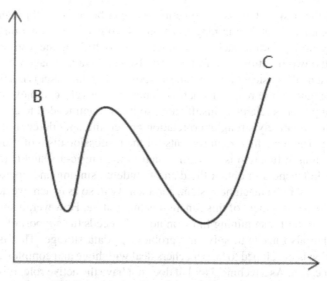

Fig. 3. Optimization process of SA algorithm

3 Design and Application of Music Assisted Teaching System

3.1 System Design

The design of music-assisted teaching system in this paper is divided into three steps, which are embedded design, functional layer development and network layer design. The details of each step are as follows.

3.1.1 Embedding Design

In order to embed the ARM terminal controller in the music-assisted teaching system, and to help the terminal controller to judge the actual results through the SA algorithm, and also to ensure the smooth implementation of the subsequent steps of the design work, the first step of the system design is to carry out the embedded design. According to the system framework, it is necessary to conduct modular development of SA algorithm in the embedded design, and this method can usually be realized by Java programming language. That is, according to the basic logic and criteria requirements of SA algorithm, Java language is used for algorithmic logic and criterion programming, and then the logic model and criterion model are combined. The priority of the criterion model is set (the priority of the criterion model is greater than that of the logical model). The SA algorithm module is loaded into the AMR terminal controller, and finally the controller is installed on the control link of the system [9, 10].

3.1.2 Functional Layer Design

The functional layer mainly integrates all the functional programs of the system, including those of the ARM terminal controller. These functions can be divided into two categories in the design. One is the function that can be realized through simple programming logic, such as data mining function. The other is the function that needs to be realized by SA algorithm, such as the function of controlling the instrument machine system. For the two functions, the former can also use Java language for programming and development, the basic way is the same as above, while the latter is not recommended to use Java language, the reason is that the latter is relatively complex, Java language interpretation power is relatively insufficient, so it is recommended to choose C++ language, which is relatively strong interpretation power, the only defect is complex logic programming. There are high requirements for the professionalism of programmers.

The data mining function is very important in the music-assisted teaching system, which can help teachers to obtain the data of students singing and operating Musical Instruments through the machine system, and identify it, so as to achieve accurate transmission, so the development of this function is imperative. However, it should be noted that the realization of data mining function not only needs the support of programming technology, but also needs to solve the problem of data storage. That is to say, data mining function is developed to help teachers deal with huge and complex data, which is also its significance. As a technical tool, it does not have the active role. It is necessary to make its large and complex data, which requires data storage. Therefore, the functional layer design also needs to set up the database, and the system database is different from other systems of the same type, need to store a large number of data, so the storage capacity of the system database should be large enough, but also take into account the data security, according to this requirement, the current requirements of the database only cloud database, the database has unlimited capacity, can store a large number of data, At the same time, firewall technology can be adopted to ensure data security. However, it is important to note that the use of the firewall technology limits the capacity of the cloud database. That is, the firewall divides the entire data space into internal space and external space to protect the data in the internal space, but also limits the capacity. Therefore, pay attention to capacity expansion when using the firewall technology. It is better to set the alarm standard according to the existing capacity. When the capacity reaches the standard, the manual will be notified, and the manual will remove the firewall temporarily, increase the storage capacity resources, and expand the capacity. Finally, the firewall can be restored.

3.1.3 Network Layer Design

In order to ensure the connection between the system and PC and APP, network layer design is required. The design of the network layer of this system is different from other systems, and it needs to take into account the characteristics of ARM terminal controller, especially in the real-time. That is, the first step of the design of the network layer is to choose the network communication protocol. Reasonable selection can ensure the real-time communication standards, and help teachers and students to interact in real time in the music assisted teaching system. From this point of view, because generally a teacher has to face dozens of students at the same time, this paper chooses the small Ethernet network protocol as the network layer basis. This network protocol is characterized by small capacity, but has certain private network attributes, only authenticated users can enter the network. These characteristics make the small Ethernet network will not have the communication congestion problem. It is beneficial to the real-time of information transmission and meets the real-time requirements of system communication. After the selection of network communication protocol, the network layout should be carried out. That is, because teachers and students usually communicate in the public Internet environment, the Ethernet layout will also be developed in this environment. The specific methods are as follows: first, the Ethernet port is developed in the Web page; Secondly, establish the identity authentication system on the port, set the teacher as the administrator, and then through the teacher set the student as the "allowed access user", so as to achieve the network layer design. In addition, the use conditions of small-sized Ethernet communication protocols are harsh and must be established in a good Internet environment. However, some colleges and universities use campus networks, which may not meet the application requirements of this communication protocol. Therefore, if small-sized Ethernet communication protocols cannot be used, other small-sized communication protocols, such as virtual private network protocols, can be considered.

3.2 Actual Application and Test

Through the above three steps, relying on ARM and SA algorithm to realize the music assisted teaching system, in order to understand the practical application of the system, but also to test it, this paper takes music singing teaching as an example to analyze. In terms of application mode, the singing teaching mainly adopts the mode of "people for accessing to people", so the teacher needs to wear relevant equipment for demonstration. During the process, the voice print data demonstrated by the teacher will be collected and then input to the computer terminal. After passing the ARM controller, it will be stopped briefly, so that the SA algorithm can calculate and recognize the data and convert it into a curve. Then the curve is transmitted to the students through the network. At this time, the students can sing according to the audio of the teacher's demonstration. During the period, according to the curve of the demonstration voiceprint data, they can judge their own shortcomings so as to improve them.

100 sets of tests were conducted according to the above methods, and the results are shown in Table 3.

Table 3. Test results of system application

Test Items	The results of
Speed of response	0.3 s~1 s
Result accuracy (refer to manual preset results)	96.1%~99.5%

Combined with Table 1,100, the worst results of system response speed and result accuracy were higher than expected, so the system was effectively applied.

4 Conclusion

To sum up, there are many tasks that teachers cannot complete and do well in music teaching, and the music assisted teaching system can help teachers complete these tasks. Therefore, it is necessary to rely on ARM and SA algorithms for system design. The system has good performance and outstanding function in practical application, which can effectively improve the efficiency and quality of music teaching.

Acknowledgements. Hebei Social Science Foundation, Knowledge Graph and Practice Paradigm of Integrating Courses for Ideological and Political Education into Music Practical Education (HB22YS046), presided.

References

1. Yang, J., Yang, D.: Design of online teaching mode recognition system for ideological and political curriculum based on hash algorithm. In: Wang, SH., Zhang, YD. (eds) Multimedia technology and enhanced learning. ICMTEL 2022. LNICST, vol. 446. Springer, Cham (2022). https://doi.org/10.1007/978-3-031-18123-8_12
2. Zhang, T., Dong, W., Shi, H., et al.: Design and implementation of teaching analysis system based on data mining. In: 2019 Chinese Control and Decision Conference (CCDC) (2019)
3. Zheng, H., Perez, Z.: Design of multimedia engineering teaching system based on internet of things technology. Int. J. Contin. Eng. Educ. Life-long Learn. 29(4), 293–305 (2019)
4. Luo, Z.: Plant slope reconstruction in plain area based on multi-core ARM and music teaching satisfaction. Arab. J. Geosci. 2021(22), 14 (2021). https://doi.org/10.1007/S12517-021-080 20-3
5. Lin, H.I.: Design of an intelligent robotic precise assembly system for rapid teaching and admittance control. Robot. Comput.-Integrat. Manufac. 64(9), 101946 (2020)
6. Song, Z., Xing, F., Mou, L., et al.: Design and application of multiple adaptability evaluation algorithms based on UHVDC digital simulation operating system. J. Phys. Conf. Ser. 2087(1), 012075 (2021)
7. Zhao, X., Liu, X., Phillips, V., et al.: Impacts of secondary ice production on Arctic mixed-phase clouds based on ARM observations and CAM6 single-column model simulations. Atmosph. Chem. Phys. 21(7), 5685–5703 (2021)
8. Jiang, Z., Dong, P., Wei, R., et al.: PSpSys: a time-predictable mixed-criticality system architecture based on ARM TrustZone. J. Syst. Architect. 2022(123-), 123 (2022)
9. Liu, H., Chen, J.: Intelligent control for new topological structure of Z-Source inverter based on ARM. Microprocess. Microsyst. 81, 103735 (2021)
10. Dong, Y.: Rural tourism development model based on arm Gpu and sensor network. Microprocess. Microsyst. 2021(2), 104067 (2021)

Author Index

© ICST Institute for Computer Sciences, Social Informatics and Telecommunications Engineering 2024
Published by Springer Nature Switzerland AG 2024. All Rights Reserved
Y. Zhang and N. Shah (Eds.): BigIoT-EDU 2023, LNICST 582, pp. 525–526, 2024.
https://doi.org/10.1007/978-3-031-63136-8

Printed in the United States
by Baker & Taylor Publisher Services